LABOR RELATIONS

second edition

LABOR RELATIONS

Arthur A. Sloane
Professor of Industrial Relations
University of Delaware

Fred Witney
Professor of Economics
Indiana University

PRENTICE-HALL, INC., *Englewood Cliffs, New Jersey*

© 1972 by Prentice-Hall, Inc., Englewood Cliffs, N.J.

All rights reserved. No part of this book may
be reproduced in any form or by any means without
permission in writing from the publisher.

13-519611-6

Library of Congress Catalog Card Number: 73–151043

Printed in the United States of America

Current Printing (last digit):

10   9   8

PRENTICE-HALL INTERNATIONAL, INC., *London*
PRENTICE-HALL OF AUSTRALIA, PTY. LTD., *Sydney*
PRENTICE-HALL OF CANADA, LTD., *Toronto*
PRENTICE-HALL OF INDIA PRIVATE LIMITED, *New Delhi*
PRENTICE-HALL OF JAPAN, INC., *Tokyo*

To
Louise, Amy, and Laura
and
Judy, Eileen, and Frank

Preface

This book has been designed as an aid to all readers who desire a deeper understanding of union-management relations. As such, it contains certain areas of focus and certain ones which must necessarily be minimized in treatment.

The volume brings in sufficient economic material to allow a basic appreciation of the labor relations process and stops at that point. We have also, throughout, tried to implement our belief that all of the various topic treatments should, as in the case of ideal girls' skirts, be short enough to be interesting (although long enough to cover the subject).

On the other hand, the book in no way *restricts* itself to what is commonly described as "collective bargaining." Its focus is on the negotiation and administration of labor agreements, with emphasis on the development and application of the more significant bargaining issues as these now appear between the covers of the contracts. But our own teaching experiences have taught us that these topics cannot profitably be studied in isolation. Labor relations, in the sense in which we shall use the term, can best be viewed as an interaction between two organizations—management and the labor union; and the parties to this interaction are always subject to various, often complex, environmental influences. Only after the reader gains an understanding of the evolving management and labor institutions, and only after he has come to appreciate the environment surrounding their interactional process, can he attempt to understand bargaining itself in any meaningful way.

The direction which this book will take is consequently an obvious one: downward, from a broad overview of the general nature of the labor-management relationship as it currently exists in the United States (Part I); through a survey of the historical, legal, and structural environments which so greatly influence contractual contents and labor relations behavior (Part II); to a close examination of the negotiation, administration, and major contents of the labor contract itself (Part III). Through description, analysis, discussion questions, and, in the later stages of this volume, selected arbitration cases drawn from our own experience, we hope to impart understanding of all these labor relations aspects to the future practitioner.

Numerous changes, primarily in the way of additions, mark this first revision of our 1967 book. Developments in the industrial relations field, even in these few years, have dictated the inclusion of new material relating to white-collar unionism, "national emergency" strikes, unionism and the black worker, coordinated bargaining, fringe benefits, and arbitration law. We have also, with the benefit now of some hindsight, substantially enlarged upon our original treatment of the Landrum-Griffin Act and considerably updated discussion of a host of other topics, ranging from wage-price guideposts to the violation of no-strike contractual clauses. Eleven new arbitration cases, as well as the retention of one case which was contained in the earlier volume, are presented. And our original clientele will also find a revised bibliography, a completely face-lifted mock negotiation problem, and the inclusion of a second appendix, dealing with the accelerating organization of governmental employees. Nonetheless, we have exercised prudence in the revision and only changes which could be defended on grounds of general improvement of our original offering have been incorporated.

We stand indebted to many people for their help in this revision, but above all our gratitude is extended to: Professor Morrison Handsaker, Chairman, Department of Economics and Business, Lafayette College; Professor Dale Yoder, Director, Bureau of Business Research, California State College at Long Beach; and Emeritus Professor E. B. McNatt, School of Commerce, University of Illinois. Through the encouragement and constructive suggestions of each of these three scholars, *Labor Relations* has undoubtedly been substantially improved. We also acknowledge our appreciation to *Personnel Journal* for permission to draw freely from a December 1969 article ("Prospects for the Unionization of White Collar Employees") by author Sloane in Chapter I, and to *Business Horizons* for permission to do the same in Chapter III with a Summer 1967 article ("National Emergency Strikes: The Danger of Extralegal Success") by the same author.

ARTHUR A. SLOANE
FRED WITNEY

Contents

PART ONE: SETTING THE STAGE   1

  **1 Organized Labor and the Management Community:
an Overview**   3

The State of the Unions Today, 6   White-Collar Employees, 9   Some Probable Explanations, 10   Some Grounds for Union Optimism, 14   Labor's Present Strategic Power, 18   Why Workers Join Unions, 19   Why Managers Resist Unions, 24   Management Philosophies toward Unions, 31   Some Concluding Remarks on the Current Qualities of Labor-Management Relationships, 38

PART TWO: THE ENVIRONMENTAL FRAMEWORK   45

  2 The Historical Framework   47

The Eighteenth Century: Genesis of the American Labor Movement, 48   The First Unions and Their Limited Successes, 50   Revival, Innovation, and Disillusionment, 51   The Laying of the

Foundation for Modern Unionism and Some Mixed Performances with It, 53   The Rise and Fall of the Knights of Labor, 56   The Formation of the AFL and Its Pragmatic Master Plan, 58   The Early Years of the AFL and Some Mixed Results, 61   Wartime Gains and Peacetime Losses, 66   The Great Depression and the AFL's Resurgence in Spite of Itself, 69   The CIO's Challenge to the AFL, 72   World War II, 75   Public Reaction and Private Merger, 76   Organized Labor since the Merger, 79   Unionism and the Black Worker, 81   An Analysis of Union History, 86

3   The Legal Framework 92

The Era of Judicial Control, 93   The Norris–LaGuardia Act of 1932, 94   The Wagner Act of 1935, 95   From the Wagner Act to Taft–Hartley, 103   The Taft–Hartley Act of 1947, 104   The Landrum–Griffin Act of 1959, 119   Some Conclusions, 125

4   Union Behavior: Structure, Government, and Operation 131

The AFL-CIO, 133   The National Union, 150   The Local Union, 164   Union Finances, 174   A Concluding Word, 175

PART THREE: COLLECTIVE BARGAINING 179

5   At the Bargaining Table 181

Preparation for Negotiations, 184   The Bargaining Process: Early Stages, 190   The Bargaining Process: Later Stages, 192   The Bargaining Process: Final Stages, 195   Crisis Situations, 197   Testing and Proofreading, 200   Coordinated Bargaining, 202   Reciprocal Character of Collective Bargaining, 204   Some Further Complexities, 205

6   Administration of the Agreement 210

Grievance Procedure, 212   Grievance Procedure: Its Flexibility, 215   Arbitration, 218   The "Trilogy" Cases, 220   Case No. 1: Time Limits Under Grievance Procedure, 236   Case No. 2: Arbitrability of Grievance, 247

7   Wage Issues under Collective Bargaining 259

Determination of the Basic Wage Rate, 261   The Truitt Decision, 270   Cost of Living: Escalator and Wage-Reopener Arrange-

ments, 273   Wage Differentials, 279   Overtime Rates of Pay, 281
Job Evaluation and Job Comparison, 284   A Final Word, 286
Case No. 3: Rotation of Overtime, 288   Case No. 4: Wage Rate
for a New Job—Job Comparison, 307

8 Economic Supplements under Collective Bargaining   322

Pension Plans, 323   Vacations with Pay, 327   Holidays with
Pay, 330   Negotiated Health Insurance Plans, 331   Dismissal
Pay, 333   Reporting Pay, 334   Supplementary Unemployment
Benefit Plans, 335   Some Final Thoughts, 340   Case No. 5:
Eligibility for Vacation Benefits, 345   Case No. 6: Payment for a
Holiday Falling on a Non-Scheduled Work Day, 355   Case No. 7:
Coverage under a Hospital Insurance Benefit Program, 362

9 Institutional Issues under Collective Bargaining   378

Union Membership as a Condition of Employment, 379   The
Checkoff, 386   Union Obligations, 388   Managerial Prerogatives, 393   Conclusions, 397   Case No. 8: Management Rights, 399

10 Administrative Issues under Collective Bargaining   409

Seniority, 410   Discharge and Discipline, 419   Safety and Health
of Employees, 422   Production Standards and Manning, 423
Automation, 426   A Concluding Word, 434   Case No. 9: Seniority: Filling of a Job Vacancy, 436   Cases Nos. 10 and 11:
Discharge of an Employee, 450   Case No. 12: Production Standards, 474

PART IV: SOME FINAL THOUGHTS   489

Concluding Statement   491

APPENDICES   497

I   Mock Negotiation Problem   499

II Labor Relations in the Public Sector   509

Index   531

LABOR RELATIONS

part one

Setting

The Stage

1

Organized Labor and the Management Community: an Overview

Our society has historically placed a high premium on property rights. Because of this, and perhaps also because the American soil has nurtured a breed of highly individualistic and aggressive businessmen, employers in this country have accepted unionism through the years approximately as well as nature tolerates a vacuum.

The evidence for this phenomenon is not in short supply. Symbolic of management sentiments in the mid-nineteenth century were, for example, the comments of the editors of the *New York Journal of Commerce* relating to current demands of the printers in that locality:

> Who but a miserable craven-hearted man, would permit himself to be subjected to such rules, extending even to the number of apprentices he may employ, and the manner in which they shall be bound to him, to the kind of work which shall be performed in his own office at particular hours of the day, and to the sex of the persons employed, however separated into different apartments or buildings? For ourselves, we never employed a female as a compositor and have no great opinion of appren-

tices, but sooner than be restricted on these points, or any other, by a self-constituted tribunal outside of the office, we would go back to the employment of our boyhood, and dig potatoes, pull flax, and do everything else that a plain, honest farmer may properly do on his own territory. It is marvelous to us how any employer, having the soul of a man within him, can submit to such degradation.[1]

Five decades later, President George F. Baer of the Philadelphia and Reading Railroad relied on God, rather than ridicule, in setting forth views which were no less representative of many employers of *his* time. In a 1903 letter, Baer replied to a citizen who had requested him "as a Christian gentleman" to make concessions to the striking workers on his railroad, as follows:

> I see you are evidently biased in your religious views in favor of the right of the working man to control a business in which he has no other interest than to secure fair wages for the work he does. I beg of you not to be discouraged. The rights and interests of the laboring man will be protected and cared for, not by the labor agitators, but by the Christian men to whom God in His infinite wisdom has given control of the property interests of the country. Pray earnestly that the right may triumph, always remembering that the Lord God Omnipotent still reigns and that His reign is one of law and order, and not of violence and crime.[2]

Sinclair Lewis used the medium of fictional satire to make his points, but real-life counterparts of his small-town businessman George F. Babbitt were sufficiently in supply to make *Babbitt* an instant success when it was published in 1922. Babbitt's opinions on the subject of organized labor were quite forthright, if not entirely consistent:

> A good labor union is of value because it keeps out radical unions, which would destroy property. No one ought to be forced to belong to a union, however. All labor agitators who try to force men to join a union should be hanged. In fact, just between ourselves, there oughtn't to be any unions allowed at all; and as it's the best way of fighting the unions, every businessman ought to belong to an employer's association and to the Chamber of Commerce. In union there is strength. So any selfish hog who doesn't join the Chamber of Commerce ought to be forced to.[3]

[1] *New York Journal of Commerce,* February 7, 1851. As quoted in Neil W. Chamberlain, *The Labor Sector* (New York: McGraw-Hill Book Company, 1965), p. 341.
[2] Herbert Harris, *American Labor* (New Haven: Yale University Press, 1939), pp. 126–27.
[3] Sinclair Lewis, *Babbitt* (New York: Harcourt, Brace & World, Inc., 1922), p. 44. (Rights for the British Commonwealth excluding Canada have been granted by Jonathan Cape Limited, Publishers, London, England.)

In our own day, management views on the subject are considerably more sophisticated and far less emotion-laden. Over the past few decades, major changes have affected the employment relationship and contributed to the lessening of overt antiunionism. The findings of the behavioral sciences, particularly industrial sociology and applied psychology, have led to an employee-centered management approach which was unknown to an earlier era. Far greater worker expectations have been fostered by a new social climate derived from the ending of mass immigration, growing levels of education, and the spread of the world's most ambitious communications network. Moreover, the old-time owner-manager, holding a major or exclusive proprietary interest in his business, has now been substantially displaced. He has been succeeded by the hired administrator, oriented toward management as a profession, as much an employee as the people far below him in the company hierarchy, and increasingly aware that profitability is not the only test of his company's performance today (and that *community* responsibilities are also prime considerations). Finally, the right of workers to organize and bargain collectively, free of employer restraint or coercion, has been protected by statute since the early 1930s.

In this new setting, progress in union-management relations has undeniably been made. Considerably more enlightened management policies toward organized labor are in effect today than was the case even twenty-five years ago. A large measure of contractual stability has been achieved in many situations. Violence in labor disputes has all but disappeared. The incidence of strikes has been almost steadily decreasing, and strikes now consume a minuscule portion of total working time, less than 0.20 percent in most recent years. A greater willingness by both parties to resort to facts rather than to power or emotion as a basis for bargaining is in evidence. And, indeed, unions have now been completely accepted by some managers, with outspoken attacks on organized labor, in general, being relatively rare from *any* employer quarter.

For all these sanguine developments, however, the fact remains that unions are still far from welcome in the eyes of the employer community. If the attacks on unionism are more muted and less belligerent than they were in the past, they nonetheless exist on a wide scale. Professor Albert Blum, an eminent observer of present-day management thinking, sums up what is perhaps the current modal situation in words which the authors believe to be wholly appropriate:

> Even if the manager does not view the union as a gang, he often still feels that they strike a discordant note in the happy home. Once there, unrest develops. A peer group outside the home becomes more important to the children than the parents; the father's powers are challenged; the child begins to think his goals are not synonymous with those of the

parents (he may even want his allowance raised); and, perhaps worst of all, he wants to have his voice heard in how the home should be run.[4]

In the face of this management enmity, on the other hand, unionism has shown absolutely no tendency to retreat. Owing primarily to the inroads of automation and its resulting employment decline as well as to changing market demands affecting the manufacturing sector, organized labor *has,* it is true, expanded its membership only moderately in the past few years. And, despite some claims by labor relations analysts that the fast-growing white-collar worker sector will soon become more hospitable to collective bargaining, it is equally true that union penetration in this area thus far has been anything but impressive. But it is no less a matter of record that almost seven times as many workers are union members today as was the case in 1932, and it is quite apparent that the 20 million employees who currently constitute the labor movement in this country exhibit no notable signs of disenchantment with it. Whatever one's speculation about the problems awaiting unionism as the nature of our labor force changes (and, as will be shown, the speculation is both optimistic and pessimistic from the union viewpoint), the labor union seems to be very much here to stay.

In this introductory chapter, then, we shall want to examine several questions. Why do workers, apparently in complete disregard of their employers' wishes, join and remain in unions? Why, for that matter, do employers so steadfastly continue to oppose the concept of unionism (beyond the extremely general reasons suggested by the preceding paragraphs)? Assuming that managers have no choice other than to deal with a labor organization, what alternative methods for this collective bargaining are open to them? And what, if any, trends in their concrete dealings with unions have managements exhibited in recent years? Before we discuss these questions, however, we must assess the current status and strategic power of the American labor movement itself.

THE STATE OF THE UNIONS TODAY

Completely reliable statistics relating to union membership in this country have never been available. Some unions in reporting their figures have traditionally exaggerated, to gain respect and influence for the union itself within the total labor movement, to make the union officers look better by showing a rise in enrollments during their term of office, or merely to hide a loss of membership. Other unions have been known to report *fewer* members than they actually have, for financial reasons (for example, to avoid paying per capita taxes to labor federations to which they may belong,

[4] Albert A. Blum, "Management Paternalism and Collective Bargaining," *Personnel Administration,* XXVI (January–February 1963), 38.

particularly the AFL-CIO), or because of bookkeeping practices which exclude workers currently on strike (or those on layoff from work) from the list of present members.

The figure of 20 million workers, offered above as constituting the present extent of union organization, is commonly accepted as an appropriate one, however. This total includes some 18.5 million United States members of national and international unions[5] and roughly 1.5 million American members of independent local unions (those not affiliated with any national or international). It excludes the approximately 1.2 million Canadians who belong to internationals with headquarters in the United States.[6]

In 1970, in terms of relative labor force penetration, the 20 million in the unionized work force represented approximately 22.8 percent of all civilian members of the labor force in the country and accounted for almost three out of every ten employees in nonagricultural establishments (where union organizing has historically been concentrated). They also constituted somewhat less than 36 percent of "organizable" American industrial employees (our nonprofessional and nonsupervisory employees, although some union representation from both the professional and supervisory sectors does exist).[7]

More specifically, just about one-half of the nation's 31 million blue-collar workers (craftsmen, operatives, and kindred workers) are now in unions. These include at least 80 percent of such workers in transportation, construction, and municipal utilities and somewhat over two-thirds of all blue-collar employees in manufacturing and mining. Almost all manual workers in many manufacturing industries—steel, automobile, rubber, aerospace, meat packing, agricultural implements, brewing, paper, the needle trades, and a few others—have now been organized. So, too, has a substantial percentage of the blue-collar employees in the printing, oil, chemical, shoe, electrical, electronic, and pharmaceutical industries.

States and cities with a high percentage of their workers in these industries show, not surprisingly, a high proportion of unionized employees. Indeed, five states alone—New York, California, Pennsylvania, Illinois, and Ohio—account for 48 percent of all union members in this country (while employing just 38 percent of the U.S. nonagricultural work force). And Washington, Michigan, and Massachusetts also have ratios of union membership to nonagricultural employment which place them well above the national average of just under 30 percent. South Carolina, North Carolina, Mississippi, and Florida, on the other hand, have ratios running only between 6 and 14 percent. Several major cities, too, which are heavily depen-

[5] The terms *national* and *international* will be used interchangeably in this volume as, indeed, they are used in practice.
[6] Unofficial data furnished by United States Department of Labor, Bureau of Labor Statistics.
[7] *Ibid.*

dent on the industries cited—Pittsburgh, Detroit, and Seattle, among others—presently have at least 90 percent of their manufacturing plant workers covered by union contract. Cities without large representation from these industries tend to show considerably lower figures.

Union strength, then, is highly concentrated—in areas which are strategic to our economy. If organized labor has thus far been notably unsuccessful in its attempt to organize such white-collar (and fast-growing) sectors as trade, services, and finance, and such remaining great pockets of non-unionism in manufacturing as the textile industry, unions *have* been cordially greeted by the workers in much of large-scale industry. Indeed, the labor movement today bargains with many of the most influential managements in the country, those which regularly take the lead in price and wage movements. By and large, as Slichter, Healy, and Livernash have pointed out, trade unions have dominant representation "where technology is most advanced, where capital is used most abundantly, where the productivity of labor is highest, and where technological progress is most rapid.... In other words, trade union membership is concentrated and strongest where strength counts most of all."[8]

Union membership related directly to industrial category also illustrates the high percentage of labor organization accounted for by the groups cited above, and the relatively small successes employed by labor organizers in white-collar industries:[9]

Industry	Percentage Unionized
Transportation, communications, public utilities	74.7%
Construction	70.9
Manufacturing	50.0
Mining	47.2
Government	14.1
Services	10.5
Trade	9.3
Finance, real estate	2.0
Agriculture	.8

Further evidence of the importance of the blue-collar industry groups to the labor movement is given in a listing of the largest unions. Ranked

---

[8] Sumner H. Slichter, James J. Healy, and E. Robert Livernash, *The Impact of Collective Bargaining on Management* (Washington, D.C.: The Brookings Institution, 1960), p. 2.

[9] Derek C. Bok and John T. Dunlop, *Labor and the American Community* (New York: Simon & Schuster, 1970), p. 44.

according to their size in 1970, the six largest internationals show their heavy dependence on blue-collar workers even in their titles. Accounting for somewhat over one-third of all union members, these internationals are:

Union	Members
Teamsters (Independent)	1,900,000
Automobile Workers (Independent)	1,400,000
Steelworkers (AFL-CIO)	1,100,000
Machinists (AFL-CIO)	900,000
Electrical Workers (AFL-CIO)*	900,000
Carpenters (AFL-CIO)	800,000

* International Brotherhood of Electrical Workers.
Source: Authors' estimates based on data published by the U.S. Department of Labor.

WHITE-COLLAR EMPLOYEES

If the labor movement is predominantly a blue-collar one, however, this is no longer true of the United States labor force itself. In 1956, the number of white-collar workers exceeded that of blue-collar workers in this country for the first time in our nation's history. The gap, moreover, has been steadily widening ever since: Such sectors as trade, services, finance, and government have continued to expand, while the blue-collar sectors—particularly manufacturing, mining, and transportation but with the construction sector as a conspicuous exception—have actually, in the face of improved technologies and changing consumer demands, shown employment declines.

More than any other factor, this changing complexion of the labor force has given organized labor cause for concern. Over the past dozen years, its inability to recruit white-collar workers on any significant scale has forced it to watch the unionized percentage of the total civilian work force slip somewhat—from over 24 percent to the approximate current figure of 22.8.

This is not to say, of course, that unions do not exert a major collective bargaining influence on behalf of some groups of white-collar workers. Such white-collar types as musicians and barbers have for years been willing joiners of labor organizations. In recent years, the Retail Clerks (with an estimated 500,000 members at the time of this writing), the State, County and Municipal Employees (300,000), and the Retail, Wholesale and Department Store Employees (190,000) have significantly increased their memberships. So, too, have such somewhat smaller white-collar internationals as the Letter Carriers (170,000), the Postal Clerks (160,000), and the American Federation of Teachers (140,000). And although substantial numbers of workers within some of these unions (in particular, the Retail Clerks and the Letter Carriers) perform such clearly blue-collar assignments as stock-handling, the percentage of pure white-collar types in each appears to have steadily climbed in the 1960s. Moreover, many of labor's largest internationals—most notably the Teamsters and the Steelworkers—do represent large numbers of white-collar employees in addition to their traditional types of constituents.

Nonetheless, there has been virtually no change in total union penetration of the white-collar field in recent years. In 1956, some 2.42 million white-collar workers were in unions; a decade later, the figure had risen only to approximately 2.7 million,[10] despite the growth of this sector by several million more jobs, to over 26 million by the late 1960s. Nor had even these modest gains of organized labor been evenly spread throughout the white-collar world. Most of them (four-fifths of the 1964–66 increases, for example)[11] had been gained strictly from the public service sector, where in many cases favorable legislation had made the enrollment of new members comparatively easy. [*Note:* See Appendix II for a detailed description and discussion of "Labor Relations in the Public Sector."]

SOME PROBABLE EXPLANATIONS

Why has the white-collar world been so relatively unreceptive to the union organizer when its blue-collar counterpart has been so hospitable to him? Many theories have been advanced by almost as many theorists. All bear some risk of oversimplification, given both the variety of ever-changing needs and wants that play on human behavior and the heterogeneity of the white-collar population itself (including as it does such dissimilar occupational categories as engineers, professional salesmen, medical and other health workers, clerical and office employees, members of the teaching profession, and governmental workers). But, among the many explanations for labor's general failure to date in penetrating the White-Collar Frontier, the following may well be the most accurate. Taken collectively, they also constitute some rather formidable grounds for union pessimism in the years ahead.

1. The public has in recent years been inundated with news of seemingly irresponsible union strikes and commensurately unstatesmanlike settlements, union leader criminality, and featherbedding situations. The resulting poor image of the labor movement, as conveyed by the mass media, may well have alienated hundreds of thousands—and conceivably even millions

---

[10] H. M. Douty, "Prospects for White-Collar Unionism," *Monthly Labor Review*, XCII, No. 1 (January 1969), 33.
[11] *Ibid.*

—of potential white-collar union joiners. In an age when even the occupant of the White House can be determined by public image, this factor—while it is not only unquantifiable but even basically unprovable—cannot be overlooked.

From the labor point of view, there is an intrinsic unfairness in such a factor. It is conflict, as more than one newsman has observed, which makes the headlines. The large majority of union agreements which are peacefully renegotiated year after year go virtually unnoticed by the reporters of the news, but the few strikes of any dimensions are treated with the journalistic zeal of a Tolstoy. The overwhelming proportion of union officials continue to lead their lives in full compliance with the laws of the land, but this seems insignificant to the news compilers in the face of the conviction of a single Jimmy Hoffa or Dave Beck, with whose blemished records all informed citizens have become amply familiar. And charges that unions demand pay for work which is not performed totally dwarf the large body of evidence that featherbedding is engaged in by only a small segment of unionized employees.

Yet what editor can justify headlines proclaiming that "Local 109 of the Hatters is a Very Statesmanlike Local," that "Business Agent Duffy Gabrilowitz of the Plumbers Union is One Hundred Percent Honest," or that "Management Says That Pulp, Sulphite, and Paper Mill Workers are Giving a Fair Day's Work for a Fair Day's Pay"? Only, it is to be suspected, a newsman with a strongly developed suicidal urge. Accordingly, the large segment of the population which allows its opinions of unionism to be molded only by those labor activities which receive wide publicity is understandably—if, for organized labor, unfortunately—less than enthusiastic about the institution. An incalculable but undoubtedly formidable number of white-collar workers—unlike their blue-collar counterparts, who are generally in a better position by virtue of proximity to perceive strengths as well as weaknesses in unionism—fall into this population category.

2. The labor movement has in recent years been distinguished in the main by uninspiring, rather bureaucratic leadership which seems only dimly aware of the white-collar problem and totally unimaginative as far as discovering any solutions. The complaint of labor scholar J. B. S. Hardman that "superannuated leaders, who have outlived their usefulness, are probably met more frequently in the labor movement than in any other militant social movement,"[12] although it was made more than forty years ago and intended to apply exclusively to the late 1920s, could fit into any typical outsider's critique of labor's current performance without doing violence to the basic theme. Hardman's words constitute, as Jack T. Conway could

---

[12] J. B. S. Hardman, *American Labor Dynamics* (New York: Harcourt, Brace & Co., 1928), p. 95.

point out in 1968, "the lingering lament of an aging officialdom, which too frequently symbolizes—to the public and to its membership—dried-up idealism and a stalled drive for reform."[13]

Nor has this condition entirely escaped the attention of labor leaders themselves. The secretary-treasurer of the United Automobile Workers, Emil Mazey, for example, has offered the observation that "some of the board members of some of the unions, when they have a board meeting, they look like a collection of a wax museum."[14] And, indeed, the UAW, which withdrew from the AFL-CIO in May 1968, at least ostensibly because of its unhappiness with what it perceived to be the federation's leadership apathy, has charged that the 130-union AFL-CIO "has become isolated from the mainstream and too often acts like a comfortable, complacent custodian of the status quo."[15] By the same token, the AFL-CIO's leadership has pointed out that UAW leadership is on vulnerable ground in making such charges, since "the UAW represents a smaller percentage of the work force in its own industry and of the total membership of the AFL-CIO itself than it did at the time of [the 1955 AFL and CIO] merger."[16]

However one judges the respective merits of the federation and UAW cases, the tremendous amount of time and energy poured into this particular battle in the past few years by the two sides constitutes to many people, as James P. Gannon has commented, "the nonproductive, self-serving task of publicly flogging each other."[17] And, since so little concrete progress in revitalizing labor's sagging fortunes has supplemented this activity, the appearance is clearly not far removed from the reality.

For those who continue to believe strongly in the potential of the labor movement as a force for accomplishment in our society, there is something quite sad about the current state of union leadership. All of the trappings of success surround the latter—as Raskin has accurately pointed out, "The hair shirt has given way to white-on-white broadcloth, imported fabrics, and custom tailoring"[18]—and the expense account perquisites of labor's major officials are totally indistinguishable in their lavishness from those of the leaders of the business community. But, somewhere in the transformation from crusader for the underdog to accepted member of the Establishment, both the sense of mission and the creative spark to imple-

[13] Jack T. Conway, "Challenges to Union Leadership in an Era of Change," in *Proceedings of the Twenty-First Annual Winter Meeting, Industrial Relations Research Association,* December 29–30, 1968, p. 183.
[14] *Wall Street Journal,* March 26, 1964, p. 8.
[15] *Business Week,* May 31, 1969, p. 77.
[16] *Business Week,* April 12, 1969, p. 78.
[17] James P. Gannon, "The Labor Movement: Sinew Turned Fat," *Wall Street Journal,* June 3, 1969, p. 22.
[18] A. H. Raskin, "The Unions and Their Wealth," *Atlantic Monthly,* April 1962, p. 89.

ment it seem to have been severely dampened by affluence. The senior citizens who constitute the bulk of current labor leadership appear, in short, to be resting quite comfortably on their hard-earned laurels, lacking motivation to re-enter the organizational arena and expend the infinite energy, money, and perhaps above all imagination which is required by such an elusive potential constituency as the white-collar sector.

3. White-collar workers possess certain unique general properties which may tend to work against unionization in any event. Any citation of these ingredients automatically incurs all of the risks of generalization alluded to earlier, but there is agreement among scholars of the white-collar population that they definitely exist.

(a) White-collar employees have long felt superior to their blue-collar counterparts and have tended to believe that joining a "union" (an institution traditionally associated with manual workers) would decrease their occupational prestige. This goes well beyond the issue of labor's currently poor image, cited above. As Sayles and Strauss have remarked, "White-collar jobs are thought to have individuality in contrast to the mass character of factory work, to be 'middle class' as distinct from working class."[19] Prior educational achievements, modes of dress and language, relative cleanliness of the work situations and even job locations within the enterprise typically also give the white-collar jobholder much more in common with management than with the blue-collar employee. Income based on salary rather than wages further weakens the potential bonds between the two submanagerial classes. Nor, clearly, can the sheer fact that society generally looks down upon manual work and places its premium upon mentally challenging employment be disregarded in explaining the superiority complex of the white-collarite.

In an economy such as ours—where for most people the more basic needs have now been relatively well satisfied—the role of such status considerations can be considerable. To ask the white-collar worker to identify by unionization with the steel worker, automobile assembly line employee, truck driver, and hod carrier—and to follow in the traditions of Samuel Gompers, John L. Lewis, Sidney Hillman, and Philip Murray (to say nothing of Jimmy Hoffa and Dave Beck)—is consequently, by its very nature, no small undertaking.

(b) However tenuous it may be, the white-collar worker can at least perceive some opportunity to advance into managerial ranks, while the blue-collar employee is typically limited in his most optimistic advancement goal to the "gray area" of the foremanship. Unlike the wearer of the white collar, the blue-collar worker senses (usually quite accurately) that educational and social deficiencies have combined to limit his promotional

[19] Leonard R. Sayles and George Strauss, *Human Behavior in Organizations* (Englewood Cliffs, N.J.: Prentice-Hall, Inc., 1966), p. 68.

avenues within the industrial world, and he can adjust to the fact that he is permanently destined to be apart from and directed by the managerial class. Since such a fate is often not nearly as clear to the white-collar worker (partially for the reasons cited in the previous paragraphs), he is understandably more reluctant to join the ranks of unionism and thus support what is potentially a major constraint on employer freedom of action.

(c) The considerably higher proportion of women in white-collar work than in blue-collar work[20] has served as a dampening force for organization. By and large, women have always been notoriously poor candidates for unionism. In many cases, the job is thought of as temporary—either premarital or to supplement the family breadwinner's paycheck (often on a sporadic basis)—and, consequently, the union's argument of long-run job security has had little appeal.[21] In other cases—perhaps as high as 25 percent at the time of this writing—the job is a part-time one, also to the detriment of the union organizer. Nor can the labor movement's traditional aura of militant masculinity be eliminated as a possible causal factor in explaining the female response to organizational attempts, although here one moves wholly into the realm of speculation.

(d) Finally, many white-collar workers with professional identifications—engineers, college professors, and institutionally employed doctors, for example—continue to believe that for them there is still much more to be gained from individual bargaining with their employer than from any form of collective bargaining. Viewing the latter as an automatic opponent of individual merit rewards, they tend to perceive the relatively few union sympathizers within their professions as either mediocrities in need of such group support or masochists.

SOME GROUNDS FOR UNION OPTIMISM

If it is thus tempting to begin sounding the death knell for the labor movement on the grounds that its failure to penetrate the critical Collar Frontier can be explained by a combination of factors which seem to be at least collectively insurmountable, realism dictates that several *other* factors also be pondered. And these additional considerations can lead one

---

[20] According to *Employment and Earnings* (August 1965, p. 10), approximately 43 percent of all white-collar workers in July 1965 were women, as opposed to only 15 percent of all blue-collar employees.

[21] As Kassalow points out, this can further work against unionism by making the promotional chances of the more stable *male* white-collar employees that much more visible to them. See Everett M. Kassalow, "New Union Frontier: White Collar Workers," *Harvard Business Review*, XL (January–February 1962), 41–52.

to an entirely different conclusion regarding the future of organized labor in the white-collar area.

1. The same newsprint, television, and radio announcements that have brought news of union misdoings to the white-collar population have also informed this primarily nonunion audience of highly impressive income improvements in the unionized sector. For example, few nonunionists are entirely unaware of the gains in the heavily organized construction sector which by 1970 were adding $3.25 per hour and more to the wages of skilled craftsmen over the next two years, or significantly more than the $2.50 to $2.75 commonly received as total hourly wages by workers in wholesale and retail trade, finance, insurance, real estate, and many other parts of the white-collar world. Contractor Donald T. Knutson's observation that "by 1971, the lowest wage for (even) a common laborer in the construction industry will be $15,000"[22] could only have been received with considerable envy by the unrepresented insurance company debit agent whose current earnings, despite his college degree, placed him at only half of this figure. And knowledge of the fact that substantial overtime opportunities at hefty premiums were also available to such unionists—as they were most frequently not to white-collar workers—could only increase the latter's flow of adrenalin.

In fairness, it must be recognized that the over-tight labor market and fractionalized bargaining structure of construction makes it a labor union extreme from the viewpoint of wage aggrandizement. But the kind of invidious comparisons engendered by the construction totals clearly extend to other situations. Consider, for example, the following gross average weekly earnings of nonsupervisory production workers for May 1969: petroleum and coal products, $172.77; transportation equipment, $160.55; primary metal industries, $158.63; mining, $154.07; machinery (except electrical), $153.15; chemicals and allied products, $142.61; and printing and publishing, $140.56.[23] In contrast to these figures—all of which pertain to heavily unionized areas—the comparable statistic for wholesale and retail trade was $89.66 ($77.63 for retail trade alone); finance, insurance, and real estate (lumped together by the Bureau of Labor Statistics) registered $107.30; and the predominantly nonunionized "textile mill products" and "apparel and other textile products" areas showed averages of $94.25 and $82.57, respectively. Nor can the white-collar population indefinitely be expected to be indifferent to truck-driver incomes (symbolically, the *International Teamster* magazine could report a few years ago that "recently a professor at ivy-covered Williams College in New England returned to the Teamsters as an over-the-road driver because he could double his

---

[22] *Business Week,* July 19, 1969, p. 90.
[23] *Monthly Labor Review,* XCII, No. 7 (July 1969), 112.

salary at Williams")[24] and to various other highly remunerated (and overwhelmingly unionized) workers such as longshoremen, tool and die makers, and airline mechanics.

The responsibility for the relatively high standards of living involved here does not rest completely with unionism. Obviously, one must also examine such a variety of other factors as skill levels, industrial ability to pay, community wage structures, imperfections in the product market, and industrial productivity (among others) in explaining these wage levels. And one can readily cite such *unionized* areas as the New England boot and shoe industry and the meat packing industry where the overall situation often allows no real wage improvement at all and, consequently, none is received by organized labor.

But the hazards of accepting the more impressive union bargaining totals at their face value are not particularly relevant in this context. Misleadingly or not, such dollar amounts often symbolize in a highly visible fashion the ability of unionism to effect dramatic wage gains. And, as the gap between the incomes of the blue-collar and white-collar worlds continues to widen, a greater willingness to consider union membership may conceivably be the result. Indeed, appreciation of the fact that snobbishness neither purchases groceries nor pays the rent seems already to have accounted for some of the increased willingness of at least teachers and—by the early 1970s—lower echelons of hospital work forces to undertake such a consideration.

2. The definite upsurge in unionism among governmental employees—while probably attributable far more to enabling legislation at not only the federal but at many state and local levels than to any pronounced rank-and-file militancy—is combining with the (lesser) emergence of collective bargaining in other white-collar areas to gradually weaken the nonmember's traditional association of organized labor with manual work. As previously inferred, the process is still an excruciatingly slow one from labor's viewpoint. But the growing presence of these higher-statused, better-educated federal civil servants and state employees (to say nothing of that paragon of brainwork, the local schoolteacher) in union ranks can only be expected to erode the older images in time. Whether this psychological change will be sufficient in itself to win over more than a fraction of the untapped white-collar market for the labor movement is another question. But certainly one of the grounds for labor's failure until now will have been dissipated.

3. It is probably also only a question of time before considerably more aggressive, imaginative, and empathetic leadership than organized labor now possesses comes to the fore, which would also make widespread white-collar unionization far more likely.

[24] *International Teamster,* September 1960, p. 16.

For all of the apparent apathy and conservatism at the highest levels of labor as it entered the 1970s, there was no dearth of individuals in the current second and third tiers of union leadership who exhibited these more positive characteristics. Far more attuned to the aspirations and values of our increasingly sophisticated labor force than were their currently more influential colleagues, they had become more and more frustrated by labor's lack of progress in recent years (as well as, often, by the tepid responses of their own memberships to the official goals of their particular unions). They fully appreciated the necessity for an immense outpouring of financial, institutional, and personal effort in the quest for the white-collarite. And, in the best traditions of Samuel Gompers and John L. Lewis, they exhibited no lack of ideas as to how such unionization could be effected, even advocating wholly different organizational structures to attain this goal should this become necessary. The vicissitudes of union politics clearly ensured that not all, or even many, of these men would ever actually achieve ascendancy in the labor movement. Those who would, however, would undoubtedly abet the chances of white-collar unionization.

4. Finally, the working conditions of white-collar employment are themselves now changing in a direction which may weaken both the superiority complex and pro-management proclivity of the white-collar wearer.

The very individuality of white-collar work is itself now disappearing from much of the industrial scene. An accelerating trend toward organizational bigness has already combined with the demands of technological efficiency to make cogs in vast interdependent machines of many clerks, comptometer operators, technicians, and even engineers, rather than allowing them to remain as individuals working alone or in comfortably small groups in these categories. And, as Kassalow has observed, "More and more white-collar workers are being routinized and bureaucratized. (Many) jobs in instance after instance become less interesting in the wake of modernization. The white-collar worker's relationship with his supervisor also becomes more remote; and, in most instances, he has no individual contact with the public. Further, since such large numbers are employed, there is a considerable blockage of upward mobility."[25]

In the years ahead, there will undoubtedly be many more such jobholders in the white-collar category. The advance of technology (particularly in the form of the computer, whose introduction into offices is now being conducted at an even faster rate than in factory atmospheres) will not only severely constrain much of the analytical and decision-making possibilities of the traditional "brain-workers," but will also cause considerable job uncertainty and most likely also a decrease in the economic value of job

---

[25] Kassalow, *op. cit.*

skills. The computer itself—since such equipment if idle constitutes an indefensible luxury—may even force many white-collar employees into one of the heretofore most distinguishing features of factory employment, shift work. But, under any conditions, these changes will serve to alter the complacent self-image of the white-collar worker by blurring the traditionally perceived differences between the nature of his work and that of his blue-collar counterpart.

And, in such an atmosphere, it may well be that what Levine and Karsh[26] have called the white-collar worker's feeling of "colleagueship" with management and his sense of "fulfillment" on the job will also evaporate, to the point of rendering the white-collarite far more susceptible than he has been in the past to the overtures of the union organizer.

Thus a case can be made for either position. And, while it is difficult to deny that future white-collar unionization does face great obstacles, it is probably no less advisable to hedge one's bets before writing off organized labor as an institution doomed to an ultimate slow death because, having long ago captured the now-shrinking blue-collar market, it has realized its only natural potential. If the grounds for union optimism as expressed above must necessarily remain speculative, nonetheless there are enough of them and there is sufficient logic to each of them to justify at least some amount of hopefulness on the part of the labor movement.

LABOR'S PRESENT STRATEGIC POWER

Other formidable obstacles also confront organized labor today. It is undeniable that unions *have* in recent years fallen from public favor, owing above all to the McClellan Committee congressional hearings, but also to their own bargaining excesses. These latter topics will be discussed on subsequent pages. Here, it is relevant to note that the publicity involved, temporarily or not, has cost the labor movement thousands of friends among the general public (and, presumably, in the ranks of potential union members). It has also led to restrictive federal and state legislation (summarized in Chapter 3) which in some ways can be construed as "antilabor." And, finally, labor has been handicapped to some extent by such current factors as: the national trend to smaller, decentralized plants, resulting in more personalized worker treatment; industry's present tendency to locate new plants in smaller, semi-rural and often Southern communities, climates not conducive to a hearty reception for the union; and the growing levels

---

[26] Solomon B. Levine and Bernard Karsh, "Industrial Relations for the Next Generation," *Quarterly Review of Economics and Business* (February 1961), pp. 18–29.

of income across the nation, stripping union promises of a "living wage" of some of their effect.

Yet, for all these adverse factors, it is still of some relevance for anyone who attempts to predict the labor movement's future that in their century and two-thirds on the American scene unions have faced even greater obstacles than these and have ultimately surmounted them. As Chapter 2 relates, the history of United States labor is in many ways a study of triumph over economic, social, and political adversity.

However one views organized labor's future, its present strategic power cannot be denied. The labor movement's concentration of membership in the economy's most vital sectors has meant that the 22.8 percent of the labor force that bargains collectively has been an extremely influential minority. One may not agree with the newspaper headlines that a particular strike has "paralyzed the economy," but it appears to be an acceptable generalization that the wages or salaries and other conditions of employment for much of the remaining 77.2 percent of the labor force are regularly affected to some degree by the unionized segment.

Thus, if the exact future dimensions and membership totals of organized labor are today in some doubt, the importance of collective bargaining is not. Neither can one dispute labor's staying power, given the labor movement's deep penetration into virtually all the traditional parts of our economy and its continuing hold upon these areas. The reports of collective bargaining's death are, as Mark Twain cabled from Europe following reports of his own demise, "greatly exaggerated." And, if the modern manager is unhappy with unionism, realism dictates not that he wait for it to vanish from the scene, but that he apply his efforts toward improving the collective bargaining process by which he is so likely to be directly affected.

WHY WORKERS JOIN UNIONS

Questions concerning human behavior do not lend themselves to simple answers, for the subject itself is a highly complex one. "Why do workers join unions?" clearly falls within this category.

In his widely accepted theory of motivation,[27] however, the late psychologist A. H. Maslow has provided us with helpful hints, although the theory itself relates to the whole population of human beings rather than merely to those who have seen fit to take out union membership.

---

[27] A. H. Maslow, *Motivation and Personality* (New York: Harper & Row, Publishers, 1954). Much of Maslow's concept was originally presented in his article "A Theory of Human Motivation," *Psychological Review*, L (1943), 370–96. See also Douglas McGregor, *The Human Side of Enterprise* (New York: McGraw-Hill Book Company, 1960), pp. 36–39, for an excellent restatement of Maslow's theory.

Maslow portrays man as a "perpetually wanting animal," driven to put forth effort (in other words, to work) by his desire to satisfy certain of his needs. To Maslow, these needs or wants can logically be thought of in terms of a hierarchy, for only one type of need is active at any given time. Only when the lowest and most basic of the needs in this hierarchy has been relatively well satisfied will each higher need become, in turn, operative. Thus, it is the *unsatisfied* need which actively motivates man's behavior. Once a need is more or less gratified, man's conduct is determined by new, higher needs which up until then have failed to motivate simply because man's attention has been devoted to satisfying his more pressing, lower needs. And the process is for most men (and, needless to say, women) unending, since few people can ever expect to satisfy, even minimally, *all* their needs.

At the lowest level in this Need Hierarchy, but paramount in importance until they are satisfied, are the *physiological* needs, particularly those for food, water, clothing and shelter. "Man lives by bread alone, when there is no bread"; in other words, any higher needs which he may have are inoperative when he is suffering from extreme hunger, for man's full attention must then necessarily be focused on this single need. But when the need for food and the other physiological essentials *is* fairly well satisfied, less basic or higher needs in the hierarchy start to dominate man's behavior, or to motivate him.

Thus, needs for *safety*—for protection against arbitrary deprivation, danger, and threat—take over as prime human motivators once man is eating regularly and sufficiently and is adequately clothed and sheltered. This is true because (1) a satisfied need is no longer a motivator of behavior, yet (2) man continues to be driven by needs, and (3) the safety needs are the next most logical candidates, beyond the physiological ones, to do this driving.

What happens when the safety needs have also been relatively satisfied, so that both of the lowest need levels no longer require man's attention? In Maslow's scheme of things, the *social* needs—for belonging, association, and acceptance by one's fellows—now are dominant, and man puts forth effort to satisfy *this* newly activated type of want.

Still higher needs which ultimately emerge to dominate man's consciousness, always assuming that the needs below them have been gratified, are in turn: *self-esteem* needs, especially for self-respect and self-confidence; *status* needs, for recognition, approval, and prestige; and, finally, *self-fulfillment* needs, for realization of one's own potential and for being as creative as possible.

All of this constitutes an oversimplification of Maslow's Need Hierarchy. Maslow himself qualified his concept in several ways, although only one of his reservations is important enough for our purposes to warrant inclusion here: he recognized that not all people follow the pattern depicted, and that both desires and satisfactions vary with the individual.

Even in the capsule form presented above, however, Maslow's contribution is of aid in explaining why workers join unions. The many research findings which now exist on this latter topic[28] basically agree that all employees endeavor to gratify needs and wants that are important to them, because of dissatisfaction with the extent to which these needs and desires have been met. They also agree that, while what is "important" among these needs and wants varies with the individual employee, much of the answer depends upon what has already been satisfied either within the working environment or outside of it. Many of these studies also support Maslow's hierarchy for the majority of workers in approximately the order of needs indicated by Maslow.

It should not be surprising that dissatisfaction with the extent of physiological need gratification is no longer a dominant reason for joining unions in this country. In our relatively affluent economy, few people who are working have any great difficulty in satisfying at least the most basic of these needs. In an earlier day, before the advent of minimum wage laws and other forms of legal protection, this was not as true and, as has already been suggested, union promises of a "living wage" were of great appeal to many workers. However, those members of the labor force who today are frustrated in trying to satisfy their minimal needs for food, clothing, and shelter are those who are *unemployed,* not the most logical candidates for union membership. The research substantiates this down-playing of the role of physiological needs rather conclusively. Significantly, one of the most thorough of the studies found that not one employee out of 114 workers in a large industrial local union became a union member primarily for this purpose.[29] (This is hardly to say that union members have lost interest in higher wages and other economic improvements. As will be shown later, the desire for these benefits persists as strongly as ever. The point is, however, that this desire now stems from *higher* need activation. Money can satisfy more than just the physiological needs.)

On the other hand, research suggests that dissatisfaction with the extent of gratification of (1) safety, (2) social, and (3) self-esteem needs—

---

[28] Perhaps the best of these studies are: E. Wight Bakke, "To Join or Not to Join," in E. Wight Bakke, Clark Kerr, and Charles W. Anrod, eds., *Unions, Management and the Public* (New York: Harcourt, Brace & World, Inc., 1960), pp. 79–85; Joel Seidman, Jack London, and Bernard Karsh, "Why Workers Join Unions," in *The Annals of the American Academy of Political and Social Science*, 274:84 (March 1951); and Ross Stagner, ed., *Psychology of Industrial Conflict* (New York: John Wiley & Sons, Inc., 1956).

[29] Seidman, London, and Karsh, *op. cit.*

in approximately that order—has motivated many workers to join unions. To a lesser extent, status and self-fulfillment needs have also led to union membership.

Unions are uniquely equipped, in the eyes of thousands of workers, to gratify safety needs. If very few of the 150,000 labor-management contracts currently in force in the United States are identical, at least this much can be said for virtually all of them: they are generally arrived at through *compromise,* and they define in writing the "rules of the game" which have been *mutually agreed upon* to cover the terms and conditions of employment of *all* represented workers for a specific future period of time. The union thus acts as an equal partner in the bilateral establishment of what the late Sumner H. Slichter called the "system of industrial jurisprudence." And, in the interests of minimizing conflict among the workers it represents, it strives to inject uniformity of treatment—particularly in the area of job protection—into the contract.

Union membership can consequently provide workers with some assurance against arbitrary management actions. The union can be expected to push for curbs against what it calls "management discrimination and favoritism" in, for example, job assignment, promotional opportunity, and even continued employment with the company. However well-meaning are a management's intentions, the company cannot guarantee that it will *not* at times act arbitrarily, for in the absence of such checks as the union places on its actions it is always acting unilaterally. Satisfaction of the safety needs—in the form of considerable protection against arbitrary deprivation, danger, and threat—is thus offered by the union in its stress on uniformity of treatment for all workers. Many employees, particularly after they have perceived "arbitrary" action by management representatives, have found the appeal irresistible.

The social needs are also known to be important, if secondary, motivators of union membership. Especially where the work itself must be performed in geographically scattered locations (as in many forms of railroad employment, truck-driving, or letter-carrying) or where the technology of the work minimizes on-the-job social interaction (as on the automobile assembly line), the local union can serve the function of a club, allowing the formation of close friendships built around a common purpose. But even when the work is not so structured, local unions foster a feeling of identification with those of like interests, often in pronounced contrast to the impersonality of the large organization in which the worker may be employed. Increasingly, unions have capitalized upon their ability to help satisfy social needs. As the latter have become more important to members of the labor force (not only because of the declining frustration of the lower needs but also because general leisure time has increased) unions have become increasingly ambitious in sponsoring such activities as vacation retreats, athletic facilities, and adult education programs for "members only." But unions have never been reluctant to publicize the social bonds which they allow: It is not by accident that internal union correspondence has traditionally been closed by the greeting "Fraternally yours," that the official titles of many unions have always included the word "Brotherhood," and that several labor organizations continue to refer to their local unions as "lodges."

Social *pressure* has also been instrumental in workers joining unions. Employees often admit that the disapproval of their colleagues would result from their not signing union application cards. Normally, the disapproval is only implied. The Seidman, London, and Karsh study, for example, unearthed such explanations from workers who had joined unions as "I can't think of a good reason except everybody else was in it" and "I suppose I joined in order to jump in line with the majority." On occasion, however, the pressure has been considerably more visible, as witness this quotation from the same study: "They approached you, kept after you, hounded you. To get them off my neck, I joined."

Other workers, at higher levels, have explained their union membership as being attributable mainly to their desire to ensure that they will have a direct voice, through union election procedures, in decisions which affect them in their working environments. Such employees tend to participate actively in union affairs and to use such phrases as "I wanted to have a voice in the system" rather freely. The underlying rationale of this behavior is a clear one: Managements do not normally put questions relating to employment conditions to worker vote; unions, however imperfectly, purport to be democratic institutions. To these workers, representation by a labor organization has appeared to offer the best hope in our complex, interdependent, and ever-larger-unit industrial society that their human dignity will not be completely crushed. On this basis, self-esteem needs can, at least to some extent, be appeased.

Finally, a relatively few other employees have found in the union an opportunity for realization of their highest needs, for status and self-fulfillment. They have joined with the hope of gaining and retaining positions of authority within the union officer hierarchy. For the employee with leadership ambitions, but with educational or other deficiencies which would otherwise condemn him to a life of prestige-lacking and unchallenging work, opportunities for further need satisfaction are thus provided.

Unionization, then, results from a broad network of worker needs. The needs for safety, social affiliation, and to a lesser extent self-esteem appear to be of primary importance to employees in contemporary America. And it would appear that these needs are being relatively well met by unions, or workers would have exercised their legally granted option of voting out unions in far greater measure than they have done.

This in no way minimizes the role of money and other economic benefits, for these emoluments—which unions have not been reluctant to seek even with their members' incomes at today's high levels—are clearly related to needs beyond the physiological. Health insurance and pensions lend protection against deprivation, for example, and wages themselves can increase not only safety but status. But it does emphasize the roles of protection against arbitrary treatment, formal group affiliation beyond the framework of the company, and—for some workers—an opportunity for participation in "the system." By definition, management can never itself satisfy either of the first two worker needs. Thus far, in unionized establishments, it has failed to satisfy employees on the last ground.

Two final remarks are in order. First, it has often been hypothesized that many workers join unions for *none* of the reasons cited above, but simply because they work where union membership is required for continued employment after their probationary period (the so-called "union shop" arrangement). While it is undeniable that some workers *do* join for this reason, the facts do not support the belief that they are numerous. Beginning in 1947, the American labor laws provided that only if a majority of workers in the bargaining unit voted for the union shop in a secret-ballot election supervised by the government would such a shop be permitted in a labor contract. In the next four years, 46,000 elections were held: 97 percent of them favored the union shop and 91 percent of the workers eligible to vote voted in favor of the arrangement. In 1951, the election provision was repealed as a waste of the taxpayer's money.

Second, although an explanation of "why workers join unions" can be reduced (as was done here) to relatively uncomplicated statements, for a specific worker the motivations may be considerably more involved, even encompassing several levels of need satisfaction at once. The summary offered is, if the research on which it is based is valid, sufficiently accurate to meet our own needs. By the same token, however, unionization is at times derived from a variety of complex variables and complete understanding of it must therefore necessarily rest on a situational foundation.

WHY MANAGERS RESIST UNIONS

Some time ago, after years of successfully withstanding union organization attempts, a small-scale New York City dress manufacturer discovered that a majority of his workers had finally become union members. Immediately thereafter, these employees struck for increased job security and improved pension benefits. On the very first morning of the strike, the manufacturer's wife—who was also the firm's bookkeeper—reported to work at her customary hour of 8 A.M. She was amazed to see her husband out on the picket line, addressing the strikers as follows: "Sam, you stand over there; Harry, you stand eight yards in back of Sam; and Leo, you come over here, eight yards behind Harry." The puzzled woman posed the natural question, "Jack, what on earth are you doing?" And the manufacturer replied, "I want they should right away know who's boss!"

The outcome of this particular labor-management struggle is unknown. But the episode nonetheless furnishes a clue as to one reason why managers are considerably less than enthusiastic about unions. As we have already seen, collective bargaining necessarily decreases the area of management discretion. Every contractual concession to the union subtracts from the scope that the company has for taking action on its own. As Bakke has put it, "A union is an employer-regulating device. It seeks to regulate the discretion of employers...at every point where their action affects the welfare of the men."[30] Yet it is the *manager* who tends ultimately to be held responsible for the success or failure of the business, and not the union. Hence company representatives feel that it is essential that they reserve *for themselves* the authority to make all major decisions, including those which the union might construe to be "affecting the welfare of the men." In short, they feel that they must still be allowed to remain, on all counts, "the boss."

Managers tend to be quite adamant on the subject. One company representative's thoughts are illustrative:

> Restriction on management freedom is a big issue.... We've got heavy responsibilities for making quick, accurate and effective decisions. Sometimes there are considerations that we can't divulge or that wouldn't be understood if we did. We're held responsible for the success of them, but the union isn't. It takes complicated maneuvering to run a business and all the parts have to be kept working together. You have to have a good deal of free play in the rope for that. Sometimes there is a particular restriction that gets your goat, but on the whole it's the over-all sense of being closed in on...that gets you. It's the cumulative effect of one area of freedom after another being reduced and the promise of still more that gives us real concern, but you make adjustments and go on to every particular one. It's not impossible, but you wonder how long it can go on and leave you able to meet your responsibilities.[31]

Behind such remarks as these is a managerial awareness, continuously reinforced for all administrators of profit-making institutions by day-to-day realities, that management hardly owes its exclusive allegiance to its

---

[30] E. Wight Bakke, *Mutual Survival: The Goal of Unions and Management* (New York: Harper & Row, Publishers, 1946), p. 7.
[31] *Ibid.,* p. 29.

employees. Clearly, employee needs are important and, for that matter, can be ignored for any length of time only with complete disregard for the continued solvency of the enterprise. But exactly the same can be said of the pressures exerted on management by the firm's customers, stockholders, competitors, and suppliers. Were those pressures not *opposing* ones management's job would be far easier than it is. Because there *are* so many points of conflict, an aggressive union can make the managerial role a highly difficult one.

The desire to retain decision-making authority is by no means, however, strictly attributable to a managerial desire for peace of mind. Unions undoubtedly do add to the personal unhappiness and consequent morale problems of managers, but the resistance to unionism is also often based on a genuine and deep concern for the welfare of *society*. Countless managers believe that only if management remains free to operate without union-imposed restrictions can American business continue to advance. And only through such progress, they believe, can it provide employment for our rapidly growing labor force, let this nation compete successfully in world markets, and increase general living standards. By decreasing company flexibility (in the form of work method controls, decreased work loads, increased stress on the seniority criterion in the allocation of manpower, and various other ways), it is argued, unions endanger the efficiency upon which continued industrial progress depends. And this is no less true, managers contend, just because these union demands are made in the name of such euphemistic goals as "job security," "equitability," and "democracy in the workplace."

A related employer fear is also held by many managers, although it is understandably given somewhat less publicity by them than is the previous argument. Such company representatives feel that in the absence of management's unhampered freedom to manage the optimum utilization of manpower will be lost to society. This argument assumes that there are strong elements of a process of natural selection at work in the industrial world and that, admittedly with some exceptions, those who rise to levels of great authority within it are those who have proven that they are best equipped to hold such places. Any attempt to undercut this authority—on the part of, for example, labor unions—consequently makes society the poorer.

On four different grounds, then—(1) that the manager must be allowed authority commensurate with his responsibility, (2) that unchecked union pressures may totally frustrate the manager in his role as the recipient of cross-pressures from many other institutional and market forces, (3) that unions limit company flexibility and thus endanger economic progress, and (4) that only by allowing managers maximum opportunity to manage is society furnished with an optimum allocation of manpower—union inroads are typically resisted by managements. There is, however, a common denominator to all four: Each argument seeks to ward off encroachments on management's *decision-making* powers.

Admittedly, even in the absence of unionism, management's ability to make decisions in the employee relations area is not an unlimited one. A widespread network of federal, state, and community legislation now governs minimum wages, hours of work, safety, and health, and a host of other aspects of employee life with complete impartiality as to whether or not the regulated firms are organized or nonunion. Moreover, where employers encounter tight labor markets (those in which new employees are difficult to recruit) they tend to accommodate at least their more visible personnel practices—wages and other economic benefits, in particular—to what the market demands. Finally, the prevalent values of our times must always be considered: The mores of society have an important influence on employers. And it is a hallmark of our ever more sophisticated society that workers expect to be governed by progressive personnel policies which are based on objective standards whenever possible. Most nonunion firms have attempted to conform to these values no less actively than have most unionized enterprises.

The fact remains, however, that managers who are not bound by the restrictions of labor agreements and who do not have to anticipate the possibility of their every action in the employee relations sphere being challenged by worker representatives through the grievance procedure have considerably more latitude for decision making than do their counterparts at unionized companies. One need not in any way sympathize with the management fear of unionism to *understand* this fear. Given the importance of the decision-making prerogative to managements, the managerial resistance to labor organizations—whether it stems directly from management self-interest or from a concern for the welfare of society—can at least be appreciated.

If the previous paragraphs help to explain the major reasons for management's jaundiced view of the labor union, they do not acknowledge other reasons which frequently *bolster* this view. There are, undoubtedly, several such reasons.

In the first place, many employers tend to look upon the union as an *outsider,* with no justifiable basis for interfering in the relationship between the company and its employees. The local union, with which the firm is most apt to engage in direct dealings, typically represents workers of many competitive companies, and hence by definition it cannot have the best interests of any particular firm at heart. Worse yet, runs this charge, the local is often part of a large, geographically distant international union, is closely controlled by the latter, and thus is not allowed to give adequate consideration to unique problems within its locality.[32] Beyond this, the union (whether local, international, or some intermediate body) has objectives and aspirations which are very different from those of the particular company: Where the company seeks to maximize profits within certain limits, the union seeks such goals as the maximization of its own membership and of its general bargaining power. These are objectives which the company can at best greet with apathy and at worst (when the pursuit of such goals is "subsidized" by the company in the form of its own concessions to the union) can view only with unhappiness.

Second, the manager may look upon the union as a *trouble-maker,* bent upon building cleavages between management and workers where none would otherwise exist. Even aside from the previously noted fact that the union grievance procedure allows all management actions which affect areas delineated in the labor contract to be challenged, and therefore regularly provides an opportunity for controversy which is normally absent in nonunion situations, there is some truth in this charge. Particularly where the union occupies an insecure status in the plant (possibly in the absence, for example, of the union shop), its leaders may find it essential to solicit grievances in order to keep the employees willing to pay union dues. But even where the labor organization does have such security, grievances may still be encouraged by union officials. Slichter, Healy, and Livernash pinpoint several possibilities:

> The purpose may be to harass management into accepting interpretations of the agreement that the union wants; or the purpose may be to develop a militant attitude among the members to help the union in negotiating new contracts. Some union representatives may stir up grievances ... in an effort to advance their political fortunes within the union or to build up interest in it. Finally, elected stewards or committeemen may lack the independence to handle weak cases.[33]

Third, many managers view unions as *underminers of employee loyalty* to the company. In order to understand this point of view one does not have to fully embrace the philosophy that high worker motivation levels depend upon appreciative employees who view the employer as a benefactor and work for him to a great extent out of gratitude. It is sufficient for the reader to imagine the reactions of any employer who has prided himself

---

[32] Not all employers lament the "outside" aspects of unionization. Many prefer the more detached viewpoints of international union representatives who *are* removed from the tensions and political considerations involved in day-by-day local labor relations. Some managers welcome, in addition, the stabilization of labor terms among otherwise competitive employers that frequently accompanies wider-scale bargaining.
[33] Slichter, Healy, and Livernash, *op. cit.,* p. 40.

on providing good wages and working conditions and showing a personal concern for the individual problems of his employees (perhaps tangibly evidenced by the voluntary payment of medical expenses to meet health emergencies and unsolicited loans to meet other financial crises) upon learning that a majority of his work force has suddenly decided to "go union." While this employer may use such epithets as "ingrates" in speaking of his *own* employees, it is more likely that the union itself will bear the brunt of his censure. It is human nature to attribute one's defeats to forces beyond one's own control ("an irresponsible union misleading our employees and turning them against the company") rather than to factors looked upon as controllable ("employee attitudes"). The previously cited facts that management can *never* itself provide either full protection against arbitrary treatment or formal group affiliation independent of the company are overlooked by company representatives at such moments. So, too, is a silver lining in the situation—namely, that it is entirely possible for workers to have dual loyalties, to the union *and* to the company.[34] In at least the early stages of the union-management relationship unions may be resisted for having subverted employee allegiance fully as much as they are opposed on the other grounds which have been noted.

A fourth root of tension, although it is applicable only to a minority of company executives, may arise simply because the previously discussed *reputation* of the labor movement has *preceded* the arrival of unionism in the plant. This has been a particularly influential factor in the resistance of some managers to collective bargaining in the recent past. Not being forced to deal with a union until now, and primarily because of this freedom knowing little more about labor unions than they have been informed by the mass media, such relatively unsophisticated employers have been alarmed by the widely publicized reports of irresponsible union strikes, union leader criminality, and featherbedding charges which have found their way onto newspaper front pages and through television antennae over the past decade. These managers have asked, in effect, "How can you expect us to welcome an institution whose representatives engage in such activities?"

Fifth, and rounding out the list of major causes of the corporate executive's opposition to organized labor, are the *major values of the labor*

---

[34] The most exhaustive study on the subject of "dual loyalties" is that of Father Theodore Purcell, conducted in the mid-1950s. Interviewing 202 workers in various departments at Swift and Company, he discovered that while at least 79 percent felt a definite allegiance to the union as an institution, 92 percent felt allegiance to the company. "Allegiance" was construed as an attitude of approval of the overall objectives of each institution, rather than strict loyalty. See Theodore V. Purcell, *Blue Collar Man* (Cambridge: Harvard University Press, 1960); and also *The Worker Speaks His Mind on Company and Union* (Cambridge: Harvard University Press, 1953), by the same author.

movement as these are perceived by management. Some of these values—a stress on seniority, work method controls, and decreased work loads—have already been mentioned in the context of "threats to decision making." There are, however, many other such shared union values which rankle management at least as much.

"Security," for example, has far more favorable connotations to unionists than it does to company representatives. Higher managers by definition have a history of successful achievement behind them and hence are willing to take chances because they are relatively optimistic as to the outcome. The average union member, feeling that the probabilities of his success in risk-taking are low and, indeed, often believing that he is running in a race that is fixed, presses the union leadership to obtain even greater protection for him in his *current* job.

"Democracy" is a hallmark of the union value structure, and union representatives who bargain with managements are usually elected through a process which at least claims to be democratic. Managers, whose hierarchy is based on merit and experience, are thus forced to bargain, often on issues with major ramifications for the company, with unionists who may have no better credentials for their role than the possession of a plurality of votes in a popularity poll.

And where the company representative speaks glowingly of "individualism" and declares that America's economic triumphs have been based upon it, the union sees itself as part of a social movement and places a premium on "group consciousness."

As for "efficiency," which scores high on the management scale of values, to the union it smacks of a callous disregard for worker dignity and even worker health. Accordingly, it is something to be regarded with deep suspicion by employee representatives and to be resisted whenever resistance is practicable.

Such comments as the above can, as was true of this chapter's treatment of "Why Workers Join Unions," be offered only as generalizations. For a specific union-management relationship, the value differences may hardly be as pronounced: The writers are personally familiar, for that matter, with several relationships where the *unions* seem to place far higher values on ability and efficiency than do the *managements*. Such value conflicts as the ones enumerated are, however, quite genuine in many union-management situations, and thus represent the realities of labor relations rather than its stereotypes. As such, they serve to reinforce management's opposition to unionism, however much this opposition may be anchored to such other reasons as the decision-making issue.[35]

[35] To this list of why employers resist unionization, some managers would probably add "status": it is, in certain management circles, quite a mark of distinction to be able to keep a union out. Such a reason is, however, somewhat less visible than are the ones outlined in the body of this section.

MANAGEMENT PHILOSOPHIES TOWARD UNIONS

Given the many different roots of management opposition, and the pervasiveness of so many of these, it is tempting to speculate that deep in their corporate hearts the basic attitude of most business enterprises must be one of intransigent hostility. Were this presumed attitude, in other words, to be stated as an official policy, it would read approximately, "We seek to weaken organized labor by any and all means at our command, to frustrate it in its demands, to grant it nothing which is not absolutely necessary, and—under no circumstances—to make any attempt at accepting the union as a permanent part of our employee relations. If we adhere to this approach consistently and with sufficient patience, our workers will see that the union offers them nothing. And they will ultimately arise and vote the union out at least as enthusiastically as they have voted it in."

There can be no denying that some executives do espouse this policy, and that at an earlier time in American labor history many managers did so. The irony of contemporary labor relations, however, is that despite management's continuing opposition to unionism and its constant resistance of new labor inroads, much of the employer community has substantially departed from such a provocative stance. It has moved instead to what Professor Lloyd Reynolds of Yale calls a "defensive endurance" philosophy: "If this is what our workers want, I guess we'll have to go along with it." In a word, the union is *accommodated,* however unwelcome and even unpalatable its presence may be. Management remains ever on guard as to "matters of principle," seeks to prevent the union from "intruding" in areas which are "the proper function of management," and frequently is highly critical of certain union actions. *But* the labor organization is taken for granted, harmony with it is sought wherever possible, and the employer can deal with the union on a day-by-day basis without feeling that conciliation has made him a traitor to his class. When one speaks of "maturity" in labor relations he is frequently thinking of this rapidly growing managerial posture—and organized labor's reciprocation of it.

A specific union-management relationship even in the early 1970's however, need not necessarily be marked by *either* employer attitude depicted above. Variety is still the essence of our labor relations system and so many variables can influence management policies that it is unrealistic to assume that the only possibilities are (1) intransigence and (2) accommodation. Variations in the abilities of managers to accurately understand the membership goals and leadership desires of the unions with which they are dealing, and in the statesmanship with which companies have met these union aspirations—to say nothing of the nature of these goals and desires themselves—have led to a wide diversity of management positions. So, too, have variations in the managers' own relative degree of security within the corporate framework, and the economic healths of the companies involved. Obviously, variations in union attitudes may be highly relevant. And the same can be said of such other variables as the past labor relationships between the parties, the technological environments of both the industry and the employer, and even the role of the government, where this is a factor. Most of these topics will receive fuller treatment in later chapters of this book. Here, it is pertinent to note the many grounds for differing attitudes toward unions among managerial groups.

Thus, although accommodation today is the dominant attitude, in many relationships having followed an era of intransigence, there are many variations on the theme of "management–labor relations philosophies." And even among the more general of these different philosophies at least six separate types (including the two above) can be distinguished.[36]

In reviewing these different possibilities for management policy, let it be clearly understood that in each case the company's ability to adopt the avenue under description depends upon a factor which is beyond its direct control: The union's own basic policy for *its* dealings with management. The labor organization, obviously, must reciprocate in kind and in the absence of such reciprocation, at least in the long run, management's chosen approach becomes a completely fruitless one. In short, the company can *work toward* each of the following approaches, but this managerial project will always be subject to some modification depending upon the union's response.

1. *Conflict,* or the intransigent, uncompromising attitude depicted previously, is now fast fading from the labor relations scene. Nonetheless, this attitude existed on a wide scale prior to World War II. Such a managerial stance arose to a great extent because many companies were newly organized before that time, and because union organizational campaigns have never been notable for their sensitivities to personal feelings. As Selekman has stated:

> The [union] organizers dramatize and make tangible [their] appeals ...by personifying whatever stands in the way of these objective as enemies who must be fought....

[36] The late Benjamin M. Selekman was justifiably considered one of the foremost theoreticians in this field, although he generally portrayed "bargaining relationships" and not merely the management "portion" of these relationships. The exposition which follows bears a strong indebtedness to his work (although it departs from it on several major points), and particularly to his *Labor Relations and Human Relations* (New York: McGraw-Hill Book Company, 1947), his "Varieties of Labor Relations," *Harvard Business Review,* XXVII (March 1949), 177–85, and his "Framework for Study of Cases in Labor Relations," in *Problems in Labor Relations,* 3rd ed., coauthored with S. H. Fuller, T. Kennedy, and J. M. Baitsell (New York: McGraw-Hill Book Company, 1964), pp. 1–11. See also Frederick H. Harbison and John R. Coleman, *Goals and Strategy in Collective Bargaining* (New York: Harper & Row, Publishers, 1951).

The organizer will of course make full use of the actual executives and supervisors in the plant if their past behavior affords substance for the antagonism he is mobilizing. But he will also evoke hostility by stereotyped images of "the other side." Behind any employer, for instance, the average worker is made to see the so-called "profit maker" ..., the inhuman corporate "interests" generally, or just the harsh figure of authority.... Employers who have long prided themselves upon fair dealing with their men only to be shaken by hostility thus unexpectedly turned toward them should probably realize that they too have been temporarily assimilated into these hate images or symbols.[37]

The union, consequently, does more than "undermine employee loyalty to the company" at such a time: it frequently goes well beyond the borders of the factual and bruises management egos in the process. Add managerial fears of decision-making encroachments and of union values which are antithetical to those of management, as well as the other grounds for management's opposition to unionism on top of such an emotion-charged atmosphere, and it should not be surprising that many companies in the period immediately following their unionization embraced a philosophy of "no acceptance" of the union. Only in the face of the law and union power could unions extract concessions from such managements, and then only quite begrudgingly and on as temporary a basis as possible.

Some companies are, of course, even today among the newly organized, since new union conquests hardly ended with the unionization of the major mass-production industries in the 1933–41 period. And it is in the labor relations of these enterprises, indeed, that one is most apt today to encounter the conflict philosophy. But this managerial attitude is not *confined* to new bargaining relationships: a minority of long-organized companies also currently adheres to it, owing to changes in management personnel, changes in union personnel, or various other factors—including the particular management's sheer refusal to abandon the hope that if unions are never really accepted by their companies they will eventually also lose acceptance from their worker-members. In recent years, various newspaper publishers throughout the country have seemed, to many observers, to epitomize this latter situation.

Such an attitude does not lead to amicable labor relations. It can also be expected to foster union militancy, as the union reacts by engaging in various pressure tactics (often including slowdowns of production and sudden "wildcat" strikes) to gain through these means what it cannot hope to procure at the bargaining table. Finally, managements embracing a "conflict" philosophy run a decided risk of being found in violation of the labor laws, particularly those involving "refusal to bargain" and discrimination against employees for the purpose of discouraging membership in a union.

[37] Selekman, *Labor Relations and Human Relations,* p. 20.

It is primarily for these reasons that many conflict philosophies have either been dismissed as realistic management alternatives in the first place, or given way to:

2. An *Armed Truce* attitude. Here company representatives are motivated by approximately the following logic: "We are well aware that the vital interests of the company and the union are poles apart, and that they always will be. But this doesn't mean that every action we take in our labor relations should be geared to weakening the union and thus forcing head-on conflict with it. Instead, since we can expect the union to firmly press to extend its fields of interest, our basic mission is to press, just as ambitiously, toward containing it *within* limits. We will honor the law immaculately, and therefore deal with the union without any subterfuges on the subjects of wages, hours, and conditions of employment; but we will hold our bargaining practice strictly within the *boundaries* of these legal obligations, and thus define our negotiation scope as rigidly as possible. Moreover, we will *strictly* interpret any agreements which emerge from these negotiations and insist upon the union observing, in its day-to-day conduct, its contractual obligations 100 percent."

Even today, many union-management relationships have made no more progress than this. The union representatives return the feelings of their management counterparts and the struggle for power goes on indefinitely. Wages, hours, and other rigidly construed employee relations areas are dealt with as their issues arise, but the more crucial question of union security versus management rights, being insoluble in such an atmosphere, continually blocks more constructive dealings. With some justification, the General Electric Company is frequently regarded as an excellent example of a company which has espoused this Armed Truce philosophy.

3. *Power Bargaining,* as an alternative, is only slightly more conducive to solving labor relations problems than is the Armed Truce approach. As is *not* the case under either Conflict or Armed Truce, managers in Power Bargaining can "accept" the union and, in fact, tend to pride themselves on their sense of "realism" which leaves them no choice but to acknowledge the union's power. (A prerequisite for this philosophy, obviously, is that the union *have* significant power.) By the same token, such executives press their own company's bargaining power to the maximum that economic and other conditions at any one time allow. To paraphrase Selekman, the managerial rationale is: "We face strong and deeply entrenched unions squarely and with an accurate perception of their power—and we accept them as sovereign spokesmen for their side. We are practical men and economic realists, not crusaders with a naïve faith in idealistic trimmings. Our task is not to pursue the fruitless approach of directly opposing and limiting the union, but to increase and then use our *own* power to offset that of the other side where we can."

Might does not necessarily make right, but it can lead to agreement at the bargaining table. And on this basis it can be argued that continued controversy is minimized in Power Bargaining. However unenthusiastically, managements in such a relationship can live with their unions, for at least the short run, in most areas affecting employee relations.

On the other hand, any relationship focused upon a balance of power is a highly tenuous one. It always contains the danger of regression to one of the earlier approaches when the power ratios change. As such, Power Bargaining has not been widespread at any one time in American labor relations, although many industries marked by small employers and highly centralized unions have at one time or another seen it. In such cases, the employers have typically associated in an attempt at a united front to counter the union's strength.

In short, for the reasons indicated, most managements in the current economy view all three previous alternatives as unsatisfactory. Since, needless to say, their unions wholeheartedly agree with them on this point, the climate for a more harmonious relationship—in the form of accommodation—exists.

4. *Accommodation*, however, is hardly the same as "cooperation." As pointed out earlier, management remains constantly vigilant as to "principle" and, as does the union, clings to such values as "orbits of respective equities and privileges." In this regard, Accommodation differs little from Armed Truce. Moreover, the management gaze is still riveted upon the traditional agenda of collective bargaining—wages, hours, and conditions of employment—and there is a selfconscious employer unwillingness to *officially* discuss anything which cannot rather rigidly be construed as falling within these topics.

The property of Accommodation which makes it unique lies in the area of everyday *practice* rather than in formal declarations. Once again, Dr. Selekman has provided a definitive description—in this case of what results in daily affairs when a management philosophy of "meeting the union halfway" is reciprocated by the labor organization:

> ... within these bounds (of "principles," "equities" and "privileges") the leaders, the ranks, and the organizations... interact within comfortable "customary," familiar patterns of behavior. They have evolved their routines of recognizing functions and settling differences. They have learned how to adjust one to another..., to accept the reduction of conflict as an accomplishment without demanding its total elimination. They have proved themselves willing to... conciliate whenever necessary, and to tolerate at all times.[38]

Note that such a definition in no way implies that the company need

[38] Selekman, Fuller, Kennedy, and Baitsell, *Problems in Labor Relations*, p. 7.

go out of its way to *help* organized labor. For that matter, opposition to the concept of unionism in general may still remain the hallmark of management's philosophy, as it frequently does. In an atmosphere of Accommodation, however, the roles of both emotion and raw power are minimized, in favor of the company's *adjusting* to the union *as it is*. Extreme legalism in at least the basic areas of wages, hours, and conditions is supplanted by compromise, flexibility, and "toleration." As such, Accommodation constitutes a considerably more positive approach to labor relations than do any of the previous alternatives.

There is ample evidence that the mainstream of American management has today entered the accommodation stage in its dealings with unions. The process of adjustment is still, as Slichter, Healy, and Livernash point out in their authoritative study, "neither complete nor uniform": Mutual accommodation of the parties' goals and policies has gone farthest in such areas as employee benefits, discipline, work scheduling, and development of grievance procedures, and least far in the areas of production standards, promotion principles, work assignment, and subcontracting.[39] And, not surprisingly, there is still wide variation in the nature and quality of contract administration among companies and even among plants within the same company. But the growth of Accommodation has quite visibly resulted in the significant development of mutually acceptable policy and in more orderly day-to-day union-management relations, results which even the great diversity of labor relations cannot obscure.

5. *Cooperation,* involving full acceptance of the union as an active partner in a formal plan, is for exactly that reason decidedly rare. It necessitates a management (as well as a union) which is willing to extend matters of everyday union-management relations beyond the traditional areas to such broader fields as technological change, waste, and business solvency. And this, in turn, calls for corporate executives who genuinely believe that unions can make definite and positive contributions to the success of the firm, through furnishing management with information which it would not otherwise have, through winning over worker support for management goals, and in various other ways.

In a formal plan for cooperation, the management supports not only the right but the *desirability* of union participation, and the union reciprocates by actively endorsing the company's right and need for an adequate return on its investment. The two labor relations parties *jointly* deal with both personnel and production problems as they occur. Suggestions pertaining to cost reduction and productivity improvement are typically solicited from all worker levels. And whatever economic gains in increased efficiency may be realized from such cooperative projects are normally shared by the company with the work force.

---

[39] Slichter, Healy, and Livernash, *op. cit.,* p. 958.

Most companies which have adopted this approach to labor relations have, by and large, been well publicized, either as participants in rather formalized "Scanlon Plans" or, as in the case of the Kaiser Steel Corporation, independently. But the very fact that so much publicity *has* been given to these plans based on the cooperative approach graphically symbolizes how few in number they have been thus far. Moreover, the approach is still so incompatible with present-day management (and, often, union) value systems that to date most such plans have been implemented only as a last resort, when the company was faced with a severe financial crisis. The word "cooperation" is frequently used in management addresses to worker groups, but in the managers' lexicon of the early 1970s it obviously has a meaning which is considerably more restricted than the one depicted here.

As different as each of the previous five approaches to labor relations is from the four others, there is a common denominator: Whichever one is selected is, subject to its ability to meet management goals, at the outset strictly the company's business. Ultimately, a Conflict approach may lead to a strike involving government intervention, or an amassing of strength in a Power Bargaining situation may have other legal ramifications, and in any of the five cases the *union* may, of course, react in such a way to make the approach unsuitable. The company can hardly do much with Accommodation if the union is Conflict-oriented. But at least at the outset the company is perfectly free to experiment with any of the various approaches.

The same *cannot* be said of one other approach, *Collusion.* If, up until now, the enumerated management alternatives can be viewed as leading to successively more union-management harmony (from conflict on the one hand to cooperation on the other), this one can be looked upon as generating "too much harmony." Our public policy, needless to say, is designed to prevent it from serving as a workable labor relations alternative.

To Selekman, alternative (6), *Collusion,* constitutes

> "cooperation" (which) generates problems that extend beyond the specific structure of relationship to affect adversely the legitimate interests of other employers, other workers, and the consuming public. For the collusive parties to collective bargaining connive to control their market, supplies, or prices, or to engage in practices of mutual interest to serve their exclusive advantage. They cooperate but through a form of jointly established monopoly which is frankly unconcerned with every legitimate interest except their own. The courts... and the watchfulness of competitors, rival unions, and public representatives no doubt will continue to curb these questionable deals.[40]

To such curbs might be added the sheer unwillingness of both companies and their unions, in all but a relatively few black-mark situations,

[40] Selekman, Fuller, Kennedy, and Baitsell, *Problems in Labor Relations,* p. 8.

to attempt such arrangements in the first place. Employer bribes to union officials to agree to substandard or "sweetheart" labor contracts and various other illegal pursuits have hardly been unknown to American labor history. But such collusion has been almost exclusively confined to narrow sectors of local market industries, with marginal and intensely competitive employers for whom a small difference in labor cost can mean the difference between solvency and insolvency and where visibility to the public law-enforcement agencies is relatively slight. Having named the least ethical sectors of the garment trades, building trades, trucking, waterfront, and entertainment industries, one has almost exhausted the list.

SOME CONCLUDING REMARKS ON THE CURRENT QUALITIES OF LABOR-MANAGEMENT RELATIONSHIPS

"Anyone," the noted arbitrator Theodore W. Kheel once remarked, "who starts a sentence by saying that 'the trouble with labor or management is' is bound to be partially right but mostly wrong."[41] Such sweeping generalizations as the one cited are highly hazardous in most areas of life, but in a field which is as varied as labor relations they are wholly unwarranted.

It is hoped that in pointing up the various "multiplicities"—of causes for workers joining unions, of reasons why managers resist unions, and of employer philosophies themselves—the dangers of being overly cavalier in *interpretation* have also been implied. Maslow's Need Hierarchy does not always fall neatly into place in linking Specific Employee X to his labor organization. And when one analyzes the motivations of "workers" as a general grouping he may be equally far off base unless he recognizes that a variety of *different* need-motivated reasons may be *simultaneously* at play. The management resistance to union inroads is, in turn, also derived from a wide array of specific causes, even though the desire to retain decision-making authority in managerial hands lies at the heart of most of them. And employer *philosophies* concerning unionism can run a gamut from intransigent hostility on the one hand to complete "togetherness" in the form of collusion on the other, although neither of these extremes is common. The various frameworks presented in this chapter can serve as useful guides for specific analyses, but a little knowledge has at times been known to be a dangerous thing. Let the student beware!

Moreover, if variations in (1) worker expectations from their unions,

[41] Theodore W. Kheel, "A Labor Relations Policy for 1964," *Personnel Journal*, April 1964, p. 181.

(2) employer grounds for resisting unionism, and (3) company attitudes in implementing this resistance account *by themselves* for much present-day diversity in labor relationships, *other* factors augment this diversity. To recall only a few which were cited in this chapter, the current financial states of the individual companies (and industries) may serve as an influential variable. So, too, may technological change confronting both the industry and the employer, *past* relationships between the parties, the goals of the leaders themselves on both sides of the bargaining table, management's degree of perception regarding labor situations; and, of relevance for some relationships, the prospects for governmental intervention, including an assessment of the form which this is likely to take.

And this is to say nothing of the differences between one union *as an institution* and another, a topic which has been intentionally deferred for extensive treatment in Chapter 4. Let it suffice to state here that unions exhibit a heterogeneity all their own. In a very important sense, indeed, there has never been a literal "labor movement" in this country. The AFL-CIO is a loose federation with very limited power. Bargaining is carried out by the highly diverse international unions, each with its particular traditions, structure, and government, and by the constituent locals and other subgroups of the internationals. Even today, despite a strong trend toward international union control over local union activities, a few international unions perform little more than bookkeeping functions, with the locals exercising almost complete autonomy. Other internationals are highly centralized and local independence in any sphere is virtually nonexistent. Organized labor is broad enough, too, to contain: (1) the Teamsters Union, which represents to many people a prime form of "business unionism," with its leaders utilizing the union as "a marketing cooperative to sell so many head of labor to employers at the highest market price"[42] and in no way being concerned with general social reform; (2) the United Automobile Workers, whose long-time president Walter P. Reuther (killed in a plane crash in May 1970) was frequently thought of as the nation's foremost "social unionist"; and (3) the garment unions, which have—through ambitious union-financed projects ranging from cooperative housing to adult education programs—made unionism for *their* constituents a "way of life." In short, there are unions and there are unions.

Any of the variables enumerated above can be crucial to the molding of a specific labor-management relationship. At any one time, several of them are apt to be at work in influencing the nature of this relationship. And, given this situation, the great variety in the subject areas, wordings, and lengths of the nation's 150,000 labor-management contracts, which

---

[42] Lester Velie, *Labor U.S.A.* (New York: Harper & Row, Publishers, 1959), p. 14.

serve as tangible (if, as will be seen, not always completely accurate) symbols of labor relationships, is understandable.

Certainly, there is no reason to expect a contract for the five waitresses in a New Hampshire restaurant to bear any resemblance to the International Brotherhood of Teamsters' nationwide trucking agreement. Any great similarity between the General Electric Company–International Union of Electrical Workers document and that negotiated by the Lace Workers and their marginal employer in Honeysuckle, Mississippi, would likewise constitute a striking coincidence.

Can *any* remarks, then, in the face of all of these variables, be applied even to merely the "majority" of the contracts in this country? Some statements can *still* be made, and even as ambitious a phrase as "the *vast* majority of all agreements" will support them.

For all their variations, almost all labor contracts today validate a particular institutional status for the union and well over two-thirds of them incorporate the union shop arrangement, requiring union membership for continued employment. The vast majority of the agreements reveal what the parties have agreed to as being "vested exclusively in the company," either explicitly (in a so-called "management rights" article) or implicitly (in indirect language which is scattered throughout the contract). They announce, in more or less detail, the increasingly broad range of wage, hour, and other economic-related employment conditions under which the employees have agreed to be governed. They incorporate a variety of administrative clauses dealing with work rules and job tenure. And they outline the procedures for settling the disputes that will inevitably arise during the life of the agreement, as well as providing for a renegotiation of the contract when its duration has been exhausted.

These are no small accomplishments. Real or imaginary threats to job security, to the union's existence, to what managers deem their "freedom to run" their own businesses, and to what employees refer to as "fair" conditions are regularly involved. Yet the signing of any contract requires some form of mutual agreement and, most often, some major concessions by both the management and the union. It is tribute to the increasing maturity of both parties that so much progress has been made in this direction over the past three decades. This is particularly true when one considers not only the drastic technological and economic changes that have taken place in our society since the Great Depression but also the many direct grounds for open conflict between labor and management which have existed ever since.

A host of other accomplishments, which will be given liberal treatment in the pages that follow, also bears testimony to the ability of the labor relations system to adjust itself to accommodate new needs and desires. The spread of the seniority principle, under which the employee with the longest service receives preference in various employment matters, has minimized employee demands for both "justice" and "objective personnel management." On these morale-building grounds it has also had considerable appeal—when used in moderation—to many managements. Moreover, the almost complete acceptance by the parties of binding arbitration by a neutral as the final step in the grievance procedure, thus normally ruling out work stoppages during the term of the agreement, has also injected much stability into labor relations. And the same can be said of the growth of long-term contracts—now commonly three years in duration instead of the traditional one-year basis. Nor can one overlook the contractual adjustments to the spread of the many new employee "fringe" benefits which have arisen in this period. Bilateral statesmanship must receive some credit, too, for the satisfactory contractual resolution, at least over time, of many knotty problems involving technological change and unionized workers.

The labor contract, admittedly, forms only the bare skeleton of the total relationship between a union and a management. As is also true of both the marriage contract and the citizen's income tax report, it is little more than a legal prerequisite to harmony: by itself it does not produce rapport. To evaluate accurately any labor relationship, one must know the degree of mutual trust and good will that lies in back of the written agreement, to say nothing of the extent to which supplementary documents and verbal understandings may affect the wording printed on the contract pages. Finally, no contract is any better than its *administration:* The contract incorporates a body of rules, but this does not guarantee that both parties will always interpret these rules in the same way. Moreover, the fact that agreements can never hope to explicitly cover all contingencies means that there will always be at least the chance for future disagreement. In short, a variety of problems affecting the relationship can surround even the most harmonious appearing labor contract.

Judged by any available standard, however, the considerable progress and increasing maturity which is at least *symbolized* by the contractual contents has marked *all* portions of union-management relations over the past very few decades. One can accept the Slichter, Healy, and Livernash verdict that the process of accommodation is "neither complete nor uniform" without in any way negating the more basic conclusions of these three scholars that

> the American collective bargaining system must be regarded as one of the most successful economic institutions in the country. In the great majority of plants it has produced rules and policies that are fair to both

sides and that permit managements to conduct operations efficiently. Although there is wide variation in the results of bargaining, the concentration of settlements that are good compromises is large ... (and) experience to date evidences a degree of social progress that few would have predicted (at the end of the 1930s).[43]

The reader is invited to postpone his own agreement (or disagreement) with these opinions until the contents of the various areas cited in the preceding paragraphs are treated more fully. Part III's six chapters are totally reserved for this latter purpose: Chapter 5, for an examination of management and union behavior at the bargaining table; Chapter 6, for the treatment of contract administration; Chapters 7 and 8, for description and analysis of the major economic issues with which collective bargaining is now involved; and Chapters 9 and 10, for a relatively detailed inspection of the basic institutional and administrative issues in the current labor-management sphere.

If one does acquiesce at this early point, however, is there also justification for assuming that the mainstream of our labor relations system today stands on the threshold of a great new era to which strikes will be entirely foreign and where "harmony" will be the universal guiding rule?

Despite all the progress to date, such a prophecy would, we think, be extremely naïve. It can be expected that managements will continue to oppose the concept of unionism and to resist new union inroads as energetically as ever, for the roots of this opposition are essentially rational ones *as judged by management values.* By the same token, there is little reason to believe that unions will not continue to press for an ever-greater narrowing of the scope of management discretion, in the interests of obliging worker wants and needs as *they* view these. Indeed, in the years immediately ahead the stresses between the parties seem destined to *grow:* The recent intensification of industrial price and technological competition has already pitted an accelerated employer search for greater efficiency against an equally determined union campaign for increased job security.

Since a labor relations millennium *is* far distant, it seems a safe prediction that occasional impasses will continue to be reached by labor and management, and that these will result in strike actions, as they have in the past.

There is both an irony and a serious threat for our system of free collective bargaining in the inevitability of future strikes. If labor relations progress has clearly been evident, the community has also increased its expectations from union-management relations. Indeed, as Livernash has pointed out, "Our level of aspiration rises perhaps more rapidly than realized progress. In this situation, there is always some feeling of impatience

---

[43] Slichter, Healy, and Livernash, *op. cit.,* pp. 960–61.

with the degree of progress of private institutions and a desire for increased governmental control."[44]

Our system of industrial jurisprudence has thus far remained essentially in private hands despite an ever deeper penetration of government regulations (described in Chapter 3). This toleration for private decision making is consistent with the dominant values of our society, particularly with its premium on maximum freedom of action for both individuals and organizations. But the possibility that a tripartite labor relations system, with the government as a full-fledged participant, will ultimately supplant the present bipartite system can never be overlooked. Whether or not what is still "free collective bargaining" will be allowed to continue will depend to no small degree on the ability of the current system to continue its progress sufficiently and in time to satisfy the increasingly high level of public expectation. The fact that there is still much room for improvement in labor-management relations makes the entire system as it currently exists a vulnerable one.

DISCUSSION QUESTIONS

1. George P. Schultz and John R. Coleman have argued that "there is at least some excuse for the inability of all of us to understand unionism as fully as we might like to: There is just too much to understand." How much knowledge and understanding of labor-management relations *does* it appear realistic to expect from the course in which this book is currently being used, and *why?*
2. "Unions have outlived their usefulness, if indeed they ever had any, for at least the many employees whose managements deal with them on the basis of enlightened, worker-oriented policies." Discuss.
3. From your own experience (first- or second-hand), which case regarding future union penetration of the white-collar field is more persuasive with you: the relatively "pessimistic" one, as advanced in this chapter, or the more "optimistic" one which has also been presented on the previous pages?
4. The authors' own qualified endorsement of A. H. Maslow's theory of motivation notwithstanding, how valuable do you personally view this theory in understanding "why workers join unions"?
5. From the viewpoint of *society,* is there anything to be said for the union's role as an "employer-regulating device," seeking (in Bakke's words) "to regulate the discretion of employers...at every point where their action affects the welfare of the men"?
6. "Even if some of the day-by-day values of management and labor are not fully compatible, in the last analysis the *basic goals* of the two parties are identical." Evaluate.
7. What *primary* standards do you feel should be adopted by anyone attempting to evaluate the current performance of labor-management relations in this country, and why?

[44] Arthur A. Sloane and E. Robert Livernash, *Note on Collective Bargaining in the United States* (Cambridge: Harvard University Press, 1961), p. 35.

8. Reflecting upon his distinguished career as vice president and general counsel of the Pittsburgh Plate Glass Corporation, Leland Hazard once wrote: "I have rarely had occasion to modify the axiom: scratch a labor problem, and you will find a management problem." What considerations might have led to this observation?

SELECTED REFERENCES

Bok, Derek C., and John T. Dunlop, *Labor and the American Community*. New York: Simon & Schuster, 1970.

Cole, David L., *The Quest for Industrial Peace*. New York: McGraw-Hill Book Company, 1963.

Harbison, Frederick H., and John R. Coleman, *Goals and Strategy in Collective Bargaining*. New York: Harper & Row, Publishers, 1951.

Healy, James J., ed., *Creative Collective Bargaining*. Englewood Cliffs, N. J.: Prentice-Hall Inc., 1965.

Maslow, A. H., *Motivation and Personality*. New York: Harper & Row Publishers, 1954.

Purcell, Theodore V., *Blue Collar Man*. Cambridge, Mass.: Harvard University Press, 1960.

Reynolds, Lloyd G., *Labor Economics and Labor Relations*, 4th ed. Englewood Cliffs, N.J.: Prentice-Hall, Inc., 1964, pp. 141–58.

Selekman, Benjamin M., *Labor Relations and Human Relations*. New York: McGraw-Hill Book Company, 1947.

Slichter, Sumner H., James J. Healy, and E. Robert Livernash, *The Impact of Collective Bargaining on Management*. Washington, D.C.: The Brookings Institution, 1960, pp. 1–26.

Wolfbein, Seymour L., ed., *Emerging Sectors of Collective Bargaining*. Braintree Mass.: D. H. Mark Publishing Company, 1970.

part two

The Environmental Framework

2

The Historical Framework

As is true of other established disciplines, there is still some controversy as to the returns inherent in the study of history. For every Shakespeare asserting that "what is past is prologue" or a Santayana who proclaims that "those who do not understand history are condemned to repeat its mistakes," there is a Henry Ford declaring that "history is a pack of tricks that we play on the dead," and that the field is, in fact, "bunk."

No one can claim to understand present-day institutions, however, unless he has at least some basic knowledge of their roots. It would make a considerable difference to those who are either hopeful or fearful that labor unions will ultimately fade from the industrial scene, for example, if unions were purely a phenomenon of the last few years (and thus potentially destined for extinction when environmental conditions change), rather than being—as they are—organizations of relatively long standing in the economy. Similarly, only by recognizing what workers have expected of their unions in the past is one entitled even to begin to pass judgment on the present performance of organized labor. This chapter thus attempts to provide the reader with a necessary working knowledge of American labor history.

THE EIGHTEENTH CENTURY: GENESIS OF THE AMERICAN LABOR MOVEMENT

If labor unions connote *permanent* employee associations which have as their primary goal the preservation or improvement of employment conditions, there were no such institutions in America until the closing years of the eighteenth century. Concerted actions of workingmen in the form of strikes and slowdowns were not unknown to the colonial period, but these disturbances were, without exception, spontaneous efforts. They were conducted on the spur of the moment over temporary grievances, such as withholding of wages. Generally unsuccessful, they were never undertaken by anything resembling "permanent" organizations.

Given the dimensions of the labor movement today and the variety of seemingly compelling reasons why workers have attached themselves to it, this total absence of labor unions for well over a century calls for an immediate explanation.

In these years of simple handicraft organization there were, in fact, at least *four* forces at work which served to weaken any motivation that workers might otherwise have had for joining together on a long-term basis.

In the first place, the market for the employer's product was both local and essentially noncompetitive. Workingmen were thus allowed close social ties with the owner, often performing their work in the owner's home. In addition, they could maintain a comparatively relaxed pace of production in such an atmosphere.

Second, both the laws of supply and demand and government regulations allowed employees a large measure of job security at this time. Labor of all kinds, and particularly skilled craft labor, was in short supply in the colonies. In addition, a series of colonial labor laws calling for apprenticeship service prior to many kinds of employment and carefully circumscribing the conditions under which employees could be discharged offered further protection to jobholders.

Third, the existence of ample cheap land in the West meant that the dissatisfied artisan or mechanic could always move on should either local adversity or the spirit of adventure strike him. Many workers did migrate to the ever-expanding frontier, allowing even more advantageous employment conditions for those who remained: incomes increased all the more in the East, to the point where by some estimates wages were twice those paid to workers in Britain.

Finally, the low ratio of labor to natural resources in the frontier nation helped ensure that price rises would lag behind the wage increases. Assistant Secretary of the Treasury Coxe, sounding very much like a twentieth-century Chamber of Commerce manager, could—even as late as 1790—assert with considerable justification that "though the wages of the industrious poor are very good, yet the necessaries of life are cheaper than in Europe, and the articles used are more comfortable and pleasing."[1]

Ironically, however, the development of the frontier laid the groundwork for the birth of bona fide labor organizations. An expanded system of transportation built around canals and turnpikes was simultaneously linking the new nation's communities and allowing the capitalists of the late eighteenth century to enlarge their product markets into the beginnings of "nationwide" ones. The merchant who was unwilling or unable to respond to the challenge was left by the wayside as competitive pressures forced each businessman to find cost-cutting devices in the newly unsheltered atmosphere. The more imaginative employers located such devices: to decrease labor costs, they introduced women and children to their workplaces, farmed out work to prison inmates, and generally cut the wages of males who remained in their employ. For good measure, they frequently increased the hours in the work day (at no increase in pay), minutely subdivided the work into more easily assimilated (but commensurately more repetitive and monotonous) operations, and hired aggressive overseers to enforce newly tightened work standards.

The less-skilled workingman could react to these unwelcome changes by moving to the frontier. Not having invested much in the way of time or education in learning his current job, he might also attempt to move occupationally to more desirable kinds of work. The skilled worker, on the other hand, had mastered his craft through years of apprenticeship and was no longer occupationally mobile.

Some skilled craftsmen did move to the frontier. But the extension of the product market meant that their new masters were still not free to ignore labor cost-cutting methods: suits tailored in Ohio competed now with those made in Boston. Nor could the craftsmen count any longer on advancing into the class of masters themselves: the scope of manufacturing was necessarily greater and to enter the employer ranks it now took capital on a scale not ordinarily available to most wage-earners. Basically, the skilled workers' alternatives were to passively accept the wage cuts, the competition of nonapprenticed labor, and the harsh working conditions, or to join in collective action against such employer innovations. Increasingly, by the end of the eighteenth century, they chose the latter course of action.

[1] Lloyd Ulman, *American Trade Unionism—Past and Present* (Berkeley, Calif.: Institute of Industrial Relations, 1961), p. 367.

THE FIRST UNIONS AND THEIR LIMITED SUCCESSES

These early trade unions—individually encompassing shoemakers, printers, carpenters, tailors, and artisans of similar skill levels—waged blunt attacks on the changes brought about by the extension of markets. Their members agreed upon a wage level and pledged not to work for any employer who refused to pay this amount. They also bound themselves not to work alongside of any employee who did not receive the basic minimum or who had not served the customary period of apprenticeship for the trade. In addition, most of these craft unions attempted to negotiate closed shop agreements, whereby only those who were union members in the first place would be employed at all. Whatever agreement was subsequently struck with the employer, little trust was placed in him by the representatives of his workers: the union sent a "walking delegate" to walk around from shop to shop on a regular basis and thus ensure that the wages and conditions of the contract were being honored. Later, "tramping committees" of union delegates performed the same function.

Generally proving themselves willing to strike, if need be, in support of their demands, the early unions were at times surprisingly successful in achieving them. And although work stoppages of the day were typically both peaceful and short in duration, the new worker aggressiveness which they symbolized was sufficient to bring on considerable countervailing action from the employers.

The masters turned to two sources: organization in employers' associations and aid from the courts. Societies of otherwise competitive master masons, carpenters, shoemakers, printers, and other employers of skilled labor were quickly established in most urban areas where union activity was pronounced, for the purposes of holding down wages and destroying labor combinations wherever these existed. Attacking on a second front, the masters also turned to the judges and urged prosecution of their workers' organizations as illegal conspiracies in restraint of trade. The jurists were quickly convinced: The Journeyman Cordwainers (shoemakers) of Philadelphia were found guilty of joining in such a conspiracy by striking in 1806, and within the next decade a variety of similar court cases had also resulted in shattering defeats for the worker organizations. Not until 1842, indeed, with the famous *Commonwealth* v. *Hunt* decision in Massachusetts that strikes could be legal if they were undertaken for legal purposes, did the judges even begin to modify the harsh tenets of the *Cordwainer* doctrine when requested to rule on union affairs by employers.

If the criminal conspiracy doctrine and the varying successes of the employer associations crimped the growth of the incipient labor movement, moreover, an economic event temporarily sent unionism into almost total collapse. In 1819 a major nationwide depression occurred and, as was to be no less the case in later nineteenth century periods of economic reversal, labor organizations could not withstand its effects. Union demands which might be translated into employer concessions when the demand for labor was high could be safely dismissed by the masters with jobs now at a premium. Employers once again cut rates with impunity and showed little hesitation in dismissing workers who had joined unions in earlier years. Under the circumstances, the worker cry was "every man for himself" rather than "in union there is strength," and virtually no union could, or did, survive such mass desertion.

REVIVAL, INNOVATION, AND DISILLUSIONMENT

The return of economic health to the country by late 1822 was paralleled by a revival in unionism. Their bargaining power restored, skilled employees in the trades which had previously been organized once again turned to union activity.

More significantly, the process of unionization now spread to new frontiers, both geographic and occupational. Aroused by the same merchant-capitalist threats to living standards and status which had previously given incentive for collective bargaining to their east coast counterparts, craftsmen in such newly developed cities as Buffalo, Pittsburgh, Cincinnati, and Louisville established trade union locals at this time. And new (and widely publicized) victories of the skilled worker unions both in the older and newer cities had by the mid-1830s generated the formation of unions among such previously nonunion groups as stonecutters, hatters, and painters. By 1836, there were fifty-eight different local trade unions in Philadelphia, fifty-two in New York, twenty-four in Baltimore, and fourteen in Cincinnati.

These years also saw other innovations made by organized labor. Prior to 1827, each local craft union had operated on its own as a totally separate organization. In that year, however, representatives of fifteen different trades in the city of Philadelphia formed the country's first central labor union, for joint action on a citywide basis. The original goal of the Philadelphia group was a ten-hour day for its trade union members, but this was soon displaced as a major demand: In 1828 the organization converted itself into a political party, endorsing "workingmen's candidates" —with only limited success—for public office.

Workingmen's parties were also organized in other eastern states in this period of Jacksonian democracy. Political associations of workers seeking such goals as universal free education and the abolition of imprisonment for debt arose in New York, Massachusetts, and Delaware. Most of their objectives were soon realized, but the workingmen's parties themselves—

often torn by internal dissension and always confronted by competition from the two major national parties—were generally short-lived.

The original form which the Philadelphia "city central" had taken—as a purely economic joint undertaking of several trade unions in a single city—had a more lasting influence on workers in other locations. Similar bodies were quickly set up throughout the East and, despite the frequent divergence of opinion among the various trades represented, showed remarkable staying-power. By the mid-1830s, at least twelve cities had such "city centrals," most of which provided their affiliated local unions with financial and moral encouragement in times of strikes and coordinated such ancillary activities as the promotion of union-made goods.

Even the beginnings of national worker organization were attempted at this time. In 1834, delegates from the city centrals of several eastern cities met in New York to form the National Trades' Union. This pioneering workers' project quickly proved fruitless—industry had not yet itself significantly organized on a national basis, and would not for three more decades—but the scope of the NTU's activities nonetheless symbolizes the ambitiousness of the worker representatives involved.

Indeed, the initiative displayed by leaders of both the city centrals and the local unions had led to impressive union membership totals by 1836. It has been estimated that there were in the country as a whole in that year 300,000 unionized workers,[2] constituting 6.5 percent of the labor force. One can only guess as to what heights the total figures would have risen had not the following year brought a national economic depression which was even more severe than the business slump of 1819.

The hard times which began in 1837 were to last for almost thirteen years. In the face of them, trade union activity vanished almost as completely as it had two decades earlier. Moreover, a new factor now arose to compound union ills: the 1840s saw waves of immigrants—themselves often the victims of economic adversity in such countries as Ireland, Germany, and England—enter the United States. American business conditions by themselves had been sufficient to wipe out most unions of the day, but this new source of job competition and low wages ensured that not even the strongest of unions could endure.

Now so severely frustrated in their economic actions and distrustful of the free enterprise system for having failed to safeguard their interests, some workers transferred their energies to a series of ambitious political schemes for redesigning the economy. "Associationists" set up socialistic agricultural communities; George Henry Evans preached the virtues of "land reform" through direct political action by workingmen ("Vote Yourself a Farm"); and still other advocates of a new social order promul-

[2] Foster Rhea Dulles, *Labor in America,* 2d rev. ed. (New York: Thomas Y. Crowell Company, 1960), p. 59.

gated producers' cooperatives—employee-owned industrial institutions—as the workingman's salvation.

None of these programs succeeded, however. As Dulles has astutely observed, they did not "in any way meet the needs of labor. In spite of the enthusiastic propaganda, the answer to industrialization did not lie in an attempt to escape from it."[3]

THE LAYING OF THE FOUNDATION FOR MODERN UNIONISM AND SOME MIXED PERFORMANCES WITH IT

With the return of prosperity in 1850, unions once again became a factor to be reckoned with. Profiting from the past, they eschewed political diversions, concentrated on such now traditional goals as higher wages, shorter work days, and increased job security, and regained much of their former membership.

The first major national unions, often superseding the economic functions of the city centrals, were also established at this time. Although the "Golden Age" of American railroading still lay ahead, the construction of the first complex rail systems was now accelerating. As a result, not only were product markets once more widening, but so too were labor markets, bringing workers within the same crafts and industries into direct economic competition with each other. National coordination to standardize wages, working conditions, membership rules, and bargaining demands was deemed necessary by labor leaders: the alternative was cutthroat competition among individual local unions, eager for new members and expanded work opportunities and therefore willing to undercut the terms of other locals (to the employer's distinct advantage). The National Typographical Union, the country's oldest permanent national, dates from 1850. By 1860 at least fifteen other crafts had organized on a national basis. In addition to the Typographers, the Machinists and the Iron Molders have continued as labor organizations to this day, although the last-named is currently anything but a giant in labor circles.

The 1861 advent of the Civil War brought a new spurt in union membership growth to a post-1836 high of over 200,000 unionists by the end of hostilities in 1865. Some of this organizational success was due to the labor shortages brought on by military mobilization: the economy's demand for labor commensurately increased, thus enlarging labor's bargaining power and union economic gains. There were undoubtedly at least two other reasons, however: (1) wartime inflation always threatened to counteract the wage increases achieved by unions, and many workers

[3] *Ibid.*, p. 81.

(somewhat unsuccessfully) looked to collective bargaining as a force for staving off this menace; and (2) organized labor was further helped by the pro-labor sentiments of President Lincoln, who firmly resisted employer and public pressure to intervene in the occasional wartime strikes and instead offered as his opinion that "labor is the superior of capital and deserves much the higher consideration."

At war's end, the labor movement still enrolled less than 2 percent of the country's labor force (as against 6.5 percent in 1836) and had yet to make any real penetration into the factories of the land and their huge organizing potential. But the foundation for the unionism of the next seventy years had now been laid. Few skilled worker types were totally unrepresented by unions in 1865: over 200 local unions, individually encompassing such widely divergent craftsmen as cigar-makers, plumbers, and barrel-makers, were founded in the war years alone. In addition, the logical necessity of forming *national* unions had now been almost universally recognized by labor leaders, and some thirty new ones had been added to the several which had preceded the war. And labor had achieved, through Lincoln, at least a measure of government support for its right to strike.

Labor's momentum, moreover, was sustained in immediate postwar years. The war-generated nationwide prosperity continued virtually unabated until 1873 and, aided by its favorable economic conditions (as in earlier business booms), labor's bargaining strength again increased. New members were attracted by announcements of new union gains, but there were now also other reasons for the increased membership totals. The broader organizational foundations which had been laid prior to 1865, particularly in the multiplication of national unions, allowed both more efficient and more varied organizing campaigns. Moreover, the post–Civil War period unleashed formidable threats to the workingman in the form of: (1) accelerated waves of immigrants (increasingly, now, from Southern and Eastern Europe) who were willing to work for low wages; (2) changing technology, with the machine downgrading many skill requirements and allowing the employer to substitute unskilled labor for craftsmen and women for men; and (3) the continued widening of the gap between wages and prices which had begun in the wartime years. Workers thus had more incentive to join in collective bargaining, and acted upon it.

On the other hand, not every union shared in these gains. Particularly unsuccessful, in fact, was the new Molders national union, whose embittered president William Sylvis now turned away from "pure and simple" collective bargaining to espouse cooperative foundries. He was totally convinced that workers "must adopt a system which will divide the *profits* of labor among those who produce them," and was soon instrumental in the establishment of a number of producers' cooperatives.

These undertakings proved no more successful than they had in the

1840s, however. By 1870 most of the worker-owned associations had been forced by competitive pressures to cut wages, hire lower-cost labor, and—in general—act very much like the management-run businesses which Sylvis had so lamented.

Sylvis then transferred his energies to a new organization which had been founded in 1866. The National Labor Union, riding the crest of union optimism at the close of the war, constituted the first major attempt at uniting all national unions, city centrals, and locals into a single central federation of American labor since the ill-fated National Trades' Union of 1834. Its first leaders, drawn mainly from the building and printing trades, had unsuccessfully urged legislative enactment of the eight-hour working day. They had also sought, again without tangible success, such further political goals as currency reform and women's suffrage.

Sylvis drew the organization even further from economic action to such new political objectives as the reservation of public lands for actual settlers only and abolition of the convict labor system. But the National Labor Union could not sustain membership enthusiasm with a credo which was so far removed from worker pocketbooks: one by one, its constituent labor organizations deserted it and by 1872 the NLU had passed from the scene.

The failures of the cooperative and political movements were harbingers of more wide-sweeping labor disasters. Business collapsed in 1873, beginning a new period of deep depression which lasted for more than five years. In its wake, most of the local unions (as well as the city centrals) once more disappeared. Many of the nationals fared no better, but the greater financial resources and more diversified memberships of these broader organizations did allow them to offer greater resistance to the slump: not only did eleven of the nationals, in fact, weather these years but eight new nationals were established during this time. Consequently, for the first time, a depression did not completely stop unionization. Nonetheless, five-sixths of total union membership did erode in the 1873-78 period: only 50,000 unionists remained in 1878.

Encouraged by the depression-caused weakening of union bargaining power, employers also turned—in the 1870s—to weapons of their own, in an all-out frontal attack on what was left of organized labor. Acting both singly and through employer associations, they engaged in frequent lockouts, hired spies to ferret out union sympathizers, circulated the names of such sympathizers to fellow employers through so-called "black lists," summarily discharged labor "agitators," and engaged the services of strikebreakers on a widespread scale.

The results of these efforts varied. Most of the labor organizations which were strong enough to withstand the depression could also frustrate the employer onslaughts. But there were at least two notable effects of the management campaign. First, several unions of this period became secret societies to avoid employer reprisal. Such esoteric groups as the Knights of St. Crispin (shoemakers) date from this era. Second, retaliating in kind to the quality of employer opposition (as well as to the widespread unemployment of the times), both unionists and nonunionized workers engaged in actions which for bitterness and violence were unequalled in American history. A secret society of anthracite miners, the Molly Maguires, terrorized the coal fields of Pennsylvania in a series of widely publicized murders and acts of arson. Railroad strikes paralyzed transportation in such major cities as Baltimore, Pittsburgh, and Chicago and, with mob rule typically replacing organized leadership as these ran their course, were most often ended only with federal troops being called out to terminate mass pillaging and bloodshed. Public opinion was almost always hostile to such activities and lacking this support the demonstrations could not succeed. It is probably also true that employers were more easily enabled, by the general resentment directed toward worker groups for these actions, to gain still another weapon in their battle against unions: the labor injunction, first applied by the courts during a railway strike at this time, was to be quite freely granted—as Chapter 3 will bring out—by the judges for more than five decades thereafter.

THE RISE AND FALL OF THE KNIGHTS OF LABOR

Prosperity finally returned to the country in 1878 and with it union growth once again resumed. Over the next ten years sixty-two new national unions (or "international" unions, as many of these were now calling themselves, in recognition of their first penetration of the Canadian labor market) were established. Locals and city centrals also resumed their proliferation. Even more significantly, the early 1880s marked American labor's most notable attempt to form a single, huge "general" union, the Noble and Holy Order of the Knights of Labor.

The Knights had actually been established before the depression. In 1869 a group of tailors had founded the organization's first local in Philadelphia. Its avowed goal was "to initiate good men of all callings"— unionists as well as those not already in unions, craftsmen and (unlike virtually all other labor organizations of the day) totally unskilled workers. It particularly desired such a broad base of membership to "eliminate the weakness and evils of isolated effort or association, and useless and crushing competition resulting therefrom." But the Knights' definition of "good men of all callings" was not all-inclusive: the founders specifically wanted "no drones, no lawyers, no bankers, no doctors, no professional politicians."

Surviving the depression as a secret society, the Knights abolished their assortment of rituals and passwords in the late 1870s and thenceforth openly recruited in all directions.

Such aggressiveness, combined with what now was the normal increase in union bargaining strength amid general economic prosperity, allowed a slow but steady growth in the Order's membership. There were roughly 9,000 Knights in 1878, and over 70,000 by 1884. Then, following a major 1885 strike victory against the Wabash Railroad, the growth became spectacular: workers of all conceivable types clamored for membership and by mid-1886 there were 700,000 persons in the wide-sweeping organization.

The aftermath of the Wabash strike was to be the high-water mark for the Knights, however. The leaders of the Order proved wholly unable to cope with the gigantic membership increase, and as the new Knights sought to duplicate the Wabash triumph with one ill-timed and undisciplined strike after another, a steady stream of union defeats ensued. The very diversity of backgrounds among the members also drained the effectiveness of the organization: the old skilled trade unionists found little in common with the shopkeepers, farmers, and self-employed mechanics who shared membership with them, and they rapidly deserted the Order. Nor did the presence of thousands of unskilled and semiskilled industrial workers, often of widely varying first-generation American backgrounds, add anything to group solidarity. Greatly discouraged by the schisms within their organization, many such workers soon followed the path set by the skilled tradesmen and left it.

While each of the above factors was undoubtedly influential in the Knights' rapid decline after 1886—to 100,000 members by 1890 and to virtual extinction by 1900—still another factor was probably even more responsible for the fall of the Order: the system of values held by the Knights' leadership was considerably at variance with the values of most rank-and-file Knights. For all their diversity and essential lack of discipline, the latter could (employers and the self-employed always excepted) at least unite on the desirability of higher wages, shorter hours, and improved working conditions. Under Knight president Terrence V. Powderly, however, these goals were significantly minimized in favor of such "social" goals as the establishment of consumer and producer cooperatives, temperance, and land reform. Even the strike weapon, despite its great success against the Wabash management and its popular appeal to Knight members, was viewed with disdain by Powderly to the end: he considered it both expensive and overly militant. The philosophical gap between leadership and followers was thus a wide one, and Powderly was forced to pay the supreme penalty for perpetuating it: ultimately, he was left with no one to lead.

By the late 1880s a wholly new organization—the American Federation of Labor—had won over the mainstream of the Knights' skilled trade unionists, and the once vast array of other membership types, disillusioned, was again outside the ranks of organized labor. Taft has written an appropriate epitaph:

> The Knights of Labor can best be regarded as a producers', and not specifically as a wage earners', organization. It had no program around which workers in industry could rally for a long campaign.... The Knights of Labor expired because it could not fulfill any function.[4]

THE FORMATION OF THE AFL AND ITS PRAGMATIC MASTER PLAN

Almost from its very inception in 1881, the American Federation of Labor was a highly realistic, no-nonsense organization.

Even in that year, the more than one hundred representatives of skilled worker unions who gathered at Pittsburgh to form what was originally entitled the Federation of Organized Trades and Labor Unions included many dissident Knights, disenchanted with Powderly's "one big union" concept and political action emphasis. The rebels were already convinced that the future of their highly skilled constituents lay completely outside the catch-all Knights. They recognized that such craftsmen possessed considerably greater bargaining power than other less-skilled types of Knights members because of their relative indispensability to employers. Consequently, they were anxious to exercise this power *directly* in union-management negotiations. Powderly's idealistic and somewhat hazy legislative goals might be appropriate for workers who could not better their lot in any other way, but they seemed to many FOTLU founders to be a poor substitute for strike threats and other forms of economic action when undertaken by unionists who were not so easily replaceable. Well versed in American labor history, these early advocates of an exclusive federation of craft unions were also well aware of the fates of earlier organizations which had subordinated economic goals to political ones.

However logical these arguments for a more homogeneous and "pure collective bargaining" federation of skilled craft unions may seem to present-day readers, the FOTLU was not immediately a smashing success. It was initially torn by both personality and philosophical schisms. More important, the built-in weaknesses of the Knights had not yet become widely apparent to the large body of American craftsmen: paradoxically, the craft confederation's ultimate triumph had to await the first real victories—and then the rapid downfall—of the Powderly organization.

[4] Philip Taft, *Organized Labor in American History* (New York: Harper & Row, Publishers, 1964), p. 120.

Indeed, the basic issue which was to split irrevocably the craft unions from the Knights involved the jurisdiction of the national unions themselves. The dramatic spurt in Knight membership following the 1885 Wabash victory threatened to entirely submerge the craft "trade assemblies," and the parent national craft unions which had thus far retained their separate identities within the Order, in a throng of numerically superior semiskilled and unskilled workers. Nor would Powderly, never the compromiser and now at the pinnacle of his short-lived success, grant any assurances that the Knights would not violate the jurisdictions of the existing national unions. Rubbing salt into the nationals' wounds, the Knights' leadership even went so far now as to organize rival national unions and to try to absorb both these and the established nationals into the "mixed" assembly and district structures of the Order.

The rupture was soon complete. In late 1886, representatives of twenty-five of the strongest national unions met at Columbus, Ohio, transformed the somewhat moribund FOTLU into the American Federation of Labor, unanimously elected Samuel Gompers of the Cigar Makers as the AFL's first president, and thereby ushered in a new era for the American labor movement. Despite their moment of glory, the Knights were soon to begin their rapid decline—with some of the impetus toward their dissolution, to be sure, being directly lent by the secession of the skilled worker nationals. For the next fifty years the basic tenets of the AFL were to remain unchallenged by the mainstream of labor in this country.

Samuel Gompers, the Dutch-Jewish immigrant who was to continue as president of the federation for all except one of the next thirty-eight years, has frequently been referred to as a supreme pragmatist, a leader convinced that any supposed "truth" was above all to be tested by its practical consequences. Careful consideration of the basic principles upon which he and his lieutenants launched the AFL does nothing to weaken the validity of this description. Essentially, Gompers had five such principles.

In the first place, the national unions were to be autonomous within the new federation: "The American Federation of Labor," Gompers proudly announced, "avoids the fatal rock upon which all previous attempts to effect the unity of the working class have split, by leaving to each body or affiliated organization the complete management of its own affairs, especially its own particular trade affairs."[5] The leader of a highly successful national himself—as were such other AFL founders as Peter McGuire of the Carpenters and P. F. Fitzpatrick of the Molders—Gompers felt particularly strongly that questions of admission, apprenticeship, bargaining policy, and the like should be left strictly to those directly involved with them.

[5] *Ibid.*, p. 117. Quoted from a speech by Gompers to the Web Weavers Amalgamated Association, March 5, 1888.

Second, the AFL would charter only one national union in each trade jurisdiction. This concept of "exclusive jurisdiction" stemmed mainly from the unpleasant experiences of the nationals with rival unions chartered by the Knights. It was also, however, due to Gompers' deep concern that such competitive union situations would give the employer undue bargaining advantages by allowing him to pit one warring union against another.

Third, the AFL would at all costs avoid long-run reformist goals and concentrate instead only upon immediate wage-centered gains. As noted above, its founders were determined not to suffer the fates of earlier, reform-centered organizations: "We have no ultimate ends," asserted Gompers' colleague Adolph Strasser on the occasion of his testimony before a Congressional committee at this time, "We are going on from day to day. We are fighting only for immediate objects—objects that can be realized in a few years."

Fourth, the federation would avoid any permanent alliances with the existing political parties and, instead, "reward labor's friends and defeat labor's enemies." Gompers was willing, however, to accept help for the AFL from any quarter with only one major exception: He had at one time been a Marxian Socialist, but familiarity had bred contempt and long before 1886 he had permanently broken with his old colleagues. At the 1903 AFL convention, he was to announce to the relative handful of Socialists present: "Economically, you are unsound; socially, you are wrong; and industrially, you are an impossibility."[6] To the end, Gompers' philosophy was firmly embedded in the capitalistic system.

Finally, Gompers placed considerable reliance on the strike weapon as a legitimate and effective means of achieving the wages, hours, and conditions sought by his unionists. Shortly before his election to the AFL presidency in May 1886, he had been one of the leaders of a general strike designed to obtain the eight-hour day. More than 300,000 workers had participated in this action, and almost two-thirds of them had achieved their objective through it. Gompers' own Cigar Makers, too, had rarely hesitated to resort to strikes when bargaining impasses had been reached. And, generally speaking, these latter demonstrations of economic strength had also been successful.

Profiting from the lessons of history, Gompers' federation thus represented a realistic attempt to adjust to an economic system which had become deeply embedded in the United States. National union autonomy, exclusive jurisdiction, "pure and simple" collective bargaining, the avoidance of political entanglements, and the use of strikes where feasible—these proven sources of union strength were to be the hallmarks of the new unionism. The federation would provide the definition of jurisdictional

---

[6] *AFL Convention Proceedings,* 1903, p. 198.

boundaries for each national, and give help to all such constituent unions in their organizing, bargaining, lobbying, and public relations endeavors. But it would otherwise allow a free hand to its national union members as they pursued their individual goals. And the stress was to be on the needs of skilled workers, not those of "good men of all callings," as the Knights had placed it: Some semiskilled and unskilled workers within a relatively few industries (such as mine workers and electricians, because of the strategic power of their national unions) were encouraged to join, but basically the AFL made no great efforts to organize workers with less than "skilled" callings and was to admit the latter only if they organized themselves and had no jurisdictional disputes with craft unions.

So successful did this master plan prove to be that, except for slight modifications which will be described later, it was not until the mid-1930s that its logic was in any way seriously questioned.

THE EARLY YEARS OF THE AFL AND SOME MIXED RESULTS

Even in the short run, the policies of the AFL were so attractive to the nationals that within a few years virtually all of them had become members of the new organization. The only notable exceptions were the brotherhoods of railroad operating employees, whose relative unwillingness to strike and emphasis on elaborate accident and health insurance plans had traditionally set them apart from other organizations of craftsmen. Given this reception, the Gompers federation grew steadily, if not spectacularly: It had counted 140,000 members in 1886; by 1898 the figure had risen to 278,000.

It is also noteworthy that the economic depression that swept the country between 1893 and 1896 did not drastically deplete union membership totals, as had been the case in earlier hard times. The new principles of Gompers, reflected at both the federation and national levels, gave labor significant staying-power. Moreover, the now centralized control held by the nationals over their locals both lessened the danger that local monies would be dissipated in ill-advised strikes and provided the locals with what were normally sufficient funds for officially authorized strikes.

On the other hand, organized labor still had a severe problem to contend with in the 1890s: the deep desire of the nation's industrialists, now themselves strongly centralized in this era of trusts and other forms of consolidation, to regain unilateral control of employee affairs. Not since the 1870s had the forces of management been as determined, as formidable, or, particularly in the case of two widely heralded strikes of the time, as successful in opposing unionism.

The first of these two union disasters involved the long-established

Amalgamated Association of Iron and Steel Workers and the Homestead, Pennsylvania, plant of the Carnegie Steel Company (predecessor of the United States Steel Corporation). Here, in 1892, the company attempted to reduce wages as part of its renegotiation of an expiring agreement with the union. When the workers refused to agree to the pay cut, the Carnegie management locked them out and imported some 200 Pinkerton detectives to safeguard 2,000 strikebreakers who had been hired to replace the Amalgamated members. In a subsequent pitched battle between detectives and unionists, ten men were killed, several on each side. But the company successfully resumed operations with the strikebreakers, aided by the presence of the state militia, and thus dealt a crushing blow to the once powerful Amalgamated: the latter's morale was badly broken and not for forty-five more years would Carnegie or most of the other fast-growing mills in the Pittsburgh area again operate under a union contract. Adding insult to injury, the Carnegie management also permanently blacklisted many of the defeated strikers and thereby denied them re-employment throughout the industry.

The Pullman, Illinois strike of 1894 was unlike Homestead in that it involved the fast-growing American Railway Union, not an AFL affiliate. Otherwise, however, it differed essentially only in degree of violence and exact method of company victory. As in 1892, it was precipitated when the company (here, the Pullman Palace Car Company) attempted unilaterally to cut wages. The workers, not originally ARU members, then walked off their jobs and requested the railway union to intervene in their behalf. The union, welcoming the opportunity for new members, promptly instituted a boycott against all Pullman cars throughout the country. In Chicago, violence ensued when the railroad executives there imported Canadian strikebreakers. Considerable railroad property was destroyed and most train operations were completely halted. When total mob rule then threatened, the United States Department of Justice intervened and obtained a federal court injunction outlawing further union activities. President Grover Cleveland also dispatched federal troops to the scene, despite the objections of the governor of Illinois. Only after a month of further violence, plant destruction, and the killing and wounding of several soldiers and rioters, was the boycott finally ended. But, as at Homestead, the defeat was a crushing one for the union. The railroads refused to reinstate the strikers and, within a few years, the union had permanently vanished from the scene.

Other managers, impressed by the triumphs of the Carnegie and railroad managements, and at times alarmed by what they felt were the overly belligerent stances of the AFL unions, also became more aggressive in their battles with labor. Employers in the metal trades formed a Metal Trades Association to defeat the Machinists in their quest for a nine-hour day, and then adopted a policy of "no outside interference" with their company operations. Builders in Chicago, no less strongly united, completely ousted their workers' union representatives and regained full control of construction activities following a one-year 1899 strike. And the employers in the job foundry industry banded together in the National Founders' Association, which successfully terminated not only long-standing Molders Union work rules but, for all practical purposes, the existence of the union itself. In addition, the general public tended to be no more sympathetic, normally, to the aims of the labor movement: symbolically, the eminent president of Harvard University, Charles W. Eliot, reportedly "went so far as to glorify the strikebreaker as an example of the finest type of American citizen whose liberty had to be protected at all costs."[7]

Moreover, magnifying union problems at the turn of the century were the effects of Frederick W. Taylor's influential "Scientific Management" movement. While many of his contemporaries lamented worker inefficiency with no more practical results than they produced when they decried the weather, Taylor was determined to take positive action. He made his life a crusade to eradicate excessive fatigue, wasted time, and lost motion from the workplace by discovering and then implementing what he called "the one best way" of performing a given operation. Two parts of the total Taylor program were particularly assailed by labor leaders: (1) the systematic breakdown of all jobs into elementary task elements and then their recombination into highly standardized "best way" procedures—which often made the new jobs so easily mastered by workers that even skilled factory employees were threatened with becoming as interchangeable and consequently as replaceable as their products; and (2) the stress on incentive methods of wage payment—which threatened to undermine group solidarity by rewarding individual initiative and to make working conditions less palatable by giving companies an excuse for instituting what workers called "speedups." Union fears proved to be justified, as the Taylor movement spread across the factory employer community. Due at least in part to the influence of "Scientific Management," too, any hopes which organized labor might have harbored for enrolling the growing army of American factory workers had to be postponed, essentially for another thirty-five years.

Despite all these adverse factors, union membership growth in this period was unparalleled. From 447,000 unionists in 1897, the figure increased almost fivefold to 2,073,000 in 1904—a rate of expansion which has never been equalled since. The figures reflect the national prosperity of the day and the success of many of the national unions (their problems notwith-

---

[7] Joseph G. Rayback, *A History of American Labor* (New York: The Macmillan Company, 1959), p. 215.

standing) in organizing their official jurisdictions along the lines of the AFL principles.

But the labor movement could not indefinitely withstand the continuing employer opposition, now augmented by a series of devastating court injunctions on the one hand and rival union challenges from leftist workingmen's groups on the other. Total union membership dropped to 1,959,000 in 1906, and even its ultimate growth to 3,014,000 by 1917 was quite uneven and—considering the fact that 90 percent of the country's labor force still remained unorganized—unspectacular.

Intensified employer campaigns for the "open (nonunion) shop," led by the National Association of Manufacturers, resulted in a number of notable union strike losses after 1904 in the meat-packing and shipping industries, among others. Violence often occurred, most drastically at the Colorado Fuel and Iron Company's Ludlow location, when in 1913 eleven children and two women were found burned to death in strikers' tents which the state militia, summoned by the company, had set afire. These were also the peak years of yellow-dog contracts (under which employees promised in writing never to engage in union activities), labor spies, immediate discharge of workers at the slightest evidence of union sympathies, and the use of federal, state, and local troops on a wholesale scale to safeguard company interests in the face of strike actions.

The courts, too, were not particularly restrained in their conduct toward unions. Injunctions banning specific union activities often appeared to unionists to be issued quite indiscriminately. As early as 1906, Gompers had been sufficiently aroused by such court orders to petition the President and Congress for relief from injunctions. His claim that the court orders represented unconstitutional usurpations of legislative power went unheeded, however, and although the AFL leader was enough moved by the rebuff to set up a lobbying agency within the federation, the injunctions continued to be forthcoming. Indeed, the judges now went considerably beyond even their restraining orders in their labor relations decisions: In 1908, the Supreme Court invalidated the pioneering Erdman Act of 1898, which had banned interstate railroads from discriminating against their union member employees, on the grounds that the act had "unconstitutionally invaded both personal liberty and the rights of property." Nine years later, the Court upheld the validity of the yellow-dog contract.

Still another threat to the established unions, in the years between 1904 and 1917, came from workers themselves. Sometimes impatient with what they considered to be the slow pace of AFL union gains, and sometimes wholly antagonistic toward the very system of capitalism, radical labor groups arose to challenge the Gompers unions for membership and influence. This was the heyday of immigration into the United States—some 14 million newcomers, mainly from Europe, arrived in the first two decades of the twentieth century—and the European political socialism which many of the radical groups espoused found some recruits in this quarter. But the most significant of these radical organizations was essentially a native American one, the colorful Industrial Workers of the World.

The IWW was founded in 1905 by a wide array of dissidents: western metal miners, loggers, and out-and-out drifters; Socialist Labor party members; and a few disenchanted AFL union leaders from locals of longshoremen and barbers, among others. Its militant organizers placed no faith in the free enterprise system and asserted in the very first line of the IWW preamble that "the working class and the employing class have nothing in common." They also: put a premium on inviting all types of workers to join (including, with a hospitality reminiscent of the Knights of Labor, farmers, industrial workers, and intellectuals); were willing to support what they called a "genuine labor party"; and strongly advocated militant direct economic action.

The "Wobblies," as IWW members were termed, achieved several tangible victories. They made major inroads among the miners and lumber workers of the West. Most notably, they assumed leadership of a spontaneous 1912 walkout of Lawrence, Massachusetts, textile workers and led them to victory in the form of wage-cut restorations, despite considerable management opposition and police intervention. But an equally bitter fight, marked by much violence, was lost the following year by the IWW-sponsored silk mill workers in Paterson, New Jersey, and from then on Wobblie membership—never more than perhaps 70,000—rapidly declined. By 1917, strongly opposing United States entrance into World War I, the IWW had lost virtually all public support, and the federal government was in the process of obtaining convictions against its leaders for sedition. Yet, despite its ultimate failure and comparatively small membership, the IWW did demonstrate in its few years of gains that many unskilled and even migratory workers were now beginning to look to collective bargaining to safeguard their interests—indeed, given no alternative by the AFL, that they would support a bargaining agency as removed from their other values as the revolutionary IWW. Gompers' original principles were still quite adequate to meet the needs of the basic labor movement, but the day would come when the concept of skilled worker paramountcy would be more seriously challenged.

For the time being, however, Gompers and the AFL could point with satisfaction to some signal gains. As previously noted these did not lie primarily in the area of overall organizational growth: In the face of the onslaughts from the employers and the courts, as well as the abortive threats of radical dual unionism, AFL union membership rose only slowly in the pre–World War I years. Rather, the gains rested to a great extent on the outstanding organizing and bargaining successes of a few specific

AFL member nationals, particularly in the building trades, the ladies' garment industry, and in coal mining. Ironically, two of these unions (the International Ladies' Garment Workers and the United Mine Workers) owed much of their new strength to membership policies which took in many semiskilled and even unskilled workers, although skilled worker needs were still emphasized (and although both of these unions were definite exceptions to AFL union practice in their actions).

The AFL's further grounds for satisfaction rested on another irony: Despite the continuation of the policy against active involvement in politics, AFL lobbying activities at both the federal and state levels had been instrumental in the enactment of significant progressive labor legislation. Among other such achievements, some thirty states by 1917 had introduced workmen's compensation systems covering industrial accidents, and almost as many had provided for maximum hours of work for women. On the federal level, the 1915 LaFollette Seamen's Act had greatly ameliorated conditions on both American vessels and foreign vessels in American ports and the 1916 Owen-Keating Act had dealt a severe blow to child labor abusers. But Gompers was destined not to be successful in what had appeared at first to be an even greater triumph: although the Clayton Act of 1914 had seemed to exempt labor from antitrust laws and the penalties of the injunction, in 1921 the Supreme Court was to interpret the Clayton Act in such a way as to render it toothless in labor disputes.

WARTIME GAINS AND PEACETIME LOSSES

From 1917 to 1920, the time of World War I and the months of prosperity following it, the AFL grew rapidly. The 3 million workers in the AFL unions on the eve of hostilities increased to 4.2 million by 1919 and to 5.1 million only one year later.

During the war, military production, the curtailment of immigration, and the draft combined to create tight labor markets and thus gave unions considerable bargaining power and commensurate gains. Real wages for employees in manufacturing and transportation increased by more than 25 percent during the war.

Even more significantly, labor received for the first time official government support for its collective bargaining activities. The rights to organize and bargain collectively, free of employer discrimination for union activities, were granted AFL leaders by the Wilson administration for the length of the war. In return, Gompers and his colleagues pledged that their unions would not engage in strikes and promised full cooperation with the war effort. Wilson was, of course, not the first chief executive to accept the idea of collective bargaining—Lincoln having done so almost six decades earlier—and the World War I President's actions were undoubtedly based to a great extent on military expediency. But where Lincoln had merely abstained from intervention on the side of the employers, Wilson's program was considerably more positive from the viewpoint of the labor movement. Although it ended with the Armistice, it undoubtedly helped to stimulate the growth of union membership during the war.

But the immediate postwar months were even more conducive to union growth than the war years. The economy's production needs remained high, now to satisfy pent-up consumer demands, and the cost of living hit an all-time high. Company profits also burgeoned, freed of artificial wartime restraints. No longer obliged to honor the no-strike pledges, unions aggressively struck in pursuit of worker wages which were attuned to both profits and cost of living and, with their bargaining power now so high, they generally succeeded. As in earlier times of demonstrated labor triumphs, victory brought further conquest: new recruits flocked into the labor movement to gain their share in prosperity through collective bargaining.

Despite this auspicious entrance into the 1920s, however, the decade was to be one of great failure for unionism. Total union membership rapidly dwindled from the 1920 peak of 5.1 million to 3.8 million three years later and, steadily if less dramatically declining even after this, hit a twelve-year low of 3.4 million at the close of the decade. The drop is even more remarkable given the fact that the economy generally continued to flourish during this period: in every prior era of national prosperity, unions had *gained* considerable ground.

Nonetheless, there were understandable reasons for the poor performance of unionism in the 1920s. A combination of five powerful factors, most of them as unprecedented as organized labor's boom period decline, was now at work.

First, after the beginning of the decade prices remained stable and, with workers generally retaining their relatively high wage gains of the 1917–20 period, the cries of labor organizers that only union membership could stave off real wage losses fell on deaf ears.

Second, employers throughout the nation not only returned to such measures for thwarting unionization as the yellow-dog contract and the immediate discharge of union "agitators" but now embarked on an antiunion open shop propaganda campaign so extensive that one contemporary observer was moved to remark that never before in its history had

> America seen an open shop drive on a scale so vast as that which characterizes the drive now sweeping the country. Never before has an open shop drive been so heavily financed, so efficiently organized, so skillfully generaled. The present drive flies all of the flags of patriotic wartime propaganda. It advances in the name of democracy, freedom, human rights, Americanism.[8]

[8] Savel Zimand, *The Open Shop Drive* (New York: Bureau of Industrial Research, 1921), p. 5.

The campaign, typically conducted under the slogan of the "American Plan," portrayed unions as alien to the nation's individualistic spirit, restrictive of industrial efficiency, and frequently dominated by radical elements who did not have the best interests of America at heart. Particularly in regard to the last of these charges, the public appeared to be impressed: It was still mindful of the IWW, and now its attention was also called, freely by the newspapers, to the relatively few other significant leftist inroads into labor circles. To many citizens, too, organizations which could even remotely be construed as going against individualism and the free enterprise system in this day of laissez-faire Republicanism were also highly un-American.

Third, but often tied into their "American Plan" participation, many companies introduced what became known as "welfare capitalism." Intending to demonstrate to their employees that unions were unnecessary (as well as dangerous), they established a wide variety of employee benefit programs: elaborate profit-sharing plans, recreational facilities, dispensaries, cafeterias, and health and welfare systems of all kinds. Employee representation plans were also instituted, with workers thus being offered a voice on wages, hours, and conditions—the companies being thereby enabled to satisfy many grievances before they became major morale problems. Although the managements could withdraw the benefits at any time, and although the employee representatives normally had only "advisory" voices, union ills were undeniably compounded by these company moves.

In the fourth place, the courts proved themselves even less hospitable to labor unions than they had been in labor's dark days preceding World War I. Having denied in 1921 that the Clayton Act exempted unions from the antitrust laws and the injunction, the Supreme Court proceeded to invalidate an Arizona anti-injunction law the same year and then struck down state minimum wage laws as violations of liberty of contract in 1923. Encouraged by the implied mandate from Washington, lower court judges now issued injunctions more freely than ever.

Fifth, and finally, some of the union losses were due to unimaginative leadership in the labor movement itself. Gompers died in 1924 and his successor, William Green, lacked the aggressiveness and the imagination of the AFL's first president. Labor's troubles were clearly not to be viewed with equanimity but Green and most of his AFL union leaders were, as Rayback has tersely commented, "content to rest upon past performances, to confine membership to the elite among workingmen, and to remain the junior partner of management in the nation's economic system."[9]

On the eve of the Great Depression in late 1929, then, organized labor remained almost exclusively the province of the highly-skilled-worker

---

[9] Rayback, *op. cit.*, p. 303.

minority, apathetic in the face of the loss of one-third of its members in a single decade, militantly opposed by much of the employer community, severely crimped by judicial actions, and often suspected by the general public of possessing traits counter to the spirit of America. It appeared to have a superb future behind it.

THE GREAT DEPRESSION AND THE AFL'S RESURGENCE IN SPITE OF ITSELF

The stock market collapse of October 1929 ushered in the most severe business downturn in the nation's history. Between 1929 and the Depression's lowest point in 1933, the gross national product dropped from over $104 billion to around $56 billion, and a staggering 24.9 percent of the country's civilian labor force was out of work by 1933, compared to an unemployment rate of only 3.2 percent in 1929.[10]

Figures which specifically relate to organized labor were equally gloomy. Between 1929 and 1933, the average twelve-month membership loss rate for organized labor accelerated to 117,000, and by 1933 union membership stood at 2,973,000—only 200,000 above the 1916 level.[11]

Given this severe loss of dues-payers, plus the necessity of sustaining strikes against the inevitable wage cuts of workers still employed, it is not surprising that many unions soon became as impoverished as their constituents. Symbolically, Ulman reports that "One forlorn strike against a small steel mill had to be called off after the contents of the strikers' soup kitchen had been depleted by a group of hungry children."[12]

It *is* surprising, however, that the mood of the workers themselves seemed to be one of bewildered apathy. The atmosphere was now marked by constant mortgage foreclosures (resulting in thousands moving into shanty towns on city dumps, which were bitterly called "Hoovervilles" after the incumbent President). It was characterized by the constant fear of starvation on the part of many of those not working, and the fear of sudden unemployment on the part of many of those still employed. Virtually all remnants of welfare capitalism were being abruptly terminated. And, under these conditions, one might have expected a reincarnation of such militant organizations as the IWW, seeking to overthrow the capitalistic system which was now performing so poorly. Some workers did indeed turn to such radical movements as communism, but in general the nation seemed to have been shocked into inaction.

It is still *more* surprising, even considering its uninspiring performance

---

[10] Stanley Lebergott, *The Measurement and Behavior of Unemployment* (Princeton, N. J.: National Bureau of Economic Research, Inc., 1957), p. 215.
[11] Ulman, *op. cit.*, p. 397.
[12] *Ibid.*, pp. 397–98.

in meeting the challenge of the 1920s, that the leadership of the AFL did not noticeably change its policies in these dark days. Through 1932, Green and the AFL Executive Council remained opposed to unemployment compensation, old-age pensions, and minimum wage legislation as constituting unwarranted state intervention. They asked only for increased public works spending from the government. So far was the AFL from the pulse of the general community at this time that although the great bulk of union officials were and had long been Democratic party supporters it refused, with scrupulous official neutrality, to endorse either candidate in the 1932 presidential election, which swept Democrat Franklin D. Roosevelt into office with what was then the largest margin in American history.

Roosevelt's one-sided victory symbolized the country's (if not the AFL's) willingness to grant the federal government more scope for participation in domestic affairs than it had ever been given before. The business community, upon which the nation had put such a premium during the prosperous years of the 1920s, was now both discredited and demoralized. It had become painfully apparent, too, to the millions who had been steeped in the values of American individualism, that the individual worker was comparatively helpless to influence the conditions of his employment environment. In short, the Depression allowed labor unions—which had been so greatly out of favor with their countrymen only a few years earlier—a golden opportunity for revival and growth, now with government encouragement.

Even before the election, such a climate had resulted in one notable gain for unions. The Norris–La Guardia Act of 1932 satisfied a demand which Gompers had originally made in his petition to the President and Congress some twenty-six years earlier: the power of judges to issue injunctions in labor disputes on an almost unlimited basis was now revoked. Severe restrictions were placed on the conditions under which the courts could grant injunctions and such orders could in no case be issued against certain otherwise legal union activities. In addition, the yellow-dog contract was declared unenforceable in federal courts.

The 1932 act marked a drastic change in public policy. Previously, except for the temporary support which unions received during World War I, collective bargaining had been severely hampered through judicial control. Now it was to be strongly *encouraged,* by legislative fiat and—after Roosevelt took office in early 1933—by executive support.

Roosevelt and the first "New Deal" Congress wasted little time in making known their sentiments. The National Industrial Recovery Act of mid-1933, in similar but stronger language than that already existing in the Norris–La Guardia Act, specifically guaranteed employees "the right to organize and bargain collectively through representatives of their own choosing...free from the interference, restraint or coercion of employers."

Green, in what for him was unusual enthusiasm, immediately praised the Act as giving "millions of workers throughout the nation...their charter of industrial freedom" and launched a moderate drive to expand AFL membership among craft workers. More remarkable, however, was the response to the NIRA by rank-and-file workers themselves: Almost overnight, thousands of laborers in such mass-production industries as steel, automobiles, rubber, and electrical manufacturing spontaneously formed their own locals and applied to the AFL for charters. By the end of 1933, the federation had gained over one million new members.

The largest single gains at this time were registered by those established AFL internationals which had lost the most members during the 1920s and could capitalize upon the new climate in public policy to win back and expand their old clientele. Both the men's and women's clothing unions fell into this category. Most impressive of all, however, was the performance of the United Mine Workers under their aggressive president John L. Lewis. Lewis dispatched dozens of capable organizers throughout the coal fields, had signs proclaiming that "President Roosevelt wants you to join the union" placed at the mine pits, and not only regained virtually all his former membership but organized many traditionally nonunion fields in the Southeast. There were 60,000 Mine Workers at the time of the NIRA's passage: six months later, the figure had grown to over 350,000.

The employers, however, did not long remain docile in the face of this new union resurgence. Terming collective bargaining "collective bludgeoning," many of them responded to the NIRA by restoring or instituting the employee representation plans of the previous decade. Such "company unions," although bitterly assailed by bona fide unionists as circumventing the law's requirements concerning "employer interference," spread rapidly: By the spring of 1934, probably one-quarter of all industrial workers were employed in plants which had them. Many other managements simply refused, the law notwithstanding, to recognize any labor organizations. On many occasions, this latter attitude led to outbreaks of violence, ultimately terminated by the police or National Guard units.

The National Industrial Recovery Act was itself declared unconstitutional by the Supreme Court early in 1935, but Congress quickly replaced it with a law which was even more to labor's liking. The National Labor Relations Act, better known (after its principal draftsman in the Senate) as the Wagner Act, was far more explicit in what it expected of collective bargaining than was the NIRA, in two basic ways. First, it placed specific restrictions on what management could do (or could not do), including an absolute ban on company-dominated unions. And, second, it established the wishes of the employee majority as the basis for selection of a bargaining representative and provided that in cases of doubt as to a union's majority status, a secret-ballot election of the employees would determine whether or not the majority existed. To implement both provisions, it established a National Labor Relations Board, empowered not only to issue cease and desist orders against employers who violated the restrictions, but also to determine appropriate bargaining units and conduct representation elections.

Considerably less than enthusiastic about the Wagner Act, many employers chose to ignore its provisions and hoped that it would suffer the same fate as the NIRA. They were to be disappointed: in 1937 the Supreme Court held that the 1935 act and its congressional regulation of labor relations in interstate commerce was fully constitutional.

THE CIO'S CHALLENGE TO THE AFL

Meanwhile, however, the AFL itself almost snatched defeat from the jaws of victory. The leaders of the federation clashed sharply as to the kind of reception which should be accorded the workers in steel, rubber, automobiles, and similar mass-production industries who had spontaneously organized in the wave of enthusiasm following the NIRA's passage. The federation had given these new locals the temporary status of "federal locals," which meant that they were directly affiliated with the AFL rather than with one of the established national unions. The workers involved, however, wanted to form their own national industrial unions covering all types of workers within their industries, regardless of occupation or skill level. And this, obviously, meant a radical departure from the fifty-year AFL tradtion of discouraging nonskilled workers and essentially excluding noncraft unions (the mining and clothing industries, as noted earlier, always excepted because of their particular situations).

John L. Lewis, who had shown such initiative in expanding the ranks of his Mine Workers in the preceding months, led the fight for industrial unionism within the federation. Allied with Sidney Hillman of the Clothing Workers and David Dubinsky of the Ladies' Garment Workers, he argued that changing times had now made skilled-craft unionism obsolete, that the AFL could no longer speak with any political power so long as it confined itself to what was (with the acceleration of mechanization and the replacement of craftsmen by semiskilled machine operators) a steadily dwindling minority of the labor force, and that, should the federation fail to assert its leadership over the new unionists, rival federations would arise to fill the vacuum. With perhaps the greatest oratorical powers ever possessed by an American labor leader, Lewis ridiculed the AFL president for not being able to decide the issue: "Alas, poor Green. I knew him well. He wishes me to join him in fluttering procrastination, the while intoning *O tempora, O mores!*" And, in a dramatic speech at the 1935 AFL Atlantic City convention, he warned that should the federation fail to "heed this cry from

Macedonia that comes from the hearts of men" and refuse to allow industrial unionism or to organize the millions still unorganized, "the enemies of labor will be encouraged and high wassail will prevail at the banquet tables of the mighty."

Lewis spoke to no avail. The convention was dominated by inveterate craft-unionists, many of whom possibly believed that Macedonia was somewhere east of Akron and who at any rate were opposed to admitting what Teamster president Daniel Tobin described as "rubbish" mass-production laborers. The demands of industrial unionism were defeated by a convention vote of 18,024 to 10,933. And Lewis, never one to camouflage his emotions for the sake of good fellowship with his AFL colleagues, left Atlantic City only after landing a severe uppercut to the jaw of Carpenter Union president William L. Hutcheson, in a fit of pique.

Within a month, Lewis had formed his own organization of industrial unionists. The Committee for Industrial Organization (known after 1938 as the Congress of Industrial Organizations) originally wanted only to "counsel and advise unorganized and newly organized groups of workers; to bring them under the banner and in affiliation with the American Federation of Labor."[13] But the AFL, having already made its sentiments so clear, was to deny the new organization the latter opportunity: almost immediately, Green's executive council suspended the CIO leaders for practicing "dual unionism," and ordered them to dissolve their group. When these actions failed to dissuade the CIO, the AFL took its strongest possible action and expelled all thirty-two member national unions.

Lewis and his fellow founders—themselves heads of such nationals, in addition to those in the garment industries, as the Textile Workers, Hatters, and Oil Field Workers—were spectacularly successful in realizing their objectives. Armed with ample loans from the rebel nationals, aggressive leadership, experienced organizers, and, above all, confidence that mass-production workers enthusiastically *wanted* unionism, the AFL offshoot was able to claim almost 4 million recruits as early as 1937.

By 1941, even more remarkable conquests had been registered. One by one, virtually all the giant corporations had recognized CIO affiliated unions as bargaining agents for their employees: all the major automobile manufacturers, almost all companies of any size in the steel industry, the principal rubber producers, the larger oil companies, the major radio and electrical equipment makers, the important meatpackers of the country, the larger glass-makers, and many others. Smaller companies which had also been unionized in this period could at least take comfort in the fact that they were in good company.

Still, the CIO's organizing campaigns were not welcomed by many

[13] *Minutes of Committee for Industrial Organization,* Washington, D.C., November 9, 1935.

of these companies with open arms. United States Steel recognized the CIO's Steel Workers Organizing Committee without a contest in 1937 (ostensibly because it feared labor unrest at a time when business conditions were finally improving). But the other major steel producers unconditionally refused to deal with unionism, the law notwithstanding: in 1941, the National Labor Relations Board ordered these companies to recognize what had by then become the United Steelworkers of America, but four years of company intimidation, espionage, and militia-protected strikebreaking—highlighted by a Memorial Day 1937 clash between pickets and police which resulted in the deaths of ten workers, injuries to many more, and substantial damage to property—had then elapsed. In other industries, characterized by similar antiunion sentiments, the workers were forced to resort to sit-down strikes—protest stoppages in which the strikers remained at their places of work and were furnished with food by allies outside of the plant. Such stoppages, now illegal as trespasses upon private property, were of considerable influence in gaining representation rights for the unions in the historically nonunion automobile, rubber, and glass industries.

Nor, more significantly, was the AFL itself placid in the face of its new competition. Abandoning its traditional lethargy, it now terminated its "craftsmen only" policy and chartered industrial unions of its own in every direction. AFL meatcutters emerged to challenge CIO packinghouse workers for members of all skill levels within the meat-packing industry. AFL paper mill employees competed against CIO paper workers. AFL electricians tried to recruit the same workers, from all quarters of the electrical industry, as did the CIO electrical union organizers. And the story was much the same in textiles and automobiles. Moreover, many of the long-established AFL unions now broadened their jurisdictions: most notable were the Teamsters, whose president had apparently become oblivious to his former charge that mass-production workers were "rubbish," and who now waged aggressive organizational campaigns among workers in the food and agricultural processing industries. Aided by the same favorable climates of worker opinion and public policy which had originally inspired Lewis, and now also helped by improving economic conditions, the AFL actually surpassed the CIO in membership by 1941. By that time, however, the CIO had paid its parent the supreme compliment: it had modified its framework to include craft unionism as well as industrial unionism and the lines separating the two rival federations had become permanently clouded.

At the time of Pearl Harbor, in December 1941, total union membership stood at 10.2 million, compared to the less than 3 million members of only nine years earlier. The CIO itself—representing some 4.8 million workers at this time—was destined to achieve little further success, as measured by sheer membership statistics: it would enroll only 6 million employees at its zenith in 1947 and then gradually retreat before the onslaught of a further AFL counterattack. But if Lewis' organization failed to live up to its founder's expectations as the sole repository of future union leadership, neither could it in any meaningful way be described as a failure. When America entered World War II in late 1941, the labor movement was not only a major force to be reckoned with but, for the first time, was to a great extent representative of the full spectrum of American workers. And for this situation, the CIO's challenge to the AFL's fifty years of dominance deserves no small amount of credit.

WORLD WAR II

As in the case of World War I, the years after Pearl Harbor saw a further increase in union strength. Although the country's economic conditions had improved considerably in the late 1930s, only after the start of hostilities and the acceleration of the draft did a tight labor market arise to weaken employer resistance to union demands.

Other factors favorable to organized labor were also present. The federal government, sympathetic enough with the goals of unionism for almost a decade, now went even further in its tangible support: in return for a no-strike pledge from both AFL and CIO leaders, labor was granted equal representation with management on the tripartite War Labor Board, the all-powerful institution which adjusted collective bargaining disputes during this period. It was also given an unprecedented form of union security—the still-utilized "maintenance of membership" arrangement, requiring all employees who are either union members when the labor contract is signed or who voluntarily join the union after this date to continue their membership for the length of the contract (subject to a short "escape" period). Finally, unions further profited in the membership area from the fast growth of such wartime industries as aircraft and shipbuilding and the reinvigoration of such now crucial sectors as steel, rubber, the electrical industry, and trucking. By the end of the war in 1945, union ranks had been increased by more than 4 million new workers, or by almost 40 percent.

By and large, labor honored its no-strike pledge during hostilities. Somewhat less than one-tenth of 1 percent of total available industrial working time was lost to the war effort through union economic action. But, with the cost of living continually rising, and with the War Labor Board nonetheless attempting to hold direct wages in check (not always successfully, and frequently at the cost of allowing such "nonwage" supplements as vacation, holiday, and lunch period pay), the incidence of strikes did increase steadily after 1942. Particularly galling to the general public were several strikes by Lewis' own Mine Workers, all in direct defiance of President Roosevelt's orders and all given substantial publicity by the mass media.

Managers themselves, regaining much of their lost stature with the stress on war production at this time, could also point to other evidence that labor had become "too powerful." The competition between the AFL and CIO, officially postponed for the duration of the war, in practice continued almost unabated. Such rivalry on occasion temporarily curtailed plant output, as unions within the two federations resorted to "slowdowns" and "quickie strikes" to convince employers of their respective jurisdictional claims. Instances of worker "featherbedding"—the receipt of payment for unperformed work—marked several industries, notably construction. And members of the Communist party, originally welcomed by some CIO unions because of their demonstrated organizational ability, had now gained substantial influence if not effective control within several of these unions, including both the United Automobile Workers and the Electrical, Radio, and Machine Workers.

The public's attention was also called, by forces unhappy with the labor movement's rapid growth, to union political strength. The AFL had not yet abandoned its traditional policy of bipartisanship, but Lewis had led the CIO actively into political campaigning and had, in fact, resigned his federation presidency (while retaining his Mine Workers leadership) when the CIO rank and file had refused to bow to his wishes and vote for Republican Wendell Willkie in 1940. Under Lewis' successor, Philip Murray, and particularly through the direct efforts of Clothing Worker president Sidney Hillman, the CIO had become even more aggressive and influential —within the *Democratic* party. It now held considerable power within most northern Democratic state organizations, and such was its influence at the national Democratic level that when a fabricated story swept the country to the effect that Roosevelt had ordered his 1944 party convention to "clear everything with Sidney" it was widely believed. So effective had Hillman's CIO Political Action Committee become by this time that attacks upon it emanated from the highest of places: the Republican governor of Ohio claimed that the PAC was "trying to dominate our government with radical and communistic schemes," and the House Un-American Activities Committee (with a membership unfriendly to Roosevelt) called it "a subversive ...organization."[14]

The American man in the street seemed to be impressed. By the end of the war in 1945, public opinion polls showed more than 67 percent of the respondents in favor of legislative curbs on union power.

PUBLIC REACTION AND PRIVATE MERGER

Organized labor fell even further from public favor in the immediate postwar period. Faced with income declines as overtime and other wartime pay supplements disappeared, with real wage decreases as prices rose

[14] Rayback, *op. cit.*, p. 386.

in response to the huge pent-up consumer demand, and with layoffs as factories converted to peacetime production, workers struck as they had never done before. While the violence of earlier-day labor unrest did not often recur, the year 1946 saw new highs established in terms of number of stoppages (4,985), number of employees involved (4.6 million), and man-days idle as a percentage of available working time (1.43).[15] The month of January 1946 alone was marked by almost 2 million workers on strike. And by the end of the year, noteworthy stoppages (many of them simultaneously) had occurred in virtually every sector of the economy, including the railroads, autos, steel, public utilities, and even public education.

Such strikes were not well received by a frequently inconvenienced public which had already voiced reservations about union strength. The sentiments that the Wagner Act and other public policies of the 1930s had been too "one-sided" in favor of labor grew rapidly, and soon became compelling. In 1947 a newly elected Republican Congress passed, over President Truman's veto, the Taft-Hartley Act.

Taft-Hartley drastically amended the Wagner Act to give greater protection to both employers and individual employees. To the list of "unfair" labor practices which already were denied employers were added six "unfair" *union* practices ranging from restraint or coercion of employees to featherbedding. Employees could now hold elections to decertify unions as well as to certify them. Provisions regulating certain internal affairs of unions, explicitly giving employers certain collective bargaining rights (particularly regarding "freedom of expression" concerning union organization), and sanctioning governmental intervention in the case of "national emergency strikes" were also enacted.

While a fuller discussion of Taft-Hartley is reserved for later pages, it might be added here that the 1947 act was at least as controversial as the Wagner Act had been. Its proponents, consistent with the views of Senator Taft, asserted that it "reinjected an essential measure of justice into collective bargaining." Less friendly observers of Taft-Hartley, including the spokesmen of organized labor, were less happy and hurled such epithets as "slave labor act" at it. That the act has proven generally satisfactory to the majority of Americans, however, may be inferred from the fact that in the early 1970s Taft-Hartley, essentially unchanged from its original edition, remained the basic labor law of the land.

Speaking with the self-assurance always allowed one who can draw

---

15 *Monthly Labor Review*, LXIV, No. 5 (May 1947), 782. Recalling this wave of strikes, one former War Labor Board member has commented that a further major factor was release from controls, "together with the economic uncertainty and even fear of a new depression. Controls were more and more difficult to maintain as time went on. It's hard to say how much longer the lid could have been kept on if the war hadn't ended, but strikes upon gaining freedom were very much to have been expected."

on hindsight, it is tempting to argue that the AFL-CIO merger of 1955 was inevitable. The issue which led to the birth of the CIO was, as noted, blunted even by the late 1930s when the AFL rapidly chartered its own industrial unions and the CIO began to recognize craft unions as part of its structure. By 1939, indeed, ten of the twenty-nine existing CIO unions were craft organizations, and the AFL encompassed possibly as many noncraft workers as it did craftsmen. But sixteen more years were still to elapse before merger became a reality and significant differences of values, political opinions, and personalities still had to be bridged in this period.

In the first place, the new unions which had been formed, first by the CIO and later by the AFL, were often meeting head-on in their quests for new members and enlarged jurisdiction. Any merged federation would have to resolve not only this kind of overlap but also the membership raiding which was frequently carried on by such rival unions. For a long while, compromise seemed impossible: the AFL tended to regard all jurisdictions as exclusively its own and to insist that the CIO unions be fully absorbed within its framework; on its part, the CIO strongly suggested that its affiliates would participate in a merger only if their existing jurisdictions were given official protection.

Second, the conservative AFL leaders displayed deep hostility toward the Communist-dominated unions within the CIO. Such unions reached a peak in the immediate postwar months when a special report of the Research Institute of America listed eighteen of them in this category. And Taft has gone so far as to assert that for a short while in that period "it was a question whether the anti-Communists in the CIO could muster a majority."[16]

Finally, personalities played a role. Murray, still influenced by his predecessor as CIO president, Lewis, and Green were mutually suspicious leaders. Each was quite unwilling to take the initiative in any merger move which would involve subordination of influence to the other.

By 1955, however, most of these cleavages had been resolved. Murray, his patience with the Communist unions exhausted as the latter became more aggressive and (in particular) strongly opposed the government's Marshall Plan, had taken the lead in expelling most such unions from the CIO in 1949 and 1950.[17] Virtually all other Communist-influenced unions, presumably taking the hint, had voluntarily left the federation shortly thereafter. Murray's move cost the CIO an estimated 1 million members, but new unions were quickly established to assume the old jurisdictions and Murray claimed to have regained most of the lost membership within the next two years.

[16] Taft, *op cit.*, pp. 623–24.
[17] Support for the 1948 presidential candidacy of Henry A. Wallace by these unions was another leading issue in this split.

Further preparing the way for ultimate merger were the 1952 deaths of Murray and Green, both suddenly and only eleven days apart. The two successors—Walter Reuther of the United Auto Workers, for Murray, and AFL Secretary-Treasurer George Meany, for Green—were relatively divorced from the personal bitterness of the earlier presidents.

And beyond these factors were growing sentiments on the part of both AFL and CIO leaders that only a united labor movement could: (1) stave off future laws of the Taft-Hartley variety; (2) avoid the jurisdictional squabbles which were increasingly sapping the treasuries of both federations; and (3) allow organized labor to reach significant new membership totals for the first time since 1947.

In December 1955, culminating two years of intensive negotiations between representatives of the two organizations, the AFL-CIO became a reality. The new constitution respected the "integrity of each affiliate," including both its "organizing jurisdiction" and its "established collective bargaining relationships." Consolidation of the rival unions was to be encouraged, but was to be on a voluntary basis. And it was agreed that the new giant federation would issue charters "based upon a strict recognition that both craft and industrial unions are equal and necessary as methods of trade union organization." Fifteen years later, as will be seen, complete harmony between the AFL and CIO wings had yet to be achieved. But with the act of merger the open warfare which had first revitalized and then damaged the labor movement passed from the scene.

ORGANIZED LABOR SINCE THE MERGER

Although some observers predicted that the original 15 million membership total (two-thirds of it provided by the AFL) of the AFL-CIO would double within the next decade, the figure had actually declined by 1970, to 13.5 million.

It is true that the united federation had expelled the International Brotherhood of Teamsters in 1957 for alleged domination by "corrupt influences," thereby depriving itself of 1.9 million members in terms of 1970 statistics. And the 1968 leaving of the AFL-CIO fold on the part of the 1.4-million-member United Automobile Workers, an action due especially to Walter Reuther's unhappiness with what he perceived to be a lack of federation leadership aggressiveness but also complicated by Meany-Reuther personality differences, must also be recognized in explaining the federation's growth failures. But the fact remains that organized labor *overall* has been anything but impressive in terms of membership growth since the merger. The current 20-million figure for all union members (counting those in unions which are at present outside the ranks of the AFL-CIO: Teamsters,

80 THE ENVIRONMENTAL FRAMEWORK

Automobile Workers, Mine Workers, railroad operating employees, and others) is, in fact, less than 2 million higher than it was in the mid-1950s. And since the nation's total labor force has been growing at a much faster clip than organized labor's membership since the merger, labor has clearly been losing ground on a relative basis. At the time of this writing, as mentioned earlier in this book, unionists made up slightly under 30 percent of America's total nonagricultural employment, the lowest percentage since 1942.

Several formidable obstacles undoubtedly serve to explain this situation. Paramount among them is, of course, the fact that blue-collar workers, traditionally comprising that sector of the labor force which has been most susceptible to the overtures of the union organizer, have now been substantially organized. And this sector has, it will be recalled, been declining as a source of jobs in recent years, due mainly to the onslaughts of automation and to changes in demand. It remains to be seen whether or not new approaches, fresh leadership, and environmental changes adversely affecting worker morale can gain for organized labor the allegiance of the growing *white*-collar sector. As the statistics in the previous chapter have indicated, however, unions to date have not been spectacularly successful in recruiting this wave of the future.

Beyond this, labor's fall from public favor, which began in the 1940s and led initially to the enactment of Taft-Hartley, had yet to be arrested a quarter-century later. Congressional disclosures of corruption in the Teamsters and several smaller unions (among them, the Laundry and Bakery Workers) in the late 1950s hardly improved labor's image. The AFL-CIO quickly expelled the offending unions, but the public seemed to be far more impressed by the disclosures than by the federation's reaction to them, as indeed had been the case following the CIO's expulsion of its Communist-dominated affiliates.

Union resistance to technological change, sometimes taking the form of featherbedding and insistence on the protection of jobs which seemed no longer to be needed (those of diesel firemen and certain airline and maritime employees, for example), also was anything but calculated to regain widespread public support. Nor was it easy to generate sympathy outside the labor movement on behalf of plumbers who threatened to strike for wage rates in excess of $10.00 per hour, electricians demanding a twenty-hour work week, and New York City transit workers seeking a 30 percent wage increase, a thirty-two-hour work week, and some seventy-five other demands. These few examples were among the extremes: most unionists showed considerably more concern for the welfare of their industries in the post-merger years. But such actions as the ones illustrated, being more newsworthy, attracted more attention. It is conceivable that, through this combination of factors ranging from corruption to excessive demands, countless potential union members had been alienated.

The continuing lack of public confidence in unionism has also led, in the recent past, to new legislation restricting labor's freedom of action. In particular, the Landrum-Griffin Act of 1959 stemmed from this climate and, directly, from the union corruption revelations of Congress which were cited above. Among its other provisions, Landrum-Griffin guarantees union members a "Bill of Rights" which their unions cannot violate and requires officers of labor organizations to meet a wide and somewhat cumbersome variety of reporting and disclosure obligations. It also lays out specific ground rules for union elections, rules which have been deemed overly inhibiting (as have most other parts of the act) by many labor leaders.

It is perhaps also true that labor's conspicuous recent lack of success has stemmed from what Lester views as still four more grounds for union concern: (1) the business leader is no longer the tyrant that he frequently was before the mid-1930s; (2) industrial employees are no longer treated as inferior citizens; (3) unionism's success has decreased its needs; and (4) an affluent society such as ours now is generates moderation and a middle-class outlook which is at odds with the laboring class viewpoint espoused by unions.[18]

But such statements as these last, as thoughtful as they all may be, tend also to be somewhat more conjectural than the earlier offered reasons for the unremarkable growth figures of American unionism over the past fifteen years.

At the very least, it was obvious that organized labor could not count the immediate post-merger period among its golden years and that many of the conditions which could explain unionism's lack of success in these years persisted at the end of this period.

UNIONISM AND THE BLACK WORKER

Inevitably, as organized labor entered the 1970s, it was also forced to devote considerable attention to an issue which was far less parochial in its thrust: the increasingly intense quest of the Negro community for genuine equality of opportunity. Employment expectations which were initially (if indirectly) raised by the landmark Supreme Court school desegregation decision of 1954 had been considerably heightened by the broad equal-employment-opportunities legislation of the Civil Rights Act of 1964. And, since even by the end of the latter decade, the gap between expectation and reality remained significant, the labor movement found itself under growing attack as frustrated blacks charged it with bigotry and racism, collusion with

---

[18] Richard A. Lester, "The Changing Nature of the Union," *New York University Thirteenth Annual Conference on Labor* (New York: Mathew Bender & Co., 1960), pp. 19–30.

an equally insensitive managerial community to exploit the Negro worker, and total inadequacy in the field of integrative social action.

Not all blacks, of course, shared this dim opinion. The Urban League's late, highly respected Whitney Young undoubtedly echoed the sentiments of a significant sector of the black world in stating that "when we look at the whole picture, labor is strongly on the side of social justice and equal rights.... All unions ought to be educating their members to the dangers of bigotry, and to the fact that racism damages white workers as well as blacks. But on the whole, organized labor is as good a friend of black efforts for equality as exists in our imperfect society."[19] Nor would objective Negroes deny not only that AFL-CIO leadership, and particularly Meany and Reuther, had been in the forefront of efforts to enact the equal-employment-opportunities provisions into the Civil Rights Act of 1964 itself, but that for a time these federation chieftains had waged this campaign almost entirely alone: as the head of the NAACP's Washington Bureau, Clarence Mitchell, could later testify in this regard, "Organized labor gave unfailing, consistent and massive support where it counted most.... The members of organized labor were always present at the right time and in the right places."[20] And most blacks would, presumably, acknowledge that the approximately 2-million-member Negro contingent within the ranks of unionism at the beginning of the 1970s constituted—as far as aggregate figures—not only roughly the same proportion as that for Negroes in the total United States population but substantial progress from 1928, when Negro membership was 2.1 percent, and even from 1956 when the figure had climbed to 8.6 percent.[21]

To the growing body of black militants, however, the Youngs and Mitchells could quickly be dismissed as Uncle Toms, whose laudatory statements only proved that they had been captured by the Labor Establishment. And the significant numerical growth in black unionists in no way touched the heart of the problem—that even where the admissions bars were down for Negroes, a highly disproportionate number of Negro jobs were at the bottom of the skills ladder, situations shunned by whites and entirely lacking in career progression opportunities. Above all, they could point with considerable bitterness to the building trades, where almost six years after the passage of the Civil Rights Act less than 4 percent of all black apprentices were enrolled in skilled craft training programs (the remainder being in the so-called "trowel trades"—general laborers, cement masons, and kindred occupations, whose pay scales averaged at least 30 percent less and

[19] "John Herling's Labor Letter," *Washington Daily News,* November 30, 1968, p. 4.
[20] Ray Marshall, *The Negro Worker* (New York: Random House, 1967), pp. 40–41.
[21] Derek C. Bok and John T. Dunlop, *Labor and the American Community* (New York: Simon & Schuster, 1970), p. 120.

whose status was lowest).[22] This was an especially jarring situation to blacks, given the increasing number of projects financed with public monies.

Thus, while black militants had increasingly espoused picketing and (on occasion) disrupted production as a protest against alleged discrimination in the automobile, steel, and appliance sectors, it was in the nation's huge construction industry that the most potentially explosive confrontations had occurred by the time of this writing. In Chicago, a black Coalition for United Community Action had demanded 25,346 skilled trades jobs and a 30 percent membership in nineteen building craft unions which had a total 1969 membership of 90,000 in the metropolitan area (according to the coalition, only 2,251 were from minority groups). It succeeded in temporarily closing construction projects involving nearly $100 million in that city, and a compromise agreement was ultimately effected whereby the unions promised "to obtain employment at once" for 1,000 qualified black journeymen (with the coalition aiding in the recruitment). Several thousand more Negro workers would also be trained and admitted over the next few years under this plan. But the coalition—which termed its original demands "realistic"—remained both bitter and restive.

In Pittsburgh, where despite the fact that Negroes constituted 23 percent of the population only four of twenty-five building trades unions had black memberships exceeding 2 percent in late 1969 and only one (the low-skilled general construction laborers local) had a Negro membership above 10 percent,[23] similar black protests—accompanied by some physical clashing with white construction workers—also resulted in compromise agreements which were received by the Negro community only with extreme reluctance. Other cities appeared destined to be forced to deal with similar protests, and quite possibly also a severe white backlash, which was already, by 1971, becoming visible in both Chicago and Pittsburgh.

The unlikely prospects for an amicable resolution of the construction employment issue may, indeed, have been accurately indicated by the enthusiastic reception accorded the president of the AFL-CIO Building and Construction Trades Department immediately after the Chicago and Pittsburgh confrontations. On this occasion, he defiantly declared to three-hundred cheering delegates at the department's convention, "We wish to make it clear that we do not favor acceptance of unreasonable demands.... We should make it clear again that the conduct, curriculum, and control of our training programs are going to remain in the hands of our crafts and our contractors. They are not going to be turned over to any coalition."[24]

Vastly compounding the construction industry problem was the deeply

---

[22] *Wall Street Journal,* September 26, 1969.
[23] *Ibid.*
[24] *Business Week,* September 27, 1969, p. 31.

embedded building trades tradition of restrictive membership, designed not only to limit competition for jobs and to increase the asking price for the existing members' performance of services, but in part also to nurture a certain amount of father-son employment situations. In support of such goals, and also because much employment in the industry had been intermittent and seasonal, hiring had historically been done through the union hiring hall. Racial intolerance itself had, indeed, not often been easily provable in the face of these other exclusionary considerations—as, presumably, in the case of the Philadelphia building trades local whose leader a few years ago countered Negro charges of discrimination with the outraged declaration that "we don't take in *any* new members, regardless of color."[25]

Adding a final complexity to the building trades issue, moreover, was the fact that, by craft union definition, journeymen cannot be created instantaneously. Skilled ironworkers, plumbers, electricians, steamfitters, and similarly highly remunerated workers by and large have emerged only after rigorous apprenticeship programs, often lasting five and more years (and paying relatively low trainee wages during the period). Only through this process, the unions had argued, could the high standards of the craft be upheld. To many blacks, who had long viewed much of the apprenticeship philosophy as primarily a restrictive device (racial or otherwise) anyhow, the unions owed the black community considerable accelerated upgrading to journeyman status as compensation for years of total exclusion. To many whites already in unions, such a concession would greatly dilute the quality of craftsmanship and thus devastate morale among the present skilled trades workers.

The gap separating the two positions by 1971 was, consequently, a very large one. And, given its dimensions, few observers predicted much success even from the federal government's limited Philadelphia Plan, which was implemented in September 1969. This innovative concept established minority group quotas for six building trades unions working on federal construction jobs in the Philadelphia area, beginning with a 4 percent quota in 1969 and scheduled to rise to a 19 percent average by 1973: it was, indeed, immediately assailed by unions and some contractors as an illegal system denying to other prospective employees equal protection of the Constitution, and thrown into the judicial arena. The building trades preferred to stress the Apprenticeship Outreach program conducted jointly by them and the U.S. Labor Department, which had indentured over 5,000 nonwhite apprentices throughout the country between its start in mid-1967 and late 1969. But—as in the Chicago and Pittsburgh controversies—this latter effort was received without applause by civil rights groups, who could

[25] Marten Estey, *The Unions* (New York: Harcourt, Brace & World, Inc., 1967), p. 68.

point out that at this rate significant progress for blacks was many decades away.

As visible as was the construction controversy at the start of the 1970s, the building trades were hardly unique in having aroused the ire of Negroes. Several of the railway brotherhoods continued to show an almost total absence of blacks on their membership rosters (a situation which could be primarily explained by the strong southern historical ties of these unions), as did some printing and entertainment industry crafts and the Air Line Pilots Association.

Yet the problem should be viewed in perspective. Generally speaking, *industrial* unions had rarely practiced membership discrimination either in admission or job assignment. They had recognized that in most industries (as opposed to crafts) large numbers of blacks already existed and that the price of discrimination in such a situation would be the sacrifice of organizing potential. Thus, even prior to the rise of the CIO, the needle trades unions and coal miners aggressively fought off efforts on the part of their more biased rank and file to restrict membership to whites, and essentially all industrial unions following the great waves of organization in the 1930s had espoused a policy of full equality regarding both admission and occupational level for Negroes. The attitude of the AFL-CIO has already been cited, in reference to the 1964 Civil Rights Act, and it is no less a matter of record that the federation had consistently upheld as a cardinal principle ever since the 1955 merger, "to encourage all workers without regard to race, creed, color, national origin or ancestry to share equally in the full benefits of union organization."[26] Nor could the effective allowances forged between labor and civil rights groups—which resulted most notably in improved conditions for black Memphis, Tennessee, sanitation workers in 1968, and one year later (under the banner of "Union Power Plus Soul Power Equals Victory") union recognition and considerable economic betterment for black hospital employees in Charleston, South Carolina—be overlooked in any summary of this more positive side of labor's efforts.

Even the federation and industrial unions, however, had been unable to uproot occasional discriminatory *practices* (as opposed to policies) within the lower levels of their hierarchies. The federation, as Chapter 4 will attempt to show, has limited powers over its affiliates and has stopped short of using its ultimate penalty of expulsion both out of considerations of "overkill" and because of a realistic fear that many craft unions might voluntarily leave the federation fold in sympathy with the disciplined organizations. And the elected leaders of local industrial unions have had, as Bok and Dunlop have accurately pointed out, "much to lose and little to gain by fighting against racial prejudice" where it does exist among their

---

[26] *AFL-CIO Constitution,* Article II, Section 4.

members at these lower levels, particularly "given the high rate of turnover in local union office, and the natural inclination to remain in power."[27] Again, however, the problem was nowhere near as blatant as in the case of the craft unions.

Perhaps it was asking too much of organized labor to exhibit a record which was above reproach in regard to its treatment of black employees, considering that no other sector of our society had performed any better—or possibly, indeed, as well. But in view of the understandable unhappiness of the Negro community with labor's performance to date, it was nonetheless obvious in the early 1970s that this issue was, for unionism, a great one.

AN ANALYSIS OF UNION HISTORY

It is impossible to explain the history of unionism in this country with a single or all-encompassing theory. Economic, structural, and philosophical factors have all been at work, in varying degrees at various times—as has, occasionally, the sheer force of circumstances.

In earlier years, the highly sporadic growth of the American labor movement depended to a great extent on the basic health of the *economy,* and one can rather closely correlate the years of union success and failure with the periods of good and bad times for general business conditions. Union bargaining power and thus the basic attractiveness of union membership was high in the essentially prosperous periods of the years immediately prior to 1819, the 1822–37 era, and in 1850 to 1873 (with the exception of brief recessions in the late 1850s): in each of these intervals union membership lists significantly rose. By the same token, it was not until the depression of 1873–78 that the labor movement could even moderately withstand the slumping demand for labor services engendered by periods of economic reversal: the depressions of 1819–22 and 1837–50 all but eradicated collective bargaining for their durations.

Nor does such a correlation end with 1878. The record fivefold expansion in union ranks between 1897 and 1904 occurred simultaneously with another economic boom period and the tight labor markets of the two world wars clearly fostered union growth and labor organization effectiveness. But after the late 1870s there are as many exceptions to this rule of "as the economy goes, so goes unionism" as there are illustrations of its accuracy. Organized labor rode out the drastic 1893–96 depression without major depletions of either its ranks or its previously acquired bargaining strength; it was forced into an ignominious retreat in the highly prosperous

---

[27] Bok and Dunlop, *op. cit.,* p. 135.

1920s; and it enjoyed its greatest successes during the most formidable of all American depressions, in the 1930s. It is clear that the analyst of labor history can take the economic conditions factor only so far.

Room must also be reserved for recognition of the pronounced *structural* changes which unionism has been willing to make throughout its existence to accommodate the changing nature of industry. Some of these attempts were premature and consequently abortive—notably the National Trades' Union of 1834, whose ambitious concept had to await the nationalizing of industry in the 1860s. But just as the widening of product markets had given impetus to the growth of local unions at the turn of the nineteenth century, the extension of labor markets following the construction of comprehensive railroad networks ultimately made the coordination of local unionism through the national union structure no less mandatory. Had labor been either unwilling or unable to establish its countervailing power in this fashion, the existence of the movement on any significant scale might have ended with the rise of the large national corporation in the closing decades of the century. It is equally tempting to speculate as to the sanguine effects for labor of the establishment of the AFL's "exclusive jurisdiction" concept: it is a matter of record, however, that the rival unionism of the pre-1886 period had proven highly detrimental to many national unions.

Above all, it is undeniable that labor faced a critical juncture in the midst of the Great Depression, when the continuing wisdom of its craft unionism structure was severely questioned—and that, however begrudgingly the peak federation moved to accommodate the millions of industrial unionist constituents who desired acceptance, an ultimate willingness to adapt to a changing situation was for labor the only logical decision. High wassail did not prevail at the banquet tables of the mighty.

Major *philosophical* decisions, too, have exerted a strong influence on the state and shape of American unionism in the early 1970s. In many ways, Samuel Gompers was not only the father of the modern labor movement but its supreme spiritual symbol. A pronounced strain of pragmatism runs, in fact, through all of labor's history, just as it motivated so many of Gompers' actions. The mainstream of labor, with or without Gompers, has *always* stressed the practical at the expense of the ideal, shunning, as he and his fellow AFL founders did, "objects that cannot be realized in a few years."

Thus such presumed social panaceas as the socialistic agricultural communities, land reform, and producers' cooperatives which were proposed by the zealous reformers of the 1840s had no great appeal to the typical workingman: their connection with his on-the-job happiness and relevancy to solving the pressing problems of industrialization were too remote to be appreciated. The same can be said of the National Labor Union's advocacy of the termination of the convict labor system, currency reform, and women's suffrage three decades later and of Terrence V. Powderly's campaign for cooperatives and temperance. Nor does the notable failure of the IWW and its revolutionary credo that "the working class and the employing class have nothing in common" detract from this common denomination. Such lofty goals as these and their latter-day reincarnations in the various radical groups which have on many occasions dotted the periphery of the labor movement have been received with total apathy by the average rank-and-file unionist.

What *has* historically concerned the union member has been more in the here and now: more economic benefits, improved working conditions, and above all else a maximum of job security. These great motivators of support for organized labor accounted directly, it will be remembered, for the rise of the first American unions and no labor organization of any lasting influence since 1800 has ever lost sight of such mundane, "bread-and-butter," but also (to the union constituent) vitally important goals.

So greatly does this stamp of "pure and simple," "more and more" unionism permeate labor history that whole schools of academic thought in the labor area have been built around it. Most notable of them is the John R. Commons–Selig Perlman, or "Wisconsin School," theory, which holds that the key to understanding union growth and survival rests primarily on understanding the American worker's "consciousness of scarcity" and of limited opportunity, which in turn fostered a deep desire for improved "property rights" on the job itself. To protect the dignity and security of the individual jobholder, collective bargaining appears to this school to have been accepted by employees as a vital first step.

History seems to support this basic Commons-Perlman thesis as at least a major further explanation of American labor history. It has not been by sheer coincidence that all major periods of union growth, excepting only wartime ones, have been marked by widespread job insecurity: this situation was as true of both 1800–19 and 1822–37, when the worker fears stemmed primarily from employer cost-cutting devices necessitated by the new scope of product markets, as it was two decades later, when the menace of inter-worker competition on a geographic basis due to widened labor markets was the major cause of alarm. It was as much in evidence when the immigrant waves from Europe accelerated in the late 1860s as in the 1897–1904 period, marked by its myriad of "Scientific Management" innovations. And the booming union totals of the 1930s coincided, of course, with the Great Depression. The fact that equally great "consciousness of scarcity" characterized other *less* successful periods for labor (for example, the 1904–16 period, when European immigration hit its peak) in no way negates the "Wisconsin School" thesis.

But just as some attention must be paid to the economic and structural factors in addition to these "philosophical" ones in understanding the growth of unionism, and just as Maslow's Need Hierarchy can hardly be ignored in dealing at least with *contemporary* unionism, so too must one recognize that some key aspects of labor history defy any theoretical generalizations at all. One can attempt to account for the huge success of AFL and CIO organizational drives in the 1930s, for example, in terms of "willingness to adjust to organizational forms" (structural) or "job-conciousness" (philosophical)—if *not* in terms of the "economic conditions" framework—but in doing so he has only a partial explanation. In retrospect, the evidence is clear that *both* of the above factors *combined* with a *variety* of special economic, public policy, and labor leadership circumstances to foster this great period of union growth, and that in many ways *each* further factor was *unprecedented* in its order of magnitude. Similarly, the adverse technological, public relations, and legal obstacles with which labor has been confronted over the past fifteen years also hinge on unparalleled conditions.

Thus what is past may not necessarily, the declaration of Shakespeare notwithstanding, be prologue. And hopes for a resurgence of union growth which are anchored only to the propositions that labor's growth has "always" been sporadic, that unionism has "always" been able to adapt itself structurally to changing needs, and that worker job-consciousness has "always" guaranteed collective bargaining a firm place in our society are not necessarily justified.

What, then, can one say about labor's future in terms of its past? Even with the high degree of uncertainty which such predictions inevitably involve, and despite all the unprecedented circumstances since the 1930s, at least one factor emerges clearly from a reading of labor history in this country, and it suggests that the current reports of unionism's impending doom may indeed be grossly exaggerated. Organized labor has been surrounded by conditions at least as bleak as those which confront it today at many times in its 170-year history, and on each occasion it has proven equal to the challenge. It has fully recovered not only from the disastrous economic depressions which at various times have wiped out most of its membership, but from the inroads of reformers who temporarily succeeded in divorcing it almost entirely from its collective bargaining functions. It has overcome devastating victories won by employers, and formidable weapons in the hands of the courts. It has incurred deeprooted public disfavor before, particularly in the 1870s and 1920s, and ultimately surmounted it. And at perhaps the two most critical junctures of all in its still-short history— (1) in the 1880s with the rapid disintegration of the Knights and their "one big union" concept, and (2) on the eve of the Great Depression, when an apathetic AFL remained almost exclusively the province of the highly skilled amid severe membership losses and concerted attacks from without— a Gompers and a Lewis could emerge to lead unionism to heights previously thought unreachable.

It is entirely possible that labor's remarkable staying-power has been due to the single fact that to many workers, from the early nineteenth century to the present, there has really been no acceptable substitute for collective bargaining as a means of maintaining and improving employment conditions. Whatever its deficiencies, the labor union has offered millions of employees in our profit-minded industrial society sufficient hope that their needs, not only as employees but as individuals, would be considered to warrant their taking out union membership. At the very least, these employees have been satisfied that the only theoretical alternative to collective bargaining—individual bargaining—has for them been no alternative at all from a practical viewpoint.

Thus the strongest of cases can be built, as the earliest pages of this book have indicated, that collective bargaining is here to stay—most probably in the highly pragmatic "bread-and-butter" form from which its successes have always emanated, and quite probably also with future structural modifications (however belated at times these may be in coming) to accommodate future institutional needs—but at least here in some form which is not dramatically different from its present character for the foreseeable future.

From this it necessarily follows that, as Kheel has pointed out, "Our objective must be not to find a substitute for bargaining but to discover ways of making it work better."[28] And the latter can be located only after one fully understands not only the labor relations process but the framework in which it operates, toward which understanding such a book as this is, of course, directed.

DISCUSSION QUESTIONS

1. "Without the rise of the merchant-capitalist in this country, there could have been no genuine labor movement." Comment.
2. It has been said that "unions are for capitalism for the same reason that fish are for water." Elaborate upon this statement, drawing from the historical record.
3. Explain the paradox that until relatively recent years skilled workers who enjoyed comparatively high levels of income and status constituted the main source of union membership.
4. "If the Knights of Labor expired because it could not fulfill any function, the American Federation of Labor succeeded because it admirably could fulfill many functions." Elaborate, qualifying this statement if you believe that qualifications are needed.
5. Richard A. Lester has offered as his opinion that "even with the New Deal ... union development experienced, not a marked mutation, but a partial alteration and expansion in leadership, tactics, and jurisdiction. The adjust-

---

[28] Theodore W. Kheel. "A Labor Relations Policy for 1964," *Personnel Journal,* April 1964, p. 181.

ment in basic union philosophy was neither profound nor completely permanent." Do you agree?
6. If a Gompers and a Lewis could emerge to rescue unionism at critical times in the past, cannot a case be made that there is nothing basically wrong with organized labor today that imaginative leadership could not cure? Discuss fully.
7. Evaluate the argument that, at least in part, unionism has become a victim of its own success.

SELECTED REFERENCES

Dulles, Foster Rhea, *Labor in America,* 2nd rev. ed. New York: Thomas Y. Crowell Company, 1960.

Galenson, Walter, *The CIO Challenge to the AFL: A History of the American Labor Movement, 1935–1941.* Cambridge, Mass.: Harvard University Press, 1960.

Harris, Herbert, *American Labor.* New Haven: Yale University Press, 1939.

Litwack, Leon, *The American Labor Movement.* Englewood Cliffs, N.J.: Prentice-Hall, Inc., 1962.

Pierson, Frank C., *Unions in Postwar America.* New York: Random House, 1967.

Rayback, Joseph G., *A History of American Labor.* New York: The Free Press, 1966.

Taft, Philip, *Organized Labor in American History.* New York: Harper & Row, Publishers, 1964.

Tyler, Gus, *The Labor Revolution.* New York: The Viking Press, 1966.

Ulman, Lloyd, *American Trade Unionism—Past and Present.* Berkeley, Calif.: Institute of Industrial Relations, University of California, 1961.

———, *The Rise of the National Trade Union.* Cambridge, Mass.: Harvard University Press, 1955.

3

The Legal Framework

As previous pages have suggested, today's manager is hardly free to deal with the union as he wishes. A growing body of federal and state laws and the judicial and administrative interpretations of these laws now govern the employer at virtually all points at which he comes into contact with organized labor. Legislation today has much to say about management's role in union organizational campaigns and its bargaining procedures in negotiating contracts once a union has gained recognition. It is also outspoken about the acceptable contents of the company's labor agreements and even its actions in administering these agreements. As is also true of the union, whose conduct is at least equally regulated by public policy, the employer can scarcely afford to be poorly informed in the area of the labor law.

If the laws have become extensive, however, they have also become complex and often nebulous. Labor lawyers have been forced to undertake Herculean tasks, not always successfully, in attempting to assess what is "legal" and what is not in the sphere of collective bargaining. And inconsistent interpretations of the labor statutes—stemming from the National Labor Relations Board, the various state and lower federal judiciaries, and the Supreme Court itself—continue to mark the field. There is, in fact, some justification for those who have termed the last major piece of federal labor legislation, the Landrum-Griffin Act of 1959, the "Lawyers' Full Employment Act."

But if it is impossible to state definitively the exact constraints on union-management relations which the law now imposes, at least what might appropriately be described as "currently useful generalizations" *can* be offered. Moreover, not only such basic principles but also their paths of development *must* be dealt with if the environment in which labor relations operate in the early 1970s is to be fully appreciated. If the lessons of general labor history have greatly influenced the nature of the bargaining process as it exists today, the ever-greater thrust of the laws has had an equally pervasive effect.

THE ERA OF JUDICIAL CONTROL

In view of the present scope of labor legislation, it is somewhat ironic that less than four decades ago employers were virtually unrestrained by law from dealing with unions as they saw fit. There was, as we have seen, almost no statutory treatment of labor-management relations from the days of the American Revolution until the Great Depression of the 1930s. Instead, individual judges exercised public control over these relations. And the courts' view of union activities was, for the most part, as unsympathetic as was that of most businessmen of the times.

The employers' traditional weapons for fighting labor organizations—such as formal and informal espionage, blacklists, and the very potent practice of discharging "agitators"—were normally left undisturbed by the judges. However, if the members of the judiciary believed that union activities were being conducted either for "illegal purposes" or by "illegal means," they were generous in extracting money damages from the unions and in ordering criminal prosecution of labor leaders.

The qualifications for "illegality" varied to some extent from court to court. In general, however, most aggressive union activities of the day —strikes to obtain agreements whereby the employer would employ only union members (the closed shop), picketing by "strangers" (those not in a direct superior-subordinate relationship with the employer), and the secondary boycott (the exercise of economic pressure against one company to force it to exert pressure on another company which is actually the subject of the union's concern)—were held to be illegal. Many courts went even further: through the 1920s such remarks as "judicial actions against even peaceful picketing are merely declaratory of what has always been the law and the best practice in equity," flowed freely from the judges. And although it was President Calvin Coolidge who asserted that "The business of the United States is business," the remark could readily have emanated from most members of the judiciary well into the third decade of this century. The courts, viewing their primary role as that of protecting property rights, allied themselves with few exceptions squarely with the employer community to neutralize the economic power of organized labor.

Fully as welcome to employers, too, was the extensive court use of the injunction. This device, a judicial order calling for the cessation of certain actions deemed injurious and for which the other forms of court-provided relief appeared to be unsuitable remedies, was often invoked by the judges following employer requests for such intervention. To unionists, such restraining orders seemed to be issued quite indiscriminately. Even the relatively detached observer of legal history, however, would very likely conclude that it did not seem to take much to convince the judges that union activities should be curbed: the jurists issued their restraining decrees almost as reflex actions; and strikes, boycotts, picketing—virtually any form of union "self-help" activity—thus ran the risk of being abruptly ended if in any way present or imminent damage to the employer's property could be shown as being threatened.

THE NORRIS—LA GUARDIA ACT OF 1932

Despite its 1932 date, the Norris–La Guardia Act is of considerably more than historical interest. As is true of the later labor laws which will be discussed in this chapter, most of its provisions are still valid and continue today to govern labor relations in interstate commerce.

At the time of its passage, however, the act was particularly noteworthy. Not only did it constitute the first major inter-industry federal legislation to be applied to collective bargaining, but—as stated earlier—it marked a significant change in public policy from *repression to strong encouragement of union activity*. Implemented in the final days of the Hoover administration, it owed its birth mainly to the widespread unemployment of the times and to a general recognition that only through bargaining collectively could many employees exercise any meaningful influence on their working environments. It also stemmed, however, from popular sentiment that justice had not been served by allowing the courts their virtually unlimited authority to issue injunctions in labor disputes.

Accordingly the act greatly narrowed the scope of the courts for issuing such injunctions. Peaceful picketing, peaceable assembly, organizational picketing, payment of strike benefits, and a host of other union economic weapons were now made nonenjoinable. Also enacted within the new law were procedural requirements for injunctions issued on other grounds.

Even more symbolic of the major shift in public policy was the act's assertion that it was now necessary for Congress to guarantee to the individual employee "full freedom of association, self-organization, and designation of representatives of his own choosing, to negotiate the terms and conditions of his employment...free from interference, restraint, or coercion of employers." All the federal labor laws passed since 1932 have embodied this same principle.

Nor was the new treatment of unionism destined to be confined only to the federal arena. Within a short period of time, twenty states (including almost all the major industrial ones) had independently created their own "little Norris–La Guardia Acts" to govern labor relations in intrastate commerce.

Norris–La Guardia and its state counterparts did not by themselves, however, greatly stimulate union growth. They clearly expanded union freedoms and placed legal limits on judicial capriciousness, but they did little to restrain employers directly in their conduct toward collective bargaining. Only the previously cited "yellow-dog" contract arrangement, whereby managements had been able to require nonunion membership or activity as a condition of employment, was declared unenforceable by the 1932 act. Otherwise, employers remained at liberty to fight labor organizations by whatever means they could implement, despite the ambitious language of Norris–La Guardia.

THE WAGNER ACT OF 1935

It remained for the National Labor Relations Act of 1935, more commonly known as the Wagner Act, to alter this situation, by putting teeth in the government's pledge to protect employee collective bargaining rights. The Wagner Act, it will be recalled, accomplished this through two basic methods: (1) it specifically banned five types of management action as constituting "unfair labor practices"; and (2) it set forth the principle of majority rule for the selection of employee bargaining representatives and provided that, should the employer express doubt as to the union's majority status, a secret-ballot election of the employees would determine if the majority existed. It also created an independent, quasi-judicial agency—the National Labor Relations Board (NLRB)—to provide the machinery for enforcing both of the previous provisions.

Employer Unfair Labor Practices

The five employer unfair labor practices, deemed "statutory wrongs" (although not crimes) by Congress, have been modified to some small extent since 1935, as noted below. They remain, however, a significant part of the law of collective bargaining to this day, and they constitute an impressive quintet of "thou shalt nots" for employers who might otherwise be tempted to resort to the blunt tactics of prior eras in an effort to undermine unionism. The Wagner Act: (1) deemed it "unfair" for managements to "interfere with, restrain, or coerce employees" in exercising their now legally sanctioned right of self-organization; (2) restrained company representatives from dominating or interfering with either the formation or the administration of labor unions; (3) prohibited companies from discriminating "in regard to hire or tenure of employment or any term or condition of employment to encourage or discourage membership in any labor organization"; (4) forbade employers to discharge or otherwise discriminate against employees simply because the latter had filed "unfair labor practice" charges or otherwise offered testimony against company actions under the act; and (5) made it an unfair labor practice for employers to refuse to bargain collectively with the duly chosen representatives of their employees.

In the years since 1935, the NLRB and the courts (to which board decisions can be appealed by either labor relations party) have had ample opportunity to make known their interpretations of all five of these provisions. In dealing with some of them, both public bodies have been quite consistent in their decisions and what the framers of the Wagner Act had in mind is no longer seriously questioned by either management or union representatives. In other cases, however, the board members and judges have had some difficulty in issuing rulings which have been perceived by the labor relations parties as being compatible with prior rulings on the same subject. But the judges have at least generally proven themselves to be reluctant to reverse the original NLRB decision when these have been appealed to the courts, and the inconsistencies would in most cases appear to stem more from the changing membership of the five-man board through the years and from inherent difficulties in the words of the laws themselves than from this "opportunity for appeal" factor.

Relatively clear-cut decisions have been rendered by the NLRB and courts in two of the five areas:

1. The interpreters of the Wagner Act have consistently held a wide variety of employer practices to be in violation of the "interfere with, restrain or coerce employees" section. Among other management actions: bribery of employees, company spy systems, blacklisting of union sympathizers, removal of an existing business to another location for the sole purpose of frustrating union activity, and promises by employers of wage increases or other special concessions to employees should the latter refrain from joining a union have all historically constituted "interference" contrary to the act. The same can be said of board and court treatment of employers who have threatened to isolate ("like a rotten apple," in one

case) pro-union workers, engaged in individual bargaining with employees represented by a union, or questioned employees concerning their union activities in such a way as to tend to restrain or coerce such employees. When satisfied that any such violations have occurred, the board has issued "cease and desist" orders against the guilty employer with no hesitation. And when it has found that employees have been discharged unlawfully in the process, the NLRB has most frequently required their reinstatement with full back pay.

Particularly in this area the courts have proven unwilling, by and large, to reverse board decisions upon appeal, moreover, and the fact that failure to "cease and desist" after the courts have called for this action constitutes contempt of court has at times dissuaded employers from carrying an appeal to the courts in the first place. However, under normal circumstances the employer who both refuses to comply with an adverse board order and decides not to appeal it (so as not to bring the matter to the court's attention) stands to gain little: the NLRB *itself* can be counted upon to take the initiative and ask the judges for an order calling for employer compliance with the original board decision.

2. The board and courts have also had no apparent difficulty in deciding what constitutes evidence of employer discrimination related to the fourth unfair labor practice. They long ago concluded that such management actions as the layoff of an employee shortly after his testimony before the board and the discharge of a woman worker immediately after her husband had filed unfair labor practice charges (on other grounds) against the company could be taken as discriminatory, and have consistently ruled in this direction ever since. The board has further concluded, apparently also without much hesitation, that a company's belief that charges filed by an employee are false in no way justifies its taking punitive action against the employee. On the other hand, considerably fewer cases have had to be decided concerning this fourth unfair practice than any of the others, presumably because employers have themselves recognized that violations here are normally quite obvious to all concerned, and have therefore refrained from taking such action in the first place.

Interpretation seems to have been somewhat more difficult when the issues have involved the three other portions of the employer unfair labor practice section.

1. The restriction on company discrimination "in regard to hire or tenure of employment or any term or condition of employment to encourage or discourage membership in any labor organization" has clearly made it unlawful for employers to force employees who are union members to accept less desirable job assignments than nonunionists, or to reduce the former type of employee's pay because of the union affiliation. Similarly, it is obvious that companies which demand renunciation of union mem-

bership as a condition of continued employment or in order to be promoted within the nonsupervisory ranks do so only at their peril. But the legality of other types of employer conduct has proven to be anything but as clearcut.

Where, for example, there is conclusive evidence that an employee has falsified his employment application and thus failed to reveal a previous criminal record, can he be properly discharged by the company for this offense? Not always, according to at least one NLRB decision covering exactly this situation. Here the board cited the company's "anti-union bias," its knowledge of the employee's union activities, and its treatment of nonunion employees who had committed comparable offenses, in deciding that the company's official reason for the discharge was only a "pretext" for discriminating against union members.[1] Cases of this kind have proven to be thorny ones for the board and the courts and have often caused considerable flows of adrenalin on the part of employers.

2. The proviso restraining company representatives from dominating or interfering with both the formation and the administration of labor unions—included because of the Congress' unhappiness with the widespread creation of employer-influenced company unions in the years preceding 1935—has been the basis of much complex litigation since that date. Falcone has tersely pointed out that "it is generally held that when an employer has control over the union sitting on the other side of the bargaining table, collective bargaining is a farce and a delusion";[2] but determining just when an employer has such control has proven to be no easy matter. Among specific management actions which the board and courts have looked unfavorably upon as evidence of employer control have been the following: the solicitation of company-union membership by supervisory employees, the company's payment of membership dues for all employees joining the union, and an employer gift to a union of $400 and the right to operate a canteen which made a monthly profit of $50 to $100—none of these company moves being especially notable for their subtlety. On the other hand, interpretations have found nothing unlawful in the mere fact that, for example, a labor organization limits its membership to employees of a single employer: the test for unfair practice pivots exclusively upon the question of which party *controls* the organization and in a case such as this only much closer inspection (and the standards for "control" established by the interpreters) can reveal whether or not the employer is in violation of the law.

3. The fact that the 1935 legislation said little more on the subject of an employer's "refusal to bargain collectively with the representatives

[1] *Photoswitch,* 99 NLRB 1366 (1962).
[2] Nicholas S. Falcone, *Labor Law* (New York: John Wiley & Sons, Inc., 1963), p. 213.

of his employees" than can be gleaned from these words perhaps guaranteed that controversies would result from this last section of the Wagner Act's "Rights of Employees" section, and this has indeed been the case. As such new topics for potential bargaining as pensions, health insurance, seniority, and subcontracting have arisen in the years since 1935, the NLRB and courts have been freely called upon to make known their opinions as to what "must" be bargained by employers, and what need not be. The courts have also been asked for a more precise definition of "bargaining" itself than the act provided. The issue is still far from resolved, and with new possibilities for bargaining constantly emerging it perhaps never fully will be. But the board and judicial decisions of the past three and one-half decades have at least ambitiously attempted to shed light on the scope for employer action in this area, and certain statements can now be made with some authority.

In brief, there are today many "mandatory" subjects of bargaining with which the employer must deal in good faith. Such objects include wages, hours of employment, health insurance, pensions, safety practices, the grievance procedure, procedures for discharge, layoff, recall and discipline, seniority, and subcontracting. Managers are *not* required to make concessions or agree to union proposals on any of these (or various other) subjects. They *are* obligated, however, to meet with the union at reasonable times and with the good-faith intention of reaching an agreement. On "nonmandatory" or "voluntary" subjects—those that are lawful but not easily related to "wages, hours and other conditions of employment"—employers are not so obligated and are free to refuse to bargain about them.

Where there is a duty to bargain, the employer must supply—upon union request—information that is "relevant and necessary" to allow the labor representatives to bargain "intelligently and effectively." The NLRB and courts have ruled, for example, that a union is entitled to information in the employer's possession concerning wage rates and increases, on the grounds that the former cannot deal intelligently with the subject without such information. Similarly, if a company claims financial inability to honor the union's demands, it must stand ready to supply the union with authoritative proof of this inability.

The employer's duty to bargain also entails the duty to refrain from taking unilateral action on the "mandatory" subjects. Companies which have announced a wage increase without consulting the employees' designated representatives or have subcontracted work to another employer without allowing their own union a chance to bargain the matter violate this portion of the law.

Yet the apparent finality of such remarks as the above is highly deceptive. Not only is considerable uncertainty left as to what *else* is a "mandatory" subject for bargaining (beyond the specific topics cited and the few others which the NLRB and judges have thus far dealt with affirmatively) and what is "nonmandatory," but the question of what constitutes "the good-faith intention of reaching an agreement" on the employer's part is left an open one.

It remains to be seen what further subjects the board and courts will ultimately assign to the "mandatory" category. A union demand for moving allowances for workers transferred by the company? A proposal that all production workers be placed on a salaried basis, rather than being paid by the hour? A request by the labor organization that all foreign production of the company's product be terminated? Guarantees by the company that pension funds will be invested in low-cost housing for union employees? Each of these demands has been raised on several occasions in actual bargaining situations in recent years. Excepting only the first, company negotiators have been notably reluctant to accommodate any of them, or numerous similarly ambitious union proposals. Yet as Fleming, who raises the possibility of all of them ultimately going before the interpreters of public policy, has pointed out, "In the changing and very real world of bargaining, all [of these, and similar demands] may be close to the felt needs of the parties...[and] deciding which of [them] falls into the mandatory category will not be an easy task. Job security and internal union affairs pose extremely delicate issues."[3]

If disposition of such issues as these must thus await future board and court treatment, it at least appears safe to predict that the books have not yet closed on the list of "mandatory" topics: most of the subjects with which employers are *now* required to deal in good faith are themselves relative newcomers to such status, and the NLRB and jurists today appear to be more activistic in this regard than ever.

The steadily increasing types of tests adopted by the board and courts for "good faith"—for example, whether or not employer delaying tactics were used in the bargaining, some evidence of management initiative in making counterproposals, employer willingness to accommodate completely routine demands (such as the continued availability of plant parking spaces) —have seemingly been attacked more for their naïveté than for the spirit behind them. As the authors of the highly respected Committee for Economic Development's *The Public Interest in National Labor Policy* have asserted:

> The limitations and artificiality of such tests are apparent, and the possibilities of evasion are almost limitless.... Basically, it is unrealistic

[3] Robben W. Fleming, "The Obligation to Bargain in Good Faith," in Joseph Shister *et al.*, *Public Policy and Collective Bargaining* (New York: Harper & Row, Publishers, 1962), p. 83; see also Guy Farmer, *Management Rights and Union Bargaining Power* (New York: Industrial Relations Counselors, Inc., 1965).

to expect that, by legislation, "good faith" can be brought to the bargaining table.[4]

At the very least, however, it is obvious that in being forced to plug the existing gaps in the Wagner Act's "refusal to bargain" interpretations, representatives of public policy have projected themselves more and more into the labor-management arena in the years since 1935, perhaps to an extent which was never contemplated when the Wagner Act was passed.

Employee Representation Elections

Despite all the interpretative difficulties which have been involved in the employer unfair labor practice provisions, the latter clearly were—and are—wide-sweeping in their implications for collective bargaining. However, they still represent an *indirect* approach to the protection of employee bargaining rights: by themselves, they clearly restrict employer action in the labor relations area, but they say nothing explicit about the key question of initial union *recognition*.

The authors of the Wagner Act were well aware of this gap and proceeded to deal directly with the latter issue in another section of the act, that pertaining to the secret-ballot election. As noted previously, the NLRB was authorized to conduct such an election should the company express doubt that a majority of its employees had chosen to be represented by any union at all. Prior to this time, a union could gain recognition from an unreceptive employer only through the successful use of such economic weapons as the strike and boycott.

As this part of the act now stands, the board can conduct a representation election if requested to do so by a single employee, by a group of employees, or by a labor organization acting for employees. In any of these three cases the petition must be supported by "a substantial number of employees" who desire collective bargaining representation and it must allege that the employer refuses to recognize such representation. *Employers* may also petition for such an election, presumably with the objective of proving that the employees do *not* desire union representation or for various reasons of scheduling strategy (such as trying to get the board to hold the election at the time least favorable to the union).

It is also possible for an election to involve two or more unions, each claiming "substantial" employee support. The employees then have the choice of voting for any of the unions on the ballot or for "no union."

---

[4] Committee for Economic Development, *The Public Interest in National Labor Policy* (New York: CED, 1961), p. 82.

If none of these choices (including "no union") wins a majority of the votes cast, a runoff election is then conducted among the two choices which have received the highest number of votes.

In administering this portion of the law, the NLRB itself ultimately framed a few further rules designed to foster labor relations stability. Should any union win an NLRB-conducted election and then execute a valid contract with the employer, rival unions may now not seek bargaining rights (through a subsequent election) for a period of three years following the effective date of the contract or for the length of the contract—whichever is the shorter. However, the victorious union is still not guaranteed its bargaining rights for this period of time: if the *employees themselves* have second thoughts about the desirability of retaining the union's services, they can—after one year—petition the NLRB for a decertification election. A majority vote in this latter election rescinds the union's bargaining agency.

Though winning an election is by far the most common way a union secures bargaining rights, there are circumstances under which the NLRB now orders an employer to bargain collectively even though it does not conduct an election. These occur when a union is successful in getting a majority of employees in a bargaining unit to sign union membership authorization cards and the employer engages in serious unfair labor practices, the effect of which destroys the union's majority. For example, the employer may discharge employees who are union sympathizers. In such situations, the NLRB theory is that a union would win the election were it not for the unfair labor practice, and the holding of the election would not reflect the actual sentiment of the employees. In 1969, the United States Supreme Court sustained this doctrine in *NLRB* v. *Gissel Packing Company* (395 U.S. 575).

Employers and management groups have bitterly criticized this NLRB policy. They contend that the NLRB should not order collective bargaining on the basis of authorization cards: the test of the union's majority should be determined only through an election. Employers contend that employees may sign cards because of social pressure or could be misled by a union organizer as to the purpose of the authorization card. Of course, employers can avoid the effect of the policy by not engaging in serious unfair labor practices during the time a union conducts its organizing campaign. In the last analysis, therefore, it depends upon employer conduct as to whether the NLRB will order collective bargaining based on authorization cards. Also, if frequency is used as a standard, the issue of bargaining orders based on authorization cards has been exaggerated. In the typical year, the NLRB orders collective bargaining on this basis in only about 1 percent of the cases. In all other cases the board determines the majority status of unions through the election process.

FROM THE WAGNER ACT TO TAFT-HARTLEY

As established by the Wagner Act, then, the scope of National Labor Relations Board activities was to be twofold. The board was charged with investigating employer unfair labor practices and it was given the authority to conduct employee representation elections.

The NLRB's members (appointed by the President, subject to confirmation by the Senate) and its various regional officials outside of Washington even in their earliest years of existence undertook both of these assignments zealously. By 1947, they had processed almost 44,000 unfair labor practice cases, running the gamut in their decisions from dismissing complaints as having no merit to issuing "cease and desist" orders against guilty employers. In the area of representation cases, the board was even more active. Almost 60,000 such cases were dealt with between 1935 and 1947. In addition to determining whether or not elections should be held and conducting such elections if the answer was in the affirmative, the NLRB often had the further duty of deciding the type of unit appropriate for the particular labor relationship (such as employer, craft, or plant).

Although its activities were necessarily controversial, as was the act sanctioning these activities, there is general agreement today that in this twelve-year period the board performed its basic mission of protecting the right of employees to organize and bargain collectively quite creditably. Even at the time, many contemporaries had been impressed: as in the case of Norris–La Guardia, "Little Wagner Acts" were soon enacted in many states to govern labor relations in intrastate commerce.

The modern labor movement in this country can, in fact, justifiably be said to have begun in 1935. Union membership totals boomed after that year, due in no small measure to the Wagner Act and its state counterparts. Other factors were, of course, also responsible: the improving economic climate, the generally liberal sentiments of the times, the keen competition between the American Federation of Labor and the newly born Committee for Industrial Organization, and dynamic union leadership. And it is equally true that prior legislation—not only Norris–La Guardia but also the ill-fated National Industrial Recovery Act of 1933—had paved the way for the new era and had independently led to much spontaneous union organization before 1935. But it is no less a fact that employers could still legally try to counteract unionism by almost any means except the yellow-dog contract and the arbitrary injunction process— up to and including sheer refusal to grant the union recognition under any circumstances—before the passage of the Wagner Act. It is extremely doubtful that organized labor could have grown as it did—from 3.6 million unionized workers in 1935 to more than 14 million by 1947—without the Wagner Act's protection.

Certainly public opinion as registered in Congress did not debate this last point. As the man in the street gradually turned against unionism in the mid-1940s he blamed existing public policy for the union excesses of the times, most notably for the postwar strike waves. As the last chapter has described, his voice ultimately became a compelling one: Congress overrode President Truman's veto and passed the Taft-Hartley Act of 1947, thereby stilling the cries that the Wagner Act had become too "one-sided" in favor of labor.

THE TAFT-HARTLEY ACT OF 1947

With the advent of Taft-Hartley, officially known as the Labor-Management Relations Act, a new period in public policy toward labor unions began: that of *modified encouragement coupled with regulation.*

Much as the Wagner Act was to a great extent designed to correct weaknesses in Norris–La Guardia, which nonetheless was not repealed and remains a part of the legal environment of collective bargaining to this day, Taft-Hartley amended but did not displace the Wagner Act. The Wagner Act, essentially as adjusted by the 1947 legislation, governs labor relations today.

Indeed, the old unfair employer practices were continued virtually word-for-word by the new legislation. The only significant changes were that the closed shop (and its requirement that all workers be union members at the time of their hiring) was no longer allowed and the freedom of the parties to authorize the *union shop* (which, as noted earlier, allows the employer to hire anyone but provides that all new employees must join the union after a stipulated period of time) was somewhat narrowed. The intention of this amendment related to the third employer unfair labor practice: in its ban on employer hiring and job condition discrimination in order to encourage or discourage union membership, the Wagner Act *had* authorized employers to enter into union and closed shop agreements. The changes clearly symbolized public policy's new attitude toward unions.

Far more indicative of the public's less enthusiastic sentiments toward unions, however, were those portions of Taft-Hartley which dealt with: (1) *union unfair labor practices,* which were now enumerated and prohibited in the same way that the employer practices had been; (2) *the rights of employees as individuals,* as contrasted with those rights which employees now legally enjoyed as *union members;* (3) *the rights of employers,* a subject which the Wagner Act had glossed over in its concentration on employer *duties*; and (4) *national emergency strikes*. To some extent, other major parts of the new law—those relating to internal union affairs, the termination or modification of existing labor contracts, and suits involving unions—also demonstrated a hardening of Congressional attitudes toward labor organizations. We shall consider these various provisions separately.

Union Unfair Labor Practices

Going the framers of the Wagner Act one better, Taft-Hartley enumerated *six* labor practices which unions were prohibited from engaging in. Labor organizations operating in interstate commerce were now officially obliged to refrain from: (1) restraining or coercing employees in the exercise of their guaranteed collective bargaining rights; (2) causing an employer to discriminate in any way against an employee in order to encourage or discourage union membership; (3) refusing to bargain in good faith with their employer about wages, hours, and other employment conditions; (4) certain types of strikes and boycotts; (5) charging employees covered by union shop agreements initiation fees or dues "in an amount which the board finds excessive or discriminatory under all the circumstances"; and (6) engaging in "featherbedding," the requirement of payment by the employer for services not performed.

As in the case of the employer unfair labor practices, interpretative difficulties have marked the subsequent treatment of some of these provisions. In addition, the six unfair labor practices directed against unions appear to have varied considerably more widely than in the case of the Wagner Act employer provisions in their effects on labor relations practice.

Two of the six provisions have perhaps had the greatest influence on collective bargaining, and undoubtedly a salutary one, in the years since the enactment of Taft-Hartley:

1. The ban on union restraint or coercion of employees in the exercise of their guaranteed bargaining rights, which also entails a union obligation to avoid coercion of employees who choose to refrain from collective bargaining altogether. What constitutes such restraint or coercion? The myriad of rulings which has been rendered by the NLRB and courts since 1947 has at least indicated that such union actions as the following will always run the risk of being found "unfair": the stating to an antiunion employee that the employee will lose his job should the union gain recognition; the signing of an agreement with an employer which recognizes the union as exclusive bargaining representative when in fact it lacks majority employee support; and the issuing of patently false statements during a representation election campaign. Union picket line violence, threats of reprisal against

employees subpoenaed to testify against the union at NLRB hearings, and activities of a similar vein are also unlawful.

This first unfair union practice also extends to the coercion of the employer in the latter's selection of his *own* bargaining representative. Post-1947 rulings have stated, for example, that unions cannot refuse to deal with former union officers who represent employers, or insist on meeting only with the owners of a company rather than with the company's attorney. On the other hand, unions have every right to demand that the employer representative with whom they deal have sufficient authority to make final decisions on behalf of the company: the interpreters of public policy have clearly understood that to have this any other way would be to frustrate the whole process of bargaining.

2. The Taft-Hartley provision which makes it unfair for a union to cause an employer to discriminate against an employee in order to influence union membership. There is a single exception to this prohibition: Under a valid union shop agreement, the union may lawfully demand the discharge of an employee who fails to pay his initiation fee and periodic dues. Otherwise, however, unions must exercise complete self-control in this area. They cannot try to force employers to fire or otherwise penalize workers for any other reason, whether these reasons involve worker opposition to union policies, failure to attend union meetings, or refusal to join the union at all. Nor can a union lawfully seek to persuade an employer to grant hiring preference to employees who are "satisfactory" to the union. Subject only to the union shop proviso, Taft-Hartley sought to place nonunion workers on a footing equal to that of union employees.

Occupying more or less middle ground in its degree of influence upon the labor relations process stands the *third* restriction on union practices, pertaining to union refusal to bargain. Here, clearly, Taft-Hartley extended to labor organizations the same obligation that the Wagner Act had already imposed on employers.

To many observers, the law's inclusion of this union bargaining provision has meant very little: unions can normally be expected to pursue bargaining rather than attempt to avoid it. Nevertheless, the NLRB has used it to some extent in the years since Taft-Hartley to narrow the scope of permissible union action. The board has, for example, found it unlawful under this section for a union to strike against an employer who has negotiated, and continues to negotiate, on a multi-employer basis, with the goal of forcing him to bargain independently. It has also found a union's refusal to bargain on an employer proposal for a written contract to violate this part of the law. To the employer community, in short, at least some inequities seem to have been corrected by this good-faith bargaining provision.

The *fourth* unfair union practice has given rise to considerable litigation. Indeed, of all six Taft-Hartley union prohibitions the ban on certain types of strikes and boycotts has proven the most difficult to interpret. Even as "clarified" by Congress in 1959, this area remains a particularly murky one for labor lawyers.

Briefly, Section 8 (b) (4) of the 1947 act prohibits unions from striking or boycotting if such actions have any of the following three objectives: (1) forcing an employer or self-employed person to join any labor or employer organization or to cease dealing with another employer (secondary boycott); (2) compelling recognition as employee bargaining agent from another employer without NLRB certification; (3) forcing an employer to assign particular work to a particular craft.

Particularly in regard to the secondary boycott provision, it does not take much imagination to predict where heated controversy could arise. To constitute a secondary boycott, the union's action must be waged against "another" employer, one who is entirely a neutral in the battle and is merely caught as a pawn in the union's battle with the real object of its concern. But when is the secondary employer really neutral and when is he an "ally" of the primary employer? The board has sometimes ruled against employers alleging themselves to be "secondary" ones on the grounds of common ownership with that of the "primary" employer and, again, when "struck work" has been turned over by primary employers to secondary ones. But board and court rulings here have not been entirely consonant.

In its other clauses, too, the Taft-Hartley strike and boycott provision has led to intense legal battles. When is a union, for example, unlawfully seeking recognition without NLRB certification and when is it merely picketing to protest undesirable working conditions (a normally legal action)? Is a union ever entitled to try to keep within its bargaining unit work that has traditionally been performed by the unit employees? On some occasions, but not all, the board has ruled that there is nothing wrong with this. The histories of post-1947 cases on these issues constitute a fascinating study in the making of fine distinctions. At least, however, the large incidence of litigation might indicate that the parties have not been able totally to overlook the new rights and responsibilities bestown upon them by Taft-Hartley (whatever these might exactly be).

Last, and least in the magnitude of their effect, stand the relatively unenforceable provisions relating to (5) union fees and dues, and (6) featherbedding.

The proscription against unions charging workers covered by union shop agreements excessive or discriminatory dues or initiation fees included, it will be recalled, a stipulation that the NLRB could consider "all the circumstances" in determining discrimination or excess. Such circumstances, the wording of the Taft-Hartley Act continues, include "the practices and customs of labor organizations in the particular industry and the wages currently paid to the employees affected." Without further yardsticks and depending almost exclusively on the sentiments of individual employees rather than irate employers for enforcement, this part of the Act has had little practical value. In one of the relatively few such cases to come before it thus far, the board ruled that increasing the initiation fee from $75 to $250 and thus charging new members the equivalent of about four week's wages when other unions in the area charged only about one-eighth of this amount was unlawful. In another case, it was held that the union's uniform requirement of a reinstatement fee for ex-members that was higher than the initiation fee for new members was *not* discriminatory under the act.

The *sixth,* and final, unfair labor practice for unions has proven even less influential in governing collective bargaining: Taft-Hartley's prohibition of unions from engaging in "featherbedding." The board has ruled that this provision does *not* prevent labor organizations from seeking *actual* employment for their members, "even in situations where the employer does not want, does not need, and is not willing to accept such services." And mainly because of this latter interpretation, the antifeatherbedding provision has had little teeth: the union would be quite happy to have the work performed and the question of need is irrelevant. Employer spokesmen for some industries, entertainment and the railroads in particular, have succeeded in convincing the public that their unwanted—but performing—workers are "featherbedding," but under the interpretation of the law as this now exists they are engaging in inaccuracies.

Even these least influential of the six union prohibitions, however, clearly indicate the philosophy in back of Taft-Hartley: in the words of the late Senator Robert A. Taft, "simply to reduce special privileges granted to labor leaders."

The Rights of Employees As Individuals

In other areas, too, the Act attempted to even the scales of collective bargaining and the alleged injustices of the 1935–47 period.

Taft-Hartley, unlike the Wagner Act, recognized a need to protect the rights of individual employees *against* labor organizations. It explicitly amended the 1935 legislation to give a majority of the employees the right to *refrain* from, as well as engage in, collective bargaining activities. It also dealt more directly with the question of individual freedoms—even beyond its previously mentioned outlawing of the closed shop, union coercion, union-caused employer discrimination against employees, and excessive union fees.

Perhaps most symbolically, Taft-Hartley provided that should any state wish to pass legislation more restrictive of union security than the union shop (or in other words, to outlaw labor contracts which make union membership a condition of retaining employment), the state was free to do so. Many states have proven themselves as so willing: nineteen states, mainly in the South and Southwest, now have so-called *"right-to-work" legislation*. Advocates of such laws, which will be discussed at greater length in Chapter 9, have claimed that compulsory unionism violates the basic American right of freedom of association; opponents of "right-to-work" laws have pointed out, among other arguments, that majority rule is inherent in our democratic procedure. There has thus far, however, been an impressive correlation between stands on this particular question and attitudes toward the values of unionism in general. Individuals opposed to collective bargaining have favored "right-to-work" laws with amazing regularity. Pro-unionists seem to have been equally consistent in their attacks on such legislation. It is still unproven, at any rate, that "right-to-work" laws have had much effect on labor relations in the states where they exist. As Hilgert and Young point out, "The general pattern emerges that existing right-to-work laws have generally been unenforceable and have accomplished little."[5] The laws are, in short, considerably more symbolic than they are of real consequence.

Also designed to strengthen the rights of workers as individuals was a Taft-Hartley provision allowing any *employee* the *right to present grievances directly* to the employer without intervention of the union. The union's representative was to be given a chance to be present at such employer-employee meetings, but the normal grievance procedure (with the union actively participating) would thus be suspended. Few employees have thus far availed themselves of this opportunity: the action clearly can antagonize the union and since the *employer's* action is normally being challenged by the grievance itself the employee may have a formidable task ahead.

Finally, the act placed a major restriction on the fast-growing *dues checkoff* arrangement. Through this device (which will also be discussed in more detail in Chapter 9) many employers had been deducting union dues from their employees' paychecks and remitting them to the union. Companies were thus spared the constant visits of dues-collecting union representatives at the workplace; unions had also found the checkoff to be an efficient means of collection. Under Taft-Hartley, the checkoff was to remain legal, but now only if the individual employee had given his own authorization in writing. Moreover, such an authorization could not be irrevocable for a period of more than one year. This restriction has hardly hampered the growth of the checkoff: it is today provided for in

[5] Raymond L. Hilgert and Jerry D. Young, "Right-to-Work Legislation—Examination of Related Issues and Effects," *Personnel Journal*, December 1963, p. 559.

over 80 percent of all labor contracts, compared to an estimated 40 percent at the time of Taft-Hartley's passage. The new legal provision has undoubtedly minimized abuse of the checkoff mechanism, however.

The Rights of Employers

In still a third area, Taft-Hartley circumscribed the union's freedom of action in its quest for industrial relations equity. In this case, it explicitly gave employers certain collective bargaining rights.

For example, although employers were still required to recognize and bargain with properly certified unions, they could now give full freedom of expression to their views concerning union organization, so long as there was "no threat of reprisal or force or promise of benefit." Thus an employer may now, when faced with a representation election, tell his employees that in his opinion unions are worthless, dangerous to the economy, and immoral. He may even, generally speaking, hint that the permanent closing of his plant would be the possible aftermath of a union election victory and subsequent high union wage demands. Nor will an election be set aside, for that matter, if he plays upon the racial prejudices of his workers (should these exist) by describing the union's philosophy toward integration, or if he sets forth the union's record in regard to violence and corruption (should this record be vulnerable) and suggests that these characteristics would be logical consequences of the union's victory in his plant—although in recent years the board has attempted to draw the line here between dispassionate statements on the employer's part and inflammatory or emotional appeals.[6] An imaginative employer can, in fact, now engage in almost any amount of creative speaking (or writing) for his employees' consumption. The only major restraint on his conduct is that he must avoid threats, promises, coercion, and direct interference with the worker-voters in the reaching of their decision. Two lesser restrictions also govern, however: the employer may not hold a meeting with his employees on company time within twenty-four hours of an election; and he may never urge his employees individually at their homes or in his office to vote against the union (the board has held that he can lawfully do this *only* "at the employees' work area or in places where employees normally gather").

Under this section of Taft-Hartley, employers can also: (1) themselves now call for elections to decide questions of representation (as noted earlier); (2) refuse to bargain with supervisors' unions (the Wagner Act

---

[6] See, particularly, the excellent article by Derek C. Bok, "The Regulation of Campaign Tactics in Representation Elections Under the National Labor Relations Act," *Harvard Law Review,* LXXVIII, No. 1 (November 1964), for a fuller discussion of these and various related organizational campaign legislative matters.

protection was withdrawn for these employees, although they are not prohibited from forming or joining unions *without* the NLRB machinery and other safeguards of public policy); and (3) file their unfair labor practice charges against unions.

Such changes, understandably, were favorably received by the employer community.

National Emergency Strikes: An Overview

Of most direct interest to the general public, but of practical meaning only to those employers whose labor relations can be interpreted as affecting the national health and safety, are the *national emergency strike provisions* which were enacted in 1947. As in the case of most Taft-Hartley provisions, these remain essentially unchanged to this day.

Sections 206 through 210 of the act provide for government intervention in the case of such emergencies. If the President of the United States believes that threatened or actual strike affects "an entire industry or a substantial part thereof" in such a way as to "imperil the national health and safety," he is empowered to take certain carefully delineated action. He may appoint a board of inquiry, to find out and report the facts regarding the dispute. The board is allowed subpoena authority and can thus compel the appearance of witnesses. It cannot, however, make recommendations for a settlement. On receiving the board's preliminary report, the President may apply, through the Attorney General, for a court injunction restraining the strike for sixty days. If no settlement is reached during this time, the injunction can be extended for another twenty days, during which period the employees are to be polled in a secret-ballot election as to their willingness to accept the employer's last offer. The board is then to submit its final report to the President. Should the strike threat still exist after all of these procedures, the President is authorized to submit a full report to Congress, "with such recommendations as he may see fit to make for consideration and appropriate action."

By 1970, the national emergency provisions had been invoked on twenty-nine occasions. They had not always been effective in bringing about settlements, however. Rees conveys the majority opinion of detached observers in pointing out that "where the fact-finders have been successful in settling disputes it is often because they have been functioning as high-level mediators, commanding more respect from the parties than the mediators ordinarily furnished by government agencies."[7] There is also evidence that the eighty-day "cooling-off" period has sometimes done no more than delay the strike for that length of time: only about one-quarter

---

[7] Albert Rees, *The Economics of Trade Unions* (Chicago: The University of Chicago Press, 1962), p. 39.

of these first twenty-nine disputes, indeed, were settled within the injunction period.

Every president since 1947 has, in fact, sharply criticized the inflexibility of the procedures. And all have proposed changes in the array of statutory tools that the law has sanctioned.

Nor, generally speaking, have men with greater professional expertise in the field of labor relations been any more enthusiastic about this portion of the law through the years. For example, W. Willard Wirtz, secretary of labor during the bulk of the 1960s, never visibly wavered from his 1959 assertion that "what Taft-Hartley comes down to is simply a polished-up, embroidered form of relief by court injunction...the real question is to get a settlement of the strike issue, and on this the injunction procedure seems to me to hurt, rather than to help."[8] George W. Taylor, a highly respected academician-arbitrator, appears adamant in his long-standing position, based to a great extent on firsthand observation, that "devices such as the injunction, designed to get production resumed prior to the settlement of a dispute, add additional complexities to the negotiating process which has already bogged down."[9] And virtually every session of Congress over the past quarter-century has been asked to consider "national emergency disputes" revision bills from those of its members with special interests and/or proficiency in the area. The procedures themselves, however, continue on the books, in their unadulterated 1947 form.[10]

It would be naïve to predict that this gap between complaint and remedial action will continue in its present dimensions for another quarter-century. Certainly a public that has greatly increased its level of aspiration as to union behavior and shouts that "there ought to be a (new) law" almost as a reflex action in the fact of public inconvenience cannot be held at bay indefinitely.

This consideration, however, cannot erase the record. In a period

---

[8] *U.S. News and World Report,* XLVII (October 19, 1959), 74.

[9] George W. Taylor, "The Adequacy of Taft-Hartley in Public Emergency Disputes," *Annals of the American Academy of Political and Social Science,* CCCXXXIII (January 1961), 78.

[10] Nor has much applause been heard for the emergency strike machinery of the Railway Labor Act of 1926, which governs the airlines as well as the railroads. General agreement exists that at least since World War II the mediation, voluntary arbitration, ad hoc emergency board appointments, and sixty-day "cooling-off" periods provided by this legislation have settled few of the major disputes in these two transportation sectors. Even worse, the parties can get the emergency boards established with relative ease—over one hundred such boards have been appointed in railroad disputes alone since 1947—and this fact has been widely blamed for depriving managements and unions involved of incentive to live up to their own collective bargaining responsibilities. Why bargain in good faith when the whole dispute can be dumped handily into the lap of the governmental boards, whose recommendations, although they may be of great help to one or the other of the parties, are not binding? As in the case of the Taft-Hartley provisions, however, the criticism continues unabated, and the emergency procedures remain wholly intact.

of unparalleled government inroads into a host of other fields of once-private endeavor (clearly including many other areas of union-management relations), our national emergency strike provisions have—with few supporters and no shortage of both influential and active antagonists—at least until now been left entirely alone.

Several reasons have been widely advanced to explain this paradox. A necessary prerequisite for altering existing legislation is the reopening of Taft-Hartley to congressional debate; a cogent case can be made that organized labor, despite its attacks upon the existing legislation, now views such action as a potential Pandora's box that might bring into the spotlight such issues as labor's present exemption from antitrust laws, a nationwide right-to-work law, and even new congressional treatment of industrywide bargaining. Nor has industry, by and large, welcomed congressional exploration of the industrial relations scene in the years since 1947. Management spokesmen have frequently voiced fears of compulsory arbitration, price control, and generally increased governmental intervention in the sphere of private enterprise. And while conjectures must remain unproven that this combined labor-management trepidation has significantly influenced the federal government in its preservation of the status quo, the joint opposition to changes in laws has undoubtedly had some restraining effect.

It is also a matter of record that agreement has been lacking as to the right solution although many have been proposed, primarily by representatives of the academic community. This, too, has presumably acted as a major deterrent to remedial action by our public officials.

And the all-but-patent futility of the task, if *balancing* the objectives of public policy is considered, must surely be thought of as a further explanation for the continuing gap between words and action in Washington. As Lloyd G. Reynolds, who has suggested that "anyone who could devise an equitable and enforceable method of handling these disputes would deserve a Nobel prize for industrial peace," has forcefully argued:

> The objective of public policy is not just to prevent strikes in essential industries. The objective is rather to prevent strikes by methods which are orderly and uniform in their application, which involve a minimum of direct compulsion, which do not impose greater hardships on one party than on the other, and which leave maximum scope for settlements to be reached through direct negotiation between the parties.[11]

Any solution falling short of satisfying all these requirements would, to most thoughtful American citizens, be deficient. Recognition that such

---

[11] Lloyd G. Reynolds, *Labor Economics and Labor Relations,* 4th ed. (Englewood Cliffs, N.J.: Prentice-Hall, Inc., 1964), p. 285.

an ideal may be impossible to achieve, however, has undoubtedly acted as an additional restraining force for public officials.

But to the explanations for the laissez-faire stance adopted, however reluctantly, by both Democratic and Republican administrations, must be added one that has been advanced with considerably less frequency: the extralegal weaponry in the hands of our presidents. It is a major irony that White House improvisation, having realized a significant amount of success throughout the past quarter-century, may also have decreased the incentive in Washington to locate something better.

National Emergency Strikes: The Weapons of Extralegality

It is not generally appreciated, particularly amid the abundance of current pleas to give the President an "arsenal of weapons" for handling national emergencies, that our chief executives do not now lack for alternative courses of action, even if these are not framed explicitly by the laws. Nor have presidents, in general, hesitated to use these weapons when political pressures to "do something" have loomed large enough and prospects of warding off or ending a strike through the machinery of Taft-Hartley (or the Railway Labor Act) have appeared sufficiently dim. And if all White House incumbents since 1947 have pressed for more wide-sweeping legalized powers, much of this pressing has presumably been geared to making their now-extralegal intervention more politically feasible and constitutionally secure, and *not* to opening up these avenues for action.

Four relatively recent examples illustrate these workings of extralegality. The 116-day 1959 basic steel strike was settled above all by high-level mediation efforts and ultimate settlement term recommendations by Vice President Nixon with the aid of Secretary of Labor Mitchell. It has been generally agreed that both Nixon's prestige and his pressure ended this dispute after the Taft-Hartley procedures had failed. The prestige was influential, as John P. Horlacher has stated, because

> in conferring with Mr. Nixon, the company and union representatives were not unaware that they were dealing with the man who could be the next occupant of the White House, the man who, in this situation, was obviously functioning as the President's alter ego.[12]

Nixon's pressure was felt through such actions as those later depicted by Mitchell in his comments upon these sessions:

> Reviewing the Waldorf [Astoria Hotel] conference, Mitchell said that Nixon did not threaten the [steel company] executives but that he did paint "a very realistic picture of what might happen" if they failed to

[12] John P. Horlacher, "A Political Science View of National Emergency Disputes," *Annals of the American Academy, op. cit.,* p. 90.

avail themselves of a chance to settle—"conjuring up many possibilities of the kind of legislation that might result."... he left "many things" to their imagination, Mitchell said.[13]

In the Lockheed Aircraft–machinist dispute of 1962, President Kennedy not only personally requested a sixty-day truce and appointed a three-man extralegal board of public citizens to assist federal mediators in negotiations but—according to Northrup and Bloom—when Lockheed "declined to accept...[this] board's recommendation for an election to determine the union shop issue, the Defense Department announced, in effect, that its defense contracts were being especially reviewed and placed on an *ad hoc* basis."[14]

Confronted with the failure of the Taft-Hartley mechanism a few months later, in the case of the 1962–63 Atlantic and Gulf Coast longshoring strike, Kennedy also appointed an extralegal board, chaired by Senator Wayne Morse. This board "in effect imposed a settlement too generous for the union to reject and which was reluctantly accepted by the employers."[15]

And President Johnson more or less duplicated his treatment of the 1964 nationwide railroad strike threat by virtually locking up the 1965 steel industry and United Steelworkers' negotiators for five days in quarters near his White House office. He constantly requested the parties during personal visits (at times with the secretaries of labor and commerce) to come to terms in the process, and ultimately provided his own "statistical referee" in the person of the chairman of the Council of Economic Advisers to institute suggestions, which led to White House recommendations accepted by both sides.

Such a list could be extended considerably. Special mediation efforts on the part of highly respected private citizens were utilized with beneficial results in the maritime disputes of 1961 and 1962. Prior to invocation of Taft-Hartley in the 1962–63 Boeing Company–machinist impasse, an extralegal board made recommendations, a privilege denied official Taft-Hartley boards. In the 1964–65 East and Gulf Coast longshoring dispute, a special panel comprising the secretaries of labor and commerce and (once again) Senator Morse did likewise after the expiration of the eighty-day injunction period, with some (although not complete) effectiveness. And the record hardly lacks for instances of presidential exhortations, made both publicly and privately for self-restraint in the face of national defense (cold war, Korean, or Vietnamese) exigencies; of executive suggestions that an unhappy Congress could be forced into drastic *ad hoc* remedial action

[13] *Business Week,* January 9, 1960, p. 28.
[14] Herbert R. Northrup and Gordon F. Bloom, *Government and Labor* (Homewood, Ill.: Richard D. Irwin, Inc., 1963), p. 369.
[15] *Ibid.,* p. 362.

(most notably carried out in the case of 1963, 1967, and 1970 railroad strike prevention orders); or of White House expressions of dissatisfaction with existing strike legislation and broad hints of less palatable laws to come should labor statesmanship not prevail on a bipartite basis.

If these extralegal weapons have not been universally successful in achieving their immediate goal of strike settlement or strike avoidance, they have at least combined with the existing labor statutes—and on many occasions with the entirely independent actions of the two contractual parties—to realize this objective. While some of the settlements may have added to unwanted inflationary movements or may otherwise have had publicly undesirable consequences, the basic mission of dissipating a national emergency dispute has always been accomplished. Extralegal avenues now open to our chief executives have invariably produced labor peace when all else has failed.

National Emergency Strikes: The Risk of Relative Success

Obviously, however, the problem can hardly be dismissed in as cavalier a fashion as the previous paragraph might suggest. At least three additional factors must be considered.

First, successful executive improvisation has often been implemented only after the "emergency" has existed for some time. The extralegal avenues performed effectively, for example, only after 116 days of strike activity (plus passage of almost the full Taft-Hartley injunction period) in the case of 1959 steel, after a three-week strike and expiration of the eighty-day period in the 1961 maritime industry dispute, and after a one-month strike following the injunction period in the case of the 1962–63 Atlantic and Gulf Coast longshoring impasse. Improvisation was tried earlier in these and many other national disputes with a notable lack of success, and the fact that such "emergencies" have not been terminated as rapidly as chief executives would have liked—with attendant adverse consequences for the economy —should not go unnoticed.

Second, although the efficacy of each of the successful extralegal weapons can hardly be debated, the question can be raised whether or not all have been consistent with the dominant values of our private enterprise society: How appropriate, for example, is a threat to deprive an aircraft manufacturer of defense contracts essentially because of the latter's presumably sincere aversion to the principle of the union shop? How advisable is the imposition of *ad hoc* compulsory arbitration in peacetime, as in the case of the railroads? And would threatened new and essentially punitive legislation, directed primarily against the party deemed by governmental representatives as the recalcitrant in the bargaining, in any way be guaranteed an objective—or equitable—basis?

Third, the fact that the extralegal actions have *until* now produced labor peace when all else has failed obviously provides no assurance that the nation will not be confronted ultimately with an "emergency" strike that no existing presidential weapon—legal or extralegal—will be able to terminate easily. It is entirely conceivable that at some future time a major labor relations impasse will combine with the imperviousness of one or both parties to existing executive weapons and the unwillingness of Congress to supply tailor-made back-to-work legislation, forcing the nation to wait until the strike burdens become completely intolerable.

In short, the existing weapons of extralegality do *not* constitute a panacea for the problem of "national emergency" disputes. And if their successful exercise in the past as a frequently used supplement to our official legislation helps explain the remarkable staying power of these all but friendless laws, the existence of the defects in the improvised weapons would still seem to make some overhaul in our present machinery highly desirable. The danger may lie in the strong possibility that the relative efficiency of these weapons in achieving their immediate purpose of ending an "emergency" is depriving us of sufficient incentive to search seriously for a better way to serve the national interest.

Other Taft-Hartley Provisions

Taft-Hartley also devoted attention to internal union affairs, the first such regulation in American history. Its impetus came not only from the previously cited Communistic taints attached to several unions but also from the fact that, in the case of a few other labor organizations, lack of democratic procedures and financial irregularities (often involving employer wrongdoing as well) had become glaringly evident. Accordingly, the act set new conditions for unions thenceforth seeking to use the NLRB's services: (1) all union officers were obligated to file annual affidavits with the board, stating that they were not members of the Communist party; (2) certain financial and constitutional information had to be annually filed by unions with the Secretary of Labor; and (3) unions (as well as corporations) could no longer contribute funds for political purposes in connection with any federal election. The affidavit requirement, judged to be ineffective, was repealed in 1959. The other stipulations were allowed to remain in force until that date, when they were only slightly amended and then substantially enlarged upon (as further discussion will indicate). Essentially, aside from what unionists vocally termed a nuisance value, the provisions are notable for the first recognition of public policy that some internal regulation of the union as an institution was in the public interest— and as a harbinger of more such regulation to come.

Another Taft-Hartley provision which has upset some union leaders involved the *termination or modification of existing labor contracts*. Applicable to both labor organizations and employers, it requires the party seeking to end or change the agreement to give a sixty-day notice to the other party. The law further provides that, during this time period, the existing contract must be maintained without strikes or lockouts. In addition, the Federal Mediation and Conciliation Service and state mediation services are to be notified of the impending dispute thirty days after the serving of the notice. Workers striking in violation of this requirement lose all legal protection as "employees" in collective bargaining, although the law also asserts that "such loss of status for such employee shall terminate if and when he is re-employed" by the employer.

In some instances, leaders of labor organizations have found it both difficult and politically unpopular to restrain their constituents from violating this provision. Unionists have also, on occasion, frankly pointed out that the scheduling prerequisites for striking have deprived their organizations of some economic power, at least insofar as the element of surprise is concerned. Yet many representatives of both parties would undoubtedly agree with Falcone that "these provisions have slowed down the calling of strikes, enabled mediators to intervene before it is too late to help and have generally provided an orderly method for resolving disputes and reaching final settlements."[16] From the point of view of the public interest, it is clearly on this latter basis that the effectiveness of the notice provisions should be judged.

Finally, Section 301 of Taft-Hartley decreed that *"suits for violations of contracts* between an employer and a labor organization representing employees in an industry affecting commerce" could be brought directly by either party in any United States district court. Labor agreements, in short, were to be construed as being legally enforceable for the first time in American history. Damage suits are not calculated to increase mutual trust or offset misunderstandings between the parties in labor relations, however, and unions and managements have generally recognized this. Consequently, relatively few such suits have come to the courts in the years since this provision was enacted. Many contracts today, in fact, contain agreements *not* to sue, a perfectly legal dodge of Section 301. The remedy of the suit, for employers confronted with union violations of no-strike clauses or for unions faced with management lockouts inconsistent with no-lockout provisions (for example), nonetheless remains an available one for both parties in the absence of any restrictive convenants.

Administrative Changes in the Law

Taft-Hartley also enlarged the NLRB from three to five members and, in the interests of a faster disposition of cases, authorized the board

---

[16] Falcone, *op. cit.*, p. 275.

to delegate "any or all" of its powers to any group of three or more members. In addition, the office of independent General Counsel was created within the NLRB, to administer the prosecution of all unfair labor practices. This last change was made to satisfy the increasingly bitter charges (particularly from employers) that the same individuals had exercised both prosecution and judicial roles.

As the NLRB machinery now operates, the board members and General Counsel delegate most of their work in processing unfair labor practice charges and conducting representation elections to thirty-one regional and two subregional offices scattered throughout the country. Each office deals with these two problems as they arise in its particular geographic area. The General Counsel supervises the work of the offices and the board members' efforts are thus saved for those issues appealed to it from the regional level. As will be recalled, board decisions can themselves be appealed to the courts (and ultimately to the Supreme Court), but thus far the judges have supported such decisions fairly consistently.

THE LANDRUM-GRIFFIN ACT OF 1959

As might have been expected, the Taft-Hartley Act generated considerable controversy. In the years immediately after its passage, labor leaders bitterly assailed the new law as being—in addition to a "slave labor act"—a punitive one, and invoked such statements in regard to its authors as "the forces of reaction in this country want a showdown with free American labor." Taft-Hartley supporters, on the other hand, have frequently referred to the act as a "Magna Carta" for both employers and employees, and widely praised its efforts to "equalize bargaining power." Unable to see any appropriateness in these latter remarks, spokesmen for organized labor, until roughly a decade ago, in turn responded by pressing for the repeal of the act—or occasionally, for its drastic amendment—in every session of Congress. Their complete failure to realize this goal and their recent unwillingness even to pursue it attests to the basic acceptance of Taft-Hartley's provisions in the recent past by the American public, as well as to labor's concern that an even less desirable law might be the outcome.

The framers of public policy themselves, however, did not long remain satisfied that existing labor legislation was fully adequate to uphold the public interest. And in 1959 the national legislature passed another significant law, the Landrum-Griffin Act (officially, the Labor-Management Reporting and Disclosure Act). This latter act was the direct outgrowth of the unsatisfactory internal practices of a small but strategically located minority of unions, as revealed by Senate investigations, and it can be said to have marked the beginning of quite *detailed regulation* of internal union affairs, going far beyond the Taft-Hartley treatment of this subject.

Under Landrum-Griffin provisions, as noted earlier, union members are guaranteed a "Bill of Rights" which their unions cannot violate, officers of labor organizations must meet a variety of reporting and disclosure obligations, and the Secretary of Labor is charged with the investigation of relevant union misconduct.

The "Bill of Rights" for union members is an ambitious and widesweeping one. It provides for equality of rights concerning the nomination of candidates for union office, voting in elections, attendance at membership meetings, and participation in business transactions—all, however, "subject to reasonable" union rules. It lays down strict standards to ensure that increases in dues and fees are responsive to the desires of the union membership majority. It affirms the right of any member to sue the organization once "reasonable" hearing procedures within the union have been exhausted. It provides that no member may be fined, suspended, or otherwise disciplined by the union except for nonpayment of dues unless the member has been granted such procedural safeguards as being served with written specific charges, given time to prepare a defense, and afforded a fair hearing. And it obligates union officers to furnish each of their members with a copy of the collective bargaining agreement, as well as full information concerning the Landrum-Griffin Act itself.

Not content to stop here in prescribing internal union conduct, the 1959 legislation laid out specific ground rules for *union elections*. National and international unions must now elect officers at least once every five years, either by secret ballot or at a convention of delegates chosen by secret ballot. Local unions are obligated to elect officers at least once every three years, exclusively by secret ballot. As for the conduct of these elections, they must be administered in full accordance with the union's constitution and bylaws, with all ballots and other relevant records being preserved for a period of one year. Every member in good standing is to be entitled to one vote and all candidates are guaranteed the right to have an observer at the polls and at the ballot-counting.

Landrum-Griffin also made it more difficult for national and international unions to place their subordinate bodies under *"trusteeships"* for pure political reasons. The trusteeship, or the termination of the member group's autonomy, has traditionally allowed labor organizations to correct constitutional violations or other clearly wrongful acts on the part of their locals. The Senate investigations preceding Landrum-Griffin had found, however, that this device was also being used by some unions as a weapon of the national or international officers to eliminate grass roots opposition *per se*. Accordingly, the act provided that trusteeships could be imposed only for one of four purposes: (1) to correct corruption or "financial malpractice"; (2) to assure the performance of collective bargaining duties; (3) to restore democratic procedures; and (4) to otherwise carry out "the legitimate objects" of the subordinate body. Moreover, the imposition of a trusteeship, together with the reasons for it, was now to be reported to the Secretary of Labor within thirty days, and every six months thereafter until the trusteeship was terminated.

The extent of Landrum-Griffin control of the internal affairs of unions is perhaps best illustrated by the act's policing of the kind of person who can serve as a union officer. Persons convicted of serious crimes (robbery, bribery, extortion, embezzlement, murder, rape, grand larceny, violation of narcotics laws, aggravated assault) are barred for a period of five years after conviction from holding any union position other than a clerical or custodial job. The period of exclusion may be shortened if the person's citizenship rights are fully restored before five years or if the United States Justice Department decides that an exception should be made.

A fair question to ask is whether or not this policy should be applied to officers of other kinds of institutions, such as business, government, universities, and churches. On the surface at least, it would appear that if government controls the moral character of union officers, it should apply the same policy across the board. To do otherwise makes it appear that union officers are being held to a higher standard of personal conduct than is required, say, of corporation officials. Should a corporation official who has been convicted of a serious crime, including violations of the nation's antitrust and pure food and drug laws, be treated in the same way as a union officer? This, indeed, could be the subject for a debate in any student group.

Though most of Landrum-Griffin was aimed at union behavior, the act does include provisions which cover employer activities. The Senate investigations had unearthed rather flagrant instances of *employer wrongdoing* as well: company bribery of union agents and, particularly, situations in which outside agents had been hired by companies to stave off union organizations by illegal means. Such agents, typically self-entitled "labor relations consultants," often acted as intermediaries in "buying off" the threat of unionization or, as a last resort, in ensuring that the union would at least extract only a minimum of concessions from the company.

Landrum-Griffin made employers responsible for reporting annually to the Secretary of Labor all company expenditures directed at influencing employee collective bargaining behavior. Employer bribery of union officers and other such blunt tactics had actually constituted federal crimes since the passage of Taft-Hartley, but the new act expanded the list of *unlawful employer actions*. Payments by companies to their own employees to bribe them so that they do not exercise their rights to organize and bargain collectively were added to the list of crimes. So, too, were many forms of employer payment aimed at procuring information on employee activities related to labor disputes. Violations by employers of their reporting obligations invite the same criminal penalties as are provided for union representatives.

In a way, the law attempts to fill the gap created by union membership apathy. It can be argued that a more effective way to promote union democracy and financial responsibility is by active participation of members in union affairs. The members of any union, local or international, have it in their power to require that their organizations adhere to democratic procedures and financial responsibility through the existing internal machinery of their unions. It is debatable that the federal government should protect union members against abuse by the organization when these members are not particularly concerned as to how their unions in fact operate.

In any event, few would now argue for repeal of the legislation. Even union opposition against Landrum-Griffin has subsided. Control of the internal affairs of unions by government is now an established feature. Possibly no law will convert unions into models of democracy. Still, the effect of the law has eliminated some of the more flagrant abuses of undemocratic practices and financial irresponsibility. For example, in 1969 the United Mine Workers held an election for its international officers. This was the first national election conducted in this union for many years. It is not likely that the election would have been held in the absence of the law's requirements. And, undoubtedly, the act has curtailed the activities of the comparatively small number of union officers who would regard the union's treasury as something to be used for their personal aggrandizement. Though probably there still exist some undemocratic practices and some corruption in the house of labor, there have been fewer flagrant instances of such conduct since the passage of the legislation. If nothing else, the law has educated union officers as to their responsibilities to their members. To this extent, the law has apparently accomplished its major objectives, and does for union members what they have failed through apathy to do for themselves.

Landrum-Griffin—Title VII

Quite apart from regulating union internal affairs and imposing obligations on employers, the Landrum-Griffin law in Title VII makes some important changes in the Taft-Hartley Act. It authorizes the NLRB to decline cases involving small employers engaged in interstate commerce, and permits the states to take jurisdiction of such cases. The theory here is that the NLRB should conserve its funds and manpower for those cases which have a substantial impact on interstate commerce.

It also closes the so-called "loopholes" which developed under Taft-

Hartley secondary boycott provisions. As we have seen, one purpose of the Taft-Hartley law was to outlaw secondary boycotts. However, the NLRB and the courts permitted unions to engage in certain types of secondary boycott activity. The reason for this was the character of the language of the 1947 law which regulated secondary boycott activities. For example, it was held lawful for a union to put pressure directly upon an employer engaged in a conflict with another union. Under the 1947 law, the union violated the boycott provisions when it directed pressure against the employees of the neutral employer for the purpose of forcing him to cease doing business with the firm engaged in the primary dispute with the union. In short, under the 1959 law Congress adopted new language which generally closed these loopholes, and under the present state of affairs a union's opportunity to engage in secondary boycott activities has been virtually eliminated.

Landrum-Griffin also outlawed the "hot cargo" arrangement. Under a hot cargo clause, an employer agrees with a union not to handle products or otherwise deal with another employer involved in a labor dispute. Accordingly, the hot cargo arrangement is a form of secondary boycott. The difference is that an employer agrees by contractual provision to engage in secondary boycotts upon receiving a signal from its union that another employer should be boycotted. Such arrangements are now illegal, and unions which force an employer to negotiate hot cargo clauses engage in an unfair labor practice. For reasons peculiar to the nature of the construction and garment industries, however, Congress excepted these two industries from the hot cargo proscription.

Title VII imposes another important restriction upon unions. It pins down and controls recognition and organizational picketing. At times, unions have found this kind of picketing effective to force employers to recognize unions and to persuade employees to join unions. Such picketing is particularly effective in a consumer business, such as a department store or a restaurant. A picket line thrown around a department store could persuade customers not to buy at the store, and this kind of union pressure could force the employer to recognize the union. Under Taft-Hartley, there was no restriction on this kind of picketing, and unions could picket for recognition and organizational purposes for an indefinite length of time.

Under the 1959 law, the opportunity for unions to picket for their purposes was sharply reduced. Such picketing activities now constitute an unfair labor practice if (1) the employer is lawfully recognizing another union; (2) a valid election has been conducted by the NLRB in the previous twelve months; and (3) no election petition has been filed with the NLRB within thirty days after the picketing began.

The latter provision is of particular importance to employers who want to be freed from the pressure of picketing. Thus, within thirty days after the start of the picketing, the union must file a petition for an election. If it loses the election, recognition and organizational picketing may not be engaged in for one year. Consequently, the opportunity of a union to picket for an indefinite period of time is eliminated.

However, there is one major qualification to this proscription. A union may picket for informational purposes after thirty days without filing an election petition. Informational picketing is defined by the law as that kind of picketing which advises the public that the employer involved does not employ members of the union or have a contract with it. Of course, the picket sign legends must be truthful. That is, they may not state that the employer does not employ members of the union if in truth he does. Also, informational picketing as distinct from recognition and organizational picketing may not interfere with pickup and delivery of products at the site of the company being picketed.

So far it would appear that the Title VII amendments to Taft-Hartley are oriented against unions. The law of 1959 authorizes the NLRB to decline cases of small employers engaged in interstate commerce, thereby eliminating the opportunity for the employees of such employers to exercise their organizational and collective bargaining rights under the federal law. If a state does not have a law similar to Taft-Hartley (thirty-eight states do not) these employees have no legal forum to protect them in their efforts to organize and bargain collectively. Unions are forbidden to engage in practically every kind of secondary boycott, and may not negotiate hot cargo agreements. And, as we have seen, the 1959 law sharply limits the opportunity for unions to engage in recognition and organizational picketing.

In only one major way did unions, indeed, *benefit* from the enactment of Title VII. The Title does redress a pro-management inequity which was created by Taft-Hartley. Under the earlier law, workers out on an economic strike (wages, pensions, seniority, and the like) were not permitted to vote in NLRB elections held during the course of a strike if the employer replaced them with other employees. What was inequitable about this provision is that the replaced economic strikers could not vote, *but the replacements were entitled to vote.* The replacements would, of course, vote to decertify the union, since if the union maintained bargaining rights it would insist as a condition of settling the strike that the regular employees be reinstated in their jobs and the replacements ("strikebreakers," "scabs," "finks" in union talk) be fired. Thus the only way that the replacements could be assured of holding their jobs would be to vote the union out. This would not be hard to do provided the employer hired a sufficient number of replacements during the strike.

Suppose the bargaining unit is composed of 500 employees, all union members. A strike takes place and the 500 employees go out on strike. The employer then hires 400 replacements and an election is held by the NLRB to determine whether the union still represents a majority of the bargaining unit. Under this illustration, *the 400 replacements vote in the election but, of the regular employees, only the 100 who have not been replaced can vote.* When the votes are counted, it should occasion little surprise that the 400 replacements vote to destroy the union. And, with this result, the employer will no longer need to recognize the union.

Indeed, under the original Taft-Hartley law some employers provoked economic strikes, hired replacements, and then petitioned the NLRB for an election. It is easy to see why organized labor looked upon this provision as a real threat to its existence.

Unions received some relief from this state of affairs in the 1959 law. Under its terms, replaced economic strikers may vote in NLRB elections, provided the election is held within one year from the start of a strike. If the strike lasts longer than one year, the replaced strikers are not eligible to vote. Under the assumption that most strikes would terminate before one year, it is understandable that the AFL-CIO stated in November 1960 that

> although most of the Taft-Hartley amendments were severely damaging to labor unions, (this one) was favorable.

SOME CONCLUSIONS

What are some reasonably safe conclusions based on the long experience of public policy recited on these pages? Can we make some predictions about the future developments in the area of labor law? The first, and perhaps the most accurate conclusion that can be made, is that public policy toward organized labor and collective bargaining has changed significantly over the years. It has moved from legal repression to strong encouragement, then to modified encouragement coupled with regulation, and finally with Landrum-Griffin to detailed regulation of internal union affairs. It seems a safe prediction not only that further shifts in this public policy can be expected but that these changes, as was not always the case in earlier times, will depend for their direction strictly on the acceptability of current union behavior to the American public.

This latter point is particularly important to the unionists of today. Especially since 1937, when it held the Wagner Act wholly constitutional, the Supreme Court has permitted the legislative branch of government the widest latitude to shape public policy. Congress and the state legislatures are judicially free to determine the elements of the framework of labor law. To most citizens, such a situation is only as it should be: our judiciary is expected to interpret law, but not to make it, and we generally expect actions of the legislative branch to be voided only when the particular statute clearly and unmistakably violates the terms of the Constitution. But since today the polls and not the courts *do* constitute the forum in which our policies toward labor are determined, and since the public *has* in the recent past apparently increased its level of aspiration as to union behavior, labor organizations have been forced to become increasingly conscious of the images which they project. Such a situation accounts to a great extent for the growing union stress on such nontraditional labor concerns as charity work, college scholarships, Boy Scout troops, and Little League teams, which will be discussed in the next chapter. It also accounts for the entire labor movement's uneasiness whenever such newsworthy strikes as the 1966 New York City transit tie-up, or the 1970 federal postal workers' strike, or such notable black marks as James R. Hoffa's jury-tampering and pension fund defrauding convictions occur. And it undoubtedly has been one major factor in leading to more maturity and self-restraint on the part of some labor leaders at the bargaining table. As Chapter 1 has noted, however, whether this progress will continue sufficiently and in time to satisfy the increasingly high level of public expectation and thereby ward off further laws of the Taft-Hartley and Landrum-Griffin variety remains an unanswered question.

Second, every law since Norris–La Guardia has expanded the scope of government regulation of the labor-management arena. To the curbs on judicial capriciousness enacted in 1932 have been added, in turn, restrictions on employer conduct, limitations on union conduct, and governmental fiats closely regulating internal union affairs. Most of the other parts of the later laws—to cite but two examples, Taft-Hartley's modification of the Wagner Act's closed and union shop provisions and Landrum-Griffin's new conditions regarding the "hot cargo" clauses—represent ever finer qualifications of the freedom of action of both parties. Given both the electorate's impatience with the progress of collective bargaining and Congress' apparently deep-seated reluctance to decrease the scope covered by its laws, future legislation can be expected to move *further* in the direction of governmental intervention. This should hold true whether the future laws are enacted with the implicit goal of "helping" *or* "hurting" unions.

Individual value judgments clearly determine the advisability of such a trend. But if one believes that stable and sound industrial relations can be achieved only in an environment of free collective bargaining, wherein labor and management—the parties which must "live" with each other on a day-to-day basis—are allowed to find mutually satisfactory answers to their industrial relations problems, there is cause for concern. Government policy which limits this freedom strikes at the very heart of the process.

This is not to say that the more recent labor statutes are entirely barren of provisions which are valuable additions to the law of labor relations. The union unfair labor practices relating to restraint and coercion of employees and to union-caused employer discrimination are clearly a move in the right direction. So, too, are Taft-Hartley's curbs on strikes and boycott activity engaged in at times by some unions for the objective of increasing the power of one union at the expense of other labor organizations, despite all of the litigation which has surrounded these curbs since 1947. Nor does the requirement that unions bargain collectively embarrass any one except the union leader who is uncooperative and recalcitrant.

At the same time, however, the government intervention in regard to such issues as union security, the checkoff, and the enforcement of the collective bargaining agreement (to cite but three) and the decreasing scope for union and management bargaining table latitude in general do raise the question of ultimate governmental control over *all* major industrial relations activities. For one who believes in "free collective bargaining," the increasing reach of the statutes may be steering labor policy in a very dangerous direction.

Third, even if one does conclude that the gains of our present dosage of government regulation outweigh its losses and inherent risks, this hardly proves that the current statutes and their interpretations constitute the most *appropriate* ones to meet each *specific* labor relations topic now being dealt with.

Consider, for as good an example as any in this connection, the current legal treatment of union organizational campaigns and representation elections. In his authoritative article on the subject, Professor Bok offers the following insightful commentary:

> Without an adequate understanding of voting behavior, disputes inevitably arise over the degree of regulation required, for it is difficult to determine how much protection the voters actually need in reaching their decision—or to determine the circumstances in which they are coerced or interfered with, to paraphrase the National Labor Relations Act. Since it would neither be reliable nor feasible to seek answers to these questions from the voters themselves, the law has been built upon inferences of "coercion" or "interference" drawn by officials far removed from the heat of the election campaign. The problems in drawing such inferences are substantial, and they do not disappear with greater familiarity and experience. Indeed, they may even become more difficult, for wider experience may simply expose the hazards of generalizing in this area. Take the discharge of union sympathizers—surely one of the most obvious and drastic techniques available to the employer. Although this tactic can often frustrate a union drive, any experienced (union) organizer knows that a discriminatory discharge may rally the voters against the employer instead of frightening them into submission. A few organizers have even provoked a discharge deliberately for this reason. Threats and other ap-

peals to fear and emotion may also seem plainly coercive but there is plenty of evidence to suggest that they too can have unintended results, and that they are often less effective in influencing voters than temperate, factual arguments on the same subject. As one moves to the subtler aspects of a campaign—restrictions on distribution, inaccurate statements, interrogation by the employer, and the like—the effects upon the election are much more difficult to gauge.[17]

In short, rather than encouraging rational voting behavior in representation elections (presumably a major legislative intention), public policy may in many instances only be compounding voting *irrationality* by fostering "martyrdom" voter considerations favoring the party which has been the object of "illegal" actions. If so, it is entirely warranted to ask whether or not we have adopted the proper regulatory policy in the first place.

Similarly, one can fully believe that labor relations disputes which imperil the national health and safety should be dealt with aggressively by the federal government even while believing that the present eighty-day "cooling-off" period *augments* the dangers to national welfare by allowing already strained union and management tempers an opportunity to further "heat up" (and contains other significant defects, as indicated above).

Uneasy considerations such as these will undoubtedly always be with us, for much speculation incapable of scientific proof is necessarily attached to them. Moreover, one can always find *some* concrete labor relations situations which will accommodate one side or the other of the debate quite amply.

It is entirely possible, however, that in being open to such charges of inappropriateness as public policy in the two illustrative areas (and there are undoubtedly other areas, depending upon how one reads labor law), a certain disrespect for labor law itself has been created. As Archibald Cox has commented: "No small part of the deep dislike which large parts of management and most of organized labor feel for lawyers in the field of labor relations is traceable to their obstructionism and insistence upon following some...legal rule, technical and unsuited to the realities of the matter at hand."[18] If this is in fact an accurate description, another unfortunate trend may be developing.

Finally, and probably also as an inevitable consequence of the increased coverage of public policy, labor laws have become anything but easy to comprehend. The inconsistent NLRB and judicial rulings which have plagued them in recent years may be based to some extent on philosophical and political differences, but they undeniably also stem from the built-in

[17] Bok, *op. cit.*, pp. 40–41.
[18] *Ibid.*, p. 58.

interpretative difficulties in the laws themselves. As Justice Felix Frankfurter could argue in this connection in 1957:

> The judicial function is confined to applying what Congress enacted after ascertaining what it is that Congress enacted. But such ascertainment ...is nothing like a mechanical endeavor. It could not be accomplished by the subtlest of modern "brain" machines. Because of the infirmities of language and the limited scope of science in legislative drafting, inevitably there enters into the construction of statutes the play of judicial judgment within the limits of the relevant legislative materials. Most relevant, of course, is the very language in which Congress has expressed its policy and from which the Court must extract the meaning most appropriate.[19]

What constitutes "refusal to bargain"? When are companies discriminating in regard to "hire or tenure of employment or any term or condition of employment" to influence union membership? What constitutes unlawful union recognition picketing? It is hard to disagree with the commonly heard lament of unionists and labor relations managers that it has become ever more risky to state definitively what is legal in bargaining relationships and what is not; and the most valuable information available to the management or labor union representative who is concerned with labor law may very possibly be the telephone number of an able labor attorney. But, given the dimensions of this law today, however unpalatable many of its tenets may be to one or the other party and whatever dangers may be inherent in present trends, the managers and unionists who are *not* concerned with public policy remain so only at their peril.

DISCUSSION QUESTIONS

1. Erect as strong a case as you can for the labor injunction. Then build as strong a case as you can *against* the injunction. Which of the two cases is more persuasive with you, and *why*?
2. "The Norris–La Guardia Act conferred no new rights on workers. It merely adjusted an inherently inequitable situation." Comment.
3. How much truth do you feel lies in the statement that "there was great need for the Wagner Act...its sole defect lay in the fact that it was not slightly broadened from time to time to regulate a few union practices of dubious social value"?
4. It has been argued that, whatever deficiencies may have accompanied the Taft-Hartley Act, it did "free workers from the tyrannical hold of union bosses." Do you agree?
5. Do you feel that the Wagner Act or the Taft-Hartley Act has been more influential in leading to the current status of organized labor in this country?
6. "In the last analysis, the public must judge the relative merits of the collective bargaining process." Discuss.
7. If all existing national labor legislation could be instantly erased and our

---

[19] *Local 1976 Carpenters Union* v. *NLRB,* 357 U.S. 93–100 (1957).

statutory regulation could then be completely rewritten, what would you advocate as public policy governing labor relations—and why?
8. Whether or not you agree with the exact scope and specific wording of the present laws, do you consider these laws to be essentially equitable to both management and labor?

SELECTED REFERENCES

Bakke, E. Wight, Clark Kerr, and Charles W. Anrod, *Unions, Management and the Public,* 3rd ed. New York: Harcourt, Brace & World, Inc., 1967, pp. 644–717.

Cohen, Sanford, *Labor Law.* Columbus, Ohio: Charles E. Merrill Books, 1964.

Committee for Economic Development, *The Public Interest in National Labor Policy.* New York: Committee for Economic Development, 1961.

Cullen, Donald E., *National Emergency Strikes.* Ithaca, N. Y.: New York State School of Industrial and Labor Relations, 1968.

Evans, Robert, Jr., *Public Policy Toward Labor.* New York: Harper & Row, Publishers, 1965.

Falcone, Nicholas S., *Labor Law.* New York: John Wiley & Sons, Inc., 1962.

Gregory, Charles O., *Labor and the Law,* 2nd rev. ed. New York: W. W. Norton & Co., 1958.

Mueller, Stephen J., and A. Howard Myers, *Labor Law and Legislation,* 3rd ed. Cincinnati: South-Western Publishing Co., 1962.

Northrup, Herbert R., and Gordon F. Bloom, *Government and Labor.* Homewood, Ill.: Richard D. Irwin, Inc., 1963.

Taylor, George W., *Government Regulation of Industrial Relations.* Englewood Cliffs, N. J.: Prentice-Hall, Inc., 1948.

Wirtz, W. Willard, *Labor and the Public Interest.* New York: Harper & Row, Publishers, 1964.

4

Union Behavior: Structure, Government, and Operation

To say that the basic philosophy of the labor movement is focused upon improving the conditions under which its members work is not equivalent to understanding its character as an institution. One must further determine how the union movement is *organized* to implement this basic objective. We have stated previously that unions are above all "pragmatic," doing each day what they feel is necessary to improve the lot of the American workingman. But it must also be understood that this pragmatism is expressed within the framework of the union movement as a dynamic and operating institution.

Indeed, unless there *is* a systematic understanding of the structure of unionism as this has emerged through the years to adapt to changing conditions, and of organized labor's functions, administrative relationships, and methods of operation, the union movement can easily appear incomprehensible and bewildering to the casual observer—for American unionism includes a *variety* of *different* functions, layers of authority, and governing practices.

For example, the AFL-CIO is a federation which contains many different sectors exercising different duties and authority. Most of the 169 national or international unions in existence in the United States belong to the federation, but 48 of them, including such mighty unions as the International Brotherhood of Teamsters, the United Mine Workers, and, since 1968, the United Automobile Workers operate independently from the AFL-CIO.[1] National unions are themselves, in turn, subdivided into regions or districts for more efficient management and administration. And although the vast majority of the country's 77,400 local unions belong to national unions, several hundred of them do not, and are thus commonly described as "independent" unions.[2] Other union groups include city and state central bodies, trade councils, and joint boards and councils. Finally, some unions are craft in character; others, industrial; and some are both craft and industrial.

Because unions are not similar in terms of heritage, the personalities of their officers, the kinds of workers who are members, their sizes, and their geographic locations, it should be expected that they will differ widely in terms not only of their governments but of their day-to-day operations. Some unions (perhaps most notably the International Typographical Union and the Newspaper Guild) both before and after Landrum-Griffin have operated very democratically, whereas a few (including most but not all segments of the International Brotherhood of Teamsters) have always maintained a highly autocratic system of internal government. Unions are different in terms of the intensity of their political activities, although events of the past quarter-century have made virtually all labor organizations conscious of a need to become relatively active in political campaigns and thus in influencing the selection of lawmakers. Some unions have engaged in considerably more "social" activities of the type alluded to in the previous chapter than have others. Above all, unions vary in terms of their internal rules, dues and initiation fees, and qualifications for membership. Thus, although in the following pages an effort will be made to present a systematic analysis of union behavior, structure, and government, one should recognize that diversity rather than uniformity characterizes the American labor movement. We must be concerned with common principles and trends, but the student should be fully cognizant that there could be many exceptions.

[1] From figures furnished by the United States Department of Labor, Bureau of Labor Statistics.
[2] A number of such "independents" nonetheless belong to the AFL-CIO as federal locals.

THE AFL-CIO

Relationship to National Unions

The decision of the former AFL and CIO to unite forces into a consolidated AFL-CIO in 1955 was made by the *affiliated national unions* of the two federations: the officers of the AFL and the CIO did not themselves have the power to bring about such a consolidation. This observation demonstrates a very important principle of the structure of the American labor movement—the *autonomy* of the national unions. The federation can exist only as long as the national unions which belong in it *agree* to stay in this labor body. Stated somewhat differently, the national unions can exist and operate independently from any kind of federation, but the federation cannot exist without the support of its national union affiliates.

In a sense, the relationship of the national unions to the federation compares closely to the relationship of member nations to the United Nations. No nation *must* belong to the United Nations; any nation *may* withdraw from the international organization at any time and for any reason whatsoever. Nor does the UN have the power to determine the internal government of any of its affiliates, the latter's tax laws, its foreign policy, the size of its military establishment, and similar national specifications. Nations affiliate and remain members of the world body for the advantages that the organization allows in the pursuit of world peace, and for other purposes, but they continue to exercise absolute sovereignty in the conduct of their own affairs.

The same is true of the relationship of the AFL-CIO to its affiliated national unions. A union belongs to the federation because of the various advantages of affiliation, but the national union is autonomous in the conduct of *its* affairs. Each union determines its own collective bargaining program, negotiates its contracts without the aid or intervention of the federation, sets its own level of dues and initiation fees, and may call strikes without any approval from the AFL-CIO (nor, conversely, can the federation prohibit a strike that an affiliated member desires to undertake).

Moreover, the federation cannot force a merger of two of its affiliates which have essentially the same jurisdiction. For example, the International Brotherhood of Electrical Workers of the old AFL and the International Union of Electrical Workers of the old CIO have what strikes the disinterested observer as virtually identical jurisdictions in manufacturing. It may seem logical that these two national unions should merge their forces. Nevertheless, the federation is powerless to compel merger.

Indeed, the constitution of the AFL-CIO, to which brief reference was made on an earlier page, states:

> Each such affiliate shall retain and enjoy the same organizing jurisdiction in this Federation which it had and enjoyed by reason of its prior affiliation with either the American Federation of Labor or the Congress of Industrial Organizations. In cases of conflicting and duplicating jurisdictions involving such affiliates the President and the Executive Council of this Federation shall seek to eliminate such conflicts and duplications through the process of voluntary agreement or voluntary merger between the affiliates involved.[3]

We have pointed out that many national unions would not have joined the federation if the merger of parallel jurisdictions *was* a condition of affiliation.

On the other hand, two or even more unions of the AFL-CIO may merge if they desire to do so on a voluntary basis. The most notable recent event of voluntary merger took place in 1969 with the formation of the United Transportation Union, composed of four of the five railroad operating brotherhoods. The Brotherhood of Railroad Trainmen, Locomotive Firemen and Enginemen, Switchmen, and Railway Conductors and Brakemen surrendered their identities and formed the new union. The Brotherhood of Locomotive Engineers, however, refused to become a part of the United Transportation Union. The new rail union is composed of 220,000 members, and is the largest AFL-CIO affiliate concerned solely with transportation.

It is likely that in future years there will be additional voluntary mergers because of the growth of the "conglomerate," a structure of business which brings under common management and ownership a variety of former companies. For example, Ling-Temco-Vought, perhaps the nation's leading conglomerate, today controls Braniff Airways, Computer Technology, Jones and Laughlin (at this writing still pending in the courts for final approval), LTV Aerospace, National Car Rental, Wilson and Company (meat packers), Wilson Pharmaceutical, and Wilson Sporting Goods. In 1969 Ling-Temco-Vought employed 123,000 workers, which made it the sixteenth largest employer in the nation. About 75 percent of the workers are members of ten different unions. Thus, to match the bargaining strength of the conglomerate, more and more unions may decide to merge on a voluntary basis.

This trend, however, would not make it any less true that authority in the AFL-CIO is *decentralized* in character: its authority is distributed among all the affiliated unions, rather than concentrated in any single

---

[3] *Constitution of the American Federation of Labor and Congress of Industrial Organizations,* 1955, Article III, Section 3.

body. The affiliated unions are masters of their own fates and each of them can pursue its own objectives, conduct its own affairs, and devise what policies and programs it desires to follow without intervention by either the federation or any other national union.

Enforcement of Federation Rules

The AFL-CIO's constitution does, however, contain certain rules of conduct which a national union must respect if it desires to *remain* a member of the federation. Each affiliate must pay to the federation a per capita tax of ten cents per member per month. No union may "raid" the membership of any other affiliate nor may it be officered by Communists, fascists, or members of any other totalitarian group. Among other rules, an affiliate is obligated to conduct its affairs without regard to "race, creed, color, national origin, or ancestry." Each affiliate is further expected "to protect the labor movement from any and all corrupt influences."

Given the preceding paragraphs, the practical question immediately arises as to what powers the AFL-CIO may exercise when an affiliated national union does not *comply* with these and various other rules of the federation. If the AFL-CIO had wide-sweeping powers over the national the federation officers could swiftly compel the errant national union to correct its improper conduct. The latter could still belong to the federation, but its violation of the federation's constitution would be abruptly terminated.

The realities of the situation, however, are such that the federation is not empowered to correct violations by exercise of such power. It can do no more than to suspend or expel a national union if the national union persists in the violation of the federation's constitution.

The expulsion weapon has been used in several instances, but never rashly. Before the AFL-CIO expelled the Teamsters Union, for example, that union was put on notice that it stood in flagrant violation of the anticorruption provision of the federation's constitution. AFL-CIO officials instructed the Teamsters that they would face expulsion unless certain of their national officers were removed, and the corrupt practices eliminated. Only when the Teamsters adamantly refused to comply did the AFL-CIO convert the threat into actuality and take the ultimate step of expelling the union from its ranks. And though the UAW actually withdrew from the AFL-CIO in 1968 because of Reuther's claim that the AFL-CIO was not doing enough in organizational work and had not been militant enough in areas of social affairs (poverty, race, and so on), the federation technically expelled the UAW only on the entirely understandable ground that the latter refused to pay its per capita dues.

Moreover, as a practical matter, the federation is compelled to use even this amount of authority sparingly and with discretion. The expulsion of the Teamsters was prompted by the corrupt practices of union officers who were highly visible to the public. The AFL-CIO could not tolerate such a situation in the light of the existing public clamor against dishonest union leadership and practices: the federation was fully aware that the retention of the Teamsters would reflect adversely on *every* affiliated union. One would be naïve, however, to believe that all unions scrupulously adhere to the letter and spirit of each rule incorporated in the federation's constitution. It is, for example, common knowledge that many affiliated unions still discriminate against Negroes, although—as has been noted earlier—in recent years progress has been made in eliminating such practices and although certain provisions of the Civil Rights Act of 1964 (which make it unlawful for unions to discriminate because of race, color, or creed) should further help in this regard. Despite all this improvement, however, some unions still prohibit Negroes from joining, fail to represent them fairly and equally in collective bargaining, and otherwise discriminate against them. Such practices, of course, conflict with the AFL-CIO constitutional proscription against racial discrimination, but the federation is faced with a major dilemma under such circumstances: if it were to expel each union found to be in any way discriminating against Negroes, the size of the federation would be drastically reduced and its influence as a labor body would be seriously impaired.[4] Indeed, to date *no* union has been expelled from the federation for racial discrimination; about all that the federation officers have done has been to use moral suasion to deal with the problem. Such an approach has not yet been particularly effective in many cases, but to do more than this would jeopardize the entire federation.

Member union autonomy is also evident from the ease with which national unions have *left* the federation *voluntarily*. The peripatetic United Mine Workers well illustrate this situation. After they were expelled from the AFL for spearheading the formation of the CIO through the efforts of their president John L. Lewis, the Mine Workers became a CIO affiliate when Lewis was elected the latter federation's first president. As part of Lewis' resignation as CIO president following the defeat of Wendell Willkie in 1940, however, the Mine Workers disaffiliated from the CIO and shortly thereafter rejoined the AFL. Yet Lewis *once again* pulled his union out of the AFL, in 1947, after he had attempted to persuade the AFL to pass a resolution to the effect that no union leader should sign the non-Communist affidavit which was then required of union officers by the Taft-Hartley law, and the Mine Workers have continued to be independent to this day.

[4] See N. F. Davis, *Trade Unions' Practices and the Negro Worker: The Establishment and Implementation of AFL-CIO Anti-Discrimination Policy* (unpublished Ph.D. thesis, Department of Economics, Indiana University, 1960), and Ray Marshall, *The Negro and Organized Labor* (New York: John Wiley & Sons, Inc., 1965).

Nor have the Mine Workers been unique in their actions. Even since 1955, several other affiliates have withdrawn from the AFL-CIO (and, in some cases, returned to it), each time pointing up the fact that the federation has no power whatsoever to force any of its affiliates to remain in its ranks.

Why, then, *do* most national unions seek to belong to the federation? Recall that each of the national unions must pay a per capita tax to remain in the federation. What do they get for their money?

Advantages of Affiliation

By far the chief benefit associated with membership is protection against "raiding." One provision of the AFL-CIO constitution states that "each such affiliate shall respect the established collective bargaining relationship of every other affiliate and no affiliate shall raid the established collective bargaining relationship of any other affiliate." This means that once an affiliated union gains bargaining rights in a company, no other union which is affiliated with the federation may attempt to dislodge the established union and place itself in the plant. Such a stricture constitutes a very important advantage of AFL-CIO membership. It frees unions from the task of fighting off raids from sister unions of the federation. Time and money conserved in this way can either be used to organize the unorganized or devoted to other union programs. Unions which violate the "no-raiding" provision of the constitution may realistically expect to be expelled from the AFL-CIO; and, because mutual self-interest of all members is involved, the amount of raiding has in fact decreased sharply since the formation of the federation.

Thus, before a union withdraws voluntarily from the AFL-CIO or engages in conduct which could result in expulsion, the officers of the union must weigh the consequences of operating outside the federation as these consequences concern proneness to raiding. Such considerations have been particularly influential in maintaining AFL-CIO membership for most smaller and weaker nationals, whom protection against raids benefits to a greater degree than it does larger national unions. But considerations of the money, time, and energy involved in counterattacking raiding attempts have also convinced most *larger* nationals of the wisdom of continued federation membership.

Federation membership involves still other advantages. With the federation as the spearhead, the union movement has comparatively more power in the political and legislative affairs of the nation—a particularly influential consideration, given the thrust of the laws today—and labor's impact upon elections and congressional voting is correspondingly greater than if each national union went its own way. In addition, by *coordinating* political efforts, the federation can use union funds and such other sources of political persuasion as letter-writing campaigns more effectively. Moreover, the AFL-CIO helps national unions in organizing campaigns, though the nationals are expected to bear the chief responsibility for new organization. And affiliated national unions also receive some help from the federation in the areas of legal services, educational programs, research, and social activities.

On the other hand, in the best tradition of Samuel Gompers, the federation does not *negotiate* labor agreements for the affiliated national unions. The federation is not equipped to render such services; nor do the autonomous national unions desire such intervention. In only one way does a national union directly benefit on the collective bargaining front by its membership in the federation: a framework is provided whereby unions which bargain in the same industry or with the same company can consolidate their efforts. A large company such as General Electric, for example, bargains with many different unions, and affiliated unions which deal with General Electric can thus more easily adopt common collective bargaining goals (such as uniform expiration dates of labor agreements and the attainment of similar economic benefits) than would be the case without the availability of federation coordination: the joint 1966 and 1969 bargaining endeavors of eleven major unions with General Electric (and subsequently with Westinghouse) were in fact conducted under AFL-CIO auspices, through the coordinating efforts of the federation's increasingly active Industrial Union Department, and this has been true of several other joint union efforts which are summarized in the next chapter under "Coordinated Bargaining."

Structure and Government of the AFL-CIO

As the accompanying chart indicates, the supreme governing body of the federation is its *convention,* held once every two years. Each national union, regardless of size, may send one delegate to the convention, and unions with more than 4,000 members can send additional delegates: the federation's constitution provides a graduated scale whereby up to nine delegates can represent unions with memberships of at least 175,000 members. Each national union delegate casts one vote for every member whom he represents, an arrangement which allows larger unions such as the Steel Workers and Carpenters more influence in the affairs of the convention.

Financial expenses of the delegates are defrayed by their individual national unions and not by the federation. Such expenses can at times be quite high and may even dissuade nationals from sending their full quotas of delegates: the convention lasts two weeks, is held in first-rate hotels in a major city, and often involves considerable travel.

The convention reflects any convention of any large group. Federation officers are elected; amendments to the AFL-CIO constitution are proposed and at times adopted; committee reports are rendered; internal policies of the federation are deliberated and at times changed; and countless resolutions which range from purely trade union affairs to such weighty topics as United States policy in Vietnam are voted upon. There are speakers and more speakers. Delegates must be able to sit for long periods and be capable of absorbing dozens of speeches.

The decisions and policies adopted by the convention are implemented by the AFL-CIO *Executive Council,* composed of the president, secretary-treasurer, and thirty-three vice-presidents of the federation. The vice presidents are elected at the convention and are usually selected from the presidents of the major affiliated national unions, although the 5,000-member Sleeping Car Porters constitutes a notable exception in this regard—primarily because of the personal respect in which its Negro president A. Philip Randolph is held. Only the president of the federation and its secretary-treasurer devote full time to the affairs of the organization, however: the vice presidents meet with the Executive Council at least three times a year, but remain as presidents of their own national unions.

Among its chief duties, the Executive Council: interprets and applies the federation constitution; plays a "watchdog" role in legislative matters which affect the interests of workers and unions; assembles, through a full-time staff of legal and economic experts, the data needed for testimony before congressional committees; keeps in contact with the many federal agencies which have authority in the labor field; and assures that the federation is kept free from corrupt or communistic influences. If it suspects that a union or its officers *are* in violation of the federation's constitution, it may investigate the matter, and if it finds that the charges are valid, it may, by a two-thirds majority, vote to suspend the guilty union. It may also recommend the ultimate penalty of expulsion of the union, but only the full convention may actually expel the union from the federation.

The Executive Council also selects six of its membership, who along with the AFL-CIO president and secretary-treasurer constitute the federation's *Executive Committee.* This smaller group meets every two months and has the major function of advising and counseling the president and secretary-treasurer on issues involving the federation and its policies. Only the president and the secretary-treasurer receive a salary for their duties—$70,000 and $45,000 per year, respectively. All other federation officers serve without salary, although they are compensated for their expenses when attending to federation business.

A fourth decision-making body within the federation is the AFL-CIO *General Board,* which consists of all members of the Executive Council and one principal officer of each of the national unions and the affiliated

STRUCTURAL ORGANIZATION of the
AMERICAN FEDERATION OF LABOR AND CONGRESS OF INDUSTRIAL ORGANIZATIONS

EXECUTIVE COMMITTEE
President, Secretary-Treasurer, 6 Vice Presidents

STANDING COMMITTEES
Civil Rights
Community Services
Economic Policy
Education
Ethical Practices
Housing
International Affairs
Legislation
Organization
Political Education
Public Relations
Research
Safety and Occupational Health
Social Security
Veterans Affairs

STATE CENTRAL BODIES
in 50 States and 1 Commonwealth

LOCAL CENTRAL BODIES
in over 774 Communities

NATIONAL CONVENTION
(Every 2 Years)

EXECUTIVE COUNCIL
President, Secretary-Treasurer, 33 Vice Presidents

OFFICERS
President and Secretary-Treasurer
Headquarters, Washington, D.C.

121 NATIONAL AND INTERNATIONAL UNIONS

60,000 Local Unions of National and International Unions

332 Local Unions Directly Affiliated with AFL-CIO

Membership of the AFL-CIO, January 1, 1970
13,500,000

GENERAL BOARD
Executive Council and one principal officer of each international union and affiliated Department

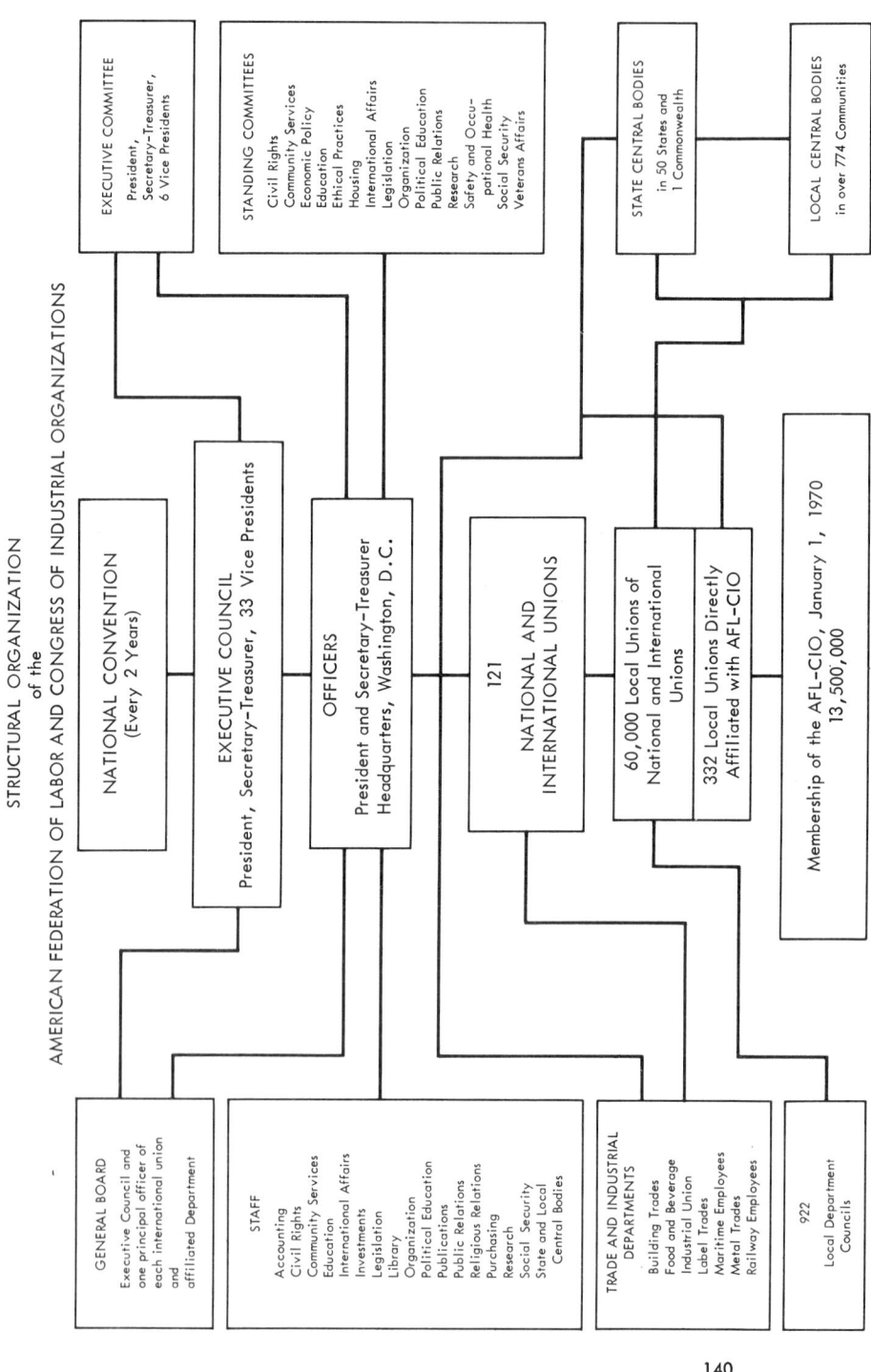

STAFF
Accounting
Civil Rights
Community Services
Education
International Affairs
Investments
Legislation
Library
Organization
Political Education
Publications
Public Relations
Religious Relations
Purchasing
Research
Social Security
State and Local Central Bodies

TRADE AND INDUSTRIAL DEPARTMENTS
Building Trades
Food and Beverage
Industrial Union
Label Trades
Maritime Employees
Metal Trades
Railway Employees

922 Local Department Councils

departments (to be described below). Usually, the affiliated national unions designate their chief officer as their representative to serve on the General Board, which must meet at least once a year and may meet more often at the discretion of the federation's president. Its chief duty is to rule on all questions and issues referred to it by the Executive Council. An important difference exists between the voting procedure of the General Board and the Executive Council, however. General Board members vote as *representatives of their unions,* and each may cast a vote based upon the membership of the union. Members of the Executive Council vote as *individuals,* which means that each member may cast only one vote and that consequently the larger unions have less influence than they do in General Board meetings.

The federation constitution also requires that the president appoint a number of *standing committees,* and AFL-CIO custom dictates that each committee chairman be president of a national union and that all members be active trade unionists. At present, such committees deal with the following issues and problems: civil rights, community services, economic policy, education, ethical practices, housing, international affairs, legislation, organization, political education, public relations, research, safety and occupational health, social security, and veterans' affairs. The growing scope of interests of the federation is illustrated by the character of these committees, most of which are relatively new and virtually all of which clearly extend well beyond "strictly trade union" affairs.

The constitution further authorizes the president to supply each committee with an adequate professional staff. These staff members, who need not be trade unionists, are professionals and experts in their fields and work under the direct supervision of the committee chairman. The committees and their staffs keep abreast of all developments in their respective areas, make reports to the federation president and Executive Council, and, when appropriate, report and make recommendations to the federation's convention. Frequently, the chairman of the committee and members of the professional staff also testify at congressional hearings.

Constitutional instructions spell out the specific duties of each committee and much of the day-to-day work of the federation is actually performed by these committees and their professional staffs. For example, the Committee on Ethical Practices has the responsibility of assisting in keeping the AFL-CIO "free from any taint of corruption or communism." Any initial investigation of alleged corruption of an affiliated union and its officers, as in the case of the Teamsters, is made by the Committee on Ethical Practices. Should the investigation disclose corruption, the committee chairman will make a recommendation to the Executive Council for appropriate action.

Departments of the AFL-CIO

A very important feature of the federation structure lies in the trade and industrial departments. In a sense, the departments are federations within the AFL-CIO. The constitution establishes seven such departments: Building Trades, Food and Beverage, Industrial Union, Maritime, Metal Trades, Railway Employees, and Union Label; and the posture of the departments in the federation structure is indicated by the wording of the constitutional provision which broadly defines them: "Each department is to be considered an official method of the Federation for transacting the portion of its business indicated by the name of the department, in consequence of which affiliated and eligible organizations should be part of their respective departments and should comply with the actions and decisions of such departments, subject to appeal therefrom to the Executive Council and the conventions of the Federation."[5] When a national union affiliates with an appropriate department, it is required to pay a per capita tax to the department based upon the number of members whose occupations or jobs fall under the department. These dues are in addition to the dues which the national union pays as a condition of belonging to the AFL-CIO.

In practice, a national union may belong to more than one department. For example, the International Brotherhood of Electrical Workers is composed of members who work in the building trades as well as those who work in factories, and the union is thus eligible for membership in the Building Trades Department and in the Industrial Union Department. The rationale behind the department structure is one of encouraging unions with common interests to work together toward common ends. By establishing an Industrial Union Department, for example, the federation encourages all national unions which have membership in mass-production industries to associate together in their joint endeavors. Thus, most former unions which belonged to the old CIO (as well as industrially oriented national unions, such as the International Association of Machinists, which belonged to the erstwhile AFL) are part of the Industrial Union Department.

Each department is concerned with problems of its particular industry. Such problems can involve collective bargaining issues, new organizational drives, legislative matters, or more specialized areas with which the unions of a particular branch of industry are uniquely confronted. Indeed, unlike the AFL-CIO, two of the departments take an active part in collective bargaining: the Railway Employees' Department, which represents the members of the craft unions who work in railroad shops, plays a major role in the collective bargaining with the railroads; and the Metal Trades

---

[5] Article XII, Section 5.

Department usually engages in the negotiations where large shipbuilding concerns are involved. The Union Label Department has as its primary objective the education of the consuming public in the desirability of purchasing union-made goods. It is composed of all AFL-CIO affiliates who stress use of a union label to show that union members produced the product: to many union members such a label is particularly persuasive before a purchase is made.

As the AFL-CIO, each department holds a biennial convention, in the same city as the AFL-CIO meeting, and immediately before the latter. Each department elects officers, adopts rules of procedure, and passes resolutions. By custom, the president of each department is elected from the ranks of presidents of the national unions affiliated with the department. Some of the departments also issue publications and conduct research of particular concern to their affiliated unions, and for this purpose maintain departmental staffs in the same building in Washington, D.C., which houses the AFL-CIO.

State and City bodies

Though most of the activities of the AFL-CIO are thus centered in Washington, the federation has also established state and city bodies to deal with problems at the state and municipal level: there are now state bodies in each of the fifty states and one in Puerto Rico, and on the city level the federation has created city centrals in more than 750 communities.

Note that these state and city central bodies are established *directly* by the AFL-CIO. They are not created by the national unions affiliated with the federation or by local unions which belong to these national unions. Local unions which belong to national unions affiliated with the AFL-CIO may join a state or a city central body, but the national union must be affiliated with the AFL-CIO; and should a national union be expelled from or withdraw voluntarily from the federation, its local unions lose membership in the state and city central bodies. Thus, when the Teamsters Union was expelled from the AFL-CIO, the locals of this union were likewise expelled from the state and city bodies.[6] The same thing occurred when the UAW forfeited its membership in the AFL-CIO. Indeed, the president of the Indiana State AFL-CIO, a UAW member, was deposed from office since the officers of the federation state and city bodies must be members of an affiliated union. Other points of importance are that national unions do not affiliate with state and city organizations (only their locals may belong to them) and that the federation does not require

---

[6] In some cases, however, Teamster locals *were* allowed to keep membership until the national officers of the AFL-CIO forced the issue.

that the locals affiliate (although most of the national unions require that their locals affiliate with the state and city bodies).

State federations, also, hold conventions at which they elect officers of the state organization. Delegates to such state conventions are elected by the affiliated local unions. Normally these delegates elect a president, vice-president, and secretary-treasurer who devote full time to the organization's business, and, of course, receive a salary for their work. At times, a state central body will also hire full-time representatives who are concerned with special matters, particularly in the field of legislative lobbying.

Similar to the AFL-CIO, also, the state and city bodies have no executive power over their affiliated unions. They do not engage in collective bargaining, call or forbid strikes, or regulate the internal affairs of their affiliated local unions. Instead, the chief concern of the state and city bodies is political and educational activities. They lobby for or against legislation, offer testimony before state legislative committees, and promote political candidates favored by organized labor. Almost all state organizations now hold schools for representatives of their affiliated unions—the classes being taught by union officials, university instructors, government officials, and on some occasions representatives of the business community. The city bodies, in addition to participating in similar legislative and educational activities, engage in a wide variety of communty service work: promoting the United Fund, Red Cross, and similar community projects, among other endeavors. In many cities and towns, such bodies have even sponsored Boy Scout troops and Little League baseball teams, as well as art institutes, musical events, day-care centers for children of working mothers, and even the purchase of seeing-eye dogs for blind people. Although genuine altruism doubtless motivates many of these good deeds, so, too, does the need for an improved public image which is today so keenly felt by many unionists.

Functions and Problems of the Federation

For all that the AFL-CIO voluntarily abstains from doing or is restricted by its constitution from attempting, there can be no denying the aggressiveness with which the federation pursues the activities which it does undertake. In the political arena this is particularly true. As do most other major interest groups in the United States, the federation now employs a large corps of full-time lobbyists whose mission is to exert pressure upon members of Congress to support legislation favored by the AFL-CIO and to oppose those bills which the federation regards as undesirable. Its principal officers themselves frequently testify before congressional committees, and make public declarations of federation political policies. And, by its very dimensions, the federation provides a powerful sounding board for all of organized labor. Ostensibly, when the president of the AFL-CIO speaks he represents more than 13,500,000 union members and their families, 121 national unions, 60,000 local unions, 51 state federations, and almost 800 citywide labor bodies. No other labor leader can claim as much attention and exert as much influence as the president of the AFL-CIO. He and other important federation officials are from time to time invited to the White House and are regularly invited by United States senators, congressmen, and heads of major federal agencies which deal with labor matters to specify labor's position on major issues of the day. And it is doubtful that representatives of any other interest group make as many appearances at the White House as do members of the AFL-CIO high command.

At times of federal and state elections, the role of the federation is equally important. The federation has created a Committee on Political Education which coordinates the political action of organized labor during such periods. This political arm of the federation operates on the national, state, and local levels, where (since the Taft-Hartley law, as we know, forbids unions to contribute union dues to political candidates) it raises money on a voluntary basis from union members. Some of this money is given directly to political candidates who are regarded as friends of organized labor; other money is expended for radio and TV programs of a political nature, the publication of voting records of candidates who have previously served in elective offices, the distribution of campaign literature, and kindred activities. Although it is difficult to assess the political impact of the federation upon the nation—the AFL-CIO having had both its successes and its failures—the fact that the federation continues to play an active role in the political affairs of the country would indicate that the victories outweigh the defeats.

The political objectives of organized labor and the federation are varied in character. The AFL-CIO supports legislation that strengthens the role of organized labor in collective bargaining, organizational drives, the strike, picketing, and boycotting. To these ends, the federation has, for example, consistently advocated such measures as the repeal of state "right-to-work" legislation, and lobbied for other changes in the federal and state laws which strengthen the use of such union self-help methods as boycotts and picketing in labor's direct relationship with business. It has also, however, regularly supported such bills as those favoring medicare, low-cost public housing, liberalized minimum wage laws, more comprehensive unemployment compensation statutes, and more effective public education—all of which measures are intended to benefit all the workers of the nation and their families rather than strictly those within the ranks of unionism. The AFL-CIO today fully recognizes that many of these less parochial objectives cannot be achieved through face-to-face union-management collective bargaining and has consequently supported such measures as the ones cited to gain additional leverage in its efforts to improve the status of the American wage-earner.

Beyond the legislative and political function, the federation carries out a massive research program—the results of which are embodied in its regular publications, such as the monthly *AFL-CIO News* and the *American Federationist,* as well as in special bulletins, briefs for the courts of the nation, and a series of pamphlets, monographs, and books. Through these varied publications, the federation tries to keep union members and others abreast of labor developments from the union point of view.

Another important function is that of promoting new organizations. Although the basic responsibility for such new organizations falls upon the national unions, the federation does organize on its own, and helps affiliated unions in their organizational drives. When the AFL-CIO organizes a union by itself, it charters such a local union directly with the federation in much the same fashion that the old AFL did in the 1930s. There are about 350 such directly affiliated labor unions now in existence and, through its field officers, the AFL-CIO bargains contracts for these local unions and aids them in time of strikes and other difficulties with management. In return, members of such locals pay dues directly to the AFL-CIO. This collective bargaining function for directly affiliated local unions should not, however, be confused with the principle already established: the AFL-CIO does not bargain collectively for affiliated national unions or for locals which belong to such affiliated national unions. Moreover, most of these directly affiliated local unions are themselves ultimately assigned by the federation to a national union which has appropriate jurisdiction over the jobs and occupations of its members.

In recent years, the American labor movement has also demonstrated increasing concern with the labor movement in foreign nations. Two major factors lie behind this development. In the first place, the increasing tempo of international trade has threatened the job security and welfare of American workers. The impact in the United States of products produced by foreign labor under conditions of comparatively lower wages and working conditions makes it more difficult for American unions to retain benefits already secured and to obtain improvements in them. American unions understand full well that benefits secured in their contracts are placed in jeopardy because of such competition from low-wage foreign nations. Hence, by strengthening the foreign labor movement, American unions not only improve the status of workers within foreign nations, but at the same time protect the advances which have been gained through collective bargaining in this country.

The second reason concerns the threat of Communist domination of foreign labor movements and, through this tactic, the possible seizure of the governments of foreign nations by Communists. Even in the United States, as Chapter 2 has demonstrated, organized labor has been faced with such a threat, although in this country it has been successfully surmounted. The 1949–50 expulsion from the CIO of the several Communist-controlled unions, and the establishment of new unions to take over the membership of such unions, dealt a telling blow to the influence of communism in the American labor movement. The AFL, too, when it was the only federation in the nation, waged a continuous and bitter battle against the left and managed to maintain its basically conservative philosophy and objectives. Happily, there are today only a handful of American labor unions, all of them relatively minor in strategic power (for example, the Furriers Union) which are even remotely believed to be dominated by Communists. But the problem is much more severe in foreign lands: in such nations as Italy and France, Communistic elements do have considerable influence in the affairs of the labor movements. And the important officers of America's labor movement, well schooled in the potential consequences of communism, believe with considerable justification that should such totalitarianism spread to the governments of these countries the first casualties would be the free labor movement, collective bargaining, and the right to strike. For such reasons, the AFL-CIO works hard to help foreign trade unions remain free from Communist domination.

Currently, the AFL-CIO participates in several international labor bodies. It is a particularly active member in both the International Confederation of Free Trade Unions and the International Labor Organization, and through these forums works with the trade unions of other free nations to promote the interests of workers throughout the world. The former organization is composed only of labor movements, while the ILO is tripartite in character and allows representation to each member government, employers, and workers.[7]

Beyond AFL-CIO participation in these labor bodies, the federation and its affiliates contribute money to aid in the organization of foreign workers, the training of foreign labor leaders, the education of foreign union members, and the promotion of a variety of similar activities. In addition, the AFL-CIO has representation on various committees of the United Nations, hosts many visiting labor delegates from foreign nations who are sent both by their governments and by higher trade union bodies in their respective nations, and even on frequent occasions itself finances the trips of these foreign labor leaders. The AFL-CIO and many of its

---

[7] When the ILO convenes annually, each member nation is allowed four voting delegates, of whom two are representatives of the government, one of the employers, and one of workers. The American delegation is composed of two representatives from the Department of Labor, one selected by employer associations, and one chosen by the AFL-CIO.

affiliated national unions have also financed trips of their *own* representatives to foreign lands to see at first hand the problems of other labor movements. Under the AFL-CIO constitution, the federation's Committee on International Affairs is charged with the responsibility of coordinating and implementing such activities.

Conflict between Craft and Industrial Unions

If the main benefit associated with federation membership is protection against raiding, one of the most important problems of the AFL-CIO is that of maintaining peace between affiliated unions in their jurisdictional disputes over jobs. Frequently, craft and industrial unions battle each other avidly over such jurisdiction, particularly in establishments where an industrial union holds bargaining rights but where there are jobs which could be carried out in a more efficient fashion by members of a craft union. Such jobs as those involving the routine maintenance of machinery or other equipment, the major overhaul or installation of equipment, and the construction of new facilities often fall into this category.

What could spark a conflict is the desire of members of craft unions whose members are *not* employees of the industrial company to do the work which is being performed by the skilled tradesmen on the payroll of the factory. At times, employers find it cheaper to hire these outside craftsmen to perform the work and therefore seek out contractor-employers who control such skilled employees. Upon other occasions, a skilled trade union, through an employer-contractor, makes overtures to the industrial employer. However, the problem could also arise from the other direction. That is, the industrial employer may have customarily subcontracted out certain maintenance work to outside skilled tradesmen. To secure this work for its own membership, the industrial union which holds bargaining rights in the factory puts pressure upon the employer to cease this practice and to award the work to his own employees who are, of course, members of the industrial union. It is not difficult to understand that when jobs are scarce, the conflict between craft and industrial unions can achieve major dimensions.

Indeed, the problem became so serious in the recession-marked first months of the 1960s that many observers predicted the imminent collapse of the entire federation through craft-industrial warfare. In the fall of 1961, the *Wall Street Journal* carried this headline: "Craft, Industrial Union Fights Grow, Threaten an End to AFL-CIO; Factions Battle Over Rights to Jobs"; and delegates to the AFL-CIO convention of December 1961 met under the most ominous of conditions.

Remarkably, however, the important leaders of the craft and industrial unions were able to arrive at a workable solution to the problem at the convention and thereby rescue the federation from such a collapse. They adopted an "Internal Disputes Plan," often also referred to as the "Live and Let Live" plan, and incorporated it in the constitution of the AFL-CIO. More technically, the constitutional amendment officially preserved the integrity of past practices in work assignments. Henceforth a union's right to jobs would depend on what relevant customs or practices had been in force where it sought such jobs. If the members of an industrial union had held jurisdiction over new construction in the past, this customary work assignment would be respected by craft unions. If an employer had customarily subcontracted out maintenance work, *this* practice was to be respected by industrial unions, who were not to put pressure upon employers to change the practice.

An elaborate procedure has been adopted to implement this new constitutional provision. In the event that a union charges that another union is violating the terms of the new policy, the AFL-CIO assigns a federation official to mediate the dispute. If this effort fails, an arbitrator is appointed to make an award. Once the arbitrator hands down his decision, the rival union is expected to abide by the award. However, the losing union has the right to appeal to a three-man subcommittee of the AFL-CIO Executive Council. This subcommittee may disallow the appeal, in which event the decision of the arbitrator is final and there is no other appeal procedure. But if the subcommittee is not fully satisfied with the arbitrator's award, it may refer the case to the entire Executive Council, which will decide the issue by majority vote. The council may uphold the arbitrator's award, reverse it, or modify it. In any event, however, the decision of the Executive Council is final and binding on the unions involved in the dispute.

If a union fails to comply with the decision rendered through this procedure, the amendment to the constitution provides that the federation may impose sanctions (described below) on the noncomplying union, and if the violation persists, the union can be expelled from the federation.

Thus far the plan has worked successfully and the threat to the federation has abated. The *AFL-CIO News,* the official publication of the federation, has detailed the results of the plan from the time of its creation in January 1962 through January 1970. In this time period, 967 complaints were filed under the plan. Of these, 581 were settled in mediation or mediation was still in progress. Arbitrators found violations of the plan in 242 cases. After the arbitrators handed down their awards, unions filed 67 complaints charging noncompliance. Subsequently, compliance was achieved in 36 cases, noncompliance was found in 16, 8 cases were withdrawn by the charging unions, and 7 noncompliance cases were pending as of February 1, 1970.

No union has ever been expelled from the federation for noncompliance. However, as of February 1970, sanctions were in effect on five affiliated national unions: Air Line Pilots Association; International Leather Goods, Plastics and Novelty Workers; National Maritime Union; Brotherhood of Railway Car Men; and the International Typographical Union. When the AFL-CIO imposes sanctions upon a union under the terms of the plan, the union may not file charges under the plan to protest that another union is violating its customary job jurisdiction; the federation will publicly give notice of the union's noncompliance; and the AFL-CIO can deny to such noncomplying union its services and facilities.

With the craft-industrial conflict now having so visibly diminished, it appears that the AFL-CIO will continue to exist as a permanent federation in the United States. At this writing, it is fifteen years old and the old antagonisms of the former members and officers of the AFL and CIO have largely subsided. It is not likely that the UAW defection will result in wholesale withdrawals from the federation. In the last analysis, the withdrawal of the UAW was the result of a personal vendetta between Walter Reuther and George Meany rather than on the basis of substantive issues. It is safe to conclude that the federation can overcome future problems, such as the election of new AFL-CIO officers, without falling apart. Moreover, union leaders understand that the collapse of the federation would seriously impair the future of organized labor in this nation. They understand that they had better "hang together" or they will hang separately. Indeed, the collapse of the federation would undoubtedly cause incessant raiding and jurisdictional strikes. Very probably, it would also result in some re-emergence of labor violence, a further decline of union membership, a possible resurgence of corruption, and other effects which would adversely affect not only unions and their members, but also employers and the general public. From the point of view of stability in industrial relations, the preservation of the AFL-CIO is a public necessity.

THE NATIONAL UNION

Relationship to Locals

If the national union is quite autonomous in the conduct of its affairs, the story is quite different when one examines the relationship between the national union and its local unions. Though there are many exceptions, most national unions exercise considerable power over their locals. Before a local union may strike, it must normally obtain the permission of the national union. And, should the local strike in defiance of national union instructions, the national union can withhold strike benefits, refuse to give the local union any other form of aid during the strike, and in extreme cases even take over the local on a trusteeship basis. In addition, consistent with the regulations of many national unions, all local collective bargaining contracts must be reviewed by the national officers before they may be put into force. All national union constitutions today contain provisions which establish standards of conduct and procedures for the internal operation of their constituent locals—usually, the dues which the latter may charge, the method by which local union officers may be elected and their tenures of office, the procedures for the discipline of local union members, the conduct of union meetings, and other rules of this kind.

Violation of these national union standards can result in sanctions placed upon the local union officers, and on the local union itself. Recently, for example, many national unions have been at least as conscious of the problem of racial discrimination within the union movement as has the AFL-CIO, and almost all national constitutions now contain a nondiscriminatory clause, designed to guarantee Negroes equal and fair treatment from the local unions. Several local unions have been seized by their nationals when they have discriminated against Negroes through such mechanisms as providing segregated local union facilities (such as washrooms and drinking facilities), or when they have failed to afford Negroes equal protection in the negotiation of labor agreements or in the grievance procedure.

In addition, within the collective bargaining process the national union is currently exercising considerably greater control and influence over the contracts which locals negotiate. This is particularly true when the members of the locals work for companies which sell their products in national product markets—an ever-increasing number. Nationals desire that companies over whose employees they have jurisdiction and which compete in national product markets operate under common labor-cost standards. They are less likely to exercise control over the unions whose members produce for local markets. This latter situation holds, for example, in the construction industry because the labor costs involved in the construction of a building in one city do not directly compete with those affecting the construction of a building in another.

Service in Collective Bargaining

The national exercises much of its influence over the local in the direct collective bargaining process through the service which the national union provides its locals in the negotiation of the labor agreements. To understand this national-local relationship, however, one should not regard the negotiation service of the national union as a function which is performed against the will of the local union. On the contrary, local unions not only generally desire and expect the help of the national union when they negotiate labor agreements with the employer, but should the national union either refuse to provide these services or perform them in an ineffective way the local union members and their officers can be counted upon to be sharply critical of the national union. The officers of the national could safely assume, in fact, that such a disgruntled local union would attempt to take political reprisal against the officers of the national in the next election of national officers.

The chief reason for the local union's desire for help from the national union in collective bargaining involves the complexities of the contemporary collective bargaining process. As will be made more evident in future chapters, many of the issues of collective bargaining have become increasingly intricate. Most contemporary collective bargaining contracts focus upon such involved items as adjustment to automation, pension plans, insurance programs, supplementary unemployment benefit plans, job evaluation, production standards, time and motion studies, and complicated wage incentive programs. Beyond the complex character of the contemporary issues, moreover, the modern collective bargaining process is obviously made more difficult because of the character of the law of labor relations. In short, it takes an expert to negotiate under current circumstances.

For effective representation, it is necessary to find people who are knowledgeable, experienced, and have a professional understanding of the collective bargaining process, and few local unions are fortunate enough to include such people in their membership. Each local union elects a negotiating committee, but the members of such committees are typically employed in the plant and work full time on their jobs. They simply do not have the opportunity to keep abreast of current developments in collective bargaining and to make a searching study of the problems involved in the negotiation of the difficult issues. On the company side, moreover, there are normally management representatives who are well trained and equipped to handle the contemporary collective bargaining negotiation. Many of them have received special training in labor relations, and some devote full time to the problems of negotiation and administration of collective bargaining contracts.

Indeed, without the services of the national union there would be a sharp disparity of negotiating talent at the bargaining table. In this light, it is easy to understand why the local union does not regard the intervention of the national union at the bargaining table as an invasion of the rights of the local, but rather views this service as indispensable to the effective negotiation of the labor agreement.

Most national unions have well-qualified people to render this service: the so-called staff representatives, who devote full time to union affairs. They are hired by the national union, paid salaries and expenses for their work, and expected to provide services to the local unions of the national.

All of them are union members, and normally reach their position of staff representative by having demonstrated their ability as union members and local union officers. They are not, however, elected to their jobs, but are hired because of their special talents.

Although the staff representatives perform a variety of duties, such as organizing new plants, engaging in political action work at times of federal and state elections, directing strikes, and representing the union and its members before the federal and state labor agencies, helping the local unions to negotiate labor agreements constitutes one of their primary functions.[8] Staff representatives gain much bargaining experience because they normally service several local unions and in the course of one year they may be called upon to negotiate many different labor agreements, thus gaining on-the-job training which serves as an invaluable asset to them when they confront a specific management at the bargaining table. Many national unions also send their staff representatives to special schools, some of which are held on university campuses and are taught by specialists in the labor education field, for additional training. Moreover, the staff representative is invariably backed up by experts within the national union. Almost every national union has several departments which concentrate on the major issues involved in collective bargaining. For example, the United Automobile Workers has departments which deal respectively with pensions, wage systems, insurance, and other critical areas. The specialists assigned to these national departments may be freely called upon by the staff representatives should their services be needed.

The Regional or District Office

Staff representatives may work out of the headquarters of the national union, but more frequently they are assigned to a regional or district office. Almost every national union divides the nation into regions or districts, and locals of the national union which are located in the geographical area or the district obtain services from their respective district offices. For example, District 30 of the United Steelworkers of America, headquartered in Indianapolis, covers most of Indiana and Kentucky and is administered by a district director elected by the local unions of the district. About twenty staff representatives are assigned by the national union to District 30, and work under the immediate supervision of the district director.

Each staff representative services about seven local unions. He attends

---

[8] A major exception to all these remarks involves craft unions in local-product market industries: here local business agents are normally elected to perform such duties.

the local union meetings, works closely with the negotiating committees, hears the problems of the workers in the plant in which the local holds control, and attempts to understand the values and objectives of the members. He is the liaison between the national union and his local union, and in this capacity can do much to influence the local in the acceptance of national union collective bargaining policies. In such a capacity, moreover, the staff representative can serve as a mediator between local unions and the national when differences arise between them.

A good staff representative wins the confidence of local officers and members, and the local union will thus rely heavily upon his counsel in collective bargaining matters. He can exert great influence upon the local to reject or accept the last offer of an employer. Indeed, frequently he can provoke a strike or prevent one by the way in which he reports to the local union and makes recommendations to the members. He is, in short, often in an excellent position to influence the decision-making process in collective bargaining.

Multi-employer Bargaining

Although most multi-employer bargaining is in relatively small bargaining units in local-product markets, at times national unions bargain with employers on a multi-employer basis. That is, a group of companies band together and negotiate with the *national* union as a unit. Employers find this structure of collective bargaining valuable because it prevents a given union from "whipsawing" each employer: usually under a multi-employer bargaining structure, each employer is comparatively small in size and unimpressive in financial resources, and the companies compete fiercely in the product market; in the absence of multi-employer collective bargaining, the union could pick off one employer at a time. Such employer association–national union collective bargaining is found in industries such as clothing, coal, and shipping—all of which contain large measures of the unstabilizing factors noted.

When multi-employer collective bargaining exists and where the product market is not a local one, the national officers themselves typically bargain for the contract and the local unions play a comparatively passive role—a situation which also holds at the other extreme, when unions bargain with the industrial giants of the nation (such as General Motors and United States Steel). The national unions negotiate the agreement in the latter instance since no one local union could possibly measure up to the strength of these companies. Bargaining logic dictates that in both cases the national union rather than the local union play the paramount labor relations role.

Additional National Union Services

Beyond providing considerable help in the negotiating of labor agreements, the national union renders other valuable services to its local unions. The national usually awards benefits to employees on strike, although the actual amount of money paid in strike benefits is usually very minimal—about $20–$40 per week to each member, on the average. More important, the national union intervenes with the strikers' creditors so that the automobiles, furniture, and other holdings of the union members will not be repossessed. And it ensures that no striking employee or his family goes hungry even if this guarantee involves the actual distribution of food to the strikers. Management should be aware that unions in these days do not lose strikes because of hunger or unpaid bills. If there are insurance premiums to be paid, doctors to see, rent to be paid, or school tuition to be met, the national unions will see to it that the worker does not suffer. This is true despite the obvious fact that the national unions themselves have financial limitations, for virtually all nationals do under normal circumstances have the resources to assure that the minimum physiological needs of their member-workers are met, and many larger unions are quite amply financed: the Automobile Workers, for example, poured out more than $12 million during the six-year 1954–60 Kohler strike to aid the members of the local engaged in that conflict. In addition, if a national union does run out of money, labor custom dictates that other national unions will lend it money to finance the strike.

The national union also aids the locals in the grievance procedure and in arbitration, both of which subjects will be discussed in detail in Chapter 6. Normally, the staff representative represents the local in the last step of the grievance procedure. Along with the local union grievance committee, he attempts to settle the grievance to the satisfaction of the complaining worker and if the case does ultimately go to arbitration, he usually directly represents the grievant. In general, whether they win or lose their arbitration cases, staff representatives present the union's case very effectively. This fact is often offered by labor leaders as one reason why unions employ lawyers less frequently than do employers when cases go to arbitration. There is no need to incur the expense if the staff representative can do the job as competently as an attorney.

Of course, at times local unions *are* in need of attorneys, as when the local union has a case which requires testimony in the courts. For example, employers may sue a union for breach of contract, or workers may be indicted because of violence in picketing. When attorneys are needed, the local union can normally obtain the services of the national union's legal staff, whose members, although invariably paid less than comparable lawyers who work for corporations, are frequently highly competent and usually quite dedicated to the union movement. Several attorneys, Clarence Darrow and Arthur Goldberg most notably, made their mark by representing labor organizations.

The fact that the local does so readily receive such services from its national constitutes the reason why the vast majority of local unions belong to a national union. Indeed, less than 2 percent of all locals are not affiliated with a national, and all these "independents" (except for the relative handful of them belonging directly to the AFL-CIO and thus enabled to make use of the federation's services) must rely upon their own resources, whereas the many local unions which *do* belong to nationals can use the considerable resources of the latter.

Other Functions of the National Union

Although national union officers and staff representatives devote the major share of their time to providing services to the local unions, the range of the national union's activities includes many other important functions. Today, the major concern of all unions is that of increasing membership in the face of the relative plateau of the past few years. Responsible labor union officials understand that the unorganized must be organized, and the chief burden for this also falls to the national union staff representatives. Although the AFL-CIO does do some organizational work, it does not have the staff to perform this function effectively; nor can the responsibility for the organization of new plants be undertaken by local union officers or members. At times, local union people help in organizational drives, but because they are full-time employees, they do not have much opportunity to carry out this function.

Accordingly, the catalyst for new organization falls to the staff representatives of the national unions, upon whom constant pressure is exerted to organize nonunion plants. Indeed, in some national unions not only the advancement but even the continued job tenure of the staff representative is determined by his success in organizing such plants.

The task is hardly an easy one. Most nonunion employers can be counted upon to wage a fierce fight against organization. Many employees who are not members of unions do not want a labor union because management provides them with many of the benefits which they would receive if organized. And the staff representative's organizing mission becomes even more difficult if he attempts to organize in the South or in small communities regardless of sectional location. In any event, the representative must make contacts among the workers, convince them of the value of unions, and dispel notions that unions are corrupt, communistic, or otherwise undesirable institutions. Many workers are ready to believe the worst about organized labor, and staff representatives often admit that these conceptions are difficult to erase.

The staff man is thus forced to use his imagination to the fullest. He may initially attempt to organize "from inside," through the informal leaders in the plant. Then he may visit workers in their homes, distribute leaflets, and arrange organizational meetings (which frequently are poorly attended). Subsequently he must counteract whatever management does to block the organizational attempt: even in today's more enlightened atmosphere, some employers warn employees of dire consequences should they organize, tell their employees that unions exist only to collect dues for the personal benefit of the union "bosses," and—the organizing tactic laws cited in Chapter 3 notwithstanding—on occasion even threaten workers with loss of their jobs if a union is established, as well as promise them benefits if they reject the union.

There are other formidable obstacles for the organizer. If the plant is located in a comparatively small community, there may be a concerted attempt among the leaders of the community to keep the union out. The target employer may have good friends who run the newspaper, the radio and TV station, the Chamber of Commerce, and the local stores, and these power centers may join forces to do what they can to keep the union from gaining a foothold. Indeed, it is not uncommon that the clergy in a town is enlisted in the fight against the union.

The organizational mission of the staff representative is thus a highly challenging one. In recent years, he probably has had more failures than successful ventures. But he is typically persistent and this tenaciousness occasionally reaps its reward: illustratively, a large company located in Kokomo, Indiana, was organized in January 1965 after the Steelworkers' Union, which carried out the organizational campaign, had been defeated in three different NLRB elections over a span of thirteen years!

Another major function of the national union concerns political action, although national unions differ widely in the vigor which they display in this regard. Some, like the Automobile Workers, are constantly engaged in politics; others, like the United Brotherhood of Carpenters, seldom exert much effort to influence elections and the subsequent actions of elected officials. Undoubtedly, however, a larger number of national unions are concerned with political affairs today than were in the past. As has already been noted, their leaders understand that the success of the union depends in large measure upon the fashioning of a favorable legal climate for new organization and for the implementation of traditional trade union weapons when conflicts arise with employers. Moreover, a growing number of national unions share the belief of AFL-CIO leaders that the political programs of organized labor in the areas of social security, medicine, low-cost public housing, full employment, and the like are in the best interests of the nation as a whole.

When the national union officers are politically motivated, they are normally aggressive in exerting pressure upon the local unions and their members to take an active role in political affairs. Their union newspapers (each national union publishes at least one monthly newspaper) are filled with political news, voting records of the candidates, and the union point of view when elections are impending. National unions also arrange political rallies, purchase radio and television time to get the national's story across to the members and the public, and issue a barrage of political leaflets and pamphlets. In some national unions, during the weeks before important elections, the staff representatives are ordered to suspend collective bargaining negotiations, grievance meetings, and arbitrations and devote their full time to political work. Given the fact that each national union employs many staff representatives—in such large unions as the Automobile Workers and Steelworkers, the numbers run into the hundreds—this serves as an important advantage; and if the staff representatives are adroit and hard-working, the favored political candidate can benefit greatly from such support.

Depending upon their sizes and leadership policies, national unions perform other functions. Some arrange educational programs for their staff representatives and local union officers. Most of the courses in these programs deal exclusively with the practical aspects of labor relations—how to bargain labor agreements, the best way to handle grievances, and the like. At times, however, the courses deal with foreign affairs, taxation, economics, government, and other subjects which are not directly related to the bread-and-butter issues of trade unionism. In addition, some national unions administer vacation resorts for their members, award university scholarships to children of members, organize tours to foreign nations, conduct publicity campaigns to acquaint union members and the public in general with the purpose of the union label, and sponsor a variety of social functions which are similar to those maintained by the state and city labor bodies but more tailored to the specific interests and aptitudes of the particular national union members.

Government of the National Union

When a national union is formed, a constitution is adopted which spells out the internal government and procedures of the union. Virtually every constitution provides that a convention should be held, and designates this convention as the supreme authority of the union. Under the rules of most national unions, each local union sends delegates to the convention, with the number of delegates permitted to each local being dependent upon the local's paid-up membership totals. Hence, as in the case of the AFL-CIO, the larger locals are more influential than are the smaller units. Within the UAW, for example, the locals range in size from somewhat over 60,000 (the local union representing Ford Motor Company workers at Ford's River Rouge plant) to a literal handful of members in some locals which have contracts with small employers.

Ordinarily, the chief officers of the local unions are elected as delegates, though in the very large locals which have the opportunity to send many delegates rank-and-file members are chosen because the quota cannot be filled by the officers alone. Being sent to a convention represents a plum to the delegates chosen. National conventions, again as the AFL-CIO conventions themselves, are usually held in large and attractive cities; when the delegates lose time in the plant because of their election, the local union normally pays their lost wages; and the convention may last as much as a week or so, allowing a welcome relief from the tedium of working in the plant. Many delegates take their wives and children, so that, along with the business of the convention, attendance at the convention may thus become a sort of work-play affair; however, the expenses involved are such that small local unions with limited funds sometimes do not send delegates to the convention even though they are entitled to do so.

Although under the terms of the Landrum-Griffin Act the delegates must be chosen by secret ballot, the officers of the nationals themselves may be selected in either of two ways. In about three-fourths of the national unions, the constitution requires that the principal officers (president, vice president, and secretary-treasurer) must be elected by the convention. In the others, the officers are elected by a direct referendum wherein each member of the union may cast a ballot. Some of the largest unions in the nation follow the latter procedure, including the United Steelworkers of America, the Amalgamated Clothing Workers, and the International Association of Machinists, but even among the larger unions most utilize the convention election system.

In addition to the election of chief officers, the convention transacts the business of the national union. Reports and recommendations of the officers are heard, and the delegates have an opportunity to deliberate them and decide whether or not to adopt them. Problems of the various locals are aired, and this provides an excellent opportunity for an exchange of ideas and experiences and for otherwise breaking down the provincialism of the local unions: delegates from a large local union located in Chicago can learn of the problems of a small local in a small southern community, for example. The convention also permits local union officers to display themselves to their best advantage. Most local union officers would like to rise in the union hierarchy, and the convention offers a testing ground for their talents. A rousing speech by a local union president may attract the attention of the delegates, and the consensus may be "here is a fellow we should watch."

The actual business of the convention may be initiated either by the national officers or by the delegates. Decision making takes the form of resolutions, proposals, and reports on which the delegates vote. As in any large convention, the officers have a distinct advantage in this respect, since the president appoints the committees which bring important issues before the delegates and is in a position to select members for these committees whom he knows are favorable to the national officers' point of view. On the other hand, a determined local union or even individual delegates who feel strongly about their cause can bring to the attention of the convention a resolution, recommendation, or even an amendment to the constitution. There is a limit, in fact, to how far any national president can go in bottling up the resentment of determined delegates. And, particularly if a delegation from a local can enlist the support of delegates from other locals, there is an excellent chance that the entire convention will hear its point of view. For all the authority and control which the nationals exert over the locals, if national officers gain the enmity of a sufficient number of local unions, the delegates of these locals can band together and cause an upheaval at the convention. And, if the issues are of extreme importance, the resentment of these locals could result in a change in national union leadership. Thus, the local unions do have a political check against their national officers. There is a line which the latter can cross only at the risk of losing their jobs.

In short, as long as the national union holds regularly scheduled conventions, the democratic process has an opportunity of working. The convention provides the forum wherein the policies, behavior, and competency of the national union officers can be evaluated, and the key to the democratic operation of a national union therefore lies in the regularity with which conventions are held. More than one-half of the national unions hold conventions either annually or biennially, and most of the rest hold them every three or four years. A small number of national unions, however, simply do not hold conventions at all, and this clearly eliminates almost entirely any practical opportunity for the local unions to participate in the government of their unions. Nothing in the Landrum-Griffin law, indeed, requires unions to hold regular and reasonably frequent conventions. The law does require that the union membership be afforded the opportunity to elect its national officers at least every five years, but a union managed by autocrats can legally avoid the holding of conventions indefinitely.

National Union Officers

The chief of the national union is, of course, its president. He administers the organization with the assistance of such other major officers as the vice president (or vice presidents), secretary-treasurer, and members of the executive board. The latter group is composed ordinarily of the district or regional directors (who, in some national unions, are also called vice presidents), and its members have a variety of official tasks: enforcing the constitution of the national, implementing its policies, filling a national officer's position when vacant, voting on important matters referred to it by the president, placing items on the agenda for deliberation and voting, and a host of related duties. Normally, the executive board of a national union meets regularly and frequently according to the provisions of a constitution, and on occasion also meets at the call of the president to deal with some pressing problem. Since the members of the executive board are from all over the nation and have direct supervision of the locals in their particular districts, the board mechanism provides an excellent way for the national union officers to learn of the problems of all locals throughout the country. Likewise, it provides a channel for communicating policies of the national union to the national union's locals and membership.

In some unions, however, executive boards merely rubber-stamp decisions of the national officers. This is true most often when a president, either by union custom or because of his particular personality, is allowed to exercise autocratic leadership. It is safe to say, however, that in most unions the executive board directs the affairs of the union and establishes the union's basic policies, which the president is then obliged to carry out. In one recent notable exception to this situation, the United Steelworkers' executive board, composed of all the district directors of that union, appeared to many members not to have much power in running the affairs of the union in the early 1960s, President David J. McDonald himself retaining it. McDonald was, however, defeated in his 1965 re-election attempt, and the perceived power imbalance has often been cited as one major reason for his ouster. The new Steelworker president, I. W. Abel, has taken pains to alter this image and to encourage the executive board to participate more fully in policymaking decisions.

A responsible, devoted, and active national union president has a difficult job. One day he may be negotiating a contract with a major corporation. The next day he is apt to be speaking at an important meeting of his union, or to the members of some other labor organization. He is also, typically, obligated to testify before congressional committees, preside over the union's executive board meetings, travel to foreign nations as a participant in international labor organization bodies, take an active role in important national political elections, constantly put pressure upon the staff representatives to organize nonunion plants, mollify companies which are disgruntled because of wildcat strikes or other forms of unauthorized union behavior, and perform a variety of other duties which may either be of major importance or strictly routine in character but which also take up his time. Indeed, the management of even a small or medium-sized national union is a difficult one; the job becomes immensely more complicated and difficult the larger the union.

The union president, moreover, is constantly torn between duties of a pressing character. In many cases, he must make the hard decision by himself and hope that the decision is the right one. As any chief executive, he bears the ultimate responsibility for the organization's efficient, honest, and prudent management. Above all, he must satisfy the membership, and at times this is a much more difficult job than dealing with management.

For the discharge of all these duties, national union presidents are moderately paid. In 1969, according to the United States Department of Labor, the average salary of national union presidents was about $26,000 per year, although this amount was normally supplemented by the payment of expenses incurred while on union business. Before the passage of the Landrum-Griffin Act, some national officers, such as Dave Beck of the Teamsters, copiously bought items of a personal nature and charged them to the union. However, the vast number of national officers are scrupulously honest in their expenses, and some, like the late Walter Reuther, have been so almost to a fault. Reuther refused to charge his union with telephone calls which were not totally related to union business, and even absorbed such costs as the pressing of his suit and kindred personal items while he was *on* union business. Reuther's salary, as president of the UAW (a union of 1,400,000 members, and thousands of locals) amounted in 1968 to only $30,861. Clearly, a corporation president managing a business of comparable size would be paid hundreds of thousands of dollars. Indeed, there are even a few college professors who earn $30,000!

Of course, workers pay the national officers' salaries, and the employee who earns $6,000 or less annually may look at the salary of his national president as being exorbitant. Rather than being too high, however, the verdict of the outside observer must be that the typical national union chief executive is underpaid. When measured by the number of members, the number of locals, and his duties, even the $86,250 salary of the Teamsters Union acting president (the highest-paid union official in the nation) does not seem unreasonable.

Though modestly paid, the national president wants to keep his job. He has power, prestige, and plays an important role in our society. Many presidents do indeed remain in office for considerable lengths of time and some of them stay in the chief executive chair for so long that memory does not recall another president. William Hutcheson was president of the Carpenters for 42 years; John L. Lewis of the Mine Workers for 40 years; Daniel Tobin of the Teamsters for 37 years; and James C. Petrillo of the Musicians gave up his job only when he grew so old and feeble that it is doubtful that he had the strength to play his instrument. A trend, however, may be developing to change this situation. With the demands on the national officers becoming ever more formidable, particularly in the field of new organization, some unions are duplicating the practice of business and requiring compulsory retirement at a certain age. In 1964, the UAW constitution was amended to require the retirement of that union's national officers at 65. Rather than work against compulsory retirement, the national officers of the UAW—including president Reuther, who was 57 years old when this amendment was passed—vigorously upheld the measure. UAW actions have frequently influenced the practices of other unions, and the 65-year compulsory retirement implementation, the first to be effected by a major international, may very well set a pattern which many other unions will follow.

There is little doubt that unions need vigorous, young, and dynamic leadership to cope with the problems of modern union affairs. Too many union leaders look with nostalgia at the past, and cherish their previous contributions to the union movement, rather than being concerned with their abilities to make future contributions. The election defeats of several union presidents in the past few years—including James Carey of the International Union of Electrical Workers, as well as McDonald and other leaders—reflect a growing restlessness among union members and a renewed emphasis on union democracy, and thus the possibility that the period of near-lifetime tenure for many national officers may now be ending.

Still, the problem exists, and the median age and years of service of national union officers remain considerable—about 63 years of age and 25 years of service. It is not difficult to explain why national union officers stay in office for so many years. Once in office, incumbent officials possess sufficient power to minimize centralized opposition and to make it extremely difficult for new candidates to present themselves to the membership in an effective manner. The point has been made that when conventions are not held regularly and frequently, it is difficult for a new face to get much backing. In addition, staff representatives are hired by the national union, and can usually be removed at the pleasure of the national officers. It would take rare courage for a paid representative to oppose the incumbent president and the tendency is, in fact, understandably in the other direction. In addition, most incumbent presidents get personal mileage out of their union newspapers. The editor of the national union newspaper is also a hired person, and subject to control of the national officers. Any upstart candidate could not expect much favorable publicity, if indeed he received any publicity at all, in the union press.

In short, the incumbent national officers have a political machine which tends to perpetuate them in office. However, it would be incorrect to believe that this is the only reason for long tenure of office. Sophisticated union members understand that frequent changes of national union officers and open displays of factionalism weaken the position of the union against management in collective bargaining. Beyond this, a national union officer may have genuinely earned re-election to office over the years because he has been doing a good job for the membership. A national union president who is devoted, honest, courageous, and competent does not need a political machine to be re-elected. Many national union officers fall within this category and representatives of management should not regard national union officers as incompetent people who hold office only because of political machination.

THE LOCAL UNION

Where the People Are

Although we leave for the last an analysis of the character and functions of the local union, it does not follow that the local union is the least important of the labor bodies in the union movement. On the contrary, it could be argued successfully that for the individual union member the local union is the most important unit of all. In a sense, the federation, the national union and its district organizations, and the other labor bodies discussed previously are administrative and service organizations. Although they are vitally important and carry out a variety of significant activities, as we have seen, no union member really "belongs" to such larger bodies. Unionists are members of these organizations only by reason of their membership in a local union, are geographically close only to the latter organization, and largely condition their loyalty toward an image of the total labor movement by what they perceive to transpire within the confines of the local union. Many union members do not, indeed, even know the names of their national and federation officers, but they do know their local union president, business agent, and stewards. They know the latter officials because they see them in the plant, and because these are the people who handle the union member's day-to-day problems.

Local Union Officers

Although some locals are formed before the employer is organized, a local union typically comes into existence when there is organization of an employer. After it has organized and secured bargaining rights a local typically applies for and receives a national union charter. This document establishes the local's affiliation with the national union, entitles the local to the services of the latter, and by the same token subjects the local to the rules and discipline of the national union. Depending upon the unit of organization, a local union may be confined to a single plant, several plants of a single company, or may include workers of a single craft, such as electricians who perform their duties in a given geographic area.

Once the local is established, the members, in accordance with their bylaws (which are usually specified in the national union constitution), elect their officers—typically a president, vice president, secretary-treasurer, and several lesser officials. Since such election procedures almost invariably allow direct participation by all union members, the local union officers are elected on a much more democratic basis than are those chosen to lead the national union. Moreover, the union member knows much more from first-hand experience about the local union candidates for office than he does about the national union officers. The vast majority of local union officers, in fact, work in the plant along with the other union members and are under constant and often highly critical observation by the latter. Both democracy and a far higher turnover rate for local officers than for the union's national officials also stem from the fact that the local union officer, unlike the national union president, has little if any patronage to dispense. He does not have a paid staff as does his national counterpart. Nor, generally speaking, can he make use of any other powers of patronage or the purse, since neither exist in any measure.

In general, the local union officers work without pay. In only the large local unions are such officers reimbursed for their work, and even then, their salaries tend to approximate the wages that they would have earned from their companies. And in the relatively infrequent instances when the local union president and secretary-treasurer do receive some small compensation for their duties even when they are full-time employees in the plant, the amount of money is comparatively small when measured against the duties which they perform.[9] For example, in Bloomington, Indiana, one local's secretary-treasurer receives $600 per year for taking care of the books, making financial reports, answering all correspondence, and assuming a volume of other miscellaneous duties. The size of his job is measured by the fact that the local has over 3,000 members, and by the union's requirement that all his duties must be conducted on his own time.

A fair question, then, is why union members desire to acquire and retain local union officer jobs. Despite their nominal or totally nonexistent

---

[9] A few, considerably more notable, exceptions involve the heads of some craft unions operating in local-product markets.

financial rewards, they must perform a variety of duties and assume considerable responsibility and they are constantly being pressured by the membership under whose direct surveillance they labor. The question is not an easy one to answer, since the motivations are obviously different with different people. A leading reason, however, is that the local union officers acquire prestige and status in the company and in the community. Virtually all people desire recognition once lower needs have been relatively well satisfied, and the attainment of a local officer's job accomplishes this objective for some workers.

Another reason may involve the local union officer's devotion and dedication to the union movement. If he really believes in unions, he has the opportunity of making the movement work by carrying out his duties in an honest and effective manner. Still other union members may genuinely court the competitive character which is associated with the office: the local union officers deal with the company on a day-to-day basis, and many of the dealings regularly involve what some workers view as "the struggle" with management. Finally, the reason may be a political one involving the future of the local union officer in his national union. As stated, national union officers are elected officers, and staff representatives are union members who are hired by the national union. Thus, to go up the ladder, the union member must normally start at the local union level: a local union officer's job is commonly the first step in the long and hard pull toward the top. The large majority of all current national union officers and staff representatives have held a local union officer's job at some earlier period of their career.

Functions of the Local Union: Relations with Management

The duties of local union officers are dependent, of course, upon the functions of the particular local union, but unless contracts are negotiated on a multi-employer basis or with a very large corporation, local union officers directly negotiate the labor agreement with the employer. If the national union staff representative often aids the local in carrying out this function and usually plays a highly visible role in the process, the fact remains that the local union officers who also are involved in the negotiations are directly responsible to the members of the local union. The staff representative, a hired hand, does not face political defeat if he exercises poor judgment or fails to negotiate a contract that the membership feels is suitable. Should a contract, however, hurt the local union members, it is very likely that in the next election the local union officers will be changed. Because of its local character, factionalism in the local is, in fact, a constant problem. It is comparatively easy for a dynamic, aggressive, and ambitious newcomer to use a poor contract as a weapon to dislodge an incumbent officer.

Another important function of the local is that of negotiating grievances. Indeed, most of the union's time is devoted to this task: the labor agreement is negotiated only periodically, but, through the grievance procedure, it must be administered every day. To this end, each local union has a number of stewards—usually one steward to a department of the company, elected by the union members of that department—who serve as administrative personnel.

In most plants, the members also elect a chief steward, to be chairman of the grievance committee. At the lower steps of the grievance procedure, the worker's complaint is handled by the departmental steward and normally the local union president or chief steward does not enter the picture until the grievance has reached the higher levels. But at the last step of the grievance procedure, the local union president and the union grievance committee (composed of the chief steward and several other stewards) will negotiate the grievance, typically with the staff representative of the national union also being present. Moreover, if a grievance goes to arbitration, the local union president and the union committee will attend the hearing and although at this forum the national staff representative usually presents the union's case, he depends heavily upon the local union officers and the committee for the data which he will present to the arbitrator.

It is difficult to overestimate the vital importance of the effective use of the grievance procedure as a function of the local union. Indeed, to the union member who has a grievance, the handling of his grievance means more to him than what the union secured in the collective bargaining agreement. This is particularly true when the grievant complains against a discharge, or against an alleged company violation of an important working condition.

In this capacity, however, the local union officers are also vulnerable. Take, for example, a grievance which, though important to the employee, does not have merit. If the local union president tells this to the union member, he risks offending a constituent. And if this happens frequently and with many different workers, the union members can demonstrate their resentment in the next election. This appears completely unfair and senseless, but it is what the local union officers have to contend with, and explains why local union officers frequently take up grievances that do not have merit.

At times, too, the local officers are forced to deal with "borderline" grievances, complaints which may or may not have merit but which for a variety of reasons the local union officers cannot persuade the company to grant. Often, the local does not want to risk losing the grievance in arbitration. It therefore refuses to handle the grievance, and the job now is to pacify the employee who may have some justification for being resentful—not an easy mission when the grievance deals with an important issue and has some basis under the labor agreement. Consequently, the local officials may change their minds and *take* such grievances into arbitration, hoping for the best: if the arbitrator denies the grievance, the local union officers can always use the arbitrator as the scapegoat. However, in spite of an effective presentation at the arbitration hearing, the disgruntled union member may still blame his officers. It is said that victory has many fathers, but defeat is an orphan. Fortunately, unions win their share of grievances in the grievance procedure and in arbitration, and in his campaign before the next election, the local union officer can point with pride to his successes and minimize or explain away his defeats.

Judicial Procedures

Another function of the local union is that of disciplining union members who are alleged to have violated union rules. As does every organization, unions have standards with which members must comply. These standards are incorporated in the national union's constitution and are duplicated in the local union's bylaws. If a union member violates any of these rules, he may be disciplined by the local union membership in the form of a reprimand, a fine, suspension, and in extreme cases, expulsion from the union.

Commonly proscribed standards of conduct which frequently merit expulsion include the promotion of dual unionism (when a union member seeks to take the local out of one national union and place it in another—true treason in unionism!); participating in an unauthorized or "wildcat" strike; misappropriating union funds; strikebreaking; refusing to picket; sending the union membership list to unauthorized persons; circulating false and malicious reports about union officers; and providing secret and confidential information to the employer. Under the official rules of some unions, a member may also be expelled because of membership in a Communistic, fascistic, or other totalitarian group. We may quarrel with the justice or fairness of one or more of these rules, but the fact remains that they must be obeyed since they have been adopted by the union at large. From the union point of view, each of them pertains to an important area of conduct.

The procedures which are used at the local level to enforce the rules of the union differ widely, but the following would probably reflect most local union procedures. Any union member may file charges against any other member, including the local union officers. When this occurs, the president has the authority to appoint a so-called "trial committee," composed of union members belonging to the local in question and normally including officers, stewards, and rank-and-file members who take an active role in the affairs of the union. The trial committee has the job of investigating the complaint, holding a hearing if it believes that the charge has substance, and reaching a decision which it will ultimately present to the entire local union body for final determination. To protect against a political situation within the local wherein favorites of the local union officers, or the local union officers themselves, may not be brought to account for a violation, the union members initiating the charge may appeal to the national union. Thus, a "not guilty" verdict, the dismissal of charges by the local union officers, or the pigeonholing of complaints does not necessarily end the disciplinary process.

After its investigation of the charges, the local union's trial committee holds a hearing at which the accused member is present. He may select another union member to act as his spokesman. As in most other private or semiprivate organizations, the union member may not hire a lawyer to defend him while the case is being processed within the union, but witnesses are called, and cross-examination is permitted. And, although no oath is administered for the same reason (since the hearing is not in a court of law), union members who deliberately lie or who grossly misrepresent the facts may themselves be charged with a violation. After the hearing, the trial committee reports its decision and the reasons for the verdict to the local union membership. At this point, the membership may adopt, reject, or modify the committee's decision. At times, the trial is in effect reheld before the local membership, since some members might desire to review the evidence that the trial committee used to arrive at its decision.

If the decision is "not guilty," the member or members who filed the charge may appeal to the executive board of the national union. By the same token, when the decision of the local goes against the charged union member, he may appeal to the national union and, under the provisions of virtually every constitution, the member can also ultimately appeal the decision of the national union officers to the national convention.

On the surface, this judicial procedure appears fair and calculated to protect the accused union member. It would seem that he receives a full and fair hearing, and gains further protection through provisions for the right of appeal. In practice, however, there have been several instances of serious abuses of the local union judicial procedure, although with more than 77,000 locals to consider it is absolutely impossible to make any kind of accurate judgment of the relative extent to which the abuse has existed and any opinion is sheer speculation.

It was because of such union actions, however, that the Landrum-Griffin Act specified that no member could be disciplined, fined, or expelled without having first received a written list of charges, a reasonable time to prepare his defense, and a full and fair hearing. Today, if these legal standards are violated, a union member may bring suit in the federal courts for relief. Under the law, the union member may not go to court before he attempts to get his case settled through union procedures, although to check dilatory union tactics the law also specifies that if the internal procedure consumes longer than four months, the union member need not exhaust the internal remedies of the union before going to court.

In 1957, the United Automobile Workers dealt with the problem of abuse in the disciplinary procedure in a more unique manner. It established a "Public Review Board," composed of seven citizens of respected reputation and impeccable integrity, and having no other relationship with the union. Usually, such men have been nationally known members of the clergy, the judiciary, or university faculties. Under the amendment to the UAW constitution which established the plan, the president of the national union selects the board members, subject to the approval of the national union's executive board and ratification by the national convention. Among other duties, this watchdog committee may reverse the decision of the executive board of the national union which has upheld the discipline of a union member, and experience has shown that the board has been quite willing to reverse the national union's executive board on the relatively few occasions when it has believed that such a reversal was justified. To date, however, only the Upholsterers International Union has followed the pattern of the UAW. If each national union were to establish such an agency, and if each agency were allowed the same freedom to act which has been granted the UAW Public Review Board, there would clearly be less need for legislation to protect the status of union members.

Political Activities

Although the AFL-CIO and national union officers and staff representatives play an effective role in lobbying and in supporting candidates in their campaigns for political office, it can be argued with much justification that the political efficiency of the union movement depends above all upon the vigor of the local. After all, the number of the Federation and national officers and staff representatives is very small in comparison with the number of local union members. And much of the legwork during the national and state elections must necessarily be performed by local union members if it is to be performed at all on any large scale. Indeed, the success of the union movement in "rewarding its friends and punishing its enemies" depends in large measure on the willingness of local union officers and members to engage in politics.

Nonetheless, the degree to which local unions participate in politics often is determined by the basic philosophy of the national union. If the national union officers do not want their union to engage in politics, or merely go through the motions of indicating such a preference, the local unions of the nationals will reflect this kind of leadership. On the other hand, when the national union officers do take an active role in the political affairs of the nation, the local unions typically respond by placing a major emphasis on such political action of their own. However, even when the national unions do cajole their locals into taking this active role in politics, the members themselves may or may not follow the instructions of the national union officers, and the national's efforts must consequently be geared in two directions: toward the local leadership and toward the local membership.

If a constant problem of the national union which is politically inclined is thus to motivate the locals to follow its example, even within the ranks of such unions as the UAW (perhaps the most active national in the political arena), there are many dozens of local unions which either refuse to participate or participate in a lackadaisical way. Locals of less politically conscious nationals often show even greater reluctance. Moreover, just because the AFL-CIO leadership or a national union president supports a candidate for elective office, this does not mean that every union member will vote that way. Some may not vote at all, of course, and postelection analyses of union member districts show that many others vote for the opposite candidate. There is no permanent "labor vote," as is sometimes claimed by people who view the political participation of the union movement as an evil.

Indeed, as long as we maintain secret elections, even the most homogeneous groups in the nation can never rest assured that their members or followers will vote as the organization urges them to. And if members of the most closely-knit of unions do not lockstep to the polls and vote in accordance with the recommendations of their leadership, members of less cohesive labor groups are often significantly divided in their election choices.

Our society is, moreover, pluralistic in character, and its countless pressure groups have their own favored candidates. Each group has the right and, indeed, the obligation to participate in the election process. These are the hallmark and the dynamics of a democratic society wherein each group seeks the votes of its members and those of the public. And, under such a system of checks and balances, any one group or organization is prevented from dominating the political life of the nation.

A union member may be a good trade unionist and support with vigor his union's collective bargaining policies and its strikes. He may enthusiastically take his place on the picket line. However, when he casts his ballot for the President of the United States, a senator, congressman, governor, and other political candidates, the vote which he casts will reflect his political heritage and his interpretation of the political situation at the time. The union member shares in common with his counterparts in a myriad of other groups the fact that he is not isolated from the multitude of pleas for his vote, arising from countless organizations and sources of political information. The daily press, radio and television, the political candidate, the worker's traditional political affiliation, and many more factors will influence his vote, and his labor organization is only one of many factors that are involved in his political determination at election time.

Nonetheless, a local union which takes an active role in politics can be of great help to a favored candidate and, in a close election, the support can tip the scales in his favor. The local union will encourage each member to register and to cast his ballot at election time. Prior to the election, it will do all in its power to "educate" the union member as to how to vote, through publications, meetings, house-to-house visits, and other forms of active political activity. In addition, the local union may legally make expenditures from union dues for such purposes as the holding of meetings of a political character and the publication and distribution of politically inspired newspapers and leaflets, although (as stated earlier) only money which is raised on a voluntary basis from the membership can be contributed directly to persons running for political office.

Other Functions and Problems

Beyond the major functions discussed above, local unions at times engage in a variety of social, educational, and community activities. Of late, as in the case of higher labor bodies, the last area has become increasingly important. Union leaders realize that the welfare of their members depends in part on a progressive and well-run community. How the schools are run, for example, is of vital interest to the local unionist who must pay taxes to operate the schools and who may have children attending the schools. As in the case of city labor bodies, representation of local union officials on United Fund Committees, Red Cross drives, and similar endeavors is also increasing in frequency. Moreover, unions recognize that the public image of organized labor, which has been tarnished in recent years, tends to improve to the extent that unions engage in such community services. Labor's various forms of participation in community service programs demonstrate that union members are not only collectively a socially oriented group, but also are individually responsible and interested citizens of the community. Likewise, the integration of unions in community work tends to lessen the tensions between management and organized labor. If a union leader can work effectively with the management representatives on the school board or in the Community Chest drive there is a better chance for harmonious labor relations in the plant.

Many local unions also conduct regularly sponsored and generally effective educational programs for the benefit of their local union officers and stewards. As noted previously, the need for these programs arises primarily from the complexity of the contemporary labor-management relationship, but it also stems to a great extent from the brisk turnover of the local union officers and stewards. Some of the programs are sponsored by the national unions, though in many cases the local itself arranges the educational program. Indeed, no union is considered "modern" today unless it has devised a well-planned educational program for its leadership. Such educational programs frequently bring to the surface workers of talent and high native intelligence. Through education, the latter not only are capable of doing a better job for their membership and acting more responsibly and rationally at the bargaining table, but education tends to make them more useful citizens. Of at least as much practical interest to many workers, union members who acquire such measures of education tend to rise more rapidly to important jobs at both the local and national levels.

One of the most important problems of the local is that of interesting the membership in attending regular monthly meetings of the union. Attendance at these meetings is frequently very poor, and the problem is not easy to solve. The vast majority of union leaders sincerely want their members to turn out at the meeting. They believe that the union has nothing to hide, and that by regular attendance and discussion at meetings, the members become more active, tend to be more devoted, and in general allow the local to deal with both employers and representatives of the public from a considerably stronger position than would otherwise be the case. The fact remains, however, that union members normally stay away from their meetings in droves; for the regular monthly meetings, only about 5 to 10 percent of the membership turns out (even a smaller percentage is common enough, especially in large locals); and one wonders why there has been so much said about union democracy when the union member himself does not seem sufficiently interested to participate in the affairs of his own union. When unions are poorly managed, when corruption exists, when leadership is second-rate, the fault essentially is that of the union member who does not care enough to attend the regular union meeting.

Thus, although from the days of the earliest unions, labor organizations have undertaken a variety of measures (ranging from more convenient hours to the incorporation of social activities into the meeting schedule) to encourage attendance, in 160 years unions have not found the solution to the problem of worker apathy toward attendance at meetings and there is every likelihood that it will persist in the future. The only notable exception involves meetings at which a strike vote is scheduled to be taken. In general, the union members will turn out at this time because this issue of striking or working is, of course, of crucial importance.

Despite poor attendance at the regular monthly meetings, management should not interpret this situation as meaning that in crisis situations the members will not support their union. In time of a showdown, the typical union member will actively support his union, and consequently a management which makes a decision to chance a strike solely on the grounds of poor attendance at union meetings makes a very unwise choice. The members invariably will rally to the union's cause when there are issues involved which vitally affect their welfare, no matter how little interest they have demonstrated in the day-to-day operation of their local at more peaceful times.

UNION FINANCES

As do all other organizations, the union makes many expenditures and must meet its financial obligations. Chief expenditures of unions include the payment of salaries for their full-time officers and staff representatives, travel expenses, clerical help, office equipment and supplies, telephones, telegrams, postage, arbitration fees, and rent or mortgage payments for office space and the union hall. Beyond this, the strike fund must be built up to pay strike benefits when needed.

At times, people are impressed by the relatively large amounts that unions collect in dues and initiation fees, but forget that the union dispenses formidable amounts of money to meet its bills. It has been estimated that the annual income of American unions from all sources amounts to about two and one-half billion dollars, most of this sum being accounted for by the regular monthly dues paid by each member, but with additional sources of income stemming from initiation fees, special assessments, and earnings from investments. To be sure, two and one-half billion dollars looks like a lot of money, but when one considers the net worth of unions a more accurate picture is gained. Bloom and Northrup, who have estimated that in 1963 the net worth of all national unions in the United States amounted to $645,431,794, have hastened to point out that "despite the enormous size of union funds, they do not approximate the wealth of corporations. The net assets of the six largest American corporations are in billions, those of the six largest unions in millions."[10] And however staggering a total the two and one-half billion dollars collected as income by unions each year may seem, it should also be remembered that a single corporation in the United States, General Motors, annually earns more than half of this amount in profits after taxes.

[10] G. F. Bloom and H. R. Northrup, *Economics of Labor Relations* (Homewood, Ill.: Richard D. Irwin, Inc., 1965), p. 129.

In general, the dues paid by union members holding semiskilled and unskilled jobs in manufacturing are less than those paid by members who work in the skilled trades. The obvious reason for this is that electricians, plumbers, carpenters, and kindred skilled employees earn higher wages than do employees whose jobs require lesser skill levels. A substantial majority of union members are probably now paying dues of about $6 per month, although in 1963 Peterson could report that 26 percent of all locals had at that time dues of less than $3, and nearly 20 percent had dues of $5 or more. These latter were "almost without exception,... relatively small unions composed of highly skilled craftsmen."[11] With respect to initiation fees, about 70 percent of new members paid in 1963 less than $25 in this form and of this 70 percent, the majority paid less than $10. Only 8 percent of union members (primarily in the building trades, airline pilot profession and similarly highly remunerated groupings) were charged more than $100 in initiation fees by their labor organizations.[12]

In the light of all that has been said about the functions of unions, the amount of money which the typical member pays is thus comparatively small. Nonetheless, like everyone else, the union member desires maximum and ever-improving services for the least cost possible. Indeed, union leadership must be very careful when it seeks to raise the monthly dues. Even a modest increase of fifty cents per month could cause an upheaval among the membership. With increasing expenses and sometimes declining memberships, unions *must* at times raise dues if they desire to maintain the same level of services to their membership, but this is a step which is normally taken only as an extreme last resort. Illustratively, during one recent period of declining union membership, the UAW laid off many staff representatives and otherwise tried to curb expenses drastically before requesting a modest dues increase.

A CONCLUDING WORD

These pages have demonstrated how the American labor movement is structured and organized to carry out its objectives. They have attempted to outline the functions of the component parts of the movement, and the interrelationships of these functions within the union structure. We have also been concerned with the major duties and problems of union officers and staff representatives, the procedures of internal union government, and the underpinnings of the theory that union members have the ultimate control of their labor organizations—however much in practice

---

[11] Florence Peterson, *American Labor Unions,* 2nd rev. ed. (New York: Harper & Row, Publishers, 1963), p. 96.
[12] *Ibid.,* p. 95.

union *leadership* has been the catalyst of the policies, programs, and operation of the union.

To be sure, the American labor movement is vast and complicated, but by this time the student should have a firm understanding of the logic of its behavior, structure, and government. Labor's elements fit together in a systematic fashion and provide the framework for the carrying out of the basic functions and objectives of the union movement.

In a day of increasing union dependence upon the sentiments of the general public, particularly as these sentiments are translated into legislative actions, these objectives have increasingly encompassed social and community activities which clearly extend well beyond labor's traditional campaigns for improved "property rights" on the job itself. These more broadly based endeavors can in no way be expected to diminish in the years ahead, for the advantages for the labor movement which can potentially be derived from them are certain to continue.

Yet this newer emphasis should not obscure either the pronounced strain of "bread-and-butter" unionism which has marked organized labor throughout its history or the internal union political considerations which continue to generate this more basic behavior. If unions are, by and large, not democratic, they are nonetheless highly political in nature. The union leader must above all be conscious of the general wishes of his constituents. And these wishes, particularly at the lower levels of the union structure where the collective bargaining process itself takes place, continue to be closely related to wages, hours, and conditions.

Just as internal political considerations have dictated national union autonomy within the AFL-CIO, so too have such considerations led to the complete responsibility of virtually all national union executives to at least the most pressing desires of local unionists and to such commonly observed phenomena as the high turnover rates of local officers themselves.

It has often been said that a union "is a political animal operating in an economic framework." No one who loses sight of this most fundamental labor relations factor can truly appreciate union behavior.

DISCUSSION QUESTIONS

1. J. B. S. Hardman has described labor organizations as being "part army and part debating society." What considerations on his part might have led to this description?
2. It has been argued in many nonlabor quarters that it is socially undesirable for unions to take the initiative in organizational campaigns and that the public interest is served only when unorganized workers initially seek out the union. Is there anything to be said for this point of view? Against it?
3. "There are both advantages and disadvantages to AFL–CIO affiliation for national unions." Comment.

4. "The increasing sophistication and enlightenment of modern top business executives in dealing with their subordinates has led to a state of affairs wherein managements today are more democratic than unions." Do you agree? Why or not not?
5. "Unions are no less private institutions than country clubs or Masonic lodges and, as such, should be no more subject to government regulation of their *internal* affairs than these other organizations." The present thrust of the laws notwithstanding, is there any validity to this argument?
6. Albert Rees has pointed out that it is "paradoxically true that the presence of strong unions may improve the operation of democratic processes in the general national or state government even if the internal political processes of the union are undemocratic." Explain this paradox.
7. Daniel Bell, the former labor editor of *Fortune* magazine, once commented that in taking over certain power from management, "The union also takes over the difficult function of specifying the priorities of demands—and in so doing, it not only relieves management of many political headaches but becomes a buffer between management and rank-and-file resentments." Is there any justification for such a comment?

SELECTED REFERENCES

Barbash, Jack, *Labor's Grass Roots*. New York: Harper & Row, Publishers, 1961.
———, *Labor Unions in Action*. New York: Harper & Row, Publishers, 1948.
Estey, Marten, *The Unions: Structure, Development, and Management*. New York: Harcourt, Brace, & World, Inc., 1967.
Lester, Richard A., *As Unions Mature*. Princeton, N. J.: Princeton University Press, 1958.
Perlman, Mark, *Labor Union Theories in America*. Evanston, Ill.: Row, Peterson, 1958.
Rosen, Hjalmar, and Ruth A. H. Rosen, *The Union Member Speaks*. Englewood Cliffs, N.J.: Prentice-Hall, Inc., 1955.
Sayles, Leonard R., and George Strauss, *The Local Union*, rev. ed. New York: Harcourt, Brace, & World, Inc., 1967.
Sultan, Paul E., *The Disenchanted Unionist*. New York: Harper & Row, Publishers, 1963.
Taft, Philip, *The Structure and Government of Labor Unions*. Cambridge, Mass.: Harvard University Press, 1954.

part three

Collective Bargaining

5

At the Bargaining Table

However much specific unions may differ in their exact structures, governments, and general operations, virtually all labor organizations share at least the same primary objective. Whatever in the way of concrete demands may be sought from the employer, the union's major goal is to negotiate with him a written agreement covering both employment conditions and the union-management relationship itself on terms which are "acceptable" to the union. But the employer, too, must be able to "live with" these terms, and it is because of this second requirement that bargaining sessions almost unavoidably contain stresses and strains: more for one party—not only in the economic areas of the contract but, as will be seen, in many of the so-called "institutional" and "administrative" areas—all but invariably means less for the other. Moreover, the labor-management tensions are *recurrent* in their nature, since contracts are regularly renegotiated—most commonly today every two, or three years. *No* contractual issue can thus ever be said to have been "permanently" resolved.

There is always a certain glamor to any interorganizational bargaining situation, particularly when such conflicts as the above can be anticipated. Labor-management negotiations constitute no exception to this rule, and, indeed, the process of arriving at a labor relations agreement has been viewed in a number of rather colorful ways.

Dunlop and Healy,[1] for example, point out that the labor contract negotiation process has been depicted as: (1) a poker game, with the largest pots going to those who combine deception, bluff, and luck or the ability to come up with a strong hand on the occasions on which they are challenged or "seen" by the other side; (2) an exercise in power politics, with the relative strengths of the parties being decisive; and (3) a debating society, marked by both rhetoric and name calling. They also note that what men do at the union-management bargaining table has, at other times, been caricatured in a somewhat less dramatic way—as (4) a "rational process," with both sides remaining completely flexible and willing to be persuaded only when all of the facts have been dispassionately presented.

In practice, it is likely that *all* these characteristics have marked most negotiations over a period of time. Occasionally, indeed, one such description seems to be extremely apt. Some bargaining sessions within the automobile industry have had all the attributes of the poker game, except that the "losers" and "winners" have not been quite as easily identifiable. No one present at negotiations between the Teamsters and representatives of the over-the-road trucking companies can fail to be impressed by the influence of the relatively far greater economic strength of the union. There are those who see a parallel between bargaining in the men's clothing industry and debating society activities. And the General Electric Company prides itself on its firm resolution to "let the facts govern," although its major union strongly disagrees that G.E. does in fact adhere to this policy.[2]

---

[1] John T. Dunlop and James J. Healy, *Collective Bargaining*, rev. ed. (Homewood, Ill.: Richard D. Irwin, Inc., 1955), p. 53.

[2] Since the late 1940s, G.E. has religiously pursued a policy of (1) preparing for negotiations by effecting what company representatives describe as "the steady accumulation of all facts available on matters likely to be discussed"; (2) modifying this information only on the basis of "any additional or different facts" it is made aware of, either by the union or from other sources, during the negotiations (as well as before them); (3) offering, at an "appropriate time" during the bargaining, "what the facts from all sources seem to indicate that we should"; and (4) changing this offer only if confronted "with new facts," (although in 1969, a long and bitter strike did motivate G.E. to adjust its offer somewhat, with the strike itself being the only visible "new fact" in the picture). A major further part of this policy, known as Boulwarism after former G.E. Vice President of Public and Employee Relations Lemuel R. Boulware, involves constant company communication to both its employees and the general citizenry of the various General Electric communities, on the progress of the negotiations as these evolve. G.E.'s primary union—the International Union of Electrical Workers—has attacked the policy on legal grounds, and

Nor, since bargaining will *always* by its very nature pit the conflicting interests of the two parties against each other, is there any reason to expect any of these factors to die out. The increasing "maturity" of collective bargaining implies enlargement of the rational process, but it is doubtful that there can ever be such a thing as complete escape from the other elements.

Moreover, a number of *additional* factors, will also, almost inevitably, have a bearing upon the conduct of the negotiations. Items such as the objectives of the parties, the personalities and training of the negotiators, the history of labor relations between the union and management, the size of the bargaining unit, and the economic environment operate to influence the character of collective bargaining negotiations.

Some negotiators try to bluff or outsmart the other side. Other negotiators would never even think of employing such tactics. Some company or union representatives try to dictate a labor contract on a unilateral basis—"take it or else"—but most bargainers recognize that such an approach is ultimately self-defeating. In most instances unions presenting their original proposals will demand much more than they actually intend to get and companies' first counterproposals are usually much lower than the managements are actually prepared to offer. In other situations, however, companies and unions do not engage in these practices to any appreciable extent and original proposals and counterproposals are relatively realistic. Representatives of companies and labor organizations differ in training, preparation, education, experience, personality, concept and standard of equity, and labor relations philosophy.

There are still other sources of variation. In some negotiations, the predominant feature might be union factionalism; in others, disagreement between management officials concerning objectives and policies. The history of labor relations in one situation might reveal that each side has had implicit faith in the other. In other negotiations, because of past experience, the bargaining might be conducted in a climate of mutual distrust, suspicion, and even hatred. Certainly, if the objective of the parties is to find a solution to their mutual problems on the basis of rationality and fairness, the negotiations will be conducted in an atmosphere quite different from one in which the fundamental objective of the union is to "put management in its place," or where the chief objective of the company is to weaken or even destroy the union. All these factors, as well

---

in December 1964, the NLRB held the company guilty of bad-faith bargaining in its 1960 negotiations with the IUE. Almost five years later, the U.S. Court of Appeals at New York upheld this NLRB ruling and shortly thereafter the U.S. Supreme Court refused to disturb this latter decision. But the facts on which these judicial actions were taken were, of course, those pertaining only to 1960, and it appeared that Boulwarism itself was far from dead.

as others, will have a profound influence upon the conduct of collective bargaining negotiations.

Two other preliminary remarks are in order. First, because so many variables do have a bearing upon the negotiations, a portion of the following discussion highlights some procedural practices that might help to reduce friction between companies and unions, to minimize the possibility of strikes, and to promote better labor relations. Nonetheless, *if* labor relations in a company have been harmonious in the past, and if collective bargaining negotiations have been conducted with a minimum of discord, there is little reason to change procedures. "Let sleeping dogs lie" is a sound principle of collective bargaining negotiations. These observations should be kept in mind throughout the following discussion.

Second, there has been a marked change in the general atmosphere of negotiations in relatively recent years. Perhaps twenty-five years ago the typical collective bargaining session involved a tussle between tablepounding, uninformed, and generally ill-equipped people. Possibly the side that came out better was the one whose representatives shouted the louder or could use overt power threats more effectively. And conceivably the typical negotiation was a matter of each side's taking the adamant position of "take it or else."

At present, however, collective bargaining is most commonly an orderly process in which employee, employer, and union problems are discussed relatively rationally and settled more or less on the basis of facts. There is less and less place in modern collective bargaining sessions for emotionalism, name calling, table pounding, and the like. Not many negotiators use trickery; distortion, misrepresentation, and deceit are not dominant characteristics of the modern bargaining session. Advantages gained through such devices are temporary, and the side which sinks to such low levels of behavior can expect the same from the other party. Such tactics will merely serve to produce bad labor relations and to encourage the possibility of industrial strife. Certainly, one objective of collective bargaining sessions should be the promotion of rational and harmonious relations between employers and unions. To achieve this state of affairs, persons to whom negotiations are entrusted should have the traits of patience, trustworthiness, friendliness, integrity, and fairness. If each party recognizes the possibility that it may be mistaken and the other side right, a long stride will be taken in the achievement of successful collective bargaining relations.

PREPARATION FOR NEGOTIATIONS

By far the major prerequisite for modern collective bargaining sessions is preparation for the negotiations. Both sides normally start to prepare for the bargaining table long before the current contract is scheduled to expire, and in recent years the time allotted to such planning has steadily lengthened. Six months or even a year for this purpose has become increasingly observable in both union and management quarters.

The now general recognition of the need for greater preparation time rests on the previously cited fact that the contents of the "typical" labor agreement have undergone a major transformation in the comparatively recent past. In recognizing and attempting to accomodate new goals of the parties, contracts have become steadily more complex in the issues which they treat.

Take, for example, wage clauses—which have appeared in almost all contracts since the days of the earliest unions. Today they make anything but easy reading. Where once such clauses noted the schedule of wages (generally the same for all workers within extremely broad occupational categories) and the hours to be worked for these wages, and usually said little more than this, over the past relatively few years they have become both far lengthier and considerably more complicated. Today subsections relating to labor-grade job classifications, rate ranges, pay steps within labor grades, differentials for undesirable types of work, pay guarantees for employees who are asked to report to work when no work is available for them, and a host of other subjects are commonplace in contracts. Moreover, most of these subsections spell out their methods of operation in detail.

Nor can the question of hours any longer be cavalierly disposed of. The extension of premium pay for work on undesirable shifts, holidays, Saturdays, and Sundays has increased the room for further bargaining. In addition, the contract must resolve the question of remuneration for hours worked in excess of a "standard" day or week: all nonexempt workers in interstate commerce today by law receive time and one-half pay after forty hours in a single week, but an increasing number of contracts have more liberal arrangements from the worker's viewpoint. And having opened *these* issues to the bargaining process, the parties must now anticipate a whole Pandora's box of further but related issues. Do workers qualify for the Sunday premium when they have not previously worked the full weekly schedule? Where employees are normally required for continuous operations or are otherwise regularly needed for weekend work (firemen, maintenance men, and watchmen in certain operations, for example) can they collect overtime for work beyond the standard week? The bargainers on both the labor and management side must prepare their answers, and their defenses of these answers, to such questions and many similar ones: all may reasonably be expected to arise during the actual bargaining. And this necessity for anticipation is no less true merely because a *previous* contract has dealt with these matters, for each party can count on the other's lodging requests for *modifications* of the old terms in the negotiations.

The same can be said concerning the wide range of employee benefits, from paid vacations to pension plans, which have increased dramatically over the past two decades. This benefit list promises to become even lengthier. Job insecurity in an age of automation should lead to increased income security devices. Collectively bargained profit-sharing and allied gain-sharing plans have received some impetus from recent single-company developments at American Motors and Kaiser Steel, respectively—and may now, after years of achieving only a foothold in industry, realistically be expected to spread. But it is even more likely that the continuous liberalization in the existing benefits and the attendant costs and administrative complexities involved in all of them which have marked the histories of each since its original negotiation will continue. No one is better aware of this fact than the experienced labor relations negotiator.

Finally, increasingly thorny problems have arisen at the bargaining table regarding the so-called "administrative clauses" of the contract. These provisions deal with such issues as seniority rights, discipline, rest periods, work crew and work load sizes, and a host of similar subjects which vary in importance with the specific industry. All these topics involve, directly or indirectly, employment opportunities. As such, treatment of them has become ever more complicated in a competitive industrial world which pits a management drive for greater efficiency and flexibility against a commensurately accelerated union search for increased job security.

Fuller discussion of all these areas is reserved for Chapters 7 through 10. Even the cursory treatment offered here, however, offers ample evidence that bargaining the "typical" contract necessitates far more sophistication than in an earlier, less technical age. Labor agreements can no longer be reduced to the backs of envelopes, and ever more specialized subjects confront labor negotiators. Accordingly, the need for thorough and professional preparation well in advance of the bargaining is no longer seriously questioned by any alert union or management.

In today's increasingly data-conscious society, much general information can aid the parties in their advance planning. The United States Bureau of Labor Statistics is a prolific issuer of information relating to wage, employee benefit, and administrative clause practices—and not only on a national basis, but for many specific regions, industries, and cities. Many employer groups stand ready to furnish managers with current and past labor contracts involving the same union with which the latter will be bargaining, as well as other relevant knowldege. International unions perform the same kind of function for their local unions and other subsidiary units, where the bargaining will be on a subinternational basis. And, for both parties, there is also no shortage of facts emanating from such other sources as the Federal Reserve Board, the United States Department of Labor, private research groups, and various state and local public agencies.

Each bargaining party may also find it advisable to procure and analyze information which is more *specifically* tailored to its needs in the forthcoming negotiations. Most larger unions and almost all major corporations today enlist their own research departments in the cause of such special data-gathering as the making of community wage surveys. On occasion, *outside* experts may also be recruited to make special studies for one of the parties: much of the bargaining stance taken by the Maintenance of Way Employees a few years ago, for example, rested on a painstaking analysis of employment trends in that sector of railroading conducted at union expense by a highly respected University of Michigan professor. Many managements have also made major use of the research services of academicians and other outsiders on an *ad hoc* basis. In multiemployer bargaining situations, whether or not an official employers' association actually handles the negotiations, the same premium on authoritative investigation has become increasingly visible.

The list of uses to which such research can be put is literally endless. Depending upon its accuracy and stamp of authority, it can be used to support any stand from a company's avowal that certain pension concessions would make it "noncompetitive" to a union's demand for increased cost-of-living adjustments. The management may find support for a desired subcontracting clause in the revelation that the union has been willing to grant the same clause to other employers. The union may gain points in its argument for a larger wage increase by mustering the bright outlook for the industry which has been forecast by the Commerce Department. On the other hand, where poker, power, or debating traits mark the bargaining, and the "rational process" of appeal to facts counts for little, the whole effort may seem a fruitless one. Most frequently, however, negotiators who approach the bargaining table without sufficient factual ammunition to handle the growing complexities of labor relations operate at a distinct disadvantage: the burden of proof invariably lies with the party seeking contractual changes and, in the absence of facts, "proof" is hard to come by.

As painstaking a task as the fact accumulation process may seem to be, farsighted managements and labor leaders recognize that considerably *more* must be done to adequately prepare for bargaining.

Increasingly, the top echelons within both union and company circles have come to appreciate the necessity of carefully consulting with lower-level members of their respective operating organizations before framing specific bargaining table approaches. Superintendents, foremen, industrial engineers, union business agents, union stewards, and various other people may never become directly involved in the official negotiation sessions;[3] and the distance separating them from the top of the management or union hierarchy is usually a great one. But the growing maturity of labor relations has brought with it a stronger recognition by the higher levels of both organizations that the success or failure of whatever agreement is finally bargained will always rest considerably upon the *acceptance* of the contract by such people. In addition, unless the official negotiators are well informed on *actual operating conditions* in advance of the bargaining, there is every chance that highly desirable modifications in the expiring agreement will be completely overlooked.

On the management side, since the daily routines of the operating subordinates require their close contact with the union, such men are in a position to provide the bargainers with several kinds of valuable information. They can be expected to have knowledgeable opinions as to what areas of the expiring contract have been most troublesome: they can, for example, provide an analysis not only of grievance statistics within their departments but of employee morale problems which may lie behind the official grievances which have been lodged. They presumably have some awareness as to existing pressures on the union leadership, and their knowledge of these political problems can help management to anticipate some of the forthcoming union demands. They may be able to assess how the union membership would react to various portions of the contemplated *management* demands.

Not to be dismissed lightly, either, is the fact that this process of consultation allows lower managers genuine grounds for feeling some sense of participation in at least establishing the framework for bargaining. The company thus stands to gain in terms of morale, as well as in information.

For the *union*, the need for thorough internal communication may be even more vital. The trend to centralization of bargaining in the hands of international unions has in no way lessened the need of the union officialdom to be responsive to rank-and-file sentiments. It has, however, made the job of *discovering* these sentiments, and incorporating them into a cohesive bargaining strategy, considerably harder; and "middlemen" within the union hierarchy must be relied upon to perform this assignment. Thus business agents, grievance committeemen, and other lower union officials can play a key role even where the negotiations themselves have passed upward to a higher union body, for only they are in a position to take the pulse of the rank and file.

---

[3] This depends upon the scope of the negotiations, however. Where the bargaining is on the local level (as opposed to areawide, industrywide or nationwide bargaining), the business agent (for example) will very likely be an active union participant in the formal sessions. The same can be said for many management superintendents.

The long list of widely varying and frequently inconsistent rank-and-file demands cannot, however, be passed upward to the international level without some adjustment. Most internationals screen these workers' proposals—inevitably giving more weight to those of important political leaders at the lower levels than to those stemming from totally uninfluential constituents—through committees composed of the subordinate officials at successively higher levels within the union hierarchy. Ultimately, a "final" union contract proposal may be placed before the memberships of each local or at least before representatives of these locals, for their official stamps of approval. And here again the support of lower union officialdom is vitally needed by the union negotiators—to rally rank-and-file support behind the finalized union demands, and to gain membership willingness to strike, if need be, in support of these demands. Aside from the fact that the local unionists may be as well equipped to help the negotiators plan their strategy as are their management counterparts, local leaders who have been bypassed in the consultation process do not typically make loyal supporters of the union's membership-rallying effort.

Finally, both legal and (on many occasions) public relations considerations now clearly demand a major place in preparation for bargaining. Specialists in both of these areas must be engaged and utilized by both sides to ensure that bargaining demands will be compatible with the labor statutes, and that public support (or, at the very least, public neutrality) will be forthcoming, if this is needed. The legal ramifications of present-day trucking contract negotiations, for example, have necessitated for the union the employment of a 400-man corps of lawyers who have become collectively known as the "Teamsters' Bar Association" and through whose high levels of remuneration Teamster president Hoffa could claim to have "doubled the average standard of living for all lawyers in the past few years," although the personal legal problems of Hoffa himself undoubtedly account for some of the high statistics. And for the importance of public relations to both parties in the railroad industry one need look no farther than to the myriad of full-page newspaper advertisements placed separately throughout the 1960s by the railroad unions and managements to state their respective labor relations cases to the general citizenry in advance of the bargaining.

For both management and union, bargaining preparation also involves more mundane matters. Meeting places must be agreed upon and the times and lengths of the meetings must be decided. Ground rules regarding transcripts of the sessions, publicity releases, and even "personal demeanor" (a designation which in labor relations can deal with a spectrum extending from the use of profanity to appropriate attire for the negotiators) are sometimes drawn up. Payment of union representatives at the bargaining table who must take time off from work as paid employees of the company must also be resolved. Only on rare occasions have the parties reached a major prebargaining impasse on such issues as these, but where relations are already strained between union and management such joint decision-making can be time-consuming and even an emotion-packed process.

THE BARGAINING PROCESS: EARLY STAGES

No manager who is prone to both ulcers and accepting verbal statements at face value belongs at the labor relations bargaining table. Negotiations often begin with the union representatives presenting a long list of demands in both the economic and noneconomic (for example, administrative clause) areas. To naïve managements many of these avowed labor goals seem, at best, unjustified and, at worst, to show a complete union disregard for the continued solvency of the employer. Although extreme demands such as the appointment of union officers to the company's Board of Directors and free transportation in company cars to and from work for all employees are rarely taken seriously, the company negotiators may be asked for economic concessions which are well beyond those granted by competitors and noneconomic ones which exhibit a greater use of vivid imagination than that shown by the late William Faulkner.

The *experienced* management bargainer, however, takes considerable comfort in the fact that the union is, above all, the *political* animal which the previous chapter has depicted: there is no sense in the union leaders alienating constituents by throwing out untenable but "pet" demands of the rank and file (beyond what the various screening committees have been able to dislodge) when the company representatives stand fully ready to do this themselves and thus to accept the blame. This is particularly true when the pet union demands originate from influential constituents or key locals within the international: alienation of such sources is a job for which the company representatives, not being subject to the election procedure, are better suited.

There are other logical explanations for the union's apparent unreasonableness. Excess demands allow leverage for trading some of them off in return for management concessions. In addition, the union can camouflage its true objectives in the maze of requests and thereby conceal its real position until the proper time—vital for any successful bargaining.

Beyond this, labor leaders have frequently sought novel demands with the knowledge that these will be totally unacceptable to managements in a given bargaining year, but with the goal of providing an opening wedge in a long-range campaign to win management over to the union's point of view. Only in this light can, for example, Walter P. Reuther's demand for supplementary unemployment benefits in the early 1950's be understood. Dunlop and Healy furnish further insight on the psychological ramifications involved, and also emphasize the increasing importance of the prebargaining research which was commented upon earlier in this chapter:

> Neither side can ordinarily be expected to concede a new demand the first time it is presented. A new idea may initially produce only opposition from the other party. The demand will be less novel and appear less outrageous a year later. The other side may have had occasion to think it through and to consider administrative problems which need mutual exploration. Thus, a pension or a health and welfare proposal introduced by the union for the first time will ordinarily receive a cool reception. Management may need several years to consider types of plans, to gather data on the age distribution and health distribution of its work force, and to get used to considering this range of issues. New contract demands ordinarily require a period of gestation, and some demands are on the list to be seasoned.[4]

Finally, since contract negotiations frequently extend over a period of weeks (and, on occasion, months), the union can gain a buffer against economic and other environmental changes which may occur in the interval. Technically, either party can introduce new demands at any time prior to total agreement on a contract, but the large initial demand obviates this necessity.

There is thus a method in the union's apparent madness. Demands which seem to managements to be totally unjustified and even disdainful of the company's continued existence may, on occasion, be genuinely intended as union demands. Far more often, however, they are meant only as ploys in a logical bargaining strategy. They are to be listened to carefully, but not taken literally.

In fact, if imitation is the sincerest form of flattery, there is ample evidence that some managements have increasingly come to appreciate the strategic value of the large demand. Many company bargainers have, in recent years, engaged in such "blue-skying" in their counterproposals, and for many of the same reasons as the union (although other companies have adamantly refused to engage in this process and even at least partially accepted a G.E.-type approach).

As a result of the premium placed on exaggerated demands and equally unrealistic conterproposals, however, the positions of the parties throughout the early negotiation sessions are likely to remain far apart.

Standing in the way of early agreement, too, is the fact that these initial meetings are often attended by a wide variety of "invited guests," from the ranks of each organization. Given a large and interested audience of rank-and-file unionists, or a union negotiating committee which is so large as to be totally unable (and unexpected) to perform the bargaining

[4] Dunlop and Healy, *op. cit.*, p. 56.

function but is nonetheless highly advisable from a political point of view, the actual union bargainers sometimes find it hard to refrain from using creative but wholly extraneous showmanship. Management representatives, too, frequently succumb to a temptation to impress their visiting colleagues as to their negotiating "toughness." And when lawyers or other consultants are engaged by either party to participate in the bargaining sessions, the amount of acting is often also significantly expanded.

Even amid the theatrics and exaggerated stances of these early meetings, however, there is often a considerable amount of educational value for the bargainers. The excessive factors still do not preclude each party from evaluating at least the general position of the other side and from establishing weaknesses in the opposing position or arguments. Frequently, indeed, if negotiators are patient and observing at this point, they will be able to evaluate the other side's proposals along fairly precise qualitative lines. Thus, during the first few sessions when each side should be expected to state its position, it often can be discerned which demands or proposals are being made seriously and which, if any, are merely injected for bargaining position. Such information will be of great help later on in the negotiations.

Actually, the principle of timing in negotiations is very important. There are times for listening, speaking, standing firm, and conceding; there are times for making counterproposals, compromising, suggesting. At some points "horse-trading" is possible; at others, taking a final position is called for. There is a time for an illustration, a point, or a funny story to break ominous tension, and there is likewise a time for being deadly serious. Through experience and through awareness of the tactics of the other side, negotiators can make use of the time principle most effectively.

THE BARGAINING PROCESS: LATER STAGES

After the initial sessions are terminated, each side should have a fairly good idea of the over-all climate of the negotiations. The company should now be in a position to determine what the union fundamentally is seeking, and the union should be able to recognize some basic objectives of management. In addition, by this time, each side should have fairly well in mind how far it will be prepared to go in the negotiations. Each party to the negotiations in secret internal sessions should establish with some degree of certainty the maximum concessions that it will be prepared to make, and the minimum levels that it will be willing to accept. Negotiators will be in a better position to bargain intelligently if certain objectives are formulated before the negotiations enter into the "give-and-take" stage. However, even at this time in the negotiations, it is not wise to take extreme positions, and to appear inflexible in the approach to the problems under discussion. Skilled negotiators who are striving to avoid a strike—and this is the attitude of the typical company and union—will remain flexible right down to the wire. It is not a good idea to climb too far out on a limb since at times it may be difficult, or at least embarrasing, to crawl back to avoid a work stoppage.

Indeed, after the original positions of the parties are stated and explained, skilled negotiators seldom take a rigid position. Rather than take a definite stand on a particular issue, experienced negotiators (often, where negotiation units are large, through the use of subcommittees to focus upon the major bargaining issues individually before these are dealt with at the main bargaining table) "throw something on the table for discussion and consideration." The process of attempting to create a pattern of agreement is then begun. In this process, areas of clear disagreement are narrowed whenever they can be, mutual concessions are offered and tentative agreements are effected. Counterproposals of companies and unions are frequently offered as something "to think about" rather than as the final words of the negotiators. In this manner, the parties are in a better position to feel one another out as to ultimate goals. By noting the reaction to a proposal thrown on the table for discussion, by evaluating the arguments and the attitudes in connection with it, a fairly accurate assessment can be made of the maximum and minimum levels of both sides.

Actually, flexibility is a sound principle to follow in negotiations because the ultimate settlement between companies and unions is frequently in the terms of "packages." Thus, through the process of counterproposals, compromise, and the like, the parties usually terminate the negotiations by agreeing to one package selected from a series of alternative possibilities of settlement. The package selected will represent most closely the maximum and minimum levels acceptable to each of the parties. The content of the various packages will be somewhat different because neither side in collective bargaining gets everything it wants out of a particular negotiation. By remaining flexible throughout the negotiation, certain patterns of settlement tend to be established over which the parties can deliberate.

The package approach to bargaining is particularly important in reference to economic issues. Once the parties obtain an agreement on a total cost-per-hour figure, it becomes a relatively uncomplicated task to allocate that figure in terms of basic wage rates, supplements to wages, wage inequities, and the like. The more difficult problem, of course, is to arrive at a total cost-per-hour figure. If, for example, through the process of bargaining, the parties established $.25 per hour as the level of agreement, the parties might finalize the money agreement in terms of a $.19-per-hour basic wage increase, $.02 per hour to correct any wage inequities, $.01 per hour to improve the insurance program, and $.03 per hour to increase pensions. Other subdivisions of the $.25 would be possible depending upon the attitudes of the parties and their objectives in the negotiations.

Trading Points and Counterproposals

In establishing the content of the alternative packages, experienced negotiators employ a variety of bargaining techniques. Two of the most important are trading points and counterproposals. These procedures are best explained by illustrations.

Let us assume that management employs the *trading point* procedure. The first prerequisite in the use of this technique is to evaluate the demands of the union. Evaluation is necessary not only along quantitative lines, but also along the line of the "intensity factor," which requires an assessment of the union demands to determine which demands the union is most anxious to secure. Management representatives should make mental notes of these strongly demanded issues as the negotiations proceed. For example, after a few sessions it may become apparent that the union feels very strongly about securing the union shop. At the same time the labor organization also demands a $.30-per-hour wage increase and nine paid holidays. The use of the trading point technique in this situation may be as follows: management agrees to the union shop but insists that in return for this concession the union accept a $.14-per-hour increase and seven paid holidays.

Labor organizations also employ the trading point technique, as illustrated by the following example. Assume that, during the course of the negotiations, the union representatives sense that management will not concede to the union demand for a reduction of the basic work week from forty hours to thirty-six. Assume further that the union feels that the issue is not worth a strike. Under these circumstances the union may be able to employ the hours issue as a trading point. Let us say that, along with the hours demand, the union has insisted upon also securing a union shop and a $.20-per-hour increase in pay. After the union presses the hours issue vigorously for some time (the union as part of the strategy may, of course, threaten a strike over the issue), the union negotiators agree to withdraw the hours demand in return for obtaining the union shop and the wage increase.

Counterproposals are somewhat different from trading points. Counterproposals involve the compromise that takes place during the bargaining sessions. As a matter of fact, the use of counterproposals is one element which the National Labor Relation Board will consider to determine whether management and labor unions bargain in good faith. However, under the established rules of the board, employers and unions do not have to make *concessions* to satisfy the legal requirement of bargaining in good faith: the implementers of public policy are more interested in whether or not there have been *compromises*. The union may request four weeks' vacation with pay for all employees. Management might counter by agreeing to two weeks' vacation with pay for employees with five years of service and one week for the remainder. A union may demand a $.22-per-hour increase, and management may agree to an $.11-per-hour increase. At times three or four counterproposals may be made before a final agreement is reached on an issue of collective bargaining.

THE BARGAINING PROCESS: FINAL STAGES

There is almost no limit to the ingenuity which skilled negotiators use in attempting to create an agreement pattern. At more sophisticated bargaining tables, even highly subtle modes of communication may do the trick, while at the same time allowing the party making a concession to suffer no prejudice for having "given in." Stevens, for example, points out that

> in some situations, silence may convey a concession. This may be the case, for example, if a negotiator who has frequently and firmly rejected a proposal simply maintains silence the next time the proposal is made. The degree of emphasis with which the negotiator expresses himself on various issues may be an important indication. The suggestion that the parties pass over a given item for the present, on the grounds that it probably will not be an important obstacle to eventual settlement, may be a covert way of setting up a trade on this item for some other. ...The parties may quote statistics (fictitious if need be) as a...way of suggesting a position, or they may convey a position by discussing a settlement in an unrelated industry.[5]

Yet, however much the gap between the parties may be narrowed by such methods, even the most adroit bargainers frequently reach the late stages of negotiations with the complete contract far from being resolved. Given the potential thorniness of many of the individual issues involved, this should not be surprising: more than both bargaining sophistication and flexibility is still generally required to bring about agreement on such delicate substantive topics as management rights, union security, the role of seniority, and economic benefits. And the fact that the bargainers seek an acceptable package which in some way deals with *all* these issues clearly makes the assignment a much more complicated one than it would otherwise be.

It is the *strike deadline* which is the great motivator of labor relations agreement. As the hands of the clock roll around, signalling the imminent

[5] Carl M. Stevens, *Strategy and Collective Bargaining Negotiation* (New York: McGraw-Hill Book Company, 1963), pp. 105–106.

termination of the old contract, each side is now forced to reexamine its "final" position and to balance its "rock-bottom" demands against the consequences of a cessation of work. And with the time element now so important, each party can now be counted upon to view its previous bargaining position in a somewhat different light.

For example, paid holiday demands—which once seemed of paramount importance to the union—may now appear less vital when pursuing them is likely to lead to the complete *loss* of paid holidays through a strike. The labor leaders may also now conclude that although the union membership has authorized the strike should this prove necessary, a stoppage of any duration would be difficult to sustain—through either lack of membership *esprit de corps* or union resources which are insufficient to match those of management.

On its part, the company may also prove more willing to compromise as the strike deadline approaches. Up until now, it has sought to increase its net income by improving its labor cost position. Now the outlook is for a *cessation* of income as operations stop.

These threats, in short, bring each party face-to-face with reality and can normally be expected to cause a marked reassessment of positions. The immediacy of such uncertainty generates a willingness to bridge differences which has not been in evidence at the bargaining table before.

The final hours before time runs out are, therefore, commonly marked by new developments. Frequent caucuses are held by each party, followed by the announcement of a caucus representative that his side is willing to offer a new and more generous "final" proposal. Leaders from each side frequently meet with their counterparts from the other side in informal sessions that are both more private and have fewer participants than the official sessions themselves. These are also likely to result in new agreements. And issues which are still totally insoluble may be passed on to a newly established long-range joint study committee, with the hope that their resolution can be achieved at some later and less pressure-laden date.

Thus, Stevens, in attempting to develop a systematic conceptual apparatus for the analysis of collective bargaining negotiation, examines the implications of the deadline in the following terms:

> The approach of the deadline revises upward each party's estimate of the probability that a strike or lockout will be consequent upon adherence to his own position... an approaching deadline does much more than simply squeeze elements of bluff and deception out of the negotiation process. It brings pressures to bear which actually change the least favorable terms upon which each party is willing to settle. Thus it operates as a force tending to bring about conditions necessary for agreement.[6]

---

[6] *Ibid,* p. 100.

Paradoxically, the imminency of the deadline can also foster positive *attitudes*, as well as positive actions, between the parties: its approach dramatically brings home to both groups that each will pay major costs, and thus emphasizes the existence of a common denominator. Walton and McKersie, illustratively, report an event occurring during the negotiations of a New Hampshire shoe company:

> The atmosphere was tense, and bargaining was definitely an adversary affair until the lights went out. Their common fate was dramatized by this incident, and the parties quickly reached settlement.[7]

Strikes do, however, occur. Sometimes the impasse leading to a work stoppage stems from a genuine inability of the parties to agree on economic or other terms: the maximum that the company feels that it is able to offer in terms of dollars and cents, for example, is below the minimum that the union believes it must gain in order to retain the loyalty of its members. Or, where rank-and-file ratification is required to put the contract into effect, the negotiators may *misjudge* membership sentiments, bargain a contract which they feel will be fully acceptable to the membership, and then see their efforts overturned by the latter's refusal to approve what they have negotiated.

On other occasions, inexperienced or incompetent negotiators fail to evaluate the importance of a specific concession to the other side, and refuse to grant such a concession where they would gladly have exchanged it for a strike situation. At times, pride or overeagerness causes bargainers to adhere to initial positions long after these become completely untenable. And, in rare instances, one or even both of the parties may actually *desire* a strike—to work off excessive inventories, to allow pent-up emotions a chance for an outlet, or for various other reasons.

The strike incidence has been almost steadily declining in the United States since the beginning of the 1960s and strikes today, as noted earlier, idle less than 0.20 percent of total available working time. As long as workers are free to strike, however, it is realistic to expect that they occasionally will do this.

CRISIS SITUATIONS

It would be strange, as a matter of fact, if there were not *some* crisis items involved in *any* particular negotiation. In the typical situation some issues will be extremely troublesome, and they will tax severely the intelligence, resourcefulness, imagination, and good faith of the negotiators.

---

[7] Richard E. Walton and Robert B. McKersie, *A Behavioral Theory of Labor Negotiations* (New York: McGraw-Hill Book Company, 1965), p. 232.

Actually, if both sides sincerely desire to settle without a strike, a peaceful solution of any problem in labor relations can usually be worked out. As previously implied, the possibility of a work stoppage is increased when both sides are not sincere in their desire to avoid industrial warfare or when one of the parties to the negotiation is not greatly concerned about a strike. If negotiators bargain on a rational basis, keep open minds, recognize facts and sound arguments, and understand the problems of the other side, crisis situations can be avoided or overcome without any interruption to production or any impairment of good labor relations.

One way to avoid a state of affairs wherein negotiations break down because of a few difficult issues is to bypass these issues in the early stages of the bargaining sessions. It is a good idea to settle the easy problems and delay consideration of the tough ones until later in the negotiations. In this way, the negotiation keeps moving, progress is made, and the area of disagreement tends to be isolated and diminished. Thus, at the early stages, the parties might agree to disagree on some of the items. If only a few items are standing in the way of a peaceful settlement toward the close of the negotiations, there is an excellent chance for full agreement on the contract. Moreover, what might appear to be a big issue at the beginning stages of the negotiations might, of course, appear comparatively insignificant when most of the contract has been agreed upon and when time is running out.

At times, crisis situations are created not as a result of the merits of certain issues, but because some negotiators make mistakes in human relations. For example, it is good practice to personalize the things that are constructive, inherently sound, and defensible, and depersonalize the items which are bad, destructive, or downright silly. Under the former situation, the union or the company, as the case may be, commends the other party, by saying "That is a good point," or "The committee certainly has an argument," or "Bill certainly has his facts straight." In the latter situation, it is sound policy to deal with the merits of a situation. Thus, in the face of a destructive or totally unrealistic proposal, the reaction of the other side might be something like this: "Let's see how this proposal will work out in practice if we put it into the labor agreement." It is elementary psychology that people like to be commended and dislike to be criticized. If this is recognized, rough spots and danger areas in the negotiations may be avoided.

Another way to avoid crisis situations is to be prepared in advance of negotiations to propose or accept alternative solutions to a problem. For example, suppose that the union desires to incorporate an arrangement in the labor agreement making membership in the union a condition of employment. In mapping its overall strategy for the negotiation, the union committee might decide first to propose a straight union shop, but be prepared, in the face of strong management resistance, to propose a lesser form of union security. Suppose, for another illustration, that the company wants to eliminate all restrictions on the assignment of overtime. It plans first to suggest that the management should have the full authority to designate any workers for overtime without any limitation. At the same time, the company is prepared to suggest some alternative solution to the problem in the event that this proposal appears to create strong resistance. For example, it may propose that seniority be the basis for the rotation of overtime insofar as employees have the capacity to do the work in question. If both sides are prepared in advance to offer or to accept alternative solutions to particular problems, there will be less possibility for the negotiations to bog down. Instead the negotiations will tend to keep moving to a peaceful climax. The momentum of progress is an important factor in reaching the deadline in full agreement on a new contract.

One additional procedure is available to minimize the chances of negotiation breakdowns. It has already been pointed out that many of the issues of contemporary collective bargaining are complicated and difficult. Issues such as working rules, pension plans, insurance systems, and production standards require study and sometimes are not suitable for determination in the normal collective bargaining process. As contract termination deadlines approach, a strike may result simply because not enough time has been allowed for *jointly* attacking these particularly complicated matters in a rational, sound, workable, and equitable manner. All the *unilateral* preparation in the world still does not dispose of this problem. The parties are, however, at liberty to consider such issues by the use of a *joint study group* composed of management and union representatives *during the existing contractual period*. At times, the management and union may see fit to invite disinterested and qualified third parties to aid them in such a project. The joint study group does not engage in collective bargaining as such; its function, rather, is to identify and consider alternative solutions. But, by definition being freed from the pressure of contractual deadlines, such a group can gain sufficient time to study these necessarily difficult issues in a rational manner.

To work effectively, the joint study group should be established soon after a contract is negotiated; it should be composed of people who have the ability to carry out meaningful research and the necessary qualities to consider objectively and dispassionately the tough issues confronting labor and management. These are no small prerequisites, but such a procedure has worked successfully in industries such as basic steel, and modified versions of it are also currently being used with beneficial results in the basic automobile, glass, rubber, and aluminum industries. There is no reason to believe that other collective bargaining parties, including those bargaining on an individual plant basis, could not also profit from it in avoiding crisis situations.

Some companies and unions have found the mediation process helpful when crisis situations *are* reached in negotiations. The Federal Mediation and Conciliation Service of the United States government and state conciliation services make mediators available to unions and companies. The Federal Service maintains regional offices in New York, Philadelphia, Atlanta, Cleveland, Chicago, St. Louis, and San Francisco, as well as field offices and field stations in many other large industrial centers. It employs several hundred mediators whose services are available without charge to the participants in the collective bargaining process.

Mediation is based upon the principle of voluntary acceptance. Suggestions or recommendations made by the mediator may be accepted or rejected by both or either of the parties to a dispute. Unlike an arbitrator, the mediator has no conclusive powers in a dispute. The chief value of the mediator is his capacity to review the dispute from an objective basis, to throw fresh ideas into the negotiations, to suggest areas of settlement, and at times to serve to extricate the parties from difficult and untenable positions. Some time ago the then General Counsel of the Federal Mediation and Conciliation Service, George E. Strong, succinctly stated some of the outstanding features of mediation and the advantages of the use of a mediator in labor disputes as follows:

> A friend in whom the parties have confidence can emphasize the mutuality of their interests. Such a mediator can assist in deflating extreme ideas and positions and sow seeds of understanding of human as well as institutional rights, duties, needs, and objectives. Of course, the climate of industrial relations created by the parties as well as by the community and the mediator can and does promote the sprouting of these seeds. However, I do not mean to imply that mediation should be utilized in every or even in a majority of negotiations, nor do I suggest that it is always a quick and certain method of avoiding strikes, lockouts, or other coercion. If the parties can settle their disputes without mediation, they should do so but they should not wait until the situation is frozen before utilizing mediation. Furthermore, if their desire is to destroy each other they should not seek mediation. If on the other hand, the parties are willing to be reasonable and seek a fair, just, and peaceful solution of their problems they will be benefited and assisted by mediation. Fortunately, enlightened self-interest usually suggests that the parties are interdependent. They know that a mutually acceptable agreement is preferable to embittered strife which injures both parties as well as the overriding interests of the noncombatant public.[8]

TESTING AND PROOFREADING

When all issues under consideration have been resolved, the contract should then be drafted in a formal document. Many unions and manage-

[8] From a lecture delivered at Indiana University on October 23, 1956.

ments permit lawyers to draft the formal contract. No objection is raised against this practice provided that the lawyer writes the document so that it can be understood by all concerned. A lawyer does not perform this function effectively if he includes in the contract a preponderance of legal phraseology. Such a contract will serve to confuse the people affected by its terms.

Regardless of who writes the final document, the author or authors should draft the agreement in the simplest possible terms. No contract is adequately written until the simplest, clearest, and most concise way is found to express the agreement reached at the bargaining table. Whoever drafts the agreement should recognize the basic fact that unfamiliar words and lengthy sentences will cause confusion once the document is put into force, and may lead to unnecessary grievances and arbitration. Hence, it is sound practice to use a word which has special meaning in the plant or in the industry. Some contracts wisely include illustrations to make clear a particular point in the agreement. And it is of particular value to explain in detail the various steps of the grievance procedure. The contract is designed to stabilize labor relations for a given period. It is not drawn up for the purpose of creating confusion and uncertainty in the area of employer-employee relations.

Before signatures are affixed to the documents, the negotiators should have the contract test-read for meaning. No person who was associated with the negotiations should be used; his interpretation will be colored by his participation in the negotiations. A better practice is to select some individual who had no part in the conference. For this purpose the union may utilize a shop steward or even a rank-and-file member. An office employee, such as a secretary, or a foreman can serve the same purpose for management. If the people who are to administer the contract were not parties to the negotiation, such individuals should also be used for testing purposes. This is an excellent opportunity for these people to determine whether they understand the provisions before they attempt to administer the document. If the testing indicates confusion as to meaning, the author must rewrite the faulty clause or clauses until the provision is drafted in a manner that eliminates vagueness.

The final step before signing is the proofreading of the document by each negotiator. Particular attention should be given to figures. Misplacing a decimal point, for example, can change a sum from 1 percent to one-tenth of 1 percent. Human errors and typographical mistakes are inevitable, and the proofreading of the contract should have as its objective the elimination of any such errors.

The signing of the contract is an important occasion. Newspapers may be notified of the event. Pictures may be taken to be inserted in union and company papers. The tensions of the negotiation terminated, the parties to the conference may well celebrate. They have concluded a job which will affect the welfare of many employees, the position of the labor union, the operation of the company, and, indeed, sometimes the functioning of the entire economy. They have discharged an important responsibility. Let us hope that they did it well!

COORDINATED BARGAINING

When the employer bargains with not just one but a number of different unions, he frequently can capitalize upon a built-in advantage to the situation. There often exists for him the possibility of dividing and conquering the various unions by initially concentrating upon the least formidable of them, gaining a favorable contract from the latter, and then using such a contract as a lever from which to extract similar concessions from the other unions. Recent corporate trends toward merger have increased such occurrences, not only by bringing together under one company umbrella a large number of unions, but also, generally, by augmenting management bargaining strength as a consequence of the greater resources now provided the company. But even without mergers, many companies have—whether because of historical accident, union rivalry, or planned and successful management strategy—enjoyed this ability to play off one union against another, often gaining even widely-divergent contract expiration dates (thus blunting the strike threat of any one union) in the process.

Increasingly, in recent years, the unions so affected have sought to offset their handicap by banding together for contract negotiation purposes in what has come to be known as "coordinated" or "coalition" bargaining. The concept, which is still so new as to lend itself to no rigorous definition but which universally denotes the presentation of a united union front at the bargaining table and often also involves common union demands, was first applied with any degree of formality in the 1966 General Electric and Westinghouse negotiations. By 1970, it had been used by organized labor as a weapon in bargaining with Union Carbide, Campbell Soup, the major companies in the copper industry, American Home Products, and Olin Mathieson, among others. It had also staged a repeat performance, at the General Electric and Westinghouse bargaining tables in 1969.

Such union attempts to change the traditional bargaining structure had, understandably, been received with something less than enthusiasm by the managements involved. Indeed, most of the endeavors had resulted in rather lengthy strikes. At Union Carbide, for example, eleven different plantwide strikes occurred, with the shortest of them lasting 44 days and the longest going 246 days. The bulk of the copper industry was shut down for more than eight months. And the 1969 General Electric negotiations were marked by a strike of more than three months' duration.[9] Nor could it be said, at the time of this writing, that particularly impressive union victories had been recorded by the new labor strategy. Generally, as Bok and Dunlop have observed, "local unions and internationals which [had] not corporated previously [had] found it difficult to withdraw their own demands to secure a concession for a relatively unknown partner."[10] In addition, the uncertain legal status of coordinated bargaining had remained a force to be reckoned with for organized labor.

At the moment, corporation between unions is, at least in the opinion of the U.S. Circuit of Appeals for the Second Circuit (New York), "not improper, up to a point." In a mid-1969 decision resulting from General Electric's refusal to negotiate with a union's bargaining committee that included—as nonvoting members—representatives of other unions of the company's employees, the court upheld an earlier NLRB finding that such an inclusion was consistent with the employees' statutory right to select their own bargaining representatives.[11] The court did, however, caution that such a labor strategy would be sanctioned only as long as there was no "substantial evidence of ulterior bad faith" and only if the negotiations were exclusively on behalf of the workers under a specific union contract. Only a few months prior to the ruling, moreover, an NLRB trial examiner had ruled that the ten-union-member bargaining coalition in the copper industry dispute *had* run afoul of the law by insisting upon common expiration dates for the (separate) labor agreements, common terms and simultaneous settlements.[12] Until an all-but-inevitable U.S. Supreme Court ruling disposes of this issue once and for all, then, the legally permissible boundaries of coordinated bargaining will remain somewhat unclear.

Generally speaking, spokesmen for those unions which have thus far used the coordinated bargaining approach seem to be encouraged by its results for their specific situations and optimistic about its general growth prospects, but at the same time they appear to be realistic in assessing its general applicability. David Lasser of the International Union of Electrical, Radio and Machine Workers is reasonably typical:

> Coordinated bargaining is no panacea for the bargaining process. It is a tool which adapts itself to the facts of modern industry and one which can be used wisely or poorly.... Certainly, the development of the skills to use the new tool are in their infancy. With the growing com-

[9] At Westinghouse, where in recent years the settlements had been patterned after those at G.E., work had continued under day-to-day extensions.
[10] Derek C. Bok and John T. Dunlop, *Labor and the American Community* (New York: Simon & Schuster, 1970), p. 258.
[11] *General Electric Co.,* 173 NLRB 46 (1968).
[12] *Business Week,* February 22, 1969, p. 108.

plexity of corporations, the diversity of the unions that deal with them, and the multiplicity of new problems, this instrument will continue to grow and will be perfected.[13]

On the other hand, many of the managements which have heretofore been recipients of the coordinated strategies have tended to share the sentiments of the Union Carbide Corporation's Earl L. Engle. He has deemed the new phenomenon "a snare and a delusion" which "puts an unreasonable amount of power in the hands of a few top union officials who probably cannot and who *will not* be responsive to the wishes of the employees (much less the best interest of the company)...."[14]

To this point, perhaps all that can be agreed upon by more detached observers of the coalition bargaining concept is that the emergence of this new approach to negotiations does seem, as economist George H. Hildebrand has pointed out, "to sustain the general thesis that bargaining arrangements, as with other institutions, are a response motivated by felt problems and needs and conditioned by ambitions and available power."[15] The certainty of further changes in these problems, needs, ambitions, and power supplies makes the new bargaining arrangements—whether or not coordinated bargaining itself has any assured future—inevitable, assuming only that the institutions involved wish to maintain their existence.

RECIPROCAL CHARACTER OF COLLECTIVE BARGAINING

The fact that collective bargaining is a two-way street is clearly evidenced in negotiation sessions. Some people hold the view that the collective bargaining process involves only the union's demanding and the company's giving. On the contrary, as earlier portions of the chapter have noted, the company frequently will resist and refuse to concede to some issues. And when the company believes that the stakes are extremely important, it will take a strike rather than concede to a particular union demand. Thus, one function of management in collective bargaining is to review union demands in terms of the functions that management must perform in the operation of the plant. It will frequently resist when it believes that the union demands could impair the ability of the company to operate on a dynamic and efficient basis. In addition, most companies play a positive role in the negotiations by making demands on the union. Skilled negotiators on both sides of the table recognize that companies do and should get something out of the negotiations.

---

[13] Industrial Relations Research Association, *Proceedings of the 1968 Annual Spring Meeting*, p. 517.
[14] *Ibid.*, p. 523.
[15] *Ibid.*, p. 531.

Management demands, of course, will be dictated by the character of a particular collective bargaining relationship. In some cases, for example, management will have reason to demand that the labor agreement be negotiated for a longer period than every twenty-four months; that the union be more responsible for the elimination of wildcat strikes; that the company have more freedom in the assignment of workers to jobs; that skilled employees get a larger proportionate increase in wages than unskilled and semiskilled employees; that certain provisions of the labor contract which have served to interfere unnecessarily with the efficient operation of the plant or which have established "featherbedding" practices, be eliminated; or that job descriptions be revised in the light of changing plant technology. Collective bargaining sessions are normally as productive in terms of protecting the basic interests of management as they are in protecting the legitimate job rights of employees. This result, however, cannot be accomplished when management remains constantly on the defensive.

Management demands need not be simulated. Over the course of a contractual period events will arise that will provide the basis for legitimate management demands. Experienced union negotiators recognize their responsibility to agree to company demands which are sound and fair, just as they expect such behavior on the part of the company representatives in reference to union demands. To the extent that companies and unions recognize in good faith that collective bargaining is a reciprocal process, the negotiation sessions and the ensuing labor agreement will be conducive to serving the interests of all concerned. In this manner, the labor contract will not be a dictated peace treaty, but a document which will establish a rational relationship between the employees, the union, and the employer.

SOME FURTHER COMPLEXITIES

Generalizations such as those offered above cannot, of course, do justice in accounting for a *specific* contract settlement or strike. To appreciate adequately the complexities and variations involved in the negotiation process, one must turn to the interdependent variables which are apt to be influential in determining bargaining outcomes.

The current healths of both the economy and industry, for example, have been of major effect in determining the relative settlements of the United Automobile Workers and major car manufacturers in several recent years. In 1955, a boom year, management resistance to union demands was weak and the UAW gains were consequently significant ones. The strike threat meant relatively little to the companies in 1958, a recession year, and the union could improve the 1955 contract only slightly and after considerable frustration. Economic conditions were somewhat better than they had been in 1958 in 1961 and the union demands of the latter year fared correspondingly better. And in both 1964 and 1967, when automobile company production and profitability set new all-time records, the management quest for uninterrupted production led the companies to grant Walter Reuther terms which dwarfed even those of 1955.

On the other hand, the shoe industry has been plagued by consistently poor economic conditions for many of its specific employers for years and, in the face of this variable and its persuasive logic, the Shoe Workers have shown considerable bargaining self-restraint for well over a decade and one half.

Technological innovations—running a wide gamut from turbojet aircraft to computerized newspaper typesetting—have been the primary cause of many major recent bargaining stalemates and subsequent strikes, as even the cursory follower of current events is well aware. In turn, job insecurity resulting partly from *improved technology in such competitive industries* as trucking and the airlines has made railroad workers a particularly touchy group to deal with in the past several years.

The influence of other major variables, all of them noted earlier in this book, can be illustrated. It took years for Swift and Company and the Amalgamated Meat Cutters to establish a *cooperative labor relationship,* but this had been generally effected at the time of this writing and the most recent negotiations between those two parties had been marked by a statesmanlike joint approach to difficult problems. By contrast, mutual trust is not the case at Armour, and resolutions of Meat Cutter–company differences there have sometimes strained the imaginations of both parties with no noticeable success. The *relative strengths of the two sides* can be decisive in particular negotiations, as in those between the aforementioned over-the-road truckers and the Teamsters Union, and in almost all recent negotiations involving the International Ladies Garment Workers Union and any of its many highly competitive and marginal employers. Some negotiations have not been easily resolved because of *political problems within the union*: the 1963 International Longshoremen's Association–East and Gulf Coast Shipping Operators bargaining was followed by a lengthy strike, due in large measure to a three-way scramble for leadership within the union and the accompanying jockeying for position of the contenders. Nor have these political problems been confined to top-level unionists. In recent years, the rank and file of an increasing number of unions—among them the previously cited UAW and Steelworkers—have supported the charges of their local leaders that the bargainers were ignoring local problems by temporarily refusing to ratify their negotiated settlements. On occasion, they have engaged in protest work stoppages as well.

The *personalities* of labor and management representatives often have a major bearing on the outcome. Despite the greater bargaining power of his union, former Teamster president Dave Beck's avowed philosophy that "for every friend I lose in the ranks of labor, I make two friends in the Chamber of Commerce" won him the wholehearted approval of many of his employers. It also made many Teamster negotiations under his presidency extremely amicable affairs. More commendably, the proven willingness of the late Pacific Maritime Association president J. Paul St. Sure and West Coast Longshoreman leader Harry Bridges to subordinate their personal goals to the welfare of their industry resulted, in the early 1960s, in a Mechanization and Modernization Agreement that represents a high level of statesmanship for both parties.

For negotiators whose bargaining can be in any way construed to affect "an entire industry or a substantial part thereof" in such a manner as to "imperil the national health or safety," there may be at least one further possible determinant. Under the Taft-Hartley Act of 1947, as Chapter 3 has explained, the President of the United States has the authority to postpone a strike consistent with the above specifications for eighty days. It will be recalled that other forms of *government intervention* may also be present in such cases: suggestions to uncooperative bargainers that restrictive legislation might be enacted should a strike take place, statements by public officials aimed at throwing the weight of public opinion to one side or the other, mediation by high-level personnel of the above-mentioned Federal Mediation and Conciliation Service or respected private citizens, and a variety of other devices. The possibility that any of these forms of intervention may be used can, of course, influence the actions of the negotiators at the bargaining table. Steelworker Union settlements in the 1960s, for example, were both peacefully arrived at and relatively mild in their economic increases (that is, "noninflationary"). Many observers have explained this situation, somewhat ironic in view of the turbulence accompanying steel negotiations as recently as 1959, by asserting that the government (which did, indeed, play a reasonably active role in all of these settlements with the possible exception of 1962–63) would have it no other way.

And the railroad operating unions, as a second illustration in this area, were widely accused of being unwilling to compromise in their long-standing work rules dispute of the past decade with the railroads. This was said to be due to their (accurate) belief that government intervenors would ultimately decide these rules anyhow—and, hopefully on better terms than the unions could extract from their employers.

The preceding examples are only a few of the many that could have been chosen to illustrate each category of variable. In any given contract negotiation, one factor might be of major importance—or of no significance at all. The degree of importance of each also, of course, changes over time. And, clearly, many (or none) of these variables can be at play at one time on the bargainers. Contract negotiation is, in short, no more susceptible to sweeping statements than are the unions and managements which participate in process.

The foregoing *has* indicated, however, that the negotiation of the labor contract in the contemporary economy is a complex and difficult job. The negotiators are required to possess a working knowledge of trade union principles, plant organization and operations, economics, psychology, statistics, and labor law. They must have the research ability to gather the data necessary for effective negotiations. Negotiators must be shrewd judges of human nature. Often, effective speaking ability is an additional prerequisite. Indeed, the position of the negotiator of the modern contract demands the best efforts of individuals possessing superior ability. Modern collective bargaining sessions have no place for the uninformed, the inept, or the unskilled.

DISCUSSION QUESTIONS

1. Assume that a large, nationwide company is negotiating a contract at the present time. What economic, political, legal, and social factors might be likely to exert some influence upon these negotiations?
2. It has been argued by a union research director that "a fact is as welcome at a collective bargaining table as a skunk at a cocktail party." Do you agree?
3. Evaluate the statement that "in the absence of a strike deadline, there can be no true collective bargaining."
4. What might explain the frequently heard management observation that "highly democratic unions are extremely difficult to negotiate with"?
5. How do you account for the fact that the joint study approach still remains confined to a relative handful of industries?
6. From the viewpoint of *society* is there anything to be said in favor of strikes?
7. Of all of the personal attributes which this chapter has indicated are important for labor relations negotiators to have, which single one do you consider to be the *most* important, and why?
8. "Successful labor contract bargaining should no longer be viewed as an 'art.' It is far more appropriate today to refer to it as a 'science.'" Discuss.

SELECTED REFERENCES

Chamberlain, Neil W., "Strikes in Contemporary Context," *Industrial and Labor Relations Review,* July 1967.
Dunlop, John T. and James J. Healy, *Collective Bargaining: Principles and Cases,* rev. ed. Homewood, Ill.: Richard D. Irwin, Inc., 1955, pp. 53–68.
Levinson, Harry, "Stress at the Bargaining Table," *Personnel,* March–April 1965.
Peters, Edward, *Strategy and Tactics in Labor Negotiations.* New London, Conn.: National Foremen's Institute, 1955.
Schelling T. C., *The Strategy of Conflict.* Cambridge, Mass.: Harvard University Press, 1960.

Siegel, Sidney, and L. E. Fouraker, *Bargaining and Group Decision Making.* New York: McGraw-Hill Book Company, 1960.

Sloane, Arthur A., "Collective Bargaining in Trucking: Prelude to a National Contract," *Industrial and Labor Relations Review,* October 1965.

Stagner, Ross and Hjalmar Rosen, *Psychology of Union-Management Relations.* Belmont, Calif.: Wadsworth Publishing Company, 1965.

Stevens, Carl M., *Strategy and Collective Bargaining Negotiation.* New York: McGraw-Hill Book Company, 1963.

Walton, Richard E., and Robert B. McKersie, *A Behavioral Theory of Labor Negotiations.* New York: McGraw-Hill Book Company, 1965.

6

Administration of the Agreement

When agreement *is* finally reached in contract negotiations, the bargainers frequently call in news reporters and photographers, smilingly slap each other on the back (as the cameras snap) and announce their satisfaction with the new contract. The exact performance, of course, varies from situation to situation. In general, however, such enthusiastic phrases as "great new era" and "going forward together for our mutual benefit" are often heard.

There is a minimum of sham in these actions. Public relations are, as has been stressed at several earlier stages in this book, important to both sides; and both management-stockholder and union leader–union member relationships are also not overlooked by the company and union participants, respectively, as they register their happiness with their joint handiwork. But typically the negotiators are genuinely optimistic about what they have negotiated: compromise and statesmanship have once again triumphed.

It will be some time, however, before one can tell whether this optimism is justified. The formal signing of the collective bargaining agreement does not mean that union-management relations are terminated until the next negotiation over contract terms. After the new labor agreement goes into effect, management and union representatives have the job of making the contract *work*. The labor agreement establishes the general framework of labor relations in the plant. It spells out in broad language the rights and benefits of employees, the obligations and rights of management, and the protection and the responsibilities of the union. But during the course of the contractual period, many problems will arise involving the *application* and the *interpretation* of the various clauses in the labor agreement.

The application of the contract is, in fact, a daily problem. Representatives of management and the union normally devote a considerably larger share of their time to the administration of the labor agreement than to its negotiation. Moreover, the climate of labor relations in the plant will be determined to a large extent by the manner in which management and union representatives discharge their obligations in the day-by-day application of the labor contract. Whether there will be good or bad labor relations depends to a significant degree on the character of the administration of the labor agreement. For these reasons, it is vital that the parties to a collective bargaining relationship understand thoroughly the problems and the responsibilities which grow out of the application of a contract.

The source for many administrative problems is in the language of the labor agreement. Owing to the conditions under which bargaining takes place, many contractual clauses are themselves written in rather broad terms. The day-to-day job in labor relations is to apply the *principles* of the labor agreement.

Many problems can arise under a single clause of the labor agreement. For example, a contract may limit the right of management to discharge for "just cause." An employee is discharged for speaking back to his foreman in harsh terms. Is this just cause within the meaning of the agreement? In another case, a seniority arrangement may provide that the employee with the longer service in the plant will get the better job, provided that he has ability to perform the job equal to that of any other employee who desires the position. Whether or not the employee with longer service *is* awarded the job is an administrative problem. Or, the parties may have agreed that employees will be expected to perform jobs falling within their job description. An emergency arises in the plant, and the company directs some employees to work outside their job description. Did the company violate the agreement? Or, as a final example, the labor agreement provides that wage rates of new jobs created in the plant are to be established in a manner which is equitable in terms of comparable jobs. Does a rate established for such a job in fact compare fairly with that for kindred jobs?

These illustrations suggest the multitude of problems that can arise in connection with the operation of a labor agreement on a day-by-day basis. Practically every provision in a collective bargaining contract can be the basis for problems that must be resolved.

GRIEVANCE PROCEDURE

Problems such as those posed above are handled and settled through the grievance procedure of the labor contract. The grievance procedure provides an orderly system whereby the employer and the union can determine whether or not the contract, in effect, has been violated. Only a comparatively small number of violations involve willful disregard of the terms of the collective bargaining agreement. More frequently, employers or unions pursue a course of conduct, alleged to be a violation of the collective bargaining agreement, which the party honestly believes to conform with its terms. In any event, the grievance procedure provides the mechanism whereby the truth of the matter will be revealed. Through it the parties have an opportunity to determine whether or not the contract has actually been violated. Such a peaceful procedure, of course, is infinitely superior to a system which would permit the enforcement of the contract through the harsh arbitrant of the strike or lockout. Each year literally hundreds of thousands of grievances are filed alleging contract violations. Indeed, industry would be in a chaotic state if the strike or the lockout were utilized to effect compliance with the contract instead of the resort to the peaceful procedures of the grievance mechanism.

The best way to demonstrate the working of a grievance procedure is through an actual circumstance. For this purpose, a case which actually occurred in industry will be utilized. Tom Swift, a rank-and-file member of Local 1000, was employed by the XYZ Manufacturing Company for a period of five years. His production record was excellent, he caused management no trouble, and during his fourth year of employment he received a promotion. One day Swift began preparations to leave the plant twenty minutes before quitting time. He put away his tools, washed up, got out of his overalls, and put on his street clothes. Jackson, an assistant foreman in his department, observed Swift's actions. He immediately informed Swift that he was going to the "front-office" to recommend his discharge. The next morning Swift reported for work, but Jackson handed Swift a pay envelope which, in addition to wages, included a discharge notice. The notice declared that the company discharged Swift because he made ready to leave the plant twenty minutes before quitting time.

Swift immediately contacted his union steward, Joe Thomas. The steward worked alongside Swift in the plant and, of course, personally knew the assistant foreman and foreman of his department. After Swift told Thomas the circumstances, the steward believed that the discharge constituted a violation of the collective bargaining contract. A clause in the agreement provided that an employee could be discharged only for "just cause." Disagreeing with the assistant foreman and the "front-office," Thomas felt that the discharge was not for just cause.

The collective bargaining contract covering the employees of the XYZ Company contained a carefully worded grievance procedure. It is through this procedure that Thomas was required to protest the discharge of Swift. The steward was aware that the requirements of the grievance procedure had to be carried out if he intended to take appropriate action to effect reinstatement of the union member. The grievance procedure provided that all charges of contract violation must be reduced to writing. Consequently, the steward and the discharged worker filled out a "grievance form," describing in detail the character of the alleged violation.

The steps in processing the complaint through the grievance procedure were clearly outlined in the collective bargaining agreement. First, it was necessary to present the grievance to the foreman of the department in which Swift worked. Both Thomas and Swift approached the foreman, and the written grievance was presented to him. The foreman was required to give his answer on the grievance within forty-eight hours after receiving it. He complied with the time requirement, but his answer did not please Swift or Thomas. The foreman supported the action of the assistant foreman and refused to recommend the reinstatement of Swift.

Not satisfied with the action of the foreman, the labor union, through Thomas the steward, resorted to the second step of the grievance procedure. This step required the appeal of the complaint to the superintendent of the department in which Swift worked. Again the disposition of the grievance by management's representative brought no relief to the discharged employee. Despite the efforts of the steward, who vigorously argued the merits of Swift's case, the department superintendent refused to reinstate the worker. Hence the second step of the grievance procedure was exhausted, and the union and the employee were still not satisfied with the results.

Actually, the vast majority of grievances are settled in the first two steps of the grievance procedure. This is a remarkable record, indicating the fairness of employers and labor unions. The employer or the union charged with a contract violation may simply admit their transgression and take remedial action. On the other hand, the party charged with violating the collective bargaining agreement may be able to persuade the other party that, in fact, no violation exists. Frequently, both parties might work out a compromise solution satisfactory to all concerned. Such a compromise may serve the interests of sound industrial relations, a state of affairs which the grievance procedure attempts to produce.

In the Swift case, however, the union refused to drop the case after the complaint was processed through the second level of the grievance procedure. Accordingly, the union appealed to the third step of the grievance procedure. Grievance personnel for the third step included, from the company, the general superintendent and his representatives, and for the labor union, the organization's plantwide grievance committee. The results of the negotiations at the third step proved satisfactory to Swift, the union, and the company. After forty-five minutes of spirited discussion, the management group agreed with the union that discharge was not warranted in this particular case. Management's committee was persuaded by the following set of circumstances. Everyone conceded that Swift had an outstanding record before the dismissal occurred. In addition, the discussion revealed that Swift had inquired of the department foreman whether there was any more work to be done before he left his bench to prepare to leave for home. The foreman had replied in the negative. Finally, it was brought out that Swift had had a pressing problem at home which he claimed was the motivating factor making for his desire to leave the plant immediately after quitting time.

The grievance personnel reached a mutually satisfactory solution of the case after all the factors were carefully weighed. Management repeatedly stressed the serious consequences to production efficiency if a large number of workers prepared to leave the plant twenty minutes before quitting time. Recognizing the soundness of this observation, the union committee agreed that some sort of disciplinary action should be taken. As a result it was concluded that Swift would be reinstated in his job, but would be penalized by a three-day suspension without pay. In addition, the union committee agreed with management's representatives that better labor relations would be promoted if a notice were posted on company bulletin boards stating that all workers would be expected to remain at their jobs until quitting time. Union and company grievance personnel were in agreement that the notice should also declare that violations would be subject to penalty. Thus the grievance procedure resulted in the amicable solution of a contract violation case.

What would have occurred, however, if the company and the labor union had not reached a satisfactory agreement at the third step of the grievance procedure? In this particular contract, the grievance procedure provided for a fourth step. Grievance procedure personnel at the fourth step included, for the company, the vice president in charge of industrial relations or his representative, and, for the union, an officer of the international union or his representative. It is noteworthy that this particular contract provided four chances to effect a mutually satisfactory disposition of a complaint alleging a contract violation.

All collective bargaining contracts do not provide for the same structural arrangements as the one described in the Swift case. Some contain only three steps. In others the time limits may be different. (NOTE: Case No. 1 at the end of this chapter, the first of twelve illustrative cases contained in the remaining chapters of this book, deals with some of the ramifications of time limits.) The particular company and union personnel participating at the different steps of the grievance procedure may be somewhat different. If their structural arrangements might vary slightly from contract to contract, however, the fact remains that the essential characteristics of grievance procedures are similar. All have as their basic objective the settling of alleged contract violation cases in a friendly and orderly manner. In each there will be provided a series of definite steps to follow in the processing of grievances. A certain time limit will be placed on each step, and an answer to a grievance must be given within the allotted time. Appeal from lower to higher steps within the grievance procedure is guaranteed to the union and the company. Finally, grievance procedure personnel are drawn from the ranks of company and union representatives who actually work in or are closely associated with the plant in which the alleged contract violation occurs.

GRIEVANCE PROCEDURE: ITS FLEXIBILITY

Since company officials and union officers make up grievance procedure personnel, people intimately connected with the plant will decide whether or not a particular pattern of conduct violates the terms of the collective bargaining agreement. Obviously, these people are in a favored position to make such a determination. Frequently, some of the people who serve as grievance procedure personnel helped negotiate the collective bargaining contract itself. Such participation in the contract-making negotiations should result in a clear understanding of the meaning of particular contract terms. Not only do grievance procedure personnel normally possess a thorough and firsthand knowledge of the meaning of the contract, but they are well aware of the character of the conduct alleged to be a violation. Grievance cases are at times complex in nature. The line dividing "lawful" from "unlawful" conduct under a collective bargaining contract is not always sharply drawn. Clearly, people actually associated with the plant in which the alleged violation occurred can best decide these difficult cases.

The local character of grievance procedure personnel serves to make this contract-enforcing technique highly flexible in character. These people are well aware of the environmental context in which the alleged violation occurred. Weight can be given to human or economic factors involved in alleged violations. This does not mean that an "explainable" violation will go unchallenged. However, the grievance procedure is a peculiarly amenable mechanism. It is probable that grievance procedure personnel might resolve an "explainable" violation in a different manner from one in which no extenuating circumstances were involved.

Since grievance procedure personnel are closely associated with the plant, they are in an excellent position to anticipate the effects of the disposition of a grievance on employers, on the union, on union leadership, and on plant operations. To promote sound industrial relations, management and union grievance procedure personnel, as noted, frequently compromise on the solution of grievance cases. It is not unknown for management to allow the union to "win" a grievance case to bolster the prestige of union leadership in the eyes of union membership. The state of industrial relations may be improved when union leaders have the confidence of the membership. On the other hand, a labor union may refuse to challenge a company violation of a contract when the employer engages in conduct absolutely essential for the operation of the plant. And, in this connection, a circumstance involving an Indiana firm and labor union might be related.

Contrary to the seniority provisions of an existing collective bargaining contract, the Indiana company laid off longer-service employees and retained shorter-service employees. Such action constituted a direct violation of the particular contract. However, the union representatives agreed with the company, when the case was resolved through the grievance procedure, that the retention of the shorter-service workers was vital to the continued operation of a crucial plant department. Union and management grievance procedure personnel concluded that had the longer-service workers been retained and the shorter-service employees been laid off, the plant, the union, and all employees of the company would have suffered irreparable damage.

It is not intended to create a false impression of the operation of the grievance procedure. Certainly, the mechanism does not function to condone employer, employee, or union violations of collective bargaining contracts. In the overwhelming number of cases disposed of through the grievance procedure, practices inconsistent with the terms of the agreement are terminated. At times retroactive action must be taken to implement rights and obligations provided for in the contract. Thus the employer may be required to reinstate with back pay a worker who had previously been discharged in violation of the discharge clause of the labor agreement. Perhaps a union caused damage to the company's property while on strike. To comply with a particular contract provision, this union might be required to pay the company a certain sum of money.

Without detracting from the fact that the primary objective of the grievance procedure is to enforce the terms of the collective bargaining contract, it remains true that this mechanism is singularly adaptable for the settlement of contract disputes to the maximum satisfaction of all concerned. Interests of all parties can be considered. Its flexible and personalized character permits compromise when this is deemed the best way to settle a particular grievance. Extenuating circumstances can be given weight. Precedent can be utilized or disregarded depending on the particular situation. Effects of the manner of disposition of a contract violation case are clearly understood by grievance procedure personnel. In short, the flexible character of grievance procedure is its outstanding merit. Solutions to problems can be reached which will serve the basic interests of sound industrial relations. These observations lead to one conclusion: resort to the grievance procedure provides management and unions with the most useful and efficient means of contract enforcement.

Grievance Procedure and Harmonious Labor Relations

As suggested above, the grievance procedure, by providing the parties to the labor contract with an excellent opportunity whereby complaints of workers, employers, and unions can be aired and discussed, may be regarded as supplying the "psychotherapy" of industrial relations. Small problems can be discussed and settled promptly before they become major and troublesome issues in the plant. Serious problems can be analyzed in a rational manner and resolved speedily, peacefully, and in keeping with the terms of the collective bargaining contract. The rights of employees, employers, and unions guaranteed in the labor contract can be protected and implemented in a prompt and orderly fashion. Not only does the grievance procedure serve as a means for the enforcement of the labor agreement but it also provides the parties with the opportunity of establishing the *reasons* for complaints and problems.

Indeed, depending upon the attitudes of the company and the union, the grievance procedure can also be used for functions *other* than the settlement of complaints arising under the labor agreement. Many parties, for example, use the grievance machinery to *prevent grievances from arising* as well as to dispose of employee, union, and employer complaints. Major grievances are viewed here as symptomatic of underlying problems and attempts are jointly made to dispose of these problems to prevent their future recurrence. In other cases, the parties may utilize the scheduled grievance meeting time, after the grievance itself has been dealt with, to explore ways of improving their general relationship and also as an avenue of bilateral communication on matters of interest to both institutions (*e.g.,* new company plans, the economic prospects for the industry, the upcoming union election).

In the last analysis, in fact, the grievance procedure should be regarded as a device whereby companies or unions can "win" a grievance only in the most narrow of senses. It should also be viewed as a means for obtaining a better climate of labor relations in a company, rather than as the machinery whereby the company or the union can exercise authority over each other. This does not mean that rights guaranteed in the labor contract should be waived or compromised, but that in discharging obligations under the grievance procedure the parties should understand the broader implications involved. Company and union representatives who regard the grievance procedure in *this* light gear their behavior, arguments, and general approach toward the objective of the *improvement of labor relations*.

This latter objective is not realized when representatives of management look upon their obligations under the grievance procedure as burdensome chores, as wastes of time, or as necessary evils. Likewise, it is not attainable to the extent that unions stuff the grievance procedure with complaints that have no merit whatsoever under the collective bargaining contract.[1] It cannot be achieved when the parties regard the grievance procedure as a method to embarrass the other side or to demonstrate authority or power. In addition, the opportunities for more harmonious labor relations through the use of the grievance procedure cannot be realized to the extent that the system is used to resolve internal political conflicts within unions or the management. If the grievance procedure does not contribute to a better labor relations climate, the fault lies not with the system, but with the representatives of unions and management who either misunderstand or distort the functions that the grievance procedure plays in the industrial relations complex.

ARBITRATION

The vast majority of problems that arise as the result of the interpretation and application of collective bargaining contracts are resolved bilaterally by the representatives of management and the labor organization. Through the process of negotiation, the parties to a contract manage to find a solution to grievances at some step in the grievance procedure. Such a record testifies to the utility of the grievance procedure as a device for the speedy, fair, and peaceful solution of disputes growing out of the application of the collective bargaining contract. It also shows rather clearly that the great majority of company and union representatives under-

---

[1] Many unions specifically instruct their stewards and grievance committeemen not to process grievances that have no merit under a labor agreement. Thus, in one union manual the labor organization instructs its stewards as follows: "After you have thoroughly investigated the case, if you decide that no grievance exists, it is your duty to the worker and the union to state this, and to take time to explain why."

stand fully the purpose of the grievance procedure and discharge their responsibilities on the basis of good faith.

Indeed, in healthy union-management relationships, the great bulk of grievances is disposed of at the lower levels of the procedure. This is as it should be: were most such complaints merely bucked up the union and management hierarchical ladders, the time and efforts of the more broadly based officials would be hopelessly drained. Lower-step settlement also helps maintain the status of lower supervision and assures that the grievance is allowed treatment by the people who are apt to be most familiar with the circumstances under which it arose.

Under even the most enviable of labor relationships, however, there undoubtedly will be some grievances that prove themselves completely incapable of being solved by *any* level within the bilateral grievance procedure. Each party genuinely believes that its interpretation of the contract is the right one, or the company and union remain in disagreement as to the facts of the case.

There may also, on occasion, be less commendable reasons for a stalemate. The union leadership may feel that it cannot afford to "give in" on an untenable grievance because of the political ramifications of doing so. Management may at times prove quite unwilling to admit that the original company action giving rise to the grievance was in violation of the contract, even though in its heart it realizes that the union's allegation is right. The union may, the remarks previously offered in this connection notwithstanding, seek to "flood" the grievance procedure with a potpourri of unsettled grievances, with the hope of using the situation to gain extracontractual concessions from the company. The company may, in turn, seek to embarrass the union leadership by making it fight to the limit for any favorable settlement. And grievances involving such thorny issues as discipline, work assignment, and management rights are sometimes accompanied by emotional undercurrents that make them all the more difficult to resolve by the joint conference method of the grievance procedure.

In short, the amount of challenge which management can expect through the grievance procedure can vary widely because of the existence of such complex variables as (1) the wisdom and extent of development of the legislated policy which is embodied in the labor agreement itself (and, no less important, the degree of operating policy development which the company has effected to supplement the labor agreement); (2) the political environment and militancy of the local union; (3) the calibre of the company's personnel administration and supervision; (4) the nature of the existing union-management relationship; and (5) economic and related variables affecting employment and working conditions.

Given all these variables, it is, in fact, a tribute to the maturity of labor-management relations that the great majority of all grievances *are* settled by the joint process.

Nonetheless, some contractual provision must be made by the parties to handle the relatively few issues for which the grievance procedure proves unsuccessful: those occasions upon which the parties to the labor contract are still in disagreement over a problem arising under the contractual terms after all bilateral steps in the grievance procedure have been exhausted.

To break such deadlocks, the parties have the opportunity to resort to the arbitration process. An impartial outsider is selected by the parties to decide the controversy. His decision is invariably stipulated in the contract as being "final and binding upon both parties."

Through the arbitrator, the dispute is resolved in a peaceful manner. In the absence of arbitration, the parties might use the strike or lockout to settle such problems, a process which is not only costly to the company, the union, and the employees, but which would tend to foster embittered labor relations. In the light of these observations, it should elicit no surprise that at present some 96 percent of all United States labor agreements provide for arbitration as the final step in the grievance procedure. This national percentage is significantly greater than it was in the early 1930s, when fewer than 8 to 10 percent of all agreements contained such a clause. And even by 1944, arbitration provisions had been included in only 73 percent of all contracts.[2]

Not surprisingly, either, the recent statistics involving arbitration case loads have been of no small order of magnitude. In 1968, for example, neutrals were called upon to make awards in no less than 30,000 labor-management disputes.[3] In an era of uncertainty as to the future growth of union membership totals, moreover, there is no collective job insecurity in the profession: by common estimate, the caseload of arbitrators keeps increasing at the rate of roughly 10 percent annually. Much of the most recent impetus for growth was provided by a major judicial decision of the late 1950s: in June 1957, the United States Supreme Court held that the federal courts may apply the Taft-Hartley law to enforce arbitration clauses. Under this ruling, an employer may not refuse to arbitrate unresolved grievance disputes when the labor agreement contains an arbitration provision.[4]

The "Trilogy" Cases

On June 20, 1960, the United States Supreme Court handed down three other decisions which provide even greater integrity to the arbitration

---

[2] "Arbitration Provisions in Collective Agreements, 1952," *Monthly Labor Review*, March 1953, pp. 261–66.
[3] *Business Week*, March 8, 1969, p. 78.
[4] *Textile Workers* v. *Lincoln Mills*, 353 U.S. 488 (1957).

process.⁵ These decisions are commonly referred to as the "Trilogy" cases. Each of them involved the United Steelworkers of America and each demonstrates that the system of private arbitration in the United States has now received the full support of the highest court in the land.

In the *Warrior and Gulf Navigation* case, the Court held that in the absence of an express agreement excluding arbitration, the Court would direct the parties to arbitrate a grievance. To put this in other terms, the Court would not find a case to be nonarbitrable unless the parties specifically excluded a subject from the arbitration process. The Court stated that a legal order to arbitrate would thenceforth not be denied "unless it may be said with positive assurance that the arbitration clause is not susceptible to an interpretation that covers the asserted dispute. Doubts should be resolved in favor of coverage."

More precisely, the courts will not decide that a dispute is *not* arbitrable unless the parties have taken care to *expressly remove* an area of labor relations from the arbitration process. This could be accomplished by providing, for example, that "disputes involving determination of the qualifications of employees for promotion will be determined exclusively by the company and such decision will not be subject to arbitration." But, needless to say, not many unions would agree to such a clause since management would then have the unilateral right to make determinations on this vital phase of the promotion process.

In so ruling, the *Warrior and Gulf Navigation* decision eliminated a course of action that some companies had followed. When faced with a demand by a union for arbitration, some employers had frequently gone to court and asked the judge to decide that the issue involved in the case was not arbitrable. On many occasions, the courts had agreed with the company, with the effect of sustaining the company position in the grievance, and denying the union an opportunity to get a decision based on the merits of the case.

In the instant case, the Warrior and Gulf Navigation Company employed forty-two men at its dock terminal for maintenance and repair work. After the company had subcontracted out some of the work, the number was reduced to twenty-three. The union argued in the grievance procedure that this action of the company violated certain areas of the labor agreement—the integrity of the bargaining unit, seniority rights, and other clauses of the contract which provided benefits to workers. On its part, the company claimed that the issue of subcontracting was strictly a management function and relied on the management rights clause in

---

⁵ *United Steelworkers of America* v. *American Manufacturing Co.,* 363 U.S. 564 (1960); *United Steelworkers of America* v. *Warrior & Gulf Navigation Co.,* 363 U.S. 574 (1960); *United Steelworkers of America* v. *Enterprise Wheel & Car Corp.,* 363 U.S. 593 (1960).

the contract which stated that "matters which are strictly a function of management should not be subject to arbitration." When the Supreme Court handled the case, it ordered arbitration because the contract did not *specifically* exclude such activity from the arbitration process. It stated:

> A specific collective bargaining agreement may exclude contracting-out from the grievance procedure. Or a written collateral agreement may make clear that contracting-out was not a matter for arbitration. In such a case a grievance based solely on contracting-out would not be arbitrable. Here, however, there is no such provision. Nor is there any showing that the parties designed the phrase "strictly as a function of management" to encompass any and all forms of contracting-out. In the absence of any express provision excluding a particular grievance from arbitration, we think only the most forceful evidence of a purpose to exclude the claim from arbitration can prevail, particularly where, as here, the exclusion clause is vague and the arbitration clause quite broad.

One additional important point must be made relative to the significance of this court decision. It does not mean that private arbitrators do not have the authority to dismiss a grievance on the basis of its nonarbitrability under a contract. Arbitrators before and after the decision have frequently held that a grievance is not arbitrable under the contract. Indeed, the authors at times after the *Warrior and Gulf Navigation* decision have upheld the arguments of companies that grievances were not arbitrable under the labor agreement. The major importance of the *Warrior and Gulf Navigation* doctrine is in its ruling that courts may not hold that grievances are not arbitrable *unless* specific and clear-cut language excludes the matter from the arbitration process. The private arbitrator is still fully empowered to dismiss a grievance on the basis of nonarbitrability. (The problem of the arbitrability of grievances is raised in Case No. 2 at the end of this chapter.)

In the second case, *American Manufacturing,* the issue of arbitrability was also involved, but in a somewhat different way from that of *Warrior and Gulf Navigation.* The American Manufacturing Company argued before a lower federal court that an issue was not arbitrable because it did not believe that the grievance had merit. Involved was a dispute involving the reinstatement of an employee on his job after it was determined that the employee was 25 percent disabled and was drawing workmen's compensation. The lower federal court sustained the employer's position and characterized the employee's grievance as "a frivolous, patently baseless one, not subject to arbitration." When the United States Supreme Court reversed the lower federal court, it held that the federal courts are limited in determining whether the dispute is covered by the labor agreement and that they have no power to evaluate the merits of a dispute. It stated:

> The function of the court is very limited when the parties have agreed to submit all questions of contract interpretation to the arbitrator. It is then confined to ascertaining whether the party seeking arbitration is making a claim which on its face is governed by the contract. Whether the moving party is right or wrong is a question of contract construction for the arbitrator. In these circumstances the moving party should not be deprived of the arbitrator's judgment, when it was his judgment and all that it connotes that was bargained for.

Essentially, this means that the courts may not hold a grievance to be nonarbitrable even if a judge believes that a grievance is completely worthless. It is up to the private arbitrator to make the decision on the merits of a case. He may dismiss the grievance as being without merit, but this duty rests exclusively with him, and not with the courts.

In the third case, *Enterprise Wheel and Car Corporation,* a lower federal court reversed the decision of an arbitrator on the grounds that the judge did not believe that his decision was sound under the labor agreement. The arbitrator's award directed the employer to reinstate certain discharged workers and to pay them back wages for perods both before and after the expiration of the collective bargaining contract. The company refused to comply with the award, and the union petitioned for the enforcement of the award. The lower court held that the arbitrator's award was unenforceable because the contract had expired. The United States Supreme Court reversed the lower court and ordered full enforcement. In upholding the arbitrator's award, the Court stated

> Interpretation of the collective bargaining agreement is a question for the arbitrator. It is the arbitrator's construction which was bargained for; and so far as the arbitration decision concerns construction of the contract, the courts have no business overruling him because their interpretation of the contract is different from his.

The significance of this last decision should be perfectly clear. It shows that a union or a company may not use the courts to set aside an arbitrator's award. The decision, of course, cuts both ways: it applies to both employers and labor organizations. Whereas the other two decisions definitely favor labor organizations, this one merely serves to preserve the integrity of the arbitrator's award. Thus, even if a judge believes that an arbitrator's award is unfair, unwise, and not even consistent with the contract, he has no alternative except to enforce the award.

Thus, the Trilogy cases demonstrate that the private arbitration system has been strengthened by the judiciary. They establish the full integrity of the arbitration process. As a result of these decisions, companies and unions must be more careful in the selection of arbitrators. This is one reason why they have increasingly voiced a desire to use seasoned and experienced arbitrators.

For the arbitrator, the decisions are equally meaningful. Private arbitrators bear an even greater degree of responsibility as they decide their cases. Not only is the post one of honor in which the parties have confidence in the arbitrator's professional competency and integrity, but the arbitrator must recognize that for all intents and purposes his decision is completely "final and binding" upon the parties. Indeed, if the system of private arbitration is to remain a permanent feature of the American system of industrial relations, arbitrators must measure up to their responsibilities. Should they fail in this respect, companies and unions would simply delete the arbitration clause from the contract and resolve their disputes by strikes or by going directly to courts. These are not pleasant alternatives, but the parties may choose these routes if they believe that arbitrators are not discharging their responsibilities in an honorable, judicious, and professional manner. Arbitrators should not feel so smug as to believe that their services are indispensable to labor unions and companies. They are as expendable as last year's calendar.

Limitations to Arbitration

If employers and unions support the arbitration process as an accepted method of disposing of disagreements relating to problems arising under the terms of a labor contract already in existence, there is almost *no* approval on the part of industry and organized labor for using arbitration as the means of breaking deadlocks in the negotiations of *new* agreements. Most employers and unions would rather have a work stoppage than refer to arbitration such latter disputes. Though many reasons are advanced in support of this position, the chief consideration lies in the parties' extreme aversion to having an outsider determine the conditions of employment, the rights and obligations of management, and the responsibilities and rights of the union. Employers and unions almost invariably believe that since the labor agreement will establish their fundamental relationship, they should have the full authority to negotiate its terms. For these reasons, the use of arbitration during the negotiation stage of a labor contract is rare. In only a very few industries do the parties surrender their rights to negotiate new contracts and establish arbitration as the method to break deadlocks.

It is also important to note that in the United States the system is one of *private and voluntary arbitration*. That is, the government does not force the parties to include arbitration clauses in their labor agreements. They do so voluntarily as they negotiate the latter. Either party can refuse to incorporate any arbitration provisions at all, as has been the case in the building construction industry, where the duration of the job is deemed too brief to make use of a neutral feasible, and in much of the trucking industry, where the Teamster hierarchy has traditionally insisted that neutrals "attempt to please both sides and actually please nobody."

Equally significant is the fact that arbitrators are private and not government officials. Most of them are lawyers and college professors. In some nations, such as Spain, arbitration is imposed by government fiat, *must* be used to resolve contractual interpretation disputes, and the arbitrators are government officials or appointees. Let us hope that the American system never takes this route. To follow the pattern of Spain and other totalitarian labor relations systems would mean the demise of the free collective bargaining system.

Characteristics of Arbitration Hearings

Since the decision of the arbitrator *is* final and binding, arbitration is quite different from mediation, a process wherein the parties are completely free to accept or reject the recommendations or suggestions of the mediator. Whether or not the arbitrator rules for or against a party to the arbitration, his decision must be accepted. This is true even when the losing side believes that the decision is not warranted by the labor agreement, by the evidence submitted in the hearing, or on the basis of fairness or justice. Frequently, an arbitrator's decision will establish an important precedent in the plant that must be followed by the company, the union, and the employees. At times the party which suffers an adverse ruling in an arbitration case will attempt to change those sections of the labor agreement which proved to be the basis of the decision during the next labor contract negotiations. Obviously, the side which is benefited by the decision will be reluctant to alter those features of the labor agreement which were interpreted and applied by the arbitrator.

These considerations tend to show the seriousness of arbitration as a tool of labor relations. When the decision to arbitrate is made, the company and union representatives are undertaking a deep responsibility. To discharge this responsibility in a competent and intelligent manner, it is necessary to put the arbitrator in such a position that he can make his decision in the light of evidence and of the relevant contractual clauses. Consequently, the parties have the obligation of preparing fully before coming to the hearing. This means the accumulation of all evidence, facts, documents, and arguments that may have a bearing on the dispute. Careful preparation also means the selection of witnesses who can give relevant testimony in the case.[6] Company and union representatives should leave no stone unturned in preparing for the arbitration.

---

[6] A competent elaboration of this topic is contained in Frank and Edna Elkouri's *How Arbitration Works* (Washington, D.C.: Bureau of National Affairs, Inc., 1960).

At the arbitration hearing each side will have full opportunity to present the fruits of its preparation. Normally, though arbitration hearings are much more formal than grievance procedure negotiations, they are considerably less formal than court proceedings. In addition, the rules of evidence which pertain in the courts of the land do not bind the conduct of the arbitration.[7] This means that the hearing can be conducted not only more informally but much faster than a case in court. However, the parties should not be deluded into believing that the arbitrator's decision will not be based upon evidence and facts. Even though the arbitration proceedings might be regarded as semiformal, the fact remains that the arbitrator's decision will most likely be based *strictly* on facts, evidence, arguments, and the contractual clauses that are involved in the proceedings. Arbitration cases are not won on the basis of emotional appeals, theatrcial gestures, or speechmaking. The arbitrator is interested in the facts, the evidence, and the parties' arguments as they apply to the issues of the dispute. Such material should be developed in the hearing through careful questioning of witnesses and the presentation of relevant documents.

The parties cannot, moreover, take too much care to make sure that they have presented *all* evidence that might support their case. Representatives of unions and companies who have dealt with a problem in the grievance procedure and who therefore are fully aware of all the facets of a case at times will not fully present their case because they believe that the arbitrator is likewise familiar with the facts and issues. Unless prehearing briefs are filed by the parties, it should be recognized that the arbitrator knows absolutely nothing about the case at the time of the hearing. It is the responsibility of the parties to educate him about the issues, the facts, the evidence, the arguments, and the relevant contractual clauses. Clearly, if the arbitration process is to have a significant positive value in the area of labor relations, the parties to the arbitration must discharge their obligations fully and conscientiously. Company and union representatives must be indefatigable in their efforts to prepare for the arbitration and must be absolutely thorough in the presentation of their case to the arbitrator.

Responsibilities of the Arbitrator

The arbitrator, of course, is the key man in the arbitration process. His is the cold responsibility for the decision in the case. He decides, for

---

[7] Thus, the rules of the American Arbitration Association provide as follows: "The parties may offer such evidence as they desire and shall produce such additional evidence as the Arbitrator may deem necessary to an understanding and determination of the dispute.... The Arbitrator shall be the judge of the relevancy and materiality of the evidence offered and conformity to legal rules of evidence shall not be necessary." *Voluntary Labor Arbitration Rules* (New York: American Arbitration Association, 1965), p. 5.

example, whether a discharged employee remains discharged or returns to work, which of two workers gets the better job, whether the company placed a correct rate on a new job, whether an employee worked outside of his classification, whether the company rotated overtime correctly, or whether an employee forfeited his seniority under the contract. Indeed, one of the most important jobs that a person can receive is the assignment by a company and a union to an arbitration case.

In discharging his responsibilities, the arbitrator is expected to adhere to a strict code of ethics. His decision must be based squarely on the evidence and the facts presented to him. He must give full faith and credit to the language of the labor contract at the time of the case. It should be recognized by all concerned that the language of the labor agreement binds the company, the union, the employees, *and the arbitrator*. It is not within the scope of the arbitrator's authority to decide whether or not a particular contractual clause is wise or unwise, desirable or undesirable. His job is to apply the language of a labor contract as he finds it in a particular case. For an arbitrator to follow any other course of action would not only be a breach of faith to the parties but would create mischief with the labor agreement. The arbitrator must regard the collective bargaining contract as a final authority and give it full respect. If a case goes against a party because of the language of the contract, the responsibility for this state of affairs lies not with the arbitrator but with the parties who negotiated the agreement.

If the language of the contract is clear-cut and unequivocal, the arbitrator's job is not too difficult. Under these circumstances, his award will favor the party whose position is sustained by the precise contractual language. Of course, there are not many cases of this type, since if the language is clear-cut and precise the dispute should not have gone to arbitration. It should have been resolved in the grievance procedure on the basis of the contractual language.

What complicates the arbitrator's problem is contractual language which is subject to different shades of meaning. That is, impartial people could find that the language involved may be reasonably interpreted in different ways. Under these circumstances, what is called "past practice" serves as the guide for construction of the ambiguous contractual language. (Past practice is the way the language has been applied in the past.) The idea behind past practice is that both parties have knowledge of the practice and both expect that the practice will be honored as the basis of administration of the relevant contractual language. Thus, when the arbitrator is confronted with contractual language which is ambiguous, he will normally base his decision on the evidence demonstrating practice. However, if the language is unambiguous and unequivocal, and the practice conflicts with the clear-cut contractual language, the arbitrator will normally base his decision upon the language rather than on the practice.

That is, unequivocal contractual language supercedes practice when the two conflict. Also, arbitrators generally recognize that past practice should not be used to restrict management in the changing of work methods required by changing conditions. Thus past practice is normally not used to prevent management from changing work schedules, work assignments, workloads, job assignments, and the number of workers needed on the job.

The key to such an arbitration principle is that *changing conditions* have made the practice obsolete. Of course, there may be written contractual language which would forbid the management making such changes in work methods. Under these circumstances, the arbitrator's decision would be based upon the written contractual language, but past practice would not normally used to block management action when conditions change. Despite these limitations, past practice is frequently used as the basis for arbitrator's decisions, particularly, as stated, when contractual language is subject to different shades of meaning.

Much has been said and written about the necessity of the arbitrator's being "fair" in his decision. A decision is fair *only* when it is based upon the evidence of a case and the accurate assessment of the relevant provisions of the labor agreement. Furthermore, fairness does not mean charity, compromise, or an attempt to please both sides. At times a company and union arbitrate a number of different grievances in one hearing. An arbitrator is not worthy of the confidence of the parties if he deliberately sets his mind to compromise or "split" the grievances. An arbitrator who is a "splitter" not only violates the ethics of his office, but causes untold confusion and damage to the parties. What companies and unions desire in arbitration is a clear-cut decision on each grievance based upon the merits of each dispute; they do not want splitting. Compromise or "horse-trading" of grievances may be accomplished in the grievance procedure. However, once grievances are referred to arbitration, each and every one of them must be decided on its own merits. Clearly, a "split-the-difference" approach to arbitration can do irreparable harm to the parties, the collective bargaining contract, and the arbitration process. Companies and unions would quickly lose confidence in arbitration if cases were decided not upon their merits but upon the determination of the arbitrator to "even up" his awards.

In fact, before hearing a case, each arbitrator normally takes a solemn oath of office that he will decide the dispute on the evidence, free from any bias. Any arbitrator who transgresses this oath by striving to decide a case on a split-the-difference formula has absolutely no business serving as an arbitrator. A famous and respected baseball umpire once said he called them as he saw them. Though umpiring a baseball game is quite different from arbitrating a labor dispute, and though the qualifications for baseball umpires are quite different from those for arbitrators in labor relations, the homely statement "call them as you see them" has real significance for arbitration of any kind of dispute.

Additional responsibilities and personal qualities are required in the person serving as an arbitrator. Not only must he be incorruptible, free from any bias, and aware of the principles of arbitration, but he must also have a deep and well-rounded understanding of labor relations. It takes more than honesty and integrity to serve effectively as an arbitrator. Arbitrators who are not trained in labor relations matters, though they be paragons of virtue, at times can cause irreparable damage to the parties by decisions which do violence to the collective bargaining contract.

At the hearing the arbitrator should treat both sides with the dignity and the respect that is characteristic of the judicial process. He should be patient, sympathetic, and understanding. Experienced arbitrators do not take advantage of their office by being arrogant or domineering. Arbitrators who have a tendency to exaggerate their own importance should be aware of the fact that arbitration, though important, plays a distinctly minor role in the overall union-management relationship. The arbitrator should permit each side to the dispute the fullest opportunity to present all the evidence, witnesses, documents, and arguments that it desires. Experienced arbitrators frequently will lean over backwards to permit the introduction of evidence which may or may not be relevant to the dispute. This procedure is better than a policy which could result in the suppression of vital information.

The arbitrator also has the responsibility of keeping the hearing moving. When the arbitrator notes deliberate or unconscious waste of time by either or both of the parties, he is obligated to take remedial action. This does not mean that the arbitrator should not permit recesses, coffee breaks, or the occasional telling of a humorous story; what it means is that the arbitrator earns part of his fee by conducting a fair, orderly, thorough, and speedy hearing. To this end, the arbitrator, though at all times demonstrating the qualities of patience and understanding, must remain in full *control* of the hearing. Individuals who unwittingly or by design attempt to take over the hearing must be dealt with courteously but firmly by the arbitrator. Of course, if the arbitrator is not experienced, is unsure of himself, or for some reason cannot or will not make definite decisions, the hearing can get out of hand.

The arbitrator also has an obligation to the witnesses called upon to give testimony in the hearing. Though witnesses should be subject to searching examination, the arbitrator should make sure that they are treated in a courteous manner by the examining party, or by the arbitrator himself if he asks questions of witnesses to clarify a point. He should not permit witnesses to be "badgered" or insulted. Even in cross-examination, where the examining party has more leeway with witnesses than it does in direct examination, witnesses should be treated with decorum.

Finally, the arbitrator has a responsibility to the parties relative to the award. Since one of the great advantages of arbitration is the comparatively fast disposition of disputes which it allows, the arbitrator has an obligation to get his decision into the hands of the parties rather quickly after the termination of the hearing. Unless unusual conditions are involved, such decisions should be forwarded to the parties in not more than thirty days after the termination of the hearing.[8] In discharge cases, the interests of the parties and the grievant may be best served by a decision rendered in about fifteen days. Of course, when the parties elect to file post-hearing briefs, the thirty-day limit starts from the date of the receipt of such briefs.

The award should be clear and to the point. There should be no question in the minds of the parties as to the exact character of the decision in the case. If the grievance is denied, the award should simply state that fact. Under these circumstances, some arbitrators in the decision also mention the contract provision or provisions that the company did not violate. For example, in a work-assignment case, the award might read as follows:

> The grievance of Mr. Elmer Beamish, Grievance No. 594, is denied on the basis that the company, under job description for Tool- and Diemakers, Class A, Code 286, and for Maintenance Men, Class A, Code 263, and without violating Article XVI of the Labor Agreement, may properly assign either category of employees to repair the classes of machinery in question in this case.

When a case is decided in favor of the union, the award should clearly and specifically direct the company to take action to bring it into compliance with the contract. In addition, to avoid any misunderstanding, the decision should require the action within a certain number of working days after the receipt of the award. For example, in a "bumping" case, the award might read as follows:

> Within three working days after the receipt of this award, the Company is directed to place the grievant, Reva Snodgrass, into the job of Spray Painter, Class "B," Labor Grade No. 7, and to make her whole for any financial loss that she suffered because of the refusal of the Company to permit her to roll into the aforementioned job on the grounds that the Company violated Article IX, Section 7, Paragraph A and B of the Labor Agreement.

---

[8] Thus, the Federal Mediation and Conciliation Service expects arbitrators appointed under its jurisdiction to make their awards within "...thirty (30) days from the date of the closing of the hearing, or the receipt of a transcript and any post-hearing briefs...unless otherwise agreed upon by the parties or specified by law."

In addition to the incorporation of a clear award, the arbitrator is charged with the responsibility of writing an opinion to support his decision. Although technically opinions are not required to explain a decision, the fact is that arbitrators almost universally write an opinion. What is more important in this connection, companies and unions *expect* their arbitrators to write them, and agencies such as the Federal Mediation and Conciliation Service and the American Arbitration Association, which submit to companies and unions the names of arbitrators, likewise tacitly expect the arbitrator to write an opinion.

In the opinion the arbitrator sets forth the basic issues of the case, the facts, the position and arguments of the parties, and the reasons for his decision. He deals with the evidence presented in the case as it relates to his decision. Arbitrators frequently are extraordinarily careful to deal in an exhaustive manner with each major argument and piece of evidence offered by the losing side. Patently, the arbitrator has an obligation to tell the losing side just why it lost the case. Since normally the losing side will be very disappointed with the decision, the arbitrator should at least indicate in a careful manner the reasons for the adverse ruling. This probably will not make the losing side feel any better, but at least an opinion which is carefully written and which covers thoroughly the major arguments and areas of evidence will demonstrate that the character of an arbitration opinion is a guide to the amount of time, energy, and thought that the arbitrator puts into the case.

Selection of the Arbitrator

After the parties decide to arbitrate a dispute, the problem of the selection of the arbitrator arises. To solve this problem, most labor agreements provide that the parties will select the arbitrator from a panel of names submitted by the above-mentioned Federal Mediation and Conciliation Service or the American Arbitration Association. When called upon by the parties to an arbitration, these agencies will supply the company and the union with a list of names. After the receipt of the panel, the parties, in accordance with a mutually acceptable formula, will select the arbitrator from the list of names. Under some labor agreements the Federal Mediation and Conciliation Service and the American Arbitration Association have the authority to select the arbitrator on a direct-appointment basis in the event that none of the names in the panel is acceptable.

The Federal Mediation and Conciliation Services is administered independently of the Department of Labor under a director appointed by the President of the United States. It maintains a steadily growing roster of experienced professional arbitrators, totalling approximately 1,300 names in 1970. Consistent with the significant growth in arbitration volume in recent years, its requests for approved panels of arbitrators have increased greatly over the past fifteen years: where in fiscal 1955, for example, the service received 1,240 such requests,[9] in fiscal 1970 the parties to agreements sought panels on over 10,000 occasions.[10] Upon the selection of the arbitrator, the service withdraws from active participation in the case and the relationship thereafter is strictly between the parties and the arbitrator.

Unlike the FMCS, the American Arbitration Association is a private organization. In its formative years, it devoted itself almost exclusively to the promotion of commercial arbitration, but since 1937 its Industrial Arbitration Tribunal has become increasingly active in labor disputes and currently has an annual load of about 5,000 cases. In addition to furnishing the parties with arbitrator selection aid similar to that of the Mediation Service, it administers arbitration hearings in accordance with a number of formalized rules. Under AAA provisions, for example, either party intending to use a lawyer must give notice to this effect prior to the hearing date; and the expenses of witnesses for either side are to be paid directly by the party producing such witnesses. The association's panel of available arbitrators currently contains about 1,500 names, although most of the work is actually done by less than 400 active arbitrators.

Other methods are utilized to select arbitrators. Some parties directly contact one of the more than three hundred arbitrators listed in the membership directory of the highly prestigious National Academy of Arbitrators, the major society of the profession and an organization to whose ranks only the most experienced of neutrals are admitted.[11] In some contracts, a person of unimpeachable integrity is designated to select an arbitrator. Under such arrangements the parties have confidence that the person so designated will select a qualified arbitrator. Thus, under some labor agreements, a federal district judge, the president of a university, or a high-ranking public official will be called upon to appoint the arbitrator.

Regardless of the method, the majority of labor contracts provide some definite procedure for the appointment of the arbitrator. At times companies and unions find that in practice they cannot agree on any arbitrator when the contract merely states that an arbitrator "mutually acceptable" to the parties will decide the dispute. It is sound procedure to incorporate some method for the selection of the arbitrators by an outside agency, when the parties are unable or unwilling to agree on an arbitrator on a mutual-acceptance basis.

Some companies and unions solve the problem of selecting the arbitrator by appointing a permanent arbitrator under the terms of a labor

---

[9] Federal Mediation and Conciliation Service, *Seventeenth Annual Report* (Washington, D.C.: Government Printing Office, 1965), p. 55.

[10] *Wall Street Journal*, June 26, 1970, p. 1.

[11] Most of the academy's members are also registered with the Mediation Service and AAA, and can be engaged by the parties on this basis as well.

agreement. Under this arrangement, a single person will decide each dispute that is arbitrated. However, companies and unions are not in agreement on the use of a permanent arbitrator as against the *ad hoc* method of selection in which a different arbitrator may be chosen for each case. Some companies and unions as a matter of policy will use a different arbitrator for each dispute. Other companies and unions find it a better practice to use the same arbitrator. The permanent arbitrator is used most frequently when a company has a number of different plants. Such a procedure makes for uniformity of labor policy within the different operating units of the enterprise. Though the permanent arbitrator is not used as frequently in single-plant situations, there is now also a growing tendency for single-plant companies and their unions to use this system.

On the other hand, the parties should never install a permanent arbitrator unless they anticipate a sufficient number of cases to justify his appointment. One of the authors was some time ago selected as a permanent arbitrator for a six-year period: in this entire length of time, he arbitrated only five grievances!

Actually, there are advantages and disadvantages to each method. Perhaps the chief argument in favor of the *ad hoc* method is that the parties will not be "stuck" with an arbitrator that they do not want. The parties can simply dispense with him if he proves incompetent or otherwise unqualified, though it appears unlikely that a company and a union would have selected such a person to arbitrate on a permanent basis in the first place. Balancing the chief advantage of the *ad hoc* system are several disadvantages. The time and effort required to select an arbitrator for each case delays the rapid disposition of the grievance, sometimes to the detriment of plant morale. At times, out of desperation, a person who has little or no experience or real qualifications is selected to serve as an arbitrator. Such a choice may be made because he is the only person available who has not handed down an award somewhere at some time that the company and the union do not like. Moreover, because each new arbitrator must be educated to the local conditions, a comparatively long period may sometimes be required to conduct the hearing. The arbitrator's fees and expenses, which are typically shared equally by the management and union, must also be considered. The vast majority of all active arbitrators today charge per-diem fees ranging between $175 and $200 and some leading members of the profession charge as much as $350.[12] On

---

[12] These amounts constituted a fairly large increase since 1954. On the other hand, the AAA's executive vice president, in announcing results of a study showing a pronounced upward trend in such fees from 1954 through 1964, appears to have been justified in stating that "the increase has certainly not exceeded the increase in the cost of living since (1954), and in fact the per diem charges of arbitrators appeared to be conservatively related to the necessary training and competence required of similar professions," and the same comments might justifiably be made in reference to more recent years. (See Robert Coulson, "Spring Checkup on Labor Arbitration Procedure," *Labor Law Journal*, May 1965, p. 264.)

this basis, it might conceivably be cheaper for the parties to adopt a permanent arrangement (such extreme cases as the personal experience cited above always excepted) and pay an annual retainer for an arbitrator's services.

Perhaps the chief disadvantage of *ad hoc* arbitration, however, is the fact that this method does not assure consistency in decisions or the application of uniform principles to contract construction. No arbitrator is bound by any other arbitrator's decisions or principles of contractual construction. Consequently, disputes involving fundamentally the same issues could be resolved in as many different ways as there were arbitrators chosen to decide cases. Thus, there is no assurance that a particular decision will bring stability to labor relations. It may have precedent value only until the next time the issues involved in the case are tested before another arbitrator.

The latter consideration indicates the greatest advantage of the *permanent* method of selection of arbitrators. The parties have the assurance of consistency and uniformity of decisions and consistent contractual interpretation. As a result, precedent will be established, the parties will know what to expect, and cases dealing with essentially the same issues as contained in a grievance which has previously been decided in arbitration can be settled in the earlier stages of the grievance procedure. In addition, the permanent arbitrator becomes familiar with the labor agreement, the technology of the plant, and the "shop language." This means that cases can frequently be expedited much more effectively than under circumstances of *ad hoc* arbitration.

Perhaps the chief *disadvantage* of the permanent selection method is that the parties involved may tend to arbitrate more disputes than are absolutely necessary, rather than first exhausting the possibilities of settling disputes in the grievance procedure. This is particularly true when the arbitrator is paid a set fee for a year and has the obligation to arbitrate any and all cases submitted to him.

This possibility, of course, is a serious charge against the permanent method of selection. As stated before, arbitration should be employed only after the parties have honestly exhausted every possibility of settling disputes in the grievance procedure. One method that might be effective in obtaining the advantages of the permanent method without incurring the possible disadvantages of excessive arbitration would be to compensate the *permanent* arbitrator on a *per-diem* or a *per-case basis* rather than on an annual-fee basis. In the last analysis, however, the amount of arbitration needed by a company and a union depends upon the attitudes of the parties rather than on the method of selection or the procedure of payment.

DISCUSSION QUESTIONS

1. Barbash has offered his opinion that the "handling of workers' grievances on the job is perhaps the single most important function of modern unionism." What considerations might have led to such a statement?
2. It is generally agreed that a low grievance rate does not necessarily prove the existence of good union-management relations, and that a high grievance rate does not necessarily prove the existence of poor relations between the parties. Why might the grievance statistics be misleading as a guide to the quality of the relationship?
3. From the company's viewpoint, what advantages and disadvantages might there be in reducing a grievance to writing?
4. Harold W. Davey has argued that "a genuine grievance requires an airing, even if it is not strictly in order under the existing contract." What considerations, again from the company's point of view, might justify this opinion?
5. Why might (a) a company or (b) a union prefer *not* to have an arbitration provision in the contract?
6. Dunlop and Healy have pointed out that although it is often said that "arbitration is an extension of collective bargaining," it is also frequently held that "arbitration is a judicial process." What are your own feelings regarding these two apparently inconsistent descriptions?
7. Given the fact that arbitrators have no compulsion to follow any other arbitrator's award or line of reasoning, how do you account for the fact that there are available at least three widely distributed publications which feature arbitration awards from all over the country? On the surface, would it not appear that such publications are a waste of time and money, since each arbitrator is in effect a "law unto himself"?
8. How could the present system of labor contract administration, as described in general terms in this chapter, be improved?

SELECTED REFERENCES

Davey, Harold W., *Contemporary Collective Bargaining*, 2nd ed. Englewood Cliffs, N. J.: Prentice-Hall, Inc., 1959, pp. 117–56.

Elkouri, Frank, and Edna Elkouri, *How Arbitration Works*. Washington, D.C.: Bureau of National Affairs, Inc., 1960.

Fleming, R. W., *The Labor Arbitration Process*. Urbana, Ill.: University of Illinois Press, 1965.

Prasow, Paul, and Edward Peters, *Arbitration and Collective Bargaining*. New York: McGraw-Hill Book Company, 1970.

Slichter, Sumner H., James J. Healy, and E. Robert Livernash, *The Impact of Collective Bargaining on Management*. Washington, D.C.: The Brookings Institution, 1960, pp. 692–806.

Smith, Russell A., "The Question of 'Arbitrability'—The Roles of the Arbitrator, the Court, and the Parties," *Southwestern Law Journal*, XVI (April 1962), 1–42.

Stone, Morris, *Labor Grievances and Decisions*. New York: Harper & Row, Publishers, 1965.

——, *Labor-Management Contracts at Work.* New York: Harper & Row, Publishers, 1961.
Trotta, Maurice S., *Labor Arbitration.* New York: Simmons-Boardman Publishing Corporation, 1961.
Witte, Edwin E., *Historical Survey of Labor Arbitration.* Philadelphia: University of Pennsylvania Press, 1952.

> As in the ten other cases which follow in subsequent chapters, the two arbitration cases below are drawn from the authors' own experiences. They are intended to shed further light on specific problems which can arise under collective bargaining and not to indicate the "appropriate" award for the specific controversy: other arbitrators would, perhaps, have ruled differently in many of these cases. To preserve anonymity, the names of companies, unions, grievants, and witnesses have been concealed, but otherwise each case is based completely on an actual situation.

CASE NO. 1

TIME LIMITS UNDER GRIEVANCE PROCEDURE

(The facts of the following case show that the grievant took a leave of absence to attend to union affairs. When his work with the union was completed, he applied to the company to return to his job. The company refused him re-employment. The arbitration case deals with the problem of whether or not the union submitted his grievance to arbitration within the time limits established by the labor agreement.

It should be noted that the arbitrator does not deal with the case's *merits,* limiting himself instead to the question of time limits. If he were to find that the demand for arbitration *was* timely, he would in *another* hearing deal with the merits of the grievance.)

On January 25, 1962, *C* filed the following grievance:

> Employee *C* on December 28, 1961, applied for re-employment with *A* Company. In a letter to Employee *C* dated January 11, 1962, the Company refused re-employment to *C* and advised him that his services with the Company were terminated.
>
> The Union contends that the Company in its refusal violated Article V, Section 2, specifically, and other pertinent sections of the Working Agreement.
>
> The Union and Employee *C* request that he *C* be re-employed consistent with the provisions of Article V, Section 2. It is further requested that Employee *C* be made whole for all benefits of employment with *A* Company, retroactive to date of application for re-employment.

RELEVANT PROVISIONS OF CONTRACT

ARTICLE XIII, Section 3, Step 4

In the event the Company and the Union are not able to adjust a grievance concerning a question of fact in dispute under the procedure above provided for, during the term of this Working Agreement, and that dispute is not settled by the Grievance Procedure, the grievance of dispute shall, on the written demand of either party, be submitted to arbitration within twenty (20) days from the date of the disposition referred to in Step 3. For the purpose of such arbitration, there shall be established for the particular grievance dispute an Arbitration Board consisting of one (1) person selected by the Company, one (1) person selected by the Union, these two to be selected within five (5) days of receipt of demand for arbitration, and a third person to be impartial chairman of this Board, to be selected by these two. In the event the appointees of the Company and the Union are unable to agree within five (5) days upon such third and impartial member of the Board, such third member shall be appointed by the following procedure.

THE BACKGROUND

This dispute is concerned with the timeliness of the union's demand to submit the grievance to arbitration. No inquiry is made relevant to the merits of the case. The arbitrator is not authorized to determine whether under the circumstances of the case the company violated Article V, Section 2, of the labor agreement as charged in the complaint. In fact, the arbitrator did not hear any of the evidence dealing with the merits of the case. Testimony and documents adduced in the arbitration dealt solely with the timeliness issue. However, the parties agreed that the instant arbitrator will hear the grievance on its merits if he finds in this proceeding that the Union's request for arbitration is timely.

As demonstrated in the chronology of the grievance, the complaint was filed originally on January 25, 1962. The parties waived the first step of the grievance procedure. On January 29, the company denied the grievance in step 2 of the grievance procedure. Subsequently the company and union held a meeting in accordance with the step 3 requirement of the grievance procedure. In this meeting, held on February 1, 1962, the parties discussed several grievances and problems, including the one involving the instant grievant. The minutes of the meeting were introduced as Union Exhibit No. 1. Relevant to the instant complaint, these minutes state as follows:

Grievance: Union Leave

The Union contends a violation of Article V, Section 2, paragraph D of the Working Agreement when *C* was denied re-employment. The

Union stated that at the time C was granted his leave he was placed on loan from the International Union and to the knowledge of the local Union C is still in the employ of the Union and entitled to re-employment. If the Company denies his request the Union will submit the grievance to arbitration.

On February 5, 1962, the company denied the instant grievance. This action constituted a denial in step 3 of the grievance procedure. Subsequently, the union wrote a letter to the company and demanded to arbitrate the employee's grievance. Such letter was dated February 26, 1962, and provides in part as follows: "Local 4-467 would like to arbitrate their disputes with the Company in the following cases; (1) the Employee Relation grievance involving C..." This letter, accepted in evidence as Company Exhibit No. 1, was handed by an officer of the union to Mr. J, manager of the company's Employee Relations Division, on February 27, 1962.

On March 1, 1962, the company wrote a letter to the union, accepted in evidence as Company Exhibit No. 2, to the effect that the company "is not required nor will it agree to submitting [this grievance] to arbitration" because of "the untimeliness of the Union's request to arbitrate [this grievance]."

BASIC QUESTION

The basic question in this case is framed as follows: Under the circumstances of this case, did the union comply with the provisions of the labor agreement establishing the time limits for arbitration?

POSITION OF THE PARTIES

It is the union's contention that the grievance should be regarded as timely for purposes of arbitration. In this respect it argues that the union demonstrated its clear intent to arbitrate the grievance and refers in this connection to Union Exhibit No. 1. Thus, it states: "We say that on February 1, 1962, as in the Company minutes of the meeting, this intent was made evident. The inclusion of Paragraph 7 shows clearly this intent. We feel that by this inclusion it was the intent of the Union to submit the issue to arbitration and any other indication of the Union to the Company does not waive the right of the Union to arbitration. If the Union renotified the Company of its intent, it merely restated its original intent." The union also contends that it made clear its intent to arbitrate the C grievance upon other occasions.

Another argument of the union involves the fact that February 24 was a Saturday, and February 25 was a Sunday. On this point the union claims that on Saturdays and Sundays there are no representatives of the company's labor relations staff available, and, therefore, "there would have been no point in bringing the letter [Company Exhibit No. 1] to the Labor Relations Department on Saturday or Sunday."

Further, the union claims that: "the written demand for arbitration was made evident by the Union's intent to arbitrate—this in itself lives up to the written demand request of the contract"; the company itself upon occasions in the past did not meet the time limits which the contract imposes on it, and the company despite such untimely conduct did not forfeit grievances; and the grievance procedure is "an amicable means to an end."

On these grounds the union claims that the request for arbitration should be regarded as timely within the meaning of the aforementioned provisions of the labor agreement.

The company claims that the request for arbitration was not timely, and, therefore, the grievance should be dismissed. Thus it states: "It is apparent that from the dates involved the request was not timely." Further, the company argues that its representatives never waived its right to invoke the time limit of the contract; the union oral declaration of its intent to arbitrate does not nullify the relevant contractual provisions; that the contract requires written notice to arbitrate and that the union did not comply with this mandate within the 20-day standard established in Article XIII, Section 3, step 4. On this basis the company requests the dismissal of the grievance.

ANALYSIS OF THE EVIDENCE

Union Intent to Arbitrate

There is no question that the union demonstrated its intent to arbitrate the C case. This intention is made apparent not only by the declaration which it made in the meeting of February 1, 1962, but by other discussions with company representatives. For example, even before the February 1, 1962, meeting, a union officer testified that "I told the Company that this case would have to go to arbitration." On another occasion, a union officer testified that the union was willing "to waive all the intermediary steps in the Grievance Procedure and proceed directly to arbitration." Indeed, the company itself was aware that the union would undoubtedly arbitrate the C complaint. J testified in this respect that "the Company recognized that this case would probably be arbitrated." Also, H, employee relations assistant, testified that "he believed that they would arbitrate the grievance."

Accordingly, the question is whether this clear intent of the union to arbitrate supersedes the undeniable fact that the union failed to comply with the time limit established in the labor agreement. As stated, the company denied the grievance in the third step of the grievance procedure on February 5, 1962. Under the provisions of Article XIII, Section 3, step 4, the union had 20 days to file a written demand for arbitration. Therefore, the time limit expired on February 25. However, the letter demanding arbitration which the union filed with the company is dated February 26, and the document was not received by the company until February 27. On the basis of these circumstances, there is no dispute that the union did not meet the time requirements agreed to by the parties in negotiations and solemnized in the labor agreement.

Written Demand within 20 Days Required

In considering the union's position that its demonstrated intent to arbitrate the grievance amounts to making its demand for arbitration timely, it is necessary to make reference to the language of step 4 of the grievance procedure. Here we find a simple, understandable, and reasonable standard of obligation written in unambiguous and unequivocal language, to which both parties agreed: The union has 20 days to file a written demand for arbitration after a grievance is denied in step 3. It says nothing about the intent to arbitrate. Rather, the parties voluntarily agreed in collective bargaining negotiations that a *written demand* must be made within *20* days after the company denies a grievance in step 3. If the parties had desired to waive this 20-day period when the union shows its intent to arbitrate, they would, of course, have adopted appropriate language to provide for this state of affairs.

In the last analysis, what the union requests is that the arbitrator shut his eyes to most clear-cut contractual language. It wants him to forget about the 20-day limitation to which the union itself agreed, and find its request to arbitrate as timely because the Union had announced its intent to arbitrate. For the arbitrator to follow this procedure would result in his rewriting of the labor agreement. Certainly, these parties, skilled and knowledgeable in labor relations, must recognize that no arbitrator is authorized to rewrite contractual language. In this case the union in effect states: Forget about clear-cut contractual language and find our request timely because we demonstrated our intention to arbitrate. Under other circumstances, would the union be content with a decision in which this arbitrator would deny an absolutely valid grievance based upon clear-cut contractual language because the company did not "intend" to violate the labor agreement? The answer to this question should be obvious to all concerned. These considerations also demonstrate the evils that can result in labor relations and to the rights of employees, employers, and labor organizations when an arbitrator simply ignores clear-cut and unambiguous contractual language.

This arbitrator does not treat contractual language which secures rights or imposes obligations in a cavalier manner. He does not believe that such language ought to be adhered to in some cases but disregarded in others. He does not believe that plain contract language should be ignored, twisted, distorted, or amended depending upon the circumstances and the expediencies of a particular case. In short, either the parties have a contract that must be honored *under all circumstances,* or else they do not have a collective bargaining contract.

Surely, this agreement between the parties must be honored in this proceeding. If the parties did not intend that the union forfeit its right to arbitrate when it does not comply with the time limit in question, they would not have incorporated an unambiguous time limit in their labor agreement. Why put a precise time limit in the contract if the union may implement the arbitration process after the time limit has expired?

Oral Declaration of Intent Does Not Comply with Contractual Standard

These considerations make wholly unacceptable the union's argument herein considered. *Oral* declaration of the intent to arbitrate simply does not constitute a *written demand* for arbitration as established by the literal language of step 4. Announcement of the intent to arbitrate is not sufficient. It is clear beyond any reasonable doubt that step 4 requires a *written* demand for arbitration. Such a demand to be timely under step 4 must be served on the company *within 20 days* after the company denies a grievance in step 3 of the grievance procedure.

Of course, the union argues that the minutes of the February 1, 1962, meeting amount to a written demand to the company within the meaning of step 4. Beyond the fact that as of February 1, the company did not yet dispose of the grievance in step 3, this position is rejected because these minutes merely reflect the union's oral declaration of intention to arbitrate. The minutes do not constitute a written demand made by the union on the company to arbitrate. This union argument would be more convincing to this arbitrator if it demonstrated that in the past the union demanded arbitration in this fashion. Undoubtedly, the practice has been that the union files a *written demand* on the company to arbitrate, and this written demand is in the form of a letter and not in the form of the minutes of grievance meetings.

Beyond these considerations is the conduct of the union itself subsequent to February 1, 1962, and subsequent to other occasions on which it orally announced its intention to arbitrate. If the union really believed that these oral declarations satisfied the requirements of step 4, how does one account for the fact that the union on February 26 did write a letter to demand arbitration? Why write the letter if oral declaration of intent is sufficient? Surely, the union recognized that such oral declaration was not sufficient, because it wrote the letter of February 26.

In this respect the union explains away the letter of February 26 by stating that it was a mere renotification of the union's demand to arbitrate, which, it argues, was timely made under the contract on

February 1, 1962. Frankly, this is not a convincing argument because why need there be renotification if the February 1, 1962, declaration of intention was timely and in the form required by step 4? Further, the union explanation ignores the heart of the problem herein considered. What did the letter of February 26 renotify? It did not renotify a *written demand* for arbitration because the declaration of the union in the February 1, 1962 meeting merely expressed an oral intention to arbitrate. And it has already been established that oral declaration of the intent to arbitrate does not measure up to the *written* obligation required in step 4. Therefore, if the letter of February 26 "renotified" anything, *it renotified the oral intention* of the union to arbitrate which in itself did not measure up to the standards of step 4.

In short, the letter of February 26 was the union's first attempt to demand arbitration in the form spelled out in step 4. Previous declarations of intent, including those of February 1, 1962, which were reproduced as part of the minutes of the grievance meeting, do not fulfill the standards established in the labor agreement.

"Saturday-Sunday" Argument Rejected

The union now argues an entirely different position in the effort to gain a favorable award in this proceeding. Thus, in effect, it instructs the arbitrator as follows: If you do not find that oral declaration of intent to arbitrate is sufficient to comply with the requirement of step 4, and if you do not find the minutes of February 1 as constituting a written demand under step 4, the union advises the arbitrator that February 24 was a Saturday and February 25 was a Sunday. Therefore, you should find the demand for arbitration as contained in the letter of February 26 as timely on this basis.

The arbitrator does not find this argument as an adequate excuse to explain why the union was late in filing its written demand for arbitration. Though it is, of course, true that February 24 and 25 were, respectively, a Saturday and a Sunday, and that members of the company's labor relations staff were not available on these two days, how does one account for the fact that the union did not avail itself of the opportunity to demand arbitration from February 5 until February 25? *Here were 20 full calendar days wherein the union could have complied with the simple task of filing a written demand for arbitration.* Still, during this entire period the union did not take advantage of its right to demand arbitration.

Furthermore, this "Saturday-Sunday" argument of the union is not convincing to the arbitrator because the parties fully intended that Saturdays, Sundays, and holidays are to be counted in computing the 20 days in which arbitration can be demanded after the company denies a complaint in step 3. This is true because the parties expressly *excluded* Saturdays, Sundays, and holidays from the calculation of the time period in which a grievance may be filed in the *first* step of the grievance procedure. Surely, if the parties had intended to exclude Saturdays and Sundays in the calculation of the 20 days under step 4 they would have adopted language similar to that found in step 1 of the grievance procedure. Since they did not do so, the clear intent of the parties is that the 20-day period constitutes calendar days which, of necessity, include Saturdays, Sundays, and holidays. Such omission cannot possibly be regarded as an oversight on their part when they specifically excluded these days from the calculation of time limits in the first step of the grievance procedure.

Company Did Not Waive Time Limits

If the company had expressly or tacitly waived the 20-day time limit in question, the case could be decided upon its merits. But the record is clear that the company did no such thing. In fact, a union official testified that "*J* did not say that he agreed to arbitrate"; and another union official testified that "I don't say that the company said that it would waive the written agreement."

Apparently the union does suggest that the company did waive the time limits under the circumstances of this case. This argument proceeds from the fact that the parties agreed to waive step 1 of the grievance procedure. However, the company's willingness to waive step 1 cannot possibly be construed to mean that it thereby waived all other requirements of the grievance procedure. This is so obvious that there is no need of further comment.

Also, the union suggests that the company waived the time limits because it was aware that the union intended to arbitrate the case, but that the company insisted that the parties go through the "formalities" of the grievance procedure. Thus, a union official testified: "*J* said 'we understand that you will have to arbitrate this case, but let's go through the formalities of the Grievance Procedure.'" Though this may be perfectly true, the arbitrator still does not see how this condition resulted in the company's waiver of the time limits. To repeat, it was the testimony of union officials that the company did not say at any time during the negotiations that "it would waive the written agreement."

Finally, the record is perfectly clear that after the union failed to meet the contractual time limits, the company refused to arbitrate the case on its merits. Its letter to the union on March 1, 1962 [Company Exhibit No. 2], and its subsequent action demonstrates without question that the company did not explicitly or implicitly waive the 20-day time limit wherein the union had the opportunity to demand arbitration.

Past Practice: Evidence Not Adequate

To buttress its case, the union argues that there were other instances wherein the company and union filed untimely grievances which nevertheless were decided on their merits. Thus a union official testified:

I recall instances in the past when other untimely acts were committed by the Union and Company. There have been times when the Company has not met the time limits of the contract. I remember once when the Company was considerably late in their answer and this Union wrote a letter to the Company about this. Since the Company was not timely, we asked whether the Company believed that the lateness meant that the Company considered the grievance granted. But the Company stated it made an honest mistake, and it was not going to grant the grievance on this basis.

Herein the union admittedly raises a significant point, and if the evidence were adequate it could have had an important bearing upon this case. But it is quite clear that the aforementioned statement does not amount to the kind of evidence which is convincing in arbitration. Specific instances are not mentioned wherein acts of untimeliness were committed. The grievances are not cited; the circumstances are not mentioned; and the dates are not spelled out.

Instead, the statement constitutes a vague generalization. Indeed, the company could not have defended itself against such ambiguous generalizations since the particulars are not spelled out. If the union desired to make a convincing point of such alleged past practice, it had the obligation to cite the particulars and the exact circumstances. In short, it would be entirely improper to base a decision on the kind of evidence which the union offers in this respect. After all, arbitration is a judicial process, and requires evidence which is concrete, precise, and definite. These standards are obviously not met, and, therefore, the arbitrator cannot possibly use such vague and ambiguous testimony as the basis for his decision.

Union Failed to Comply with Time Limit

No matter how one regards the circumstances of this case, it simply is not possible to find the union's demand for arbitration to be timely under the labor agreement. The only way that this can be done would be for the arbitrator to shut his eyes to the words "20 days" and "written demand" spelled out in step 4 of the grievance procedure. Such conduct on his part would be wholly indefensible and would amount to a breach of the obligations of his office.

Of course, the arbitrator understands that the union in this case probably made an innocent error—an error, however, which cannot be overlooked in arbitration. The union had a clear obligation to demand arbitration in *writing* and *within 20 days*. The hard and cold fact is that it did not meet this obligation, and regardless of the valiant attempt which the union made in this proceeding, this failure on its part cannot be ignored or explained away. Rather, the failure of the union to comply with the contractually stated time limits must stand as the determining feature in this proceeding.

Precedents

The issue involved in this case is not a novel one in arbitration. Many cases have been decided wherein the question of timeliness of the filing of grievances and demands for arbitration have been involved. In this respect, professional and seasoned arbitrators have normally denied grievances wherein unions have failed to meet clearly defined time limits. Thus, as stated in a standard volume on arbitration: "If the agreement does contain clear time limits for filing and prosecuting grievances, failure to observe them generally will result in a dismissal of the grievance if the failure is protested."[13] Many arbitration decisions underscore this principle in arbitration:

International Harvester, 10 LA 525 (1948)[14]
Northeast Airlines, 37 LA 741 (1961)
Valley Dolomite, 11 LA 98 (1948)
Barbet Mills, 19 LA 677 (1952)
Phillips Petroleum, 7 LA 595 (1947)
Jones & Laughlin Steel Corp., 17 LA 277 (1951)
Tim Processing Corp., 26 LA 732 (1956)
Bethlehem Steel Co., 6 LA 397 (1947)
Standard-Coosa-Thatcher Co., 4 LA 79 (1946)
Southeastern Greyhound Lines, 4 LA 459 (1946)
Kaiser Aluminum & Chemical Co., 32 LA 704 (1959)
Kroger Co., 36 LA 270 (1960)
Olin Mathieson Chemical Corp., 37 LA 588 (1961)
West Penn Power Co., 31 LA 297 (1958)
Square D Co., 25 LA 225 (1955)
Truitt Manufacturing Co., 27 LA 157 (1956)
Walker County Hosiery Mills, 13 LA 387 (1949)
Bauer Bros., 15 LA 318 (1950)
Walter Kiddie & Co., 16 LA 369 (1951)

A review of these precedents demonstrates that many of them were decided by respected and seasoned arbitrators, including Ralph Seward, Peter Kelliher, and Whitley McCoy; several of them involved cases wherein employees were terminated from their jobs; and in some cases the union failure to comply with time limits amounted to a very short period of time. Thus, in *Olin Mathieson Chemical Corp.,* 37 LA 588 (1961), which involved the discharge of an employee, the arbitrator in that case dismissed the grievance because the labor organization was two days late in complying with grievance procedure time limits.

These precedents are cited to show that the arbitrator's decision

---

[13] Elkouri, *op. cit.,* p. 105.
[14] Bureau of National Affairs, ed., *Labor Arbitration Reports,* X (Washington, D.C.: Bureau of National Affairs, Inc., 1948), 525.

in this case is in keeping with an accepted principle of labor arbitration. He understands, of course, that these precedents are not binding upon him, but still it is very significant that arbitrators have established the principle that failure of unions to comply with clear-cut time limits results in forfeiture of the right to arbitrate grievances on their merits.

To be sure, there have been some instances wherein arbitrators have found grievances to be timely submitted over the protest of the company. In these cases, however, there were involved extenuating or special circumstances which prompted the arbitrators to hold the grievances to be timely. For example, in *Levinson Steel,* 23 LA 135, the arbitrator held that the United States Post Office was responsible for the union's failure to meet the time limits; in *Lapham-Hickey,* 3 LA 327, the arbitrator found that the company waived time limits by its action of discussing the case on its merits *after* time limits had run out, and did not mention time limits during these negotiations; and in *United States Pipe and Foundry,* 28 LA 777, the issue was found to be arbitrable because time limits in the contract were ambiguous. Clearly, the circumstances of the instant proceeding are distinguishable from these cases.

CONCLUSIONS AND AWARD

The arbitrator is fully aware of the significance of his decision. What it means is that C cannot get his job back, and he cannot even have the benefit of an arbitration hearing wherein the merits of his case can be determined. Unless the company, despite this decision, elects to arbitrate the C case on its merits, the employee's job is terminated. Naturally, the arbitrator is sympathetic to the grievant. After all, it wasn't the grievant who caused his complaint to be dismissed without even so much as a hearing to examine its merits.

The arbitrator is frank enough to state that he reaches his decision with real and deep regret. He would have preferred to hear the case on its merits, since here we have an employee terminated, not because of the substance of his claim, but because of a procedural issue.

Further, the arbitrator passes no judgment on the wisdom of the company's insistence that the grievance be dismissed because of the failure of the union to comply with contractual time limits. As the union states, the grievance procedure is designed to promote the "amicable" disposition of disputes arising between the parties. What the union really is saying is that the dismissal of this grievance on the basis of time limits does not resolve the actual problem which gave rise to the dispute in the first place, and, further, it suggests that the real purpose of the grievance procedure is not effectuated by the company's stand in this proceeding.

Still the fact remains that the arbitrator cannot find in the evidence that the union's demand for arbitration was timely within the meaning of the labor agreement. Since it was not timely, the union forfeited the right of the grievant to have his case heard on its merits. The arbitrator is bound by the written labor agreement which the parties negotiated. Part of this agreement is the requirement that the union demand arbitration *in writing within 20 days* after a grievance is denied in step 3 of the grievance procedure. Regardless of how one looks at the evidence in this case, the cold and hard fact is that the union did not comply with this precise and clear-cut statement. Since it did not comply, this arbitrator has no choice except to deny the grievance. The alternative would be for the arbitrator to blatantly disregard a clear-cut contractual standard, voluntarily agreed to by the union and the company. Such conduct on his part would amount to the forfeiture of the trust and faith reposed in him by the parties and to a repudiation of the best and accepted standards of arbitration.

After carefully considering the evidence, including the relevant provisions of the labor agreement, and in his best judgment, the arbitrator makes the following award:

The grievance of *C*, dated January 25, 1962, is denied on the grounds that the union's demand for arbitration was not timely within the meaning of Article XIII, Section 3, step 4 of the labor agreement.

QUESTIONS

1. How would *you* have decided the case? Justify your decision with cogent arguments.
2. Would the integrity of the time limits included in the labor agreement be jeopardized if the decision went for the Union?
3. Should a discharged employee be denied a hearing on the merits of his case because someone in a union does not comply with time limits established in a contract?

CASE NO. 2

ARBITRABILITY OF GRIEVANCE

(In this case, decided long after the Supreme Court's decisions in the "Trilogy" cases, the arbitrator was asked to rule whether or not the issue was arbitrable on its merits, and whether the grievance had or had not been properly processed under the grievance procedure. The case involves a distinguished symphony orchestra and the union representing its musicians. As you read it, you may want to speculate as to why the musicians did not file a grievance, and why the union filed one on their behalf.)

Involved in this case is the claim by the union that the association should pay orchestra members *G* and *J*, contracted flutists, a so-called "doubling fee" for a concert played by the symphony orchestra on November 30, 1968. When the association refused to make this payment, the union filed a grievance dated December 16, 1968, which states:

> This is to call your attention to the fact that G and J have not received doubling pay for playing piccolo at the concert of November 30.

The association denied the union's claim on the grounds that under the circumstances of the dispute the doubling fee is not warranted, and further on the grounds that the grievance was not properly filed under the relevant provisions of the grievance procedure.

Relevant to the dispute are the following provisions of the labor agreement:

ARTICLE II

Section 2.3. The parties also recognize that members of the Federation are subject to all rules and regulations of the union as now in effect.

ARTICLE XII

Section 12.1. Any member of the Orchestra is entitled to be represented by the Union in the presentation and processing of any complaint which he may have relating to his employment.

Section 12.2. During the term of this Agreement, both parties shall, if either party so requests, discuss and attempt to agree upon improvements in the existing procedures for handling such grievances (and for handling any grievances which the Union, as an entity, may file, claiming a violation of the Union's rights as an entity under the Agreement, as distinguished from the rights of individual members). At present, the parties have agreed to continue the existing procedures which include:

> *Step A.* An initial informal discussion for the purpose of enabling the member to present the complaint, and, if possible, to resolve the problem immediately. It is agreed that the number of participants in this informal discussion should be limited, so as not to unduly prolong the process of adjustment. The persons present at such a discussion should be the grievant himself, a Union representative, if he so requests, and the General Manager of the Symphony Orchestra or a representative of the Orchestra's management designated by him. The Union will notify the General Manager of the Orchestra of the name of the person authorized by the Union to serve as the representative for any particular case.
>
> *Step B.* In any case in which such a conference demonstrates that the complaint includes a difference of opinion as to the proper interpretation of the Collective Bargaining Agreement, or involves a discharge or the non-renewal of a member's contract of employment, and the grievant is not satisfied with any adjustment reached, additional review procedures will be available, provided that the grievant promptly (in no case later than one week from the first discussion unless otherwise mutually agreed) submits to the Manager a written statement of his grievance containing a brief description

of the nature of the complaint. Upon receipt of such a written grievance, the Manager shall prepare the Association's written answer to the grievance and promptly submit a copy of the same to both the grievant and the Union....

ARTICLE XVII

Section 17.3. Doubling: A player who is called upon and agrees to play an extra instrument in any week will receive in addition to his regular salary twenty-five dollars ($25.00) per performance for that work week. This price includes all rehearsals necessary for said performance(s). Each of the following shall be considered a separate instrument:

flute

Instruments not herein mentioned shall be considered separate, and doubling fees shall be paid.

THE BACKGROUND

This dispute arises as a result of a concert played by the symphony orchestra on November 30, 1968. On the day of the concert, *L*, personnel manager of the symphony orchestra, posted a list of encores scheduled for the performance. One of the scheduled encores was "The Stars and Stripes Forever." As *N*, union steward, testified:

Q. This encore listing, which included "The Stars and Stripes Forever," was posted on what day?
A. On the day of the concert.

Also, *N* testified that the number was not rehearsed.

When "The Stars and Stripes" is played by the symphony, the flutists not only play their own instruments but also at appropriate times play the piccolo. Under the labor agreement, this is known as "doubling." In this respect, *N* testified:

Q. What is doubling?
A. Doubling is a case where a man who is contracted to play a specific instrument, such as Mr. *G* and Mr. *J* were contracted to play the flute and getting paid for playing the flute only, these people—
Q. They are basically contracted as flutists, is that correct?
A. As flutists. In some cases where a piece calls for another instrument, these people, if they happen to play that instrument, are asked to play that instrument also, with the proper fees payment for that instrument at the end of the week. In this case, it was the piccolo.

Thus, *G* and *J*, contracted as flutists, were alerted on the day of the concert that "The Stars and Stripes" was scheduled for an encore, and that in keeping with customary procedures they would be expected to play the piccolo as well as the flute.

It so happened, however, that the piece was not played in the concert. Apparently, it was not played because the reaction of the audience did not warrant the playing of the number as an encore. In any event, "The Stars and Stripes" was not played, and G and J did not actually play the piccolo. On this basis, the association refused to pay them the doubling fee provided for in Article XVII, Section 17.3 of the labor agreement.

G and J, the flutists involved, did not file a grievance requesting the doubling fee. Rather, it was the union which filed a claim for the doubling fee. As union counsel states: (T. 8)

> I will point out, as I understand the facts, that neither of the flutists... are present today or are otherwise participant in this grievance, except as they are involved through the grievance as filed by the Union as a whole.

BASIC QUESTIONS

The basic questions involved in this proceeding are framed as follows:

1. Is the grievance arbitrable under Article XII of the labor agreement?
2. If it is arbitrable, did the association violate Article XVII, Section 17.3 under the circumstances of this case?

PARTIES' ARGUMENT

With respect to the issue of arbitrability, the union contends that the grievance is properly before the arbitrator for decision on its merits. In this respect, union counsel argues:

> Although the Association seeks to evade its obligation under the contract by taking refuge in a procedural question, the Union submits that the procedural question provides no shelter for the Association. It is true that neither G nor J filed grievances in their own behalf, but the Union is charged under the law with the protection of the rights of *all* members of the Orchestra and, if the Arbitrator permits the Association to avoid the merit question in this case, the Association will then be in a position where it can argue in any ensuing similar grievance that such grievants have no right to doubling fees because in this grievance none were found to be due.
> The Union submits that if a member of the Union is reluctant to pursue his rights or concludes not to pursue them, such action should not militate against the rights of other members of the Orchestra. The Union is deeply concerned that if it does not protect the doubling fee rights to the full extent of the contract for these employees, it will tend to erode the rights of other members of the Orchestra similarly situated.
> The Union therefore submits that with or without grievances filed

by the individuals directly involved, the Union may nevertheless process such grievance as a general grievance. The rights of every member of the Orchestra are involved when the rights of any individual are impaired.

On the other hand, the association believes that under the relevant contractual language, the grievance is not properly before the arbitrator and should be dismissed without any inquiry as to its merits. In defense of this position, association counsel contends that

> in the instant case, neither of the flutists made any complaint, filed any grievance, participated in any informal discussion, or filed any written statement of the grievance asking for an appeal to Step B. There is, therefore, no proper grievance before the Arbitrator for decision.

Beyond the issue of arbitrability, the parties are also in disagreement on the merits of the grievance. In his argument that the grievance has merit, union counsel stated:

> During the concert in question, both flutists brought to the stage their piccolos and were prepared to play them if the encore was performed. The contract language clearly calls for payment of the doubling fee under such circumstances, and the Union submits that the *playing is not the criterion* for payment but rather the criterion for payment is in *being prepared* and *required* under direction from the Personnel Manager to play such instrument. It follows that had the flutists not been prepared to play the piccolo in the encore, they would have seriously failed in their duty and may have even been subject to disciplinary action for the failure to perform required duties.

In contrast, association counsel argues:

> The very simple answer to the grievance, on the merits, is that the two flutists did not perform the services for which doubling pay is intended as compensation, did not earn any doubling compensation, and therefore were properly paid no doubling compensation.
> Only an artifically strained reading of the provisions of Section 17.3 could produce the result contended for by the Union. A fair reading of the section reveals that the $25.00 per performance amount is intended to compensate the musician for performing a special service. If he does not perform that service, surely it cannot be said that he has earned his pay.

Additional comments and arguments of counsel, if required and appropriate, will be made in the subsequent portion of this opinion.

ANALYSIS OF THE EVIDENCE

The Issue of Arbitrability

Before the arbitrator may reach the merits of the grievance, it is first necessary to determine whether or not the grievance is properly before him for decision on the substance of the claim. An arbitrator may not make a determination on the merits of a grievance unless it has been properly processed through the grievance procedure. Hence the first obligation is to find whether or not under the relevant contractual language the grievance has standing before the arbitrator.

In this respect, it is incontrovertible, of course, that the orchestra members involved, *G* and *J*, are not a party to the grievance. They did not file a grievance; did not participate in any step of the grievance procedure; and failed to appear at the arbitration hearing. Whatever their reason for not participating in the grievance, it is of no importance for purposes of this case. Whether out of mere neglect, fear, or believing that they had no valid claim under the doubling fee provision, the fact remains that the flutists at no time exercised rights they have under the grievance procedure. Instead, the union itself instigated the grievance, processed it through all steps of the grievance procedure, and elected to invoke the arbitration process.

It is not uncommon in labor relations for labor organizations to file grievances on behalf of employees. This occurs where the labor agreement itself provides for such filing, or where the employer raises no objections. Hence, what is involved in this case is not the novelty of the union filing a grievance on behalf of the two musicians involved, but whether or not under the relevant contractual language, the union may properly file a grievance on their behalf.

Unambiguous Grievance Procedure Language

Unless the arbitrator wishes to undermine the integrity of the grievance procedure, agreed to by the parties and incorporated in plain and unequivocal contractual language, he must find that the grievance has not been properly processed in the grievance procedure. Since this is the case, the grievance has no standing under the arbitration clause.

Throughout the entire grievance procedure the parties placed certain obligations upon musicians who wish to protest against actions of the association. In step A it is stated:

> An initial informal discussion for the purpose of enabling the member to present the complaint.... The persons present at such discussion should be limited to the grievant himself, a Union representative, if he so requests, the General Manager of the Symphony Orchestra...

The key words are, of course, that the *member* presents his complaint, and the *grievant himself* should be present at the discussion contemplated by the first step of the grievance procedure. *G* and *J* neither presented their claim, nor did they attend the discussion established under step A of the grievance procedure. They had an opportunity to do so, but failed to exercise the right afforded them under the grievance procedure.

Here the language is clear-cut, unambiguous, and unequivocal. The orchestra member must originate his complaint, and attend the hearing held on his grievance.

If the results under step A of the grievance procedure do not satisfy the orchestra member, step B provides for an appeal to the second level of the grievance procedure. What is important here is that the member bears the burden to implement the procedures specified in step B. Note the clarity of the language in this respect:

> ... [if] the *grievant* is not satisfied with any adjustment reached, additional review procedures will be available, provided the *grievant* promptly... submits to the Manager a written statement of *his* grievance... (emphasis supplied).

Unless words do not mean what they plainly say, the parties place the obligation on the musician to effectuate the second level of the grievance procedure. It does not state *either the union or the grievant*. Rather, the language is restricted to the grievant himself.

G and *J*, of course, neither appealed to step B nor did they file a written complaint. If they had done this, they could, of course, have elected to have a union representative help them in their complaint. However, the impetus of the appeal must come from the musician, and not from the union.

So, the facts are plain that the flutists involved did not carry out their obligations under either step of the grievance procedure. They presented no complaint to start up the machinery of the grievance procedure, and, of course, made no appeal to the second level.

Legal Obligations and Rights of the Union

Despite all of this, the union argues that it may properly submit a grievance on behalf of *G* and *J*. To defend this position, the union argues that

> the union is charged under the law with the protection of the rights of *all* workers of the Orchestra.

It is true, of course, that the union is the bargaining agent of the employees. In this respect, it represents them in collective bargaining. In the discharge of this obligation, the union along with the association agreed upon a carefully drawn up grievance procedure to handle the complaints of the orchestra members. In this procedure, as the plain language shows, the parties agreed that the members must originate complaints and appeal unsatisfactory settlements. This is how the union discharged its legal obligations in matters of the processing of grievances.

However, now the union says that despite the unambiguous language, it still may file grievances on behalf of the employees because it is legally obligated to represent the employees of the bargaining unit. This argument is not acceptable since once the union and the association have agreed upon a certain way in which grievances are to originate and be processed, these procedures are binding on all concerned.

Indeed, if the union argument relating to its legal obligation to represent the members is carried to its logical conclusion, the integrity of all provisions of the labor agreement would be threatened. The union and the association have agreed to a multitude of items in the contract. To say, depending upon circumstances, that the language does not mean what it says would render the contract worthless as a means of providing industrial relations stability. Why should grievance procedure language be an exception to the other agreements reached by the parties wherein the union discharged its legal rights and obligations of representation? The union discharged its legal obligations by negotiating certain salary scales. May the union now successfully argue that such an agreement is not binding and attempt to alter the salary scales in midstream of the contract? By the same token, may the association successfully argue that in midstream the agreements which it reached with the union should be changed?

What the union really argues here is that after it discharged its legal obligations and negotiated a clearly defined and unambiguous grievance procedure, its requirements should be ignored and the union be permitted to file grievances on behalf of orchestra members. To accept this union argument would fly in the face of the very agreement which the union itself negotiated.

Union's Right to File Grievances

Additional analysis of the grievance procedure reinforces the arbitrator's conviction that the instant grievance was not properly filed under its terms. The grievance procedure does permit the union to file grievances under certain circumstances. The circumstances under which it can file grievances are those when association conduct allegedly violates the union's rights *as an entity*. Grievance procedure language specifically draws a distinction between association conduct which is calculated to impair the union's rights as a whole as distinct from action which may violate members' rights as individuals. Note the following language contained in Section 12.2:

> ... for handling any grievances which the Union, as an entity, may file, claiming a violation of the Union's rights as an entity under the Agreement, *as distinguished from the rights of individual members*... (emphasis supplied).

What this provision tells us is that the union has the right to file grievances under certain specific circumstances. It may file a grievance when the interests of the union as a whole may be in issue. For example, the union may properly file a grievance under circumstances when the association refuses to recognize the union as the bargaining agent or refuses to honor the labor agreement's union security language. There could, of course, be other situations wherein the union may properly file a grievance under the aforecited language. The key to such a finding, however, must be some action taken by the association which would threaten the union as an institution. In the instant case, the refusal of the association to pay doubling fees could scarcely threaten the union as an entity. Only two employees are involved, and the refusal of the association to pay the fees requested simply does not threaten the status of the union as an entity. To find otherwise would place a construction on the word "entity" which would be highly unrealistic.

In short, it is clear from the language that the parties' scheme for the use of the grievance procedure separates grievances into two broad categories. It contemplates that certain action of the association could undermine the status of the union as an entity. It also contemplates that certain association action may impair the rights of employees as individuals. Under the former category, the Union may properly file grievances. In the latter category, the individual employees must file grievances, and if they fail to do so, the union may not properly file grievances on their behalf.

Application of Article II, Section 2.3

Before reaching his final decision in this case, the arbitrator considered the language of Section 2.3 and the union rules contemplated by its terms. Section 2.3 states:

> The parties also recognize that members of the Federation are subject to all rules and regulations of the union, as now in effect.

Union Exhibit No. 1 is a document styled "Rules and Regulations for Symphony Orchestra Union Representative and Alternate." In this regard, the union refers to Sections 3 and 5 of these rules. Such rules state:

> Sec. 3(a). The Steward shall be empowered to settle all disputes with the Symphony Management arising under the provisions of the current collective bargaining agreements by consultation with the Personnel Manager, the Manager of Operations or the General Manager of the Symphony Orchestra as the case may be.
> (b) The Steward, in the event he is unable to settle any dispute described in Section 3(a) herein, shall refer such dispute to the Vice President of the Local. The Vice President shall thereafter advise the President and/or the Board of Directors of all disputes referred to him by the Steward for disposition.
> Sec. 5. The Steward shall hereinafter be empowered to invoice the Orchestral Association for the payment of salaries, extra rehearsal fees,

overtime fees, or per diem where the Steward finds such monies to be due and not paid. If the amount invoiced is disputed by the Orchestral Association, they shall refer the matter to the Board of Directors of the Local.

After due reflection of the aforecited contractual language and rules, the arbitrator does not find that they supercede the language of the grievance procedure. What the rules do is to confer certain powers upon the union steward. However, the rules do not relieve members of the orchestra from their obligations under the grievance procedure. Despite whatever powers are provided the steward, employees still must file their own grievances when they believe their individual rights have been violated by the association. Clearly, the rules do not provide stewards with the authority to file grievances on behalf of employees when the employees fail to file their own claims. It is true that Section 3(a) provides the steward with the power

> to settle all disputes with the Symphony Management arising under the provisions of the current collective bargaining agreements....

For purposes of the grievance procedure, what this means is that the steward is empowered to settle a grievance with the association. However, his power of settlement is not the same thing as the filing of a grievance in the first place. In short, the powers of the steward come into play *after a grievance is properly filed by a member*. In the instant case, the steward had no power to settle the grievance because no grievance was filed by G or J.

Indeed, it would be a masterpiece of error on the part of the arbitrator to read into the cited rules the authority of a steward to file a grievance on behalf of an employee when the employee refuses to file a grievance in the first place. In the instant case, we are not concerned with the *settlement* of a dispute; rather, we are concerned with the issue of the proper filing of a grievance.

Neither can Section 5 of the rules convert the instant grievance to a proper one for determination on its merits. This rule empowers the steward to invoice the association for monies due and not paid. In the instant case, there is no money due because G and J did not raise a claim for the doubling fee. If they raised no claim, how can such fees be due and not paid?

No Precedent Established on Merits of the Grievance

There is another feature of the union's position that is worthy of consideration. It attempts to demonstrate that if the arbitrator does not deal with the merits of the union-filed grievance, *the rights of all members* of the orchestra could be placed in jeopardy. For sure, if the arbitrator were satisfied that his failure to deal with the merits of the dispute would result in such a situation, it would follow that the rights of the union as an entity would be involved. Under these circumstances, the arbitrator would not hesitate to deal with the grievance on its merits. This would be a matter of common sense and in keeping with the language and intent of the grievance procedure. If the rights of *all* members of the orchestra are threatened, it would be logical to conclude that the rights of the union as an entity would be in issue. Under such a situation, the rights of employees would be indivisible from the rights of the union.

To be specific, the union claims that unless the arbitrator deals with the grievance on its merits, a precedent would be established wherein no member of the orchestra could ever raise a similar kind of complaint. That is, whatever protection is afforded by the doubling fee provision would be forfeited by all employees under the circumstances that involved *G* and *J* on the day of the concert in question. In this respect, union counsel argues:

> ... if the Arbitrator permits the Association to avoid the merit question in this case, the Association would then be in a position where it can argue in any ensuing similar grievance that such grievants have no right to doubling fees because in this grievance none were found to be due.

With full deference to the union and its counsel, the arbitrator's decision in this proceeding establishes no precedent whatsoever on the merits of the grievance. It is denied for only one reason—it was not filed properly in the grievance procedure. Nothing in the arbitrator's decision applies, nor is it meant to apply, to the merits of the instant grievance.

Indeed, the union is on record as to its position on the merits of this case. It believes that musicians should be paid doubling fees as under the circumstances of this case when a musician is directed to double on an instrument but actually does not play the instrument. With clarity, union counsel sets forth the issue on the merits of the grievance:

> Whether under the terms of the contract a player who is informed that he must play an extra instrument in any week is entitled to an additional payment of $25.00 per performance, whether he actually plays such extra instrument or not.

It would labor the obvious to point out that this arbitrator makes no decision whatsoever on the merits of the issue as presented by union counsel. Should the situation arise again as was involved under the circumstances of this case, any member of the orchestra may file a grievance to test the application of the doubling fee provision.

Indeed, to allay any fears of the union on the issue of precedent, reference is made to the following statement of the association:

ARBITRATOR: Just one question. How would you answer the argument that if the Union didn't proceed to represent these people it would establish an adverse practice that might injure other employees under the same circumstances?

ASSOCIATION COUNSEL: I think in the very first beginnings of this matter the Union has made its position clear that it believes the doubling fee should have been paid under these circumstances. And I think it is that alone that would preserve its position. There could be no claim made subsequently that the Union agreed to, tacitly or otherwise, what was done here. It would be free to assert that claim or to represent a member asserting that claim in a future case, but in this case there is no grievant; and, therefore, there is no grievance.

In other words, any member of the orchestra in the future may file a grievance to test the applicability of the doubling fee provision under the same circumstances which involved G and J during the concert of November 30, 1968. Such a grievance would be arbitrable on its merits.

CONCLUSIONS

On the basis of the language of the grievance procedure and in the light of the facts of this case, the arbitrator must of necessity hold that the instant grievance was not filed and processed properly under the grievance procedure. Therefore, the arbitrator must dismiss it because it is not arbitrable. Arbitrators and the courts generally prefer to deal with a dispute on its merits. Indeed, the arbitrator would have preferred to deal with the grievance on its merits. It raises some interesting points of contractual interpretation.

In any event, the arbitrator would abuse his authority and breach principles of the arbitration process if he went to the merits of the grievance after finding that it has no standing under the grievance procedure. It is stressed that the merits of the grievance may be treated in another grievance, provided that members of the orchestra, as distinct from the union, file a similar kind of complaint.

QUESTIONS

1. How would you have decided this case on its merits?
2. What if the symphony orchestra association had refused to arbitrate? Do you believe that if the union had gone to court to demand that the association arbitrate, the court would have directed arbitration under the Trilogy doctrine?
3. Would you conclude that the arbitrator has ruled once and for all that no musician is entitled to "doubling fees" unless he actually plays his extra instrument in a concert?

7

Wage Issues Under Collective Bargaining

Almost all contract negotiations pivot upon, and most grievances and arbitration procedures thus ultimately deal with, four major areas (1) wages, and issues which can be directly related to wages; (2) employee benefits, or economic "fringe" supplements to the basic wage rate; (3) "institutional" issues, dealing with the rights and duties of employers and unions; and (4) what might be most appropriately described as "administrative" clauses, treating such subjects as work rules and job tenure. In this chapter and the three which follow it, each of these areas will be discussed in turn. As in the previous chapter, arbitration cases also will be used, where appropriate, to illustrate particular problems.

Probably no issues under collective bargaining continue to give rise to more difficult problems than do wages and wage-related subjects. When negotiations reach a stalemate, they frequently do so because company and union representatives are not able to find a formula to resolve wage disputes. And wage controversies are, for that matter, by far the leading overt cause of strikes: in the years from 1964 through 1968, for example, they accounted for 44 percent of all such work stoppages.[1]

This record highlights the vital character of wage negotiations in collective bargaining, and also suggests that in the area of wages much can be done to decrease management–labor conflict substantially. In any area of human relations, ignorance breeds suspicion, distrust, and conflict; this principle of human behavior is fully applicable to wage negotiations under collective bargaining. To the extent that understanding is substituted for ignorance there will be a greater opportunity for peaceful settlement of wage controversies, even if conflict of interest in such matters will never disappear.

It is not difficult to understand why wages do play such an important and controversial role in labor relations. For workers, wages are normally the only source of income, and the standard of living of the employee and his family is determined almost exclusively by this source. For workers' families, the weekly paycheck establishes the character and quality of their dwelling, food, clothing, education, recreation, and of all other items which are included in the concept of *standard of living*.

But if from the point of view of the worker, wages are income which establishes a standard of living, from the viewpoint of the *company,* wages are a cost of production. And here is the heart of the wage controversy. On one hand, employees press for higher and higher wages with the objective of raising their standard of living. On the other hand, employers are confronted with increasing pressures on the cost of production. When wages are a significant element of cost of production, when wage increases are not offset by such economic phenomena as increased efficiency, and when the union has been unable (or unwilling) to extract equal wage concessions from all competitive firms, wage increases tend to place the firm in an undesirable economic position. A company so placed might not be able to survive for long in the competitive struggle. Under such a state of affairs, union wage policy, instead of advancing the standard of living of its members, could plunge them into economic oblivion.

As a result of the difficult and controversial nature of wage problems, it is crucial that they be dealt with in an intelligent and sound manner. Perhaps as does no other area of collective bargaining, wage problems test the skill, understanding, and attitudes of negotiators. The latter are, as we know, now confronted with a *legion* of wage issues, including the establishment of the basic wage rate, wage differentials, overtime rates, and wage adjustments during contractual periods, as well as with the thorny problems involved in the negotiation of the so-called "fringe" or supplemental wage payments which will be discussed in the next chapter. It is

---

[1] Data furnished by Bureau of Labor Statistics, U.S. Department of Labor.

hoped that the following discussion of some of the principles, practices, and trends concerning these several wage and wage-related areas will contribute to better understanding of them.

DETERMINATION OF THE BASIC WAGE RATE

If union and management representatives are exhibiting an ever greater willingness to deal with factual information at the bargaining table, there is still no single standard for wage rate determination which has anything approaching a "scientific" base. Both of the bargaining parties, indeed, commonly utilize at least *three different* such standards, each of which has definite advantages from the viewpoint of achieving an "equitable" settlement but also significant limitations: the "comparative-norm," ability to pay, and standard of living criteria.

Comparative-norm Principle

To a great extent, company and union negotiators make use of the "comparative-norm principle" in wage negotiations. The basic idea behind this concept is the presumption that the economics of a particular collective bargaining relationship should neither fall substantially behind nor be greatly superior to that of other employer-union relationships, that—in short—it is generally a good practice to keep up with the crowd, but not necessarily to lead it.

The outside observer would very likely agree with this principle, at least on the surface. When a firm is operating with a highly competitive product or in highly competitive labor markets, there is safety for employee relations in keeping labor costs and wage rates consistent with the local and industrial pattern, but not necessarily any need to exceed this pattern. Unions tend to maintain harmony and contentment among the rank and file as long as wage conditions are uniform; on the other hand, it is at times quite difficult and embarrassing for union leaders to explain to the membership why their economic terms of employment are *not* at least equivalent to those of other unionists (particularly where one local of an international union falls substantially behind another local of the same international). In short, the comparative-norm principle is often valid for economic, sociological, and psychological reasons.

Thus companies and unions frequently make a careful and comprehensive study of the community and industry wage structure before negotiations begin and then compare these rates to the rates in existence in the plant involved in the negotiations. The strategic implications of such comparisons, already cited in Chapter 5, are quite obvious. If the plant rates are below the community or industry pattern, the union can be expected to argue for a wage increase on this basis. When the plant rates are in excess of the community or industry pattern, the company has an argument *against* a wage increase.

Notwithstanding these considerations, there are limitations to this approach to the bargaining process. All firms do not have the same capacity to meet economic demands. This is the case not only for firms in different industries but also for companies operating within the same industry. Though economic forces are at work which tend to place firms operating within the same industrial grouping on the same economic footing, many other factors—such as imperfections in the product market, technological differences, location, stage of economic development, and financial resources—*may,* at any one time, place such firms on different economic levels. From this it follows that at any one time firms may be quite different in their individual capacities to meet economic demands and that the optimum wage level for one firm of a particular industry could be quite low (or quite high) in comparison with that of the industry in general.

Negotiations in the steel industry serve to illustrate this point. Most of the basic steel manufacturers, whether large or small, are organized by the United Steelworkers of America. So, too, are most steel fabrication firms, which purchase their steel from the basic steel companies, fabricate it, and then sell the resultant steel products directly to other industrial plants or to private consumers. The membership of the union is, in fact, divided about equally between employees who work in these two sectors of the steel industry.

In negotiations with the basic steel companies, the union's highest national officers deal directly with a small employer committee agreed upon by the larger of these companies (United States Steel, Bethlehem, Republic, Jones and Laughlin, and similar large producers). From this key negotiation, a "pattern," or comparative norm is established. The union then officially tries to gain about the same wage settlement individually from the smaller basic steel plants and the steel fabrication firms. Clearly, however, the financial and market circumstances of the large basic steel producers are quite different from those confronting the other types of managements—and the inevitable result is a wide variety of different degrees of pattern following and pattern deviation in what is nonetheless still referred to as the "steel industry."

Many other examples could be used to demonstrate the same principle. Within the rubber industry, the economic conditions, and thus the wage-paying abilities, of the large firms oriented toward the rubber-tire market are quite different from those of the smaller footwear manufacturers. And highly competitive rubber-heel plants, for example, normally settle with the Rubber Workers for considerably less than the rubber-tire pattern established with Firestone, Goodrich, and similar rubber-tire titans, even though many of the latter firms also manufacture footwear. Large meatpackers (such as Swift and Armour) are generally in better positions to allow higher wage levels than are their smaller competitors. In the automobile industry, there are obviously significant economic differences between General Motors and American Motors. These considerations must be recognized before one accepts the proposition that the comparative-norm principle of wage determination should be used as the exclusive, or the most desirable, standard for wage settlements in collective bargaining.[2]

There are at least four other factors to be considered in regard to the comparative-norm principle. *First,* not only do firms within a given industry at any given time have unequal capabilities to meet economic demands, but frequently it is quite difficult to *classify* a firm in a particular industrial grouping for wage comparison purposes. Some firms may logically be classified in two or more industries because of the products they manufacture or the services they provide. Likewise, even if a firm is classified within a particular industry, there are frequently highly meaningful subgroupings in each major industrial classification. Within the oil industry, for example, there are large, medium, and small producers of oil, and producers can be classified considerably further in terms of exact product and nature of operations. Such complicating circumstances illustrate the difficulty of classifying a particular firm in a particular industry or in a segment of an industry for purposes of wage determination.

A *second* limitation involved in the use of the comparative-norm wage principle for collective bargaining is the fact that it is at times misleading to compare employees within a particular job classification, because the content of jobs may be substantially different among plants within the same labor market. The duties of an employee classified as a "subassembler, B" in one plant may be quite different from those carried out by an employee classified identically in another plant. The fact is that job classifications within industry have not been standardized. As long as this situation exists, and there is reason to believe that it will continue to exist, the usefulness of the comparative-norm wage principle is proportionately reduced.

This wage criterion is limited in its applicability by still a *third* complication. It is difficult to use the principle when comparing workers who

[2] Recognition of the differences between firms and industries should also be taken into account when the *nonmoney* items of collective bargaining are negotiated. A seniority system, for example, which is suitable for one employer-union relationship, may not fit the needs of the employer and employees of another plant. Union security formulas, checkoff arrangements, managerial prerogative systems, grievance procedures, discharge and disciplinary arrangements, and the character of union obligations should be geared fundamentally to the particular collective bargaining relationship. Company and union representatives are at times astonished to learn of the contractual arrangement of another employer-union relationship. The fact is, however, that such a formula frequently can be explained logically in terms of the environment of that firm.

are within the same job classification but who are paid by different systems of wage payments. Some workers are paid on a straight hourly-rate basis, others under an individual incentive system, and still others on a group incentive plan. The kind of wage system in operation can in itself have a significant impact upon wage rates.

Briefly described, incentive wages constitute a method of wage payment by which earnings are geared more or less directly to actual output instead of to time spent on the job. Employees are thus granted a relatively clear-cut financial motivation to increase their outputs, essentially by increasing the effort on which such outputs depend.

On the other hand, determination of the actual rate of pay for each "piece" or unit of output is, of course, open to union-management controversy: the company's conception of an appropriate rate is typically somewhat less liberal than is the union's. And the problem is compounded when the original job on which the rate has been set is in any way "modified" (as virtually all jobs ultimately are, because of a host of factors ranging from worker-implemented short cuts to management job re-engineering) and each party seeks a new rate which is beneficial to its own interests.

Some unions have historically opposed such plans from their inception, through fear of management rate-cutting (for example, artificial reconstruction of the job in order to pay it a lower rate) and because of a deeply harbored suspicion that there is nothing "scientific" to *any* established rates. But managements which have yielded too *readily* to union requests for higher rates have *also* suffered, in inequities between earnings and effort, and in consequent problems involving not only finances but also employee morale. Increased automation of industry to the point where many workers cannot control their output rates has caused some further de-emphasis of incentive plans in recent years. However, about one-quarter of all production-plant workers in the United States continue to be paid under such plans, and it is obvious that the presence of such workers can make the comparative-norm principle severely misleading.

Fourth, and finally, consideration must be given to the existence of the wide variety of fringe benefits previously cited. These benefits are not distributed equally throughout industry. Thus it could be wrong to conclude that workers in different plants are not equal in terms of net economic advantage where one group earns a lower basic wage rate but surpasses another group in terms of paid holidays and vacations, retirement, social insurance, and the like.

These considerations do not mean that the comparative-norm principle is of no value in collective bargaining. Its utility is demonstrated by its widespread use. But bargainers who utilize this avenue of wage comparisons without recognition of the several problems and limitations involved in its implementation do so only at their peril.

Ability to Pay

A second leading criterion involved in wage determination under collective bargaining is the ability of the firm or industry to pay a wage increase. Frequently the outcome of wage negotiations will be shaped by this factor, and many strikes do occur where there is disagreement between company and union negotiators relative to the wage-paying capacity of the enterprise. Careful consideration and better understanding of this factor of wage determination is no less imperative for reducing the area of disagreement between industry and organized labor than is familiarity with the comparative-norm factor.

The level of profits is one indicator of the wage-paying ability of the firm involved in the negotiations. If a firm is earning a "high" rate of profit, union representatives will frequently claim that the company can afford all or most of the union wage demand. If the firm is earning a "low" rate of profit, management negotiators will frequently argue that the firm does not have the financial capacity to meet the union's wage demands. But the heart of this controversy is, clearly, the determination of what constitutes a rate of profits sufficient to meet a given union wage demand. Unfortunately, there is no economic formula which can answer this question with precision and exactness.

As in the case of the previous criterion, the problem is complicated by further considerations. In the first place, it is not certain whether a given rate of profits earned by a company over a given time in the past will hold for the future. Future profits may fall or rise depending upon the behavior of a number of economic variables, which are themselves uncertain: changes in sales, output, productivity, price, managerial efficiency, and even the state of international relations will all bear upon the future profit experience of a particular firm or industry. Thus a wage rate negotiated in the light of a given historical profit experience may not be appropriate in the future. Moreover, if profits are to be used as an indicator of the firm's ability to meet a given wage demand, consideration must be given to anticipated government tax structures. The wage-paying ability of the firm may be quite different before and after the payment of the federal income tax, as many business administrators can testify. There are additional elements of the never-static national and state tax programs which tend to have an impact on the wage-paying ability of industry.

Second, the use to which a company intends to put its profits also has a vital bearing upon this problem. Since profits frequently are used to promote plant growth and improvement, the future plans of the enterprise itself must receive consideration by the negotiators. The problem of whether profits should be used for plant growth and improvement, for lower commodity price, or for higher wages is one of the most troublesome issues in industrial relations. The complexities of the problem involve such highly controversial matters as business-cycle theory, the orderly and sound growth of the economy, adequate purchasing power to buy the goods that industry produces, the varying expansion needs of different firms and industries, the justice or the injustice of plant expansion instead of wage increases, the specific amount of the profits which should be used for wages, and alternative methods of financing growth and plant improvement other than the use of profits. These are only some of the secondary problems involved in the use of profits as an indicator of the ability of a company or industry to meet union wage demands. Clearly, the multitude of problems and questions that come to light in this connection demonstrates the difficulty of the utilization of this determinant of wages.

Third, though the level of profits is an important factor in the determination of a firm's ability to pay wages, it is not the only factor. Other considerations which have an important bearing on the problem are: the ratio of labor costs to total costs, the amount of money expended for the financing of fringe benefits, the character of the product market in which the firm operates, the degree of elasticity of demand for the firm's product, and the ability of the company to increase productivity.

The ratio of labor costs to total costs particularly conditions the ability of a firm to afford increased wage rates. An employer is in a better position to grant higher wages when the firm's labor costs represent a comparatively small part of the total costs. For example, a 10 percent increase in wage rates will result in a 1 percent increase in total costs when wage costs are 10 percent of total costs (as they are, for example, in portions of the petroleum industry). Where, however, wage costs are 50 percent of total costs (as in segments of the leather industry), a 10 percent increase in wage rates will result in a 5 percent increase in total costs. This illustration, of course, is based upon the assumption that there is no increase or decrease in labor productivity after the wage rates are negotiated. If output increases faster than the wage rise, labor cost per unit of production tends to decrease. The reverse would be true where labor productivity does not increase with higher wages.

Moreover, the ratio of labor cost to total cost cannot by itself be taken as conclusive evidence of the wage-paying ability of a particular firm. Firms with a low labor cost do not necessarily have the capacity to pay higher wages. By the same token, it would not be accurate to conclude that firms with a high labor cost can never afford wage increases. All that can be said with some degree of accuracy is that if all economic variables were held constant, a firm with a low labor-cost ratio could afford to pay higher wages more easily than a firm with a high labor-cost ratio.

As in the case of the comparative-norm principle, it should also be re-emphasized that an employer's total wage bill includes not only direct wage costs but costs incurred in providing employees with so-called "fringe" benefits. Though basic wages constitute the major labor cost, industry each year pays a considerable amount of money in financing supplements to the basic wage bill. Into this category fall such items as sickness, accident, hospital, and dental insurance, pensions, severance pay, and paid holidays and vacations.

Industry's payments for such benefits have been rising rapidly. In a comprehensive survey conducted by the United States Chamber of Commerce for 79 identical companies, for example, it was estimated that these benefits rose from an equivalent of about 15.1 percent of total payroll in 1947 to about 30 percent of total payroll in 1967, an increase of almost 100 percent. Even more impressive were the *absolute* gains revealed by the chamber: fringe benefits increased from 21.7 cents per payroll hour in 1947 to about $1.05 in 1967 (or virtually quintupled) and from $439 per employee in 1947 to almost $2,200 per employee in 1967 (for almost an exact fivefold growth in this twenty-year period).[3]

The ease with which a company can pass on the costs of a wage increase in the form of higher prices to other firms or to the consuming public is still another determinant of its wage-paying ability. Some firms (in the brewing and cigarette industries, for example) operate in a highly competitive selling market. Under these circumstances it is very difficult, if not impossible, for an employer to shift the burden of a wage increase to the consumer. Even a slight increase in price could result in a significant decrease in sales, since consumers would simply buy from other sellers. To the degree that a firm sells its products in a highly competitive market, it will find strong consumer resistance to price increases. In contrast, some companies (for example, newspaper publishers in single-newspaper cities) operate in monopolistic markets. Under these circumstances, companies have a greater degree of freedom to raise prices without experiencing a sharp decrease in sales. This would be particularly true where the product in question is sold under conditions of inelastic demand. Such a demand characteristic would apply to goods which are necessities or to those for which there are few satisfactory substitutes. Thus, if a company is operating in a monopolistic market and selling a product for which the demand is relatively inelastic, it has an excellent opportunity to shift the costs of wage increases to other firms or to the general public in the form of higher prices.

Negotiators at times take advantage of such an economic environment. Wage increases are agreed upon and the result is higher prices. From the public point of view it would be much more desirable if unions and

[3] Economic Research Department, U. S. Chamber of Commerce, *Fringe Benefits, 1967* (Washington, D.C.: U. S. Chamber of Commerce, 1968), p. 28.

employers could work out an arrangement whereby wages could be increased without price increases. Certainly, a wage agreement which increases the prices of basic economic commodities and thereby generates a general inflation of the price level cannot be regarded as socially sound.

For a few years in the 1960s, as it had on other occasions in the nation's history, the federal government made its feelings on this latter point abundantly clear. Starting in January 1962, the President's Council of Economic Advisors argued that labor cost increases should be limited to the nationwide annual rise in labor productivity (as measured by output per man-hour). Over the prior few years, according to CEA statistics, this annual productivity increase for the economy had averaged 3.2 percent, and the council consequently urged that contract settlement, through "voluntary restraint" by the bargaining parties, remain below this figure, or at a level which would presumably negate the need for price increases. Consistent with the sentiments of former CEA chairman Walter W. Heller that "the public interest today, more than ever, requires that the stability of our costs and prices be protected,"[4] the council guideposts (or "guidelines," as they were also called) were viewed by government officials as a mechanism for advancing national prosperity, aiding the nation in its balance of payments problems, and generally protecting the broader public interest.

Neither managements nor labor organizations, generally speaking, gave much endorsement to these wage-price guideposts. Managers tended to view them as a not-very-subtle form of government intervention, and even as a harbinger of ultimate price controls. Company spokesmen also argued that the CEA's recommendations would stifle business initiative and that, in addition, the current national levels of unemployment, unused plant capacity, and domestic and foreign competition were sufficient in themselves to ward off inflation. Symbolically, one steel executive commented that the guidelines were "based on the economics of the Potomac, not the economics of the steel industry."

To many unionists, the guideposts appeared to ignore "special situations," such as that existing in the automobile industry prior to the 1964 negotiations there: with auto profits at record highs in that year, the UAW leadership vociferously argued that the industry could pay considerably more than 3.2 percent to its workers and still cut prices, thereby making a settlement noninflationary. The union finally settled for about 4.8 percent. Labor spokesmen also attacked the guideposts as inequitably "freezing" worker shares in the income distribution pie at their pre-1962 levels, in the absence of a convincing reason why such wage income shares should not be *increased*. And, as their counterparts on the management side, they

[4] T. R. Brooks, "A Look Ahead to the Auto Negotiations," *The Reporter,* May 21, 1964, p. 27.

also viewed with some alarm the increased government intervention implicit in the guideposts. It was, symbolically, commented by one leading unionist that the 3.2 percent guideposts were "as welcome to organized labor as 3.2 beer."

Indeed, in February 1966, the AFL-CIO Executive Council officially condemned the guidelines. At that time, federation president George Meany, in characteristically blunt language, stated that

> labor does not, cannot, and will not accept the guidelines. We see no way it can be applied equitably in an economy such as we have. We just don't like the guidelines. It destroys our collective bargaining. It works only one way—against us.[5]

Given this meaningful wave of opposition, it is doubtful that the guideposts ever had any significant influence on inflation. As President Nixon's Council of Economic Advisors could comment in reviewing these earlier years from the vantage point of 1970, the policy was applied during "years of considerable slack in the economy, relatively high unemployment, and stable or declining farm prices"—conditions that independently tended to favor price stability. When inflationary pressures—due particularly to the exigencies of the war in Vietnam—increased after mid-1965, the guidepost policy "clearly did not work...Labor and business were being asked to act as if prices were not rising, when in fact they were. As it became evident that steps necessary to keep prices from rising were not being taken, it also became more obviously unrealistic and inequitable to make these requests in specific cases."[6] By late 1965, indeed, settlements reached in the can, aluminum, rubber, textile, oil, and construction industries—among others—had all breached the 3.2 figure in varying degrees and a few months after this the guidepost policy, being widely perceived as unsuccessful, was allowed to quietly fade away.

From 1966 through at least the time of this writing, governmental efforts to combat a wave of inflation which had accelerated to a 6 percent annual average by 1970 emphasized strictly fiscal and monetary policy—not the guideposts. The conspicuous lack of success of these latter tools in curbing the upward spiral of prices had motivated few in governmental positions of influence to suggest a restoration of the unimpressive guidepost policy so soon after its recent poor performance.

Yet there is little doubt but that the labor relations parties themselves could do considerably more than many have been willing to, in the recent past, in devoting their efforts toward minimizing the price rise. If management and workers strive for greater productivity and efficiency, it is possible that some of the costs of an increased wage bill can be offset by

[5] *Christian Science Monitor,* February 26, 1966, p. 4.
[6] *Monthly Labor Review,* March 1970, p. 2.

increased output and by the reduction of nonlabor costs. Many companies and unions have not fully examined the possibilities of joint cooperation in eliminating waste and scrap, decreasing absenteeism and tardiness, and reducing industrial accidents. Management may be able to increase its efforts to purchase raw materials at cheaper prices, modernize machine technology, decrease material-handling costs, improve plant layout, or otherwise innovate for greater efficiency. Unions might examine their policies with the view of eliminating those which retard production, interfere with the efficient operation of the plant, or otherwise operate to curtail output. Indeed, at times unions can do much to improve the capacity of a company to produce without jeopardizing the health and safety of their members or impairing the members' legitimate job rights.

The preceding analysis indicates that many factors condition the ability of a firm to pay additional wages. This wage determinant cannot be applied automatically or in a whimsical manner. Its importance to intelligent and peaceful wage negotiations is counterpoised by its complexity and difficulty in application. All the factors bearing upon the wage-paying ability of a company must be weighed accurately and fairly. In this manner, wage negotiations can be conducted on a factual basis with minimized controversy and industrial strife.

THE TRUITT DECISION

In April 1956, the United States Supreme Court handed down an important and still applicable decision dealing with the legal obligation of employers who argue that they cannot afford wage increases.[7] At times a company which is confronted with a wage request by a union will claim that it lacks the financial capacity to meet such a demand. When an employer takes this position, labor organizations will ordinarily request that the company furnish them with information bearing upon the company's wage-paying ability. In the *Truitt Manufacturing Company* case, the Supreme Court held that when the employer argues that he lacks the economic ability to meet a particular wage demand, he must make financial information available to the union. In justifying this policy, the high court stated:

> Good faith bargaining necessarily requires that claims by either bargainer should be honest claims. This is true about an asserted inability to pay an increase in wages. If such an argument is important enough to present in the give and take of bargaining, it is important enough to require some sort of proof of its accuracy.

[7] *NLRB* v. *Truitt Manufacturing Co.,* 351 U.S. 149 (1956).

The *Truitt* decision, of course, does not mean that the company must capitulate to union wage demands. In fact, the company can refuse to meet the union request even if the information induced by the union shows conclusively that it *has* the ability to pay the wages demanded by the union. In addition, the Supreme Court did not specify that the employer must automatically produce proof in every instance where he pleads inability to pay. The Court held that each case must turn upon its own merits. Thus, in this connection it declared:

> We do not hold ... that in every case in which economic inability is raised as an argument against increased wages it automatically follows that the employees are entitled to substantiating evidence. Each case must turn upon its particular facts. The inquiry must always be whether or not under the circumstances of the particular case the statutory obligation to bargain in good faith has been met.

Finally, the *Truitt* decision did not establish a hard and fast rule as to the character of evidence that the employer must show when he pleads lack of ability. As is apparent from the general tone of the Court's decision, this determination would also be made on a case-by-case basis, as indeed has been the case in the years since *Truitt* was decided. These considerations, however, do not detract from the important principle established in the *Truitt* decision. The fact is that employers who argue economic inability to meet union wage demands must now generally be prepared either to produce relevant evidence to substantiate this position or to face charges of unfair labor practice.

Standard of Living

Orientation of the plant wage structure to community and industry levels and ability to pay are not the only criteria utilized for wage determination in contemporary industry. Many management and particularly labor representatives are concerned with the problem of the *adequacy* of wages to guarantee workers "a decent standard of living." Disagreements arise, however, as to what constitutes such a standard.

The problem is most often resolved by personal judgment and opinions of the negotiators. More objective information is, however, at the disposal of the parties, and it has frequently been used to support demands and counterdemands at the bargaining table.

At the present time, the most widely publicized source of standard-of-living information is that published by the United States Department of Labor's Bureau of Labor Statistics. First developed in 1946–47 at the request of Congress, and revised periodically since that time, the BLS's "City Worker's Family Budget" attempts to describe and measure a "modest but adequate standard of living." It is necessarily selective, restricting itself to a measurement of the income needed by a family of four (a 38-year-old employed husband, a wife not employed outside the home, and two children of school age—a 13-year-old boy and an 8-year-old girl) living in a rented dwelling in a large city or its suburbs. By studying the prices of a "representative list of goods and services" presumably purchased by such families, for twenty major cities (weighted according to their populations), the BLS endeavors to show the cost of "a level of adequate living standards prevailing in large cities of the United States in recent years."

Although the income required by the City Worker's Budget varies widely from one city to another, the overall weighted average of $9,076 at the time of this writing was sufficiently beyond that earned by most workers to make the budget an attractive bargaining weapon for union negotiators. Labor spokesmen had not been hesitant about arguing the "need" for substantial wage increases to reach the budgeted levels, while also pointing out (as the official AFL-CIO monthly magazine had done) that the overall weighted average "is required to meet the necessities of life, pay taxes, and enjoy a few of the amenities of life—but with no allowance for luxuries or savings."[8]

Employers, equally logically, had taken bitter exception to this most recent City Worker's Budget. They had argued that the items used in computing the budget were far too generous to warrant the description "modest but adequate": frequently cited in this regard were the budget's $145 annual allowance for gifts and contributions, and certain of its provisions for furniture, appliances, automobiles, and recreation. In addition, they pointed out that wage earners do not have uniform responsibilities in terms of dependents (with many, of course, having no dependents) and that many families have more than one wage earner.

The arguments and counterarguments can be expected to continue indefinitely, without mutual agreement as to their validity: the line of demarcation between "luxury" and "necessity" has never been susceptible to exact location and the concept of "decency'" allows much room for emotion. Moreover, despite the increasingly frequent use of the standard-of-living criterion at the bargaining table, it does not carry as much weight as the other wage factors analyzed in the previous sections of this chapter. After all, an employer who truthfully cannot pay wages which will realize the "modest but adequate standard of living" may be entirely sympathetic to his worker's needs, but the cold realism of economic life will not persuade him to grant the additional wages. Likewise, a union will not stop at the level of wages required of the budget if it can get more from the employer because of the operation of the other wage criteria;

---

[8] "The Income Needs of the City Worker's Family," *The American Federationist,* May 1965, p. 16.

indeed, under these circumstances, the union will probably argue that the items of the budget are too meager.

But use of such standard-of-living information as that provided by the BLS—and by such other sources as the Census Bureau, Federal Reserve Board, Department of Commerce, and independent studies of the parties themselves—is still to be preferred to *total* recourse to personal opinion on the subject. The data may not be accepted, but even in rejecting it the recalcitrant party is forced to deal with information which is more objective than mere individual sentiment.

COST OF LIVING: ESCALATOR AND WAGE-REOPENER ARRANGEMENTS

In addition to the comparative-norm, ability-to-pay, and standard-of-living principles, experienced negotiators pay close attention in wage negotiations to the status of the *cost* of living. This economic phenomenon is important because trends in the cost of living have an important bearing upon the real income of workers. Increases in the cost of living at a given level of earnings result in decreased capacity of workers to buy goods and services. By the same token, real income tends to increase with decreases in the cost of living at a given wage level. Real income for a particular group of workers also increases for a time when money wages increase faster than the cost of living.

It is beyond the scope of this volume to analyze the multitude of factors which influence the cost of living in the American economy. This cost is affected by a variety of forces, including the general climate of business activity, productivity, financial and monetary policies followed by financial institutions, the rate of new investment, and the propensity of consumers to spend money, as well as by the wage policies which are followed under collective bargaining itself. Government policies relating to interest rates, tariffs, the lending capacity of national banks, taxation, and agriculture also have an impact upon the cost of living.

The uncertain character of the forces which determine the cost of living makes it very difficult to predict with certainty its future trends. The difficulty inherent in using the cost of living as a determinant in wage negotiations is simply this: wages are negotiated for a future period, whereas cost-of-living data are *historical* in character. It is a comparatively simple task to adjust wages for historical trends in the cost of living if this is the desire of the negotiators. The criterion is of limited usefulness, however, in the attempt to orient wage rates to *future* trends in the consumer price index. The capricious character of the index makes forecasting extremely hazardous. In any event, for intelligent utilization of this wage determinant it becomes necessary not only to have accurate information of historical trends, but also to make an assessment of the future trends of the factors which determine the consumer price index.[9] It cannot be emphasized too much that such predictions are fraught with difficulties and uncertainties.

Some companies and unions have, however, adopted one or both of two procedures—escalator clauses and wage reopeners—which take into account the capriciousness of the cost of living and likewise recognize the importance of trends in the consumer price index as they relate to the real income of employees and to the financial position of companies.

Escalator Clauses

The philosophy behind the incorporation of so-called "escalator clauses" in labor agreements is that wages of workers should rise and fall automatically with fluctuations in the cost of living. The escalator arrangement first attained national prominence in the 1950 General Motors–United Automobile Workers collective bargaining agreement. As a result of the anticipated price inflation growing out of the Korean War, many other companies and unions soon negotiated similar arrangements and by 1952 such arrangements covered about 3.5 million workers—concentrated mainly in the automobile, railroad, textile, aircraft, agricultural implement, and flat-glass industries. They also appeared in a wide variety of other manufacturing and nonmanufacturing industries.

To date, however, the spread of escalator arrangements has not been impressive. Since 1952 use of the wage escalator clause appears to have depended to a great extent on the upward movement of the cost-of-living index. By 1955, for example, three years of comparatively steady prices had elapsed and the number of workers covered by such escalator clauses had dropped considerably, to about 1.7 million.[10] In 1956, on the other hand, the Consumer Price Index moved strongly forward, and a study which was conducted late in that year estimated that approximately 3.5 million workers were once again covered by escalator arrangements.[11] The incorporation of an escalator formula in the 1956 basic steel contract—covering 600,000 workers—alone accounted for almost one third of this increase.

---

[9] The price index that is almost universally utilized in collective bargaining by employers and unions is the one prepared and published by the Bureau of Labor Statistics. It is called the "Consumer Price Index" (CPI) and appears each month in the Bureau's *Monthly Labor Review.*

[10] "Wage Escalation—Recent Developments," *Monthly Labor Review,* LXXVII (March 1955), 315.

[11] Bureau of National Affairs, ed., "What's New in Collective Bargaining Negotiations and Contracts," No. 300 (November 30, 1956), p. 4.

With relatively modest annual price movements from 1956 through mid-1965, interest in the escalator once more temporarily waned. By 1965, the railroads, electrical industry, and (ironically) basic steel had completely abandoned the device, and only about 2 million workers—concentrated mainly in automobiles and automobile parts, farm and construction equipment, trucking, and meatpacking—were covered by escalator clauses in the latter year.[12] On the other hand, the significant surge in the price level after mid-1965 had brought another half-million employees under coverage by 1969 and doubtless more would enter the fold when figures postdating 1969 were officially announced.

Perhaps the greatest single reason why the above figures are anything but spectacular, even for the pronounced United States inflation following 1965, lies in the intense historical management opposition to the escalator concept. Employers have voiced fears that prices could not be commensurately raised without undesirable effects on profits. They have also argued what they view as the inequities of a system which allows workers to benefit without effort of any kind on their part: one mid-1960s increase in the cost-of-living index, for example, was attributed by government spokesmen primarily to increases in sugar and cigarette prices—a situation which even the most sugar-consuming and chain-smoking work force could not noticeably influence. Still other managers have stressed the potential inflationary ramifications of the escalator in opposing its use. Above all, however, employers have attacked the constant "freezing" of cost-of-living allowances into basic wage rates: most labor contracts ultimately make such allowances a permanent part of rates when the agreements are renegotiated and to many workers the allowances are, consequently, really additional wage increases temporarily couched in other terms.

Managements could, understandably, be expected to generate greater enthusiasm for the escalator in the event of a prolonged national period of markedly *downward* prices, but this appears an unlikely possibility for the foreseeable future. Even in the continuing absence of such a situation, however, and even if one disregards the current aggressive attempts of unions to gain the escalator device in the face of the strong upward price movements now operative, it is possible that *some* impetus will be provided for the escalator in the general gradual lengthening of the terms of labor contracts.

The evidence that contracts are becoming longer is persuasive. Where in 1948 about 75 percent of collective bargaining agreements were for one year or less, by 1963 the proportion of contracts running for longer than one year had increased sharply—to as much as 86 percent, by some

---

[12] "Deferred Increases Due in 1965 and Wage Escalation," *Monthly Labor Review*, LXXXVII, No. 12 (December 1964), 1384. Some employees in chemicals, retail trade, and public transit also remain covered by escalator clauses.

estimates,[13] and by 1970 as many as 90 percent of all contracts may have been for more than one year. Longer-term contracts lend greater stability to labor relationships, and by definition they reduce the problems of negotiation and the traumas of frequent strike threats. However, as contracts are negotiated for longer periods of time, negotiators must recognize the necessity of providing some method for the adjustment of wages during the contractual period. Some authorities believe that increasing awareness of this situation, together with the *continuation* of the trend to contracts of longer duration will lend greater allure to the escalator formula, even in the face of continuing managerial opposition to the whole idea and despite the unconvincing escalator statistics of the moment.

Although there is a wide variety of escalator arrangements, all contain a number of common principles. The most significant characteristic of the escalator formula is its automaticity. For the duration of the labor agreement, wage changes as related to cost of living are precisely determined by the behavior of a statistical index—almost always the Bureau of Labor Statistics' "Consumer Price Index." Wages are increased or decreased in accordance with comparatively small changes in this index. For example, the labor agreement might provide, as many recent ones have, for a $.01-per-hour adjustment of wages for every 0.4-point change in the CPI.

Escalators frequently work on a quarterly basis. Under this arrangement, used until recently by the automobile industry (among others), the cost-of-living index is reviewed every three months and wages are changed in accordance with the escalator formula. On the other hand, the over-the-road trucking industry currently provides for essentially annual determination, and several other sectors which use the escalator operate it on a semiannual basis. In addition, the escalator arrangement often specifies the floor to which wages can fall in response to changes in the cost-of-living index: under the contract, for example, wages might not be decreased if the CPI falls lower than 125.0 (1957–59 = 100). However, the escalator formula does not usually contain a *ceiling* on wage increases occasioned by increases in the CPI.

Finally, the escalator principle of wage adjustment is often accompanied by a definite and guaranteed increase in wages on an annual basis. This feature of the wage contract is popularly referred to as the *annual improvement factor*. Under the 1964–67 auto contracts, for example, wages were to be increased in 1965 by 2½ percent or $.06 per hour (whichever

[13] See, for example, "Agreement Duration, Renewal, and General Wage Adjustments," published jointly by the School of Business of Indiana University and the Indiana State Chamber of Commerce (Bloomington, Ind., 1963). *Labor Relations Reporter* (June 29, 1959), pp. 198–225, found that even by 1959 only 24 percent of all contracts were for one year or less.

was the greater), continuing the same formula for these three-year contracts that had been applied to each year except 1964 (when the formula was suspended to allow increased fringe benefits) of the 1958–61 and 1961–64 automobile contracts. In 1966, however, there was to be a change: the annual increases would be advanced to 2.8 percent, with a minimum of 7 cents. And under the 1967–70 contracts a more complicated formula took over (e.g., workers with a straight-time hourly rate of less than $3.17 would receive an annual improvement factor increase of 9 cents per hour; those earning between $3.17 and $3.49, 10 cents, etc.). Workers were guaranteed this increase regardless of fluctuations of the CPI during the contractual period.

Wage Reopeners

A second method for wage adjustments during the life of a labor agreement involves a provision which permits either the company or the union to *reopen* labor agreements *for wage issues* at stated intervals. Where such a procedure is employed, labor agreements normally provide that contracts that are negotiated for one year may be reopened for wage issues after six months. Contracts that are written for two-year periods or longer customarily are open for wage negotiations once each year.

Two major characteristics of the wage-reopening clause arrangement distinguish it from the escalator principle as a method of wage adjustment. The most important involves the fact that whereas the escalator arrangement provides for an *automatic* change in wages based upon a definite formula, the parties must *negotiate* wage changes under wage reopeners. This could be an advantage or a disadvantage, depending upon the particular circumstances of a given collective bargaining relationship. In addition, the wage-reopener arrangement can be utilized to take into account determinants of wages other than the cost of living. The fact that both the escalator and the reopener arrangements are frequently found together in industry indicates that *both* procedures apparently fill the needs of employers, employees, and unions. What may be suitable for one collective bargaining relationship, however, clearly might be unsuitable for another company and union.

To invoke a wage-reopening clause, collective bargaining contracts require that the party which desires to change wages give a written notice to the other party within a specified period. Under the terms of the Taft-Hartley law, as we know, a party to a collective bargaining agreement desiring to modify or terminate the agreement must give 60 days' notice of its intention to do so. Following such notice, the law declares that there may be no lockout or strike "for a period of sixty days...or until the expiration date of such contract, whichever occurs later." Employees who engage in a strike during this period lose their status as employees under Taft-Hartley and have no legal right to be reinstated.

These provisions of the Taft-Hartley law are important in connection with this discussion because wage-reopening arrangements invariably provide that a union may call a strike over wage issues if a settlement is not reached during the negotiation period. Such a strike takes place after the negotiation period as provided for in the wage-reopening clause but before the termination date of the entire contract. The question therefore arises as to whether or not a strike under these circumstances is lawful under the Taft-Hartley law. It is stressed that the law provides that no strike may take place during the 60-day notice period or until the date the contract expires, *"whichever occurs later."*

The National Labor Relations Board dealt with this question of whether or not a strike called pursuant to a wage-reopening clause is consistent with Taft-Hartley in 1954, and held that such a strike is lawful even though it occurs before the terminal date of the entire labor contract, provided that the 60-day notice requirement of the Taft-Hartley law is met.[14] In reaching this decision, the board was compelled to interpret that portion of Taft-Hartley which forbids a strike during the 60-day notice period or until the date of expiration of a contract, "whichever occurs later." It held in this connection that for purposes of the law the term *expiration* date refers not only to the terminal date of the entire collective bargaining contract but also to the date agreed upon in the contract when the parties can effect changes in its provisions. On this point, the board declared,

> the term "expiration date" as used in Section 8 (d) (4) thus has a twofold meaning: It connotes not only the terminal date of a bargaining contract, but also an agreed date in the course of its existence when the parties can effect changes in its provisions.

Upon a review, a circuit court of appeals, however, rejected the meaning attributed by the board to the term "expiration date." In this court's view, the term must be held to mean "termination" date, and all strikes for modification before the contract's actual termination are unlawful. Concluding that the labor agreement had not been "terminated" within the meaning of the Taft-Hartley Act at the time of the strike, the court ruled that the employees in the strike lost their status as employees for purposes of the law and that they could be discharged by the company. Because of the obvious importance of the issues involved in the controversy between the National Labor Relations Board and the circuit court, the board appealed to the Supreme Court for a review of the case. In

---

[14] *Lion Oil Co.,* 109 NLRB 680 (1954).

January 1957, the Supreme Court sustained the position of the board and held that the Taft-Hartley law permits a strike, after a 60-day notice, during the life of collective bargaining contracts that contain wage-reopening clauses. To the date of this writing, labor relations continued to be governed by such a principle.

WAGE DIFFERENTIALS

Under certain circumstances collective bargaining contracts provide for different rates of wages for different employees performing the same kind of work and holding down the same type of jobs. Such differentials are completely lawful, except when used by the parties to discriminate on the basis of race, color, religion, sex, or national origin; as of July 2, 1965, the latter practices were forbidden under the terms of Title VII of the Civil Rights Act of 1964.[15] To many employers (as well as to unions), moreover, utilization of the "nondiscriminatory" differentials appears mandatory to ensure an adequate supply of willing employees for work under arduous or otherwise unpleasant conditions.

The most common of these differentials involves premium payment for work on relatively undesirable shifts—in the late afternoon, evening, night, and early morning hours. Within industry as a whole 98 percent of workers in plants running such late shifts were by the mid-1960s receiving extra pay for this work.[16]

In addition, under most contracts there is now a graduated increase in compensation for working the second and third shifts. All but a tiny fraction of workers in establishments where there is a third, or "graveyard," work schedule now receive a rate for it which is higher than that received by second-shift workers. But second-shift workers themselves have received relatively significant premiums for their acceptance of these working hours: Premium rates for second-shift work are now most commonly at least five cents per hour, and often as high as 10 percent above first-shift rates. Premiums of at least 15 cents per hour, and often up to 10 percent of second-shift rates, are the general rewards for the graveyard-shift workers.

The rationale for the shift differential is quite easy to understand. When an employee works a less common shift, there is obvious interference with his family life and with his full participation in the affairs of society. In Western society the school system, recreational activities, cultural pursuits, and the like assume that employees work during the day. Since working the odd hours tends to interfere with the employee's family and

[15] Title VII did, however, grant exemptions to work forces of less than 25 persons.
[16] Bureau of National Affairs, ed., *Facts for Bargaining*, II (Washington, D.C.: Bureau of National Affairs, Inc., June 4, 1965), 522.

societal affairs, the premium is designed to compensate him for this sacrifice. And although it is a fact of industrial life that some employees because of certain conditions may actually *prefer* to work the afternoon or midnight tour (under these circumstances, the employee reaps a net benefit for the shift differential premium), because the overwhelming number of employees prefers the day shift, the shift differential will undoubtedly always be a common feature in the collectively bargained wage package.

Under many collective bargaining contracts, special premiums are also provided for workers who handle: certain supervisory or instructional duties; especially demanding tasks; or particularly hazardous, dirty, or undesirable work. For these jobs, extra pay is again granted as a premium to the basic wage rate of the worker concerned. For example, under one current Midwestern agreement a $.60-per-hour premium is paid to employees who are engaged in "dirty work." Such work is spelled out in the labor agreement and includes, among other possibilities for premium-rate reimbursement, "work in oil tanks where not cleaned out." Another labor agreement provides for the regular overtime rate for employees engaged in hazardous work. This provision covers employees working at elevations "where there is danger of a fall of fifty feet or more."

In addition to these *premium* rate practices, many collective bargaining contracts allow *lower* differentials for other situations. A number of agreements provide lower rates for workers who are handicapped, superannuated, temporary, or learners. Such differentials are rooted in the belief that these qualities make workers comparatively less productive and even the federal government, recognizing the persuasive economic logic involved, has gone along with this employer argument to the extent of exempting such workers from the minimum wage laws. Abuses have occasionally been in evidence, however: some "temporary" employees turn out, upon closer inspection, to be deserving of twenty-five-year pins; and some "handicapped" employees appear to have nothing more than color-blindness. Such situations notwithstanding, employer good faith in regard to these workers is far more the rule than the exception and the differential can be defended on the grounds that the alternative to a lower rate of remuneration for such employees is, most often, unemployment.

Until passage and implementation of the Civil Rights Act, some contracts also contained lower wage rates for women than for men and for Negroes than for white employees. For women, the practice was traditionally defended on such presumed grounds as a lesser productivity of women than men, a female inability to do all the tasks performed by men in accomplishing a job, and the argument that the employment of women at times involves extra costs not incurred when men are employed. Racial discrimination *per se* appears to have motivated the Negro differential, although some of the lower-productivity claims used to defend lower women's wages were also heard. Since mid-1965, neither type of differential is, understandably, promulgated by labor contracts which are governed by the act, although whether or not the *practices* involved will continue is subject to employer and union compliance which goes well beyond the official wording of their agreements. At least for women, one convenient and perfectly legal dodge has been available to recalcitrant managers: the *alteration* of certain jobs—often by removing some minor portion of the original job sequence—and then rewarding such work to qualified women applicants as "female work."

OVERTIME RATES OF PAY

Collective bargaining agreements invariably establish a standard number of hours per day and per week during which employees are paid their regular rate of pay. For hours worked in excess of the standard, however, employers are required to pay employees overtime rates. By far the most common standards found in labor agreements are eight hours per day and 40 hours per week, with only a fraction of labor agreements establishing standards differing from this formula. In the wearing apparel, printing, and publishing industries a number of agreements do provide for a basic 7- to 7½-hour day and 35-hour work week, and in the food-processing, retail, and service industries some contracts establish a standard 44-hour week, but these remain the exceptions.

The fact that the Fair Labor Standards Act provides a basic 40-hour week undoubtedly has caused the adoption of a 40-hour standard work week under collective bargaining. Labor agreements which provide for a basic work week in excess of 40 hours without premium overtime pay presumably do not fall within the scope of this legislation, or within the reach of the several state wage and hour laws which regulate this activity within certain states for their intrastate commerce. On the other hand, nothing in the federal wage and hour law prohibits employers and unions from negotiating a work week of *less* than 40 hours and (although thus far with more potential than actuality) the shorter work week as a partial answer to the unemployment threats of automation loomed as a new labor relations issue in the early 1970s, after years of relative quiescence. In addition, the Fair Labor Standards Act places no restriction on employers who desire their employees to work *more* than 40 hours in a work week, other than that the employees who work more than 40 hours must be paid at least one and one-half times their regular rate of pay for all hours in excess of 40.

The vast majority of labor agreements provide overtime rates of exactly one and one-half times the regular rate of pay for employees who work in excess of 40 hours per week, thus offering a not surprising conformity to the minimum provisions of the Fair Labor Standards Act, but a relatively small number of labor agreements do call for overtime rates of greater than time-and-one-half pay, most frequently double-time. With respect to hours worked in excess of the *daily* standard, most labor agreements also provide for time-and-one-half, although some labor agreements provide for double-time after a certain number of hours are worked or after a stipulated hour of the day or night. For example, some employers and unions have agreed that double-time rates should be paid if employees work more than four hours' overtime on any one workday. In this connection it should be noted that—since the Fair Labor Standards Act does not establish a basic work*day*—if employees are to be paid for working hours in excess of a certain number per day, the parties to the collective bargaining contract must negotiate this objective.

In addition to establishing standard workdays and work weeks and providing the rate for hours worked in excess of these standards, collective bargaining contracts deal with other phases of the hours and overtime problem. Most labor agreements prohibit the *pyramiding* of overtime. This means that weekly overtime premiums are not required for hours for which daily overtime premiums have already been paid; moreover, many contracts provide that only one type of overtime premium can be paid for any one day. And in many collective bargaining relationships the company also has the unlimited authority for *ordering* overtime.

As in the case of the shorter work week, this latter issue of overtime scheduling authority also promised to become a major collective bargaining issue at the time of this writing. Because of the economy's growing unemployment totals—which had reached a ten year high of 6 percent by 1971 and appeared to be going higher—and because of the constant menace of ever greater displacement through automation, some unions were pressing for a flat prohibition against overtime in an attempt to preserve job opportunities. Few unions had thus far succeeded in this goal, although several bargaining units in the wearing apparel industry did enjoy such a situation, but under some other agreements employees did have the right to *refuse* overtime without any penalty.

It seemed a reasonable speculation that both the mounting union drive for outright overtime prohibition and sanction for the independent employee refusal to work overtime would grow—despite often fierce employer antagonism to both developments—should the numbers of unemployed continue their upward path. Nor, indeed, could one discount the possibility of new governmental action in the overtime arena—perhaps along the lines of an abortive 1964 proposal of the Johnson administration that minimum overtime pay rates in selected industries be increased to double-time (with the goal of lessening the national unemployment figures of that time by encouraging new hiring).

The Johnson proposal immediately incurred heated opposition from the business community, Chase Manhattan Bank president David Rockefeller typifying the general management reaction in declaring that

> the claims made for the Administration's proposal are unjustified, the economics unsound, and the penalties unreasonable.... The Administration's plan... would penalize employer, employee, and consumer, and would not create any substantial number of new jobs. It aims at creating jobs not by making it more attractive to hire additional workers, but by making it less attractive to assign overtime.... The plain fact is that unemployment can be reduced only through the achievement of an economic growth rate high enough to sustain full employment with a "full" work week.[17]

The intensity of this kind of reaction caused the Johnson administration to shelve its project. But a persistent belief on the part of governmental economists that a considerable increase in overall employment could be obtained by such an action remained alive even in the Nixon era. And certainly, given particularly the continuing hold of the time-and-one-half overtime-pay arrangement in collective bargaining agreements, it was at least obvious that any government regulation adopting double-time as the minimum standard would be widesweeping in its effects, and that in many cases it would render the employer's typical authority to order overtime an essentially valueless prerogative.

Even without government limitations, moreover, the employer's overtime authority has rarely been an unrestricted one. About one half of all collective bargaining contracts provide that overtime work must be shared equally within given classifications of employees, or that at least this obligation of the employer is binding to the extent that overtime is to be rotated equally "as far as is practicable." Some agreements limit overtime to regular employees as against seasonal, temporary, part-time, or probationary employees. A number of labor contracts require that the employer give some advance notice of overtime work, the time period of this notice varying from early in the workday in question to early in the work week during which the overtime is to be done; failure to provide such notice normally relieves the employee of the obligation to work overtime (or at least assures him of special meal pay).

By the same token, however, under many collective bargaining agreements, penalties may be assessed against employees who refuse to work overtime. Such penalties range from discharge to ineligibility to work overtime at the next opportunity. For all that has been said regarding union pressures for overtime discouragement, the premium earnings even of overtime at time-and-one-half remain sufficiently attractive to individual employees on most occasions to make the ineligibility penalty a meaningful one.

---

[17] *Wall Street Journal*, February 18, 1964, p. 3.

Indeed, a prolific source of grievances and even arbitration is the employee complaint that the employer has improperly, under the labor agreement, failed to offer him the opportunity to work overtime. Where the grievance is found to have merit, the employer typically has the obligation of paying the employee the amount of money which he would have earned on the overtime tour of duty.

The employee, of course, has nothing to lose by filing such grievances, even if he would have refused the assignment had he been *offered* the opportunity to work overtime. If the opportunity has *not* been offered him, he can file his grievance and possibly get paid for work which he never intended to do in the first place. For these reasons, employer representatives are very careful to assure that eligible employees are afforded the opportunity to work the overtime. Where a foreman, for example, makes an error in this regard, the company may be faced with the situation of paying for the same work twice and at *premium rates*. To say the least, the company controller would take a dim view of this state of affairs! (NOTE: Case No. 3 at the end of this chapter deals with the problem of rotation of overtime.)

JOB EVALUATION AND JOB COMPARISON

Thus far we have been dealing with general changes in the level of wages under collective bargaining. The comparative-norm, ability-to-pay, standard-of-living and cost-of-living principles—as well as the principles relating to wage differentials and overtime rates—rather than affecting any *particular* jobs, apply either to all jobs within the plant or to all jobs which fall within certain widely delineated areas (for example, night work, "dirty work," and overtime work).

Another important problem, however, involves the establishment of *relative* wage rates (or rate ranges) for each particular job so that wage differentials are rationalized (jobs of greater "worth" to the company are rewarded by greater pay) and the overall wage structure is stabilized on a relatively permanent basis.

Essentially, companies adopt one of two methods to achieve the above goal: (1) job evaluation; and (2) what, for lack of a universally accepted descriptive designation, might be best described as "job comparison."

Job evaluation in its broadest sense is actually used by all companies. As French argues,

> [it] is a universal phenomenon in organizations which pay wages. For example, if the owner of an insurance brokerage decides that the receptionist should be paid more than the typists, job evaluation has occurred.

Thus, job evaluation occurs whenever decisions are made about relative worth of jobs and it is therefore an inescapable factor in organizational life.[18]

In the more technical sense in which it is used here, however, job evaluation requires a more *systematic* approach than that presumably adopted in French's brokerage example. Briefly, job evaluation—through the use of thorough job descriptions and equally detailed analyses of these descriptions—attempts to rank jobs in terms of their (1) skill, (2) effort, (3) responsibility, and (4) working requirement demands on the jobholder. *Each job* is awarded a certain number of points, according to the degree to which each of these four factors (or refinements of them) is present in it, and the total number of points consequently assigned to each job (usually on a weighted-average basis, depending on the importance of each factor) determines the place at which the particular job falls in the job hierarchy of the plant. Wage rates or ranges are then established for all jobs falling within a single total point spread (usually called a "labor grade") of this hierarchy. All jobs awarded between 250 and 275 points, for example, might constitute labor grade 4 and be paid whatever wages are called for by this labor grade.

Many managements have found the appeal of such a system to be irresistible. In addition to simplifying the wage structure through the substitution of a relatively few labor grades for individual job listings, it allows the company a basis for defending particular wage rates to the union and provides a rational means for determining rates for new and changed jobs (through using the same process for *these* jobs, and then slotting their point totals into the hierarchy of labor grades). At least three quarters of all American managements probably make use of such a system today.

This growth of job evaluation, at least for unionized companies, has nonetheless been accomplished only in the face of rather adamant union opposition. Only a few unions—most notably the Steelworkers—have done anything but strongly attack the system. Virtually all others have voiced deep suspicion of the technique itself and have decried the reduced possibilities for union bargaining on individual wage rates allowed by job evaluation.

Why, then, has this method of evaluation spread so pervasively to industry? Livernash conveys an authoritative opinion:

> In part, unions have been bought off. Objection was not strong enough to turn down evaluation if an increase in the rate structure was

---

[18] Wendell French, *The Personnel Management Process* (Boston: Houghton Mifflin Company, 1964), p. 240.

also involved.... In part, unions became willing to accept less bargaining over individual job rates.... Unions found that job evaluation did not freeze them out of a reasonable voice in influencing the wage structure and continuous wage grievances became a union problem. Particularly when accompanied by formal or informal joint participation in the evaluation process, the technique became acceptable.[19]

Thus, as the same observer concludes,

> Clearly union practice indicates a far higher degree of acceptance of and tolerance for evaluation than do official [union] pronouncements.[20]

Job comparison is, in many cases, the manager's answer to intransigent union opposition to job evaluation where this *remains* a force. It also has been utilized by many companies whose job structures do not appear complex enough to warrant job evaluation, or (in some cases) where the management itself is divided on the efficacy of the evaluation technique. Although it has certain refinements, it most frequently involves (1) the establishment of an appropriate number of labor grades with accompanying wage rates or ranges, and (2) the classification of each job into a particular labor grade by deciding which already classified jobs the particular job most closely resembles. The systematic approach of the evaluation method is, in short, dispensed with—and so are the many subsidiary advantages of such an approach. By the same token, however, whatever deficiencies the management or unions see in evaluation are also bypassed. The procedure, a not-too-satisfactory compromise between evaluations and individual rates for each job, is not now common in industry and, for the reasons indicated in the discussion of evaluation, can probably be expected to become increasingly less so in the years ahead. (Case No. 4 deals with job comparison.)

A FINAL WORD

As this chapter has demonstrated, wage rates and allied wage issues pose highly difficult collective bargaining problems. But if the resultant complications do make wage controversies the leading overt cause of strikes, the fact remains that such strikes take place in only a comparatively few instances. Although the stakes can be very high and the problems formid-

---

[19] Sumner H. Slichter, James J. Healy, and E. Robert Livernash, *The Impact of Collective Bargaining on Management* (Washington, D.C.: The Brookings Institution, 1960), pp. 563–64.
[20] *Ibid.*, p. 564.

able, employers and unions in the vast majority of cases ultimately find a peaceful solution in the wage area as in other areas of bargaining.

Some of the settlements, admittedly, may not be the kind which would be advocated by economists, and some clearly fail to adjust the issues in a way which reflects equity and fairness. But the parties, most often, do resolve their wage disputes in a manner which proves generally satisfactory to all concerned.

It should be remembered that these wage problems are not resolved in an antiseptic economic laboratory where wage models may be constructed. If the settlements do, at times, offend the economic purist, it must be appreciated that these issues are dealt with in the practical day-to-day world, wherein pressures, motives, and attitudes cannot be isolated from the negotiations. Given such realities, it is to the credit of both parties that mutual accommodation has become increasingly visible.

DISCUSSION QUESTIONS

1. Both industry *A* and industry *B* are extensively organized by militant and honestly run labor unions. Still, since 1947, the wages within industry *A* have risen at about three times the rate of those in industry *B*. How might you account for the difference in the wage situation between these two industries?
2. "Though the actual wage rate which will be negotiated in a particular negotiation is not determinable, it is certain that the set of arguments which union and management representatives will use to support their respective positions will not change from negotiation to negotiation." To what extent, if any, do you agree with this statement?
3. Compare the methods available for the adjustment of wages during the effective period of a labor agreement and defend what you would judge to be the most desirable arrangement.
4. "From the employer's point of view, it is inherently inequitable to require the payment of equal wages to women and to men for performing the same job." Construct the strongest case that you can in support of this statement and then balance your case with the most convincing *opposing* arguments that you can muster.

SELECTED REFERENCES

Lester, Richard A., *Economics of Labor*. New York: The Macmillan Company, 1964.

Morgan, Chester A., *Labor Economics,* 3rd ed. Austin, Texas: Business Publications, Inc., 1970.

Phelps-Brown, E. M., *The Economics of Labor*. New Haven: Yale University Press, 1962.

Rees, Albert, *The Economics of Trade Unions*. Chicago: University of Chicago Press, 1962.

Ross, Arthur M., *Trade Union Wage Policies*. Berkeley, Calif.: University of California Press, 1948.

Taylor, George W., and Frank C. Pierson, *New Concepts in Wage Determination.* New York: McGraw-Hill Book Company, 1957.

Tolles, N. Arnold, *Origins of Modern Wage Theories.* Englewood Cliffs, N. J.: Prentice-Hall, Inc., 1964.

CASE NO. 3

ROTATION OF OVERTIME

(In this case, the company believed that it did not violate the labor agreement's overtime equalization clause. The arbitrator found otherwise, and awarded the grievants the wages that they would have earned had they worked the overtime. He did this even though the company argued that the arbitrator had no authority to award back wages as a remedy for the company's violation. Hence, squarely involved in this case is the issue of the authorized power of the arbitrator. Keep this in mind as you read the case.)

This dispute involves the issue of overtime assignments. In protest against the company action involved under the circumstances of this case, the union filed two grievances. Grievance No. 68–160, dated November 28, 1968, was filed by the union on behalf of employees *S, E, T,* and *W*. They are classified as maintenance men. It states:

> Overtime was required on the 3:00 to 11:00 P.M. Shift 11–28–68. These low men on overtime were not offered the overtime.

On November 28, 1968, the union also filed grievance No. 68–161 on behalf of employees *P, K, G,* and *B*. They are assistant maintenance men. It states:

> Overtime was required on the 3:00 P.M. to 11:00 P.M. Shift 11–28–68. The low asst. maint. men on overtime were not offered the overtime.

As a remedy for each of the grievances the union requests that the company pay each of the grievants eight (8) hours' pay at two and one-half (2½) times the employees' regular rate of pay.

In step 2 of the grievance procedure the company denied each of the grievances stating that

> the Company will make every effort to distribute overtime so that the Grievant shares in the appropriate overtime as equally as possible.

In step 3 of the grievance procedure the company denied both grievances stating

> the Company is making every effort to distribute overtime as equally as possible among the employees who customarily perform work where

overtime is required. Payment as requested in this grievance, in lieu of overtime assignments is denied.

Having failed to resolve the grievances in the grievance procedure, the parties have submitted them to arbitration for their final and binding determination.

Involved in this dispute are following provisions of the labor agreement:

ARTICLE V

Section 2. An employee shall be compensated at the rate of 1½ times his basic rate of pay for all time worked by him
- a) in excess of 8 hours in any one work day; or
- b) in excess of 40 hours in any one work week (excluding hours paid for under Section 2[a]); or
- c) on the 6th consecutive work day worked by him in any one work week.

An employee shall be compensated at the rate of 2 times his basic rate of pay for all time worked by him on the 7th consecutive work day worked by him in a work week.

Any employee must work a minimum of 4 hours on each day for it to constitute a day worked for the purpose of computing overtime for work performed on the 6th and 7th consecutive work days worked in a work week.

Section 4. When overtime is required in a department, area or classification, the Company will make every effort to distribute the overtime as equally as possible among the employees who customarily perform such work. A record of the overtime worked in each department, area or classification shall be posted daily, to the extent possible, Monday through Friday.

When in quest of an employee to perform overtime work a supervisor will, where reasonably possible, contact or attempt to contact the six (6) employees lowest in overtime. If the supervisor is unsuccessful in his attempts to contact the six (6) employees he can assign the overtime to anyone qualified and available provided a Union member has been given the opportunity to be present when the calls are made, but there shall be no such requirement for a Union member to be present when such calls are made from outside the Plant.

ARTICLE IX

Section 1. The following shall be considered paid holidays for each employee:
New Year's Day
Good Friday
Memorial Day
Fourth of July
Labor Day
Thanksgiving Day
Friday after Thanksgiving Day
Christmas Eve (December 24)

Christmas Day.

An employee who works on any of the holidays mentioned in this Section shall be entitled for all time worked by him on such day, including time worked in excess of eight (8) hours, to compensation at the rate of two and one-half (2½) times his hourly base rate.

ARTICLE XI

Section 2. The impartial umpire shall have the authority only to interpret and apply the provisions of this Agreement, and he shall not have authority to alter or to add to in any way any of such provisions. An award of the impartial umpire shall not in any case be made retroactive to a date prior to the date on which the subject of the grievance occurred.

THE BACKGROUND

This dispute involves the assignment of maintenance employees to overtime work which occurred on the 3 P.M. to 11 P.M. shift on Thanksgiving Day, November 28, 1968. All the grievants are either classified as maintenance men or assistant maintenance men. Under the labor agreement Thanksgiving Day is considered a paid holiday, and employees who work on a holiday are to be paid at two and one-half (2½) times their regular hourly rate. At the time of the circumstances of this case the company employed 340 maintenance employees.

On November 27, 1968, at about 2 P.M. the company informed *F*, a maintenance foreman, that a conveyor system had to be repaired on the next day. Thereupon, the foreman phoned and requested a man who was in charge of overtime*

to get people to work on Thanksgiving to repair the equipment.

F testified that this man told him he could not get anybody to do the work. The man told him that at least six maintenance employees refused to work on Thanksgiving. The foreman testified that he asked the man if the refusals were such that he

could ask the employees that worked directly for me to do the job.

F declared further that the man told him he could do this, and, thereupon, *F* testified:

So I contacted the people working for me and got eight people to agree to work the next day. At this time, I realized that the job would run to excess of 8 hours and asked these people about working more than eight hours.

---

* *F* did not testify as to the name of this man. He testified he did not know who he was, though he spoke to him over the telephone.

In any event, the eight employees whom *F* contacted on November 27 reported for work at 7 A.M. on Thanksgiving Day. The repair job in question required four maintenance men and four assistant maintenance men. *F* assigned them to the repair job.

Also reporting at 7 A.M. on Thanksgiving Day were twenty-eight maintenance employees who had been previously scheduled for work on that day. The record is not clear as to whether or not the eight-man repair crew selected by the foreman was included in this figure of twenty-eight men. However, this confusion is not important for the proper determination of the dispute involved in this case. In any event, scheduled for Thanksgiving Day maintenance work were the eight grievants involved in this proceeding. They were not assigned to the aforecited repair crew, but were among those maintenance personnel scheduled for Thanksgiving Day.

F testified that the repair job on the conveyor system was not completed at 3 P.M., the normal quitting time for first-shift employees. With the exception of one man, *F* elected to keep the repair crew working after 3 P.M. The employee who left at 3 P.M. was replaced by another maintenance employee. The replacement was not one of the grievants involved in this case. The repair crew worked until 11 P.M.

X, a maintenance man, worked on Thanksgiving Day. Apparently he was one of the employees who was selected for the repair crew in question. *X* testified:

> I worked the day turn (7 A.M. to 3 P.M.) on Thanksgiving Day. At the end of the shift, I saw that we would not finish the repair job. I discussed this with *F*. I said he should get the men with the lowest amount of overtime in the yard* to work after 3 P.M. He told me "I am going to use the same crew that I had."

The parties stipulated that the grievants

> had a lesser amount of overtime than those who actually did the repair work.

The record demonstrates that a considerable amount of overtime is worked by the Maintenance Department. Also the record shows that a considerable amount of overtime is refused among the maintenance personnel. Thus, Company Exhibit No. 1 shows that for the month of November 1968 the Maintenance Department employees, maintenance men and assistant maintenance men, worked 8,965 overtime hours. For the same month the document demonstrates that maintenance personnel declined 4,677½ overtime hours.

Company Exhibit No. 2 depicts the grievants' overtime hours of

---

* By the men in the "yard" is meant those maintenance personnel who were working in the plant area on Thanksgiving Day.

November 28, 1968, and June 28, 1969, as compared to the average amount of overtime in the grievants' respective classifications. The document states:

Name	November 28, 1968 Overtime Hours	November 28, 1968 Classification Average	June 28, 1969 Overtime Hours	June 28, 1969 Classification Average
B	100	$104\frac{1}{2}$	213	$203\frac{1}{2}$
G	$106\frac{1}{2}$	$104\frac{1}{2}$	198	$203\frac{1}{2}$
K	$99\frac{1}{2}$	$104\frac{1}{2}$	$208\frac{1}{2}$	$203\frac{1}{2}$
P	88	$104\frac{1}{2}$	203	$203\frac{1}{2}$

Name	November 28, 1968 Overtime Hours	November 28, 1968 Classification Average	June 28, 1969 Overtime Hours	June 28, 1969 Classification Average
E	100	103	215	210
S	99	103	$217\frac{1}{2}$	210
T	$84\frac{1}{2}$	103	206	210
W	$93\frac{1}{2}$	103	215	210

BASIC QUESTION

The basic question involved in this proceeding is framed as follows: Under the circumstances of this case, did the Company violate the overtime provisions of the Labor Agreement? If so, what should the remedy be?

POSITION OF THE PARTIES

It is the position of the company that the grievances should be denied. In defense of this position the company argues:

> It is the position of the Company in these grievances that there has been no contract violation. There is no contractual provision for payment for time not worked and no contractual *time limit* for the equalization of overtime distribution.
> In neither of these cases does the Contract require that the employees lowest in overtime be given the overtime assignment under all circumstances, nor does it require that overtime be equalized at a specific time. Neither does the Contract require or permit the Company to pay for a differential in the amount of overtime worked. It does require that overtime be distributed as equally as possible, thus providing for inequities to be resolved by distribution rather than by paying for time not

worked. None of the Grievants have suffered any loss; all currently are in a relatively average position in their sharing groups.

Where necessary and appropriate, additional company arguments and observations will be cited in the subsequent portion of this opinion.

It is the position of the union that the grievances should be granted. In defense of this position the union argues:

> The Union feels the Company has an obligation to contact the six employees with the least amount of overtime when reasonably possible. The parties have worked out an accommodation which takes into account the difficulty of making all the necessary contacts in the Company's spread-out facilities. The present Contract does not demand that overtime be in exact balance at all times: it gives the Company a degree of flexibility by requiring it to contact only the six employees who are lowest in overtime. That is the standard both parties have agreed upon for determining whether the Company has complied with its obligation to "make every effort to distribute the overtime as equally as possible among the employees."
>
> From the language in the Contract as well as the bargaining history, it is held that the offering of a subsequent overtime opportunity to a bypassed employee named in the grievance is not an adequate remedy.

Where necessary and appropriate, additional union arguments and observations will be cited in the subsequent portion of this opinion.

ANALYSIS OF THE EVIDENCE

The Time Period Involved: 3 P.M. to 11 P.M.

To place this dispute in its correct perspective, it may be stated at the outset that the controversy does not center on the maintenance personnel who reported at 7 A.M. on Thanksgiving Day. Though there was some testimony in the arbitration hearing and some reference in the parties' post-hearing briefs of how the employees for the repair job were selected by F in the first place, the fact is that their initial selection is not at the core of the case. Note the grievances deal exclusively with the time period between 3 P.M. and 11 P.M. Actually, the grievants worked the day turn, 7 A.M. to 3 P.M., and, of course, have no claim for overtime work during this period of time. Rather the grievances charge improper assignment of overtime work for the time during which the repair crew worked after 3 P.M. The union believes that the grievants should have been afforded the opportunity to perform the repair work which took place between 3 P.M. and 11 P.M. on the grounds that they had lower overtime hours as compared to the eight employees whom F kept on after 3 P.M. As stated, the parties stipulated that the grievants had less overtime hours as compared to the eight employees who F directed to perform the repair work between 3 P.M. and 11 P.M. on the day in question.

F and the "Overtime Contact" Provision

Article V, Section 4* contains the provision that when a supervisor has need for an employee to work overtime, he will

> where reasonably possible contact or attempt to contact the six (6) employees lowest in overtime.*

It also requires that when such a contact is made, or attempted to be made, a union member shall have the opportunity to be present, provided the contact is made in the plant.

The present version of the overtime contact clause was adopted for the first time in the current labor agreement. In the previous contract the supervisor had the obligation only to contact three employees among those lowest in overtime. This provision stated: (Labor Agreement dated August 4, 1965 to August 1, 1968)

> If in quest of an employee to perform overtime work, a supervisor has contacted or attempted to contact three employees without success, he shall not be obligated to continue trying to obtain an employee from among those lowest in overtime, but can assign the overtime to anyone qualified and available provided a Union member has been given the opportunity to be present when the calls are made, but there shall be no such requirement for a Union member to be present when such calls are made from outside the plant.

Thus, the current version of the overtime contact clause is much more precise and unambiguous. What it tells us is that before a supervisor can assign overtime work to anyone qualified and available, *he must contact or attempt to contact the six (6) employees lowest in overtime.* Obviously, the parties adopted the new and current version of the overtime contact clause in order to place a more definite and objective obligation on the foreman who desires employees to work overtime. Under the previous contract, the obligation placed on the foreman was comparatively vague and uncertain. To correct this situation the parties adopted a definite, precise, and objective standard. The six employees lowest in overtime must be contacted or attempted to be contacted by a supervisor before the supervisor is permitted to assign the overtime work to other employees. Here then we have a simple, concrete, and objective obligation placed on the supervisor.

Deliberate Violation of Overtime Contact Clause

In this light it should be perfectly obvious to all concerned that F deliberately violated the current version of the overtime contact

* For convenience this provision will be referred to hereinafter as the overtime contact clause.

clause. He made no attempt whatsoever to contact the six employees with the lowest amount of overtime among the maintenance personnel who were working the day shift on Thanksgiving Day. If he did, the grievants would have been selected for the work between 3 P.M. and 11 P.M.; there would have been no dispute; and we would not be in arbitration. The grievants were available; they were qualified; and they were low in overtime hours as compared with the employees whom F kept on the repair job after 3 P.M.

When X told F to get the men lowest in overtime who were in the yard to work after 3 P.M., his reply was that he was going to carry on with the same crew. X testified that after it became apparent that the repair job was not going to be finished by 3 P.M., he (X) discussed the problem with F. He testified without contradiction that he (X) told F that he "should get the lowest men in overtime."

To this the foreman replied: "I am going to use the same crew I had." Hence, not even a warning or counsel by X deterred the foreman in his disregard of the overtime contact clause.

Note that the overtime contact clause relieves a supervisor from the obligation to contact the six employees with the least amount of overtime when such a procedure would not be "reasonably possible." Under the circumstances of this case it would be a masterpiece of error to find that such a contact would not be reasonably possible. At the most there were thirty-six maintenance personnel working the day shift on Thanksgiving Day. Certainly with such a comparatively small number of employees at work, it would have been a simple matter for F to comply with the overtime contact clause.

What, however, impresses the arbitrator most about F's conduct is that he made no attempt to comply with the provision in question. Indeed, in his testimony developed in the arbitration hearing, he made no effort even to explain why he did not contact or attempt to contact the grievants. As stated, a foreman need not contact the six employees with the least overtime or even attempt to contact them where there are circumstances which would make such contacts unreasonable. However, F did not even explain why he refused to make the contacts. Here we do not have an inadvertent error on the part of the foreman; here we do not have any confusion in the state of the mind of the foreman; here we do not have evidence that there were some circumstances involved which would make the contact unreasonable; here we do not have evidence of some sort of an emergency or pressing need that justified the foreman not to contact or attempt to contact the six employees with the lowest amount of overtime.

Rather what we have here is incontrovertible evidence that *F proceeded as if the overtime contact clause were not in the labor agreement.* This was his action despite the fact that he was warned and counseled by X to follow the procedure which the parties adopted in contract negotiations and solemnized in crystal-clear and perfectly understandable language. In short, what we have here is a deliberate, conscious, and flagrant violation by *F* of a plain, unambiguous, and understandable procedure adopted by the parties.

In its argument the company states: (Company Post-Hearing Brief, p. 7)

> At the Hearing, the Union attempted to make an issue of an alleged violation of Article V, Section 4, Page 10, Paragraph 2 [the overtime contact clause]. *This is a procedural matter in which there is no complaint contained in the grievance before the Arbitrator.*

To the contrary, and with full deference to the company, the fact is that F's complete disregard of the requirements of the overtime contact clause is at the very heart of this proceeding. Indeed, his deliberate violation of the procedure is at the essence of the grievants' complaint. They grieve because *F* disregarded the procedure outlined in the contact clause, and thereby deprived them of the opportunity to work the overtime hours in question. To argue that the foreman's deliberate violation of the overtime contact clause is a mere "procedural matter" and not within the scope of the grievance before the arbitrator is to ignore a fundamental issue involved in this proceeding.

In short, the arbitrator finds on the basis of the incontrovertible evidence that *F* deliberately violated that standard of the overtime provisions which requires a supervisor to contact, or attempt to contact, the six (6) employees with the least amount of overtime before the foreman may assign the overtime to anyone he desires.

At times, a supervisor violates overtime assignment language in error; because of some sort of an emergency or pressing need; or because of some confusion as to which employees should be contacted for overtime work. Any employer's obligation to rotate overtime, and distribute overtime equally, should be viewed with a measure of sympathetic understanding. The arbitrator recognizes that under the pressure of production, to get things done, a supervisor may make an error. This would be particularly true in the instant company wherein the amount of overtime is considerable and because the amount of refusal of overtime is likewise considerable.

Thus, arbitrators at times give sympathetic understanding to extenuating circumstances which have resulted in the failure of supervisors to comply with overtime distribution procedures. At times, arbitrators have held that under the circumstances of a particular case, it is not practical or reasonable for a supervisor to comply with overtime language.

What is impressive, however, in *F*'s conduct is that none of these observations applies. *He offers no explanation as to why he did not even attempt to comply with the standards outlined in the overtime contact clause.* Indeed, F persisted in his deliberate violation of the overtime contact clause despite being warned and counseled by a union member. In short, as stated, he proceeded in his conduct as if the overtime contact clause were not even in the labor agreement.

If the arbitrator did not consider such conduct on the part of the foreman in the assessment of the grievants' claim, he would destroy the integrity of the clause in question. Indeed, if the arbitrator did not regard F's conduct as a central feature of this case, he would in effect read the provision out of the contract.

Expansion of the Company Position

If the arbitrator understands the position of the company and the sense of its argument, it is that despite the obvious violation by F of the overtime contact clause the grievances still do not have merit. Its argument is that the violation of the overtime contact clause does not mean that the company violated the overtime equalization provision which requires the company to make

> every effort to distribute the overtime as equally as possible.

Beyond this, the company argument is expanded one step further. Thus, even conceding that under the circumstances of this case the company is held to violate the overtime contact clause and the overtime equalization provision, the arbitrator has no power to issue an award to direct back pay. A money remedy, the company argues, is not authorized under the labor agreement even though it may be held that the company on Thanksgiving Day violated the overtime provisions.

In defense of this position the company contends that at the most the proper remedy would be the assignment to the grievants of overtime opportunities in the future. However, the company's main point is that by June 28, 1969, the grievants' overtime status compared favorably with the other employees in the Maintenance Department, and, therefore, there was no violation of the overtime equalization provision, and, consequently, no remedy whatsoever would be proper. That is, since the overtime equalization provision contains no time limits as to when overtime must be equalized, no remedy would be required since by June 28, 1969, the company had equalized overtime for the grievants.

To repeat the central company argument:

> It is the position of the Company in these grievances that there has been no contract violation. There is no contractual provision for payment for time not worked and no contractual *time limit* for the equalization of overtime distribution.
> In neither of these cases does the Contract require that the employees lowest in overtime be given the overtime assignment under all circumstances, nor does it require that overtime be equalized at a specific time. Neither does the Contract require or permit the Company to pay for a differential in the amount of overtime worked. It does require that overtime be distributed as equally as possible, thus providing for inequities to be resolved by distribution rather than by paying for time not worked.

None of the Grievants have suffered any loss; all currently are in a relatively average position in their sharing groups.

It emphasizes that by June 28, 1969, the grievants' overtime assignments were comparatively equal to the average amount of overtime in the Maintenance Department. In this regard the company states:

The Company is distributing overtime as equally as possible recognizing the circumstances of its size, operational complexities, amount of overtime worked, personnel distribution and availability. *This is illustrated by the Grievants' opportunity to work overtime subsequent to the circumstances upon which these Grievances are based, and it is further illustrated by the Grievants' current overtime status.*

With respect to the demand by the union for a money remedy, the company argues:

The Union has taken a position that the Company is obligated to pay the Grievants for time not worked. Article V, Section 2 specifically provides for time *worked* by an employee. The contract does not provide, in any applicable provision related to this situation, payment for time not worked. Article V, Section 4 provides only for the distribution of overtime and does not require equalization at all times. If the parties had contemplated payments as requested in these grievances, they would have so provided as they specifically did in Article V, Section 2 and 6 for other instances when an employee should be compensated for overtime and the amount to be received.

It is apparent that in the absence of a specific Contract provision relating to payment for an overtime imbalance, no such provision may be implied. In the absence of such language, we believe the Union is asking the Arbitrator to modify the terms of the Contract as negotiated.

For the Arbitrator to grant the Union's demand for payment for time not worked would not be just or proper, or even permissible under the terms of the Contract. The Company submits that a much more reasonable and practical remedy is available and that is distributing overtime as equally as possible. The Company's obligation, and the Contract's intent and purpose is to distribute overtime as equally as possible, not to pay for time not worked.

In defense of its position the company refers to the D arbitration award which involved the instant parties, and which decision was rendered on December 6, 1962 (Company Exhibit No. 4). In his award Arbitrator D stated:

There is no provision in the Agreement for payment of overtime not worked. The Agreement provides that the overtime shall be distributed as equally as possible among the employees in the department or division but it gives no time limit on such equalization.

On the basis of the D award, the company states:

This position and practice was upheld in a previous arbitration between the parties (Grievance No. 62–9, FMCS File No. 62A/3456), the award of which was presented as Company Exhibit 5. In this award, Arbitrator *D* said:
"There is no provision in the Agreement for payment of overtime not worked. The Agreement provides that the overtime shall be distributed as equally as possible among the employees in the department or division, but it gives no time limit on such equalization."
The basic language of this provision is unchanged in the present contract. An examination of the Contracts in effect since 1960 will show that the following language is essentially the same:
"When overtime is required in a Department, Area, or classification, the Company will make every effort to distribute the overtime as equally as possible among the employees who customarily perform such work."

The D Award

It is true that the overtime equalization language has remained the same since the *D* award. Such language reads exactly the same in all contracts since the award, including the current labor agreement. Certainly this arbitrator is fully aware that an arbitration decision interpreting and applying contractual language is binding upon subsequent arbitrators where the issue in arbitration involves the same contractual language. Indeed, upon occasion, the instant arbitrator has used this principle to deny grievances. However, for two reasons the instant arbitrator does not find controlling the *D* decision for purposes of the instant case. In the first place, it should be noted that in Arbitrator *D*'s decision he held that the company's failure to assign the available overtime to an employee low in overtime was attributable in part to an "honest error." In this connection he stated:

> The Company is understandably trying to distribute the overtime as equally as possible and the incident of this grievance was the result of an honest error on the part of an employee in the bargaining unit. (p. 5)

In short, one reason for the denial of the grievance by Arbitrator *D* was the fact that the low overtime man was bypassed by an "honest error." In the instant case, it would ignore the incontrovertible evidence to find that *F*'s refusal to offer the overtime work available on Thanksgiving Day to the grievants resulted from an "honest error."

In the second place, the instant arbitrator does not regard the *D* decision as binding upon him because when his decision was made the labor agreement which governed his decision did not contain the overtime contact clause as it appears in its present form. Instead it contained the old, vague, and ambiguous language which appeared in previous contracts. As we know, the instant labor agreement changes the requirement by the adoption of plain, objective, and understandable language. In short, the present version of the overtime contact clause makes it absolutely certain what a supervisor must do when he seeks employees to work overtime. Such language simply did not appear in the labor agreement which was in existence when Arbitrator D made his decision. In summary, we do not know what Arbitrator D would have ruled had there been no "honest error" and if the present form of the overtime contact clause were included in the labor agreement under which he rendered his decision.

Simultaneous Violation of Overtime Equalization Provision

Thus, the arbitrator does not find that the D decision is binding upon him under the circumstances of this case. With this finding made, the next issue to be determined is whether or not the company's violation of the overtime contact clause results in a violation of the overtime equalization provision. By the "overtime equalization provision" is meant that language which states:

> When overtime is required...the Company will make every effort to distribute the overtime as equally as possible....

It is true, as the company argues, that there are no time limits contained in the provision as to when overtime is to be equalized. On this basis the company contends that it did not violate this provision of the labor agreement, since by June 28, 1969, the grievants' overtime status compared substantially favorably to other employees in the Maintenance Department. In other words, the company position is that even though the overtime contact clause was violated by F this does not mean that the overtime equalization provision was violated. In effect, the company position is that the two provisions should be read separately and independently. The violation of one does not mean that there was a violation of the other provision.

Under the circumstances of this case, the arbitrator finds this reasoning to be unacceptable. Note that the overtime equalization provision states that the company will make "every effort" to equalize overtime. *Clearly, F did not make any effort whatsoever to equalize overtime when he deliberately violated the overtime contact clause.* The overtime contact clause was obviously adopted by the parties in its present form for the purpose of making more sure that the Company will make "every effort" to equalize overtime. If this were not the fundamental purpose of this provision, the arbitrator wonders what was the purpose of the parties.

In short, under the circumstances of this case, it must be held that F's violation of the overtime contact clause resulted in a simultaneous violation of the overtime equalization language. For purposes of this case, both provisions must be read together and not separately. The fact that the grievants' overtime status as of June 28, 1969, compared favorably with the other employees in the Maintenance Department does not erase the fact the F on Thanksgiving Day did not make "every effort" to equalize overtime. In fact, he made no effort whatsoever, and his action resulted in a greater disparity of overtime hours of the grievants as compared to the employees whom the foreman kept on the job.

The Proper Remedy

So far we have found that the company under the circumstances of this case has violated the overtime provisions of the labor agreement. It violated the overtime contact clause and the overtime equalization provision. What remains, therefore, is to determine whether or not the grievants' claim for back pay is a proper remedy under the labor agreement. As demonstrated before, the company position is that the arbitrator has no authority to direct back pay. As it states:

> For the Arbitrator to grant the Union's demand for payment for time not worked would not be just or proper, or even permissible under the terms of the Contract.

At the most, the company contends that the proper award could be that the grievants should be permitted to make up the overtime which they lost on Thanksgiving Day sometime in the future; that is, the makeup of overtime work is the only remedy authorized in the labor agreement.

Certainly this arbitrator is conscious of any limitations of powers placed on him under the labor agreement. He has always been respectful of any limitations which a contract places upon his authority. He understands that his powers flow from the contract, and to go beyond those powers would constitute an abuse of arbitral authority.

Keeping all of this in mind, and after carefully considering the argument of the company, the arbitrator is still fully satisfied that under the labor agreement he has the authority to direct back pay under the circumstances of this case, and further, that a back pay award constitutes the only adequate remedy for the willful violation of the overtime provisions by Foreman F.

If the arbitrator did not direct back pay under the circumstances of this case, it would mean that there would be no meaningful and adequate way to enforce the overtime contact clause. In the absence of a back pay award, supervisors in the future could violate its terms with impunity. Thus, to maintain the integrity of contractual language the arbitrator of necessity must direct back pay. Not to do so under the circumstances of this case would license supervisors to violate the overtime contact clause which would mean that there would be less assurance that overtime would be equalized.

In its defense that it would not be proper or even permissible for the arbitrator to direct back pay, the company stresses that the overtime provisions do not expressly provide for such a remedy and that such a remedy should not be implied. The company also argues that under the overtime provisions it is only obligated to pay for overtime which is worked. It is not obligated to pay for overtime which is not worked, the company contends.

If this is true, how do we account for the fact that the company has paid two grievances for overtime violations of the labor agreement? Thus, the record demonstrates that the company itself paid two grievances when it was charged with violation of the overtime provisions. In Grievance No. 67–79, dated September 7, 1967, the company paid an employee for eight hours' overtime at double and one-half his regular rate because the company violated the overtime provisions (Union Exhibit No. 3). In Grievance No. 67–127, dated December 5, 1967, the company paid an employee eight hours of pay at time and one-half his regular rate for an overtime violation (Union Exhibit No. 4).

With respect to the monetary settlement of these two grievances, the company states: (Company Post-Hearing Brief, p. 10)

> Out of the hundreds of thousands of overtime manhours worked at the facility since the Company has had a contractual obligation to distribute overtime, the Union can only point to two incidents (one involving complications by holiday schedule) where the Company has paid for time not worked, although a Union witness testified there have been many disputes. It is an understatement to say that it would be incredulous to consider this a "precedent" or "practice."

It is true that two instances do not constitute a "past practice" as this concept is used in arbitration. However, this is not the point for purposes of this case. The importance of the monetary settlement of the two aforecited grievances is that such a remedy under appropriate circumstances may be made under the contract. This was done by the company itself on two comparatively recent occasions. It did so under the same overtime language which appears in the instant labor agreement. Thus, if the company has itself fashioned a money remedy, does it not follow that the arbitrator has the authority to direct the same kind of remedy under proper circumstances? In short, the company action itself demonstrates that there can be occasions under which a back pay award is authorized for violations of the overtime language. If a money remedy were not permitted by its terms, it is extremely doubtful that the company would have paid the aforecited grievances.

In defense of its position that the arbitrator is not empowered to direct a money remedy for violation of the overtime provisions, the company refers to past negotiations in which the union without success attempted to negotiate specific language to authorize money payments for overtime violations. It points out that in the 1962 contract negotiations, the union unsuccessfully attempted to negotiate an amendment to the overtime provisions which stated: "Overtime errors will be paid the aggrieved employee."

Also it points out that in the negotiations which resulted in the current labor agreement the union committee stated, as testified to by *R*, a member of the union committee:

> The overtime issue was brought up in the last negotiations. In the event the Company did not abide by the contract on overtime, we wanted the Company to pay. This was brought up several times in negotiations.

It would, of course, be true that if the union were successful in these attempts the labor agreement would make more clear the company's obligation under proper circumstances to pay back wages for overtime violations. About this there is no question, and the arbitrator is candid enough to recognize this fact. However, the unsuccessful attempts of the union in this respect do not mean that it forfeited rights of employees which they already have in the labor agreement. The company argues that with these unsuccessful attempts there is no specific language authorizing back pay. However, it is also true that there is no specific clause in the labor agreement which forbids the awarding of back pay. The failure of the union's attempt merely left things as they were and subject to the construction of the relevant contractual language as to whether or not back pay under proper circumstances is permitted under the labor agreement. And did not the company itself tend to resolve this issue when it paid the two aforecited grievances wherein there was a violation of the overtime provisions? Note that these grievances were paid *after* the first attempt of the union to negotiate specific language, and it paid the second one *under language which is exactly the same as appears in the current labor agreement.*

Arbitration Precedents

In its argument the company states:

> The Union, by its demand for time not worked is seeking to impose a penalty against the Company for which no contractual provision exists and which is contrary to vast arbitral authority.

To the contrary, there exists a significant body of arbitration precedent in which respected and professional arbitrators have directed a money remedy when the employer violated overtime equalization language which is essentially the same as found in the instant labor agreement. They have done so under the facts of a particular case when in the judgment of the arbitrator a money remedy was the only practical and meaningful remedy.

The same argument which the company advances in this case was raised by Pittsburgh Plate Glass in an arbitration case decided by Arbitrator *S* (32 LA 622). In that case, the overtime language reads as follows:

> The Company will endeavor to divide overtime equitably among regularly scheduled qualified employees within a department who regularly perform such work.

Thus, the language is quite similar to that which we find in the instant labor agreement.

Like the company in this case, Pittsburgh Plate Glass argued that the arbitrator was not empowered to award a remedy in favor of back wages. Thus, it is stated by Arbitrator S:

> There is another basic issue that is generic to all these grievances, and that concerns the remedy to be applied, if and when it appears that the overtime has been allocated improperly. The Company argues that in such an eventuality this Board should require that the resultant disparity in overtime hours be corrected at the earliest possible time by affording the successful grievant an opportunity to work it out, and that to do otherwise is to inflict a penalty without the Agreement.

Arbitrator S rejected the argument advanced by Pittsburgh Plate Glass, and granted a back pay award in many of the grievances before him. While doing so he stated:

> The Company's suggestion that it merely be required to give the successful grievant the next, or an early, opportunity to work overtime *finds very little support in the reasoning of arbitrators considering this problem throughout industry* (emphasis supplied).

And:

> *The overwhelming predominance of views expressed by arbitrators, however, is in favor of granting pay for the overtime lost* (emphasis supplied).

Note also that in *Pittsburgh Plate Glass,* the contract did not contain a specific and clearly drawn up overtime contact clause as is present in the instant labor agreement. Also, in the precedent case, there is no showing as in this case that the supervisors deliberately and flagrantly engaged in a violation of the overtime provisions.

In *Bendix Aviation* (26 LA 540), Arbitrator K applied a contract which stated that overtime should be equalized

> within a classification or a shift insofar as practicable.

Back pay was directed, and Arbitrator K stated in defense of his decision that

> it is the Company's position that all it is required to do under the language of Section 6 is to equalize overtime. The Company's remedy would not prevent violations of the Collective Bargaining Agreement.

A right is of no value unless an adequate remedy exists (emphasis supplied).

In *Standard Lime & Cement Co.* (26 LA 469), Arbitrator *D* had before him an overtime provision which stated:

> It is recognized that overtime cannot always be offered to the man entitled to the same at the time overtime is needed, but the Company will attempt insofar as practical to equalize the same during the one (1) year term of this contract.

While directing back pay, Arbitrator *D* stated:

> The right and privilege of performing overtime work is to be exercised at the time it arises and may not be substituted by a later assignment. The fact that the overtime assignment section does not specify any penalty against the Company [*this is exactly the argument in the instant proceeding*] in the case of failure to assign overtime to the proper employee is of no significance since the section expressly affords a right and the remedy in the event of a violation is inherent in the grievance procedure.

In *U.S. Rubber* (13 LA 839), Arbitrator *A*, while directing back pay under an overtime equalization clause, stated:

> Affording an employee an opportunity to make up improperly lost hours at a later date is not an adequate remedy. He is entitled to work those hours at the time they are available, not at a later time more convenient to the employer. Furthermore, there always remains the possibility of termination of an employee between the time he is improperly denied available hours and the time when the employer decides to make additional hours available to him.

There is no need to add to the list of precedents. Contrary to the company's argument that back pay under overtime equalization language would be "contrary to vast arbitral authority," the fact is that arbitral authority demonstrates that arbitrators under proper circumstances have directed back pay. As in the instant labor agreement, the contracts before the cited arbitrators did not contain specific language authorizing them to direct back pay. However, the arbitrators have directed back pay in order to make meaningful and effective the overtime equalization distribution language. And what is significant is that the precedent cases do not contain an element present in the instant case—the deliberate and conscious refusal of *F* to honor the overtime contact clause. Indeed, a deliberate violation by a supervisor resulted in the payment of back pay under the following overtime language (*Kimberley Clark*, 39 LA 216):

> Any errors in the assignment of overtime should be corrected through the assignment of future overtime hours.

Despite this plain language, which appears to forbid the payment of a money remedy under any circumstances whatsoever, the arbitrator in *Kimberly Clark* directed back pay because of a deliberate and conscious violation of the overtime provisions by supervision.

CONCLUSIONS

Under the circumstances of this particular case, the arbitrator concludes that a back pay award is the only adequate and meaningful remedy for F's willful violation of the overtime provisions. The overtime contact clause was designed to protect employees in their overtime rights. It makes more meaningful the company's obligation to make "every effort" to distribute overtime as equally as possible. Here we do not have an honest error on the part of the foreman, or confusion, or some pressing need to bypass the overtime contact clause. Rather, we have here a deliberate, conscious, and flagrant disregard of a contractual provision which the parties adopted in their recent negotiations.

Certainly, the foreman did not make "every effort" to distribute overtime equally. Hence, his violation of the overtime contact clause resulted in a simultaneous violation of the overtime equalization language. That by June 28, 1969, the grievants compared favorably in overtime work with other employees in the Maintenance Department does not erase the fact that on Thanksgiving Day the foreman did not contact the six (6) employees with the least overtime so that overtime equalization would be implemented.

To refuse to direct a back pay award under these circumstances would literally wipe out a contract provision. It would mean that in the future any supervisor could ignore the overtime contact provision with impunity. In the absence of a back pay award, this provision would be rendered worthless. Supervisors could proceed, as F did, as if the provision were not in the labor agreement. Such conduct would make it less likely that employees would be protected in their overtime rights.

As to the authority of the arbitrator to direct back pay, he stresses that if he did not award back pay there would be no effective way to maintain the integrity of the overtime contact clause. In addition, there is no specific language in the labor agreement which forbids the arbitrator to direct back pay under proper circumstances. Also, the fact is that the company itself on two occasions awarded back pay for violations of the overtime provisions. If the contract forbids such payment, the company itself would scarcely have paid out money for the two grievances.

In short, the arbitrator, after due consideration of the contractual language involved and the facts of this case, is fully satisfied that he has the authority to direct back pay. His judgment in this respect is reinforced by the weight of arbitration authority.

As the published and unpublished arbitration awards of this arbitrator have demonstrated, he has not hesitated to deny grievances which have no merit. Indeed, locals of this national union have been involved in cases before this arbitrator in the past and have frequently received unfavorable awards. This statement is made for the sole purpose of demonstrating that the instant arbitrator does not grant grievances unless there is a sound and genuine basis. He does not take arbitration lightly, and grants or denies grievances only when he is satisfied that his decision is justified by the evidence and the contractual language involved.

In the instant case, the arbitrator is fully satisfied that the union has presented meritorious grievances. He is equally satisfied that under the relevant contractual language and under the facts of this case, he is authorized to direct back pay, and that the award of back pay is the only adequate remedy for the foreman's deliberate and conscious violation of the overtime provisions.

QUESTIONS

1. Do you believe that the arbitrator exceeded his authority in this case? Assume that the company refused to comply with the award and the union went to federal court to require payment to the grievants. What do you believe the court would do?
2. How do you account for the foreman's refusal to comply with the overtime clause? Do you believe that top management criticized him (even fired him!) after the award came down?
3. Do you believe that the arbitrator's decision would have been the same if the company had not paid two grievances of similar character in the past?
4. Why did the arbitrator deal extensively with arbitration authority in his decision?

CASE NO. 4

WAGE RATE FOR A NEW JOB—JOB COMPARISON

(Where job comparison is used to set a rate for a new job, the judgment of the parties is involved. If the dispute goes to arbitration, of course, the arbitrator's judgment is also called for. In this case, the company originally offered $3.11 and the union demanded $4.50. Later on, in direct negotiations, the spread became smaller, but the parties still could not reach agreement and arbitration was used to settle the dispute.

What complicates this case is that the company at one time offered $3.43 and the union refused the offer—and that later on the union was willing to accept the $3.43 but the company refused and posted and filled the job at $3.29. Note that in this case the arbitrator made a physical inspection of the jobs being compared. Indeed, about four hours were spent in the physical inspection and only about three hours in the hearing room.)

GRIEVANCE

This dispute involves the establishment of the wage rate for the operator of the Travelift, a material handling piece of equipment. In protest against the company's rate for the job, the union filed a grievance, dated December 17, 1968, which states:

> The undersigned hereby grieves the rate of pay established by the Company for the Travelift job. The Union feels the rate should be four dollars and fifty cents per hr.

THE BACKGROUND

The Travelift was acquired by the company in late 1968. It is a new piece of equipment, and the rate structure in the labor agreement does not provide a rate of pay for the operator of the Travelift. The Travelift was produced by the *D* Manufacturing Company, and it is described as a "rubber tired, all hydraulic mobile overhead crane and transporter." Its load capacity is 25 tons, it straddles the material to be lifted, and the products are attached to the crane by means of two chains and hooks which are secured to the products. The Travelift has the capability of operating on two planes. That is, the material can be lifted and lowered, and swung from right to left. Its speed is about 4.2 miles per hour. The operator is located in a cab stationed in the left and rear of the equipment. The cab is about 15 feet above the ground. To operate the Travelift, he makes use of levers and pedals located in the cab. A helper or "ground-man" assists the operator. The function of the helper is to affix the chain to the product, and guide the operator as he moves the equipment within the yard.

On December 5, 1968, a meeting was held between representatives of the company and union to deal with the wage rate of the Travelift operator. Before discussions started as to the rate, the parties agreed upon a job description for the Travelift operator. The pertinent features of the job description are as follows:

General Description:

> Operates Travelift equipment in the yarding and loading of products and in moving forms, materials and equipment.

Duties:

The following outlines in general terms the essential duties of this classification, but is not intended to describe these duties in detail.

1. Operate Travelift in proper and efficient manner.
2. Make minor adjustments as needed to Travelift and daily lubrication check.
3. Yard and load products with Travelift.
4. Move forms within storage area, and between plant and storage area.
5. Move raw materials and equipment within storage area and between plant and storage area.
6. Maintain yarding and loading records and submit required (reports) records.
7. Check product for obvious defects such as chips, cracks, etc., and report such defects in accord with standard procedure.
8. Maintain general work area (Travelift Roadways) in a clean, safe manner.
9. Perform other related duties are required within the general framework of this classification.

With regard to the rate, the union first proposed that the operator be paid $4.50 per hour. The basis for this proposal is the fact that the locomotive crane operator receives $4.50 per hour. As C, president of the union, stated:

> We proposed $4.50 per hour by comparing the Locomotive Crane Operator. As the Locomotive Crane, the Travelift handles enormous products like the Giant T's, which are 80 feet long and weigh up to 22 tons.

The company rejected the $4.50 per hour rate, and asked the union to suggest a figure which would be in the "ballpark." The union then proposed $3.75 as the rate. In turn, the company proposed $3.11 per hour. In part, this company proposal was based upon the area rates for the operators of D Travelift. In this respect, F, industrial relations administrator, testified:

> We searched out what other companies were paying. We found out that other employers were paying $3.11 or less for the operator of the Travelift.

To substantiate the area rates for the equipment, the company presented letters written to it on May 26, 1969, by the M Company, B Company, and SS Corporation. Such letters state as follows:

M Company:

> This is to confirm our telephone conversation of May 26th, during which I stated that prior to February 24, 1969, the rate range for our

Yard Crane and Engine Man classification was $2.77 to $3.07 per hour. This classification operates several types of material moving equipment. One of which is a *D* Travel Lift 500 Al. This classification is represented by the International Association of Machinist and Aerospace Workers Local 1281.

B Company:

We are the owners of 3 500-A *D* Travelifts used in the manufacture and loading of concrete. We are members of ... Union Local and have been in operation for a period of 5 years. The rate of pay for our Travelift operators is $2.70 per hour as of December 31, 1968 with a 15¢ per hour increase for the year 1969. Our scale for common laborers is $2.40 per hour.

SS Corporation:

The *SS* Corporation owns and operates a *D* Travelift, Model 500-Al. The Travelift is used for the loading and yarding of heavy structural beams, bridge girders, fabricated steel plate, and steel coils. The operator of the *D* Travelift is classified as a Crane Operator and is paid Three Dollars and Six Cents ($3.06) per hour in accordance with [this] agreement effective as of the 30th day of June, 1968.

The union was not persuaded by the company's effort to establish the wages for the Travelift operator based upon area rates. Consequently, the December 5 meeting ended with the parties poles apart on the wage rate for the job. The union requested $3.75 and the company proposed $3.11 when this meeting was adjourned.

Another session was held on December 6, 1968, attended by representatives of the parties. In this meeting the company originally offered $3.29 for the job in question. *F* testified that

on the basis of the rate structure in the Labor Agreement, and on the basis of what other employers were paying, we offered $3.29.

On its part the union trimmed its request to $3.50 per hour. This meeting was adjourned without an agreement on the wage rate. The parties were twenty-one (21) cents apart.

A third meeting was held on December 9, 1968. When this meeting started, *F* testified that "our position was still $3.29 per hour."

However, he declared that during this meeting, *D* a superintendent of the company, stated:

"We would go to $3.43 if this would settle the issue once and for all. It would be out-of-line and be above the maximum rates of my operation."

With regard to what *D* stated, *C* testified:

> He offered $3.43, and said "this is the maximum that the Company could go. This is as high as we can go."

C also testified that the company

> might have said, "look to settle this thing, to get it out of the way, we will offer $3.43."

In any event, the union rejected the offer of $3.43, standing pat on its proposal of $3.50. The meeting ended on this basis. At this time, the parties were seven (7) cents apart.

On December 12, 1968, the company posted the job with a top rate of $3.29 per hour. Apparently the company had difficulty in keeping the job postings on its bulletin board. They were removed by some person or persons. The rationale for posting the job at $3.29 per hour was explained by *F* as follows:

> We were at an impasse. We had to post the job. We posted it at $3.29 on the grounds that is the rate for the Sewer Pipe Gasoline Crane. We felt it was an equitable rate based upon the rate schedule of the Labor Agreement, and what outside firms were paying.

On January 5, 1969, *C* stated to the company that the union would accept $3.43. This was the rate that the company offered in the December 9, 1968, meeting. In this respect, *C* testified:

> I told the Company we would accept $3.43 to settle the issue to avoid additional trouble.

The company refused the union proposal to accept $3.43 as the rate for the job. Before the union agreed to accept $3.43 on January 5, 1969, the union filed the instant grievance on December 17, 1969, and *F* testified that the company received a request from the union for the arbitration of the rate on December 29, 1969.

On January 30, 1969, the company posted the job once again with a top rate of $3.29. However, along with this second posting, the company posted another notice the effect of which was to inform the employees that the rate would be arbitrated and that the company agreed to pay the rate established by the arbitrator. In pertinent part this notice states:

> The Company and the Union have now gone thru all steps, except arbitration, provided for in the contract in an attempt to establish a rate of pay for the Travelift Operator Classification.
> Since no agreement has been reached on a rate of pay, the Union has

requested this be settled by arbitration. The Company agrees to abide by the arbitrator's decision as stated in Article 15.4 of the contract.

BASIC QUESTION

The basic question to be determined in this arbitration is framed as follows: What should the rate of pay be for the Travelift operator's job?

Thus, the job was posted with a top rate of $3.29. It was filled by S, the successful bidder, and he has held the job since February 26, 1969. The purpose of this arbitration is to determine the rate of the Travelift operator's job. In this respect, the parties agreed that the arbitrator, if he believes it proper, may establish a rate below $4.50, the rate requested by the union in its grievance, and above $3.29, the rate placed on the job by the company. That is, the rate which he will establish need not be either $4.50 or $3.29 per hour. It may fall between these rates. To put it in other terms, the parties by mutual agreement affirmed that the arbitrator is not restricted to establish either $4.50 or $3.29 as the rate for the job.*

PARTIES' ARGUMENTS

In the first place, the union argues that the company demonstrated bad faith under the circumstances of this case. This charge is based upon the company's rejection of the union's proposal to accept $3.43 per hour for the job, the rate which the company offered in the December 9, 1968, meeting. In this regard, union counsel argues:

> The Company showed bad faith and the facts show it. The Company witness testified that $3.43 would have settled this dispute. This was the highest the Company would go. This was a final offer by the Company. We asked to settle at $3.43 and the Company refused. There is no answer for this Company rejection except that it was stubborn. If it believed that $3.29 was the highest rate, why did the Company offer $3.43? Here is bad faith of the worst kind.

Beyond these observations, the union believes that the rate of $3.29 is not proper in terms of comparable jobs and in the light of the rate structure established in the labor agreement. In this regard, union counsel states:

> We offered a rate of $4.50 per hour to avoid intraplant wage inequities between jobs involving large pieces of equipment and comparable skills.

---

* The arbitrator raised this issue in the arbitration, since at times parties in wage rate cases of the kind involved herein restrict an arbitrator to select either the rate proposed by the employer or the union.

Also, the union directs attention to the rate paid for the operation of the Ross-Carrier, which is another piece of material handling equipment. The operator of the Ross-Carrier is paid $3.39 per hour. Its argument here is that the operation of the Travelift is much more difficult, responsible, and involves a higher order of skills than the Ross-Carrier. Thus, union counsel argues:

> The Travelift operator must have greater skills and responsibility than the operator of the Ross Carrier.

Also, the union contends that the company purchased a large piece of equipment, the Travelift, to increase its efficiency, but will not pay a proper rate despite the increase in efficiency.

On its part, the company position is that $3.29 is the proper rate for the job, and requests that this rate not be increased in this arbitration. Relative to the union charge of bad faith, the company argues that it did not display bad faith when it rejected the union offer to accept $3.43 as the rate for the job. In this respect, company counsel states:

> We did not demonstrate bad faith. We bargained with the Union. An impasse was reached. We acted in good faith by establishing a rate for the job, recognizing that the rate could be arbitrated. We tried to establish a rate in negotiations which was fair, proper, and one which compares equitably for comparable jobs and what other firms are paying. This does not add up to bad faith.

In addition, the company argues that the arbitrator should consider the area rates for the Travelift job; the Travelift operator has a helper and the Ross-Carrier operator does not; the operation of the Ross-Carrier is more difficult, has a greater speed capability, and there is more danger to people and property in the operation of the Ross-Carrier as compared to the Travelift. Moreover, the company avers that the Ross-Carrier is operated over the road and the Travelift is restricted to the company's yard.

Also the company believes that the locomotive crane operator's job is not comparable to that of the Travelift, and that the arbitrator should give controlling weight to the rate paid to the sewer pipe gasoline crane. It also directs attention to the lift truck operator's Over Ten Ton job which pays $2.96.

ANALYSIS OF THE EVIDENCE

Events in the Negotiation of the Rate

At the outset it is necessary to determine whether or not the arbitrator should establish the rate for the job at $3.43 on the grounds that the company offered this rate in the December 9 meeting. At that time the union rejected the offer, but later on agreed to it. The company refused this offer of the union, and on this basis the union charges that the company displayed bad faith.

In short, it is the union's contention that the arbitrator should establish $3.43 as the rate because the company had offered it during the December 9, 1968, meeting. When it refused the union's subsequent acceptance, the union charges bad faith and on these grounds it avers that the arbitrator should determine the rate at $3.43 per hour.

In evaluating this union position, it is clear that the evidence demonstrates that the company made the offer in an effort to settle the grievance so as to avoid arbitration. Even *C* testified that the company in the December 9 session

> might have said, "look to settle this thing, to get it out of the way, we will offer $3.43."

Such a declaration corroborates the unequivocal testimony of *F* who testified:

> We [the Company] would go to $3.43 if this would settle this issue once and for all.

What the evidence demonstrates is that the company made the offer in the effort to settle and compromise the dispute. It was purely and simply a compromise offer. It was made to get the dispute out of the way and to avoid arbitration with its attendent risks, time, and expense.

In this light, what the substantive issue of this feature of the case amounts to is the weight to be given in arbitration to an offer made in the grievance procedure to compromise or settle a dispute. This is not a novel issue. It has been treated frequently in arbitration by professional and experienced arbitrators, including the instant arbitrator. What has been established as a cardinal and uniform rule is that little or no weight is given in arbitration to offers of settlement made in the grievance procedure. The reason for this principle is easy to understand. If arbitrators regarded as binding offers of settlement and compromise in the grievance procedure, this forum could not operate effectively for the settlement of grievances. If either unions or employers feared that an offer of settlement would be binding in arbitration, they would be reluctant to offer compromises in the grievance procedure. Under these circumstances, the grievance procedure could not perform its fundamental function as a method to settle grievances. The result would be constant arbitration to the detriment of all concerned.

Recently in a discharge case handled by the instant arbitrator, the company involved submitted evidence that the union in the grievance procedure proposed that the employee be reinstated without back pay. The company argued that such an offer on the part of the union established the guilt of the employee. The arbitrator refused to accept as conclusive the offer of the union as proof of guilt, and dealt with the case on its merits. He flatly refused to accept the offer made by the union as proof that the employee was guilty of the charge made by the company

In the instant case, the company attempted to settle and compromise the wage dispute at $3.43. Unless the instant arbitrator desires to depart from an accepted and sensible rule, and by doing so establish a precedent that would tend to make the grievance procedure a sterile device for the settlement of disputes, he cannot find that the offer made by the company is binding upon it, and is the governing factor in this case. In short, this arbitrator refuses to establish a precedent that could conceivably destroy the grievance procedure as an effective forum for the settlement of grievances.

As stated in a standard volume on arbitration:

> Offers of compromise and admissions made in attempting settlement of "rights" disputes prior to submission to arbitration may be received but probably will be given very little, if any, weight by arbitrators. It is recognized that a party to a dispute may make an offer with the hope that a compromise may be reached and the dispute ended. Even the mere introduction of such evidence may impair future attempts at dispute settlement.*

In short, the company made an effort to compromise the dispute. During grievance procedure negotiations, it offered $3.43. The union originally refused the offer. The effort of the company to compromise the differences between the parties failed. Though the union subsequently agreed to the offer, the fact is that before that time the company, aware that its effort to compromise the dispute failed, posted the job in question at $3.29. Under these circumstances, and in line with a sensible principle of the arbitration process, the arbitrator refuses to regard as controlling for his decision the offer of the company to settle the dispute at $3.43 per hour.

Area Rates

Neither does the arbitrator regard as material and governing the evidence introduced by the company establishing area rates for the operation of the Travelift. Fundamentally, the basic issue in this case is to determine a rate of pay for the job which will establish the job in a proper and equitable manner under the wage structure of the instant labor agreement. The rate should place the job in a wage slot that would be realistic and fair in terms of the rates paid for comparable jobs within the bargaining unit of the instant company.

Surely, reference to area rates is not a proper guide to make such a determination. True, the evidence the company submits in this con-

---

* Elkouri and Elkouri, *How Arbitration Works*, rev. ed., 1960, p. 195.

nection establishes that the rates paid for the job by other companies is substantially lower than the rate proposed by the company. Also, the arbitrator notes that the employers cited in the company's evidence are all organized by strong labor unions. However, to rely on this evidence as a guide would not be proper since the rate to be established must be oriented properly to the wage structure established by the instant labor agreement.

In short, the issue in this case is not a determination of a rate which would be comparable to the rates paid within the area, but to establish a rate which would be equitable in terms of comparable jobs within the bargaining unit of the instant company. It is to this task that we now turn our attention.

Evidence Establishing Rates for Comparable Jobs

Before proceeding with the evaluation of the evidence in this portion of the case, the arbitrator will affirm that the establishment of rates for new jobs in arbitration is a very difficult assignment. Regardless of how conscientious an arbitrator is in the evaluation of the evidence, and regardless of his determination to be fair, the fact is that the parties are better equipped to establish a rate than any arbitrator. The establishment of rates for new jobs is best left to the parties. Still, the parties have not agreed upon a rate, and the task has been turned over to this arbitrator. He recognizes that his responsibility is great, since to establish a rate which is too high or too low would have an adverse effect upon the wage structure, and with implications involving earnings of the employees, worker morale, and company costs. In any event, the arbitrator shall do the best he can to evaluate the evidence, and to determine a wage rate for the job which will be sensible and equitable in terms of comparable jobs.

Locomotive Crane

In the grievance the union has requested that the rate for the job should be $4.50 per hour. The basis for this request is that the locomotive crane operator rate is $4.50. In other words, the union's contention is that the Travelift and the locomotive crane operator jobs are comparable for purposes of this case.

In this respect, the arbitrator rejects this union argument as being without merit. In the first place, the locomotive crane is used essentially as a production piece of equipment. It is an integral part of the productive process. In contrast, the Travelift is used strictly as a material handling piece of equipment. In the second place, the jobs are not comparable in terms of skill, responsibility, and possibility of damage to persons and property. In the third place, the facts demonstrate that an employee can operate the Travelift in a reasonably efficient manner after about a 30 day training period. This was established by both company and union witnesses. On the other hand, the evidence shows that employees assigned to the locomotive crane will be given up to a six month training program. Certainly, jobs are not comparable in terms of skill, responsibility, and complexity if one calls for a training program of about 30 days and the other requires a training program of up to six months. In short, the arbitrator finds that the Travelift and the locomotive crane operator jobs are not comparable for purposes of the establishment of a rate of pay for the Travelift job.

The Sewer Pipe Gasoline Crane

The sewer pipe gasoline crane pays $3.29 per hour, and that is exactly the rate which the company established for the Travelift job. It would appear that the company argues that these two jobs are so comparable in character that they should be paid at the same rate. There is an important defect in the company's argument herein considered. It is that the sewer pipe gasoline crane is not a piece of material handling equipment as compared with the Travelift. As the evidence demonstrates, the crane is used directly in the productive process of sewer pipe. In fact, as one company witness testified, the crane "paces the work" of the production workers involved in the manufacture of sewer pipe. Like the locomotive crane, the sewer pipe gasoline crane, therefore, is an integral part of the productive process. In effect, it is a production piece of equipment, whereas the Travelift is strictly a material handling piece of equipment. The Travelift is not used directly in the manufacture of the products of the company. True, the sewer pipe gasoline crane handles material. It lifts sewer pipe out of the forms, and places the pipe on the ground at designated locations. However, the pipe could not effectively be manufactured without the use of the crane. From this point of view, it is production equipment, and not a piece of material handling equipment like the Travelift.

It is stressed that the task before the arbitrator is to establish a rate for the Travelift in terms of comparable jobs. He believes that the comparison between the Travelift and the sewer pipe gasoline crane or the locomotive crane would not be proper because the essence of these jobs is not the same. The Travelift is used strictly as a piece of material handling equipment. Therefore, the proper comparison should not involve equipment which plays an integral part in the manufacture of products, but with jobs which are exclusively involved in material handling. In all candor, the arbitrator believes that he would undermine the wage structure of the labor agreement if he used as the basis for his decision a comparison of jobs which are unlike in terms of fundamental functional purposes.

Lift Truck, Over Ten Ton

As established in the wage structure, the operator of the lift truck, Over Ten Ton, is paid $2.96. Unlike the sewer pipe gasoline crane, and similar to the Travelift, the lift truck is a piece of material handling equipment. Like the Travelift it is operated in the yard, and performs the same basic function as the Travelift. In fact, it handles some of the same material handled by the Travelift. What is more, the skill and the responsibilities of the Travelift and lift truck operators are somewhat comparable in terms of difficulty and complexity. So here we have a valid basis of comparison for the establishment of the rate of the Travelift job.

However, the spread between the company's position of $3.29 for the Travelift and the rate of $2.96 established in the wage structure for the lift truck is so substantial that the comparison of these jobs does not constitute a valid basis for the establishment of the rate for the Travelift job. If the company believed that the two jobs are so comparable in terms of skill, responsibility, and complexity, it surely would not have placed a $3.29 rate on the Travelift job. Company counsel stated that the rate for the Travelift job should be "somewhat higher" than that of the lift truck operator's job. However, since the spread between the rate of the lift truck operator's job at $2.96 and the company's established rate of $3.29 for the Travelift job is so great, a comparison between the jobs for purposes of the case would be far too nebulous in character as a valid basis for wage determination.

Ross-Carrier

If one thing is made clear from the evidence, and as physical inspection by the arbitrator demonstrated, it is that the realistic basis for comparison is between the Ross-Carrier and the Travelift. As H, plant manager, testified:

> The skill levels are somewhat parallel for the Ross Carrier and the Travelift. The skill levels of the Ross Carrier would be closer to that of the Travelift.

Here we have two pieces of material handling equipment which perform the same function. Indeed, as company witness D declared: "The Travelift will phase out the Ross Carrier."

In all candor, the arbitrator believes that the rate of the Travelift should be established in and around the rate of the Ross-Carrier which is established at $3.39 per hour. This certainly would be a rate which would be within the "ball park."

In the evaluation of the evidence dealing with the Travelift and the Ross-Carrier, there are some major reasons to establish a rate for the Travelift which would be the same as the Ross-Carrier, or somewhat below this figure. The Ross-Carrier operator works without a helper, and the Travelift operator has a helper. Without a helper, the Ross-Carrier operator must from time to time climb down from his cab to secure and disengage hooks. This task is performed by the helper assigned to the Travelift. The operator does not have the inconvenience and need not engage in the physical discomfort of climbing in and out of his cab to perform this duty. Also the helper is available to guide the operator of the Travelift as he moves his equipment. In contrast, the Ross-Carrier operator is on his own, and must use his judgment and discretion as he moves around the yard to avoid injury to persons and damage to property.

In the second place, the Ross-Carrier can operate at about 12–15 miles per hour (or faster, as the arbitrator and the parties noted during the lunch break!), while the Travelift rate of speed is only about 4 miles per hour. With comparatively greater speed, it follows that the Ross-Carrier operator must be more careful to avoid injury to persons and damage to property. In the third place, the Ross-Carrier may operate over the road. This capability is not within the scope of the Travelift. *M,* vice president of the union, testified that from time to time

> the Ross Carrier moves material to the dump from the yard. It goes on the street—one long block—a quarter of a mile distance.

In this respect, the Ross-Carrier operator has the responsibility to avoid injury to persons and damage to property when he takes his equipment down the street.

In addition, there is the danger that the Ross-Carrier may topple if loads are not properly centered on the runners, or if for some reason the operator hauls a load beyond the weight capability of the equipment. In comparison, the Travelift straddles the products and it would be impossible to topple the equipment.

As against these considerations, the evidence demonstrates that there are important reasons to establish a rate for the Travelift job which would be equal to that paid to the Ross-Carrier operator, or a rate which would be somewhat higher. Important in this respect is that the Travelift operates on two planes—it lifts and lowers material and moves the products suspended on chains from right to left. These movements may be performed simultaneously by the operator in accordance with job needs. In contrast, the Ross-Carrier operates on one phase—it only lifts and lowers.

In addition, the Travelift operator has one important task which is not required of the Ross-Carrier operator. Note that the two chains of the Travelift which are separated quite a distance apart are attached to the products being handled. The operator must make sure that these two chains are kept at the same level or the material being handled can fracture. As *M* testified:

When I assembled the Travelift, I spoke to the factory [D] representative. He said that both hooks [one attached to each chain] had to be operated simultaneously or the product can fracture.

No such problem exists for the operator of the Ross-Carrier. He simply places his runners under the banks upon which the product rests and lifts the banks and the product. In short, the Travelift operator must perform a task which the Ross-Carrier operator does not. He must make sure that the chains are in balance to avoid the fracture of the product being handled. Here is a task which requires judgment, discrimination, and coordination.

Though the arbitrator agrees fully with company counsel that the amount of weight lifted does not require any additional effort on the part of the operator, it is material that the Travelift has a load capacity of 25 tons while the Ross-Carrier has a load capacity of 15 tons. True, as company counsel states, it is the machine that lifts the weight, and not the operator. In either case, "he just presses a button" to activate the lifting mechanism. From this point of view, it would not be proper to base a wage rate on the comparative weight lifting capacity of the Ross-Carrier and the Travelift.

On the other hand, the fact is that the Travelift operator is responsible for the handling of heavier and proportionately more expensive loads. The company would probably suffer a greater loss if the Travelift operator damaged a product weighing 25 tons as compared to damage to a product weighing 15 tons.

CONCLUSION

After careful reflection of the evidence dealing with the operation of the Travelift and the Ross-Carrier, the arbitrator is of the judgment that the operation of the Travelift is somewhat a more responsible job in terms of skill, dexterity, coordination, judgment, and possible damage to products. In this light, it is the conclusion of the arbitrator that the rate for the Travelift should be established at $3.41 per hour. This, of course, is the arbitrator's judgment, and in cases of this sort everyone concerned with the case could have a different judgment. That is why an arbitrator is placed in a vulnerable and unenviable position in rate setting cases.

In any event, the arbitrator has been faithful to the evidence the best he could, and believes that the rate which he has set places the Travelift job in an equitable, fair, and realistic place in the wage structure of the bargaining unit in terms of comparable jobs.

QUESTIONS

1. Why did the arbitrator refuse to settle this case at the rate of $3.43, the rate which the company at one time offered?

2. Do you believe that the arbitrator was justified in refusing to use area rates as a guide for his decision?
3. Do you think that—following their experience in this arbitration—the parties will be more or less inclined to settle rate cases by themselves without resort to arbitration?

8

Economic Supplements Under Collective Bargaining

We have indicated that the incorporation of employee supplementary economic benefits—from paid vacations to pension plans—in collective bargaining contracts is widespread throughout American industry. Such benefits have increased dramatically since World War II, in both their value to the employee and their variety. And, since these supplements to the basic wage rate are now commonly equivalent to as much as 30 percent of payroll, it is understandable that some managers express hostility when the once accepted designation *"fringe* benefits" is used to describe this area.

Many of these benefits are not new to personnel administration and, indeed, some of them were introduced by employers on a unilateral basis before the advent of unionism. However, such benefits now play a much more important part in labor relations than was ever the case in the past. By the end of World War II, many unions had succeeded in bargaining vacations and holidays for their members; the federal government's regulation of wages during 1942–45 had proven influential in guiding the labor negotiators in this direction. And in the quarter-century since the war, many other benefits have found their way into labor documents with increasing regularity and employer largesse: pension plans; various health insurance arrangements, including life insurance and hospital and other medical benefits; accidental death and dismemberment payments; and dismissal and reporting pay, among many others. Supplementary unemployment benefit plans, a comparatively recent major collective bargaining issue, also may properly be regarded as a supplement to the basic wage rate.

PENSION PLANS

Pension plans became a significant issue in labor relations and collective bargaining in the period immediately following World War II. Many factors operated to make them a major feature of the bargaining process, particularly the 1949 ruling of the United States Supreme Court which held that employers and unions have the obligation to bargain over this issue.[1] The Court rejected the point of view that pensions were not covered as a bargaining issue under national labor law. But other factors, particularly in more recent years, have also contributed to the growth of pension plans: the modest character of the benefits provided under the federal social security program; the fact that employees are increasingly expected to live considerably longer and to have more years of retirement after the termination of their industrial lives than in the past; the spread of union-sponsored seniority and related provisions (to be discussed in Chapter 10), making it all but impossible to terminate employment for older employees *except* by pension; and a growing managerial awareness of a company *obligation* to employees after their retirement. On the last point even in 1949 one public commission could comment that

> pensions should be considered a part of normal business costs to take care of ... permanent depreciation in the "human machine" in much the same way as provision is made for depreciation and insurance of plant and machinery. This obligation should be among the first charges of revenues.[2]

From a modest beginning in 1946, pension plans in American industry have grown phenomenally. Negotiated pension plans are today found in about 73 percent of all labor agreements. Even this total, moreover, under-

---

[1] *Inland Steel Co. v. United Steelworkers of America*, 336 U.S. 960 (1949).
[2] These conclusions were incorporated in the report of the Steel Fact-Finding Board appointed by President Truman in July 1949 to inquire into the facts of and to make recommendations in the dispute which was then taking place relative to pensions between the United Steelworkers of America and the steel corporations.

states the degree of growth: The coverage of pension plans doubled during the period 1950–60, and is expected to double again by 1980.[3]

As might be expected, there is a wide variety of plans in existence, but a number of common characteristics are found in almost all of them.

Whereas the earliest bargaining pensions integrated their benefits with payments received from the operation of the federal social security program—and thus, in the late 1940s and early 1950s, enabled employers to realize considerable savings as the benefits of the Social Security Act were liberalized, there has been a distinct trend away from this practice in recent years. One method of thus passing the statutory increases directly along to the worker has been the establishment of a flat monthly payment per year of service, regardless of the amount the retired worker receives from the federal government. Thus, as of 1969, automobile workers under the Ford-UAW agreement then in effect—by way of example—were to be credited with $5.50, $5.75, or $6.00 per month (depending on hourly rates of pay) for each year of service upon normal retirement and anything obtained from the operation of the public system would be in addition to this amount. Automobile workers fared considerably better than most other workers covered by negotiated pensions, however: the amount of private plan benefits now ranges from $20 a month to more than $200 (depending on not only the generosity of the plan but also, of course, the length of service of the worker) but, on the average, monthly payments to employees with thirty years' service are between $100 and $110 per month, exclusive of social security.

Under most plans, the mandatory retirement age is set at 65, and although many companies still permit workers upon mutual annual agreement to stay on their jobs until they are 70 years of age, there has been some move away from this flexibility in recent years. Many manufacturing employee unions (in steel and rubber, for example), influenced by the size of the unemployment figures in their sectors of the economy, have generally not opposed this increasing trend toward compulsory retirement at 65. In fact, labor organizations have increasingly sought to open up further job opportunities in the face of automation and changing market demands by a new emphasis on early retirement *before* age 65, and some provision for this benefit is now made under the pension stipulation of many contracts.

By and large, voluntary early retirement (as opposed to retirement necessitated by permanent disability) carries with it reduced benefits for the employee. This typically amounts to a reduction of more than one third in monthly benefits for a worker retiring at age 60 and of more than 20 percent for an employee who chooses to retire at age 62. Under a few agreements in which the negotiating parties have actively sought to

[3] "Characteristics of the Private Pension Structure," *Monthly Labor Review,* LXXXVII, No. 7 (July 1964), 774.

encourage early retirement, however, the employee can gain considerably more income than these modal figures would indicate. In 1965, for example, under a new plan of the Chrysler Corporation, that company's workers reaching age 60 with 30 years of service and a wage of $3 per hour could receive $110.54 in basic pensions (actuarially reduced from the age 65 level) plus a supplement of $253.46, for a $364 monthly total; the basic pension would be a lifetime one, but the supplement would be ended when the retired employee reached age 65, to be replaced by Social Security payments at a lower figure. Two years after these and similar Chrysler provisions went into effect in early 1965, the plan had already succeeded in realizing its goal of creating new job opportunities for other workers: in these two years, almost 11 times as many Chrysler workers retired as in all 1964 and the plan—pronounced a success—has been liberalized and extended in later Chrysler-UAW contracts. Nor was it necessarily inevitable that *any* income decrease would be suffered by early retirement: under contracts in the clothing, maritime, and mining industries, to name only three of a fast-growing number, the benefits are identical for all retired workers—regardless of age—subject only to their meeting minimum service requirements. In general, however, the service requirements remain rigid: no employee is eligible for a full annuity until he has served with a company for at least 20, and most often 30, years.

Under plans which provide for pension benefits to workers who have been permanently disabled and who have not reached the normal retirement age, it is also usually required that such workers have a specified number of years of service with the company to be eligible for such benefits. Under many of these contracts, 10 to 15 years of service is required before an employee may expect to draw pension benefits because of permanent disability.

The question of who is to finance the pension plans—the employer alone or the employer and the employee jointly—has been an important issue ever since collectively bargained pensions attained prominence, and it continues to pose problems at the bargaining table. At the present time, employers finance the entire cost of retirement benefits (and the plans involved are therefore called "noncontributory," in recognition of the lack of expense to the employee) in about three out of four plans, with the remainder being financed jointly (and thus on a "contributory" basis).[4] Jointly financed plans remain common in some manufacturing industries (notably textiles, petroleum, and chemicals) as well as in the nonmanufacturing area (finance, for example).

In favor of *noncontributory* plans, the usual arguments are that: (1) the average employee cannot afford to contribute; (2) the employee is

[4] *Ibid.*, p. 778.

already contributing toward part of his retirement under the social security program; (3) (consistent with the previously cited statement of the public commission in 1949) costs of pensions should be borne exclusively by the employer on the ground that this expense is no less important than depreciation expenses for machinery and plant; (4) the return to the employer from the plan in terms of lower labor turnover rates and increased efficiency justifies the cost; and (5) although employers can charge contributions to pension plans against taxes, employees cannot. Proponents of *contributory* pension plans, on the other hand, claim that: (1) since there is a definite limit to the economic obligations that employers can assume at any given time, employee contributions assure better pensions; (2) requiring employees to pay for a share of their pensions tends to educate employees in the knowledge that retirement programs must be paid for by someone; (3) employees will take a far greater interest in plans to which they contribute and hence will advocate better administration, sounder funding, and less waste; and (4) when employees contribute, they have a stronger claim to their pension as a matter of right.

Regardless of whether pension programs are financed on a contributory or noncontributory basis, however, the program must be financed and funded in a manner which positively guarantees employees the benefits provided for by the plans upon their retirement. There is no need to dwell upon the catastrophe that would befall a worker who upon retirement finds that the pension he expected is not available. Funded plans—those in which pensions are paid from separated funds, isolated from the general assets of the firm—ensure that such benefits are in fact guaranteed, whereas unfunded plans must necessarily depend upon employer ability and willingness to comply with the pension provisions of the labor agreement. In addition, employers may currently minimize their federal income taxes by obtaining tax credits as they make fund contributions, rather than waiting until the pensions are actually paid, and the earnings of the pension trust fund are also exempted from income taxes. Because of these considerations, there is an unmistakable preference among employers and unions for a fully funded and actuarially sound plan: only 7 percent of all workers covered by private pension arrangements belonged to unfunded plans even as early as 1960,[5] and the figure is undoubtedly even smaller today.

Finally, recent contract renegotiations have seen a marked increase in "vesting" allowances for workers covered by pensions—giving, with more or less qualifications concerning years of service and sometimes age, the employee the right to take his credited pension entitlement with him should his employment terminate before he reaches the stipulated retirement age. Only 25 percent of plans studied by the Bureau of Labor Statistics in

[5] "Unfunded Private Pension Plans," *Monthly Labor Review,* LXXXVI, No. 12 (December 1963), 1414.

1952 allowed vesting, but 67 percent of those examined in 1963 did so, however much the vesting privilege remained qualified,[6] and by common estimate the figure is probably close to 75 percent today. Considerations of equity, worker morale, and the displacement threats in many industries have given unions the incentive to push hard for the expansion and liberalization of this benefit over the past decade. So, too, has an equally cogent argument for meaningful vesting rights: in the absence of such rights, the individual worker's ever-increasing stake in pension plan entitlement may stifle desirable labor mobility and thus result in the underutilization of manpower. Workers who *can* take their pension privileges with them are afforded maximum opportunity for employer-to-employer and industry-to-industry movement, a situation which is presumably a desirable one from the viewpoint of our not only efficiency-minded but democratically-oriented society.

VACATIONS WITH PAY

Vacations with pay for production workers constitute, as was noted earlier, a comparatively new development in American industry. Prior to World War II only a fraction of workers covered by collective bargaining contracts received pay during vacation periods and, at that time, other employees were permitted time off only if they were willing to sacrifice pay. At present, vacations with pay are a standard practice in practically every collective bargaining contract and this has been true for some time. As far back as 1957, in fact, a Department of Labor study of 1,813 agreements, each covering more than 1,000 workers, found that only 8 percent of these contracts did not provide some form of paid vacation;[7] and the employer not furnishing this type of pay for time not worked *today* is a true individualist.

In addition to the influence of the National War Labor Board's wage controls in spearheading the spread of paid vacations, a growing recognition on the part of employers, employees, and unions of the benefits of such a policy (in terms of worker health, personal development, and productivity) has contributed to the growth.

Paid vacations have also undergone steady *liberalization* as a worker benefit. In recent years, an annual five-week vacation (normally requiring 20 years of service or more) has been bargained by the parties in some situations, and while this length of paid leisure time is still anything but

[6] "Vesting Provisions in Private Plans," *Monthly Labor Review*, LXXXVII, No. 9 (September 1964), 1014.
[7] U.S. Bureau of Labor Statistics, *Paid Vacation Provisions in Major Union Contracts, 1957*, Bulletin No. 1233, June 1958.

commonplace, it is relevant that such a vacation was all but nonexistent until the late 1960s. Four-week vacations (usually after at least 18 years) are today included in a majority of all agreements, or more than half again the 1960 frequency. Of more significance to shorter-term workers is the three-week vacation, provided for in almost 90 percent of contracts (as against 78 percent in 1960) and most frequently requiring 10 years of service (where 15 years was the modal prerequisite a very few years ago). Virtually all employees, moreover, can count on a two-week vacation after building up five years of seniority, and contracts increasingly allow this length of time off after only two or three years of service. The only stagnation which has occurred, is, in fact, in the one-week vacation area: one year of service has entitled most employees to a single week of vacation with pay for well over a decade now, and the next frontier relating to the one-week vacation will probably be its total abolition in favor of the two-week vacation after one year—an arrangement which is even now granted by perhaps as many as one-fifth of all agreements.[8]

An innovation which thus far has not spread appreciably beyond the scope of influence of the United Steelworkers of America is considerably more imaginative than the mere liberalization denoted by the above statistics. In 1962, the Steelworkers and metal can manufacturers negotiated a "sabbatical" paid vacation of thirteen weeks' duration, allowed all employees with fifteen or more years of service *every five years,* and the basic steel industry incorporated essentially the same agreement for the senior half of *its* work force the following year. The rationale behind this device is a twofold one: greater leisure time for employees (with, at least in theory, greater attendant benefits to worker health, personal development, and productivity than under less liberal vacation allowances) *and* the creation of new jobs through the major immediate need for additional employees brought about by the sabbatical. After several years, the plan had received mixed evaluations: it was particularly hard to isolate the effects of the plan from such other employment-increasing factors as a strengthened market demand for the products involved in most of those years; and the fact that many eligible employees had exercised an option of accepting extra pay in lieu of some of the time had also to be reckoned with. It was at least apparent that, if the "sabbatical" was to achieve either of its objectives, employees would be obliged to actually take their vacations—and also to abstain from taking other paid work during the vacation period. It also seemed clear that bargainers in other industries were awaiting more conclusive proof of the benefits of the plan before pushing for its incorporation in their contracts.

[8] All information cited in this paragraph is based on data furnished by the Bureau of Labor Statistics, U.S. Department of Labor.

In qualifying for vacations, most labor agreements require that an employee must have worked a certain number of hours, days, or months prior to the vacation period, and failure of the employee to comply with such stipulations results in the forfeiture of the vacation benefits. (Case No. 5 deals with the eligibility of an employee for vacation pay.) The rate of pay to which the employee is entitled during his vacation is ordinarily computed on the basis of his regular hourly rate, although (in a comparatively small number of agreements) vacation benefits are calculated on the basis of average hourly earnings over a certain period of time preceding the vacation and, in some agreements, vacation pay is calculated as a specified percentage of annual earnings; usually this latter figure amounts to between 2.0 and 2.5 percent of the annual earnings.

A problem arises involving the payment of workers who work during their vacation periods. In some contracts—as in the case of the steel and can provisions alluded to previously—the employee has the option of taking the vacation to which he is entitled or of working during this period. Other labor agreements allow the company the option of giving pay *instead of* vacations if production requirements make it necessary to schedule the worker during his vacation period. No less than in the case of the sabbaticals, when employees work during their vacation periods either upon their own or the company's option, the principles upon which paid vacations are based (health, productivity, etc.) are, of course, violated. In any event, the question arises as to how to compensate employees for their vacation time when they work during this period. In most labor agreements, employees under these circumstances are given their vacation pay plus the regular wages which they earn in the plant. In a few cases, particularly when the employer schedules work during a vacation period, the wage earned by the employee working on his job during his vacation period is calculated at either time-and-one-half or double the regular rate. Such earnings are in addition to the employee's vacation pay.

In a majority of contracts, management has the ultimate authority to schedule the vacation period. Under an increasingly large number of agreements, however, the company is required to take into consideration seniority and employee desires. A fairly sizeable number of labor agreements permit management to schedule vacations during plant shutdowns.

An additional vacation problem involves the status of employees who are separated from a company before their vacation period. In some collective bargaining agreements, these employees are entitled to accumulated vacation benefits when they leave the employment of companies under certain specified circumstances, such as permanent layoff, resignation, and military duty. In a comparatively small number of contracts, workers discharged for cause may also claim vacation benefits.

HOLIDAYS WITH PAY

Similar to paid vacations, paid holidays for production workers was not a common practice before World War II. When a plant shut down for a legal holiday, the workers simply lost a day of work. And, also as in the case of vacations with pay, the National War Labor Board permitted employers and unions to negotiate labor agreements providing for paid holidays under its wartime wage regulations. As a result paid holidays became a common feature in collective bargaining contracts during World War II and the practice continued after hostilities terminated. By 1948 about 70 percent of all labor agreements provided for paid holidays, and at present nearly 100 percent of all labor agreements incorporate some formula for paid holidays.

The modal number of such holidays granted in 1970 was eight. There was almost universal agreement among the contracts on at least four of these specific holidays: more than 98 percent allowed paid time off for Independence Day, Labor Day, Thanksgiving, and Christmas. And well over 94 percent of all contracts paid for holidays on New Year's Day and Memorial Day. Wider variation takes place where more than six holidays are sanctioned, but half days before Thanksgiving, Christmas, and New Year's Day are frequently specified, and in an increasing number of cases a seventh (or eighth, ninth, or tenth) holiday is oriented on an individual basis—such as the employee's birthday. Under this latter arrangement, the company by definition is not penalized with whatever inefficiencies may result from a plant shutdown. Many agreements also recognize any of a variety of state and local holidays, ranging from Patriot's Day in Massachusetts to Mardi Gras in parts of the South. Company—and even union—picnics are declared occasions for paid holidays in a somewhat smaller number of contracts.[9]

Most labor agreements place certain obligations upon employees who desire to qualify for paid holidays, with the common objective in this respect being that of minimizing absenteeism. The most frequently mentioned such requirement is that an employee must work the last scheduled day before and the first scheduled day after a holiday. The obligation is waived when the employee does not work on the day before or after the holiday because of illness, authorized leave of absence, jury duty, or death in the family. Under some collective bargaining relationships, illness must be proved by a doctor's certificate, by nurse visitation, or by some other device.

Production requirements and emergency situations at times require

[9] *Ibid.*

that employees work on holidays, and such circumstances raise the problem of rates of pay for work on these days. About three-quarters of all labor agreements provide for double-time for work on holidays, and a small number of contracts now call for triple-time. In the continuous-operation industries such as the hotel, restaurant, and transportation sectors, labor agreements frequently substitute another full day off with pay for a holiday on which an employee worked.

An additional problem involves payment for holiday time when the holiday falls on a day on which the employee would not ordinarily work. For example, if a plant does not normally work on Saturdays, and if in a particular year July 4 (a paid holiday under the collective bargaining agreement) falls on Saturday, the question arises as to whether employees are entitled to holiday pay. Another aspect of the same general problem involves a paid holiday falling during an employee's vacation period. Some unions claim that pay for holidays constitutes a kind of vested benefit to employees, regardless of the calendar week on which the holiday occurs. Thus, if the holiday falls on a regular nonworkday, some unions ask that another day be designated as the holiday or that the employee be given a day's wages; or if the holiday falls during an employee's vacation period, that he receive another day's paid vacation or wages for the holiday. The opposing view holds that payment for holidays falling on a day on which employees do not regularly work violates the basic principle underlying paid holidays, which is protection of employees from loss of wages. Many labor agreements reflect the thinking of labor unions on this issue and designate, for example, another day off with pay if a holiday falls on a nonworkday, but a large number of labor agreements do not treat the problem one way or the other, and frequently because of the nature of the language establishing holidays with pay, controversies in this respect are settled in arbitration. (Case No. 6 concerns itself with this issue of holiday pay.)

NEGOTIATED HEALTH INSURANCE PLANS

Health insurance plans are now a common feature of collective bargaining contracts. These plans provide for one or more of the following: life insurance or death benefits; accidental death and dismemberment benefits; accident and sickness benefits; and cash or services covering hospital, surgical, maternity, and medical care. Recently the boundaries of the package have been extended to such areas as major medical insurance (often defraying all such expenses up to 80 percent of their total), dental insurance, and psychiatric treatment benefits. By 1970 the vast majority of workers under collective bargaining contracts were covered, although in considerably varying degrees, by some or all parts of this overall insurance mechanism.

A number of factors provide the basis for the spread of insurance plans under collective bargaining. Insurance programs were also a major fringe issue in the period of wage control during World War II, although to a far smaller extent than were vacations and holidays. Many employers and unions have, moreover, increasingly recognized that industrial workers—particularly with health costs rising rapidly in recent years—are not prepared to meet the risks covered by such plans. The Internal Revenue Service has also given incentive to the spread of such insurance, by permitting employers who contribute to these programs to deduct payments as a business expense, for tax purposes, where such plans conform to the standards of law for tax relief. In addition, group insurance permits purchasing economies not available to individuals. Finally, the fact that the federal social security program has not provided protection for most risks covered by these insurance plans has made the private insurance system a widely sought one.

Today's typical bargained health and welfare package is of no small dimensions. There is a strong likelihood that it includes: group life insurance for an amount which approximates 90 percent of the employee's annual salary; disability and sickness benefits of at least $70 weekly for six months; semiprivate hospital room and hospital board for as long as ninety days—together with such add-ons as drugs and medicines, X-ray examinations, and operating room expenses (under either Blue Cross or a private insurance company plan); surgical expenses up to a $400 maximum for contingencies not covered by workmen's compensation legislation; and coverage for the employee's dependents as well as himself for all or most of the above benefits. And, as in the cases of pensions, vacations, and holidays, these emoluments are continuing their own process of liberalization, with discernable trends in recent years involving: an increase in the amount and duration of the benefits; the extension of the benefits to retired workers, as well as to those dependents not yet covered; defrayal of the expenses of at least some medically related drugs; and the added protection for catastrophic illnesses and accidents and addition of dental and mental health benefits which were cited previously. (NOTE: Case No. 7 deals with one part of this package in some depth, focusing upon a problem involving hospital benefits under a group insurance policy.)

There has been a commensurately strong trend toward exclusive employer financing of the health benefit package: 21 percent of all unionized employers paid the full cost in 1949; roughly 40 percent did so in 1956;[10] and it is very likely that over 50 percent currently pay all expenses for the greatly enlarged package of the early 1970s. With the continuing union

[10] U.S. Department of Labor, Office of Welfare and Pension Plans, *Welfare and Pension Plan Statistics, 1960* (Washington, D.C.: Government Printing Office, 1963), pp. 3–4.

emphasis on health expense defrayal, no reversal of this trend seems to lie on the horizon.

DISMISSAL PAY

Unlike all the wage supplements discussed above, dismissal, or "severance," pay is still not a common product of collective bargaining. A recent study of 1,773 major (1,000 workers or more) and thus presumably more liberal agreements found only 30 percent of these contracts providing such a benefit.[11] And on an industrywide basis the practice remains largely confined to contracts negotiated by the Steelworkers, Auto Workers, Communications Workers, Ladies' Garment Workers, and Electrical Workers—although many sectors of the newspaper and railroad industries also have such plans.

Dismissal pay provisions normally limit payments to workers displaced because of technological change, plant merger, permanent curtailment of the company's operations, permanent disability, or retirement before the employee is entitled to a pension. Workers discharged for cause and employees who refuse another job with the company normally forfeit dismissal pay rights, as do workers who voluntarily quit a job.

The amount of payment provided for in dismissal pay arrangements varies directly with the length of service of the employee. The longer the service, the greater the amount of money. Ordinarily a top limit is placed upon the amount that an employee can receive. Although labor agreements vary in respect to the payment formula, as a general rule low-service workers receive one week's wages for each year of service prior to dismissal, with higher than proportional allowances for high-service employees (up to 60 weeks' pay, for example, for 15 or more years of service, and as high as 105 weeks' pay for workers with 25 or more service years).

A problem involving dismissal pay is the situation wherein an employee is subsequently rehired by the company. There is little uniformity in collective bargaining contracts relative to the handling of this problem. Actually, a large number of labor agreements which provide for dismissal pay are silent on whether the employee must make restitution to the company upon being rehired or whether he may keep the money paid to him when his employment was originally terminated. Some agreements, however, specifically provide that such an employee must return the money; for example, one telephone industry collective bargaining contract stipulates that such employees must repay to the company any termination

[11] "Severance Pay and Layoff Benefit Plans," *Monthly Labor Review,* LXXXVIII, No. 1 (January 1965), 27.

payment either in a lump sum or through payroll deduction at a rate of not less than 10 percent each payroll period until the full amount is paid.

Since the dismissal provision is designed to cushion the effects of employment termination through technological change, merger, and cessation of business (as well as through involuntary retirement due to personal health misfortunes), it is logical to conclude that this benefit, too, will spread in the years ahead. The acceleration of technological and business operations changes beginning in the 1950s and continuing through the 1960s was itself responsible for a considerable increase in the dismissal pay statistics in those years: only 10 percent of labor agreements had such a provision in 1949.[12] Given the continuing presence of these causative factors, there is little reason to believe that the spread of dismissal pay has run its course.

REPORTING PAY

Under the provisions of approximately 90 percent of the collective bargaining contracts currently in force, employees who are scheduled to work and who do not have instructions from the company *not* to report to their jobs, are guaranteed a certain amount of work for that day or compensation instead of work. Issues involved in the negotiation of reporting pay arrangements are the amount of the guarantee and the rate of compensation, the amount of notice required for the employer to avoid guaranteed payment, the conditions relieving the employer of the obligation to award reporting pay, and the conditions under which such pay must be forfeited by employees.

Labor agreements establish a variety of formulas for the calculation of the amount of the guarantee. Reporting pay ranges from a one-hour guarantee to a full day. About 50 percent of labor contracts dealing with this issue provide for four hours' pay; approximately 10 percent call for eight hours' pay. These rates are calculated on a straight-time basis. However, under circumstances where workers are called back to work by management outside of regularly scheduled hours, such employees are frequently compensated at premium rates, ordinarily at time-and-one-half the regular rate. Such reimbursement, popularly styled "call-in" pay, might be awarded a worker, if, for example, he is called back to work before he has been off for sixteen hours. Thus, if he regularly works the first shift and is called back under some emergency condition to work the third shift, the labor agreement might require that he be paid at premium rates.

---

[12] "Dismissal Pay Provisions in Union Agreements, 1949," *Monthly Labor Review*, LXX (April 1950), 384.

In the event that the employee reports for such work only to find that the company no longer has need for his services he will still be entitled to a certain number of guaranteed hours of pay calculated at premium rates.

In most agreements providing for reporting pay an employer is relieved of the obligation to guarantee work or to make a cash payment to employees when he notifies his employees not to report to work. Contracts frequently provide that such notice must be given employees before the end of the worker's previous shift, though in some cases the employer may be relieved of the obligation if he gives notice a certain number of hours before employees are scheduled to work. Eight hours' notice is provided in many labor contracts. In addition, employers are relieved of the obligation to award reporting pay when failure to provide work is due to causes beyond the control of the company. Thus, when work is not available because of floods, fires, strikes, power failures, or "acts of God," in most contracts employers either are fully relieved of the obligation to award reporting pay or the amount of the pay is substantially reduced. Of course, there are many questions of interpretation involved in this situation. For example, does power failure resulting from faulty maintenance relieve the employer of the obligation to award reporting pay? As in so many previous cases, such questions are resolved through the grievance procedure and at times through arbitration.

Under certain circumstances employees forfeit reporting pay. If employees, for example, fail to keep the company notified of change of address, reporting pay is forfeited under many labor agreements. Other forfeitures might result if employees refuse to accept work other than their own jobs, leave the plant before notice is given to other employees not to report to work, or fail to report to work even though no work is available.

SUPPLEMENTARY UNEMPLOYMENT BENEFIT PLANS

One of the most interesting developments in collective bargaining during recent years is the supplementary unemployment benefit (SUB) plan. This new issue of collective bargaining attracted national attention in 1955, when a supplementary unemployment benefit plan was negotiated by the United Automobile Workers and the basic automobile manufacturers, and again in 1956 when the basic steel corporations and the United Steelworkers of America included such a plan in their new labor agreement. There is not much evidence of plans protecting workers' income during periods of unemployment prior to 1955, although a few such arrangements had been established in sectors of the consumer goods industries.

Essentially SUB plans constitute a compromise between the "guaranteed annual wage" demanded by many unions in the late 1940s and early 1950s, and a continuing management unwillingness to grant such relatively complete job security as the "guaranteed wage" designation would indicate. The plans are geared primarily to two goals: (1) supplementing the unemployment benefits of the various state unemployment insurance systems; and (2) allowing further income to still-unemployed workers after state payments have been exhausted. And they implicitly recognize at least one weakness in the state system: since the states started paying benefits in the late 1930s, the average ratio of these benefits to average wage levels of employees when working has steadily dropped from approximately 40 percent three decades ago to somewhat less than 35 percent today.

About 3 million employees are now covered by negotiated supplementary unemployment benefit plans. By far the largest numbers of these (perhaps two-thirds) are concentrated in the basic auto and steel industries, but such plans are now also in existence in such other widely divergent sectors of the economy as aluminum, aerospace, glass, farm equipment, retail trade, electrical, can, rubber, apparel, printing and publishing, and the maritime industry, and the vast majority of these plans have some major elements of similarity.

All SUB plans, for example, require that an employee have a certain amount of service with the company before he is eligible to draw benefits; the seniority period varies among the different plans—with a one-year requirement in the basic auto and can contracts contrasting with a five-year prerequisite (the most extreme) under a current agreement between the Minnesota Mining and Manufacturing Company and the Oil, Chemical and Atomic Workers Union. In addition to seniority stipulations, virtually all plans require that the unemployed worker be willing and able to work. The test in this latter connection is, most often, the registration for work by the unemployed worker with a state unemployment service office; for example, under the automobile plan a worker is not qualified to obtain benefits unless he registers for work with the appropriate state office and does not refuse to accept a job deemed suitable under such a state system. Beyond this, the plans invariably limit benefits to workers who are unemployed because of layoff resulting from a reduction in the work force by the company. Workers who are out of work because of discipline, strikes, or "acts of God" cannot draw benefits. Nor can workers whose curtailment of employment is attributable to government regulation or to public controls over the amount or nature of materials or products which the company uses or sells, do so.

Under the most prevalent type of SUB agreement, all employees (including those just hired) start to acquire credit units at the rate of one-half unit for each week in which they work. When they complete enough service to qualify for the benefits (the one to five years cited in the previous paragraph) they are officially credited with these units, which they can then trade off for SUB pay when unemployed up to a maximum unemployment duration. Most plans now have set this maximum at 52 weeks and consequently an automobile or steel industry worker with two years of continuous employment has achieved the maximum amount of SUB coverage. Under about half of the current plans, however, the ratio of credit units to weeks of benefit can be *increased* when the SUB fund falls below a certain level, thereby shortening the duration of benefits. Another common variation is to adjust the ratio in such a way that laid-off workers with long service are protected for a proportionately longer length of time than are shorter-service employees.

Almost universally, employees are entitled to draw benefits only up to the amount of credits that they have established, and can receive no benefits—no matter how large the amount of their credits—during the first week of unemployment, a stipulation which is consistent with the one-week waiting period under most state unemployment insurance plans. In addition, credit units are canceled in the event of a willful misrepresentation of facts in connection with the employee's application for either state or SUB income.

Benefit formulas under most layoff plans currently set a normal level of payments at 60 to 65 percent of "take-home" pay (gross pay minus taxes) for all eligible employees. This level comprises payments from both the negotiated benefit plan and the state system. If, for example, a worker whose normal take-home amount is $120 is laid off, a plan which calls for 65 percent of his take-home pay allows him $78. And if his state unemployment compensation totals $45 weekly, the SUB plan would then pay him the weekly sum of $33 to make up the difference. There is some debate even among the most rabid advocates of SUB plans as to whether the level should be pushed much beyond this 65 percent figure, for even at this percentage, several plans have experienced the ironic situation of workers preferring total layoff to work. The recent experience of the major automobile companies, indeed, has dramatized the potential consequences of *liberalizing* such a situation: under the 1967–70 UAW contracts in that industry, workers with at least seven years of seniority actually received 95 percent of their after-tax wages while on layoff (minus $7.50 for such work-related expenses as transportation, work clothing, and lunches) for up to 52 weeks—and almost invariably preferred such a well-remunerated enforced leisure period to their normal work assignments! Given the typical influence of auto industry contracts on labor settlements outside of the automobile sector, it seems a safe prediction that other SUB industries will ultimately experience this problem of unionists demanding to be laid off.

To establish the fund for the payment of supplementary unemployment benefits, most plans require that the company—which invariably exclusively finances all SUB plans—contribute a certain amount of money per work hour. Many agreements call for a cash contribution of five cents per hour, although several go as low as two cents and about the same number require ten cents. The payment into this fund most often represents the *maximum* liability of the company, however. Typically a maximum size of the fund is defined and company contributions for any one contractual period stop completely when this limit is reached and maintained: the objectives, aside from relieving the companies of overly rigorous payments, are to prevent too large an accumulation of fund money and to encourage the companies to stabilize their employment levels. On the other hand, when fund finances fall below the stipulated amount—because of SUB-financed payments—the employer must resume payments at the rate required by the plan. In addition, many SUB plans—including most of those negotiated by the Steelworkers—require a further company liability: when the SUB fund reaches the "maximum" level, companies *continue* to make contributions—first to a Savings and Vacation Plan (to keep *its* benefits fully current) and then once again to the SUB fund—until approximately $250 per employee is accumulated. Only at the latter point do company contributions cease.

The foregoing indicates a number of fundamental characteristics of supplementary unemployment benefit plans of the type currently in force in the basic steel and automobile-manufacturing industries. Such plans are the most common in industry and apply to the vast majority of workers covered by arrangements protecting workers' income during periods of unemployment. In summary, the basic elements of these plans are as follows:

1. They provide a definite and predictable liability against the company.
2. Payments are made solely out of the fund established by the employer contributions.
3. Laid-off employees have the responsibility to accept suitable employment as provided for under state employment service programs.
4. Employees must be eligible to receive state unemployment compensation benefits as a prerequisite to obtaining payments from a supplementary unemployment benefit plan.
5. There is a specified limit to the contributions by the company to the fund.
6. Benefits are paid only to those employees laid off because a company is unable or unwilling to furnish work; such benefits are not available to employees whose employment terminates for any other reason.

THE "GLASS" TYPE PLAN

Although plans of this type are the most popular at the present time, another procedure calculated to protect employees' income during periods of unemployment has also been adopted by some companies and unions. This approach establishes for individual workers income security accounts that are financed by company contributions and from which the employee can draw benefits. Such a plan was adopted in 1955 by some glass companies and the United Glass and Ceramic Workers of North America (AFL-CIO). Under this kind of plan the company makes a contribution of $.05 per hour into the employee's account. Once an individual has accumulated a $600 reserve, the contribution is paid into a separate vacation account, from which the worker can draw to supplement regular vacation pay. If the employee is laid off, injured, or sick, he can withdraw from his account up to $30 per week, but not more than 10 percent of the balance of his account at any one time. Unlike the automobile and steel arrangements, the "glass plan" endows the individual worker with a vested interest in his account. Thus, if the worker is discharged, or is retired, or quits, he receives any balance in his account.

Basic differences are evident in the two types of plans. The automobile and steel plans are based upon a pooled fund, whereas the income security account plan establishes a fund for each employee. Under the glass-plan arrangement there is no integration with state unemployment compensation systems and funds in the individual worker's account may be used independently of the state program; an employee need not be eligible for unemployment compensation to draw upon his account. Finally, whereas the auto and steel plans operate only to provide workers with income for periods of unemployment which stem from the employer's being unable or unwilling to provide an employee with work, the individual income security plan can be used to provide an employee with benefits during periods of unemployment because of illness or injury, or to supplement regular vacation pay. This feature of the plan could make it attractive to workers with high levels of seniority who may never realize any tangible benefits under the supplementary unemployment benefit plans of the kind negotiated in the auto and steel industries.

With the passing of time the impact on the social and economic fabric of the nation of the operation of plans calculated to protect workers' incomes during periods of unemployment will become more evident. Since these plans are still comparatively new and cover a relatively small percentage of the labor force there is insufficient empirical data to determine their effects on the critical elements of the socioeconomic environment. There seems to be little question that they made some contribution to mitigating individual hardship, as well as to maintaining consumer purchasing power, during the general recessions of 1957–58, 1960–61, and 1970. But additional evidence is needed to establish their impact upon features such as the growth of industry, the level of employment and unemployment, the mobility of labor, the incentive of employees to work, the relations between management and union, the operation and character of state unemployment compensation plans, and technological changes within industry. Much speculation and deductive argument has been advanced in this respect. Unfortunately a large share of the discussion has been initiated on a purely partisan basis and hence has only served to confuse and distort the issues. As in other areas of labor relations, scientific investigation of the effects of this new development of industrial relations is required.

The fact remains, however, that—in strong contrast to virtually every other economic benefit discussed in this chapter—the growth of SUB plans since their negotiation in the automobile and steel industries in the middle 1950s has been far from impressive. Most craft unions continue to greet such a device with total apathy, preferring to substitute other economic improvements for its introduction. And seniority protection appears to have thus far satisfied workers in many noncraft industries sufficiently so that SUB has not become a major union demand there. But the continuing hold of SUB upon the several major industries in which it was originally negotiated, and the constant improvement of SUB allowances there, remain facts which cannot be ignored, either in assessing the creativity of the collective bargaining process or in judging the potential impact of this "guaranteed annual wage" compromise should the employment instabilities which have always characterized most industries in which SUB has now been implemented spread to other parts of the economy. If SUB extensions have not been impressive in total, SUB today does exist in sectors where it is needed—namely, in cyclical industries.

SOME FINAL THOUGHTS

Whether or not SUB arrangements will ultimately achieve the universality of pension plans, health insurance, paid vacations, and paid holidays (and such various other widespread but considerably lesser benefits as paid time off for obligations stemming from death in the family, jury duty, and voting) thus remains an open question. Yet, *even* in the case of SUB, a broader issue does not. It appears to be all but axiomatic to collective bargaining that *any* benefit, once implemented by the parties, becomes subject through the years to a process of continuous liberalization from the workers' viewpoint. Even supplementary unemployment benefits have undergone this process in the years since 1955, when the automobile industry's maximum of $30 weekly for no more than twenty-six weeks was considered generous.

Many of these benefits continue to allow the same cost advantages to the parties, in terms of both "group insurance" savings and tax minimization, that they did at the times of their various inceptions. Generally tight labor markets have further led employers to amass attractive benefit packages, to be placed in the front window as recruitment devices. And considerations of worker retention and productivity and pure pride have also undoubtedly stirred both managers and union leaders in their bargaining on these economic supplements. As the new worker needs and wants in the benefit area have become active, the collective bargaining parties have clearly responded to the challenge.

However, neither for the bargaining parties nor for the nation as a whole is this situation an unmixed blessing. Increasing caution from both managements and unions will, in fact, be required as the liberalization process continues, and at least six caveats appear warranted.

In the first place, many improvements in the benefit portfolio automatically present potentially troublesome sources of union grievances which would otherwise be absent. Increasing latitude for employee choice of vacation time, by the incorporation of a "seniority shall govern, so far as is possible, in the selection of the vacation period" contractual clause, for example, carries far more potential for controversy than a clear-cut statement reserving vacation scheduling strictly for company discretion. As a second example in this area, with two weeks the maximum vacation allowance, there is usually no question of carryover credit from year-to-year: the worker is not confronted with "too much of a good thing" and normally does not seek to bank unwanted vacation time until it may be worth more to him. Under a more liberal allowance, however, the question does arise, as many companies and unions can testify—and policies must be both established and consistently adhered to if problems on this score are to be averted.

The list of such newly created grievance possibilities could be extended considerably to virtually all of the benefit sectors. Who qualifies as a dependent under an expanded health insurance plan which now accommodates such individuals? What religious credentials must be established to authorize paid time off "as conscience may dictate" on Good Friday or Yom Kippur? Is a suddenly decreed national day of mourning an "act of God," relieving the company of an obligation to grant reporting pay, or do its circumstances compel the employer to pay such monies? How many hours or weeks of work—and under what conditions—constitute a year, for purposes of calculating pension entitlement within a system granting a flat monthly payment "per year of service"? In a less generous age, these and obviously a myriad of similar questions were automatically excluded.

Second, even on the now-rare occasions upon which the benefits are not formally liberalized, many of them automatically become more costly simply because *wages* have been increased. All wage-related benefits fall into this category, and a twenty-cent-per-hour wage increase will thus inevitably elevate total employment costs by considerably more than this face amount because of the simultaneous rise in the worth of each holiday, vacation period, and any other allowance pegged to the basic wage rate. This industrial relations truism would hardly be worth citing were it not so often ignored in union-management bargaining rooms, in favor of accommodating only wage increases to increases in productivity (for example) rather than wage increases plus wage-related benefit increases. The degree of danger in overlooking these inflationary ramifications, moreover, obviously rises with the increasing value of the benefit itself.

In the third place, one suspects that managements have—at least at times—generated *negative* employee motivation by implementing benefits without either participation or approval of work force representatives in the process. The day of company paternalism, fortunately, now lies far in the past for the large mainstream of American industry. But the arousal of employee ego-involvement is all the more imperative in today's sophisticated industrial world. Few people have dealt with the penalties of oversight in this regard more cogently than has Leland Hazard. Describing a deep and enthusiastic interest in unionization on the part of employees at a large Pittsburgh plant "that was well known as having excellent wages and working conditions, and supposedly had almost perfect employee relationships," he quotes the following remarks of "one attractive girl" to explain the general sentiment:

> It's about time something like this happened. We have got to stand on our own feet. They do everything for you but provide a husband, and I even know girls who they got a husband for. And them what ain't got time to get pregnant, they get foster kids for.[13]

Related to this question of negative motivation, but isolable as a fourth potential problem, must stand the very real alternative possibility of *no* employee motivation whatsoever. Not being as a class masochistic, employers logically expect some benefits from their expenditures in the wage supplement area—particularly, more satisfactory worker retention figures, an improved recruitment performance, and—above all—generally increased employee productivity. Without such returns on the benefit investment, companies would be engaging in clear-cut wastage.

One can readily locate situations where employee benefits have obviously achieved at least some of these desired results. Particularly in those areas where benefit entitlement expands with increasing seniority (pensions and vacations, for example), greater worker retention has undoubtedly often been fostered. Yet there is to this moment no convincing proof that benefits have significantly affected employee motivation on any large-scale basis in American industry—and, for that matter, the few scholarly treat-

---

[13] Leland Hazard, "Unionism: Past and Future," *Harvard Business Review*, March-April 1958.

ments of this topic that have cropped up in the literature indicate that the extent of employee *knowledge* as to exactly what the benefits *are* is something less than awesome.[14] There is a critical need for far more research by employers and other interested parties into this subject than has thus far been conducted, for the possibility that industry may be undergoing an ever-increasing expense which may be returning very little in the way of concrete worker performance cannot as yet be safely dismissed.

Fifth, it is possible that overall employment has suffered—and conceivably will continue to suffer—from the continuation of benefit expansion of the type described in this chapter. As in the previous case, the evidence thus far is not fully conclusive. But the increasing cost pressures and personnel administration complexities involved appear to have combined with related factors to push in this direction. Certainly Garbarino, whose exploration of such a possibility for manufacturing employees is perhaps the most thorough of its kind to date, does not dispute this point. He deems it "reasonable to conclude" that the cost and administrative considerations, as well as uncertainty as to future labor requirements and other management problems, have "contributed to minimizing employment expansion without necessarily leading to a major expansion of overtime scheduling."[15] Aside from the basic issues of society's optimum utilization of manpower and the dashed aspirations of the consequently unemployed or underemployed individuals which are always presented by such an outcome, Garbarino's conclusion—if, in fact, "reasonable"—clearly contains further pungent considerations related to urbanized ghetto America today.

Finally, unlike wage increases (which can often be at least partially negated by such mechanisms as job re-evaluation and incentive rate implementation or modification), the benefit package has a strong tendency to remain a permanent part of the landscape. Except in extreme cases of corporate financial crisis, it is quite immune from disintegration. And if any significant *positive* effect of benefits on employee motivation thus far remains to be proven, the annals of industrial history are replete with examples of companies which have encountered surprisingly intense worker resistance in attempting to dismantle even such relatively minor portions of their benefit packages as child-care programs or banking facilities. Downward revisions of the leisure time, health, and pension offerings remain several miles beyond the realm of the conceivable. In short, once the parties introduce a benefit, they can expect to be wedded to it for life, with

[14] See, for example, "Relationship Between Attitude and Knowledge in Employee Fringe Benefit Orientation," by James L. Sheard in *Personnel Journal*, November 1966; and "Employee Benefits: In One Ear and Out the Other?" by Arthur A. Sloane and Edward W. Hodges in *Personnel*, November-December 1968.

[15] Joseph W. Garbarino, "Fringe Benefits and Overtime as Barriers to Expanding Employment," *Industrial and Labor Relations Review*, XVII, No. 3 (April 1964), p. 439.

the only meaningful questions focusing on the timing and degrees of the subsequent benefit liberalizations.

For all of the reservations expressed in the above paragraphs, employee benefits hardly warrant an evaluation similar to that given by the old railroad baron James Hill to the passenger train ("like the male teat, neither useful nor ornamental"). They do provide considerable security at minimal cost to the covered employees (whether or not the latter explicitly desire such protection in lieu of other forms of compensation), at least at times abet the employer's recruitment and retention efforts in a tight labor market, and minimize the tax burdens of both company and worker. If there is room for doubt that they also allow the employer any significant return in the form of worker morale and productivity, these other reasons alone are probably sufficient to justify their dramatic spread during the past quarter century.

And because the benefit package has become so relatively standardized between companies in this time interval, too, the wage supplements probably also perform a further (if less constructive) function for managers and the unions with which they deal. Their presence in anything approaching the typical dimensions *prevents* invidious comparisons by both current and potential employees in evaluating the desirability of the company as an employer. The extent of worker knowledge of specific benefits may fall far short of perfection but in the early 1970s, because corporate pattern-following has been so prevalent in this area, the absence of seven or eight paid holidays, a three-week paid vacation after no more than ten years of service, significant medical coverage for all members of the family, meaningful pensions, and any of the various other parts of the generally conspicuous benefit portfolio are often grounds for workers' dissatisfaction.

Thus it can be predicted quite fearlessly that the years ahead will see a continuation of the benefit growth. As indicated, it appears to be all but axiomatic to industrial relations that any benefit, once implemented, through the years becomes subject to a process of continuous liberalization from the worker's viewpoint. And, while variety in these economic supplements has now become increasingly difficult to achieve, there is also little doubt but that new ones (perhaps most emphatically in the areas of income stabilization and employment relief) will join the already-crowded ranks.

Possibly, however, increasing awareness on the part of "fringe" benefit implementors as to the various problem areas outlined here will result in some slowing down of the continuous liberalization process and restrain the introduction of new types of benefits until thorough investigation—tailored to the needs of *individual* companies and unions—has taken place. At the very least, the future demands considerably more research into these areas than has thus far been carried out. And such an omission seems particularly blatant when one realizes that there remain few *other* aspects of industrial relations which have *not* been subjected to searching scrutiny. But one must be a pessimist on these latter scores: thus far both the research and the benefit deceleration have been notably absent.

DISCUSSION QUESTIONS

1. Which set of arguments as expressed in this chapter's section on pensions carries more weight with you: the case *for* contributory plans, or the case *against* them?
2. "SUB plans of the type negotiated in the automobile and steel sectors are wholly undesirable. They discourage employees in the incentive to work, replace state unemployment compensation systems, discriminate against the worker not represented by a union, place an undetermined but intolerable burden on management, are financially unsound, and can actually cause permanent unemployment among some workers." In the light of your understanding of the character of these SUB plans, evaluate this statement.
3. Paul Pigors and Charles A. Myers have argued that "management should offer employee benefits and services, not because [it has] to, not only within legal limits, and not as a camouflaged form of bribery, but because such benefits and services are in line with the whole personnel program." Do you agree? Why or why not?

SELECTED REFERENCES

Bloom, Gordon F., and Herbert R. Northrup, *Economics of Labor Relations,* 5th ed. Homewood, Ill: Richard D. Irwin, Inc., 1965, pp. 613–720.

Garbarino, Joseph W., "Fringe Benefits and Overtime as Barriers to Expanding Employment," *Industrial and Labor Relations Review,* XVII, No. 3 (April 1964), 426–42.

Slichter, Sumner H., James J. Healy, and E. Robert Livernash, *The Impact of Collective Bargaining on Management.* Washington, D.C.: The Brookings Institution, 1960, pp. 372–489.

Sloane, Arthur A., and Edward W. Hodges, "Employee Benefits: In One Ear and Out the Other?" *Personnel,* November–December 1968.

CASE NO. 5

ELIGIBILITY FOR VACATION BENEFITS

(This is an interesting case because it involves a compulsory maternity leave of absence as it applies to the eligibility for vacations. The grievants argued that they were entitled to paid vacations even though they were on leave of absence for six months because of pregnancy. As you read the case, you will note that the arbitrator denied their claim under the relevant contractual provisions even though he passed no judgment as to whether or not their exclusion from paid vacations was fair, just, or wise.

Frequently, the issue of equitability is involved in arbitration cases, but arbitrators do *not* use such a standard for decisions when contractual language requires a decision which [on the surface at least] does not appear to be in fact equitable. After you have digested this case, you may wish to speculate as to whether or not this principle of arbitration is a sound one.)

GRIEVANCES AND CONTRACT PROVISIONS

This dispute involves the vacation rights of female employees who are required to be absent from their jobs for six (6) months because of pregnancy. The company denied their vacation privileges and, in protest against such company action, five (5) employees filed grievances.* Illustrative of the five (5) grievances is the one filed by Mrs. B, dated June 15, 1966.

> Off October 8 till April 4, 1966 because of pregnancy. They [the Company] told [me] that [I] did not have a vacation coming.

Similar grievances were filed by Y, R, L, and F.

Having failed to resolve the grievances in the grievance procedure, the parties have instituted this arbitration for their final and binding settlement.

Relevant to the dispute are the following provisions of the labor agreement:

ARTICLE VIII

Section 1. Employees who have been continuously employed in the Company's plant for a period of one (1) year or more, shall be entitled to receive one (1) week's vacation with pay for forty (40) hours at his or her average straight-time hourly earnings for the last five (5) weekly pay periods preceding his or her vacation. Any employee who has been laid off from work or away from work because of illness and then rehired and who would otherwise have been continuously employed for a period of one (1) year, shall be given the same consideration with respect to such vacation as an employee who has continuously worked for a period of one (1) year or more, and be entitled to a vacation as aforesaid, provided such lay-off or absence because of illness does not exceed sixty (60) days during such year....

ARTICLE IX

Section 2. In case of maternity, a female employee shall have the right to receive a leave of absence for six months without pay, and her

---

* From the record it appears that vacation rights were denied other employees under the same circumstances. The parties stipulated that the decision in this case will serve as the precedent for the disposition of other grievances falling within the same category.

seniority rights in such event shall not be impaired. Said employee will be required to vacate her job three months prior to delivery and will not be reinstated until three months after delivery.... Temporary lay-offs due to lack of work, illness of the employee or leaves of absence granted by the Company shall not constitute interruption of an employee's continuous service with the Company as such term is used in this Agreement....

THE BACKGROUND

Of the some 260 employees of the company, the vast majority are women. For the first time, the parties agreed in the instant labor agreement that in the case of pregnancy, the employee shall be required to vacate her job three months prior to the delivery of the infant and shall be required to vacate her job until three months after delivery. This agreement is incorporated in Article IX, Section 2, the so-called "maternity clause."

After the execution of the instant labor agreement, one employee, absent because of pregnancy, was denied a vacation by the company. The denial resulted in a work stoppage, and it terminated only after the company agreed to pay her under protest with the understanding that the issue involved in this proceeding would be submitted to arbitration.

Hence, this arbitration is sparked by the denial by the company of vacation benefits when an employee has vacated her job for six (6) months under the "maternity clause" of the labor agreement.

BASIC QUESTION

The basic question in this case is framed as follows: Under the circumstances of this case, did the company violate the labor agreement?

PARTIES' ARGUMENTS

On its part, the union believes that the company is in violation of the labor agreement when it refuses to grant a paid vacation to employees who have vacated their jobs under the maternity clause of the labor agreement. It argues that

> a maternity leave of absence is *not* an absence because of illness within the meaning of Article VIII of the contract. The Union's position [is that a maternity leave of absence] did not constitute an interruption of an employee's continuous service with the Company.

It argues further that when the maternity clause was incorporated in the instant labor agreement, it can be assumed with certainty that the effect the Company now urges it should have on Article VIII, Vacations, was not discussed. Had the difficulty which now arises in the administration of the vacation plan, i.e., the effect interruptions of service had on such privileges, been fully explored, either the difficulty would have been eliminated or the contract would not have been executed.

However, it refers to the testimony of *S*, secretary-treasurer of the union, who declared in the arbitration hearing that it was his understanding when the negotiations were concluded that the "required maternity leave of absence would not have this effect on an employee's vacation."

In support of its position, union counsel cites *Milwaukee Spring Company* and *American Machine Foundry Company*.

On these grounds, the union requests that the grievances be granted.

In contrast, the company urges that the grievances be denied. It argues that

"it is well established that seniority rights have no correlation to vacation rights."

That is, the fact that seniority rights are not impaired because of the maternity leave of absence does not automatically qualify an employee for vacation benefits. Further, the company argues that

the contract here involved is clearly premised on the concept that a vacation is a reward for actual work performed. In this connection it is important to note that in the "Vacation" clause, Article VIII, it is provided that if an employee is "laid off from work or away from work because of illness" the employee shall be given the same consideration in determining continuous employment for vacations as an employee who "continuously worked," provided such layoff or absence because of illness does not exceed sixty (60) days during the vacation year.

In support of the company's position, company counsel cites *Berg Metals Corporation* and *Kelly* v. *Montour Railroad Company*.

On these grounds, the company requests that the grievance be denied.

EVALUATION OF THE EVIDENCE

Construction of Article VIII

For a sound decision in this case, it is first necessary to understand the basic meaning of Article VIII, Section 1. It is this area of the labor agreement which establishes the vacation formula negotiated by the parties. In this provision, the parties stipulated that employees who have been *continuously employed* in the company's plant for one year or more shall be entitled to a week's vacation with pay. After so agreeing, the parties then tackled the problem of vacation pay eligibility for employees who do not work within the year because of being laid off or absent because of illness. If an exception were not made for these employees, absences of this sort would disqualify them for vacation pay because the first sentence of the provision speaks in terms of a worker being "continuously employed." That is, under the first sentence any break in employment could disqualify an employee if special considerations were not stipulated in the provision.

Therefore, for those employees who are not continuously employed because of illness or because of being laid off, the parties agreed that an exception should be made to the stipulation that workers must be continuously employed for a year to qualify for vacation pay. For these employees—those not continuously employed in the year because of illness or layoff—the provision states that they are to be regarded as continuously employed.

If nothing more were added to the provision, there would be no question that the grievants would be entitled to vacation pay. However, the parties placed a limitation on the duration of absence caused by layoff or illness. In language which is precise and unambiguous, the parties agreed that such absence may not exceed sixty (60) days if employees so absent are to qualify for vacation pay. There is no doubt about the clarity of the language in this respect:

> ... provided such layoff or absence does not exceed sixty (60) days during such year.

Thus, what the parties agreed to is this: if an employee is absent for sixty (60) days or less because of illness or layoff within the vacation year, he or she will be regarded as continuously employed for purposes of vacation pay. However, if any such absence is longer than sixty (60) days, the employee will not be regarded as continuously employed, and, therefore, not eligible for vacation pay. Up to this point, there should be no question as to the intent of the parties or the construction of the contractual language. The language is unambiguous and unequivocal.

Absence Because of Maternity

As stated, when the instant labor agreement was executed, the parties stipulated in Article IX, Section 2 that employees who are pregnant are required to take a six (6) month leave of absence. That is, they will be required to vacate their jobs three months prior to and three months after delivery. This requirement is set forth in the second sentence of Section 2. In the first sentence of Section 2, the parties agreed that in cases of maternity the employees may take "a leave of absence for six months." Apparently, this was incorporated in the previous labor agreements, and the innovation of the current contract is that such leaves of absence are compulsory upon the mother.

If we read both sentences together, the absence for maternity is a *leave of absence* for maternity purposes. Though the second sentence speaks in terms of the vacating of the job, the first sentence speaks in terms of a leave of absence; and since the second sentence is the newly adopted language, there is little doubt that what the parties intended was that pregnant women are to be compelled to take a six month leave of absence.

Section 2 also provides that when an employee is laid off due to lack of work, illness of the employee, or leaves of absence granted by the company, such absences shall not constitute "interruption of an employee's continuous service...." That is, there is no break in the employee's seniority. Should an employee be absent for six (6) months, say, because of an approved leave of absence, the employee will still earn seniority credits for the period in which he did not work.

Is Enforced Six Month Leave a Layoff under Article VIII?

The preceding observations provide the framework for the determination of the basic problem involved in this case. Thus, is an employee on an enforced six (6) month leave of absence for maternity purposes eligible for a vacation under the terms of Article VIII? To put it in other terms, is such an employee "laid off from work or away from work because of illness" for longer than sixty (60) days within the vacation year?

The arbitrator recognizes that the union argues that maternity is not an illness, and, therefore, the absence of the grievants was not because of illness. Hence, they are entitled to vacation pay. Without prejudice to this union argument, the arbitrator will first deal with the issue of whether or not an employee on an enforced six (6) month maternity leave of absence is "laid off" within the meaning of Article VIII? If she is "laid off" within the meaning of Article VIII, she is not entitled to vacation benefits. On the other hand, if she is not "laid off" within the meaning of Article VIII, she would be entitled to vacation pay, provided that her six (6) month absence is not due to illness. Therefore, the arbitrator will hold in abeyance the question of whether or not pregnancy is an illness until he resolves the question of whether or not a maternity leave of absence is a layoff within the meaning of Article VIII. If this question is determined in the affirmative, there would, of course, be no need to reach a decision on whether or not pregnancy and/or maternity is an illness.

In determining whether or not an enforced six (6) month maternity leave amounts to a layoff within the meaning of Article VIII, the arbitrator is impressed with the first sentence of Article VIII. As stated, what sets the tone for eligibility for vacation pay is that an employee must be *continuously* employed in the company's plant for a period of one year. That is, he or she must be actively employed for a period of one year. This is unambigous language which must be given full faith and credit. It does not merely state that the employee must be on the seniority roster of the employer for the year, or in a state of *continuous service* of the company. Frequently, employees are on the seniority roster or in continuous service of an employer but are not on the active payroll or *continuously employed*. In the instant contract, this would be true if employee is on a company approved leave of absence, laid off because of lack of work, or ill. These employees accumulate seniority credits—there is no break in their continuous service or seniority—but they are not on the active payroll or continuously employed.

Clearly, the intention of the parties upon the adoption of the first sentence of Article VIII is that vacation benefits will be limited to employees who are on the active payroll of the company—*continuously employed*—during the vacation year in question. In this light, it follows logically that employees on an enforced maternity leave of absence for a six (6) month period are not entitled to a vacation. They are not entitled to a vacation because they are not continuously employed. In this sense, an employee on a maternity leave of absence is laid off within the meaning of Article VIII.

In reaching this conclusion, the arbitrator considered that the words "laid off" as used in Article VIII could mean something different from an absence due to pregnancy. That is, "laid off" might refer to an absence caused by lack of work. Such an interpretation is not possible, however, because the provision does not spell out what "laid off" means. It does not state "laid off" because jobs are not available. Since this is true, and particularly since the first sentence of Article VIII clearly means that vacations are to be limited to those employees who are continuously employed, the arbitrator would add language to Article VIII if he held that a six (6) month absence because of pregnancy did not disqualify an employee from vacation pay.

After all, the sense of Article VIII is that vacations are to be a reward to the employees for *continuous employment*. In this sense, the employer benefits from the continuous work of the employee, and he, in effect, shares this benefit with the employee in the form of a paid vacation. In all candor, if the arbitrator did not deny the grievance, there could be discrimination against other employees. Thus, the union probably would not argue that an employee who takes a six (6) month leave of absence for personal reasons, say, to run a business, or for political work, union service, or attendance in school, would be entitled to a paid vacation. Indeed, if the union argument is carried to its logical conclusion, such an employee would be entitled to a paid vacation. Certainly, this is not the intent of the language of Article VIII.

Continuous Service v. Vacation Rights

One of the most important arguments of the union is that Article VIII provides that approved leaves of absence, illness, or layoffs due to lack of work, do not constitute an interruption of an employee's continuous service. Thus, since the grievants' continuous service is not broken by the maternity leave of absence, they are entitled to a vacation. As stated previously, this argument is not meritorious because there is a vast difference between the protection of an employee's seniority rights under a collective bargaining contract and his eligibility to obtain vacation benefits. True, the grievants' seniority rights are not impaired because of their maternity leave of absence, but it is still true that when they took these leaves of absence they were not *continuously employed* during the vacation year. Suppose an employee is elected to public office, and he obtains an approved leave of absence just short of one year. During this time his seniority is protected as if he were working. However, it would be a most tortuous construction of Article VIII to hold that he is entitled to a paid vacation during this year in which he performed no service to the employer. If he should be denied a paid vacation, it follows logically that the grievants should be likewise denied a paid vacation. Both have their seniority protected, but both were absent from their jobs for longer than the sixty (60) day period specified in Article VIII.

S, secretary-treasurer of the union, testified that it was his understanding that employees would not be disqualified from vacations because of the enforced six (6) month maternity leave of absence. He testified that this was his "recollection" of the negotiations. However, as the arbitrator reads the record in this case, it is quite clear that the basic issue involved in this case was not even discussed in the negotiations. Note, union counsel argues that

> had the difficulty which now arises in the administration of the vacation plan, i.e. the effect interruptions of service had on such privileges, been fully explored, either the difficulty would have been eliminated or the contract would not have been executed.

This assertion plus the uncertain testimony of *S* leads this arbitrator to believe that the parties did not discuss the impact of the maternity leave on vacation rights.

In this light, the arbitrator must be bound by the written language of the labor agreement. If the language as contained in the labor agreement is to be followed, the grievances have no merit. Surely, the arbitrator has no authority to speculate on what might have occurred if the problem were raised in negotiations. And, surely, he has no power to legislate terms of the labor agreement.

PRECEDENTS

On behalf of the grievants, union counsel cites *American Machine Foundry* (38 LA 1085) and *Milwaukee Spring Company* (39 LA 1270). The arbitrator read both of these cases carefully, but finds that these decisions cannot be used effectively to support the basic claim of the union in the instant case. Indeed, even if these decisions are read in the most favorable light for the grievants, the arbitrator simply does not see how they can support their claim in this proceeding. Even union counsel recognizes that in *American Machine Foundry*

> the agreement in that case allowed the Arbitrator to base his decision on the language of the contract, and the custom and practice of the parties.*

In the instant case, there is not one scrap of evidence which establishes practice. Therefore, the dispute must be decided on the basis of the contractual language involved. Furthermore, as union counsel recognizes with respect to both cases,

> the labor agreement and the circumstances in the above [cited] cases are different from the one in question.†

In short, the arbitrator cannot possibly find for the grievants on the basis of the precedents cited by union counsel, though he recognizes that they were cited in good faith and not represented to him as precedents which are four-square to the instant case. In fact, the candor of union counsel in this respect is truly commendable, since he does not attempt to delude the arbitrator that his cited cases are the same in circumstances and contractual language as those in the instant dispute.

CONCLUSION

In the last analysis, the union requests that the arbitrator ignore clear-cut contractual language and the intent of the parties, and write a

---

* In *American Machine Foundry,* the arbitrator based his decision on past practice. He held that the language of the contract pertaining to the issue of maternity leaves as they relate to forfeiture of vacation eligibility lacked the "necessary clarity," and, therefore, required "resort to custom and practice to determine the meaning intended by the parties." On the review of the evidence, the arbitrator held that the past practice of the parties supported the employees' position.

† In *Milwaukee Spring,* the arbitrator held that maternity leaves are not to be computed as "time off for illness" as time worked for purposes of vacation eligibility. He held that the parties abrogated a past practice and negotiated new contractual language which "does not provide for computing time off due to pregnancy as time worked for the purpose of determining vacation eligibility." Moreover, in this case, there was no issue which is basically involved in the instant proceeding in the determination of whether or not an employee on maternity leave is laid off for purposes of vacation eligibility. In addition, the vacation clause in the precedent case is quite different from that involved in the instant labor agreement. The former provided a minimum number of hours worked in the vacation year to qualify for employee vacations; in the latter, the formula requires that an employee be continuously employed with the exception that 60 days absence for illness or layoff shall not disqualify an employee for vacations.

new provision into the labor agreement. As we all know, such conduct on the part of the arbitrator would be indefensible. After all, the authority of an arbitrator is limited to the construction of contractual language as agreed to by the parties. He may not legislate new language, since to do so would usurp the role of the labor organization and employer.

In the instant case, the arbitrator finds that the contractual language involved does not support the claim of the grievants. Under these circumstances, he has no choice except to deny the grievances. If the union believes that denial of vacation benefits to employees who take a maternity leave of absence is inequitable, the proper forum to seek a remedy is at the bargaining table and not in arbitration. Of course, this arbitrator passes no judgment as to whether the present state of affairs is right or wrong, just or unjust, wise or unwise. He limits his decision to the contractual language involved, and, thereby, attempts to justify the faith and trust of the parties in his integrity and competency when they selected him to serve in this case.

One final observation, however, may be in order. The employees of this company received a substantial benefit when their union negotiated the maternity leave clause. What this means is that their jobs are automatically protected while they are pregnant and after the delivery of the infant. The company *cannot refuse* such leaves of absence, as can other employers under collective bargaining contracts.* By making the leave of absence compulsory, the union and the company have taken into consideration the health and safety of the mother and the infant. This is a substantial benefit which this union has conferred upon their members.

What the grievants really attempt in this case is to add to this benefit by requesting vacation pay even though they provide no service to the employer for a six (6) month period. Undoubtedly, the grievants believe they are entitled to such vacations and seek this benefit in good faith. Their claim, however, is not justified on the basis of the contractual language involved, and, further, the arbitrator is somewhat disturbed that they attempt (in good faith) to add a benefit —paid vacations—to a real and substantial benefit, the protection of their jobs during and after pregnancy and the safety and health of the mother and the infant. The arbitrator trusts that should the grievants read this opinion, they will share the arbitrator's judgment that under the contractual language they are not entitled to vacations.

---

* See, for example, *Texas Company* (19 LA 709) where it was held that discharge of an employee who was unable to work because of pregnancy was for "proper cause" within the meaning of the contract. Contention of the employee that employer was required to give employee leave of absence, instead of discharging her, was rejected. It was held that the contract permits the employer to grant leaves of absence at his discretion, and he refused to grant leaves of absence for pregnancy.

QUESTIONS

1. If the arbitrator had held that the grievants were not "laid off" from work within the meaning of Article VIII, he would then have been required to determine whether or not pregnancy is an illness. How would you rule on this issue?
2. Why did the arbitrator hold that, even though the grievants' seniority was protected during the maternity leave, they still were not entitled to vacation benefits?
3. As in many arbitration cases, the parties cited several other arbitration awards as authority for their respective cases. How adequately did the arbitrator distinguish the cases cited by the union from the case before him?

CASE NO. 6

PAYMENT FOR A HOLIDAY FALLING ON A NONSCHEDULED WORKDAY

(This case involves a county highway department and a typically fast-growing public employee union. It deals with the issue of holiday pay when a holiday falls on a nonscheduled workday—Columbus Day, in this instance, falling on a Saturday. The county had laid off the employees with pay on the Friday preceding the Saturday in question, and then did not pay them for Columbus Day. The employees protested, arguing that they were entitled to holiday pay for Saturday and that the county had violated the labor agreement by its action.

Complicating the story somewhat is the fact that the policy which the county followed was in effect before the union came into the picture. This is the first contract between the parties.)

GRIEVANCE AND CONTRACT PROVISIONS

This dispute involves the issue of holiday pay for Columbus Day, October 12, 1968. In protest against the action of the county taken under the circumstances of this case, the union filed a grievance, dated November 4, 1968, which states:

> On Fri. Oct. 11, 1968 we were supposed to work as one day of our guaranteed work week. On Thursday, Oct. 10 we were told to take off Oct. 11, 1968 to celebrate Oct. 12, 1968 which is a paid holiday. By doing this we are short 8 hours pay at the hourly rate. We are asking that all employees receive this money.

Relevant to the case are the following provisions of the labor agreement:

ARTICLE IV

It is agreed that all conditions of employment relating to wages, hours of work, overtime differentials and general working conditions, shall be maintained at not less than the highest standards in effect at the time of the signing of this Agreement, and the conditions of employment shall be improved wherever specific provisions for improvement are made elsewhere in this Agreement.

ARTICLE VI

Section 1. The County Highway Department agrees that the standard guaranteed hours of work shall be eight (8) hours per day or forty (40) hours per week, and that the work week shall start on Monday and end on Friday. All employees shall be paid the first and third Monday of each month.

Section 4. All regular employees covered by this agreement will be guaranteed a weekly pay that will not be less than the equivalent of forty (40) hours at straight time rate, provided the employee reports for work on each day of the work week.

ARTICLE XX

The following named holidays shall be paid for at the rate of eight (8) hours' pay for the holiday in addition to any monies the employee may earn on such holidays: New Year's Day, Memorial Day, Fourth of July, Labor Day, Thanksgiving Day, Christmas, Washington's Birthday, Lincoln's Birthday, Columbus Day, Veteran's Day and the two election days in the year of the election. To be eligible for election holidays' pay the employee must vote in the election.

THE BACKGROUND

On July 1, 1968, the instant labor agreement went into effect, and is the first labor contract negotiated by the county and union. Before the collective bargaining relationship was established, the county followed the policy of laying off the employees with pay on Friday when a holiday fell on Saturday and Sunday. For example, if July 4 fell on a Saturday, the employees did not work on the Friday immediately preceding the Saturday holiday and were paid for Friday. That this policy was in force before the labor agreement went into effect was stipulated by the county and union.

Columbus Day is designated as a holiday under Article XX of the labor agreement. In 1968, this holiday fell on Saturday, October 12. The county followed the aforecited policy which was in effect before execution of the labor agreement. Thus, the employees did not work on Friday, October 11, and were paid for this day. However, the county did not pay them holiday pay for October 12, Columbus Day.

In short, the employees did not work on Friday and Saturday of the work week in question, and were paid for Friday but not for Columbus Day.

C, business agent of the union, testified that he learned of the county's intention to take such action on Thursday afternoon, October 10. He declared that he attempted to reach *H*, garage superintendent, on Thursday evening but was not successful. *C* also testified that he did not attempt to contact any member of the Board of Commissioners.

A county-union meeting previously had been scheduled for Friday, October 11. The meeting started at 9 A.M. on that day, and in attendance were *C* and stewards of the union and *H*, representing the county. In this regard, *C* testified:

> *H* said he was instructed to work this way because this was the way it was worked before the signing of the contract. I advised *H* that the County was not following the contract. I told him to call the employees in and have them work the balance of the day. My Stewards said the men were ready to go to work. I told *H* that he could still call the men in to finish the day, but he refused.

BASIC QUESTION

The basic question involved in this dispute is framed as follows: Under the circumstances of this case did the county violate article XX of the labor agreement?

PARTIES' POSITIONS

It is the union's position that the county violated the holiday provision of the labor agreement. Union counsel argues that

> our position is that the men should have received the 40 hours guaranteed pay for the week, and holiday pay for Columbus Day.

In contrast, the county position is that there is no violation of the labor agreement under the circumstances of this case. County counsel argues that

> the County followed the established policy by laying off the employees with pay on Friday, and not paying them extra for Columbus Day.

Both attorneys presented additional arguments in defense of their respective clients. Where appropriate and necessary, such arguments are dealt with in the succeeding portions of this opinion.

ANALYSIS OF THE EVIDENCE

What this dispute amounts to is a determination of the basic question in the light of the relevant contractual language. Bulking large in the county's argument is the contention that the relevant language is ambiguous and for this reason the county policy which was in force before the labor agreement became effective should govern its construction. In this respect, county counsel argues:

> We have a contract here which is ambiguous and not clear. That is why the previous policy should govern what the intent of the parties was when they negotiated the labor agreement. This is the reasonable way to construe the contract.

If the relevant provisions are found to be ambiguous, as county counsel argues, there would be a sound basis to regard the previous policy as controlling in their construction. To this extent the county raises a meritorious argument. To test the validity of the argument, however, there must be a careful analysis of the relevant provisions of the labor agreement.

In this respect, attention is first directed to Article VI, Sections 1 and 4, which provide a guaranteed weekly pay program for the employees. Section 1 provides that

> the standard guaranteed hours of work shall be eight (8) hours per day or forty (40) hours per week, and that the work week shall start on Monday and end on Friday.

There is nothing ambiguous about this provision of the labor agreement. Employees shall be guaranteed 40 hours of pay per week, and such work week starts on Monday and ends on Friday. What this means is that the county may work the employees for 40 hours within this span of time. If it does not, the employees still will be paid for 40 hours.

Understandably, Section 4 provides a restriction to the 40 hour guaranteed pay program. Employees must report for work each day of the work week. If an employee does not report to work, he will not be paid for that day.*

In short, when we read Sections 1 and 4 together, the clear conclusion is that employees are guaranteed 40 hours of pay for the work week provided they report to work each day.

As the facts show, the employees did not work on Friday, but were paid for this day. They received 40 hours' pay as required by the rele-

---

* Subsequently there will be a discussion as to whether the employees would have reported for work on Friday, October 11, except for the county's laying them off on this day.

vant language of Article VI. Hence, the county did not violate these provisions of the labor agreement. It was the prerogative of the county not to work the employees on Friday provided, of course, the county paid them for the Friday, which it did.

Does the county's compliance with the guaranteed pay provision mean that the county complied with the holiday clause of the labor agreement? Is there an ambiguity in this provision which would justify the construction of this language on the basis of the county's previous policy? These are the pertinent issues involved in this proceeding. In this respect, it is first necessary to note that the guaranteed pay provision established in Article VI and the holiday provision established in Article XX have separate and different objectives. They are treated in different provisions of the labor agreement, and must be read independently for purposes of the case. That these provisions have different objectives, and serve to protect employees in different phases of their working conditions, should be clear to all concerned. One provision establishes that employees will be guaranteed 40 hours of pay. The other provides for paid holidays. Hence, it would not be proper to leap to the conclusion that just because the county complied with the guaranteed pay provision, it likewise complied with the holiday provision. In other words, the holiday pay provision must stand by itself in the determination of whether or not the county violated its terms.

Article XX states that

> the following named holidays shall be paid for at the rate of eight (8) hours pay for the holiday in addition to any monies the employees earn on such holidays: ... Columbus Day ...

With full deference to county counsel, the arbitrator sees no ambiguity in its terms. It states simply that Columbus Day is a paid holiday. Surely the provision does not state that employees are not entitled to holiday pay just because they are not scheduled for that day; and it equally does not state that they are to lose holiday pay just because during the work week they had received 40 hours of pay. Rather it states that employees are to be paid holiday pay for Columbus Day and there are no limitations placed on the right of the employees to receive this benefit.

In 1968, Columbus Day fell on Saturday, October 12, and the clear language of the provision requires that the employees be paid for the holiday on this date. At no place in the holiday provision do we find that the county has the authority to designate different days for the holidays listed in its terms. In effect, what the county did was to designate Friday as the paid holiday for Columbus Day. But where do we find contractual authority for such county action? All that Article XX provides is that Columbus Day is a paid holiday. Columbus Day did not fall on Friday, October 11. It fell on Saturday, October 12. If the parties intended that the county may switch the days for those holidays specified in its terms, it would follow that the parties would have adopted appropriate language to confer this right on the county.

Moreover, the county's action to switch days for holiday purposes is not consistent with the language of Article VI, Section 1. Note that this provision states that the

work week *shall* start on Monday and end on Friday (emphasis supplied).

This means that these days are workdays on which employees must work unless, of course, a holiday specified in Article XX falls on one of these days. In the absence of such a holiday, this language contemplates that the county is without authority to convert a work day to a paid holiday.

Unless the arbitrator is prepared to read into Article XX language which is not there, he must of necessity hold that employees are entitled to holiday pay on the day upon which the holiday falls. This is the agreement the parties reached when they adopted the holiday provision. They did not agree that the county may designate a different day for the holidays specified in its terms. In all candor, the arbitrator simply does not see how Article XX can be read in any other way. Its language and intent are clear-cut, unequivocal, and precise. To accept the county's position would mean that the arbitrator would deny employees a benefit which the parties conferred upon them. Indeed, the county is no more authorized to designate a different day for the holidays specified in Article XX than the union and/or employees are authorized to designate a different day for holiday purposes. Would the county, for example, argue that the employees may designate Friday as the day for a holiday when the holiday by the calendar falls on a Tuesday? To raise this question is to provide the obvious answer. Under the language of Article XX, neither party is permitted to switch the days for purposes of holiday pay.

There is no need to prolong the discussion on this feature of the case. Purely and simply, the parties stipulated in Article XX that Columbus Day is a paid holiday. In 1968, this holiday fell on Saturday, October 12. It is on this day that the employees must be paid their holiday pay. Rather than being ambiguous and equivocal, the language is precise and clear cut. In this light, the arbitrator cannot accept the argument of the county that the previous policy should govern the construction of the holiday pay provision. Such a policy was changed when the parties adopted Article XX of the labor agreement. To reach any other conclusion would distort the language contained in Article XX.

Additional County Arguments

Before reaching his final conclusion in this case, the arbitrator carefully considered additional arguments offered by the county. In this regard county counsel argues:

In this case, the Stewards and C knew before Friday what the County's position was. They knew about it before Friday when the County policy could have been changed, and the men called to work on Friday. Now we are asked to pay not only for this day, but for an additional day off. We are now being asked to pay for a six day week, with the employees being off on two of these days.

This argument is rejected as being without merit because C testified without contradiction that he advised H early on Friday morning that the employees were prepared to work, and that they should be called to work the remainder of the day. H refused. This was his choice after the union warned him that the county was not following the labor agreement. It was not a case where the union in bad faith led the county down the primrose path only to betray the county. The union did not "sandbag" the county. It warned the county; and, indeed, requested the county to call the men to work on the Friday in question.

True, C did not contact a member of the Board of Commissioners about the problem. Instead, he spoke to the superintendent, a person having the authority to call employees to work, and who dealt with the union on matters of the labor agreement. Moreover, C took prompt action to warn him that the County was in violation of the labor agreement.

County counsel argues that the philosophy of a holiday is to provide employees with rest and rejuvenation, and that a paid holiday should not constitute a "windfall" for employees. Still the fact remains that Columbus Day is a designated paid holiday in Article XX, and must be celebrated with pay on the calendar day upon which it falls. If the employees received a "windfall" because they were off two days and paid for both of them, this was a condition of the county's own making. It could have required the employees to work on Friday. It was the county and not the union or employees who contributed to this state of affairs. The men were prepared to report to work on Friday, but the county refused to call them to work. In short, the county provided the basis for the windfall.

In addition, county counsel argues that to grant the grievance would mean that the employees would be required to work on each holiday that falls between Monday and Friday. In all candor, the arbitrator does not see the merit of this argument. Article XX requires that the designated holidays be celebrated on the calendar days upon which they fall. It is on these specific days that the holiday is to be celebrated. Indeed, without contradiction, union counsel stated that the employees were off for a holiday on Friday, May 30, 1969, the Memorial Day holiday.

Finally, the county argues that Article IV, the Maintenance of Standards provision, authorizes the county's action. Nothing could be further from the truth. This provision guarantees employees that benefits which exceed contractual terms shall remain in effect during the life of the contract. In this case the county seeks to deprive the employees of a benefit which is established in the labor agreement.

CONCLUSIONS

What this case boils down to is the preservation of the integrity of contractual language. Article XX specifies certain paid holidays. In the absence of language to the contrary, this provision requires that the paid holidays be celebrated on the calendar days upon which the holidays fall. The language does not provide either the county or the union with the authority to designate a different day for holiday purposes.

Hence, the arbitrator cannot accept the county argument that the policy in force prior to the execution of the labor agreement should govern the construction of its terms. Such policy was changed by the clear-cut language of Article XX. It would be a masterpiece of error on the arbitrator's part, a clear distortion of the terms of the holiday provision, for him to hold that the county under Article XX may switch days for holiday purposes.

QUESTIONS

1. What was the economic motivation behind the county policy involved in this case?
2. Why did the arbitrator say that to hold for the county would deprive employees of a benefit which they have under the labor agreement?
3. What must the county accomplish in the next contract negotiations to obtain contractual authority for the action taken by it in this case? Do you believe that the union would sympathize with such an effort on the part of the county?
4. Do you believe that the arbitrator would have ruled for the county if the guaranteed weekly pay program were not in the contract?

CASE NO. 7

COVERAGE UNDER A HOSPITAL INSURANCE BENEFIT PROGRAM

(In this case, the parties were in disagreement as to the extent of coverage for employees who receive treatment in the "emergency room" of a hospital located in the city involved. The union contended that even treatment for the common cold should be paid for by the company. On the other hand, the company contended that it was liable for payment only when there was treatment for an injury or where surgery was performed. The job of the arbitrator was to rule on what kind of treatment was covered by the emergency room provision of the hospital insurance program. The case was complicated by contradictory testimony regarding what was said or not said by a company representative when the provision was adopted.)

CHARACTER OF THE DISPUTE

What is involved in this dispute is a determination of the insurance benefits to which employees are entitled when they or their dependents receive treatment in the emergency room of *K* Hospital. Physicians staff the emergency room, and the facility operates on a 24 hour, seven day a week basis. In the instant labor agreement, the parties negotiated an insurance plan which covers the use of the emergency room.

In the previous labor agreement there was no provision for insurance benefits in the use of the emergency room. The company's insurance plan is carried with the *CL* Insurance Company. It is the carrier for all insurance benefits provided to the employees, including the use of the emergency room. However, as far as this case is concerned, the dispute is between the company and union. The insurance carrier is not a party to the labor agreement.

The insurance benefit for the use of the emergency room is included in Article XXVI which in pertinent part states:

> The Company will provide insurance for the employees which will include the benefits outlined below and explained more fully in a booklet, copies of which will be distributed to all employees....
>
> MAXIMUM HOSPITAL BENEFITS—EMPLOYEES and DEPENDENTS
> 1. Hospital daily room and board: Semi-private room accommodations in full, or an allowance toward daily cost of private room equal to the price charged by the hospital for the most common of its semi-private rooms.
> 2. Maximum confinement per disability ....120 days
> 3. Miscellaneous hospital charges ....Unlimited
> 4. Maternity—Maximum hospital allowance $200.00
>   Doctor Fee for Regular Delivery $150.00
>   Doctor Fee for Caesarean Section $300.00
> 5. In-hospital doctor's fee—$5.00 per visit
>   and maximum of $600.00
> 6. Surgical Benefits—In or out of hospital $300.00
> 7. Polio insurance $5,000.00
> 8. Emergency room coverage ....Unlimited

Following the execution of the current labor agreement, the company refused to pay for certain kinds of treatment received by employees and their dependents in the emergency room. Joint Exhibit No. 2

demonstrates 80 claims which the company refused to pay. The caption of Joint Exhibit No. 2 states:

> The following is a list of claims that were filed by employees for Emergency Room treatment, which will not be processed.

The document is dated February 12, 1969, and includes the names of the employees making the claims and the reason for the treatment received by the employees or their dependents. Such reasons are:

Chest X-ray
Cold, Pharyngitis
Flu
Tonsillitis
Gastro Intestinal Spasm
Foot Sprain
Gastritis
URI with Pharyngitis
Croupy, Cough
Asthma
Respiratory Infection
Diaper Rash
Vomiting
Headache
Diabetes
Stomach Pain
Colitis
Nerves
Pain, L. Side
Sore Throat
Red Throat
Dizziness & Nausea
Bronchiolitis
Fever & Diarrhea
Eye Infection
Possible Colic

After the company refused to pay the claims indicated in Joint Exhibit No. 2, the employees involved and the union filed a grievance for each individual case. Such grievances were not submitted in evidence in this arbitration, and no attempt was made to establish the circumstances surrounding the disability treatment in the emergency room. Hence, there is no specific grievance before the arbitrator, and, instead, the parties submitted the following question to be determined in this arbitration:

What is covered by Sub-Section 8 of Article 26 of the contract?

PARTIES' ARGUMENTS

It is the union position that employees should be paid for any kind of treatment which is received by them or their dependents in the emergency room. This position is made clear by S, president of the union, who testified:

> We believe that any condition is covered by item 8 [of Article 26]. We believe that any treatment in the emergency room is covered. Anytime a person is admitted to the Emergency Room and receives treatment, it is covered. Any type of physical condition warrants coverage under item 8 if it requires medication.

Also, C, a member of the Union Negotiating Committee, stated the position of the union:

> We believe that if an employee or his dependent goes to the Emergency Room for any condition whatsoever, it would be covered.

To defend this position, the union argues that the term "unlimited" found in item 8 of Article XXVI means that the company agreed to pay for any kind of treatment received in the emergency room. In this regard, the union states:

> We would like to draw the Arbitrator's attention to the Company's contention from opening statements that the "Unlimited" portion of Emergency Room Coverage Unlimited had reference to the amount of money for payment if an Emergency existed, was not confirmed by testimony from any of the witnesses. In fact all witnesses testified that there was very little discussion on the subject during contract negotiations.

In other words, in the union's view, the term "Unlimited" does not refer to money, but rather its meaning is that there is unlimited coverage as to the kind of treatment received in the emergency room.

In the second place, the union argues that it was the intent of the negotiations that the provision in contention cover any kind of disability treated in the emergency room. In this respect, it argues that D, manager of manufacturing, stated in the negotiations that item 8 would cover a "common cold." As to this point, the union refers to the testimony of union witnesses who declared that in answer to a question of a union representative as to what is covered by item 8, D replied:

> "As far as I am concerned, it would cover a common cold."

On this basis, the union argues:

It is the Union's position that in clarification of the contract in the last days of negotiations that *D* made the statement that as far as he was concerned the Emergency Room would cover a common cold. Therefore, we conclude that the Union Negotiation Committee was satisfied that there would be no limits or conditions that an employee would be denied use of the Emergency Room Service.

On these grounds, the union requests that to the parties' submitted question the arbitrator reply that item 8 covers any and all kinds of treatment received by an employee or his dependent in the emergency room.

Needless to state, the company does not share the position of the union. Rather its position is that an employee is covered by item 8 only when he or his dependent is treated for an emergency condition. In this respect, it points out that an emergency condition is defined in the insurance booklet referred to in the opening sentence of Article XXVI. In this regard, the company states:

> The requirements for qualifying for hospital benefits are stated in the first paragraph of that page, as follows:
>
> "WHEN BENEFITS BEGIN.
>
> To qualify for hospital benefits, confinement must last at least 18 hours in a legally constituted hospital with the recommendation of a qualified physician or surgeon. However, benefits start immediately in case of emergency following injury or whenever surgery is required."
>
> It is noted that to qualify for hospital benefits, two separate and cumulative conditions must be met, viz.:
>
> 1. Hospitalization must be "with the recommendation of a qualified physician or surgeon."
> 2. Confinement must last at least 18 hours, except in emergencies. In "emergencies" benefits start at once and are not subject to the 18-hour requirement.
>
> Requirement No. 1 is obvious, as otherwise any irresponsible person, or child, could on his own responsibility commit himself to a hospital for hospital treatment (at the employer's expense) for a condition which no qualified physician or surgeon would consider an emergency requiring immediate hospitalization, such as an ordinary common cold or headache.

In other words, the company position is that for purposes of emergency room coverage, an employee or his dependents must be treated for an injury or receive surgery.

The company stresses that the arbitrator is constrained from adding to the language of the labor agreement under Article VII, Section 4, which in pertinent part states:

> The Arbitrator shall not have the authority to add to or subtract from, or to modify any of the terms of this Agreement.

In this connection, the company argues:

> In short, anything which would in effect modify any term of the Agreement or which would in anywise add to its present provisions is specifically reserved to the negotiating principals themselves. Aside from requiring that hospitalization must be upon recommendation of a physician (who presumably would determine whether an emergency requiring hospital treatment exists), the present Agreement and booklet do not define what type of cases constitute an emergency of that character. In this situation, an Arbitrator, the same as the Court's in construing the Labor Acts, would have to proceed on a case-by-case basis and be governed by the total relevant facts in each case. He cannot, under the restrictions of this Agreement, add to the present Agreement any general term or provision which will automatically determine all future claims which may be presented. However, an arbitrable Grievance might have been presented by the Union, by grieving in a specific borderline case which they conceive to illustrate their theory of an emergency covered by the Agreement. In a hearing on such a specific claim, an Arbitrator, within the jurisdictional restrictions of this Agreement, might still determine, upon all the facts and circumstances of that case, whether a situation there existed which constituted an "emergency" for which the employee qualified for this benefit. But while disposing of the case then at hand, this would not settle the parties' continuing problem, which would recur in each subsequent claim and require ascertainment of all the relevant facts and circumstances of each.
>
> The final solution apparently will have to be a negotiated agreement between the parties themselves of some sort of addition to the language of the present Agreement providing some sort of "guide line" for evaluating future claims, if that is found practicable. An Arbitrator cannot make such an addition to the Contract.

In addition, unlike the union, the company contends that the term "Unlimited" found in item 8 refers exclusively to dollar coverage and has nothing to do with the kind of treatment contemplated by the emergency room provision. Also, it denies that D stated that it would cover even a common cold.

On these grounds, the company would have the arbitrator reply to the parties' submitted question that the provision covers only treatment for an injury or when a person receives surgery.

ANALYSIS OF THE EVIDENCE

No Specific Grievances Before the Arbitrator

At the outset it should be pointed out that the arbitrator does not have a specific grievance before him for decision. He understands that there are many grievances pending dealing with the issue involved in this case which the parties intend to dispose of in the light of the decision in this proceeding. Be that as it may, the arbitrator, of course, does not decide any of those grievances, since they are not before him for decision. In this way, this case is quite different from the normal arbitration in which an arbitrator makes a decision in the light of the facts and circumstances of a particular grievance as it may relate to particular contractual language.

Rather than a grievance in the ordinary sense of the term, the parties have submitted to him a question to be determined in these proceedings. It is hopeful, of course, that his determination of this question will provide the necessary basis for the disposition of these grievances. However, the arbitrator wants it perfectly clear that the grievances awaiting his decision are not before him, and his decision will not in this arbitration necessarily grant or deny any of them. It will be the job of the parties to dispose of them in the light of the arbitrator's determination of the question submitted to him for decision.

Jurisdiction of the Arbitrator

If the arbitrator understands the basic position of the company, it is that employees are covered by item 8 of Article XXVI only when they receive emergency care in the emergency room because of injury or where surgery may occur. The basis of this position is that item 8 itself does not define what an emergency is, and the only reference to "emergency care" is contained in the booklet referred to in the opening sentence of Article XXVI. This reference is contained in the following paragraph on page 13 of such booklet:

WHEN BENEFITS BEGIN

> To qualify for hospital benefits, confinement must last at least 18 hours in a legally constituted hospital with the recommendation of a qualified physician or surgeon. However, benefits start immediately in case of emergency care following injury or whenever surgery is required.

In short, the company argues that the concept of emergency care for purposes of item 8 is defined in the booklet. Its argument is that emergency room coverage pertains only to an injury or surgery. If an employee is treated for anything else, he must pay the charges and not the company. As N, manager of industrial relations, testified:

> We do not pay for outpatient care. Outpatient care is someone coming into the Emergency Room for treatment for something other than an injury or an operation. An emergency is spelled out on page 13 of the booklet—injury or surgery.

To illustrate this point, N testified that an employee would not be covered by item 8 if he brought his child into the emergency room with a 102 degree fever on a Sunday or Thursday afternoon when doctors are not available. (In X city the testimony is that doctors are not available in general on Thursday afternoons.) He testified that this disability constitutes outpatient care, and not an emergency situation within the meaning of item 8. Hence, the employee would be required to pay the bill, and not the company.

In short, the company's view is that the concept of emergency—injury or operation—is spelled out in the insurance booklet for purposes of item 8, and the arbitrator under the arbitration clause has no power to add to the concept. It refers to Section 4 of the grievance procedure which states that

> the Arbitrator shall not have authority to add to or subtract from, or to modify any of the terms of this Agreement.

Thus, if the arbitrator accepted the company argument he would reply to the parties' submitted question as follows:

> Subsection 8 of Article 26 covers only those conditions where an injury or surgery is involved.

If this kind of a decision which the company apparently believes is the only one the arbitrator has the authority to make does not satisfy the union and employees, the company suggests that the parties themselves negotiate a broader concept for purposes of item 8. To this suggestion, the union points out:

> As for the Company's request that the Union and the Company should Re-Negotiate, the Emergency Room coverage Unlimited clause in our present contract wouldn't be a workable solution to our problem. To strike a Company is the ultimate weapon of a Union. We have two years remaining of our current contract, therefore negotiations could continue for a period of two years, as the list of at least one hundred claims would continue to grow.

Needless to state, the first duty of any arbitrator is to be sure that he has the jurisdiction and authority to make a decision. Indeed, if an arbitrator makes a decision which flagrantly violates his jurisdiction under a labor agreement, such a decision is reversible in the courts. Not even the celebrated "Trilogy Cases" decided by the United States Supreme Court in 1960 would preserve an arbitrator's decision which clearly exceeds his authority under the powers conferred upon him under a collective bargaining contract. Beyond these observations, the instant arbitrator firmly believes that as a matter of principle an arbitrator should not exceed his authority. As many of his decisions have demonstrated, the arbitrator is of the conviction that the parties must write their own collective bargaining language. This is the primary responsibility of the parties, and not that of an arbitrator whose responsibility is to apply and interpret contractual language.

Thus, the arbitrator understands fully the company's argument involving his jurisdiction and allowable powers. This is an important argument, and one to which the arbitrator has given full and long consideration.

In the instant case, however, the arbitrator is of the judgment that he does not violate his jurisdictional limitations when he holds that the emergency room provision covers more than injury and surgery. After serious and long consideration, the arbitrator is not altogether certain that the parties intended that the injury and surgery statement appearing on page 13 of the insurance booklet applies to the emergency room provision. This statement provides:

> However, benefits start immediately in case of emergency care following injury or whenever surgery is required.

Note that this sentence was also contained in the insurance booklet issued pursuant to the terms of the previous labor agreement. As the facts show, such a booklet was prepared and issued pursuant to the hospital insurance plan under the old contract. This booklet contained the very same language which appears on page 13 of the booklet issued pursuant to the current labor agreement. The same statement is repeated in the current booklet which was issued pursuant to the instant labor agreement which contains the emergency room benefit. There is, however, no specific reference in either company or union witnesses' testimony that the injury and surgery statement contained in the current booklet is to apply to emergency room coverage. That is, we have no direct and unequivocal testimony from any witness that in negotiations the parties agreed that the emergency room provision covers only injury or surgery. What the company really argues is that this was the intent of the parties. For sure, this is a reasonable assumption, but still the arbitrator is not fully satisfied that this was the intent of the parties. At no place in the record do we find testimony that in the negotiations which resulted in emergency room coverage a company representative made a statement such as this:

> Look, to qualify for Emergency Room coverage, the employee or his dependent must have been injured or had surgery performed. Nothing else is covered.

We find no such statement in the record of this case. Instead, the parties negotiated emergency room coverage, but did not agree as to the circumstances under which an employee will be covered by its terms.*

After the provision was negotiated and the current labor agreement

---

* Subsequently, there will be a discussion of the issue involving the alleged statement of *D* that he told the union that item 8 would cover even a common cold.

went into effect, a dispute arose as to the proper coverage of the emergency room provision. Now the company argues that the aforecited injury and surgery statement contained in the booklet governs the scope of the provision. Only by inference, albeit a reasonable one, does the company reach such a conclusion.

It is true, of course, that the injury and surgery statement appearing in the booklet speaks in terms of "emergency care." On this basis, the company argues that since the emergency room provides for "emergency care," it follows that employees must have been injured or have received an operation, before they qualify for benefits under the emergency room provision. This is indeed a reasonable and logical inference of the language. However, the injury and surgical statement may have been adopted for an entirely different purpose. That is, when a person is injured or has had surgery performed, he is relieved from the 18-hour confinement clause appearing in the sentence immediately preceding the one which contains the injury and surgical statement. In other words, we know for sure that such a statement has this specific purpose—the relief of the 18-hour confinement requirement as a condition for the receipt of hospital benefits. However, what we do not know for sure is that the parties intended that the same statement conditions and limits emergency room coverage.

As a matter of fact, the company itself is not sure that the emergency room provision is limited only to injuries and surgery. By its own action, the company has paid emergency room claims which did not involve injuries or surgery. Note the following testimony of D in this regard:

> "We are willing to give consideration to cases which are emergencies other than injuries, accidents, and surgery. We have broadened the coverage beyond the booklet [i.e., the injury and surgical statement]. I do not know how far we have broadened it."

In other words, the company by its own action has paid for claims under the emergency room provision which did not involve injury or surgery. Hence, it follows that the company believes that there can be situations other than those which involve injury and surgery which fall within the scope of the emergency room coverage provision. Indeed, if the company by its own action has construed the provision in this fashion, the arbitrator is of the judgement and the conviction that he does not breach his authority or jurisdictional limitations when he holds that the provision under proper circumstances covers persons who receive treatment in the emergency room for conditions other than injuries or who have received surgery.

In short, the arbitrator is called upon in this case to construe the coverage of the emergency room provision contained in item 8 of article XXVI. After long and deep reflection, and for the reasons expressed above, he finds that under proper circumstances this provision covers persons who are treated in the emergency room for disabilities other than injuries or surgery.

The Basic Union Position

At the other end of the scale, the union's fundamental position is that the emergency room provision covers treatment for any kind of illness or condition provided for in the emergency room. It believes that the company should pay for all items specified in Joint Exhibit No. 2. As union witnesses testified, the provision covers "any condition whatsoever," and

> we believe that any treatment in the Emergency Room is covered. Any time a person is admitted to the Emergency Room and receives treatment, he is covered. Any type of physical condition warrants coverage under item 8 if it requires medication.

If the arbitrator accepts this position of the union as the basis of his decision in these proceedings, he would reply to the parties' submitted question as follows:

> Subsection 8, Article 26 covers any and all treatment received in the Emergency Room.

How does the union defend this position?

The Meaning of Word "Unlimited" in Item 8

In the first place, it argues that its position is supported by the literal language of item 8, Section 26, pointing to the word "Unlimited" which appears adjacent to the phrase "Emergency Room Coverage." It believes that the word "Unlimited" means that any and all treatment is covered by the insurance program. That is, coverage is unlimited as to the type, kind, and reason for treatment.

Such construction of the word "Unlimited" is rejected as without merit, since it should be clear to all concerned that the word "Unlimited" refers to the *amount of money* for a claim and not to the kind of treatment involved in the use of the emergency room. In all items preceding item 8 dollar limits are referred to in the same column as the word "Unlimited" appears for item 8. For example, immediately above item 8, we find the following:

> 7. Polio Insurance $5,000.00

This means, of course, that if an employee or his dependent is stricken with polio the insurance program will pay up to a maximum of $5,000.00 to cover the illness. In Article XXVI, we find other kinds of benefits and adjacent to each one there is a particular amount of money representing the company's liability.

In short, the union would place a construction on the word "Unlimited" which is completely inconsistent and at variance with its obvious meaning and purpose. What is clearly meant by this term is that when an employee or dependent is treated for a disability covered by the phrase "Emergency Room Coverage," there is no limit to the company's liability as far as money coverage is concerned.

In addition, the arbitrator's construction of the word "Unlimited" is supported by testimony offered in the hearing. *Without contradiction, N* testified that under the previous labor agreement employees used the emergency room, but that the employees and the company shared the costs. He testified further and without refutation that the employees were dissatisfied with this arrangement and desired the company to assume the full burden of the payment.

Thus, *N* testified:

> There were complaints of the Union during the negotiations that employees had to pay part of the fees for the use of the Emergency Room. The Union wanted to change this practice. It wanted the Company to pay the full costs.

Note that such testimony was not contradicted or refuted by any union witness. The union complained about the cost-sharing practice, and wanted this changed to the extent that the company should assume the full burden. This is exactly what was accomplished in the negotiations when the parties inserted the word "Unlimited" adjacent to the phrase "Emergency Room Coverage." The company's liability is now unlimited for the treatment of a disability which is properly covered by item 8.

Thus, in the light of the positioning of the word "Unlimited" in item 8, and in view of the background which resulted in the adoption of the term, the arbitrator is fully satisfied that the word "Unlimited" as it appears in item 8 refers to *money coverage* and not to the kind of treatment received in the emergency room.

The Common Cold Statement

In further support of its position, the union argues that company witness *D* made a statement in the negotiations which the union construes as meaning that item 8 covers any and all kinds of treatment obtained by an employee or his dependent in the emergency room. Each union witness, *S, A,* and *C,* testified that he participated in the negotiations which resulted in the adoption of the emergency room coverage provision. Each testified that the union raised the following question in the negotiations:

> In your own words, what would be covered by item 8?

All union witnesses testified that to this question *D* replied:

> "As far as I am concerned, it would cover even a common cold."

On this basis, the union argues that it was the intent of the parties that all and any kind of treatment received in the emergency room be fully covered by the emergency room coverage provision. Thus, it states:

> It is the Union's position that in clarification of the contract in the last days of negotiations that Mr. *D* [manager of manufacturing and spokesman for the Company] made the statement that as far as he was concerned the Emergency Room would cover a common cold. Therefore, we conclude that the Union Negotiation Committee was satisfied that there would be no limits or conditions that an employee would be denied use of the Emergency Room Service.

D, N, M, and *G* were the company witnesses in this proceeding. Each participated in the negotiations, and each witness testified that he was present at the time that *D* allegedly made his "common cold" statement.

In this regard, *G* testified:

> I do not recall that such a question was put to *D* or that he said that item 8 would cover even a common cold. I never heard *D* say this.

M declared:

> I do not recall *D* making this statement. I did not hear *D* make this statement.

In this regard, *N* testified:

> I was sitting next to *D* in the negotiations. I don't remember any such question or answer being stated. I heard everything *D* said, and my notes and my personal recollections show nothing to that effect.

And *D* testified:

> I was not asked such a question. I did not make such a statement. It would have expanded the coverage [i.e., every kind of treatment covered by item 8]. I would have had to receive permission to negotiate such a coverage. It would increase the cost of the insurance quite a bit. I don't recall the Union asking me what it would cover, and I don't remember making such a statement.

With regard to *D*'s testimony, the union argues that

> he did not flatly deny making the common-cold statement. His testimony was that he could not remember. This leaves the possibility that he could have made it.

On the other hand, *D* testified categorically in direct examination that

> I was not asked such a question. I did not make such a statement.

True, on cross-examination, he stated he could not remember that such a question was put to him, and he could not recall that he made such a statement.

In any event, the testimony on the issue herein considered is in a hopeless state of confusion and contradiction. It places the Arbitrator in an unenviable position, since to accept one version would imply that the witnesses testifying to the other version were telling a deliberate lie. Frankly, the arbitrator cannot determine from the record who was telling lies and who was telling the truth. All witnesses testified under oath, and each was equally motivated to testify as he did. Unfortunately, there was no evidence presented except the oral testimony of the witnesses. Neither the company nor the union presented any notes or other memorandums which might have objectively resolved the issue.

Under these circumstances, and without resolving with finality the issue of the truthfulness of the witnesses, all the arbitrator can do is hold that the proofs do not adequately demonstrate that *D* made the statement in question. In reaching this conclusion, the arbitrator does not necessarily doubt the veracity of the union witnesses. It very well could be that *D* made the statement in question, and the union witnesses are telling the full truth of the matter. Indeed, the arbitrator is candid enough to recognize this possibility.

Still, what can the arbitrator do under the circumstances which are involved in this feature of the case? What is involved is contradictory oral testimony. No written notes or memorandums were presented to him. Thus, under the state of the record, all that the arbitrator can do is find that the proof is not adequate that *D* made the statement in question. He may or may not have made it. In other words, the state of the record does not demonstrate categorically and objectively that he made it. It is stressed that this finding is made without reference to a determination of the veracity of the testimony. All that the arbitrator finds is that it was not proven satisfactorily that *D* stated that the emergency room coverage provision covers "even the common cold."

Coverage of Treatment Not Involving Surgery or Injury

As previous analysis has demonstrated, the arbitrator is satisfied that the emergency room coverage provision covers treatment received in the emergency room for disabilities other than injuries or surgery. On the other hand, in the light of the foregoing analysis, the arbitrator is satisfied that the proof is not adequate that the parties intended that the provision covers any and all kinds of treatment received in the emergency room. If the union position in this regard is carried to its logical conclusion, it would mean, for example, that an employee would be covered if he walks into the emergency room and complains to the attending physician that he has a headache. The treatment could consist of only giving the employee a couple of aspirins. This is the extent of the treatment, and still the union's position is that any charge for this kind of treatment would be covered by the provision.

Construction of Emergency Room Provision

Common sense alone would dictate that this could not possibly be the intent of the provision. Note that it states *"Emergency* Room Coverage" (emphasis supplied). Common sense would tell us that the treatment must be of an emergency character. There must be a sense of urgency involved which means that unless the person receives immediate medical attention his health would be imperiled. Thus, the disability must be of an emergency character—a disability which arises of a serious character which requires immediate medical attention.

In this proceeding, it would be improper, and indeed impossible, for the arbitrator to specify the details of this standard in the application of item 8. Each case must be treated on its own merits, and under its own set of circumstances. The key to the application of the provision is this—does an emergency exist in the sense that the person's health would be imperiled unless he receives immediate medical attention? If such a disability exists, item 8 would apply to a claim growing out of this state of affairs.

The parties themselves in good faith and using common sense must apply this standard for the application of item 8. The arbitrator has confidence that the parties possess the qualities of fairness, common sense, and good faith that would make the administration of the provision a realistic benefit to the employees, without at the same time burdening the company for charges involving disabilities of a minor, trivial, and non-emergency character.

CONCLUSIONS

In short, the arbitrator finds it within the scope of his jurisdiction to construe the emergency room coverage provision in this way:

1. It does not cover each and every kind of medical treatment received in the emergency room.
2. It covers treatment involving injuries or surgery.
3. It also covers treatment of disabilities, not involving injuries or surgery, for which the lack of immediate medical attention would imperil the health of a person.

As stated, the arbitrator in this proceeding does not resolve any of the grievances which await this decision. Not only would it be improper for the arbitrator to do so since the particular grievances are not before him for decision, but what is more, before any such grievances are determined, there must be consideration paid to the facts and circumstances of each particular case. However, the arbitrator is fully confident that the parties can resolve the grievances in the light of his construction of the emergency room coverage provision. If they cannot, the good offices of this arbitrator are available for the final determination of any of the pending grievances.

QUESTIONS

1. Since the company had previously paid for treatment in the emergency room which did not involve injury or surgery, how do you account for the company's position in this case that its liability involves only injuries or surgery?
2. Flatly and unmitigatedly contradictory testimony, such as that pertaining to D's alleged "common cold" statement is not uncommon in arbitration. Do you approve of the way in which the arbitrator handled this issue in the case? Why did not the arbitrator hold that D made the statement on the grounds that the company did not prove with irrefutable evidence that D did *not* make the statement?
3. Note that in this case the arbitrator did not settle any of the 80 grievances which provoked this arbitration. In the light of the standards laid down by his decision, how would each of these grievances be settled? (Apparently the arbitrator's confidence in the parties being able to settle these 80 grievances *was* justified. At least he was not asked after this decision was rendered to arbitrate any of these 80 grievances.)

9

Institutional Issues Under Collective Bargaining

The modern collective bargaining contract encompasses many issues which do not fall into the general category of wages or "fringe" supplements. Such subjects, rather, deal with the rights and duties of the employer, the union, and the employees themselves. Some of them—such as seniority and discharge—most directly serve to protect the job rights of workers and might be most appropriately thought of as "administrative" concerns. They will be treated in such a manner in Chapter 10.

Other subjects, however, tend to supply the institutional needs of either the labor organization or the particular management—through "compulsory union membership" clauses, for example, or by provisions explicitly allowing the company the right to make decisions for the direction of the labor force and the operation of the plant. These matters will be dealt with in the paragraphs which follow in this chapter.

In considering this institutional dimension of collective bargaining, it must be recognized that the topics which it encompasses can on occasion give the negotiators considerably more trouble than do the wage or fringe issues. There can, indeed, be deeply rooted conflict over basic philosophies of labor relations, the rights of management, and the rights and obligations of unions. And it is, for example, at times infinitely easier to compromise and settle a wage controversy than to resolve a heated difference of opinion as to whether or not a worker should be compelled to join a union as a condition of employment. For all the thorniness of many wage and wage-related issues, some of the longest and most bitter individual strikes have had as their source conflicts dealing with the institutional issues of collective bargaining.

This chapter will inspect, in turn: union membership as a condition of employment, the so-called "checkoff" mechanism, union obligations, and managerial prerogatives.

UNION MEMBERSHIP AS A CONDITION OF EMPLOYMENT

Prior to the passage of the Wagner Act in 1935, there was essentially only one way in which a union could get itself recognized by an unsympathetic management: through the use of raw economic strength. If the labor organization succeeded in pulling all or a significant part of the company's employees out on strike, or in having its membership boycott the production or services of the company in the marketplace, it stood a good chance of forcing the employer to come to terms. Lacking such economic strength, however, the union had no recourse—even if *all* the company's workers wanted to join it—in the face of management opposition to its presence.

The 1935 legislation, as we know, greatly improved the lot of the union in this regard. It provided for a secret-ballot *election* by the employees, should the employer express doubt as to the union's majority status. It also gave the union the exclusive right to bargain for *all* workers in the designated bargaining unit should the election prove that it did indeed have majority support. As Chapter 3 has indicated, these new ground rules for union recognition continue to this day.

Legally fostered recognition has not been synonymous with any assured status for the union as an institution, however. Indeed, in the many years since the Wagner Act, unions have still been able to find three grounds for insecurity. For one, the law has given the recognized labor organization no guarantee that it could not be dislodged by a rival union at some later date. For a second, there have still been many communication avenues open to antagonistic employers who choose to make known to their employees their antiunion feelings in an attempt to rid themselves of certified unions after a designated interval following the signing of the initial contract. And for a third, the government has not granted recognized unions protection against "free riders"—employees who choose to remain outside the union and thus gain the benefits of unionism without in any way helping to pay for those benefits. Under the law the union clearly has not only the *right* but also the *obligation* to represent all employees in the bargaining unit, regardless of their membership or nonmembership in the union. Unions have particularly feared that the "free-rider" attitude could become contagious, resulting in the loss through a subsequent election (in which nonmembers as well as members can vote) of their majority status and thus of their representation rights.

Consequently, organized labor has turned to its own bargaining-table efforts in an attempt to gain a further measure of institutional security. By and large, such attempts have been successful: by the 1970s, possibly as high as 83 percent of all contracts contained some kind of "union security" provision.[1]

Such provisions, which are frequently also referred to as "compulsory union membership" devices, essentially are three in number: the closed shop, the union shop, and the maintenance-of-membership agreement.

Brief reference has already been made to each of these mechanisms. A common denominator to all is that in one way or another membership in the union is made a condition of employment for at least some workers. They differ, however, in the timing for the requirement of union membership and in the degree of freedom of choice allowed the worker in his decision about joining the labor organization.

The closed shop and union shop are dissimilar in that under the former the worker must belong to the union *before* obtaining a job, whereas the latter requires union membership within a certain time period *after* the worker is hired. Under a maintenance-of-membership arrangement, the worker is free to elect whether or not he will join the union. Once he does join, however, he must maintain membership in the union for the duration of the contract period or else forfeit his job.

These forms of compulsory union membership can also be viewed as differing with respect to the freedom of the employer to hire workers. Under the closed shop he must hire only union members. This allows the union in effect to serve as the employment agency in most situations, and to refer workers to the employer upon his request. Under union-shop and maintenance-of-membership arrangements, the employer has free access to the labor market. He may hire whomever he wants and the union security provision becomes operative only after the worker is employed.

A final significant feature of union security is, of course, that it has received considerable attention from both the United States Congress

---

[1] Based on unofficial information furnished by the Bureau of Labor Statistics, U.S. Department of Labor.

and state legislatures. The laws which both bodies have enacted must be taken into account at the bargaining table, and union security provisions which disregard these relevant public fiats do so only at a definite risk.

As in many other areas of collective bargaining, there are several different approaches to the union security problem. The elasticity of the process is clearly demonstrated in the varied methods which employers and unions have adopted to deal with the issue.

The *closed shop,* obviously the most advantageous arrangement from labor's point of view, appeared in 33 percent of the nation's agreements in 1946.[2] Prohibited for interstate commerce by the Taft-Hartley Act of 1947, it visibly decreased in its frequency in the years immediately thereafter and an elaborate study of 1,716 collective bargaining contracts which was conducted by the Bureau of Labor Statistics in 1954 revealed that by the latter year less than 5 percent of all agreements researched contained such a provision.[3] No exhaustive investigation on the subject has been conducted since 1954, but there is reason to suspect that the closed shop's decline is somewhat exaggerated in the bureau's figures. Not only was the study confined primarily to agreements governed by the Taft-Hartley Act and hence not completely representative, but—as Slichter, Healy, and Livernash could argue even in the 1960s—"many enterprises subject to the Taft-Hartley Act, which nominally have the union shop, in fact have the closed shop either because the employer finds it advantageous or because the union is too strong for the employer and dictates the terms of the contract."[4] Even some industries subject to Taft-Hartley, moreover, have refused to accept the law's closed-shop verdict—notably building construction, which bluntly flouted it until 1959, when the Landrum-Griffin Act recognized the special characteristics of that sector and officially allowed it a stronger form of union security which approximates the closed shop.

Nonetheless, there can be no denying that closed-shop arrangements received a severe setback with the passage of Taft-Hartley, and that presumably at least the bulk of the closed-shop provisions which continue in force have been negotiated by companies and unions which are not within the scope of the national labor law.

With the decrease in usage of the closed shop, the *union shop* became the most widespread form of union membership employment condition. After being part of only 17 percent of all contracts in 1946,[5] it appeared in

[2] Theodore Rose, "Union Security Provisions in Agreements, 1954," *Monthly Labor Review,* LXXVIII, No. 6 (June 1955), 646.
[3] *Ibid.*
[4] Sumner H. Slichter, James J. Healy, and E. Robert Livernash, *The Impact of Collective Bargaining on Management* (Washington, D.C.: The Brookings Institution, 1960), p. 29.
[5] Rose, "Union Security Provisions in Agreements, 1954," *op. cit.*

about 64 percent of all labor agreements in 1959 and the figure is at about the 70 percent level today.

The *maintenance-of-membership* arrangement, originating in the abnormal labor market days of World War II, is still fully legal, but is utilized relatively infrequently. After appearing in about one quarter of all contracts in 1946, it had steadily lost ground thereafter and only 8 percent of all contracts studied in 1966 made provision for it.[6] Much of the loss was undoubtedly absorbed by the gains of the union shop, which maintenance-of-membership employers, having already taken *this* step toward accommodating the union, have rarely resisted very adamantly.

Two other brands of union security, both relatively infrequent, constitute compromises between the union's goal of greatest possible security and the management's reluctance to grant such institutional status. Under the *agency shop*, nonunion memberships of the bargaining unit must make a regular financial contribution—usually the equivalent of union dues—to the labor organization, but no one is compelled to join the union. The money is, in fact, at times donated to recognized charitable organizations. Nonetheless, the incentive for a worker to remain in the "free-rider" class is clearly reduced in this situation, and the union thus gains some measure of protection. The *preferential shop* gives union members preference in hiring, but allows the employment of nonunionists and its efficacy seems to depend on how the parties construe the word *preference*.

Though the straight union shop thus appears to be the most popular form of union security, some employers and unions have negotiated variations of this species of compulsory union membership. Under some contracts employees who are not union members when the union-shop agreement becomes effective are not required to join the union. Some agreements exempt employees with comparatively long service with the company. Under other contracts old employees (only) are permitted to withdraw from the union at the expiration of the agreement without forfeiting their jobs. Under this arrangement a so-called "escape period" of about fifteen days is included in the labor contract. If an employee does not terminate his union membership within the escape period, he then must maintain his membership under the new arrangement. Newly hired workers, however, are required to join the union.

Whether the straight union shop or modifications of it are negotiated, the Taft-Hartley law forbids an arrangement which compels a worker to join a union as a condition of employment, unless thirty days have elapsed from the effective date of the contract or the beginning of employment (whichever is later). In administering this section of the law the National

---

[6] *Basic Patterns in Union Contracts,* Bureau of National Affairs, 1966, 87:1–87:3. Part of the decline is, however, not entirely real: some arrangements have adopted the name of "union shop" but modified the latter in practice to equate or nearly equate to maintenance of membership.

Labor Relations Board has held that the thirty-day grace period does not apply to employees who are already members of the union.[7] However, it interprets the provision literally for workers who are not union members on the effective date of the contract or who are subsequently employed. Thus, in one case a union-shop arrangement was declared unlawful because it required workers to join the union on the twenty-ninth day following the beginning of employment.[8] Another union security arrangement was held to be illegal because it compelled employees to join the union if they had been on the company's payroll thirty or more days: in invalidating this latter agreement, the board ruled that it violated the law because it did not accord employees subject to its coverage the legal thirty-day grace period for becoming union members *after* the *effective date* of the contract.[9]

Whereas some negotiators have adopted variations of the straight union shop, others have devised a number of alternatives to the maintenance-of-membership arrangement. Only at the termination of the agreement are employees under most maintenance-of-membership arrangements permitted to withdraw from the union without forfeiting their jobs, and usually only a fifteen-day period is provided at the end of the contract period during which time the employee may terminate his union membership. But many agreements have a considerably less liberal period of withdrawal, from the worker's viewpoint, and some contracts allow more than the modal fifteen days. If an employee fails to withdraw during this "escape" time, he must almost invariably remain in the union for the duration of the new collective bargaining agreement.

Under some labor agreements, maintenance-of-membership arrangements also provide for an escape period after the *signing* of the agreement to permit withdrawals of existing members from the union. Other agreements do not afford this opportunity to current members of the union but restrict the principle of voluntary withdrawal to newly hired workers.

These modifications are fully consistent with the law in all but the 19 "right-to-work" states, which ban any form of compulsory union membership, but certain other arrangements are not. Reference has already been made to the terms of Taft-Hartley under which an employee cannot lawfully be discharged from his job because of loss of union membership unless he loses his membership in a union because of nonpayment of dues or initiation fees. In spite of the existence of an arrangement requiring union membership as a condition of employment, expulsion from a union for any reason other than nonpayment of dues or initiation fees *cannot* result in loss of employment. The National Labor Relations Board will order the reinstatement of an employee to his job with back pay where

---

[7] *Charles Krause Milling Co.*, 97 NLRB 336 (1951).
[8] *Chesler Glass Co.*, 92 NLRB 1016 (1950).
[9] *Continental Carbon, Inc.*, 94 NLRB 1026 (1951).

this feature of the law is violated. Depending upon the circumstances of a particular case, the board will require the employer or the union, or both, to pay back wages to such an employee.

The board has, in fact, applied a literal interpretation to this feature of Taft-Hartley. In one case[10] the board has held that a worker actually does not have to *join* a union even though a union-shop arrangement may be in existence. His only obligation under the law is his willingness to tender the dues and initiation fees required by the union. In this case three workers were willing to pay their union dues and initiation fees but they refused to assume any other union-related obligations, or even to attend the union meeting at which they would be voted upon and accepted. As a result the union had secured the discharge of these workers under the terms of the union security arrangement included in the labor agreement. The board held that the discharge of workers under such circumstances violated the Taft-Hartley law, ruled that both the union and the company engaged in unfair labor practices, and ordered the workers reinstated in their jobs with full back pay.

The "right-to-work" laws themselves, of course, serve as formidable obstacles to union security arrangements in the primarily Southern and Southwestern states in which, through 1970, they remained on the books. On the other hand, not only has their effect on labor relations in these states been highly debatable, but in its 1965–66 sessions the United States Congress came close to repealing the relevant Taft-Hartley Act passage permitting the enactment of such state laws (Section 14b),[11] and there was at the time of this writing some likelihood that the repeal efforts would soon be resumed on Capitol Hill.

Were Congress to remove Section 14b, this action would nullify all right-to-work laws as far as these laws apply to interstate commerce because of the *federal pre-emption* doctrine, which forbids states to pass laws in conflict with a federal statute. And in this event the right-to-work laws existing in Alabama, Arizona, Arkansas, Florida, Georgia, Iowa, Kansas, Mississippi, Nebraska, Nevada, North Carolina, North Dakota, South Carolina, South Dakota, Tennessee, Texas, Utah, Virginia, and Wyoming would have application only in the area of *intra*state commerce. They would cease to have any effect upon firms engaged in interstate dealings.

Regardless of the fate of right-to-work legislation, however, it seems very likely that the question of whether union security provisions should

[10] *Union Starch & Refining Co.,* 87 NLRB 779 (1949).

[11] The repeal measure passed the House by a 20-vote margin, but a filibuster led by the late Senator Everett M. Dirksen of Illinois prevented the bill from being formally considered by the Senate. AFL-CIO officials, nonetheless, claimed that as many as 56 senate votes, or more than the majority needed, would have been forthcoming in favor of repeal had the measure been brought to a vote.

be negotiated in labor agreements will remain a controversial one for some time to come—among the general public and some direct parties to collective bargaining, if not among the large segment of unionized industry which has already granted such union security.

This controversy actually contains three major elements: morality, labor relations, and power.

Whether or not it is *morally* right to force an employee to join a union in order to be able to work is not an easy issue to resolve. Unions and supporters of unionism often argue that it is not "fair" to permit an employee to benefit from collective bargaining without paying dues, given the fact that the union must under the law represent all workers in the bargaining unit. And the argument is not without logic. Improvements obtained in collective bargaining *do* benefit nonunion members as well as union member employees, and the union *is* compelled by law to represent nonunion bargaining unit employees even in the grievance procedure in the same fashion as it has the duty to handle grievances of union members. Against this argument stands the equally plausible one that employees should not be forced to join a union in order to work. Such compulsion seems to many people to be undemocratic, immoral, and unjust. Almost everyone, however, has different ideas on what is "morally" correct in this controversy. Indeed, even the clergy has been drawn into the fight, and its members have exhibited the same lack of unanimity in their opinions as have other people. If these stewards of God are not certain what is morally correct, how can college professors make a judgment which will once and for all resolve the moral issue?

Some observers claim that union security is the key to *stability in labor relations*. It is argued that a union which operates under a union shop arrangement will be more responsible and judicious in the handling of grievances and in other day-to-day relations with its employers because of its guaranteed status. Again, there is some strength to this argument. At times, conflict between union members and nonunion employees does hamper the effective operation of the plant, and on this basis, some employers may welcome an arrangement which forces all employees to join the union, as a way of precluding such conflicts. Moreover, unions can also claim that in the absence of a union security provision, the union officers must spend considerable time in organizing the unorganized and keeping the organized content so that they will not drop out of the union. Proponents of this position justifiably declare that if union officers are relieved from this organizational chore, they can spend their time in more constructive ways which will be beneficial not only to the employees but also to the company.

On the other hand, other debators point out with equal justification that unions which *do* enjoy a union security arrangement sometimes use this extra time to find *new* ways to harass the company. The solution to *this* particular controversy appears to an outsider to depend upon the character of the union involved and on its relationship with the employer. Clearly, no one would blame an employer if he resisted granting the union shop to a union which had traditionally engaged in frequent wildcat strikes, continually pressed grievances which had no merit and, in short, sought to harass management at every turn.

At times, finally, employers and unions themselves argue along morality and labor relations lines to conceal a different purpose—their respective desires for *power* in the bargaining relationship. It is self-evident that the union *does* have more comparative influence in the negotiation of labor agreements and in its day-to-day relationship with the employer when it operates under a union shop. And, by the same token, the employer has more comparative influence when employees need not join the union to work and may terminate their membership at any time. Or, in short, the parties may speak in terms of morality merely as a smokescreen to conceal an equally logical but less euphemistic power issue.

But "power" still remains a rather nebulous term. Depending upon the assumptions one makes, a union could have infinitely more power than a company, and the *reverse* would be true under a different set of assumptions and circumstances. Given this elusiveness, as well as the unhappy connotations often placed on the word, it is perhaps not surprising that the verbal controversy over union security continues to be waged along the other lines described as well as those of power.

THE CHECKOFF

Checkoff arrangements are included in the large majority of collective bargaining contracts. This dues collection method, whereby the employer agrees to deduct from the employee's pay the latter's monthly union dues (and in some cases also his initiation fees, fines, and special assessments) for transmittal to the union, has obvious advantages for labor organizations, not only in terms of time and money savings but also because it further strengthens the union's institutional status. For the same reasons, many managers are not enthusiastic about the checkoff, although some have preferred it to the constant visits of union dues-collectors to the workplace. Once willing to grant the union shop, however, employers have rarely made a major bargaining issue of the checkoff *per se*. And the growth of this mechanism has been remarkably consistent with that of the union security measure: where in 1946 about 40 percent of all labor agreements provided for the checkoff system of dues collection, by

1954 this percentage had increased to about 75 percent[12] and the figure is, as we know, somewhat over 80 percent today.

Taft-Hartley, as was also pointed out earlier, regulates the checkoff as well as union security: under the law the checkoff is lawful only on written authorization of the individual employee. It is further provided that an employee's written authorization may not be irrevocable for only one year or for the duration of the contract, whichever is shorter.

Soon after the Taft-Hartley law was enacted the question arose as to the lawfulness of a collective bargaining provision under which an employer deducts initiation fees, special assessments, and fines as well as regular monthly membership dues. In addition, a question was raised as to whether it was required under the national law that each employee personally sign a new authorization card each year. On May 13, 1948, the assistant solicitor general of the United States issued an opinion which has served to clarify these questions somewhat.[13] He ruled that the term *membership dues*, as utilized in the law, includes initiation fees and assessments as well as regular periodic dues. On the other hand, he made no reference to fines assessed against union members for the violation of union rules. The assistant solicitor general further offered as his opinion the ruling that checkoff arrangements which provide an employee the annual opportunity to rescind a written authorization did not appear to be a "willful" violation of the Taft-Hartley law. This meant that arrangements between employers and unions which give such an opportunity to employees but which do not actually involve the signing of a new authorization each year are valid.

As a result, many checkoff provisions now allow for the deduction of initiation fees and assessments as well as for regular monthly membership dues. In addition, it is a common practice in industry for employees to sign one authorization card. However, under the latter arrangement, both the collective bargaining contract and the authorization card clearly state that the employee has an annual opportunity, usually lasting for 15 days, to rescind his written authorization. If he does not avail himself of his opportunity, the authorization card remains in force for another year.

Checkoff provisions frequently deal with matters other than the specification of items that the company agrees to deduct. Some arrangements specify a maximum deduction that the company will check off in any one month, require each employee to sign a new authorization card in the event that dues are increased, indemnify the company against any liability for action taken in reliance upon authorization cards submitted

[12] Rose, "Union Security Provisions in Agreements," *op. cit.*, p. 657.
[13] "Coverage of Checkoff Under Taft-Hartley Act," *Monthly Labor Review*, LXVII (July 1948), 42.

by the union, require the union to reimburse the company for any illegal deductions, and provide that the union share in the expense of collecting dues through the checkoff method. Not all these items, of course, appear in each and every checkoff arrangement; many labor agreements, however, contain one or more of them.

From the foregoing, it appears rather clear that though the checkoff is an important issue of collective bargaining, it does not normally constitute a crucial point of controversy between employers and unions. It does not contain the features of conflicting philosophy which are involved in the union security problem, falls far short of other problems of collective bargaining as a vexatious issue between the parties, and has rarely by itself become a major strike issue since the stakes are not that high. As a matter of fact, though the checkoff serves the institutional needs of the union, employers often find some gain from the incorporation of the device in the collective bargaining agreement. This would be particularly true where the labor contract contains a union security arrangement. Not only does the checkoff obviate the previously noted need of dues collection on company premises with the attendant impact upon the orderly operation of the plant, but it avoids the need of starting the discharge process for employees who are negligent in the payment of dues. Frequently, without a checkoff, an employee who must belong to a union as a condition of employment will delay paying his dues, and the employer and union both are then faced with the task of instituting the discharge process, which is most commonly suspended when the employee (faced with loss of employment) pays his dues at the last possible minute. The checkoff eliminates the need for this wasted and time-consuming effort on the part of busy employer and union representatives.

Even when the union shop is not in effect, moreover, the checkoff need not necessarily be given permanent status. The employee obligates himself to pay dues for one year only, and if he desires to stop the checkoff he may do so during the "escape period." But, under any circumstances, if the management believes that the union with which it deals is so irresponsible as not to deserve the checkoff, it need not agree to it as its part of the renegotiated contract, and the mechanism is consequently also "revocable" from the company's point of view.

UNION OBLIGATIONS

The typical collective bargaining contract contains one or more provisions establishing certain *obligations* on the part of the labor organization. By far the most important of these obligations involves the pledge of a union that it will not strike during the life of the labor agreement.

Most employers will, in fact, refuse to sign a collective bargaining contract unless the union agrees that it will not interrupt production during the effective contractual period.

The incorporation of a no-strike clause in a labor agreement means that all disputes relating to the interpretation and the application of a labor agreement are to be resolved through the grievance and arbitration procedure in an orderly and peaceful manner, and not through the harsh arbiter of industrial warfare. The pledge of the union not to strike during the contract period stabilizes industrial relations within the plant and thereby protects the interests of the employer, the union, and the employees. Indeed, a chief advantage that employers obtain from the collective bargaining process is the assurance that the plant will operate free from strikes or other forms of interruption to production (slowdowns, for example) during the contract period.

Companies and unions have negotiated two major forms of no-strike provisions. Under one category, there is an *absolute and unconditional* surrender on the part of the union of its right to strike or otherwise to interfere with production during the life of the labor agreement. The union agrees that it will not strike for any purpose or under any circumstances for the duration of the contract period. Employers, of course, obtain maximum security against strikes by this approach to the problem.

Under the second major form, the union can use the strike only under certain *limited* circumstances. For example, in the automobile industry the union may strike against company-imposed production standards. Such strikes may not take place, however, before all attempts are made in the grievance procedure to negotiate production standard complaints. Other collective bargaining contracts provide that unions can strike for any purpose during the contract period but only after the entire grievance procedure has been exhausted, when the employer refuses to abide by an arbitrator's decision, or when a deadlock occurs during a wage-reopening negotiation. The union cannot strike under any other conditions for the length of the contract.

In the vast majority of cases, labor organizations fulfill their no-strike obligations, just as most unionized companies fulfill all their contractually delineated responsibilities. However, in the event that violations do take place, employers have available to them a series of remedies. In the first place, under the terms of the Taft-Hartley law employers can sue unions for violations of collective bargaining contracts in the United States district courts. And although judgments obtained in such court proceedings may be assessed only against the labor organization and not against individual union members, additional remedies are provided for in many collective bargaining contracts. Under some of them, strikes called by a labor union in violation of a no-strike pledge terminate the entire collective bargaining contract. In others, the checkoff and any agreement requiring membership as a condition of employment are suspended.

In addition, the employer may elect to seek penalties against the instigators and the active participants or either group in such a strike. Many contracts clearly provide that employees actively participating in a strike during the life of a collective bargaining contract are subject to discharge, suspension, loss of seniority rights, or termination of other benefits under the contract, including vacation and holiday pay. The right of an employer to discharge workers participating in such strikes has been upheld by the United States Supreme Court.

Finally, arbitrators usually will sustain the right of employers to discharge or otherwise discipline workers who instigate or actively participate in an unlawful strike or slowdown. Such decisions are based upon the principle that the inclusion of a no-strike clause in a labor agreement serves as the device to stabilize labor relations during the contract period and as a pledge to resolve all disputes arising under the collective bargaining contract through the orderly and peaceful channels of the grievance procedure.

In June 1970 the United States Supreme Court provided employers with a powerful legal weapon to deal with strikes which violate a no-strike clause contained in a collective bargaining contract. At that time, the high court by a 5–2 vote in *Boys Markets* v. *Retail Clerks* (38 U.S. L.W. 4462, June 1, 1970) held that when a contract incorporates a no-strike agreement and an arbitration procedure, a federal court may issue an injunction to terminate the strike. This decision permits employers to go into court to force employees back to work when a labor agreement contains a no-strike pledge and an arbitration clause. The idea behind the decision is that the grievance procedure and arbitration should be used to settle disputes which arise during the course of a collective bargaining contract.

Though the decision of the United States Supreme Court could be defended on the grounds that employees should not strike to settle their grievances when arbitration is available, the 1970 decision astonished many observers of the labor relations scene. They were astonished because in 1962 the United States Supreme Court ruled that federal courts could not issue an injunction to stop a strike called in violation of a no-strike clause (*Sinclair Refining* v. *Atkinson,* 370 U.S. 195 [1962]). In the 1962 decision, the high court held that injunctions could not be issued because the Taft-Hartley law did not make such strikes illegal. Since they were not made illegal, the Court reasoned that such strikes, though in violation of the labor agreement, constituted a labor dispute within the meaning of the Norris–La Guardia Act. We have learned from the study of this law that federal courts are forbidden to issue injunctions when a labor dispute exists within the meaning of the statute.

Thus, after an eight-year period, the Court changed its position full circle. Some people believe the Court was wrong in this switch of policy because Congress did not seek to change the 1962 decision through legislation. As the *Wall Street Journal* observed on June 5, 1970:

> As a matter of fact such legislation was introduced, but Congress so far has not seen fit to act. Congressional action, of course, would have been much the better way. However desirable the result, the Supreme Court still should restrain itself from assuming the tasks that properly belong to the legislators.

Such criticism of the *Boys Markets* decision does not, of course, mean approval of strikes in violation of no-strike agreements. As a matter of labor relations stability and to preserve the integrity of agreements made at the bargaining table, employees and unions should resort to arbitration to settle disputes with their employers and not to the street. Rather, the source of the criticism is the change in Supreme Court policy after an eight-year period during which Congress did not see fit to reverse the 1962 *Sinclair* decision. As the minority opinion stated:

> Nothing at all has changed except the membership of the court and the personal views of one justice.

Regardless of one's judgment of the Supreme Court change in policy, the fact remains that it has provided employers with a potent weapon to stamp out strikes which violate no-strike agreements. It is highly likely that employers will make widespread use of the weapon placed in their hands by the high court.

At times, strikes and other interruptions to production that are *not* authorized by the labor organization occur. These work stoppages, commonly known as "wildcat strikes," are instigated by a group of workers, sometimes including union officers, without the sanction of the labor union. Under many labor agreements, the employer has the right to discharge such employees or to penalize them otherwise for such activities.

A special problem has been created by the Taft-Hartley law in reference to wildcat strikes. Under this law a labor union is responsible for the action of agents even though the union does not authorize or ratify such conduct.[14] Thus, an employer may sue a union because of a wildcat strike even though the union does not authorize or ratify the work stoppage. As a result of this state of affairs, unions and employers have negotiated the so-called "nonsuability clauses" which were discussed in Chapter 3.

---

[14] Section 301(e) states: "... For purposes of this section, in determining whether any person is acting as an 'agent' of another person as to make such other person responsible for his acts, the question of whether the specific acts performed were actually authorized or subsequently ratified shall not be controlling."

Under these arrangements, the company agrees that it will not sue a labor union because of wildcat strikes provided that the union fulfills its obligation to terminate the work stoppage. Frequently, the labor contract specifies exactly what the union must do in order to free itself from the possibility of damage suits. Thus, in some contracts containing nonsuability clauses, the union agrees to announce orally and in writing that it disavows the strike, to order the workers back to their jobs, and to refuse any form of strike relief to the participants in such work stoppages.

Other features of some collective bargaining contracts also deal with strike situations. Under many labor agreements, the union agrees that it will protect company property during strikes. To accomplish this objective, the union typically pledges itself to cooperate with the company in the orderly cessation of production and the shutting down of machinery. In addition, some unions agree to facilitate the proper maintenance of machinery during strikes even if achieving this objective requires the employment of certain bargaining unit maintenance personnel during the strike. Finally, it is not uncommon for unions to agree in the labor contract that management and supervisory personnel entering and leaving the plant in a strike situation will not be interfered with by the labor organization.

Many collective bargaining contracts place other obligations upon unions extending well beyond the area of strikes and slowdowns. Under many agreements, for example, the union obligates itself not to conduct on company time or on company property any union activities that will interfere with the efficient operation of the plant. The outstanding exception to this rule, however, involves the handling of grievances: meetings of union and company representatives which deal directly with grievance administration usually are conducted on company time. Some agreements also permit union officials to collect dues on company property where the checkoff is not in existence. And another exception found in many contracts involves the permission given to employees and union officers to discuss union business or to solicit union membership during lunch and rest periods.

Another frequently encountered limitation of union activity on plant property involves restrictions of visits to the company by representatives of the international union with which the local is affiliated. Still another denies unions permission to post notices in the plant or to use company bulletin boards without the permission of the company. Where the union is allowed to use bulletin boards, many labor contracts specify the character of notices that the union may post: notices are permitted, for example, only when they pertain to union meetings and social affairs, union appointments and elections, reports of union committees, and rulings of the international union. Specifically prohibited on many occasions are notices which are controversial, propagandic, or political in nature.

MANAGERIAL PREROGATIVES

That collective bargaining is in many ways synonymous with limitations on managerial authority is an observation which was offered in the earliest pages of this book. A fundamental characteristic of the process is restriction on the power of the company to make decisions in the area of employer-employee relations, and much of the controversy about collective bargaining grows out of this factor. On the one hand, the labor union seeks to limit the authority of management to make decisions when it believes that such restrictions will serve the interests of its members or will tend to satisfy the institutional needs of the union itelf. On the other hand, the responsibility for efficiency in operation of the enterprise rests with management. The reason for the existence of management, in fact, is the overall management of the business, and executives attempt to retain free from limitations those functions which they believe are indispensable for the successful operation of the business. Since the responsibility for efficiency of the enterprise rests upon the shoulders of management and not of the union, companies feel that they must retain for themselves the authority to make certain decisions free from control of the bargaining process. Consequently, controversy in collective bargaining occurs when the desire of unions to achieve an objective through the bargaining process is in conflict with the determination of management to exercise a particular function on a unilateral basis.

The problem is, moreover, hardly disposed of simply because most union leaders assert—and normally, in good faith—that they have no intention of interfering with the "proper functions of management." Years of witnessing official union interest expand from the historical wages and hours context into such newer areas as those outlined in this portion of the book have led managers understandably to conclude that what is "proper" for the union depends on the situation and the values of the union membership.

Nor do employers find much consolation in the fact that the managerial decision-making process is already limited and modified by such economic forces as labor market conditions, by such laws as those pertaining to minimum wages, and by the employee-oriented spirit of our society. If unionism is not by any means the only restriction on company freedom of action in the personnel sphere, it is nonetheless a highly important one for companies whose employees live under a union contract.

Beyond this, finally, the controversy is hardly *confined* to the personnel area, for managers can point to numerous (although proportionately infrequent) instances of strong union interest in such relatively removed fields as finance, plant location, pricing, and other "proper" management functions. In recent years, for example, some railroad unions have constantly blamed their employers' high degree of bonded indebtedness for depriving railroad workers of "adequate" wage increases; legal representatives of the Ladies' Garment Workers as well as those of several other unions have become familiar faces in courtrooms, to protest plant relocations of their unions' employers; and the United Automobile Workers' interest in the pricing of cars is now all but taken for granted in automobile industry bargaining rooms (although the UAW's freely offered advice on this subject has yet to be accepted by the automobile manufacturers). Given the present state of the government's "legal duty to bargain" provisions, as Chapter 3 has indicated, no one can assert with complete confidence that such examples will not multiply in the years ahead.

In many ways, in fact, ramifications of the subject extend far beyond the two parties to collective bargaining. There is justification, indeed, for arguing that the "managerial rights" issue really pivots upon the broader question of what the appropriate function of labor unions in the life of our nation should be.

Managements have frequently translated their own thoughts on the subject into concrete action. Approximately one half of all labor agreements today contain clauses that explicitly recognize certain stipulated types of decisions as being "vested exclusively in the Company."[15] Such clauses are commonly called "management prerogative," "management rights," or (more appropriately, to many managers), "management security" clauses.

Fairly typical of management prerogative provisions is the following, culled from the 1970–73 agreement of a large Midwestern durable goods manufacturer:

> Subject to the provisions of this agreement, the management of the business and of the plants and the direction of the working forces, including but not limited to the right to direct, plan, and control plant operations and to establish and to change work schedules, to hire, promote, demote, transfer, suspend, discipline, or discharge employees for cause or to relieve from duty employees because of lack of work or for other legitimate reasons, to introduce new and improved methods or facilities, to determine the products to be handled, produced, or manufactured, to determine the schedules of production and the methods, processes, and the means of production, to make shop rules and regulations not inconsistent with this agreement and to manage the plants in the traditional manner, is vested exclusively in the Company. Nothing in this agreement shall be deemed to limit the Company in any way in the exercise of the regular and customary functions of management.

[15] See, for example, "Management Rights Provisions in Major Agreements," *Monthly Labor Review*, LXXXIX, No. 2 (February 1966), 171.

Some rights clauses, by way of contrast, limit themselves to short general statements. These are much more readable than the above, but considerably less specific (for example, "the right to manage the plant and to direct the work forces and operations of the plant, subject to the limitations of this Agreement, is exclusively vested in, and retained by, the Company").

No matter which way management injects such clauses into the contract, however, two industrial relations truisms must also be appreciated: (1) the power of the rights clause is always subject to qualification by the wording of every other clause in the labor agreement; and (2) consistent administrative practices on the part of the company must implement the rights clause if it is to stand up before an arbitrator.

According to one point of view, moreover, the inclusion of such a clause in a labor agreement is *unnecessary* and, of course, many agreements do not make any reference to managerial rights. This practice of omission is often based upon the belief that the employer retains all rights of management which are not relinquished, modified, or eliminated by the collective bargaining contract. Thus, in the absence of collective bargaining, according to this view, the employer has the power to make *any* decision in the area of labor relations that he desires (subject to considerations of law, the market place, etc.). This right is based upon the simple fact that the employer is the owner of the business. For example, the employer's right to promote, demote, lay off, and rehire may be limited by the seniority provisions of the collective bargaining contract. And the contract may stipulate that layoffs be based upon a certain formula. However, to the extent that such a formula does *not* limit the right of the employer to lay off, it follows that management may exercise this function on a unilateral basis. (Case No. 8 deals with management rights in a dispute which involved seniority.)

This concept of management prerogatives is sometimes called the "residual theory" of management rights. That is, all rights "reside" in management except those which are limited by the labor agreement or conditioned by a past practice. Where a management embraces the residual theory, it most commonly takes a stiff attitude at the bargaining table relative to union demands which would tend further to limit rights of management. With more elements of an "Armed Truce" than an "Accommodation" philosophy, it views the collective bargaining process as a tug of war between the management and the union—management resisting further invasions by the union into the citadel of management rights, which are to be protected at all costs as a matter of principle.

Such companies are not particularly concerned with the merits of a union demand. *Any* demand which would impose additional limitations on management must be resisted. For example, such a management, regardless of the merits of a particular claim, would typically resist the incorporation of working rules into the labor agreement—rules dealing with such topics as payment to employees for work not actually performed, limitations on technological change or other innovations in the operation of the business, the amount of production an employee must turn out to hold a job, and how many men are required to perform a job. One can also safely predict that a residualist management would strongly resist any demand that would limit its right to move an operation from one plant to another, shut down one plant of a multiple-plant operation, subcontract work, or compel employees to work overtime. In addition, such a management would quite likely try aggressively when the occasion seemed appropriate to *regain* "rights" which it had previously relinquished.

Indeed, today many employers *are* striving to reclaim the right to make unilateral determinations of working rules. The 116-day steel strike of 1959, as well as many other important strikes of recent years, was waged because management desired to erase from the bargaining relationship working rules to which it had agreed in previous years. It is understandable why labor organizations resist these attempts of management: with the elimination of working rules, employees could more easily be laid off, for example. Since automation and changing market demands constitute in many relationships constant threats to job security, it is no mystery why some unions would rather strike than concede on this point.

The opposing view of the theory of residual rights is based upon the idea that management has responsibilities other than to the maximization of managerial authority. It proceeds from the proposition that management is the "trustee" of the interests of employees, the union, and the society, as well as of the interests of the business, the stockholders, and the management hierarchy. Under the "trusteeship theory," a management would invariably be willing to discuss and negotiate a union demand on the merits of the case, rather than reject it out of hand because the demand would impose additional limitations on the operation of the plant. Such a company would not necessarily *agree* to additional limitations, but it would be completely amenable to discussing, consulting, and ultimately negotiating with the union on any demand that the latter might bring up at a collective bargaining session. Exhibiting an attitude of "Cooperation," the trusteeship management does not take the position that the line separating management rights from that of negotiable issues is fixed and not subject to change. Rather, it attempts to balance the rights of all concerned with the goal of arriving at a solution that would be most mutually satisfactory. As such, the "trusteeship" and "residual" theories are poles apart in terms of management's attitude at the bargaining table and even in the day-to-day relationship between the company and the union.

There is no "divine right" concept of management in the trusteeship theory, a statement which cannot be made for the residualist camp. No better summary of the differences between the two theories on this score has ever been made than that offered many years ago by the eminent Arthur J. Goldberg, then general counsel of the United Steelworkers of America:

> Too many spokesmen for management assume that labor's rights are not steeped in past practice or tradition but are limited strictly to those specified in a contract; while management's rights are all-inclusive except as specifically taken away by a specific clause in a labor agreement. Labor always had many inherent rights, such as the right to strike; the right to organize despite interference from management, police powers, and even courts; the right to a fair share of the company's income even though this right was often denied; the right to safe, healthful working conditions with adequate opportunity for rest. Collective bargaining does not establish some hitherto nonexisting rights; it provides the power to enforce rights of labor which the labor movement was dedicated to long before the institution of arbitration had become so widely practiced in labor relations.[16]

It is impossible to determine how many companies follow the residual theory of management rights and how many follow the trusteeship theory. Crosscurrents are clearly at work: the previously mentioned management attempt to regain work-rule flexibility, and the equally visible trend to more employee-centered management which was described in Chapter 1. The relative infrequency of Cooperation philosophies would, however, indicate that trusteeship managements remain in the distinct minority. Moreover, there is no universal truth as to which would be a *better* policy for management to follow, or whether some compromise between the two might form the optimum arrangement. The answer to this problem must be determined by each company in the light of the climate of the particular labor relations environment.

CONCLUSIONS

If unions and management are viewed as institutions, as distinct from the individuals whom they represent, the issues considered in this chapter take on special meaning. Institutions can survive long after individuals have perished, and in a real sense the problems of union security, union obligations, and management rights are related to the *survival* of the bargaining institutions. Union security measures preserve the union *per se* (although in so doing they may also allow it to do a better job for the

[16] "Management's Reserved Rights under Collective Bargaining," *Monthly Labor Review*, LXXIX, No. 10 (October 1956), 1172.

members of the organization). Similarly, to survive and function as an effective institution, management must be concerned with its prerogatives to operate the business efficiently. It must also be concerned with union obligations as *these* might affect its continued effectiveness.

In principle, therefore, the devices of collective bargaining which feed the institutional needs of the union and the firm are cut from the same cloth. They are designed to assure the long-run interests of the two organizations. The objectives of labor unions and companies are quite different, but the fact remains that to carry out their respective functions both need security of operation. Business operates to make a profit, and thus must be defended against encroachments of organized labor which might unreasonably interfere with its efficiency as a dynamic organization in the society. And although firms clearly differ in their philosophical approach to this problem, as witness the sharp differences between the residual and trusteeship concepts of management rights, the typical management position is the fundamental one that the business unit must be permitted to operate as efficiently as possible within the collective bargaining relationship. Its insistence upon management prerogatives stands as a bulwark of defense in this objective.

But unions *also* justify themselves as institutions on the American scene in their attempting to protect and advance the welfare of their members, and union security arrangements are an important avenue toward the realization of *this* objective. Although there may be philosophical objections to compulsory union membership, there cannot be any question that union security arrangements serve the long-run survival needs of organized labor.

If we view in retrospect the labor relations environment over the years, the conclusion appears irrefutable that business and unions have been relatively successful in reconciling these fundamental objectives, however much the verbal controversies continue to rage. Businesses which have engaged in collective bargaining relationships have by and large not only been able to survive but have often flourished. Many of the most influential and prosperous firms in this country have, as we know, been highly unionized for years. Likewise, organized labor has not only survived but has grown appreciably in strength over the years, the contemporary unexciting performance of union membership totals being accountable chiefly from causes other than management destruction. Moreover, if institutional survival and growth of unions is measured by the quality of employee benefits, one would have to conclude that in most relationships unions have succeeded in defending and promoting the welfare of their members. Although the objectives of the two institutions are quite different, and although occasional major impasses are reached by unions and managements in their bargaining on these issues, meaningful protection for both organizations has been provided in the vast majority of unionized industry.

DISCUSSION QUESTIONS

1. Arguing in favor of "right-to-work" laws, a publication of the National Association of Manufacturers has expressed the view that "No argument for compulsory unionism—however persuasive—can possibly justify invasion of the right of individual choice." Do you agree or disagree? Why or why not?
2. "From the viewpoint of providing maximum justice to all concerned, the agency shop constitutes the optimum union security arrangement." To what extent, if any, do you agree with this statement?
3. Which of the two management prerogative concepts, residual or trusteeship, do you personally tend to favor, and why?
4. Evaluate the opinion of former Steelworker Union president David J. McDonald that "nothing could be worse than to have ... management appease the union, and nothing could be worse than to have the union appease management," relating these remarks to the areas of management rights and union security.

SELECTED REFERENCES

Chamberlain, Neil W., *The Union Challenge to Management Control.* New York: Harper & Row, Publishers, 1948.

Chandler, Margaret K., *Management Rights and Union Interests.* New York: McGraw-Hill Book Company, 1964.

Meyers, Frederic, *Right to Work in Practice.* New York: Fund for the Republic, 1959.

Pulsipher, Allan G., "The Union Shop: A Legitimate Form of Coercion in a Free-Market Economy," *Industrial and Labor Relations Review,* July 1966, pp. 529–32.

Stone, Morris, *Managerial Freedom and Job Security.* New York: Harper & Row, Publishers, 1963.

CASE NO. 8

MANAGEMENT RIGHTS

(Although, on the surface, this case appears to involve a seniority type of grievance, actually it deals with the management's right to operate the plant and direct the labor force.

The company refused to permit a "leadman" to be bumped on the basis of seniority. The arbitrator agreed with the company, the effect of the decision being that the company's right to designate a leadman was not to be disturbed on the basis of seniority. Interestingly enough, the contract did not contain a management rights clause but—as we know—even in the absence of such a provision management has the right to operate the plant and direct the work force unless limited by contractual language.

Moreover, you will discover that under the contract the company has the unilateral right to designate leadmen. It was to protect this right of the company and make it viable that the arbitrator refused to permit the company-designated leadman to be bumped by a senior employee.)

GRIEVANCE AND CONTRACT LANGUAGE

This dispute involves the exercise of seniority by an employee, classified as a tool and die maker, who desired to bump from the night to the day shift and into the leadman classification. The company refused this request, though it did permit the night shift employee to displace another tool and die maker on the day shift. Believing that the employee had the right to bump into the leadman classification on the day shift, the union filed a policy grievance, dated September 29, 1967, which states:

> The Company takes the position that Leadman is a classification and is not subject to seniority in regard to bumping rights. All we want [the Union] is for the Company to go by the seniority list.

Having failed to resolve the dispute in the grievance procedure, the parties have instituted this arbitration for its final and binding settlement.

Central to this case is Article IV, Section 3:

> All employees covered by this Agreement, who work on the second shift shall be paid ten percent (10%) extra compensation. An employee having greater seniority may bump an employee on another shift but after exercising bumping rights he shall remain on that shift for a minimum of six (6) months. Employees with the greatest seniority shall be given preference of shift assignments when vacancies occur. In case no employee desires the night shift, the Company may at its discretion assign to the night shift the employee having the least seniority in the particular classification, but not less than one (1) year seniority, provided no new employee is hired to replace him on the day shift.

THE BACKGROUND

W, classified as a tool and die maker, was working the night shift and requested to exercise his seniority to move to the day shift. He made this request in writing in the latter part of September 1967. *W*'s seniority date for purposes of the labor agreement is April 14, 1954. *L*, classified as a leadman or group leader, was assigned to the day shift and his seniority date is October 8, 1964. Also, on the day shift was *P,* a tool and die maker, who had less seniority than *W*. Under the terms of the labor agreement, leadmen receive ten (10) cents more per hour than their regular rate or ten (10) cents more per hour than any employee under their leadership, whichever is greater. The leadman in effect is the assistant to the foreman, and may assign work to employees, check out their work, answer their questions, and generally assist the foreman. *L* served as the leadman over the day shift tool and die makers. He was originally hired as a tool and die maker.

When *W* made his request to move to the day shift, he desired to bump *L,* the leadman. The company refused this request, and stated that *W* could use his seniority to displace *P,* a day shift tool and die maker. The dispute arises because the union contends that *W* has the right under the labor agreement to bump *L,* the leadman, who has less seniority than *W*. Eventually *W* did bump *P* on the day shift, but the union still pressed its grievance, alleging that the company violated the labor agreement when it refused *W* the opportunity to bump into leadman classification on the day shift.

The parties stipulated that leadman is a classification for purposes of the labor agreement, and that from time to time W served temporarily as a leadman over the tool and die makers.

BASIC QUESTION

The basic question to be determined in this dispute is framed as follows: Under the circumstances of this case did the company violate Article IV, Section 3, of the labor agreement?

PARTIES' ARGUMENTS

It is the union's position that *W* had the right to bump *L* under the terms of Article IV, Section 3, of the labor agreement. To support this position, the union argues that under this provision

> an employee has the right to bump an employee on another shift.

In addition, it avers that the labor agreement does not provide language which

> excludes Leadmen from the bumping process. No exceptions are provided for in the contract. By the Company excluding Leadmen from the bumping process, it is the same as conferring upon this group a superseniority status. In the contract, we do not even provide superseniority for Stewards or Shop Committeemen.

The union points out further that W had served as a leadman and was never disqualified from this job when he was so assigned. Also, it stresses that a leadman may bump into the tool and die maker classification if for some reason his job as a leadman is terminated. So, it argues:

> if a Leadman can bump down, he may himself be bumped by an employee with greater seniority.

On these grounds, the union requests that the grievance be granted.

At the heart of the company's contention is the argument that a leadman may not be bumped by an employee in a lower classification. It stresses that leadman is a separate classification for purposes of the labor agreement, and that under the contract and as a matter of historical practice the company has the right to appoint leadmen. It argues that

> for Management to agree with the Union's position in the instant grievance would be tantamount to agreeing that a lesser qualified person would be satisfactory on this important [leadman] job.

It avers further that

> never in the past has the Union ever contended that this important classification [leadman] was bumpable for shift preference or even for layoff purposes.

For these reasons, the company requests the denial of the grievance.

ANALYSIS OF THE EVIDENCE

Literal Language

Standing alone, the second sentence of Article IV, Section 3, supports the basic position of the union in this dispute. It states:

> An employee having greater seniority may bump an employee on another shift....

W, the tool and die maker, has much greater seniority than L, the leadman, and the literal language of the above cited provision would appear to provide W with the right to bump L.

Further, as the union argues, there is no limitation on bumping rights in the expressed language of the second sentence. It does not place leadmen in a special and privileged category protected against being bumped by a senior employee who desires to exercise his seniority rights to claim shift preference. In short, if the second sentence were to be used as the exclusive basis for the determination of this grievance, the union position has merit. W is "an employee" within the meaning of this language. L is "an employee" within its meaning, and since W has more seniority it would follow that he can bump L and move to the day shift.

The Company's Right to Designate Leadmen

To reach a sound decision in this case, however, it would not be proper to read the second sentence of Article IV, Section 3, as separate and independent from other provisions in the labor agreement and in isolation from the historical practice of the parties. To get at the true intent of the parties, it is necessary to read the labor agreement as a whole. Thus, in a standard work on arbitration, the authors state:

> It is said that the primary rule in construing a written instrument is to determine, not alone from a single word or phrase, but from the instrument as a whole, the true intent of the parties and to interpret the meaning of a questioned word or part with regard to the connection in which it is used, the subject matter and its relation to all other parts or provisions.
> Similarly, Sections or portions cannot be isolated from the rest of the agreement and given construction independently of the purpose and agreement of the parties as evidenced by the entire document. The meaning of each paragraph and each sentence must be determined in relation to the contract as a whole. This standard requiring the agreement to be construed as a whole is applied very frequently.*

What would make it particularly improper in this case to base the decision solely on the second sentence of Article IV, Section 3, is the fact that the parties in another provision in the labor agreement state that the company has *the unilateral right to designate leadmen.* Thus, in Article IV, Section 6, we find the following:

> *Employees who are designated as Leadmen by the Company* shall receive ten (10) cents per hour more ... (emphasis supplied).

Further, the evidence clearly establishes that the company as a matter of historical practice has exercised its right to designate the leadmen on a strictly unilateral basis. Such a right may be exercised without reference to seniority. To put it simply, the company may choose any employee it desires to serve as a leadman, and such appointments are not subject to protest on the part of the union. It is indeed significant that in the case at hand the company designated L as leadman over the tool and die makers even though his seniority is quite

---

* Elkouri and Elkouri, *How Arbitration Works,* rev. ed. (Bureau of National Affairs, 1960), pp. 207–208.

limited, dating back only to October 8, 1964. Presumably, other employees in this classification, for example, W himself, possessed far greater seniority than L when the company designated L for the leadman job.

Thus, the second sentence of Article IV, Section 3, must be placed in juxtaposition to the right of the company to designate which employees are to serve as leadmen. Both of these provisions must be read together to arrive at the true intent of the parties. If a senior employee were permitted to exercise his seniority for shift preference and displace a leadman designated by the company to serve in this capacity, it would follow that such a state of affairs *would negate and cancel out* the right of the company to designate leadmen under Article IV, Section 6, of the labor agreement. Under such circumstances, the clear-cut contractual right of the company to appoint leadmen would be negated. In other words, it is the judgment of the arbitrator that when the parties agreed to the second sentence of Article IV, Section 3, they did not intend that the exercise of seniority for shift preference would cancel out a right of the company to designate leadmen, a right which is clearly established in the labor agreement and supported by the historical practice of the parties.

Of what value would this company's right be if another employee exercised seniority to bump a leadman designated by the company to this classification? Its right in this connection would for all intents and purposes be stricken from the labor agreement.

In the instant case, the company designated L to serve as the leadman on the day shift. Presumably, it designated him because in the judgment of the company he was the most qualified individual to fill this post. It made this appointment pursuant to a stipulation agreed to by the parties and stated in unequivocal terms in the labor agreement. Now, along comes W, senior to L, who desires to bump L. If the arbitrator permitted this bump, he would in effect wipe out of the labor agreement the right of the company to designate leadmen whom it believes most qualified to serve in this capacity. The arbitrator cannot possibly permit this bump and remain true to the obligations of his office and to the faith and confidence which the parties have placed in him. It is his conviction that when the parties agreed to the second sentence of Article IV, Section 3, they did not intend that the exercise of seniority for shift preference could be used to displace leadmen, which the parties stipulated to be a separate and distinct classification under the labor agreement.

The union argues that the contract by express language does not confer superseniority upon leadmen, or for that matter on any employee regardless of his position in the union. Though this is true, the fact remains that when the union agreed that the company may designate leadmen it thereby protected the employee in this classification from being bumped by senior employees who desire to exercise their seniority for purposes of shift preference. This is the crux of this case, and the standard upon which this decision must be based. When the union agreed with the company in contract negotiations that the employer may unilaterally designate leadmen, it also agreed that the seniority rights of employees established in Article IV, Section 3, are limited by this company right.

As stated, of what value would this right be to the company if employees have the right to bump them off the leadmen jobs after the company designated them as leadmen? Assume as of a Monday, the company designates an employee to serve as a leadman pursuant to a right which it has under the labor agreement, and a right supported by past practice. On Tuesday, another employee, with greater seniority than the appointed employee, bumps him off the job because he wants to work the shift on which the leadman is designated. Surely, this could not have been the intent of the parties when they agreed to Article IV, Section 3 and Section 6. Indeed, if it were the intent, the parties, in effect, would have made the company's right to designate leadmen on a unilateral basis a barren academic exercise.

Leadman May Bump Down

The arbitrator considered seriously the union argument that a leadman, if his job is eliminated, may bump down to a lower classification. That is, if for some reason L's job as leadman were eliminated, L could then bump into the tool and die maker classification. As the union argues, if a leadman has the right to bump under these circumstances, it would appear reasonable that he himself should be subject to being bumped. On the surface, this appears to be a logical and fair argument. It would appear equitable to permit the leadman to be bumped, if the leadman himself has the right to bump into a lower classification. The arbitrator considered this argument at length because of the equities that are involved. Indeed, for a time the arbitrator contemplated granting the grievance on this basis because the union argument herein considered appeared to him to be fair and logical.

Still, after due and long reflection, the arbitrator rejected this course of action. It was rejected because to permit a leadman to bump down does not impair the right of the company to designate leadmen. However, to permit a leadman to be bumped by another employee for shift preference basis would be inconsistent with this company right protected by the labor agreement.

In other words, the parties agreed that the company may designate leadmen. If the leadman's job is eliminated, and if this employee bumps to a lower classification, this bump does not negate this contractually stated right. On the other hand, to permit the leadman to be bumped would in effect negate and cancel out this company right. The arbitrator admits that on the surface it does appear unfair to permit the leadman to bump on the basis of seniority, and at the same time to protect him against being bumped by an employee with greater seniority. To be frank about it, this does appear to be inequitable but still the arbitrator cannot permit this consideration to erase from the labor agreement the right of the company to designate leadmen, a right which the union has agreed to in the labor agreement and condoned as a matter of historical practice.

A System of Job Rights Based on a Classification System

Added to these considerations, there is still another line of analysis which reasonably could be used to deny the grievance. That is, when the labor agreement is read as a whole there is some reason to believe that the parties agreed to a system of job rights based upon a classification system. It is true, of course, that when the parties agreed to the second sentence of Article IV, Section 3, they did not stipulate that to exercise seniority rights for shift preference the employee must exercise this right in terms of a classification. The word "classification" is not included within the second sentence and the arbitrator fully understands this union argument. He understands the union when it argues that since the second sentence is not qualified by the word "classification" an employee under this sentence may exercise his seniority to gain shift preference even if he bumps into a different classification. Hence, though W desired to bump from the tool and die maker classification into the leadman classification which is separate and independent from the tool and die maker classification, as agreed to by the parties, he has this right in the union's judgment because the parties did not specify in the second sentence that the exercise of seniority for the purpose of shift preference must be limited to a classification basis. This is a sound argument and duly considered by the arbitrator.

Still, when the labor agreement is read as a whole, it becomes rather clear that the system of the exercise of job rights is oriented to job classification. Indeed, this kind of system is common within bargaining units which are composed of craftsmen as distinguished from semiskilled and unskilled workers. Craftsmen are proud of their skills and desire recognition for the time (in many cases, years of training) in the acquiring of the skills of their craft. For these reasons, it is quite common that bargaining units composed of skilled craftsmen vigorously establish craft classifications as the basis of the operation of job rights.

In the instant labor agreement, we note several references to the prerequisites of classification as the basis for the operation of job rights. Whatever may be the meaning of Article II, Section 1, the fact is that layoffs *are based upon a classification system* and not on a bargaining unit basis. Even in the third sentence of Article IV, Section 3, we find that the company discretion to assign employees to the night shift is based upon a classification system. (It is noteworthy that though the parties did not specify classifications within the second sentence, they used the term in the third sentence.) In Article IV, Section 4, the provision for the filling of job vacancies, it specifically states that job openings shall be posted and in the posting the shift and *classification* will be stated. Thus, the successful bidder will bid into a classification. In Article IV, Section 5, a regular day shift employee may be transferred to the night shift while a new employee works the day shift for a maximum of 60 days to determine his qualifications, but the parties agreed that the day shift employees so transferred to the night shift must be in the *particular classification* involved. In Article IV, Section 12, the parties establish a system for the distribution of overtime. Once again we see the paramount importance of classification. Thus:

> No employee shall accumulate more than 20 overtime hours over employees in the Tool room *within the classification* (emphasis supplied).

Within Article IV, Sections 6 and 15, the parties based their wage agreements upon a classification system.

In short, what we have here is a system of job rights, some of them based upon seniority, oriented to a classification system. They are not based in terms of the bargaining unit, but upon classifications. Such an intention so clearly expressed in many provisions of the labor agreement makes it unreasonable to hold that the parties deliberately omitted the word "classification" in Article IV, Section 3 so that the exercise of seniority for shift preference could be based upon an interclassification basis. Perhaps they did, and the arbitrator acknowledges that he does not know for sure. However, the intent of the parties to orient job rights, including those of a seniority nature, to classifications so clearly spelled out throughout the labor agreement would make it entirely reasonable to believe that the parties intended that the second sentence of Article IV, Section 3 be likewise based upon a classification system.

CONCLUSIONS

In any event, even if the analysis in the immediately preceding section is rejected as speculative and not sound, the arbitrator still is fully satisfied that the second sentence of Article IV, Section 3 does not permit seniority to be used to displace a leadman designated by the company. He is of the firm conviction that seniority rights may not be used to negate and cancel out a right specifically conferred upon the company in Article IV, Section 6. Perhaps we do not know for sure whether or not the parties intended that seniority for shift preference purposes may be used on an interclassification or solely on an intraclassification basis. However, this we do know for sure: the company without reference to seniority or protest from the union may designate leadmen on a unilateral basis. About this there is no speculation or conjecture. Accordingly, this contractual stipulation, not subject to doubt, must be taken into account when the second sentence of Article IV, Section 3, is applied. Therefore, the conclusion must be that a leadman designated by the company, without reference to seniority, may not be bumped because a more senior employee desires to claim his shift. To hold otherwise would in effect render worthless a company right to designate leadmen.

To say the least, the arbitrator recognizes that this decision will probably be very unpopular with the bargaining unit and the union because seniority rights have not been recognized. No one need instruct the arbitrator as to their importance to workers and the part they play in labor relations. He fully recognizes the great contribution of organized labor in protecting job rights on the basis of seniority.

Still, the arbitrator must be resolute in his determination to give full faith and credit to *all the language agreed to by the parties.* He cannot get it out of his mind that under the labor agreement the company has the right to designate leadmen without reference to seniority. It exercises this right on a unilateral basis, and to this extent the union itself has compromised the seniority principle. Having agreed to this, the arbitrator is of the firm conviction that the union cannot now argue successfully that this right may be negated by the operation of seniority rights under the second sentence of Article IV, Section 3.

QUESTIONS

1. Do you believe that the arbitrator's decision would have been the same in the absence of Article IV, Section 6, which gives the company the right to designate leadmen?
2. Why did the arbitrator take considerable care to point out that the general posture of job rights as established in the contract is based upon a classification system? Would you have found it necessary to have done this had you been the arbitrator?
3. Why did the company refuse to grant this grievance, even though W (the senior employee) appears well qualified to serve as leadman, having already served in this position from time to time?

10

Administrative Issues Under Collective Bargaining

Provisions relating to seniority, discipline, employee safety, and the various other "administrative" areas of the labor relationship have, as in the case of institutional provisions, the common characteristic of falling into the noneconomic classification of collective bargaining. It should not, however, be concluded that they do not have a profound influence upon the economic operation of the plant or the economic status of the employees.

The character of a seniority clause, for example, can have a vital impact upon the efficient operation of the productive process. Similarly, the protection afforded an employee as a result of the discharge clause can be of much greater importance than any of the rights he enjoys as a result of the negotiation of wage rates or fringe benefits. It matters little to the worker who has been discharged for an obviously unfair reason that the wages called for by the labor contract are very generous.

Moreover, at the present time the problem of automation rivals the importance of most wage issues for many collective bargaining relationships. In a real sense, in fact, the adjustment to automation through contract negotiations cuts across the entire gamut of bargaining. Currently, the overriding concern of many employees and unions is with job security, a posture resulting from the fact that each day many hundreds of jobs are eliminated by innovations in the technological structure of industry. Already there has been mention of union demands which are rooted at least partially in the automation problem: early retirement of workers, severance pay, and supplementary unemployment benefit programs, for example. As will be demonstrated, many administrative demands of unions also flow from worker fears that jobs are vulnerable because of automation.

In short, as important as the negotiation of economic issues may be, one cannot ignore these nonwage administrative issues of collective bargaining. Both are interwoven in the contemporary labor relations environment and to ignore or slight either—or, clearly, the institutional area of the contract, as well—would represent a distortion and an incomplete picture of present-day labor relations in the United States.

The following discussion indicates the nature of these problems, the manner in which employers and unions handle them in collective bargaining, and recent trends in administrative clause negotiations.

SENIORITY

The principle of seniority, under which the employee with the greater length of company or company subunit service receives increased job security (and, commonly, greater entitlement to employee benefits), is not a new one for American industry. The railroads and printing trades, for example, have emphasized it for many decades.

For at least four reasons, however, seniority has received increasing stress in labor contracts over the past three decades.[1] In the first place, both management and employee representatives have become convinced that there is a certain amount of justice to the arrangement, especially in terms of work contraction or recall opportunities after layoffs. Second, the application of seniority is an objective one, calculated to avoid arbitrariness in the selection of personnel for particular jobs and consequently less irksome for the labor negotiators to deal with than alternative devices. Third, the employee benefit programs which have mushroomed in these years have been geared almost exclusively to seniority—often, to make them more acceptable to the companies by restricting the number of employees entitled to the benefits. And fourth, outside agencies, notably government labor

---

[1] For an excellent full description, see Sumner H. Slichter, James J. Healy, and E. Robert Livernash, *The Impact of Collective Bargaining on Management* (Washington, D.C.: The Brookings Institution, 1960), pp. 104–41.

boards and impartial arbitrators, have tended to weigh seniority heavily in their decisions.

Almost every labor agreement now includes some seniority formula, and this practice has become a deeply imbedded feature of the collective bargaining process. It is a chief method whereby employees obtain a measure of security in their jobs. It also limits the freedom of management to direct the labor force and influences considerations of plant efficiency. A seniority structure which approaches the ideal would be one which affords protection to employees in their job rights and at the same time does not place unreasonable restrictions on the right of management to make job assignments without sacrificing productivity and efficiency in the plant. This objective can best be realized to the extent that a seniority system is constructed to fit a particular plant environment. It must be tailored to fill the requirements of the technology, the kinds of jobs, the skills and occupations of the employees, and the character of labor relations of a specific company. A seniority formula that might be desirable in one industrial situation might not be suitable to another plant environment. In addition, perhaps no other phase of the collective bargaining relationship demands so much of company officials and union leaders in terms of common sense, good faith, and reciprocal recognition of the problems of management, the labor organization, and the employees.

As a result of the nature of the seniority principle, many problems are inherent in the formulation and application of a seniority structure. Among the major problems, beyond the crucial determination of the phases of the employment relationship which are to be affected by the length-of-service principle, are: establishment of the unit in which employees acquire and apply seniority credits; identification of circumstances under which employees may lose seniority; determination of the seniority status of employees who transfer from one part of the bargaining unit to another or who leave the bargaining unit altogether; and the fixing of certain exceptions to the seniority system. As can be expected, these problems are handled in a multitude of fashions in collective bargaining relationships. Some labor agreements, moreover, attempt to cover all of these issues and some deal with only certain ones of them.

Virtually all labor agreements, for example, provide that seniority play a part in the determination of layoffs, in rehiring, and in promotions. But, as discussed below, the same labor agreement might use one seniority system to govern layoffs and rehiring and a different one in connection with promotions (where considerations of ability and physical fitness are often as important as, and in many cases more important than, length of service). Where a fixed-shift system exists in a plant, labor agreements may permit workers their choice of shifts on the basis of seniority, and factors such as personal convenience, wage or hour differentials, and the kind of job itself may dictate the senior worker's choice in this respect. Under other contracts, however, seniority plays no role in shift assignments.

Units for Seniority

There are three major systems relating to the unit in which an employee acquires and applies his seniority credits: company- or plantwide, departmental or occupational, and a combined plant and departmental seniority system.

Under a *company- or plantwide seniority system*, the seniority status of each employee equals his total service with the firm. Thus, transfers from job to job within the establishment or transfers from one department to another have no effect on an employee's seniority standing. Subject to other features of the seniority structure, an employee under the company- or plantwide system will apply his seniority for purposes covered by the seniority system on a strictly company- or plantwide basis. In actual practice this system is not used in companies in which it would be necessary for an employee to undergo a considerable training period when he takes a new job to replace a worker with less seniority. It is practicable only for companies where the jobs are more or less interchangeable. A companywide system obviously gives the greatest protection to employees with the longest length of service. On the other hand, depending upon the other features of the seniority structure, it could serve as a deterrent to the efficiency and productivity of the plant.

Under *departmental or occupational seniority systems*, separate seniority lists are established for each department or occupational grouping in the plant. If such a system does not have any qualifications or limitations, an employee can apply his seniority credits only within his own department or occupation. Such a system facilitates administration in large companies employing a considerable number of workers. It minimizes the opportunity for large-scale displacement of workers from their jobs in the event of layoffs or discontinuation of particular jobs because of technological innovations, or because of permanent changes in the market for the products of the company. On the other hand, additional problems arise as the result of the use of this kind of seniority system. If layoffs in one department become necessary or if certain jobs in such a department are permanently discontinued while other departments are not affected, a state of affairs could develop wherein employees with long service in a company would find themselves out of a job while employees with less seniority were working full time. In addition, under a strict departmental seniority structure, transfers between departments tend to be discouraged because a transfer could result in complete loss of accumulated seniority.

As a result of the problems arising from a strict company or departmental seniority system, many companies and unions have negotiated a number of plans combining these two types of seniority structures. Under a combination system, seniority may be applied in one unit for certain purposes and exercised in another unit for other purposes. Thus, seniority may be applied on a plantwide basis for purposes of layoffs, whereas departmentwide seniority is used as the basis of promotion. A variation of this system is to permit employees to *apply* their seniority only within the department in which they are working, but to *compute* such seniority on the basis of total service with the company. In addition, although the general application of seniority is limited to a departmental basis, employees laid off in a particular department may claim work in a general labor pool in which the jobs are relatively unskilled and in which newly hired employees start out before being promoted to other departments. At times a distinction is drawn between temporary layoffs resulting from lack of business or material shortages and permanent layoffs resulting from changes in technology or permanent changes in the products manufactured by the company. Under the former situation seniority may be applied only on a departmental basis, or seniority might not govern at all (as in autos), whereas under the latter circumstances employees have the opportunity to apply their seniority on a plantwide basis. Other variations of the combination system are utilized within industry as determined by the circumstances of a particular plant.

Limitations Upon Seniority

Regardless of the type of system under which seniority credits are accumulated and applied, many collective bargaining agreements place certain limitations and qualifications upon length of service as a factor in connection with layoffs. Possibly as many as one third of all agreements in existence may include such limitations. In some cases, seniority systems provide for the retention of more senior employees only when they are qualified to perform the jobs which are available. In considerably fewer labor agreements, a senior employee will be retained in the event of layoffs in a plant only when he is able to perform a job available "as well as" other employees eligible for layoff.

Although a large number of labor agreements permit employees scheduled for layoff to displace less senior employees, limitations on the chain displacement or "bumping" process are also included in many labor agreements. Employers, unions, employees, and students of labor relations recognize the inherent disadvantages of seniority structures which permit unlimited bumping. Such disadvantages are manifested in many ways. Bumping could result in serious obstacles to plant efficiency and productivity to the detriment of all concerned, could cause extreme uncertainty and confusion to workers who might be required to take a number of different jobs as a result of a single layoff, and could result in serious internal political problems for the labor organization.

For these reasons, careful limitations usually are placed on the bumping process. Many labor agreements allow an employee to displace a less senior worker in the event of a layoff only when the former employee has a minimum amount of service with the company. Other contracts circumscribe the bumping process by limiting the opportunity of a senior employee to displacement of a junior worker from a job that the employee with longer service has already held. Under this system, the worker comes down in the same fashion that he went up the job ladder. Under other seniority systems the area into which the employee may bump is itself limited. Thus, it may be stipulated that employees can bump only on a departmental or divisional basis, or can displace workers only within equal or lower labor grades. In addition, the objective of limiting the displacement process is achieved by permitting the displacement of only the *least* senior employee in the bumping area and not of any other less senior employees.

Most labor agreements provide for rehiring in *reverse* order of layoffs —the last employee laid off is the first rehired. In addition, laid-off employees are given preference over new workers for vacancies that arise anywhere in the plant. However, such preferences given employees with longer service are frequently limited to the extent that the employee in question is competent to perform the available work. In this connection the problem of the re-employment of laid-off workers becomes somewhat complicated when a straight departmental seniority system is used. In such a case, although a labor agreement might provide for the rehiring of workers in the reverse order of layoffs, production might not be revived in reverse order to the slack in production and thus employees with shorter service might be recalled to work before employees with greater seniority. To avoid such a state of affairs, some labor contracts provide the older employee in terms of service with the opportunity of returning to work first, provided he has the ability to carry out the duties of the available job.

Length of service as a factor in promotion is of less importance than it is in layoffs and rehiring, and in only a relative handful of contemporary labor agreements is length of service the *sole* factor in making promotions. The incidence is low because all parties to collective bargaining realize that a janitor, for example, in spite of many years of service in this position, is not qualified to be promoted to, say, a tool- and die-maker's job. But if such a criterion is rarely the sole factor in the assignment of workers to higher-rated jobs, the vast majority of labor agreements now require that seniority along with other factors be given *consideration*. In many contracts seniority governs promotions when the senior employee is "qualified" to fill the position in question. Under other collective bargaining agreements seniority becomes the determining criterion in promotions when the senior employee has ability and physical fitness for the job in question "equal to that" of all other employees who may desire the better job. Under the latter seniority structure, length of service is of secondary importance to the ability and physical fitness factors, however.

In practice, management makes the decision about which worker among those bidding for the job gets the promotion and in the vast majority of cases this decision of the company is satisfactory to all concerned. This is the case many times because the senior employee *is* best qualified for the job in question or because the company is completely willing to give preference to him when ability differences among employees are not readily discernible. At times, however, when the company passes over a senior employee in favor of an employee with shorter service in making a promotion, the union may protest the action of the company through the grievance procedure. For example, the union may argue that the senior employee bidding for the better job has equal ability to that of the worker whom the company tapped for the promotion. The problem in such cases is to evaluate the comparative abilities of the two workers. Such a determination involves the study and appraisal of the entire work record of both workers. Consideration here is usually given to such items as the previous experience of the workers on the actual job in question or on closely related jobs; the education and training qualifications of the workers for performing the job in question; production records of the employees; and absenteeism, tardiness, and accident records when relevant. Ordinarily, such disputes are resolved between the union and the company on the basis of these considerations. At times, however, the parties are still in disagreement and the matter is then most often referred to an impartial arbitrator who will make the decision in the case. (NOTE: Case No. 9 deals with this kind of issue.)

Seniority in Transfers

Another seniority problem involves the seniority status of employees who *transfer* from one department to another. As stated above, interdepartmental transfers do not create a seniority issue under a straight plantwide seniority system. To the extent that seniority is acquired or applied on a departmentwide basis, however, the problem of transfers becomes important to employers, unions, and employees: reference has been made to the fact that interdepartmental transfers are discouraged when employees lose all accumulated seniority upon entering a new department. Some contracts deal with this problem by allowing a transferred employee to retain his seniority in his old department, while starting at the bottom of the seniority scale in the new department; under these circumstances such an employee would exercise seniority rights in his old department in the event he were laid off from his new department. Some contracts even permit such an employee to further accumulate seniority for application in his old department in the event that he is laid off from his new department. Another approach to the problem permits the transferred employee to carry his seniority acquired in the old department to the new department. This is a common practice where the job itself is transferred to a new department, where the job or the department itself is permanently abolished, or upon the merging of two or more departments.

Still another seniority problem arises under the circumstances of an employee's transferring entirely *out of the bargaining unit*. This issue is particularly related to the seniority status of workers who are selected by management to fill foremen's jobs. There are three major approaches to this problem. Under some contracts a rank-and-file employee who takes a supervisory job simply loses accumulated seniority. If for some reason his supervisory job is terminated and he desires to return to a job covered by the collective bargaining contract, he is treated as a new employee for purposes of seniority. Another method is to permit such an employee to retain all seniority credits earned earlier when he serves as a foreman. Under this latter approach, if the employee transfers back to the bargaining unit, he returns with the same number of seniority credits as he had when he left. Finally, under some contracts, an employee taking a supervisor's job accumulates seniority in the bargaining unit while he serves as a foreman. If he returns to the bargaining unit, he comes back not only with the seniority credits that he acquired before he took the supervisory job, but with seniority credits accumulated while he served as a foreman. Rank, at times, does have its privileges.

Obviously, the seniority status of foremen is not a problem when management fills its supervisory posts by hiring outside the plant. On the other hand, the problem is a real one when the company elects to fill such jobs from the rank and file. It is apparent that a worker with long seniority in the bargaining unit would hesitate to take a foreman's job if he would lose thereby all his accumulated seniority. In recognition of this situation many employers and unions have agreed that workers promoted from the bargaining unit to supervisors' jobs at least may retain the seniority they accumulated while covered by the labor agreement. Whatever approach unions and companies take to this problem, it generally would be desirable to spell out the method in the labor agreement. Confusion, uncertainty, and controversy could arise when the contract is silent on this issue.

Exceptions to the Seniority System

Under many collective bargaining contracts there is provision for some *exemptions* from the normal operation of the seniority structure. One of these involves the issue of "super-seniority" for union officers. Some companies and unions have agreed that designated union officers may have a preferred status in the event of layoffs. Such employees are protected in employment regardless of their length of service with the company. They are entitled to such consideration strictly by virtue of the union office which they hold, however, and lose their super-seniority status when their term of office is terminated.

One obvious problem involved in the negotiation of a super-seniority clause is the designation of the employees who are to have this status. Frequently, labor agreements limit this protection to the comparatively major local union officers. If too many employees are covered by a super-seniority status, the effective and fair operation of the seniority structure might be prevented. In any event it is common practice to specify exactly which officers of the union are to be included under the super-seniority clause.

Another problem concerns the bumping rights of employees protected under such an arrangement. Contracts usually are clear as to just what job or jobs such employees are entitled to when they are scheduled for layoff. In addition, it is common practice to make clear the rate of pay that the employee will earn in the new job. Thus, if a worker protected by super-seniority takes another job which pays a lower rate than his regular job to avoid layoff, the contract specifies whether or not he will get the rate of the job that he is filling or the rate of his regular job. Obviously, when these problems *are* resolved in the labor agreement, there is less chance for controversy during the hectic atmosphere of a layoff itself.

Some labor agreements also permit management to retain in employment during periods of layoff a certain number of non-union-officer employees regardless of their seniority status. Such employees are designated as "exceptional," "specially skilled," "indispensable," or "meritorious" in collective bargaining contracts. As in the case of super-seniority, problems growing out of this exception to the seniority rule normally are resolved in the collective bargaining contract. Problems in this connection involve the number of employees falling into this category, the kind of jobs that they must be holding to receive such preferential status, their bumping rights (if any), and the rate of pay they shall earn in the event that they are retained in employment in jobs other than their regular ones.

Another general exception to the normal operation of a seniority system involves newly hired workers. Under most labor agreements such workers must first serve a probationary period before they are protected by the labor agreement. Such probationary periods are frequently specified as being from about thirty to ninety days, and during this period of time the new worker can be laid off, demoted, transferred, or otherwise assigned work without reference to the seniority structure at all. However, once such an employee serves out his probationary period, his seniority under most labor agreements is calculated from the first day of hire by the company.

Under the terms of many collective bargaining contracts, employers may lay off workers on a *temporary* basis without reference to the seniority structure. Such layoffs are for short periods of time and result from purely temporary factors, such as shortages of material, power failures, and the like. It is, of course, vital in this connection that the labor agreement define the meaning of temporary layoff. At times, contracts incorporate the principle that employers may lay off without reference to seniority on a temporary basis but fail to specify what is meant by the term *temporary layoff*. Some agreements define the term as any layoff for less than five or even ten working days. Other contracts, however, specify that the seniority structure must be followed for any layoff in excess of twenty-four hours. Whatever time limit is placed on the term, the labor agreement should specify the duration of a temporary layoff. By this means, a considerable amount of future argument will be avoided. Of course, once the temporary layoff period has been exhausted, a laid-off employee can then exercise his seniority rights in accordance with the seniority structure of the labor agreement.

Finally, virtually all seniority structures specify circumstances under which an employee *loses* his seniority credits. All employees should fully understand the exact nature of these circumstances and the significance of losing seniority credits. Under the terms of most collective bargaining contracts an employee loses his seniority if he is discharged, voluntarily quits, fails to notify the company within a certain time period (usually five working days) of his intentions to return to work after he is recalled by the company after a layoff, fails to return to work after an authorized leave of absence, neglects to report to work within a certain period of time (usually ninety working days) after discharge from military service, or is laid off continuously for a long period of time, usually from about twenty-four to forty-eight months.

A Concluding Comment

However qualified it may be in particular situations, there can be no denying the current acceptability of the seniority criterion in regulating potential competition among employees for jobs and job status. The traditional arguments that seniority fosters laziness, rewards mediocrity, and crimps individual initiative are no longer automatically brought into play by managers to oppose this length-of-service criterion. And the on-balance benefits of seniority, both in improving employee morale and in minimizing administrative problems, are no longer seriously questioned by progressive companies, *if* length of service is limited by such other factors as ability when these are meaningful. Although it is probably true that in general a seniority system tends to reduce the efficiency of the plant operation to some extent, if care is taken to design a system to the needs of the particular company, and if length of service *is* appropriately limited in its application, the net loss to plant efficiency is normally not very noticeable.

Beyond this, many would argue that efficiency, despite its obvious importance, should not be the only goal of American industry. The advantages of providing a measure of job security to employees, and thereby relieving them of the frustrations of discrimination and unfair treatment, cannot be easily quantified. But human values have become the increasing concern of modern management, and the judicious use of seniority clearly serves the human equation.

Discharge and Discipline

In the absence of a collective bargaining relationship, an employer may discharge or otherwise impose penalties upon an employee without any limitations except those imposed by law. An employee may be discharged for any reason, or, indeed, for no reason. The power of discipline in a nonunion situation remains fully and completely in the hands of the employer.

Once a collective bargaining relationship is established, however, the employer's prerogative to discipline employees is invariably limited by the labor agreement. The nature of such a restriction is not that the company loses its right to discharge or otherwise discipline employees; rather, it is that the employer's right in this connection is restricted to the extent that he can inflict discipline on employees only for sufficient and appropriate reasons.

Thus, most collective bargaining contracts contain the general statement that an employee can be discharged only for "just cause." And the critical interpretation of just cause is accomplished through industrial practice, through the results of the grievance procedure existing in the particular plant, through common sense, and through arbitration decisions.

Frequently companies and unions agree that a particular infraction by an employee constitutes a proper reason for discharge and there is no litigation on the issue. On the other hand, in many cases the employer and the union are in disagreement as to whether an offense by an employee constitutes a valid basis for discharge. Under these circumstances, the issue is discussed and debated between the company and the union in the grievance procedure. If the parties fail to reach an agreement through this process, the dispute is frequently submitted to an arbitrator for final decision.

It is understandable that a large percentage of arbitration cases involve discharge. Discipline, of course, is required to run an efficient business. If every worker were free to do what he wanted, the productive process could hardly be carried out effectively; such a state of affairs would operate to the distinct disadvantage of the employees, the employer, and the union. Accordingly, the right of the employer to discipline becomes an indispensable prerequisite to the operation of a successful business. On the other hand, to the worker and to his family, the loss of a job by discharge is very serious. Not only does it result in the loss of a man's immediate livelihood, but the stigma of discharge is likely to make it more difficult for an employee to find another job. From this point of view, a discharge has much more serious consequences to the worker and his family than does a permanent layoff. In addition, a discharged employee frequently loses part of his coverage under most state unemployment compensation laws. Thus, because the implications of discharge are so profound, this feature of collective bargaining has frequently proven both highly challenging and quite controversial for both labor relations parties.

Although the majority of contracts contain only the previously noted general and simple statement that discharge can be made only for just cause (or "proper reason"), many labor agreements list one or more specific grounds for discharge: violation of company rules, failure to meet work standards, incompetency, violation of the collective bargaining contract (including in this category the instigation of or participation in a strike or a slowdown in violation of the agreement), excessive absenteeism or tardiness, intoxication, dishonesty, insubordination, wage garnishments, and fighting on company property. Labor agreements which list specific causes for discharge normally also include a general statement that discharge may be made for "any other just or proper reason."

In addition, many contracts distinguish between causes for immediate discharge and employee offenses which require one or more warnings. For example, sabotage or willful destruction of company property may result in immediate discharge, whereas a discharge for absenteeism may occur only after a certain number of warnings. In recognition of the fact that not all employee infractions are grave enough to warrant discharge, lesser forms of discipline are imposed at times under collective bargaining relationships. Into this category fall oral and written reprimand, suspension without pay for varying lengths of time, demotion, and denial of vacation pay. Frequently, union and management representatives in the grievance procedure will agree upon a lesser measure of discipline even though the employer presumably has the grounds to discharge an employee for a particular offense. At times the union and the employee in question will be willing to settle a case on these terms rather than risk taking the case to arbitration.

A very large number of collective bargaining contracts specify a distinct procedure for discharge cases. Many of them require notice to the employee and the union before the discharge takes place. Such notification generally is required to contain the specific reasons for the discharge. A hearing on the case is also provided for in many labor agreements and in this respect the typical labor agreement requires not only the presence of the worker in question and an appropriate official of the company, but also a representative of the labor organization. Frequently, collective bargaining agreements provide for a suspension period before the discharge becomes effective. The alleged advantage of this latter procedure is that it provides for an opportunity to cool tempers and offers a period of time for all parties to make a careful investigation and evaluation of the facts of the case.

Part of the procedure for discharge cases is provided for in the general grievance procedure of the collective bargaining contract. As suggested, almost every labor agreement provides for appeal of discharge cases and this appeal is taken through the regular grievance procedure, since the appeal is looked upon as a grievance. If, for example, the labor agreement provides that the employee or the union must appeal a discharge within a certain number of days, such appeal must be made during this period or the discharge may become permanent regardless of the merits of the case. Likewise, a company which neglects its obligation to give an answer to the appeal within the stipulated number of days may find that it has lost its right to discharge a particular worker regardless of the justice of the situation.

Frequently, labor agreements also provide that a discharge case has a priority over all other cases in the grievance procedure. Some of them even waive the first few steps of the grievance procedure and start a discharge case at the top levels of the procedure. In these arrangements, companies and unions recognize the fact that it is to the mutual advantage of all concerned to expedite discharge cases. The worker wants to know as quickly as possible whether or not he has a job in the plant. The company also has an interest in the prompt settlement of a discharge case because of the disciplinary implications involved and because labor agreements normally require that the company award the employee loss of earnings where a discharge is withdrawn.

From the foregoing, it should be clear that under a collective bargaining relationship, the employer does not lose his right to discipline or discharge. What is involved, however, is that it is more difficult for management to exercise this function. There must be just cause, a specific procedure must be followed, and, of course, management must have the *proof* that an employee committed the offensive act.

If cases do go to arbitration, in fact, the arbitrator will be particularly concerned with the quality of proof that management offers in the hearing. The occasions on which employers have lost discharge cases in arbitration because the evidence which they have presented is not sufficient to prove the case for discharge are many in number. At times, the company's case against the employee has simply been poorly prepared; at other times, the management has not been able to assemble the proof despite the most conscientious of company efforts (one difficulty in this latter regard, as all arbitrators are well aware, is that employees dislike to testify against other employees who are charged with some offense).

If the arbitrator did not demand convincing proof before sustaining discipline, however, the protection afforded employees by the labor agreement would be worthless. The same situation prevails in our civil life, wherein juries have freed criminals because the state has not proven its case. Such courses of action reflect one of the most cardinal features of our system of justice, the presumption that a man is innocent until proven guilty, and this hallmark of our civil life plays no less a role in the American system of industrial relations. Though this situation has undoubtedly resulted in the reinstatement to their jobs with full back pay for employees who are in fact "guilty," it is beyond argument that an employer bears the obligation to prove charges against employees whom it has displaced. In the absence of such an obligation, this most important benefit allowed employees under a collective bargaining contract, protection against arbitrary management treatment is obviously negated. (NOTE: Cases No. 10 and 11 at the end of this chapter involve the discharge of employees under a collective bargaining contract.)

SAFETY AND HEALTH OF EMPLOYEES

Few people would argue that employees do not have a real interest in the area of industrial safety and health. After all, it is the worker and his family who suffer the most devastating consequences of neglect in this area, in terms of accidents, sickness, and even death. And although most employers can sincerely claim that they, too, are deeply interested in safe and healthy working environments, such concern cannot restore to life a man killed on the job or restore his limbs, or succor his family when an employment-caused accident or illness disables an employee for long periods of time. Indeed, this consideration is at the root of a long-standing policy of the National Labor Relations Board that safety and health demands of unions are mandatory subjects of collective bargaining. Thus, employers must bargain on these issues even though company working conditions are also subject to the many safety regulations imposed by federal and state statutes.

Not surprisingly, then, most collective bargaining contracts contain explicit provisions relating to the safety and health area, although such provisions take one of two routes depending upon the particular contract.

On the one hand, many contracts merely state in *general* terms that the management of the plant is required to take measures to protect the safety and health of employees. At times the term *measures* is qualified by the word *reasonable*. When a contract contains such a broad and general statement, the problem of application and interpretation is obviously involved and disagreements between the company and union in this regard are commonly resolved through the regular grievance procedure, or by the operation of a special safety committee.

The second category of contracts provides a *detailed and specific* listing of safety and health measures which obligate the company. Thus, many agreements stipulate that the company must provide adequate heat, light, and ventilation in the plant; that it will control drafts, noise, toxic fumes, dust, dirt, and grease; that it will provide certain safety equipment, such as hoods, goggles, special shoes and boots, and other items of special clothing; and that it is responsible for placing guards and other safety devices on machines. In addition, under many contracts, the company must provide first-aid stations and keep a nurse on duty. Of course, whether or not a collective bargaining contract contains safety rules, a company must comply with the state safety and health laws applicable to its plant.

Many labor agreements impose obligations on employees and unions as well as on employers in the matter of safety. Such provisions recognize the fact that safety, despite the individual employee's crucial stake in it, is a joint problem requiring the cooperation of the company, employees, and the union. Under many labor agreements, employees must obey safety rules and wear appropriate safety equipment, and employees who violate such rules are subject to discipline. In some labor agreements the union assumes the obligation of educating its members to comply with safety rules and procedures of the plant. And some labor agreements in the interest of safety also establish a joint union-management safety committee. Many of these committees serve as advisory bodies on the general problem of safety and health. Other committees, however, have the authority to establish and enforce safety and health rules, allowing the union a considerably more active role.

PRODUCTION STANDARDS AND MANNING

Certainly one of the most important functions of management is that of determining the amount of output that an employee must turn out in a given period. So important is this area to management's objective of operating an efficient plant that employers will at times suffer long strikes to maintain this right as a unilateral one.

It is easy to understand why employers have such a vital interest in production standards. To the degree that employees increase output, unit labor costs decline. With declining labor costs, employers make a larger profit, or else they can translate lower labor costs into lower prices for their products or services with the expectation of thereby increasing the total volume of sales and strengthening the financial position of the company.

There is still another way to look at production standards in the operation of the firm. If employees produce more, the employer will have to hire commensurately fewer additional employees, or may even be in a position to lay off present employees on a temporary or permanent basis. Indeed, with a smaller labor force, the management could also save on the number of foremen needed to supervise the work of its employees.

Production standards are thus directly related to the manning of jobs, or to the question of how many employees are needed to carry out a specific plant assignment. But even where contractual commitments or past practices obligate the company to assign a certain minimum number of workers to a given operation at all times, significant economies can be realized by management if it is able to impose higher production standards upon this inflexible crew.

If the interest of management in production standards is understandable, however, it is no less understandable that employees and their union representatives have an equal interest in ensuring "reasonableness" and "fairness" in this phase of the firm's operation. Before the advent of unions, employers could require employees to produce as much as management directed. Failure to meet these production standards could result in the summary dismissal of the employee. At times, employees suffered accidents, psychological problems, and a generally shortened work life in meeting the standards of the employer. And although modern and enlightened management does not normally impose production standards that employees cannot reasonably attain, unions and employees are nonetheless still vitally concerned with the amount of production that an employee must turn out in a given length of time because of the patent ramifications for job opportunities and union membership.

There is no simple solution to the problem of how much an employee must produce to hold his job or to earn a given amount of pay. At times, the determination of a solution is purely subjective in character: a foreman or superintendent's individual judgment is the criterion adopted to resolve the problem. To this, unions argue that the judgment of employees or labor union officers is as good as that of the management representatives.

More sophisticated methods of determination are available, but these techniques, too, are hardly so perfect or "scientific" as to end the controversy. Such techniques fall under the general title of time and motion studies. That is, having been shown the most efficient method of performing a job, so-called "average" employees who are presumably thus working at average rates of speed are timed. From such a study, management claims that the typical employee in the plant should at least produce the average amount in a given period. Where incentive wage systems are in effect, as we know, the employee receives premium pay for output above the average. However, production standards are important even when employees are paid by the hour, since failure to produce the average amount could result in employee discipline of some sort—ranging from a reprimand to discharge, with the intervening levels such as a suspension or a demotion to a lower-paying job. Unions are far from convinced that time and motion studies constitute the millennium in the resolution of the production standards problem. They claim that the studies are far from scientific, since they still involve human judgment, and that employees who are timed are often far better than average (and that the rate of speed of the studied employees is consequently unrealistically fast).

With few exceptions (most notably in the garment industries), unions have pressed for an effective means of *review* of employer establishment of production standards, rather than toward seeking the right to establish such standards initially. Organized labor has generally believed that employee and union institutional interests are served as effectively, and without the administrative and political complexities of initial standard establishment, if there is a union opportunity for *challenge* of the management action either through arbitration or by the exercise of the right to strike *during the contractual period* in the event of unresolved production standards disputes.

Some unions have historically preferred the right to strike to arbitration in this area. The United Automobile Workers has, for example, steadfastly refused to relinquish its right to strike over production standards disputes, and although the UAW now agrees to arbitration on virtually all other phases of the labor agreement, it is adamant in its opposition to the arbitration of standards. The international neither distrusts arbitrators nor challenges their professional competency. Rather, it believes that a union cannot properly prepare and present a case in arbitration which can successfully challenge production standards. It contends that the problems are so complicated, the proofs so difficult to assemble, and the data so hard to present in meaningful form that arbitration is not the proper forum to resolve production standards disputes. In essence, it claims that employers have an advantage in any arbitration dealing with production standards, and the union does not intend to turn to this process because it would jeopardize the interests of its members.

On the other hand, most unions have now agreed to the arbitration of production standards. Beyond reflecting the general contemporary acceptance of the arbitration process itself, this course of action has behind it a highly practical reason: frequently, production standards are protested by only a small group of employees in the plant. For example, the employer may have changed (because of improved technology, equipment, or methods) the standards in one department, but left unaltered at least temporarily the standards in all other departments. Without arbitration, the only way in which the affected employees could seek relief would be for the entire labor force to strike—at times, a politically inopportune weapon for the union to use because the employees in the other departments are satisfied and do not care to sacrifice earnings just to help out employees in a single department. Arbitration avoids this situation, while still allowing a final and binding decision on the grievance of the protesting employees. (NOTE: Case No. 12 deals with production standards or, as called in the case, "work loads.")

There is, however, probably no area of labor relations wherein management and organized labor still stand any further apart than in production standards. There is no magical solution to such controversies when they arise. Standards lie at the heart of the operation of the plant, and are vital to the basic interest of the employees and unions. To say that they should be established "fairly" and "reasonably" is a most idle statement to make, falling in the category of "we should all love our mothers." In the give and take of day-to-day operations, wherein production standards may be changed, deep and bitter circumstances are perhaps even *bound* to arise. The stakes are very high, and as long as management seeks efficiency and the union seeks to protect the welfare of its members, there exists no easy way out of the problem. Certainly nothing approaching a panacea for it has yet been discovered by the parties to collective bargaining.

At least, however, if companies and unions fully recognize the apparent inevitability of standards disputes, the fact that no dispute in this area will perhaps ever be settled in such a way that all involved in it will be fully satisfied, and the high degree of sensitivity of this labor relations issue, the point of realism will have been reached. Once these basic propositions are understood, the parties are in a position to fashion workable production standards compromises without jeopardizing the broader collective bargaining relationship.

AUTOMATION

As stated at the beginning of this chapter, the problem of automation cuts across much of the contemporary collective bargaining process. Most of the methods which the private parties have employed to ease the adjustment to this new technology are administrative and institutional in nature, insofar as they deal with the job rights of workers, the institutional needs of labor organizations, and the rights of management in directing the work force. But such previously discussed "economic" issues as severance pay, pension-right vesting and supplemental unemployment benefits also are increasingly being geared to cushioning the labor-saving and displacement effects of automation. It is thus quite unrealistic to view this problem as falling exclusively within one descriptive category. Indeed, one is fully justified in looking at this final portion of the chapter as a synthesizer of many current trends in collective bargaining, providing the capstone of the "administrative" segment but actually extending well beyond it.

Broadly defined, automation is the control of the elements of production through a system of automatic devices which integrate the entire productive process. Not only is the human hand not needed, but the process also makes less necessary a major feature which distinguishes human beings from animals: judgment. Automated computers are now able to determine optimally what product to produce in the first place, the color and design of the product, where the goods should be sold, and even the pricing of the product.

Even today, automation affects, to some extent, almost all segments of the work force. Although the industrial blue-collar worker, and particularly the unskilled and semiskilled factory worker, has thus far been hardest hit, examples abound to show the impact of automation, even at this relatively early stage in its history, in other sectors of the economy. In railroading, for example, robot track-laying equipment and the automatic handling and dispatching of freight cars have made many jobs obsolete. The same can be said of many forms of retail trade, as symbolized by one mail-order house in which a computer now handles 90,000 tallies each day, keeping an automatic inventory record of the 8,000 items sold by the firm in the process. Nor has government employment been immune from automation's inroads: the 450 United States Treasury clerical workers who were recently replaced by a computer designed to accommodate the 350 million checks issued by the federal government every year are far from unique among the casualties of automation in that sector.

The fact remains, however, that the blue-collar worker in mass production industry—unionism's strongest bastion—has been the most visible victim of the advent of automation. In the modern automobile plant, 154 engine blocks now run through the production line in one hour, requiring 41 workers; under older methods, the same amount of production required 117 men. In the typical automated radio-manufacturing establishment, only two employees produce 1,000 radios per day, where standard hand assembly required a labor force of 200. And, perhaps most dramatic of all, fourteen glass-blowing machines, each operated by a single worker, have for some time produced 90 percent of all glass light bulbs used in the United States, as well as all the glass tubes used in radio and television sets except for the picture tubes![2]

[2] Edward B. Shils, *Automation and Industrial Relations* (New York: Holt, Rinehart & Winston, Inc., 1963), p. 179.

For all these labor displacement and related skill rating and wage payment effects, there are clearly offsetting advantages offered by automation. Certainly, the automating *employer* benefits, either by gaining a competitive edge or by closing a competitive gap, in making this form of technological change. Of far more general benefit, national living standards are raised immensely by the increased productivity allowed. It is now estimated, for example, that the average family income in the United States at constant dollars will be $15,000 annually in the year 2000, up from only about half that figure today.

There are, moreover, still other advantages to automation: greater safety, resulting from the use of modern methods of materials handling and from the elimination of other hazardous jobs; a frequent improvement in product quality, since the automatic machine has little room for human error; and even an improved defense posture for the nation, modern methods of warfare having as their common denominator an automation base. Most important of all, it can be argued with considerable justification that every one, *in the long run,* benefits from the needs and wants created by improved technology. There are infinitely more men working in the automobile production and servicing industries than there ever were blacksmiths, for example. And the number of employees associated with the telephone industry vastly exceeds the highest labor force totals ever achieved by the town-crier profession.

All these arguments, however, are of small consolation to the employee actually being displaced or threatened by automation. Just as logically, he can echo the irrefutable statement of Lord Keynes that "in the long run, we are all dead." And he can often balance the fact that automation has generally improved working conditions by pointing to undesirable features of the problem which have an impact upon the workers in the plant: greater isolation of employees on the job, with less chance to talk face to face with other workers and supervisors; a greater mental strain, particularly since mistakes can now be much more costly; the deterioration of social groups, since it requires considerably less teamwork to run the modern operation; and the fact that jobs in the automated plant (or office) are fast becoming much more *alike,* with less on-the-job variety also often the case, and attendant psychological and social implications stemming from this situation.

But most worrisome of all to the industrial worker is the threat of displacement, or at least of severe skill requirement downgrading, through *future* automation. The results of one employee survey with which the authors are personally familiar showed almost three quarters of all respondents replying in the negative as to whether they believed that "automation is a good thing for workers" (and many of them added that the new methods constituted a "real job threat"). Such findings have been echoed in countless other studies.

The fears appear to be well grounded. If automation undeniably creates new jobs and even industries, the possibility remains that at the present time automation is destroying more jobs than it creates. Even placing all government and private estimates at their rock-bottom minima, it is likely that 4,000 jobs are eliminated *each week* in this manner. And however many of the displaced are ultimately reabsorbed into the employed labor force, the increasing skill requirements of an automated world leave little room for at least the unskilled worker to join their ranks: at the time of this writing, with a national rate of unemployment seemingly inflexibly fixed in the 5.5 to 6.0 percent range, the rate for unskilled workers had steadily exceeded 15 percent in recent years.

Thus, if by far the greatest *organizational* problem of unions involves the organization of the white-collar sector in the face of the automation-caused changing complexion of the work force, within the *current arena of collective bargaining,* organized labor—both as the blue-collar worker's representative and for its own institutional preservation—has inevitably been forced toward the promotion of *measures minimizing job hardship for blue-collar workers.*

Accordingly, unions have in recent years pushed hard, and with much success, for several devices geared explicitly to cushioning the employment impact of automation. In addition to such previously discussed areas as SUB, pension vesting, severance pay, extended vacation periods, and early retirement provisions (which have frequently been negotiated for reasons other than adjustment to automation), several such devices deserve attention.[3]

1. *Advance Notice of Layoff or Shutdown:* Such advance notice, impracticable for management in the case of sudden cancellation of orders and various other contingencies, is far more feasible where automation is involved, since many months may be required to prepare for the automated equipment and processes. An increasing number of agreements now call for notice considerably in excess of the few days traditionally provided for in many contracts, with most of the liberalizations now providing for three to twelve months.

Managements independently have often agreed with the advisability of such liberalization—to maintain or improve community images, to dispel potentially damaging employee rumors, and, frequently, because of a desire to develop placement and training plans for displaced workers. Very often, in fact, the actual notice given by management exceeds that stipulated in the contract. There seems to be little doubt, however, that unions have been

[3] Some of the following exposition is based upon information provided in a comprehensive 1964 review by the United States Department of Labor's Bureau of Labor Statistics, *Methods of Adjusting to Automation and Technological Change.* See also Shils, *op. cit.,* and Gerald G. Somers, Edward L. Cushman, and Nat Weinberg, eds., *Adjusting to Technological Change* (New York: Harper & Row, Publishers, 1963).

instrumental in inserting longer advance-notice provisions in some contracts —as in portions of the meat-packing and electronics industries—which might otherwise not have modified traditional practices.

2. *Adoption of the "Attrition Principle":* An agreement to reduce jobs solely by attrition—through, in other words, deaths, voluntary resignations, retirements, and similar events—by definition gives maximum job security to the present jobholder, although it does nothing to secure the union's long-run institutional interests. As a compromise, it has appealed to many employers as an equitable and not unduly rigorous measure. Managements have proven particularly amenable to this arrangement when the voluntary resignation rate is expected to be high, when a high percentage of workers is nearing retirement age, or when no major reduction of the labor force is anticipated in the first place (and the number of jobs made obsolete by automation is consequently small to begin with). In other cases, unions have been the major force behind introduction of the principle—usually, however, with some modifications more favorable to the union as an institution placed upon it. Thus, the current agreement between the Order of Railroad Telegraphers and the Southern Pacific Railroad places an upper limit of 2 percent upon the jobs which can be abolished for any reason in a given year. Good faith is obviously required in such cases as the latter, however; as Bok and Kossoris comment,

> If [employers] are bound to follow attrition by agreement, temptation may arise to hasten the departure of employees by imposing more onerous working conditions or otherwise making the job less attractive. Further controversy may result if the agreement does not answer such questions as whether employees must agree to transfer or to accept more demanding positions and assignments in order to remain on the payroll.[4]

3. *Retraining:* An expanding but unknown number of bargaining relationships now provide opportunities for displaced employees to retrain for another job in the same plant or another plant of the same company. The same protection is also increasingly being extended to employees for whom changes in equipment or operating methods make it mandatory to retrain in order to hold their current jobs. Often such retraining opportunity, which is most commonly offered at company expense, is limited to workers who meet certain seniority specifications. General Electric workers, for example, must have at least three years of continuous service in order to qualify. At other times, preference but not a promise for retraining is granted senior workers, as in one Machinist Union contract which provides that such employees "shall be given preference for training on new equipment, provided they have the capabilities required."

Where such provisions have significantly mitigated displacement, not

[4] Bureau of Labor Statistics, U.S. Department of Labor, *Methods of Adjusting to Automation and Technological Change,* p. 5.

unexpectedly, they have been implemented by companies whose operations have been expanding in areas other than those causing the initial displacement. "Retraining for *what*?" is a meaningful question when such expansion is not in evidence, or at least is not highly likely. Lack of employee self-confidence or lack of worker intelligence levels which are sufficient to meet the new skill requirements have also been known to make the retraining opportunity an essentially valueless one for employees permitted to utilize it. Yet, there is much to be said for retraining in the absence of such adverse factors; as the personnel director of Inland Steel has stated,

> Retraining makes maximum use of manpower and contributes to the long-range security of the individual.... We think this is smart because it minimizes resistance to change, enables us to get up production faster than when people fear they won't keep their jobs, and gives us a quicker return on our investment.[5]

4. *Automation Funds:* Ironically, the several "automation funds" which have sprouted in a variety of industries in the recent past do little or nothing to aid employees who are actually displaced. They do, however, tend to make it easier for management to implement change, both by gaining the cooperation of the *retained* workers and by strengthening the union's institutional status through providing benefits for present and future union members. Such funds as those negotiated by the United Mine Workers, American Federation of Musicians, West Coast Longshoremen, New York Longshoremen, and Amalgamated Meat Cutters with various employers are essentially devices for sharing the savings of automation with retained employees—through such means as free medical care, guaranteed weekly pay provisions, early retirement allowances, and lump sum "bonus payments."

In addition to the political and public relations advantages which they allow to the various unions, there are specific advantages in the funds from management's point of view. Kennedy believes that perhaps the major such advantage

> is that it impresses more strongly on the employees the reason for the benefits which they are receiving. When the benefits are paid from an "automation" fund, it is clear that they are being paid out of the savings of automation and that the employees are expected to cooperate with the automation process in return for such benefits. On the other hand, when the savings of automation are shared through higher wage rates or through improved fringe benefits without a fund, the service of the benefits as well as the reason for giving them may not be so evident in the beginning and are much more easily forgotten with time.[6]

---

[5] *Wall Street Journal*, August 23, 1961, p. 6.
[6] Thomas Kennedy, *Automation Funds and Displaced Workers* (Boston: Graduate School of Business Administration, Harvard University, 1962), pp. 351–52.

On such a pragmatic basis, automation funds can probably be expected to continue their spread.

5. *Restrictions on Subcontracting:* Subcontracting, the term which stands for arrangements made by a company (for reasons such as cost, quality, or speed of delivery) to have some portion of its work performed by employees of another company, obviously can have major work-opportunity ramifications for the first company's employees. There is probably no completely integrated company in the nation, and some measure of subcontracting has always been accepted by all unions as an economic necessity. But when the union can argue that union member employees *could* have performed the subcontracted work, or that such work *was* previously done by bargaining unit employees, it can be counted upon to do so. And when disputes do arise over this issue, they are, as Chapter 4 has pointed out, often of major dimensions. In the face of automation-caused job insecurity, there has been an observable recent trend toward union control over many types of subcontracting; the battle has tended to move from open interunion competition to the union-management bargaining table.

So thorny is the subcontracting problem that more than 75 percent of all major contracts still make no direct reference to it in a special contractual section. But an increasing number of contracts are incorporating in various of their other sections (ranging from union recognition clauses to seniority articles) or in separate "memoranda of understanding" certain limitations on the procedure.

The limitations are of several kinds: (1) agreements that subcontractors will be used "*only*" on special occasions (for example, "where specialized equipment not available on company premises is required," "where peculiar skills are needed"); (2) no-layoff guarantees to present employees (as in "no Employee of any craft, which craft is being utilized by an Outside Contractor, shall be laid off as long as the Outside Contractor is in the plant doing work that Employees in such craft are able to do"); (3) provisions giving the union veto power over any or all subcontracting; and (4) requirements that the company prove to the union that time, expense, or facility considerations prevent it from allowing present employees to perform the work.

Slichter, Healy, and Livernash have summed up the present situation as follows:

> [Unlike many other collective bargaining areas] subcontracting remains an area of conflict in labor relations. Where adjustment has been achieved by the adoption of workable contract language, it has usually had the effect of limiting management's flexibility to a considerable extent. Seldom has explicit language been adopted affirming management's right

to subcontract without challenge from the union. The trend has been in the opposite direction.[7]

Only when more adequate solutions to the problems of automation are formulated can one expect the conflict in this area to abate.

6. *Other Measures:* Unions have also unilaterally attempted to minimize the administrative, institutional, and other problems of automation through increasingly successful if still limited bargaining table campaigns for: (a) shorter work weeks, often with a prohibition against overtime work when qualified workers are on layoff or where the overtime would result in layoffs; (b) the requirement of joint labor-management consultation prior to the introduction of any automated change; (c) the overhauling of wage structures with job upgrading to reflect the "increased responsibility" of automated factory jobs; and (d) special job and wage provisions for downgraded workers, to minimize income losses suffered by such workers, or to offset these entirely. In addition, unions have in some cases sought to facilitate new employment through the development of their own training, placement, and referral services. And, perhaps most visibly, they have often waged highly ambitious political lobbying campaigns (both on the international and AFL-CIO levels) for: a vast array of employment-generating public works programs; far-reaching tax programs and expanded social security benefits (to increase consumer purchasing power and lessen the burden on those most likely to be displaced); and innovative federal and state training programs.

As judged by short-run goals—the insertion of the various contract provisions within labor agreements and, in the latter case, the enactment of the lobbied-for legislation—unions have achieved a considerable measure of triumph. And the fact that they have frequently been aided in such campaigns by increasingly social-minded employers in no way detracts from this success. Although union aggressiveness and creativity has varied widely, there can be no denying that many unions have considerably alleviated the burdens of automation for many workers.

Yet neither singly nor in combination have these measures, or the host of other automation-adjustment methods cited earlier, provided anything approaching a full solution for the basic problems with which they deal. The displacement and displacement threats continue, now actually in accelerated form, as automation continues to prove that it is both a blessing and a curse for society. Indeed, a case can be made that a vicious circle is involved: virtually all these measures increase labor costs for the companies concerned, giving the employer even further motivation

---

[7] Slichter, Healy, and Livernash, *op. cit.,* pp. 315–16.

for automating, and often thus causing the represented employees to lose jobs all the more rapidly.[8]

There appears to be rather general agreement among all segments of our society on at least three relevant points, however. First, most of us concede that automation is a product of society. It is not caused only by individuals, single firms, or groups of firms, but rather it is an expression of our cultural heritage, of our educational system and of our group dynamics. As such, unlike other problems affecting collective bargaining, it requires not only a private (labor-management) solution but a supplementary public (government) one. Second, we are essentially in agreement that no single group should bear the entire burden of automation. Rather, we admit that we should all bear the burden by making sure that the benefits of the increased productivity allowed by automation are shared by all. Without such a philosophical basis, automation would mean that some would make spectacular gains, and others would shoulder the full burden. We do not want automation to divide the nation into the "haves" and the "have nots." Third, we share general unanimity that this is a time for daring innovation in social dynamics and social engineering and that, although the problem is great, we fortunately have within our capacity the power to deal with the issues within a system of free enterprise. Since old methods will not work, we must innovate and pioneer.

The increasing attention being given to automation at the bargaining table (and by the bargaining parties in the public arena) can thus be viewed as recognition of a great but not necessarily insurmountable challenge.

A CONCLUDING WORD

The mutual accommodations and adjustments to the hard issues of collective bargaining which the parties have displayed in regard to wages, employee benefits, and institutional issues is no less in evidence when one inspects the current status of the administrative issues in our labor relations system. Management has increasingly recognized the job-protection and working-condition problems of the industrial employee and has made important concessions in these areas. At the same time, however, there has been reciprocal recognition on the part of unions that the protection of the employee cannot be at the expense of the destruction of the business firm. The axiom that employees cannot receive any protection from a

---

[8] This is, of course, true only if the costs are incurred in any event. If they occur *only* if one automates, they reduce the saving and in some cases could make automation unprofitable.

business which has ceased to exist appears to have been fully appreciated by all but the extreme recalcitrants of the labor movement, and workable compromises have been possible with respect to the areas of seniority, discipline, and the various other dimensions discussed in this chapter no less than in the case of previous topics.

Clearly, there is considerable room for future progress, and on occasion the conflicts between the parties on the administrative issues can be very serious. Production standards and subcontracting remain two highly visible sticking points. And strikes do, of course, at times result. There should be no illusion that the sensitive matters of collective bargaining are adjusted *without* painful struggle. Such an observation would not be realistic and would run contrary to the contemporary scene. Even standing alone, however, this chapter demonstrates rather irrefutably that managers and unionized employee representatives have increasingly recognized each other's position. It offers additional evidence of the growing maturity of the American labor relations system.

DISCUSSION QUESTIONS

1. It has been generally agreed that the increased use of the seniority concept in industrial relations has lessened the degree of mobility among workers. What can be said (a) for, and (b) against, such a consequence?
2. "The typical labor agreement's disciplinary procedures contain as many potential advantages for management as they do for unions and workers." Comment.
3. Jack Barbash has commented that "management's perception of technological change is producing an offensive strategy; the union's perception is in general producing a defensive strategy." Confining your opinion to automated changes, do you agree?
4. The several devices noted in the last section of this chapter constitute the major existing avenues for minimizing employee resistance to automation. Can you suggest other measures which might be utilized in an attempt to realize this goal?

SELECTED REFERENCES

Kennedy, Thomas, *Automation Funds and Displaced Workers*. Boston: Graduate School of Business Administration, Harvard University, 1962.

Phelps, Orme W., *Discipline and Discharge in the Unionized Firm*. Berkeley: University of California Press, 1959.

Simler, Norman J., "The Economics of Featherbedding," *Industrial and Labor Relations Review,* October 1962.

Slichter, Sumner H., James J. Healy, and E. Robert Livernash, *The Impact of Collective Bargaining on Management*. Washington, D.C.: The Brookings Institution, 1960, pp. 104–371, 624–62.

Somers, Gerald G., Edward L. Cushman, and Nat Weinberg, eds., *Adjusting to Technological Change*. New York: Harper & Row, 1963.

U.S. Department of Labor, Bureau of Labor Statistics, *Methods of Adjusting to*

Automation and Technological Change. Washington, D.C.: Government Printing Office, 1964.

Weinstein, Paul A., ed., *Featherbedding and Technological Change.* Boston: D.C. Heath, 1965.

CASE NO. 9

SENIORITY: FILLING OF A JOB VACANCY

(The problem in this case was to determine whether or not the grievant, the senior employee, had ability relatively equal to that possessed by the junior service employee whom the company selected for the leadman job. As you read the case, you will note that the union charged discrimination on the basis of favoritism and union membership. In addition, the grievant was black and the employee selected for the job was white.

The locale of the case was a community located in a Southern state and the union involved was one which has been frequently cited for racial discrimination.

Although there were probably some undercurrents of serious tension attached to the case, the hearing was very orderly and the parties conducted themselves with dignity, showing due respect to the arbitrator. After the decision was handed down, the arbitrator learned that the company fully and promptly complied in good faith with this decision.)

GRIEVANCE AND CONTRACT PROVISIONS

This dispute involves the filling of a job vacancy. G, senior to F, who was selected to fill the job in question, filed a grievance, dated June 19, 1968, which states:

> I have seniority on the man that filled Vacancy. Know how to operate Walkie-Talkie radio. Am qualified to perform the work in this department. Have worked in this department since the time it was first set up.

As a remedy, the grievant requests that he be placed in the job which has been filled by the junior service employee.

Relative to the dispute is the following provision of the labor agreement:

SECTION 17(B) (In pertinent part)
In all cases of promotions...or..., when vacancies occur...preference shall be given employees with the greatest length of continuous service,

subject to their relatively equal ability to perform the work in question. In determining an employee's ability, the past performance in regard to quality and accuracy of work done by such employee shall be considered....

THE BACKGROUND

The job in question in this dispute is the one styled "leadman" in the Material Handling Department.* A vacancy in this job was created when D, who held the job, retired from the company. It was filled with F on June 17, 1968. D had twenty-six (26) years of service with the company before he retired, the last three (3) years of his service being in the leadman's job. For purposes of this case, the grievant's seniority dates from January 25, 1951, and that of F dated from December 19, 1960.

Within the Material Handling Department, there are five (5) employees assigned in addition to the leadman. This group of five employees includes three tow motor, or fork lift operators; one tractor operator; and one employee who operates a mobile crane. Fundamentally, the leadman instructs the employees under him as to the movement of material. Normally, the production departments call the storeroom for material, and the employee receiving the order in the storeroom relays the information to the base station. The base station operator by radio contacts the leadman who assigns employees in his crew to pick up and deliver the material to the production departments. When material is received by the company from suppliers, the storeroom contacts the base station which in turn relays the information to the leadman. The leadman then directs members of his crew to pick up the material for delivery to the proper storage area of the plant.

Communication between the leadman and his crew is either through radio or by personal contact. Also, the leadman performs some record-keeping duties involving material delivered or received by the use of his crew.

D related the essential duties of the leadman as follows:

> As a leadman, I had to keep a record of all material. I checked the material delivered, and handled the paper work in these deliveries. I gave instructions to my men and directed the men under me. My job as leadman required that I had to see to it that the material was delivered. It consisted mainly of knowing the material; where it was to be delivered and seeing that the material went to the proper department. I would tell my men by radio or personally the kind of material to be delivered, and where to take the material.

* Actually, the Material Handling Department technically falls within the Inspection Department. That is, it really is a section of the Inspection Department. However, during the hearing the parties referred to it as the Material Handling Department, and the arbitrator shall use this term in this opinion.

At the time that the vacancy was filled, G was assigned as a tow motor operator in the Material Handling Department, and had served in this capacity for many years. G testified that he worked for the company for about twenty (20) years with fourteen (14) of these years in the Material Handling Department. When the vacancy was filled, F was classified as a utility man and assigned to the so-called "utility gang." It has the responsibility for general plant housekeeping and maintenance, clean-up work, painting, repair work, and moving of equipment. O was the direct supervisor over F, and from time to time he assigned F as the leadman over the utility gang on a temporary basis. According to Company Exhibit No. 1, F served as a temporary leadman of the utility gang from October 26, 1964, to March 15, 1965; from April 18, 1966, to May 9, 1966; from June 14, 1966, to June 27, 1966; from April 17, 1967, to May 15, 1967; from May 22, 1967, to April 8, 1968.

About two weeks before D retired, F was assigned to the Material Handling Department. In this regard, D testified on direct examination:

> Prior to my retirement, F was transferred to my department. I trained him myself. He had to be trained in the location of material; the identification of material; the storage of material; and made acquainted with the foremen of the department with whom he had to deal. I trained F in the operation of the radio.

On cross-examination, D testified: "F was familiarized with the job rather than trained."

From time to time, when D was absent from his job as leadman because of vacation or sickness, the company did not fill his job on a temporary basis. B, a foreman with authority over the Material Handling Department, testified in this respect:

> When D was out for a vacation or sick, I replaced him. I doubled up. The men knew their job pretty good. They performed their jobs without a leadman. They got their orders from the Base Station. If there was a conflict between movements, which was the first or second to move, I would resolve it or T* did.

For some time, O directed F to drive his car into the plant area and park it so that both of them could get away as soon as possible after quitting time. O and F were in a car pool. Under company rules, the bringing of automobiles into the plant area is prohibited. A, assistant plant manager, stopped the practice when he learned about it. He testified:

> I put a stop to this when I heard about it. This was during the week F was promoted to leadman. This car thing may have been going on for several weeks or months before the promotion.

---

* T is a foreman over several departments, including the Material Handling Department.

O testified with regard to the car-parking incident:

> I ordered F to bring in his car because he worked for me. When I give an employee an order, I expect him to carry it out.

When the company placed F on the job, employees in the plant filed eighty-eight (88) grievances. Many of them were filed by employees with lesser seniority than F. In any event, all grievances except that of G were dropped.

The company was aware that D was to retire sometime before the vacancy actually was created. F was selected during a management meeting attended by the plant manager, the assistant plant manager, the personnel director, T, and B. A testified that

> other men were considered for the job, but I can't recall the names.

He also testified that

> we were looking for leadership qualities; effective communication; a good atmosphere to control the behavior of the employees; emotional stability; and our desire to select a man to achieve the goals of the job.

With reference to the management meeting in question, B testified:

> We considered the Grievant for the job, but he was not qualified in my opinion; he or any other employee in the Material Handling Department.

Apparently, F is not a member of the union while G is a union member. With respect to this situation, C, personnel director, declared that X is a so-called "right to work" law state, and the company cannot control whether or not employees join the union. He also declared that within the plant are thirty-six (36) leadmen, of whom nineteen (19) are union members, and seventeen (17) are not union members.

BASIC QUESTION

The basic question in this case is framed as follows: Under the circumstances of this case, did the company violate Section 17(B) of the labor agreement?

PARTIES' ARGUMENTS

In its answer to the grievance in question, the company stated:

> It is true the grievant holds some of the qualifications for the job, but we feel there are certain intangible qualifications for this semi-supervisory

position which the employee placed in the job possesses to a degree to make the grievant's ability not relatively equal. An example of these qualifications would be leadership skills.

It is the company's obligation to provide our employees with the best possible leadership, without which all our jobs would suffer.

It also argues that F worked as a leadman before, and demonstrated leadership qualities, and G has not made these qualities known to the company. The company stresses that they

are talking about a leadman and we must consider qualities other than the skills of the job. It is a leadman job in question.

Though the company argues that G is a good tow motor operator, it argues that there are requirements of the leadman's job which the grievant does not possess—

ability to lead others, motivate them, communicate effectively, and direct them efficiently.

It also refers to certain testimony of company supervisors which is calculated to cast doubt upon the fitness of the grievant to fill the leadman job.

With respect to the charge of favoritism, the company argues that the decision to promote F was made as a result of a group decision participated in by high management officials. Thus

we have established that O was not a party to the decision of promoting F.

It believes that the filing of eighty-eight (88) grievances was a "harassment" tactic used by the union, based upon the mistaken idea that the company showed favoritism to F because of his relationship to O, manifested by the car-parking incident. Also, the company argues that the decision to promote F was "misunderstood" by the union and/or employees, not only on the mistaken idea of favoritism, but because the company does not promote by seniority alone, but only when the senior employee has relatively equal ability in accordance with the contract.

In short, the company denies favoritism, and argues that

the evidence shows that the Grievant's qualifications are not relatively equal to those of F in terms of the requirements of the job.

On these grounds, the company requests that the grievance be denied.

In support of the grievant, the union argues that his claim should be granted because G had relatively equal ability to perform the job in question compared to F. It points out that F

never worked as a leadman in the Material Handling Department, did not know the material, the employees, or the foremen.

It argues also that the company has practiced

> favoritism because of the non-union status of employees, and that the Company is using the temporary assignment clause in the contract as a means of selecting and training employees more or less on the same basis as F.* The Company tells us they can assign any employee on a temporary basis without reference to seniority or union membership.

With reference to the comparison between G and F, the union argues further that

> we are weighing seniority of about 20 years as against 8 years and weighing experience and ability of a man who worked day to day in the Material Handling Department as against a man who worked in the Utility Gang performing janitorial work, painting, and digging duties.

It points out that 88 employees felt that the assignment of F was wrong, and that they expressed "their dissatisfaction the only way they could by filing grievances"; and "that every man dropped his grievance in favor of G."

On these grounds, the union requests that the grievance be granted.

ANALYSIS OF THE EVIDENCE

Charges of Discrimination and Favoritism

The union argues in part that the company filled the job in question on a discriminatory and favoritism basis. The company denies these charges, stating that they selected F for the job because the grievant's ability to fill the job in question was not relatively equal to that of F when it filled the job. Hence, his selection was proper under the labor agreement. After due consideration of the evidence, the arbitrator does not find the necessary proof that the company discriminated against G when the job was filled. It is probably true that there was more than a foreman-employee relationship between Foreman O and F, as manifested by the car-parking incident. Still, there is no adequate proof that the company selected F because of the relationship between the foreman and F. The available evidence demonstrates that F was selected as a result of a management meeting attended by the highest officers of the company. A, assistant plant manager, testified that employees other than F were considered during the meeting, though he could not recall the other names. Foreman B, who also

---

* Under Section 10(C) "the Company may, at any time, temporarily assign any employee or employees, to a class of work other than that on which he, she, or they are normally employed...."

attended the meeting, testified that the grievant was considered for the job, but he was not deemed qualified for the job. O denied that he recommended F for the position, though when he was asked by a company official whether or not F would make a good leadman, O replied in the affirmative. This was a natural response since O on several occasions selected F as the temporary leadman over the utility gang.

Also, the record does not demonstrate that the company bypassed the grievant and selected F because of the union membership issue. C, personnel director, declared that out of the thirty-six (36) employees assigned as leadmen in the company, nineteen (19) are union members and seventeen (17) are nonunion members. Also, as C declared, X has a so-called "right to work" law and the company has no control over the decisions of the employees to join or not to join the union.

In addition, the charge of discrimination levied by the union against the company is not proved by the fact that 88 employees filed grievances protesting the selection of F. Under the labor agreement, the company has the right to select employees to fill vacancies, and its decisions in this respect are not subject to a ratification process on the part of the bargaining unit. Apparently, the choice made by the company was not popular with the employees, but this feature of the case simply does not add up to the evidence needed to prove the charge of discrimination or favoritism. Frequently employers make decisions which are not popular with the employees, but this does not nullify or limit the employer's decision-making powers. As long as an employer's decision conforms with the labor agreement, it may make it regardless of the popularity of its action with employees.

In short, the evidence does not establish that the company made its decision to promote F and not G on a discriminatory or favoritism basis. The union speculates and believes that this is the case, but speculations, beliefs, or innuendos do not provide proper grounds for a decision in arbitration.

Analysis of Section 17(B)

In the last analysis, therefore, what this case amounts to is a determination of whether or not the company filled the vacancy properly under the pertinent language of Section 17(B) of the labor agreement. To make this determination, there must be an analysis of the language involved, and a careful examination of the evidence as it applies to the relative ability of F and G to fill the job in question.

As the clear language of Section 17(B) tells us, the parties did not agree to a so-called straight seniority system in the filling of job vacancies. This provision states that the employee with an edge in seniority will be given preference only when the abilities of the junior and senior employees are relatively equal.

By the same token, the senior employee is not required to offer superior qualifications as compared to the junior employee. His ability need only be comparatively equal to claim the job. To put it in other terms, under Section 17(B), the junior service employee may be placed on the job provided that his qualifications are relatively or comparatively better than the senior employee.

G, therefore, is not entitled to the job just because he had many more years of seniority as compared to F. For his grievance to have merit, the evidence must show that at the time the company filled the job his ability was comparatively or relatively equal to that of F.

In considering this evidence, the cutoff point is *at the time* the company filled the vacancy. In this light, the arbitrator considers as irrelevant the performance of F after he was selected for the job. If we believe the testimony of union witnesses, F made errors after he received the promotion. If we believe the company witnesses, he did an excellent job. One company supervisor, R, even declared that F did a better job than D who held the job for three years.

All of this evidence is not relevant to the construction of the promotion language. What is relevant is the evidence demonstrating comparative qualifications of the grievant and F when the job was filled. How F performed on the job after he received the promotion does not constitute evidence, one way or the other, as to the qualifications of the two employees when the company placed F in the job.

Thus, the grievance will be denied if the evidence demonstrates that, at the point of the promotion, the grievant's qualifications were not relatively or comparatively equal to F. It will be granted if the evidence demonstrates that the ability or qualifications of G were comparatively or relatively equal to those of F when the latter employee was selected to fill the job vacancy in question.

Analysis of Evidence Demonstrating Qualifications: Technical Knowledge

The job in issue is the leadman job in the Material Handling Department. At the core of the job is the direction and supervision of five employees in the movement of material. As D, the retired leadman, declared:

> It [the job] consisted mainly of knowing the material; where it was to be delivered and seeing that the material went to the proper department. I would tell my men by radio or personally the kind of material to be delivered, and where to deliver the material.

When the promotion was made, the evidence is incontrovertible that F had no knowledge of the technical requirements of the job. He never worked in the Material Handling Department either as a member of the crew or as a leadman. F's ignorance of the job skills is made clearly manifest by the fact that two weeks prior to D's retirement, F was placed in the department to receive instruction. Whether or not one terms this instruction period as a "training program" or a "familiarization" period, the fact is that F's assignment to the department for two weeks prior to D's retirement is evidence that F knew nothing about the technical requirements of the job. Without contradiction, D testified:

> Prior to my retirement, F was transferred to my department. I trained him myself. He had to be trained in the location of the material; the identification of the material; the storage of material; and made acquainted with the foremen of the department with whom he had to deal. I trained F in the operation of the radio.

Since F was never assigned to the department, it is, of course, crystal-clear that when he received the promotion he was comparatively ignorant of the skills of the job. The two weeks in question during which F was assigned to the department do not count in his favor because when he was so assigned the company in effect had made up its mind that F was to receive the job. If it had not, it would not have assigned F for instructional purposes in the first place. Thus, whatever knowledge of the technical requirements of the job he gained in the two week period has no weight for purposes of Section 17(B).

In contrast to F, the evidence demonstrates that the grievant had full knowledge of the technical requirements of the job in question. In this regard, D testified without contradiction:

> If G replaced me, he would need no training except in the use of the Base Station.

In other words, by virtue of G's long service in the department, he had complete knowledge of the kind of material to be moved; the identification of the material; the location of the material; the operation of the radio; and he was acquainted with the foremen of the departments with whom he had to deal.

There is no need to prolong this feature of the case. The evidence is incontrovertible that when the promotion was made the grievant not only had ability relatively equal to F in terms of the technical requirements of the job, but he had vastly superior qualifications in this respect within the meaning of Section 17(B).

Leadership Considerations

If the arbitrator understands the basic position of the company, it is probably prepared to concede that the ability of G involving the technical characteristics of the job was at least equal to that of F, but that the latter employee has an edge in terms of qualification because F frequently served as a leadman of the utility gang and G has never served as a leadman in any capacity within the plant. Therefore, the company would appear to argue that despite the deficiency of F in the technical knowledge of the job requirements, he was properly placed in the job instead of G because what is at stake is a leadman job. As the company argues:

> We are talking about a leadman and we must consider qualities other than the skills of the job. It is a leadman job in question.

In other words, F had demonstrated his leadership qualities before the promotion was made, and G had not. Therefore, whatever edge G may have had in the technical skills of the job is outweighed by the fact that F had demonstrated leadership qualities and G had not. This could be regarded as a convincing argument, and it surely was considered at great length by the arbitrator. In fact, for a time, the arbitrator considered denying the grievance on this basis, since it is customary in arbitration to sustain an employer's selection of employees to fill job vacancies unless there is a showing that the employer's decision is unreasonable under the facts of a case.*

Upon close examination of the evidence, however, the arbitrator is not persuaded by the company's argument herein considered. In the first place, the junior employee's leadership qualities were not demonstrated in the Material Handling Department. They were demonstrated in the utility gang operation, the function of which is completely different than the function of the Material Handling Department. In the second place, before F could demonstrate his leadership qualities in the Material Handling Department, he was required to learn the technical and skill requirements of the job, qualities already possessed by the grievant when the promotion was made.

Clearly, one test for the comparison of qualifications or ability among employees for a leadman's job within the meaning of Section 17(B) is consideration of evidence dealing with their technical knowledge of the job. The evidence is clear that as prerequisite for the proper execution of the duties of leadman in the Material Handling Department the employee so-assigned must know the material to be moved; the location of the material; the identification of the material; the operation of the radio; and must have familiarization with the foremen with whom he must deal. F had no such knowledge when he was selected for the position. Despite his previous leadman assignments, how could it be possible for him to carry out a leadership role in the Material Handling Department in the absence of such knowledge? How could he have effectively and intelligently given directions to the members of the crew in the absence of the knowledge involving the technical skills of the job? It would be as if a person with demonstrated

---

* For example, see the instant arbitrator's award in *Thiokol Chemical Corporation,* Huntsville, Alabama, and the *International Association of Machinists,* when the arbitrator sustained the employer's decision to bypass a senior employee in the filling of a job vacancy (68–2 Arb. 5810–5818, September 4, 1968).

leadership qualities but who knew nothing about the game were selected as a football coach.

In the third place, the company argument herein considered breaks down because the evidence does not show that G could not have filled the leadman's job effectively if he were given the opportunity. In addition, other than the grievant's knowledge of the technical skills of the job, there is evidence that demonstrates that he possesses some of the qualities needed for the execution of the job in its leadership aspect.

In an effort to cast doubt upon the grievant's capacity to fill the leadman's job, the company refers to certain portions of the testimony of supervisors R and B. R supervised the grievant in the period 1960–63. He testified that on

> occasions in giving him instructions, he had the tendency to want to discuss my instructions. I consider this as giving me conversation. He was at times resentful about my orders.

However, R testified that during this period of time, the tow motor operators were not radio dispatched. The supervisor declared that because of this circumstance

> anyone in the shop could stop the drivers without notifying the storeroom. It was a hectic period for drivers. There was a lot of pressure on them. So I tried to understand the circumstances. The other two drivers did not give me conversation about my orders.

R testified that the tow motor operators became radio dispatched in 1965. Hence, whatever difficulties the grievant had with R were attributable to the circumstances of the times. In any event, there is no evidence that the grievant was insubordinate to R, or to any other supervisor for that matter.

B testified that he supervised the grievant for three or four years, and declared

> he takes instructions every day pretty good, but could be irritated if given 2 or 3 jobs to do at any one time. He would complain to the Base Station that he was already doing one job.

On the other hand, B testified that

> we get minor complaints all the time. A lot of people complain. No one is perfect.

Thus, it would appear that the grievant's conduct was no different from other employees. And, of critical importance, B declared:

> I have known the Grievant for 20 years. He does a good job. There is no record of insubordination to me or to any other foreman.

Frankly, when viewed realistically and objectively, the testimony of the two supervisors does not add up to evidence which would disqualify the grievant from the leadman's job.

On the other hand, there is evidence which demonstrates that the grievant possesses some of the qualities needed for effective leadership within the Material Handling Department. *A,* plant manager, testified that

> we were looking for leadership qualities; effective communication; good atmosphere to control the behavior of the employees; establish stability; and desire to achieve the goals of the job.

Certainly, what with about seventeen years of service with the company, *and in the absence of any discipline whatsoever,* it would appear on this basis that the grievant possesses a great deal of emotional stability. It takes a lot of emotional stability for an employee to work for seventeen years with any employer and to achieve such a spotless record. Also, the evidence demonstrates that the grievant can communicate effectively. As part of his daily work, the grievant communicated with his leadman through the radio and by personal contact. Certainly, the leadman job requires frequent and effective communication. The grievant demonstrated this quality in his day to day work.

Of great importance, the evidence demonstrates that the grievant has had no difficulty in getting along with the members of his crew. Surely, to achieve the "goals of the job," and to provide a "good atmosphere to control the behavior of the employees," there must be a harmonious and respectful relationship between the leadman and the members of the crew. *Without contradiction, D* testified:

> During the last three years, I was over *G* and had no complaints about his attitude or his work. He had no trouble with any employee in my department.

He testified further that

> of the five men in my department *G, M,* and *Y* are Negroes, and *Z* and *X* are white. There was no resentment in my department either way because of race.*

In short, the incontrovertible evidence demonstrates that the crew members get along with *G,* respect him, and, therefore, they would be prepared to carry out his orders and instructions.

Thus, what the evidence discloses is a virtual absence of evidence which would disqualify the grievant from the leadman job, and

---

* *Z* testified that he filed a grievance for the job in question, but that he dropped it after *G* filed his grievance. He declared that he dropped it because "I felt he was more qualified because he had 20 years of service."

evidence which demonstrates that the grievant was capable of filling the job in terms of its leadership characteristics.

Previous Arbitration Cases

Before reaching his final decision, the arbitrator considered the previous arbitration cases between the company and the union. There were three such cases accepted in evidence in this proceeding. Each case was decided in favor of the company.

One of the cases was handled by Arbitrator H with the decision being made on September 10, 1968. He denied the grievance, but the issue in that case is not similar to the instant dispute. In the H case, the issue was whether or not under the labor agreement a vacancy existed. H held that no vacancy existed and denied the grievance. In the instant case, a vacancy existed, and, hence, the issue is quite different than the one presented to H.

A second case was decided by Arbitrator I on July 10, 1967. In that case, a vacancy existed for a leadman job over welders. The company promoted the junior service employee over the senior employee, and the selection of the company was upheld by I. However, there are important distinguishing characteristics between the I case and the one presented to the instant arbitrator. In the I case, both employees were skilled welders. In the instant case, F was totally unfamiliar with the technical skills involved in the job in contention. Also, and of critical importance, in the I case the grievant, S, had the opportunity to fill a leadman job and a subforeman position. I held that the evidence demonstrated that he failed to execute these jobs properly. While denying S's grievance I stated:

> So the issue here is: Does the grievant have the same relative ability to be a Leadman as L, the employee management picked? If he does, seniority should prevail and S should get the job. First of all, both S and L are, from the record, technically qualified as excellent welders and on this ground alone S, because of his greater seniority, should prevail.... Testimony of two of the grievant's supervisors shows that he was passed over because of his inability to communicate, his lack of leadership and his failure to handle men. The assistant plant manager testified without contradiction that when the grievant acted as a Leadman ten years ago he lost control of his men and had to be removed.

In contrast, in the instant case G has had no opportunity to serve as a leadman, and there is evidence that if given the opportunity he could fill the job effectively. Certainly, if there were evidence that the grievant had served in a leadman's job, or some other leadership role, and failed to execute the leadership function effectively, the arbitrator would not hesitate to deny the grievance. Or even if there were substantial evidence that the grievant could not fill the leadership role effectively, the grievance would be denied. The only adverse evidence offered in this respect was the statements of R and B, but, as stated above, their testimony in this respect would be a very weak reed upon which to deny the grievance.

The third case was decided by Arbitrator K on January 21, 1967. In that case, the issue involved the filling of a *temporary* vacancy in the welder leadman job. In the instant case, what is involved is the filling of a permanent vacancy. Also, in the K case the junior and the senior employees were both skilled welders. In the instant case, the grievant had full knowledge of the skills of the job in question, and the junior service employee was totally unfamiliar with the technical skill requirements.

Thus, the three previous arbitration cases do not serve as precedent for the instant case. Those cases are clearly distinguishable in terms of facts and issues from the instant case.

CONCLUSIONS

On the basis of the entire record, the arbitrator is convinced that the company decision to bypass the grievant was unreasonable under the facts of the case. When viewed objectively and realistically, the evidence demonstrates that the grievant's ability to fill the job was relatively equal to that of F when the position was filled. This being the case, the grievant should have been selected for the job since a senior employee under Section 17(B) has preference when his ability to do a job is relatively equal to a junior employee.

In reaching this decision, the arbitrator carefully considered the common principle in arbitration that an employer's selection to fill a job vacancy should be sustained unless the evidence discloses that an employer made a demonstrable error in the consideration of the facts. Indeed, the arbitrator has frequently denied grievances on this basis, as his published and unpublished decisions abundantly demonstrate. In the case at hand, however, the arbitrator is fully satisfied that the record demonstrates that the company decision was unreasonable under the facts. It failed to give sufficient consideration to the comparative abilities of the two employees in terms of the technical requirements of the job. It failed to recognize that F would be required to learn the technical skills of the job before he could demonstrate his leadership talent. Also, it failed to give sufficient consideration to evidence which demonstrates that the grievant possesses qualities required for the leadership feature of the job aside from his unquestioned competency in the technical skills of the job.

In short, after a most careful, dedicated, and serious consideration of the evidence, the arbitrator is fully satisfied that under the circumstances of this case, the company made a decision which is unreasonable under the facts when it bypassed the grievant and filled the job with the junior service employee.

QUESTIONS

1. Would you say that the arbitrator's reasoning and decision are consistent with his reasoning and decision in Case No. 8 (where the job in question was also that of leadman)?
2. Do you believe that the company discriminated against G on the grounds of race, favoritism, or his union membership? What did the arbitrator find on the issue of discrimination?
3. How did the arbitrator distinguish between the instant case and the three arbitration cases presented by the company as precedent? Since these three cases rather clearly did not parallel the instant case, how do you account for the company's action in calling them to the attention of the arbitrator?

CASES NO. 10 AND 11

DISCHARGE OF AN EMPLOYEE

(The following two cases involve the discharge of an employee. Such cases are obviously very important to all concerned, and are among the most difficult ones for an arbitrator to decide. The basic question in each is whether or not, in the light of the entire record, the discharge was for just cause.

In Case No. 10, the arbitrator ruled for the employee and reinstated him in his job with full back pay. The company involved operates a TV station, and it discharged the grievant—a union officer —because he refused to reveal the name of an employee who wrongfully removed a log sheet from the company's transmitter.

In Case No. 11, the arbitrator upheld the company's discharge of the grievant. The employee had engaged in a fight on company property.)

GRIEVANCE AND CONTRACT PROVISIONS

This dispute involves the discharge of S. In protest against his discharge, the union filed a letter with the company dated May 26, 1969, which in pertinent part states:

> The matter the Union wishes to grieve is the suspension and discharge of Mr. S....
> Since we both decided in our latest telephone conversation to set aside the two items the Union sought to arbitrate on Monday, June 9th and instead substitute the discharge of S on this date for arbitration, I assume

that we both agree that Section 3.02 (b) of the agreement between the Union and the Company has been complied with. This letter merely fulfills the desire to go on record as formally grieving on the Company's action in the discharge of Mr. S. . . .

I believe we both understand the reason for the discharge and, of course, we are not in agreement as to the validity of the reason. As we agreed during our last telephone conversation, the issue will be disposed of one way or another on June 9th by arbitration.

The arbitrator finds that the dispute is properly before him, the procedural requirements for arbitration spelled out in Section 3.02 having been complied with by the company and union.*

Relevant to the dispute are the following provisions of the labor agreement:

ARTICLE III

Section 3.03: Authorized representatives of the Union shall be allowed access at reasonable hours to the premises of the Employer where members of the Union are employed under this Agreement in order to inspect or investigate operations of the Employer including inspection of time sheets and schedules for compliance with the terms and conditions hereof. This provision is not to be construed so as to permit investigation of the Employer's financial or confidential records.

ARTICLE VIII

Section 8.04: The Employer shall have the right to discharge any Staff Employee for just cause. The dismissal, except for insubordination, drunkenness, or dishonesty, shall be preceded by two (2) weeks written notice thereof, stating the reason for such discharge, or two (2) weeks pay in lieu thereof. If the Union believes any discharge to be unjustified, the matter shall then be considered as a grievance and shall be handled as stated in Article III of this Agreement. . . .

ARTICLE XI

Section 11.01: The Union reserves the right to discipline its members for violations of its laws, rules, and agreements.

Section 11.02: The Employer will not discriminate against any Employee for anything said, written, or done in furtherance of the authorized and legal policies and aims of the Union. Nothing in this Article shall be construed to permit the Employee to neglect the duties to which he is assigned.

THE BACKGROUND

Before his discharge S was employed as a licensed engineer by the company. He worked in its studio located about ten miles from the

---

* As company counsel states: "On May 26, 1969, the Union wrote to the Company asking for a grievance meeting pertaining to the suspension of Mr. S. The parties stipulated at the hearing that there are no procedural issues and that the matter is properly before the arbitrator for disposition."

company's transmitter. For several months before his discharge, the grievant served as the chief steward of the union.

On May 11, 1969, *P*, chief engineer of the company, received a phone call at about 7 A.M. and was notified that no engineer was present at the transmitter to put the station on the air. He went to the transmitter, located near his home, and activated the transmitter. The union alleged that *P* violated the labor agreement when he performed this task.

As required by FCC regulations, the company maintains a log book describing the day-to-day activities of the station. It is kept at the transmitter. As part of his investigation of *P*'s alleged violation of the labor agreement, *S* instructed an engineer or engineers to make a copy or to take a picture of the log sheet for May 11. In this respect, the grievant testified:

> I asked some of the engineers who either worked at the transmitter, or who lived near there, to get a copy of the log sheet or to make a polaroid picture.

He testified that he made this request on either May 15 or May 16.

On Sunday, May 18, at about 7 P.M. the grievant received a phone call at his home informing him that the "information which he wanted" was at the studio. He went to the studio, and was handed a paper bag by an unnamed person.* *S* testified that when the bag was handed to him the person stated: "Here is the information which you want."

S testified that without examining its contents, he placed the bag in his locker. Sunday and Monday were the grievant's days off. He reported for work at 6:15 P.M. on Tuesday, May 20. At this time he opened the bag and discovered that the bag contained the original of the log sheet for May 11, 1969. *S* testified:

> I recognized at this time that the log sheet should be taken back to the transmitter as soon as it could be.

He requested *W*, an engineer who lives near the transmitter, to return the log sheet. *W* returned it at about 4:30 A.M. on Wednesday, May 21. Before this was done *S* had copies made of the log sheet on company copying equipment.

At about midnight on May 20, *P* had occasion to visit the transmitter. He was concerned with an overtime problem, and desired to check the signoff time of the station for May 11. While checking the log book, he discovered that the sheet for that date was missing. He

---

* As subsequent discussion demonstrates, the grievant was discharged because he refused to identify the person who gave him the paper bag which contained the log sheet of May 11.

asked *K*, the transmitter supervisor, about the missing sheet. *P* testified that *K* replied that he did not know it was missing. While *P* was at the transmitter, he overheard a phone conversation in which *K* was engaged. In this regard, *P* testified:

> *K* got a phone call from the studio and hearing his end of the conversation, I surmised that someone was coming to replace the missing document.

Thereupon, *P* remained in the vicinity of the transmitter from about 2:30 A.M. to 4:30 A.M. on Wednesday, May 21. At about 4:30 A.M. *W* drove up and entered the transmitter building. He stayed there for about 15–30 minutes and left. *P* then entered the building, inspected the log, and discovered that the missing log sheet had been returned.

When *W* reported for work on May 21, *P* interviewed him in his office. *H*, station manager, was present during the conversation. *P* accused *W* of having removed the log sheet in question. *W* denied that he had taken it, and stated that *S* had asked him to return the log sheet. Also *P* testified that *W* stated to him that

> "they asked me to take the log sheet, but I would not do it because I knew it would be illegal."

P testified that *W* did not identify who "they" are. Before *W* reported for the interview, *P* had his pay check prepared for him. That is, *P* believed on the basis of his observations of the previous night that *W* had removed the document, and his check was prepared in anticipation of *W*'s discharge. When *W* disclosed that it was *S* who asked him to return the log sheet, *P* did not suspend or discharge him. Company counsel states that no action was taken against *W* because of "his frankness and honesty."

After *W* left *P*'s office, *S* was summoned for an interview. *H* remained in the office. *P* told *S* that *W* had just informed him that *S* had given *W* the log sheet to return to the log book. *P* accused *S* of having removed the sheet. *S* denied that he had taken the document. *P* then asked him to identify the person who had given him the log sheet. *S* replied that he was not "at liberty" to name the person who had given him the log sheet.

Relative to his refusal to name the person, *S* testified:

> I could not name the person who gave me the log sheet because I am a Shop Steward of the Union. The Union by-laws forbid me to discredit a brother. I believed that if I had named him his job would be in jeopardy because *P* told me that the removal of the log sheet was a serious offense and there would be an FCC investigation, and that my own job was in jeopardy.

After S refused to name the person, P suspended the grievant. On this point P testified:

> I then told him [S] that he was suspended for an indefinite period of time if he refused to tell me who was guilty of taking the log.

S told P that under the labor agreement he could not be suspended. With regard to this feature of the case, P testified:

> S argued that I could not suspend him and he attempted to argue the case of whether the Labor Agreement provided for suspension. I refused to enter into an argument, and told him until I could investigate the matter further he was suspended.

After this interview ended, S contacted D, the business agent of the union. P and D held a meeting on May 22. In this meeting D

> urged [P] to either lift the suspension or discharge the man.

After the P-D meeting, the company discharged the grievant. On May 22, 1969, P sent a discharge letter to the grievant which states:

> You are hereby notified that your employment will be terminated June 7, 1969. The current suspension will be continued through that date.

P testified that the reason for the grievant's discharge was the same as the reason for his suspension. He testified:

> I discharged S because he refused to cooperate in the effort to discover who took the log.

Additional material relevant to the case may be outlined at this time. As stated, the company, being a TV station, is subject to the regulations of the FCC. Such regulations which are applicable to the dispute follow: (Company Exhibit No. 1)

> *73.669 General requirements relating to logs.*
> (a) The licensee or permittee of each television broadcast station shall maintain program, operating and maintenance logs as set forth in 73.670, 73.671, and 73.672....
> (b) The logs shall be kept in an orderly and legible manner, in suitable form, and in such detail that the data required for the particular class of station concerned is readily available....
> (c) No log or preprinted log or schedule which upon completion becomes a log or portion thereof shall be erased, obliterated, or willfully destroyed within the period of retention provided by the provisions of this part....
>
> *73.673 Retention of logs.*
> Logs of television broadcast stations shall be retained by the licensee or permittee for a period of 2 years: ...

73.674 Availability of logs and records.
The program, operating, and maintenance logs shall be made available upon request by an authorized representative of the Commission.

Being a licensed engineer, S successfully passed a test on FCC regulations. The grievant testified: "I am familiar with the FCC rules in question"; and further declared: "I am aware that FCC examiners come to the station without prior notice or warning."

During the time that the log sheet was missing, FCC investigators did not inspect the station's log. P testified:

> An FCC inspector did not come in to see the log. The station was not cited because of the removal. It did not come to the knowledge of the FCC so they could not cite us.

In February 1969, P discovered an item in *Broadcast Engineering*, a trade journal. After he read the item he sent it to the transmitter for posting with the following note on it:

DON'T LET THIS HAPPEN TO US.

The item was posted on the transmitter bulletin board and states:

> An AM licensee in the Washington, D.C. suburbs has been fined $10,000 and threatened with the loss of his license for numerous technical and non-technical rule violations; among other things, the operator on duty was two hours behind in his transmitter log, and was "catching it up" with false readings when the R.I. walked through the door....

On May 26, 1969, the grievant wrote the following letter to the K FCC field office which administers the activities of the TV station involved:

> Engineer in Charge
> FCC Field Office
>
> Dear Sir:
>
> I would like to know if the removal of the T.V. station transmitter log, and transmitter maintenance log, all or part from the transmitter site to the studio and back is a violation of any FCC rule or regulation? If so, please let me know what rule or regulation has been violated.

On June 4 the field officer replied to him as follows: (Union Exhibit No. 2)

> The moving of the logs from the transmitter to studio location and back is not a violation of any Rule.
>
> Sincerely,
> (Engineer in Charge)

BASIC QUESTION

The basic question in this case is framed as follows: Under the circumstances of this case did the company discharge S for just cause within the meaning of Section 8.04 of the labor agreement?

POSITION OF THE PARTIES

The position of the company is that the grievance should be denied, and the union position is that it should be granted. In support of their respective positions, counsel for company and counsel for union offer a series of arguments. Such arguments where necessary and appropriate will be presented in the subsequent portions of this opinion.

ANALYSIS OF THE EVIDENCE

Reason for Discharge

To set this dispute in its proper perspective, it is necessary to stress the reason why the company discharged the grievant. As P testified:

> S was discharged because he refused to cooperate in the effort to discover who took the log.

That is, he refused to tell P the name of the person who gave him the log sheet. This is the sole reason for his discharge. No other charge was made by the company against him.

In this light, it is pertinent to note the issues which are not involved in this case. S was not charged with the removal of the log sheet in question, nor that he directed that it be removed by some other person. Indeed, there is no evidence in the record that he committed either of these offenses. S's uncontradicted testimony was that he gave instructions that a copy or a picture be made of the document. Accordingly, the arbitrator rejects as without merit the company argument that S "himself was primarily responsible for the entire affair." He would have been responsible for the entire affair if he had taken the sheet, or instructed someone to remove the document. S is not charged with either of these offenses, and no evidence establishes that he did commit either of them.

Also the arbitrator rejects as without merit the company argument that S's "entire course of conduct was dishonest and he knew it."

Indeed, in the light of the arbitration precedents which are presented by the company, it would appear that the document was stolen by someone and that the company discharged the grievant because he refused to name the person who had stolen the document. In this connection the company cites:

Mailing Service, 13 LA 1360
Aurora Gasoline, 33 LA 497
Southern Greyhound Lines, 43 LA 113
Simoniz Co., 44 LA 658
Chesapeake & Potomac Telephone Co., 51 LA 457

The arbitrator read each of these cases, and finds that the arbitrators involved in these cases sustained the penalties of employees because they refused to tell the employers the name of a person who stole company property. Though the removal of the log sheet was not proper, it does not follow that the sheet was stolen. Even the person who removed the sheet had no intent to steal the document. It was removed so that a copy could be made, and after that was done the sheet was to be returned. By no stretch of the imagination could such conduct be branded as a theft. Therefore, the arbitration precedents argued by the company are not applicable to the case at hand. There is a vast difference between a situation wherein an employee refuses to name the person who has stolen company property as compared to the circumstances of this case.

In short, there is nothing in the record to establish that the grievant was dishonest in the sense that he committed a theft, aided in a theft, or blocked the company in an investigation of a theft. He simply refused to name the person who gave him the log sheet. However one may describe this conduct of the grievant—stubbornness, courage, foolishness or what—it does not add up to dishonesty. He shielded a person who certainly would have been discharged if he had identified him to the company.

It may be argued that the grievant acted foolishly and showed poor judgment. If he had asked the company for the information contained on the log sheet, it would have given such information to him. Indeed, under Section 3.03 of the labor agreement the company would have been obligated to provide the information to him. In this light, *S* testified:

> I did not ask the Company permission to copy it. I'm sure that the Company would have given me a copy, but I didn't believe that I had to ask the Company for permission. I did not believe that I did anything illegal or immoral.

Thus, it could be argued that *S* exercised poor judgment. However, the exercise of bad judgment does not add up to a theft, or the conspiracy to commit a theft, or that he blocked a company investigation of a theft. In short, he was not discharged for a display of bad judgment, or for conduct connected with the theft of company property. As the company states:

> The Company was thoroughly justified in disciplining him for his failure to cooperate with the Company in its attempt to ascertain the identity of the person or persons who had removed the log.

It must be reiterated that there is no evidence whatsoever that the grievant told someone to remove the original of the log. He issued instructions that a copy or picture be made of the log sheet in question. This is an important fact of this case. If the grievant had given instructions that the original be removed, the reason for his discharge would undoubtedly be different than the one which the company presents as the only basis for his discharge. The fact is that the evidence does not show that the grievant gave instructions that the original document be removed from the log book. Despite this feature of the case, the company still argues:

> The Grievant's instructions to someone else to get the log, his receiving and admittedly having it in his possession for over two full days and his arranging to have another person replace it in the middle of the night make the grievant an accessory before the fact, to the fact and after the fact.

As stated, the evidence does not show that S gave instructions to "someone else to get the log." Moreover, he was not even discharged for this reason. In addition, the grievant was not discharged for having the original of the log in his possession, or for instructing someone else to return it in the middle of the night. It would appear that the company after discharging the grievant for refusing to divulge the name of the person from whom he received the log sheet now seeks to broaden the charge against him. This is not proper, if indeed the company now seeks to broaden the basis for the grievant's discharge. It is a cardinal rule of the arbitration process that a discharge

> must stand or fall upon the reason given at the time of the discharge. (*West Virginia Pulp & Paper Co.,* 10 LA 117, 118.)

See also *Penn-Dixie Cement* (29 LA 457), wherein the arbitrator stated:

> The determination of reasonable cause must be made as of the time when the disciplinary action was taken.

Along the same lines, see *Borden's Farm Products,* 3 LA 607, 608; *Swift & Co.,* 12 LA 108; *United States Potash Co.,* 30 LA 1039.

As the evidence demonstrates in the instant case, the discharge of S was effected by the company because he refused to divulge the name of the person who gave him the log sheet. This was the only reason for his discharge as the record plainly shows. It was the sole reason, and the company's case must stand or fall on the basis of this reason. It would not be proper for the arbitrator to find that the discharge was for just cause on other grounds. In short, the fundamental issue involved in this proceeding is whether or not the company had just cause to discharge S because he refused to name the person from whom he received the log sheet. This is the central question involved, and stands as the heart of the dispute.

Seriousness of Removal of Log Sheet

Before dealing with the central issue, the arbitrator will affirm that the removal of the log sheet was a very serious offense. In this respect, he agrees fully with company counsel when he argues:

> At the outset it should be emphasized that removing the log from the transmitter was a serious offense. The admitted facts are that it had been taken from the transmitter by sometime during the day on Sunday, possibly earlier, and was not returned until 2:00 a.m. Wednesday morning. This meant that the page was missing from the transmitter for two full ordinary work days, Monday and Tuesday. During that period of time the licensee, the Company, was certainly not in compliance with the FCC regulation 73.669(b) which required that the log's information on the logs be "readily available." Had an FCC examiner turned up at the transmitter on Monday or Tuesday, the log would have been missing and the Company could not have made it available to the examiner, since the Company did not know where it was.

To minimize the importance of the removal of the log sheets union counsel argues:

> Undoubtedly the Company will argue that while it wasn't investigated by the F.C.C., it could have been; and it was possible that the Station could have gotten a citation from the F.C.C. While almost anything is "possible," the Union submits that such speculation is without merit and most surely should not be the basis for upholding a discharge.

The fact is that the log sheet is company property. It was removed without the knowledge of the company and without its permission. FCC regulations state that the log book "shall be made available upon request." The sheet was missing for at least two regular working days, during which time the company could have been checked by the FCC. In the event of such a check, the company would not have known where the missing log sheet was. Clearly, the offense of the removal of the sheet in such an unauthorized way cannot be condoned on the grounds that the company suffered no actual harm.

The exchange of letters between the grievant and the K Field Office of the FCC does not condone the removal of the sheet. What *S*'s letter does not disclose is that the removal was made without the approval of the company and without its knowledge. True, it was taken from the transmitter to the station, but the arbitrator is fully satisfied that the answer from the FCC would have been different had it been informed that the log sheet was removed without the authorization and the knowledge of the company. Undoubtedly the FCC answered as it did because it assumed that the removal was authorized and known to the company.

In short, regardless of the arbitrator's determination of the central question involved in this case, he wants it perfectly clear for all to understand that the removal of the log sheet was a grave and serious offense. Regardless of the reason for its removal, and despite the fact that the company suffered no harm, the person committing the act engaged in conduct which clearly warrants discharge. The arbitrator wants this perfectly clear so that his ultimate decision whatever it may be will not establish a precedent for the removal of a log sheet or the log book without the knowledge and the authorization of the company.

Having said this, however, the evidence does not show that *S* removed the log sheet, or that he instructed another person or persons to do this. The company did not discharge him for these reasons, and the evidence does not establish that he engaged in such conduct.

The Central Question

We now turn to the determination of the central question involved in this case: Was the company justified in discharging the grievant because he refused to divulge to it the name of the person from whom he received the log sheet?

If the evidence disclosed that *S* instructed the person to remove the log sheet, there would be grounds to sustain the discharge. However, the available evidence demonstrates that the grievant instructed the unnamed person to make a copy or take a picture of the document. Such person did not follow instructions and instead removed the original log sheet. The arbitrator does not believe that *S* should be discharged because of the failure of such person to follow his instruction.

However, this finding only serves to focus attention upon the grievant's refusal to name the person who failed to follow his instructions. To say the least, this is not an easy question to determine. If it were, this case would not be before the arbitrator for decision.

It is understandable why the company desires to learn the identity of the person who removed the original document. The seriousness of this offense has already been established in the previous portion of this proceeding. Undoubtedly, the company would have discharged him, as witness the company action in preparing the pay check for *W* when the company believed he was the one who had committed the offense. In his interview with *P, S,* of course, understood that the company would discharge the person should he divulge his identity. This was the dilemma in which *S* found himself. Either he named the person who would certainly be discharged by the company, or face discharge himself.*

If it were not for the fact that *S* is a union officer, and the document was removed in connection with union business,† *S*'s refusal to name the person could amount to an act of disloyalty to his employer and discharge could be an appropriate penalty. Arbitrators have frequently sustained the discharge of employees who engage in disloyal acts against their employers. Indeed, on February 17, 1969, the instant arbitrator sustained the discharge of an employee who committed a disloyal act against his employer in a case involving the *ST* company and Union *M*.‡ In short, the arbitrator is fully aware that an act of disloyalty against an employer is a grave employee offense and discharge is sustainable in arbitration.

It could be argued that the grievant was disloyal to the company. The person who removed the document committed a very serious offense. The company wanted to know the name of the person. *S* was aware of his identity, and refused to divulge his name to the company.

On the other hand, *S* was chief steward of the union when the circumstances of this case arose. The document was removed in connection with union business, though it was wrongfully removed *and removed against the instructions of the grievant.* This is the complicating feature of this case and one which the arbitrator reflected upon for a considerable length of time. After much soul-searching, the arbitrator does not believe that the company was justified in discharging *S* under these circumstances. Here we have a union officer who certainly would have caused the discharge of an employee if he had identified him to the company. Should he reveal the name, *S* would violate the obligations of his union office. The company failed to give due consideration to the predicament in which *S* found himself. It failed to understand that *S* as a union officer had an obligation to keep the person's name in confidence. The document, though wrongfully taken, and against the specific instructions of *S,* was nevertheless attained in connection with the investigation of an alleged violation by the company of the labor

---

* Actually, there is no practical difference between the company action in suspending *S* for an indefinite period of time and his discharge. In either case *S* would be in the same situation. He would remain on indefinite suspension until he named the person. This would amount to a discharge for all practical purposes.

† It is stressed that *S* did not instruct the person to take the original document.

‡ The circumstances of this case involved conduct of the employee which jeopardized the employer's ability to secure government contracts. The discharged employee informed a U.S. government agency of what he believed to be defective parts being sold to the government.

agreement. A grievance investigation properly falls within the scope of Section 11.02 which forbids the company to discriminate against an employee, and particularly a union officer, in "furtherance of the authorized and legal policies and aims of the Union."

The arbitrator, of course, understands that the policies of the union may not be furthered by the unauthorized removal of the log sheet. As the facts show, however, this offense was committed by a person other than S. The grievant did not remove the log sheet or give instructions that the original should be removed. Once it was removed, however, S would betray this employee and violate the obligations of his union office if he identified him to the company.

In short, the company failed to give due consideration to the circumstances in which S found himself. It failed to give consideration to the fact that S was a union officer. It was not as if S's refusal to divulge the name was for some flimsy or arbitrary reason. His refusal was not motivated by sheer stubbornness or for the sole purpose of defying the company. To the contrary, S, a union officer, had a moral obligation to keep the name in confidence. As a union officer he occupies a position of trust and integrity. Thus, if S divulged the name of the person who wrongfully removed the document, but in connection with union business, S would have committed a flagrant violation of the obligations of his union office. These are the considerations which the company failed to take into account, and therefore, the arbitrator is of the judgment that S's discharge was not for just cause.

QUESTIONS

1. What options were available to the company in handling the problem short of discharge?
2. What arguments did the company offer in support of its position which did not deal with the sole reason which it presented for the discharge?
3. What would you have done had you been in the shoes of the grievant?

GRIEVANCE AND CONTRACTUAL LANGUAGE

This second dispute involves discharge because of fighting on company property. A fight took place between employees B and N in the company's parking lot on July 6, 1967. Both employees were discharged for violating a plant rule against fighting. B filed Grievance No. 67–6, dated July 7, 1967, protesting the discharge. It states:

> I feel I was unjustly discharged as I was not fighting but merely protecting myself as he had made threats around the plant and was causing a lot of friction in our department. I told my foreman about this report and he did nothing so when he smarted off again to me I told him watch his mouth and leave me alone. He then waited for me

after work with a club and attacked me. I feel this was justified protection of myself and ask I be reinstated on my job and some other way of punishment would be acceptable to me, such as time off to be determined by the company and union or some other means of correction.

N elected to accept the discharge and is not a grievant in this proceeding.

Having failed to resolve the dispute in the grievance procedure, the parties have instituted this arbitration for its final and binding determination.

Relevant to the case are the following provisions of the labor agreement:

ARTICLE II

The right to manage the business and the plant of the Company and to direct the employees includes the right to hire, promote, transfer, suspend or discharge for proper cause, and the right to relieve employees from duty because of lack of work or for other legitimate reasons.

ARTICLE IV

Section 2. Grievances of a contractual nature, such as those involving plant safety, rules and regulations, those involving the employees of more than one classification, and etc., may be taken up first under Step 3 of this Procedure.

Section 4. GRIEVANCE ON DISCHARGE. Any employee who is discharged shall be notified in writing. If such employee desires to protest such discharge, he shall submit a written grievance to a member of the Shop Bargaining Committee within two (2) work days after he is notified of the discharge. The notice of discharge shall contain the specific reason for the action. A copy of the notice shall be given to the Chairman of the Shop Bargaining Committee or his designated representative at the time it is given to the employee unless no such person is then working, in which case it shall be delivered at the start of the first shift thereafter when such person is available at work. Any grievances submitted under this Section shall start in Step 3 of the Grievance Procedure.

If it is determined that the employee has been unjustly dealt with, the Company agrees to pay the employee for all loss of earnings. He shall be returned to his job with all former rights and privileges restored unless it is found that some other disciplinary measure rather than discharge was in order.

THE BACKGROUND

The circumstances of this case took place on July 6, 1967, in the company's *G* Street plant. *B,* hired by the company on January 7, 1965, and *N* were employed as fork lift truck operators during the day shift on July 6. At about 12:30 P.M. an argument took place between the two employees regarding the placement of a skid of material. *N* was

COLLECTIVE BARGAINING

helping two quality control employees when *B* arrived on the scene. He requested *N* to place some skids of material at a certain place. *N* replied by stating that if *B* wanted to locate them in the place designated by *B* that he (*B*) could put them there himself.

On July 7, *E*, director of industrial relations, conducted an investigation of the circumstances of this case. As part of the inquiry, he sought to determine the circumstances of the argument between *N* and *B* concerning the placement of the skids. In this investigation, he interviewed several employees, including the participants in the fight. During the interview *M*, chairman of the Union Bargaining Committee, was present. *M* was also present at the arbitration hearing, though he did not testify. After each employee was questioned by *E*, the results of the interviews were reduced to writing and the content of the document was read back to the employee being interviewed to assure accuracy. In each case, the person who made the statement to *E* responded that the written statement was correct.

The statement which *N* made to *E* was accepted as evidence as Company Exhibit No. 4. This statement was not signed by *N*, and the employee did not appear at the arbitration hearing. Consequently, the union vigorously objected to the introduction of the aforecited company exhibit on the grounds that *N* did not sign the statement and that he was not present at the arbitration to identify the document. However, *M* was present at the arbitration hearing, read the contents of the document during the arbitration hearing, and did not take the witness stand to dispute the accuracy of the exhibit. Consequently, the arbitrator finds that Joint Exhibit No. 4 accurately relates the information which *N* told *E* on July 6. It is reasonable to believe that it did, since *M* did not take the witness stand to dispute its accuracy. It is emphasized that *M* was present when *N* was being interviewed by *E* and was present at the arbitration at which time he read the statement before it was accepted as evidence in this proceeding.

In Joint Exhibit No. 4, the *N* statement, we find the following:

> I was helping some Q.C. girls unload some skids and *B* came up and told me to put the skids there, pointing to a location. I told him "———on you, put them there yourself." He then told me, "If I meet you outside tonight you won't be here tomorrow because I'm going to put you in the hospital."

When *B* testified at the arbitration hearing, he admitted that an argument took place between *N* and himself relating to the placement of the skids. He declared that the exchange of words lasted about two minutes. With respect to this incident, *B* testified that

> I do not recall what I said to *N* during this exchange of words about the skids. I was very disturbed. I could have said "I'm going to put you in the hospital."

As stated, *E* interviewed *B* during the investigation. Relating to this interview, *B* testified in the arbitration as follows:

> I recall that the Director of Industrial Relations questioned me and read my statement back to me. I said in the statement "he [*N*] better be long gone after 3:30 P.M." I was pretty much overheated during the exchange of words about the skids.

After this argument between *N* and *B*, they saw each other at least once more in the plant. *B* testified that "I saw him again in the plant, but no more words were exchanged."

In *N*'s statement to *E*, we find the following:

> The second time he [*B*] saw me he said; "Remember what I said."

The day shift ended at 3:30 P.M. Either shortly before or after this time, *N* obtained a slat of wood 3 feet long, 1 inch thick, and tapered from 1 to 4 inches. *B* testified that while he was in the clock-out line, an employee, *W*, told him: "*N* is waiting for you. He has a club."

The fight between *N* and *B* took place in the company's parking lot in the vicinity of *N*'s car. It took place at this location shortly after the employees clocked out. Both *B* and *N* had their automobiles parked in the lot. The arrangement of the cars in the lot was such that *B*'s car was closer to the plant building than that of *N*. *N*'s car was in the row back of the one which contained *B*'s automobile. Separating the rows of cars is a driveway which is about 10 feet in width. In short, to get to *N*'s car, *B* passed his own and also had to cross the driveway.

When *B* left the plant, and arrived in the parking lot, he saw *N* standing at his car. As *B* testified:

> The parking lot is a few feet away from the building. When I got to the lot, I saw *N*—he was standing at his car. His car was parked directly behind my car.

B proceeded to *N*'s car, and at this point there was first an exchange of words between the two employees. After this, the fight took place, the circumstances of which are considered in a subsequent portion of this opinion. *D*, a bargaining unit employee, was a witness to the fight, and he testified at the arbitration hearing.

On July 7, 1967, the day following the fight, *E* conducted the investigation as described above, and on this basis the company discharged the grievant. He was given his discharge notice which stated as follows:

> Violation of Company Rules Group III, Rule #7, Fighting on Company Property. This violation calls for immediate dismissal. You are dismissed as of 3:30 P.M. Friday, July 7, 1967.

BASIC QUESTION

The basic question involved in this case is framed as follows: Was *B* discharged for proper cause under the circumstances of this case?

PARTIES' ARGUMENTS

It is the position of the company that the grievant was discharged for proper cause. To support this position, the company argues that

> fighting on company property is a serious offense which fully justifies application of the discharge penalty. Arbitrators have long recognized that employees who lack self-control to handle their affairs without resorting to physical violence are a menace not only to their own safety and well-being but also to that of their fellow workers.

Relating to the union's chief line of defense of the grievant, company counsel avers:

> The Union's principal contention appears to be that *B* was not the aggressor in the fight, but acted only in self defense. We assert that the evidence conclusively demonstrates that is not the fact. *B* implied that *N* had provoked him by his comments in the plant prior to the time they completed work on July 6. Even assuming that *N* was responsible for the argument and assuming further that his act of arming himself with a stick was intended to provoke *B* rather than dissuade him from an attack, *B* cannot be held blameless. Provocation alone does not constitute justifiable self-defense. One claiming self defense is limited to the use of the force required to repel his attacker. Moreover, he must seize upon the first opportunity to terminate the attack.

On these grounds, the company requests that the grievance be denied.

On behalf of the grievant, the union raises a series of arguments:

1. No Company personnel actually saw any part of the altercation between the two employees *B* and *N*. The Company learned of the incident from some employees the next day.
2. *D*, the Company's only witness to the altercation, was somewhat confused at the start of his testimony in being able to relate the incident in the order of the way the events occurred. However, after he finally related the chain of events it became obvious that the altercation actually got under way when *N* put the club to his shoulder and prepared to wield it upon *B*. Mr. *D* in his testimony indicated that each time *B* and *N* made any kind of body contact it appeared

that *B* was merely holding *N* in order to protect himself. Even in the last action when *B* finally did put his knee into *N*'s stomach he walked away to his car after throwing the club away. If *B* had been the aggressor or had he wanted to continue the fight he would have waited for *N* to get up once again.
3. Mr. *N* went to an out of the way area and secured a club prior to leaving the plant. It was also pointed out by both *D* and *B* that *N* was standing at his car waiting for *B* to arrive at his car which was parked directly in front of *N*'s. It further was pointed out that *N* had time and enough room to have gotten in his car and at least been headed out of the parking lot before *B* got out to his car.
4. The Union realizes that the Company can't allow employees to engage in fighting on company property. However, it must also be recognized that on some occasions both parties engaged in an altercation can't be equally to blame and as a result both receive the same discipline. In the case of *B* the Union feels that he was merely protecting himself from bodily harm and was not an equally aggressive participant in the dispute. The Union further points out that under Article IV, Section 4, the arbitrator is given the power to impose a lesser penalty if he feels warranted.

On these grounds, the union requests that the grievance be granted.

ANALYSIS OF THE EVIDENCE

Fighting on Company Property

That a company may discharge employees for fighting on company property has been underscored by countless arbitration decisions. Citation of precedents is not necessary since employers, unions, employees, and arbitrators understand that fighting between employees on company property is not consistent with the operation of an orderly plant. Indeed, fighting between employees on company property is among the most serious offenses that can be committed in our system of labor relations. There is no need to belabor this point. A plant is for work where the productive processes may be carried out in an orderly way for the benefit of all concerned. It is not a place to test courage, manhood, and the like, by resorting to violence. It is not a place where bad blood or friction between employees is to be resolved by fighting.

Reflecting this principle of labor relations, the company had posted for many years a rule against fighting. Such a proscription against fighting is incorporated in Group III, Paragraph 7 of the company rules, in a clearcut reference to

Fighting or deliberately injuring another employee on company property.

Though the company rules were not negotiated between the company and the union, no one can seriously contend that such a rule may not unilaterally be established by an employer. It is a most reasonable rule calculated to preserve peace and order in the plant. Such a rule need not be negotiated. Indeed, a company would be derelict in its responsibilities if it did not establish and enforce such a rule. It is designed not only to promote the interests of the employer, but also serves the best interests of the employees.

Though an anti-fighting rule may be established unilaterally by any employer, it is worthwhile to note that by implication the union has conceded that the company may establish and enforce reasonable rules. Note that in the grievance procedure, the parties agreed that

> grievances of a contractual nature, such as those involving plant safety, *rules and regulations* ... may be taken up first under Step 3 of this Procedure (emphasis added).

Thus, it is clear that the parties contemplated that the company may unilaterally establish reasonable rules to govern employee conduct. The arbitrator does not know of a more reasonable rule than one which prohibits fighting on company property.

What remains, therefore, in this proceeding is not further discussion of the company's right to establish and enforce a rule against fighting, but whether or not it enforced it in the instant case in a proper manner. Just because an employer has the right to establish such a rule does not mean that its enforcement is proper under all circumstances. Thus, to arrive at a sound decision in this case, a careful analysis of all the circumstances of this case must be made. The arbitrator understands the seriousness of this case to the grievant, the company, the union, and the plant's employees. Surely, to discharge his responsibilities, the arbitrator must give careful attention to the evidence as it relates to the unhappy events of July 6. The discharge cannot be sustained just because a fight took place. Under proper circumstances, arbitrators, including the instant arbitrator, have limited the right of an employer to discharge employees because of a fight on company property. Fighting or altercations between employees do not mean automatic endorsement of the discharge of employees in arbitration.*

The Argument between B and N

As the facts show, an argument took place between *B* and *N* on the afternoon of July 6 concerning the placement of the skids of material. This argument is quite relevant to the fight which took place

---

* See, for example, the instant arbitrator's decision in *American Machine & Foundry Co.* and *International Association of Machinists,* 62–1, *Labor Arbitration Awards,* pp. 3806–12.

in the parking lot. It is relevant because the evidence demonstrates that B threatened N with bodily harm after the close of the regular shift. In short, it was these threats which induced N to obtain the club which became a factor in the fight. Note the comparative weight and heights of the two protagonists. B weighs about 230 pounds and is 6′5″ tall and N weighs about 150 pounds and is 5′8″ tall. Faced with the threat of bodily harm, N secured the club. If he were not so threatened, N would have no reason to arm himself with a weapon. The arbitrator, of course, does not condone N when he obtained the club. However, for purposes of this case, the important fact is that in essence it was the threat of bodily harm by B which placed this club in the hands of N. If N was wrong in securing the weapon, it is still true that B's threat to him induced N to secure it.

That the grievant threatened N with bodily harm is substantiated by the evidence. N did use ugly and colorful language when B requested that N move the skids to a particular location. Though the arbitrator understands that N's reply irritated and provoked B, the fact is that this lack of dignity of N's language does not condone a threat of bodily harm. What is important is that after N replied in this manner to the request by B the grievant did use coercive language which added up to threat of violence to the person of N.

Note the testimony of B in this connection. He testified that he told N "he [N] better be long gone after 3:30 P.M."

When asked what he meant by this statement, B declared in the arbitration that

> I can't say what I meant by it [the "long-gone" statement]. It might have been an indirect threat. I think that it was a warning.

Also, it is important to note that B *did not deny* that he told N

> "if I meet you outside tonight you won't be here tomorrow because I'm going to put you in the hospital."

In the arbitration, B testified: "I could have said it."

Aside from the fact that N told E during the investigation that B threatened to put him in the hospital, and independent from the fact that B did not deny that he made such a coercive statement, it is important to note that during the argument the grievant was very angry and upset. B testified that during the heated exchange of words between N and himself about the skids, "I was very disturbed. I was pretty overheated."

Considering such a state of mind of the grievant, it is quite likely, though not absolutely positive, that B told N that

> "if I meet you outside tonight you won't be here tomorrow because I'm going to put you in the hospital."

However, even if we discount the threat as not being 100 percent proved, there is the admission by the grievant that N "had better be long gone after 3:30 P.M." B admitted that he made this statement, and even the grievant admits that such words at least constituted an "indirect threat—a warning."

In short, a reasonable and realistic analysis of the evidence relating to the argument between the two employees leads to the conclusion that B threatened bodily harm to N. This finding squares with the evidence. If N was wrong in obtaining the weapon, B was equally at fault when he used threatening and coercive language which induced N to obtain the club. Surely, in the analysis of the anatomy of the fight, an important factor is the threats which the grievant used to induce N to get the club in the first place.

Failure to Avoid Fight

B testified that while he was in the clock-out line an employee told him that "N is waiting for you—he has a club."

Despite being informed of this, the grievant entered the parking lot area. If he wanted to avoid a confrontation with N, it is only reasonable that he should not have gone to the parking lot area. He could have told someone in management that he was informed that N was waiting for him with a club. Certainly, if the company was so informed, it would have taken appropriate action to assure the safe conduct of the grievant to his car, and the disarming of N. He did not so inform management at this point which would have assured that there would not have been a fight. Instead, B, with knowledge that N had a club, proceeded to the parking lot. By such action, it appears that B was eager for a confrontation, verbal or physical, with N.

Even when B entered the parking lot, he could have taken proper action to prevent a fight from taking place. Note the testimony of B relating to his entrance to the parking lot:

> When I got to the lot, I saw N. He was standing at his car. Just before I got to my car, he stepped out behind an open door of his car. I saw him while he was stepping out from behind the door and he held the club over his shoulder like a baseball bat.

In other words, when B stepped into the parking lot, he saw N waiting for him with a club held in an apparent attack position. If he desired to avoid a confrontation with N, all the grievant had to do was to go back into the plant and alert the management. Here was an excellent opportunity to display conduct which would have avoided any fight whatsoever. Instead of doing this, the grievant continued to walk to N's car. It would, appear, therefore, that the grievant was eager to make good his threats to N which he made a few hours before 3:30 P.M.

An employee has the responsibility to avoid a fight by displaying proper conduct. If he does not do this, he becomes a direct party to the fight. B had two opportunities to avoid the fight but did not do so. As stated before, the plant is no place to demonstrate courage and elements of manhood. It is no adequate defense to the grievant to argue that if he retreated he would not display courage. There are many places and modes of conduct to display courage in this life. However, one of these places is not in a plant where the demonstration of this quality results in a fight on company property.

Surely, B knew of the danger which he himself helped create by his threats and coercive statements made to N in the plant. He was aware of this danger when he proceeded to the parking lot. By his own testimony, he saw N there armed with a club. Instead of retreating to the plant to avoid a fight, we find B walking to N's car. Would it not be most unreasonable to find that the grievant is guiltless in this situation? By his threats he induced N to get the club; and he did not take proper action to avoid the fight when he saw N standing in the parking lot armed with a club.

In this case, it would appear that the union's chief argument on behalf of the grievant is that of self-defense. Clearly, the best way possible that the grievant could have defended himself was to retreat into the plant when he saw N in the parking lot armed with a weapon. It is not that N rushed at the grievant with the club at the very instant that B entered the parking lot. Under these circumstances, the grievant, of course, could have taken proper action to defend himself. If the events occurred this way, B could have then used physical force to disarm N so as to prevent injury to his person.

However, the events did not develop in this way. N was waiting at his car with the club in his hand. As stated, the best defense for the grievant under these circumstances was to retreat into the plant. If he had done this, there would not have been a fight and this unhappy case would not have taken place. Instead of displaying this prudent conduct, we find the grievant walking into the parking lot and toward N.

In short, before the actual fight took place, we find that the grievant had two opportunities to avoid the fight. He made no use of these opportunities. If N was wrong to wait for the grievant armed with a club, B was equally at fault because he did not take advantage of the opportunities to avoid the confrontation. It would be most unrealistic, therefore, to find that the grievant was guiltless and the entire blame for the fight rested with N.

For sure, the arbitrator is well aware of the rule that the aggressor in a fight between employees bears the greatest burden of guilt. But, who is the aggressor in this proceeding? Is it N, who waited for the grievant armed with a club? Or is it the grievant, who approached the area with full knowledge of danger, and who by his threats induced N to get the club in the first place? Who is most at fault, the lion in the cage or the person who knowingly enters the cage and then is attacked by the lion? It would appear to this arbitrator that B was as much the aggressor as N because the grievant did not take prudent action to avoid the fight, and played a leading role in setting the stage of the fight by his threatening and coercive remarks.

The Fight

As the facts show, the grievant passed his own car, crossed the ten-feet-wide driveway, and approached N who was standing by his own automobile. B testified that he did not get into his car because the door was locked and he would be required to lean over to unlock the door. Apparently, he believed that if he did this, N would hit him with the club. On his behalf, B also testified that N was stepping toward him starting to cross the driveway separating the rows of cars.

It would have been very helpful to the grievant in this proceeding if he made some attempt to enter his car. This would have been overt evidence that he was not seeking a confrontation with the other employee. He did not do this, and justifies this failure on the grounds that if he did try he was fearful of being struck by the club held by N. It is emphasized that B himself testified categorically that he saw N armed with the weapon *"before I got to my car."* It was at this point that the grievant could have retreated so as to avoid the fight. As stated, his failure to stop and retreat at this point leads one to believe that he was willing and eager to confront the other employee. The fact is that he passed his own car and confronted N at the site of N's automobile. B did not go there at the invitation of N, and to say the least, he did not go there to bid him good-bye.

In any event, the two employees argued again at the site of N's car. D^* the employee who witnessed the fight, testified that "when I got to my car they were just arguing."

He also testified that N had the club over his shoulder, which corroborates the testimony of B, who declared: "During the course of the argument the board was still over his shoulder."

---

* In its brief, the union argues that no company personnel actually saw the fight. If by this argument the union means that an employer cannot discharge employees for fighting unless his representatives actually see the conflict, such an argument is rejected as without merit. In the instant case there was a fight. Incontrovertible evidence demonstrates that there was a heated argument between the two employees in the plant during which B threatened N with bodily harm. The fight flared up from this state of affairs, and in this case whether or not a company representative saw the actual fight is not important. Indeed, the arbitrator does not even rely very much on the testimony of D, a bargaining unit employee. Rather, the decision is based upon a realistic analysis of the facts of this case which are largely not subject to dispute.

For purposes of this case, it is not important to determine who struck the first blow or to ascertain what exactly and immediately stimulated the first blow. In his defense, B testified that

> N seemed to raise his arm as to swing. I put one hand on his hand and the other on the club and then N let go of the club and the club fell to the ground.

D testified that

> N had the club first. B took the club away—then the grievant grabbed N by the throat.

By this time, the battle was joined. B testified that N rushed him "like a bull" and for sure in N's statement he admits striking B with his fists. D also testified that he saw N strike B with his fists after the grievant made N drop his club. Indeed, at one point, D testified that there was "some" reason to believe that B was trying to defend himself from the club. This is undoubtedly true at this point in the conflict, but this does not erase the fact that it was threats of B which induced N to get the club in the first place and does not blot out the fact that B approached N knowing that he had a club.

The two employees then fought and wrestled for a time, and N again secured the club and hit B across the back of the legs. The fight apparently ended when B kicked or kneed N in the groin.

As stated, it is not vital to determine who struck the first blow, or who immediately perpetrated the first physical contact when the two employees were standing at N's car. The union argues that it was "self-defense" for the grievant to disarm N. In the course of this disarmament procedure, the first physical contact was made and the fight was on. What is important for purposes of this case is that N got the club because of the threats which the grievant made to him in the plant. What is of importance is that when the grievant saw N waiting for him with a club he did not take prudent action to avoid the fight. B knew that N had the weapon when he was still in the plant. He saw N waiting for him with the club when he entered the parking lot. He could have returned to the plant, even if we accept his testimony that he did not get into his car for fear that N would attack him with the club while he was leaning over to unlock the door.

CONCLUSIONS

To grant the instant grievance, it would be necessary to find that B was guiltless in the events of July 6. Such a finding would be entirely improper in the light of the conduct of the grievant at the time of the argument in the plant and his failure to take prudent action to avoid the fight. If *N*'s conduct helped bring about the fight, it is likewise true that *B* played an equally leading role in the conflict. To find the grievant guiltless would be a most incredible interpretation and application of the evidence. One would have to shut his eyes to the evidence to hold that the grievant did not play a leading role in the events which resulted in the fight between the two employees.

On the grievant's behalf, the union points out that under the labor agreement

> the Arbitrator is given power to impose a lesser penalty if he feels warranted.

For sure, the arbitrator did consider this course of action at length because he understands the seriousness of a discharge to any employee. However, the arbitrator cannot in good conscience lessen the penalty the company assessed against the grievant. His conduct on July 6 helped result in a fight between employees on company property. This is a most serious offense in our labor relations system. To reinstate the grievant to his job would indicate to the employees of the bargaining unit that fighting on company property would not lead to discharge. If discharge is not warranted in this case the arbitrator would encourage the employees of the bargaining unit to settle their differences by physical violence. Under these circumstances, the company could become a jungle, and not a plant for the efficient and orderly carrying out of production, and where employees can work without fear of physical harm. This arbitrator does not want to be a party to any such state of affairs.

QUESTIONS

1. Do you believe that the arbitrator should have reinstated the grievant on the grounds that he engaged in conduct to defend himself against attack from employee *N*?
2. Would you have sustained the discharge of the grievant had the fight taken place away from the company's property?
3. Supposing that employee *N* had not accepted the discharge, would you have reinstated him if his case were arbitrated before you?

CASE NO. 12

PRODUCTION STANDARDS

(This case involves the production standards or work loads of employees. The union proved that the work load of the concerned employees did increase during the relevant time period. However, the grievance was denied, the arbitrator holding that under the contractual provision involved the union had proven only 50 percent of its case.

Note that, as in some other cases presented in this volume, the arbitrator used past practice as part of his justification for his decision. By this time, it should be appreciated that past practice is an important standard for contractual construction. As in this case, it is used to give meaning to contractual language which is vague and ambiguous.)

GRIEVANCE AND CONTRACT PROVISIONS

This case involves the issue of whether or not there has been an increase of workload in the wool plant within the meaning of Section 110 of the labor agreement. Charging that there has been an increase in the work load in the wool plant under this provision, employees assigned therein filed a grievance, dated February 20, 1969. Such grievance, No. OH 160–69, signed by thirty-eight (38) employees, states:

> We the undersigned feel that there have been several increases in work loads even dating back to when we went off of bonus. Nothing has been said but it has went up little by little, day by day; we feel it is now time to increase our wages.

Relevant to the case are the following provisions of the labor agreement:

ARTICLE II

Section (5) The Union agrees that insofar as possible, it will cooperate with the Company and support its efforts to assure a fair day's work by all employees, that it will discourage absenteeism and any other practice which restricts production. The Union further agrees that it will support the Company in its efforts to maintain and improve machine speeds and efficiencies, and to eliminate waste in production, conserve materials and supplies, improve the quality of workmanship and prevent accidents.

ARTICLE X

Section (109) Section 1: Any grievance or dispute arising over the interpretation or application of the terms of this Agreement shall be determined through the following procedure, providing such grievance is submitted within seven (7) calendar days following the alleged act.

Section (110) Exception: A grievance may be entered in connection with a change in work load resulting from a major change rather than within the seven calendar days limitation.

Section (115) Note 1: The arbitrator shall limit his decision to an interpretation of this Agreement and shall have no authority to add to, change, modify or amend any of its provisions nor to adjust, increase or change wage rates.

THE BACKGROUND

Involved in this case is the production of rock wool in the wool plant of the company's facilities. To produce wool, a cupola is charged with various kinds of ingredients. The loading of a cupola is called a "charge." A charge consists of slag, coke, and other ingredients. Once in the cupola, the material is melted for a proper length of time. After the melting process is completed, wool is produced. The material is then loaded in either large or small bales and sent to the warehouse. Generally, the company operates three (3) cupolas in the wool plant, though at times only two are used in the production process.

Assigned to the wool plant are several classifications of employees. One is the "charger" who is responsible for the charging of the cupolas. Another is the cupola operator who is responsible for the melting process.

Before May 25, 1961, the employees in the wool plant were paid on the basis of a bonus system. At that time the parties elected to abandon the bonus system, and since that date the employees have been paid under a straight hourly rate system.

According to the testimony of H, union president, the employees were required by the 1960–61 contract to file a grievance dealing with a change in the workload resulting from a major change within sixty (60) days. He testified that starting with the contract negotiated on May 21, 1961,

> we changed this where we would have no time limit to enter a grievance on a major work load change.

Both parties provided testimony and documents dealing with the number of charges and the tons of wool produced in the wool plant. The analysis of such evidence as it pertains to the dispute will be treated in a subsequent portion of this opinion.

On April 12, 1969, the union requested a panel of arbitrators from the Federal Mediation and Conciliation Service. In this letter the union stated:

> International Union, and the representative of the Company, wish to request a panel of arbitrators. Nature of the grievance OH-160-69 concerning changing in work load in accordance to Article 10 Section 1 para 110.

BASIC QUESTIONS

The basic questions to be determined in this case are framed as follows:

1. Is the grievance arbitrable under the relevant provisions of the labor agreement?
2. Has there been a change in the work load resulting from a major change within the meaning of Section 110?

POSITION OF THE PARTIES

In the first place, the company position is that the grievance is not arbitrable under the labor agreement. To defend this position the company refers to Section 115 of the contract which forbids the arbitrator "to adjust, increase or change wage rates." In this connection the company also refers to the grievance which in part states:

We feel that it is now time to increase our wages.

In the light of the limitation on the authority of the arbitrator in the matter of wages, and in the light of the request of the employees covered by the grievance for an increase in wages, the company argues:

Examination of the Grievance, Joint Ex. 2, clearly states that what the grievants are seeking is a wage increase and, having failed to do so in the preceding steps of the grievance procedure, they are now attempting to circumvent the clear statement of Par. 115 by resorting to the subterfuge that all they seek is a determination by the Arbitrator of whether, under the Agreement, a change in work load has occurred and if so, how much of a change has occurred. For the Arbitrator to rule on this issue would be tantamount to decreeing that a change or amendment to the wage rates should occur.

Other than arbitrability, the company also contends that

the Union failed to show a "change of work load resulting from a major change" as that phrase is used in the Agreement.

On these grounds, the company contends that the grievance should be denied. If necessary and appropriate, additional arguments and comments by the company will be used in the subsequent portions of this opinion.

In contrast, the union contends that the grievance should be granted. With respect to the issue of arbitrability, the union contends that all it seeks in this proceeding is a determination by the arbitrator of whether or not the workload in the wool plant has been increased, and, if so, by what percentage. In this connection it refers to the testimony of H who declared:

The letter to the FMCS [Union Exhibit No. 4] specifies that the motive of the grievance is added work loads. It does not say anything about wages. We want you [the arbitrator] to determine the rate of the increase of the work load—not wages.

With respect to the merits of the grievance, the position of the union is that there has been an increase in the work load of the employees of the wool plant. In this regard, the union argues:

> The employees in the Wool Department do have an added work load. The added work load of some shift units has increased some fifty percent or more. The overall average has, according to the Company records, increased ten percent. Added workloads throughout the Plant is a continuing process and is recognized as such by the Company as proven by the settling of grievances in the Union's favor concerning added work loads. The continuous adding of new machinery and the modernization of machinery by the Engineering staff of the Company is the reason for added production and the increase in the work load.
>
> We hope and pray that the Arbitrator will find for a reasonable amount of percentage increase in the workload and a reasonable amount of retroactivity in reference to when that increase began.

On these grounds, the union requests that the grievance be granted. If necessary and appropriate, additional arguments and comments of the union will be used in the subsequent portions of this opinion.

ANALYSIS OF THE EVIDENCE

The Issue of Arbitrability

If the sole request of the union in this arbitration is an increase of wages, the arbitrator, of course, would dismiss the grievance as being nonarbitrable. Indeed, if this were the case, the decision would be terminated at this point without any further inquiry into the merits of the claim. This would be the case since under Section 115 of the labor agreement the arbitrator is strictly forbidden to "adjust, increase, or change wage rates."

It is true, of course, that when the employees filed their grievance they did state:

> We feel that it is now time to increase our wages.

However, the grievance also speaks in terms of "... several increases in work loads."

When the employees submitted their grievance and mentioned therein an increase in work loads and an increase in wages, they did not know for sure that it would go to arbitration. They filed the claim under Section 110 of the labor agreement, and they knew in the past that the company did increase wages under this provision of the labor agreement. Thus, the union submitted in evidence sixteen (16) grievances wherein the company increased wage rates of employees. (Union Exhibit No. 1) Almost all of these grievances were filed under the same language which is currently incorporated in Section 110. In short, grievances were previously filed under Section 110 for a wage increase, and the Company did adjust wage rates. Note that though the labor agreement forbids the arbitrator to deal with wages, the company, of course, may increase wage rates under circumstances involved in Section 110.

In other words, when the employees filed their grievance, they were merely doing what has always been done in the plant. They believed that their work loads have increased within the meaning of Section 110 and asked the company for a wage increase. They did not know when they filed their grievance that the grievance would necessarily go to arbitration. Hence, in the grievance they charge a work load increase under Section 110, and requested the company to increase their wages. The company, of course, has refused to adjust the wages and that is why we are in arbitration. But now the company argues that the grievance should be denied by the arbitrator without an inquiry into its merits because the grievance in part requests a wage increase.

It should be noted, however, that beyond wages the employees charge that their work loads have increased within the meaning of Section 110. To this extent the grievance is arbitrable because the labor agreement, though forbidding an arbitrator to change wage rates, does not forbid him to make a decision involving work load issues which arise under Section 110. Furthermore, the request by the union to the Federal Mediation and Conciliation Service for arbitration specifies that the arbitrator will deal with work loads. It does not specify wage rates. In addition, the union made it perfectly clear in the arbitration hearing that the arbitrator should deal strictly with the work load issue and not wages. This was made crystal-clear by the testimony of *H,* the union president.

Of course, the arbitrator is not so naïve as to believe that if the union receives a favorable award in this case on the issue of work loads it would not use such a decision as a basis to request a wage rate increase from the company. That is why the company argues:

> For the Arbitrator to rule on this issue would be tantamount to decreeing that a change or amendment to the wage rates should occur.

In other words, the company argument is that if the arbitrator finds that the employees in the wool plant experienced a work load increase within the meaning of Section 110, he would imply that he believes a wage increase should be given. Hence, there would be pressure on the company to increase the wage rates of the employees covered by the grievance. As stated, the union undoubtedly would use a favorable award on the issue of work loads as a tool to gain a wage increase from the company. Indeed, in Union Exhibit No. 3 the union states:

> We would like for the Arbitrator to rule what percentage of an increase

[work load] or if any. We also feel that if there is an increase, the Company should apply to our wages according to the increase.

This is a convincing company argument, but it should be noted that the arbitrator would have no jurisdiction of the case or over the parties after he determines the work load issue. Whatever happens after his decision, whatever it may be, would be up to the parties. They can make of it as they will. The arbitrator would perform no role whatsoever after he makes his decision in this case.

Beyond this, the arbitrator would place a restriction on his authority which the parties themselves did not incorporate in the arbitration clause if he held that work load issues arising under Section 110 are not arbitrable. Note that the parties forbid arbitration over wage rates. This proscription is clearly spelled out in Section 115. However, no such limitation is placed upon the arbitrator's authority under Section 110. If the parties had intended to remove this provision from the arbitration process, they would have done so by the adoption of appropriate language. That they did not would indicate that the work load issue under Section 110 is properly a subject for arbitration.

For these reasons, the arbitrator finds that the grievance is arbitrable as far as it deals with the work load issue under Section 110 of the labor agreement. On the other hand, it is not arbitrable insofar as it requests a wage increase.

Work Load Issue—Time Period Involved

Under Section 110 of the labor agreement, the union and/or employees may file a grievance

... in connection with a change in work load resulting from a major change....

Under Section 109 a grievance must be filed within seven (7) days following the alleged violation of the labor agreement.

However, with respect to work load issues, the parties made an exception to the seven-day time limitation. H testified that at one time grievances dealing with work loads had to be filed sixty (60) days after the alleged change in work loads took place. However, even this limitation was dropped in 1961, and Section 110 has no time limit incorporated in its terms.

Probably because Section 110 contains no time limits, the union presents evidence as far back as 1962 for purposes of this case. Union witness T, a veteran in the plant of 42 years of service, and who has served as a charger for 6 years, testified:

In 1962, there were 19 charges per cupola per shift. There was not much of a change in 1963. In 1964, the Company started to speed up, and now we are getting as high as 35 charges per shift.

Also *H* testified that

> we used to get 19 charges per shift, and that was considered high. Today we are getting as high as 35 charges per shift per cupola.

In addition, Union Exhibit No. 3 states:

> Our high charge used to be as high as 19 charges per unit per shift. The Company thought at that time [presumably 1962] this was a good run. Now the charges have gotten up to as high as 35.

Also Union Exhibit No. 3 refers to tons of rock wool produced. In this respect it states:

> The Company considered when a run was 680 to 700 bales per shift that it was really a good run. Now we are running as high as 1068 bales per shift.

Also it should be noted that the grievance itself speaks in terms of a work load increase "even dating back to when we went off bonus." This would be back to 1961.

In other words, if the arbitrator understands the union presentation, it desires the arbitrator to consider the work load issue starting in 1962. That is why it presents data dealing with the number of charges per cupola per shift and tonnage of wool produced starting with 1962.

This would be entirely improper, despite the fact that Section 110 contains no time limit for the filing of a grievance dealing with changes in work loads. For purposes of this case, the proper starting time is the date upon which the current labor agreement became effective. This date is May 25, 1968. To start before this date would ignore the fact that in the negotiations of the current labor agreement the union had every opportunity to raise the workload issue for the employees in the Wool Department for whatever purpose it desired. In other words, if the employees in the Wool Department believed prior to the negotiation of the current labor agreement that their work loads had increased to the extent of justifying special treatment for them, they should have alerted their union committee to their problem. Apparently they did not, and the wage rates for the classifications in question were set and agreed to in the light of the work loads which they were carrying when the labor agreement went into effect on May 25, 1968. In short, the existing rates for the classification were based upon the work load of May 25, 1968. The wage rates reflected a certain job content and a certain work load. For the arbitrator to deal with the period prior to the effective date of the instant labor agreement would in effect place the employees in a position wherein they might obtain from arbitration benefits which they did not seek in contract negotiations.

Apparently this is a very serious grievance as far as the employees in the wool plant are concerned. They sincerely believe that their work loads have increased sharply over the years. They believe themselves to be treated unfairly and inequitably. In the light of these considerations, the arbitrator frankly wonders why the issue of their work loads was not raised in the negotiations which resulted in the instant labor agreement. There is no testimony from union or company witnesses that the issue was even raised, let alone a special wage adjustment made for them because of their alleged complaint. Instead, the parties negotiated the current wage structure in the light of the job content and the work loads of the employees in the Wool Department existing at the time the current contract became effective. As T testified:

> While I was a Charger, we never got an increase in wages except the general wage rate increase. We never got a classification increase.

In this light, it would be a masterpiece of error on the arbitrator's part to start his inquiry of the work load issue before the date upon which the current labor agreement went into effect.

Let us be frank about what this case is all about. The union does not conceal its purpose. In Union Exhibit No. 3, it makes its motive for the case perfectly clear:

> We feel that the work load has increased from 40 per cent to 60 per cent [presumably from 1962 to the present]. We have not received any money for this increase at all. We feel that the Company is trying to gain something through an arbitrator that they could not get in negotiations of May 25, 1968. We would like for the Arbitrator to rule what percentage of an increase or if any. We also feel that if there is an increase, the Company should apply to our wages according to the increase.

In other words, the union would have the arbitrator deal with the work load issue for many years prior to the adoption of the current labor agreement so that he might pave the way for the union to make a wage request from the company. This would be absolutely improper, since the union had an opportunity to raise the issue during the negotiation of the current labor agreement. Instead of saying the "company is trying to gain something through an arbitration that they could not get in negotiations of May 25, 1968,; it would be accurate to say that for the time period prior to May 25, 1968, *the Union is trying to get something in arbitration which it did not get in negotiations.*

The arbitrator reaffirms his finding that work load issues under Section 110 are a proper subject for arbitration. However, in the light of the declared intention of the union to use arbitration as a vehicle to get a wage increase, and in the light of the fact that the union and/or employees in the wool plant did not request or gain special treatment in the negotiations which resulted in the current labor agreement on the basis of increasing work loads, it would be improper for the arbitrator to give any consideration to the work load issue except as it is a factor under the current labor agreement.

Work Load Data, May 25, 1968, to Date of Arbitration

On the basis of the foregoing considerations, the proper time period to deal with the employees' claim of an increased work load is from May 25, 1968, the effective date of the labor agreement, until July 14, 1969, the date of the arbitration. Technically, the arbitrator should not consider any evidence dealing with the time period after February 20, 1969, the date upon which the grievance was filed. Normally in arbitration, evidence dealing with events after the filing of a grievance is not considered. Indeed, upon occasion, arbitrators will not even accept in evidence events which occurred after the filing of the grievance which sparked the arbitration.

However, for this case the arbitrator will depart from the normal rule and consider work load data up to the date of the arbitration hearing. He shall do so because he was impressed with the union's statement that the filing of the grievance alerted the union to the collection of data which bears upon the issue, and some of this material postdates the filing of the grievance. In this respect H testified:

> The Grievance was filed and the Union Committee then got the information.

Also, he notes that both parties submitted into evidence data which reflects work loads in the wool plant after the grievance was filed.

Work Load Has Increased

The evidence shows that the number of charges and wool tonnage increased during the period of time under consideration. T kept a daily running account of the number of charges made during this period of time. His testimony did not cover every working day in the period, but the data which he collected does demonstrate an upward trend. Likewise, Company Exhibit No. 1 shows the same tendency. This document presents the number of charges per cupola per shift by month. It demonstrates that on the average the number of charges increased from about 22.5 to about 23.65. Also the amount of wool tonnage increased somewhat during this period of time. The union attempted to show the trend by demonstrating that the amount of tonnage increased in terms of certain tonnage standards which the company uses as a guidepost for the operation of the wool plant. There was considerable discussion of these standards during the arbitration hearing. However, the arbitrator does not believe it necessary to deal with this aspect of the case in depth since the company concedes that there was an increase in tonnage. Thus, B, plant manager, testified:

> With a given amount of charges, we are producing more wool.

Moreover, Company Exhibit No. 1 demonstrates that tonnage has increased from about 15 tons of wool per cupola per shift to about 15.30 on the average for the time period under consideration.

In short, the union has proved that from the date upon which the labor agreement became effective until the date of the arbitration hearing the employees in the wool plant make more charges per shift, and that the amount of wool production has also increased.

To this extent it follows that the work load of the employees has increased. As B testified:

> It takes more effort on the part of employees to make 30 charges than 20 charges. This is an added work load. The employee is doing more work.

It is a matter of common sense that when employees make more charges and produce more tonnage of work they are working harder, expending more effort, and are carrying a heavier work load.

Application of Section 110

To this extent the union has proved its case. It has demonstrated that the wool plant employees have experienced a heavier workload during the time period under consideration. However, before the arbitrator can find that there has been a "change in work load" within the meaning of Section 110 there must be an inquiry as to the causes of the increased workload. This inquiry is required because of the way the language reads in this provision of the labor agreement. Note that it states:

> A grievance may be entered in connection with a change in work load resulting *from a major change...* (emphasis supplied).

What this language tells us is that a grievance filed under Section 110 would have merit only if an increased work load resulted from a major change. It is not sufficient for the union only to show that the employees' work load has increased. The language is specific that the union must not only demonstrate a change in work load, but it must also show that such a condition resulted from a major change. In this respect, the language is clear and unambiguous. A *major change* must be the cause for the increase in work load.

What complicates the application of Section 110 is that the concept "major change" is not defined in the labor agreement. It does not tell us just what constitutes a major change. That is, it does not instruct us as to what must change for a grievance to have merit under Section 110.

Past Construction of Section 110

Since the labor agreement does not designate what must change for a grievance to have merit under Section 110, the arbitrator has no choice except to find as controlling the way in which Section 110 has been used in the past. As Union Exhibit No. 1 demonstrates, employees have received wage increases under Section 110. Thus, the company has agreed that under certain circumstances employees have experienced an increase in work load which has resulted from a major change. Inspection of these grievances incorporated in Union Exhibit No. 1 therefore is evidence of what has constituted a major change within the meaning of Section 110. The arbitrator has spent considerable time in analyzing the grievances incorporated in Union Exhibit No. 1, since the settlement of these grievances provides the key for the construction of the concept of "major change" found in Section 110.

In Union Exhibit No. 1 there are 16 grievances. They are comparatively recent grievances, having been filed in the last few years. In most of the grievances the union has contended that employees have experienced an increased work load which resulted from a major change within the meaning of Section 110 and, therefore, the employees deserved a wage increase. The company granted these grievances, and did increase the wages of the employees covered by them.

Now, what these grievances demonstrate is that in each case the "major change" involved a major change in equipment, technology, method of production, or new and additional duties performed by the grievant employees. There is no need here to detail each of these grievances since they are part of the record and were carefully examined by the arbitrator. The common denominator of the grievances demonstrates that a wage increase was granted because the increase in work load resulted from a major change of equipment, technology, or method, or there was a change in the sense that the company added to the employees new and important duties.

In March 1955, the parties received an arbitration award handed down by Arbitrator S (Union Exhibit No. 2). He ruled in favor of the union on the grounds that the employees involved experienced an increase in work load. However, what is significant for purposes of the instant case is that the basis for his ruling was that the evidence demonstrated that the increase in work load resulted from a *major change in process equipment*. At one point in his decision, Arbitrator S stated:

> On the basis of the available evidence, the Arbitrator is satisfied, beyond a reasonable doubt, that the "fair days work" has substantially, and not merely slightly, been increased for all employees in the Tile Department

...*as a result of a major change in the productive process, or process equipment* (emphasis supplied).

Causes for the Increased Work Load

Thus, on the basis of the settlement of the grievances incorporated in Union Exhibit No. 1, and in the light of the S decision, it is clear that what the parties mean by a "major change" for purposes of Section 110 is that a grievance filed dealing with an increase in work load has merit only if the increase in work load has resulted from a major change in equipment, method, technology, or the addition of new and important duties to employees. In the absence of evidence to the contrary, the arbitrator must hold as controlling such a construction of Section 110. This is the way the provision has been applied in the past, and the arbitrator must of necessity follow such precedent.

In short, the arbitrator will find that for purposes of Section 110 there has been an increase in work load in the wool plant under the circumstances of the instant case provided that the evidence demonstrates that such an increase in work load resulted from a major change in technology, equipment, method, or the addition of new and important duties to the employees. In this respect, the evidence plainly shows that whatever work load increase was experienced by the wool plant employees did not result from a major change in technology, method, equipment, or the addition of new and important duties to the employees.

Note the testimony of T on this point:

Q. From January, 1968, has there been any change in equipment or mechanical change in the operation?
A. No.

Likewise, company witness B testified that there has been no change in the technology of the cupolas.

Indeed, there is not a scrap of evidence in the testimony offered by the union witnesses that the increase in work load resulted from the factors which the company has used to grant grievances under Section 110.* In short, the increase in work load of the wool plant employees did not result from a major change in technology, methods, equipment, or the addition of new and important duties to employees. Rather, the increase resulted from other factors, as testified to without

---

* In the union post-hearing brief, it states that "the Company has made major changes in production by the installation of new and more efficient machinery." (Union Post-Hearing Brief, p. 2) This assertion is not supported by the testimony of either company or union witnesses. Possibly these changes, if made, were put into effect prior to the effective date of the current labor agreement. If so, they are not relevant to the case.

contradiction by the plant manager. He declared that the wool plant operates more efficiently resulting in the increase in the number of charges and wool tonnage because of

(1) a reduction of downtime;
(2) better procedures for the startup day;† and
(3) better maintenance.

In other words, these are factors which have resulted in the making of more charges, and which have resulted in more wool tonnage. Thus, the union has proved only 50 percent of its case for purposes of Section 110. It has proved that employees have experienced an increase in work load; but it has failed to show that such an increase in work load resulted from a major change in technology, method, equipment, or the addition of new and important duties to the employees.

CONCLUSIONS

The crucial language of Section 110 is that an increase in work load must result from a major change. The concept "major change," as applied and interpreted by the parties in the past, and as affirmed by Arbitrator S, is that a major change must involve technology, method, equipment, or the addition of important and new duties to employees. *These factors are not present in the instant case.* True, the employees have experienced an increase in work load. They do expend more effort and work harder. But before a grievance has merit for purposes of Section 110 the evidence must show that the increase in work load must result from a major change in technology, method, equipment, or the addition of new and important duties to the employees. What has happened during the time period under consideration is that the increase in work load is attributable to other factors. Consequently, the arbitrator of necessity must find that there has not been a "change in work load resulting from a major change" within the meaning of Section 110.

Having reached this conclusion, the arbitrator has applied Section 110 exactly as it has been applied in the past. There is no evidence that Section 110 grievances have been deemed meritorious when a work load increase has resulted from factors other than those which involve major changes in technology, method, equipment, or the addition of new and important duties to employees. Rather, the evidence is

† The startup day, the first day of the work week, usually results in less production than the other days of the week. Thus, T testified: "The first day of the week is the startup day. We used to get only 12–14 charges on the first day. Now we get 16–20 charges on the startup day."

clear that under Section 110 grievances have been granted when the increase in work load has resulted from one or more of these factors.

In essence, what the union requests the arbitrator to do is to shut his eyes to critical language contained in Section 110. It desires that he rule in favor of the union on the grounds that the employees have experienced an increase in work load. To be faithful to the obligations of his office he must apply the *entire* language of Section 110, and construe it as the parties have applied it in the past.

If the parties desire to change the language of Section 110 to the extent that a grievance under its terms would have merit when employees experience an increase in work load, regardless of the factors which result in such an increase, the proper forum to make such a change is the bargaining table. It cannot be changed in arbitration. For the arbitrator in this case to rule in favor of the union would destroy the integrity of Section 110 of the labor agreement.

QUESTIONS

1. To what extent did the arbitrator find the grievance to be arbitrable on its merits? Why did the company argue that the grievance was *not* arbitrable?
2. Construct a contractual provision which would have formed the basis for a favorable award for the union.
3. Do you believe that the arbitrator's basis for denial of the grievance was the correct one?
4. What was the arbitrator's reason for considering evidence only from May 25, 1968? Do you share his confidence that this was an appropriate course of action?

part four

Some Final Thoughts

Concluding Statement

The productive potential of the United States depends upon many factors, including the status of employer-employee relations. Our nation has been extremely fortunate in being endowed with a highly favorable natural environment for the encouragement of the productive process. Its virtually inexhaustible stores of natural resources, advantageous geographic location, and population growth constitute a sound basis for an expanding and dynamic economy. Despite these considerations, the fact remains that the fruitfulness of the productive process of our nation depends fundamentally upon the creativeness of the managerial function, the economic and political system in which business and labor operate, and the industry and the spirit of the labor force. Other nations which have not attained the level of industrial development of the United States can match to an extent our natural resources. Few people, however, equal the vigor and the creativeness of the American people in implementing the productive process. In the last analysis, the level of the standard of living of a nation depends not so much upon its stores of iron ore, coal, oil, and the like, as upon the motivation and the energy of its people, and the system of government and economics within which the productive process is accomplished.

A fundamental if implicit thesis of this volume has been that an important prerequisite for the increasing productivity of the American nation is the status of its employer-employee relations. Since we are a nation practicing free enterprise, what has thus far remained (despite a highly visible trend to increasing government interest in labor relations) an essentially private employer-employee relationship is by far the dominant characteristic of the industrial relations environment. The character of this relationship determines to an important extent our productive capabilities. A wholesome labor relations environment that encourages maximum efforts of labor and management will do much toward improving our standard of living. In contrast, the productive process will be obstructed to the extent that the employer-employee relationship is implemented in a hostile framework. From this it follows not only that the best interests of employers and employees are dependent upon the establishment of a harmonious industrial relations climate, but that the entire nation likewise has a stake in the accomplishment of this objective.

In retrospect the evidence is clear that collective bargaining relations in the United States have improved remarkably over the years. It is well to recall in this connection that widespread collective bargaining is a comparatively recent development in this country. The earliest unions date from 1800, and unionism can hardly be viewed as a new phenomenon, but even 40 years ago only a relatively few employers and employees were involved in the process, virtually none of the vital industries of the nation were characterized by collective bargaining, and unionism had not yet penetrated the major mass-production sectors. During the period of growth of collective bargaining, union-employer relations in these industries were far from satisfactory and not conducive to high levels of industrial productivity. Since the process was new and virtually untried, there was much distrust and suspicion on both sides of the bargaining table. Many employers questioned the methods and the ultimate objectives of labor unions and in general aggressively resisted the development of unions. In some cases unions moved too fast in their development and failed to take into consideration the legion of problems involved in establishing collective bargaining within new industries. On a number of occasions, labor-management relations deteriorated into prolonged and violent strikes resulting in loss of life, in physical injury, and in destruction of company property. It may be argued with some validity that these events probably were unavoidable because of the newness of the collective bargaining process. Such happenings might be regarded as the "growing pains" of a new and potentially important area. Notwithstanding these considerations, the fact remains that some of the history of the development of industrial relations

—particularly prior to the 1930s but even as late as World War II—is not pleasant to recall.

With the passage of time, labor relations handled under the collective bargaining process have improved enormously. As noted earlier, violence during strikes has virtually disappeared from the American industrial scene. To appreciate this, one has only to compare the bloody Memorial Day, 1937, Little Steel incident with the Ford Motor Company strike in the fall of 1967. In the steel industry strike ten lives were lost, scores of people suffered serious physical injury, and there was severe damage to property. In the automobile strike only token picket lines were manned by the union, and there was no violence and no damage to property. The latter strike was so "civilized," indeed, that some of the plants involved in it supplied power for the TV sets viewed by employees serving on "picket-line duty."

The virtual demise of the role of violence is, however, only one of many developments attesting to the greatly improved state of labor relations in recent years. The earliest pages of this volume indicated that there has been similar progress along almost every basic labor-management dimension, and it is hoped that by this point in the book the reader stands in fundamental agreement. The facts show not only that in an overwhelming number of instances the parties have been able to negotiate under a strike deadline without reaching a stalemate, but that with respect to unauthorized, or "wildcat," strikes the record is similarly impressive. Instead of resorting to industrial warfare as the means of adjusting and settling disputes arising over the interpretation and application of an existing contract, employers and unions settle these problems through the grievance and arbitration procedure, thereby lending considerable further stability to their relationships.

Running through the preceding pages are testimonials to other types of success—from a stress on considerably more informed bargaining sessions to the attainment of a far larger measure of contracts that constitute "good compromises," and from the almost complete disappearance of Conflict philosophies to the great growth of Accommodation (if not Cooperation) ones.

Indeed, under some management-union relationships there is now a genuine feeling of mutual trust and respect between the parties. Although contract negotiations, grievances, and arbitration cases are treated with vigor by both the company and the union, the problems are handled within a general framework of friendliness and of bilateral trust and confidence. It is obvious that such a state of development of industrial relations fosters high levels of productivity, profits, wages, and quality of product. It means that all parties to the collective bargaining process, including the public, derive benefit.

Such progress in labor relations did not develop by accident. There are cogent reasons for the great strides that have been made in the union-management relationship. Developments in management and union attitudes, in philosophy, and in procedures have been responsible for this trend.

On the part of companies, there is general acceptance, even if this is in many cases given begrudgingly, of the process of collective bargaining. In contrast to the state of affairs three decades ago, the typical management today has no open quarrel with the existence of collective bargaining. However much it might prefer a nonunionized work force (and however greatly it might continue to oppose the union in theory), it is now preoccupied with the practical problem of *getting along with* its labor organization on a day-by-day basis, while preserving at the same time those managerial prerogatives needed to operate an efficient and productive enterprise. Many companies operating under collective bargaining contracts sincerely believe that the protection of job rights of their employees by a labor agreement is desirable. Though at times protection of job rights obtained through collective bargaining might diminish plant productivity, most companies and unions have found the collective bargaining contract sufficiently elastic to accommodate the objectives of both efficiency of production and the protection of job rights. The pliability of the collective bargaining process has thus far provided chances for the reconciliation of both objectives and it is to be suspected that even the thorny problems of automation will ultimately be resolved in the same way (although, here, most likely in conjunction with government actions).

In addition, many companies have taken a realistic approach to the institutional character of unionism. They are aware that to an extent the collective bargaining process tends to supply the needs of the union as an institution, as well as to provide the mechanism whereby the terms of employment of workers are established. Many contractual provisions are agreed to by management on the theory that a union secure in its status may be more judicious in its behavior at the bargaining table and in grievance negotiations.

Management's recognition of the problems and needs of employees likewise is an important element in the establishment of sound relations under collective bargaining. Relations between companies and unions are bound to be more harmonious as management exhibits a genuine understanding of the problems confronted by the individual employee. A union will tend to be more aggressive and attempt to impose more limitations on the managerial function to the extent that a company, through its general behavior and personnel policies, demonstrates an unsympathetic attitude toward employees' problems and objectives. Indeed, one major reason for the establishment and the expansion of unions is that in the past some companies did not give sufficient attention to the needs of employees. At present the evidence is quite clear that the business community in general is vitally concerned with the welfare of its workers. One of the primary bases of the science of personnel management is the development of techniques and procedures which have at their core the sympathetic consideration of employee problems. In many companies the needs of employees are given equal weight and attention with the problems of finance, production, sales, and quality control. And executives are, in fact, assigned to personnel departments to no small extent because of their ability to understand sympathetically employees' problems and their capability to deal with employees on the basis of sound human relations. This development means that a solid foundation exists for more harmonious relations between companies, unions, and employees.

There is also a growing tendency on the part of industry to place the operation of labor relations in the hands of qualified and professional managers. There is scarcely a major company in existence that has not established a department to handle labor relations and personnel problems. More important, in many companies the industrial relations department has equal prestige and status with any other division or department within the enterprise. Such a development likewise fosters better relations at the bargaining table. But because collective bargaining negotiations and the administration of labor agreements constitute a most difficult and highly responsible job, it is necessary that companies entrust such a function to executives who are qualified in terms of training, motivation, skill, and personality. Companies which delegate these duties to unqualified personnel or impose the duties as additional responsibilities on already busy executives cannot expect to acquire a labor relations climate conducive to high levels of productivity.

It is also noteworthy that companies are increasingly conducting classes and other training programs involving the problems of contract administration for *first-line supervisors*. This appears an indispensable part of a sound company industrial relations program. Frequently, grievances arise because first-line supervision has not been adequately trained in the principles of labor relations and in the meaning and application of the collective bargaining contract. With the growth of the science of industrial relations, and particularly as this is cast within the framework of collective bargaining, it is imperative that a company's labor relations program be executed and administered correctly by all levels of supervision. To the extent that this has been recognized by the business community, the cause of harmonious and sound labor relations has been proportionately advanced.

Not only does the evidence, finally, reveal that employers in increasing numbers are giving sympathetic understanding to the problems of employees and unions, but there is also a growing awareness by *union* members and their leaders of the problems of management. At present many union leaders, although they are representatives of organizations that are above all political, are fully conscious of the fact that in the last analysis the welfare of employees depends upon the economic prosperity of the firm. The leaders understand further that the collective bargaining process is conditioned by the economic framework surrounding the particular negotiations, and that the overall economic character of a firm or an industry relative to its competitive position, sales, profits, capital equipment, expansion requirements, and quality of production necessarily determines the economic benefits which can be provided to employees. There is increasing awareness that a company has obligations not only to its employees but also to its investors, management, and customers. These considerations do not mean that unions are less militant in collective bargaining. Negotiations are not conducted in a tea-party atmosphere. What these observations do mean is that labor relations generally improve to the degree that collective bargaining negotiations are based upon factual information and rationality, and carried on in a general atmosphere of reciprocal recognition of problems and in a spirit of genuine good faith and mutual respect. Clearly, guesswork, emotionalism, preconceived notions of equity, and intransigence, whether displayed by a company or a union in collective bargaining negotiations, are not conducive to good labor relations.

Collective bargaining literally means the joint determination of the terms of employment. The process does not *create* the problems of the employment relationship; issues such as wages, hours and overtime, vacations, holidays, discipline, job classification, promotions, and employee safety and health exist with or without collective bargaining. Problems growing out of the employment relationship must be solved, in one way or another. In the absence of collective bargaining they are handled and determined by the employer on a unilateral basis. His decisions in this respect are final; they have as their frame of reference his own standards of fairness and are limited only by the marketplace and the law.

But if collective bargaining does not create the problems of the employment relationship, it *does* establish a definite procedure wherein they are handled and resolved. Employers and employees, through their respective representatives, negotiate the terms of employment and provide the mechanisms by which these terms can be administered throughout the contractual duration. Whatever deficiencies remain in the present system, the considerable progress which has been made in the past few decades augurs well for the future productive potential of the nation, assuming only that we can exercise sufficient patience in having our expectations for collective bargaining translated into action.

Appendices

Appendix I

Mock Negotiation Problem

The purpose of this problem is to familiarize students with the negotiation of a labor contract. The problem is strictly a hypothetical one and does not pertain to any actual company or union. It is designed to test in a practical way the student's understanding of the issues of collective bargaining studied during the semester and the strategy of the bargaining process. The strategy and techniques of negotiations are treated in Chapter 5 and the issues of collective bargaining are dealt with primarily in Chapters 7 through 10. Before the actual mock negotiation, the student should carefully reread these chapters.

PROCEDURE AND GROUND RULES:

1. Class will be divided into labor and management negotiation teams. Each team will elect a chairman at the first meeting of the team.

2. Teams will meet in sufficient number of planning sessions to be ready for the negotiations. Each participant will be required to engage in necessary research for the negotiation.
3. In the light of the following problem, each team will establish *not more* than 8 items *nor less* than 6 which it will demand. *All demands must be based upon the problem. No team will be permitted to make a demand which is not based upon the problem.* For purposes of this problem a union wage demand and all fringe issues, if demanded, will be considered as only *one* (1) demand.
4. Each team should strive to negotiate demands which it believes to be most important. This requires the weighing of the alternatives in the light of respective needs of the group the team is representing.
5. Compromises, counterproposals, trading, and the dropping of demands to secure a contract will be permitted in the light of the give and take of the actual negotiations.
6. Each team should strive sincerely and honestly in the role playing to do the best job possible for the group which it represents. This is a *learning* situation and to learn there must be sincere dedication to the job ahead.
7. *Absolutely no consultation with any of the other teams, regardless of whether company or union, will be permitted. Each team must depend entirely upon its own resources.*
8. Chairmen should coordinate the planning of each team, decide on the time and place for planning sessions, and assign work to be done to members of the team. Chairmen, however, are not to do all the talking in the actual negotiations. To maximize the learning situation, each member of the team should positively participate in the negotiations.
9. There must either be a settlement of all issues in the negotiation or a work stoppage. *No extension of the existing contract will be permitted.* It is a question of either settlement or work stoppage.
10. Someone on each team should keep track of the settlements. Do not write out the actual contractual clauses agreed to. It will suffice only to jot down the substance of agreements.
11. There will be a general discussion of the problem after the negotiation. Each team chairman or his representative will make a brief statement to the entire class as to the final outcome of the problem.

Herein follows the problem upon which the demands will be based and which provides the framework for the negotiations. *Read the problem very carefully to size up the situation. Base your demands only upon this problem.*

Representatives of the Auto Products Corporation of Indianapolis, Indiana, and Local 5000, United Metal Workers of America, are in the process of renegotiating their collective bargaining contract. The current contract expires at the close of today's negotiations. (*Instructor should set the date of the mock negotiation, and the exact clock time that the contract* *expires.*) The negotiations cover the Indianapolis plant.* Auto Products also owns a plant in Little Rock, Arkansas, but the southern plant is not organized and is not a part of the current negotiations. The current contract which covers only the Indianapolis plant was negotiated for a three-year period. The time of the negotiation is the present, and accordingly the parties are conditioned by current elements of economic trends, patterns of collective bargaining, and labor relations law.

The Indianapolis plant has been in business for 46 years and has steadily grown in size. At present, 3,800 production and maintenance employees are in the bargaining unit for the Indianapolis plant.

Except for the depression years, 1929–36, the financial structure of the company has been relatively good. For the current year, the sales of the Indianapolis plant amounted to $56 million. Sales totaled $52 million in the previous year, and $53 million for the first year of the current contract period. During the last fiscal year the Indianapolis plant's profits amounted to $2 million after taxes; $1.8 million the previous year; and $1.9 million in the first year of the labor agreement. At present, its assets in the Indianapolis plant amount to $18 million, including an inventory of $400,000 of unsold goods. Over the three-year period the company distributed 75 percent of its net profits in dividends; 20 percent was held as retained earnings; and 5 percent was used to improve and expand facilities in the Indianapolis plant. (All the above financial data apply exclusively to the Indianapolis plant.) The company's stock is listed on the New York Stock Exchange. It has no bonded indebtedness, though last year it borrowed $4.3 million from the First National Bank of Chicago. The rate of interest on the loan amounts to 6.9 percent. The proceeds of the loan were used to expand the Little Rock plant. The loan is scheduled for liquidation in ten years.

The company manufactures a variety of auto accessory parts. Such products include auto heaters, oil pumps, fan belts, rear-view mirrors, piston rings, and in the last year the company has also started production of auto air conditioners. About 65 percent of its sales are to the basic auto companies (General Motors, Ford, Chrysler, and American Motors); 25 percent to auto repair facilities; and the rest to government agencies. The plant operates on a two-shift basis. A three-cent-per-hour premium is paid to employees who work the second shift.

The employees of the company were not formed in a union until 1937. In that year, as a result of the CIO campaign to organize the mass production industries, the union was formed. In August of that year, the union was victorious in an NLRB election. As a result of the election,

* The location of the plant may be shifted to your own area to provide more local relevancy.

certification was awarded to Local 5000 on August 17, 1937. From that date, Local 5000 has represented the production and maintenance workers of the company. The first collective bargaining agreement between the company and Local 5000 was signed on November 14, 1937.

Only one contract strike took place since the union came into the picture. It occurred in 1940. The issues of the strike were the union's demands for a union shop, increased wages, and six paid holidays. The strike lasted six weeks. When it terminated, the union obtained for its members a four-cent hourly wage increase, retroactive to the day of the strike (the union had demanded seven cents), and four paid holidays. The union failed in its attempt to obtain any arrangement requiring membership in the union as a condition of employment. Also, the current contract does not include a "checkoff." At the time of these negotiations, all workers in the bargaining unit, with the exception of 400, are in the union.

The average wage for the *production workers* in the Indianapolis plant is $3.87 per hour. Of the 3,800 employees, there are 175 skilled maintenance employees (electricians, plumbers, carpenters, mechanics, and tool and die makers) and their average rate is $4.43 per hour. The existing contract contains an "escalator" clause providing for the adjustment of wages in accordance with changes in the Consumer Price Index. It provides a 1-cent increase in wages for each 0.5 point change in the CPI. During the past three years, employees have received a 12-cent increase in wages as a result of the escalator clause. Also, the employees have received a 5-cent-an-hour wage increase in each of the two previous years. This has resulted from the operation of the so-called "annual improvement" feature of the contract. The current wage rates existing in the plant include the increases generated from the escalator clause and the annual improvement factor.

The Little Rock plant was built five years ago. It started with a modest size labor force, but during the past three years the southern plant expanded sharply and now employs about 1,500 production and maintenance workers. Efforts to organize the southern plant have so far been unsuccessful. The union lost an NLRB election last year by 300 votes. Of the 1,500 employees, 1,300 cast ballots, with 800 voting against the union and 500 voting for the union. The average wage in the Little Rock plant is $2.85 per hour. During the last eight months, 300 employees in the Indianapolis plant have been laid off. It is no secret that a chief reason for this has been the increase of output in the Little Rock plant. Another reason for the layoffs has been a slight decrease in sales at the Indianapolis plant.

In general, the relations between the management and the union have been satisfactory. There have, of course, been the usual disagreements, but all in all relations have been rather harmonious. However, last month there was a "wildcat strike," the first one since the union came into the picture. It occurred in the Oil Pump Department, and the alleged cause was the discharge of the steward of the department on the grounds that he shoved a foreman while he was discussing a grievance with him. The union disclaimed all responsibility for the strike and its officers stated that they did all they could to get the men back to work. However, the employees in the Oil Pump Department picketed the plant and the incident, which lasted two days, shut down all production in the plant for these two days. There is a no-strike clause in the contract which states that

> there will be no strikes, slowdowns, or other interruption of production because of labor disputes during the contract period. Employees who engage in such prohibited activity are subject to discharge.

The company threatened to sue the union for damages under the Taft-Hartley law, but finally decided not to go to court after the employees returned to work. No employee was disciplined because of the strike; however, at present, the steward remains discharged, and the union has demanded his return to his job. Under the contract, the company has the right to discharge for "just cause." The steward is 63 years old, and was one of the leading figures in the organization of the union.

The existing contract contains a standard grievance procedure and provides for arbitration for all disputes arising under the contract, except production standards. Management has the unilateral right to establish production standards. During the last contractual period (three years), 275 written grievances were filed by employees protesting "unreasonably" high production standards. As required by the contract, the company negotiated the production standard grievances but the union did not have the right to appeal to arbitration or to strike over them. In three cases sparked by the production standard grievances the company reduced the standards. In all other cases, the company denied the grievances. The management rights clause states in effect that the company retains all rights except as limited by express provisions of the labor agreement.

Provided in the contract are a series of fringe benefits: six (6) paid holidays; a pension plan patterned after the one in basic auto; a very good hospitalization and surgical benefits insurance plan; and a vacation plan wherein employees receive one week vacation for one year of service and two weeks for five or more years of service. The total costs of all these fringe benefits amount to 49 cents per hour. The current contract does not require that employees retire when eligible for pension.

With respect to the seniority clause, it provides for promotions based on length of service and ability. That is, seniority governs when the senior employee has qualifications reasonably equal to those of junior employees who bid on the job. During the contract period, 21 grievances were filed by employees who protested against the company filling jobs with junior service employees. The company's position in these grievances was that the junior employees had far more ability than the senior employees. Five of these grievances went to arbitration, the company winning four and the union winning only one. Promotions are bid for on a department basis.

The seniority area of the existing contract provides for plantwide application of seniority credits for layoffs and recalls. During the recent period in which layoffs occurred, the company as required by the contract laid off many junior employees rather than senior employees because of the plantwide system. Foremen have complained to management that in many cases the junior employees who had been laid off were more efficient than the senior employees who had to be retained because of the plantwide system.

Also, the current contract provides that an employee whose job goes down, or whose job is preempted by a more senior employee, may bump any junior employee in the plant provided he has the qualifications to fill the job. During layoff periods the company became aware that this situation caused a great deal of expense because of an unreasonable amount of job displacement. Also, the current contract does not contain a temporary layoff clause. This means that a displaced employee may exercise his bumping rights based upon his plantwide seniority regardless of the length of the layoff. Foremen have complained to the management that employees should be laid off without regard to seniority when the layoff is for a short period of time.

The existing contract provides for "super-seniority" for stewards and other union officials. This provision protects the stewards and union officials only from layoffs. There are 60 stewards in the plant. Last year stewards spent, on the average, about 10 hours each per week on grievance work for which they were paid by the company. There are no limitations on stewards for grievance work. Foremen have complained that some stewards are "goofing off," using "union business" as a pretext not to work. All stewards deny this. In fact, the stewards claim that it is the unreasonable attitude of foremen that provokes grievances and complaints. Also, the stewards claim there cannot be a true measure of their time on the basis of the number of written grievances filed (a total of 185 were filed last year) since they say that a good share of their time is spent discussing grievances on an oral basis with employees and supervision before a written grievance is filed. There is no record to show how many of these oral discussions ended problems without written grievances being filed.

Last year, because of an unexpected order from the government, the plant worked Saturday and Sunday overtime for a period of two weekends. Under the existing contract, the company has the right to require overtime.

About 200 employees refused to work overtime, and did so only because the company threatened to fire them if they refused. These 200 employees have been raising a lot of trouble in the union about this overtime affair. Also, the company has the right to select the employees to work overtime. Some (other) employees have claimed that foremen are not fair, giving their personal friends the opportunity to earn the extra money and discriminating against the other employees.

For many years, by custom, each skilled tradesman has worked only within his trade. There are five maintenance trades: mechanics, carpenters, tool and die workers, plumbers, and electricians. Five months ago the company required a mechanic to do a job normally performed by a plumber. The employee and union filed a grievance, and the case went all the way to arbitration. The arbitrator sustained the position of the union on the basis of the "past practice" principle.

Some maintenance people have been affected by the current layoff, with twenty-five laid off. They charge that the company has been subcontracting out skilled work which could be done by them. Last year, the company, for example, subcontracted out electrical work while three electricians were on layoff. The subcontract job lasted six days. Under the current contract, there is no restriction on the company's right to subcontract.

The present contract, as stated, was negotiated for a three-year period. Both sides indicated that in the future they may want to move away from this long-term arrangement for a variety of reasons. However, there is no assurance that this attitude indicated the parties' sincere position, or merely was an expression of a possible bargaining position.

With respect to the current layoffs, the facts show that of the 300 employees laid off, 75 of them had exhausted their benefits under the Indiana Unemployment Compensation Act. The present contract does not provide for a supplementary unemployment benefit program.

Automation has been a problem in the company for a period of several years. About 250 workers have been permanently separated because of automation. Union and management meetings to deal with the problem during the past several years have proved fruitless. Previous discussions have centered around the rate of automation, the problem of income for the displaced employees, and training of employees for the jobs created by automation. All indications are that the next wave of automation will cost about 390 bargaining unit jobs. The 250 employees who have been permanently separated are in addition to the current 300 employees who are on layoff because of the southern situation and the slight recent drop in sales.

There has been considerable controversy over the problem of temporary transfers. Under the existing contract, the company may not transfer an employee to a job not in his job classification.

There are also problems regarding other working rules. These include: a 15-minute rest period every four hours; a stipulation that no supervisor may perform bargaining unit work regardless of circumstances; no change in crew size; paid lunch periods of 20-minute duration; and paid "wash-up" time for 10 minutes prior to quitting time. The company contends that these "working rules" are costing it a lot of money. Whenever this issue has been brought up in the past, the union has refused any change.

Company records show that 60 percent of the workers have seniority up to 10 years; 30 percent between 10 and 20 years; and 10 percent more than 20 years. The average age of the employees in the plant is 39 years of age. About 5 percent are over 65 years of age. About 20 percent of the bargaining unit are women; and 15 percent are blacks. Some black employees have complained that they have not been given equal opportunity to get better jobs. They have threatened to file complaints against both the company and the union under Title VII of the Civil Rights Act and Taft-Hartley. They have retained an attorney for this purpose.

(For the Instructor)

HOW TO USE MOCK NEGOTIATION PROBLEM

We have used the preceding mock negotiation problem with great success for several years. Students are uniformly enthusiastic about the problem, and there exists a friendly rivalry among the students during the weeks before the negotiation. Here are some suggestions on how to use the problem most effectively:

1. The class should be divided into union and management negotiation teams about the middle of the semester. Each management and union team should include from three to five students. The teams could be selected in random fashion, but a better method is to distribute the better students among the different teams: by the middle of the semester the instructor should have a good idea of the capability and the potential of the students. Each student should be assigned to a specific team, and each team should elect a chairman as rapidly as possible.
2. The teams should be instructed to conduct the research necessary to collect the data and formulate the arguments to be used in the negotiation. The chairman of each team should be encouraged to divide the research among the members of each team. For example, one member may be responsible for the problem of wages; another for answering the other team's demands for changes in the seniority structure, and so on. Depending upon the number of students on each team, and the number of issues that are likely to be negotiated, one student may be required to research more than one issue. The idea here is that each member of each team should be involved in the research, and

the task of research should be divided as equally as possible among all members of the team. The instructor should advise students where the information can be found. The more helpful sources include: the *Monthly Labor Review,* of the U.S. Department of Labor; the Bureau of National Affairs' *Collective Bargaining Negotiations and Contracts;* special reports of the United States Department of Labor; existing collective bargaining contracts; the AFL-CIO *Federationist;* the *AFL-CIO News;* publications of the American Management Association and other management sources; *Labor Law Journal; Industrial and Labor Relations Review; Business Week;* and the *New York Times* and *Wall Street Journal.*

3. Experience has shown that each team should meet in its private planning sessions about five times for about two to three hours for each session before the negotiation. This is in addition to research conducted on an individual basis. Because of the time involved, the negotiation could be used instead of the traditional term paper.

4. The instructor may, if he desires, attend some of the planning sessions, although in recent years we have not been doing this on the grounds that the full responsibility for planning should be assumed by the students. If visits are made, the instructor should not shape the over-all strategy of the team but merely consult with the team on particular problems.

5. We have found that the negotiation session should last about four hours. It could be held on an evening or a Saturday morning. Announce the date well in advance of the actual negotiation—at least six weeks.

6. The negotiation should be held toward the end of the semester so that the students can use the knowledge gained during the semester. We have usually scheduled the exercise during the second to the last week of the semester.

7. The number of negotiations depends upon the number of students in the class. In one semester, the class included sixty-six students, and, hence, there were six negotiations going on simultaneously. Be sure to arrange for the rooms in which the negotiations are to be held well in advance of the exercise. If possible, the room should be of the conference type, though any room will do provided that chairs can be arranged around a table so that the teams face each other.

8. The instructor should visit each negotiation and his time should be divided equally among the groups. If some technical problem arises during the negotiation, the instructor should deal with the issue. Other than this, the instructor should remain silent as he observes the negotiation. *Do not give any help to any team while the negotiation is underway.* At times, we have had management and organized labor representatives visit the negotiations. Uniformly they have been impressed with the success of the students and their competency at the bargaining table.

9. The teams should be instructed that the sessions must end promptly at the specified time. If the negotiations are to end at 10 P.M., they should end at 10 P.M. Do not extend the time since to do so would result in lack of uniformity for the different teams.

10. When the negotiations are over, all students should meet in one room for a wrap-up session. Each chairman should report on whether there was a strike or settlement, the major difficulties and problems of the negotiation, and other highlights of the negotiation. The chief purpose of this session, however, is for the instructor to make observations based on his visits to the negotiations. This session should not exceed forty-five minutes. This meeting is usually charged with emotion, some horseplay, and friendly criticism of each other by the students. If there is not a definite time limit, it could go on indefinitely. In the instructor's analysis, the students should be treated kindly. They have worked hard and deserve congratulations and a pat on the back. Remember that this is their first experience and mistakes will be made. These should be pointed out, but in a strictly impersonal manner.
11. Other suggestions are that (1) some arrangements should be made for the students to have coffee during the negotiations; (2) if possible, smoking should be permitted; (3) to pacify the janitorial staff, the rooms should be cleared of debris, and chairs and tables rearranged when the negotiations are ended; (4) the instructor should permit some poetic license during the actual negotiation, but cut off a student or a team which invents too much; and (5) he should not discourage some of the fun which the students develop during the negotiations.

Appendix II

Labor Relations in the Public Sector

The issue of public employee collective bargaining reached unprecedented proportions in the decade of the sixties. Measured by union membership, the greatest rate of growth in the labor movement has occurred among unions which represent public employees. In 1961, the State, County, and Municipal Employees Union claimed 210,000 members located in 1,561 local unions; by 1970, its membership had increased to about 300,000 members and 1,700 locals. The American Federation of Teachers by 1970 increased its membership to 140,000 members, from 56,156 in 1961. And this trend is more remarkable when it is noted that many unions in the private sector have suffered a *decline* in membership. The sharp rate of growth of public employee unions demonstrates clearly to many observers that the public employee desires the same organizational and bargaining rights enjoyed by employees in the private sector.

Other than the evidence that in general the public employees' working conditions have not kept pace with those of their counterparts in the private sector, the changing composition of employment in the United

States provides an explanation for the sharp increase in the rate of growth of public employee unions. In 1930, only about 6 percent of the civilian labor force was engaged in public employment. In 1968, government employees constituted nearly 17 percent of the nonagricultural work force. At the close of 1968, federal, state, and local governments employed a total of 12,202,000 workers.[1] Government employment has more than doubled since 1947 when it totaled 5,474,000.[2] However, the greatest gains have been at the state and local levels—not in federal jobs, as is often mistakenly believed: in the twenty-one-year 1947–68 period, federal employment rose by about 50 percent while state and local employment increased nearly 300 percent. State and local employment in 1968, indeed, accounted for 9,465,000 of the total of the 12,202,000 government employees. If the current trend continues, nearly 16 million persons will be employed by all levels of government by 1975.

EXECUTIVE ORDER NO. 10988

In 1961, President John F. Kennedy appointed a six-member task force to study the problem of employee-management relations in the federal service. The group, headed by Labor Secretary Arthur J. Goldberg, submitted its findings on November 30, 1961, and reported in part that

> at the present time, the Federal Government has no Presidential policy on employee-management relations, or at least no policy beyond the barest acknowledgement that such relations ought to exist. Lacking guidance, the various agencies of the Government have proceeded on widely varying courses. Some have established extensive relations with employee organizations; most have done little; a number have done nothing. The Task Force is firmly of the opinion that in large areas of the Government we are yet to take advantage of this means of enlisting the creative energies of Government workers in the formulation and implementation of policies that shape the conditions of their work.[3]

Thus it was deemed improper for the government to fail to extend to its own employees the same privileges enjoyed by workers in private enterprise as a result of federal action. Moreover, the task force believed that responsible unions would strengthen and improve the federal service.

In January 1962, President Kennedy responded to the report by issuing

[1] *Monthly Labor Review*, XCII, No. 5 (May 1969), 99.
[2] *Ibid.*
[3] Report of the President's Task Force on Employee-Management Relations in the Federal Service, *A Policy for Employee-Management Cooperation in the Federal Service* (Washington, D.C.: Government Printing Office, 1961), p. III.

Executive Order No. 10988, which established the basic framework within which collective bargaining was to take place in agencies under the executive branch of government. In October 1969, President Nixon issued Executive Order No. 11491, which substantially changed President Kennedy's order. The new order became effective on January 1, 1970.

First we shall examine President Kennedy's executive order and then show how the new order changes the union organization and collective bargaining rights of federal employees. The key to understanding these orders is that for the first time federal employees have the protected right to join unions and engage in collective bargaining with the agencies (Post Office Department, Department of Defense, Labor Department, Agriculture Department, etc.) for which they work. And the corollary is that these agencies under proper circumstances *must* recognize and bargain collectively with unions representing government employees. Thus, what the federal government has done is to attempt to provide organizational and bargaining rights for its employees in essentially the same way as these rights are established for employees in the private sector by Taft-Hartley.

Under Executive Order No. 10988, federal employees were free to decide to join or not to join any employee group. Union bargaining rights depended upon the extent of employee membership in the organizations. Three types of union recognition were provided. These were informal, formal, and exclusive.

INFORMAL RECOGNITION. This form was extended to any employee organization that did not qualify for either the formal or exclusive forms. Management was not required to seek the views of such organizations in personnel matters. This form of recognition, therefore, did not amount to much, since a union which secured this kind of recognition need not be consulted by government management in the establishment of conditions of employment. A head of a government agency might consult with such a union on a voluntary basis, but there was nothing compulsory about it. To secure informal recognition, a union did not have to show any specific amount of union membership. The AFL-CIO termed this form of recognition "virtually meaningless."[4]

FORMAL RECOGNITION. Formal recognition was permitted if a union demonstrated a stable membership of at least 10 percent of employees in the bargaining unit. Unlike the condition that prevailed under informal recognition, a federal government agency was obligated to consult with a union securing formal recognition on personnel policies and practices. In addition, such a union had the right to raise such matters for discussion with the appropriate government management representatives. It follows,

[4] *AFL-CIO News,* November 11, 1969.

therefore, that formal recognition was a more meaningful form of recognition than the informal type.

EXCLUSIVE RECOGNITION. The most important and meaningful type of recognition under Executive Order No. 10988 was exclusive recognition. To secure exclusive recognition for a group of federal employees, a union had to show that it represented at least 10 percent of the employees involved, and then be selected or designated by a majority of employees within the bargaining unit. When a union obtained exclusive recognition, it represented all employees in the bargaining unit without regard to union membership. Of crucial importance, such a union was authorized to negotiate collective bargaining contracts, and the government agency was compelled to meet with such a union in collective bargaining. Thus President Kennedy's order stated:

> When an employee organization has been recognized as the exclusive representative of employees of an appropriate unit it shall be entitled to act for and to negotiate agreements covering all employees in the unit and shall be responsible for representing the interests of all such employees without discrimination and without regard to employee organization membership. Such employee organization shall be given the opportunity to be represented at discussions between management and employees or employee representatives concerning grievances, personnel policies and practices, or other matters affecting general working conditions of employees in the unit. The agency and such employee organizations, through appropriate officials and representatives, shall meet at reasonable times and confer with respect to personnel policy and practices and matters affecting working conditions, so far as may be appropriate subject to law and policy requirements. This extends to the negotiation of an agreement, or any question arising thereunder, the determination of appropriate technique, consistent with the terms and purposes of this order, to assist in such negotiation, and the execution of a written memorandum of agreement of understanding incorporating any agreement reached by the parties.

To this extent, unions which obtained exclusive recognition had similar rights as unions under the Taft-Hartley law representing employees in the private sector. Also, when exclusive recognition prevailed, the government agency had obligations similar to those imposed under Taft-Hartley for private employers.

Additional Characteristics of Executive Order No. 10988

There were several other major characteristics of Executive Order No. 10988. An employees' association was not a lawful organization if it (1) asserted the right to strike against the United States government; (2)

advocated the overthrow of the United States Consititution; or (3) discriminated with regard to membership on the basis of race, color, creed, or national origin. In other words, a union which did not conform to these standards had no rights or standing under the executive order. If, for example, a union advocated the right to strike against the United States government, it could not represent federal employees, and a government agency would be forbidden to recognize such a union for the purposes of collective bargaining. Also, the order prohibited any arrangement requiring union membership as a condition of employment. Thus, under the order no government employee is obligated to join a union as a condition of employment. Note that in the private sector federal law permits the union shop and maintenance-of-membership agreements.

Other items were removed from the scope of collective bargaining under Executive Order No. 10988. It prohibited negotiations regarding the mission of a federal agency and its structural organization. Also forbidden were negotiations on the budget of an agency, the assignment of personnel, and the technology under which its work is carried out. For example, no union representing federal employees could negotiate an agreement limiting the right of a federal agency to automate its operation. As expected, negotiations could not result in changes of salaries or wages established by an act of Congress.

Despite these limitations on the scope of collective bargaining, there was a considerable range of matters which might be lawfully negotiated and reduced to a collective bargaining contract. Indeed, even with these limitations, and taking into consideration that federal employees and their unions were (and, of course, still are) forbidden to strike, the issues negotiated and included in written collective bargaining agreements covering federal employees under No. 10988 are truly impressive. Such issues include the following: overtime; callback and call-in pay; shift differentials; upgrading of an entire job classification; rest periods; shift scheduling; apprenticeship programs and career development; qualifications for promotions and the posting of open jobs upon which employees may bid; transfers; vacation scheduling; safety programs; assignment of disabled employees; use of bulletin boards; and training programs for new employees and refresher courses for senior employees. Many of these items are included in labor agreements covering private employees.

Also, and of significance, is the fact that the voluntary checkoff of union dues was lawful under Executive Order No. 10988. Unions which held formal or exclusive recognition rights could negotiate dues checkoff arrangements. Federal employees, however, have had the opportunity to rescind the checkoff authorization twice a year. In contrast, under Taft-Hartley, employees who authorize their checkoff of union dues may rescind their authorization only once per year.

President Kennedy's order also permitted the negotiation of a grievance procedure to apply the terms of an existing labor agreement. Not only could employees or unions protest that a government agency violated working conditions established by the contract, but they could also file a grievance protesting the discipline, including discharge, of a federal employee. In this respect, there is a great similarity between private labor agreements and those negotiated for federal employees. However, there existed an important difference between grievance procedures established in the private sector as compared with those negotiated under Executive Order No. 10988. We know that the capstone of the grievance procedure under private contracts provides for final and binding arbitration. In contrast, the order established only *advisory* arbitration for federal employees. Thus, for example, if a union representing federal employees elected to arbitrate an unresolved grievance protesting the discharge of an employee (an arbitration thus similar to one taking place in the private sector) the head of the government agency was not bound by an award issued by the private arbitrator. He could view it as only a recommendation, as *advice*. If the agency head refused to honor an award issued by an arbitrator in favor of the discharged employee, there was no recourse for the employee or the union.

In two other ways the system of collective bargaining established for federal employees differed from that which prevails in the private sector. When a private employer and a union agree to a collective bargaining contract, it goes into effect without further approval (ratification by union members excepted). However, in the federal sector, the head of a government agency had the right to approve a labor agreement negotiated by a union and government agency representative. For example, the United States postmaster general had the authority to rescind all or part of a labor agreement negotiated by a union and the postmaster of the post office located in Rutland, Vermont. Under these circumstances, the union would have no recourse from the decision of the postmaster general.

Finally, the issue of handling an impasse in the negotiation of a labor agreement differed greatly as compared to the private sector. We know, of course, that a strike can take place when a private employer and a union reach an impasse in negotiations. In the private sector this is par for the course. However, federal employees are forbidden to strike and this weapon cannot be used to achieve a settlement of the issues in dispute. Moreover, arbitration of any kind, advisory or final and binding, was forbidden under Executive Order No. 10988 as a forum to break a deadlock in negotiations. Hence, there was no effective way to break an impasse in negotiations. Mediation was permitted, but a recommendation by a mediator is not binding on the union or agency.

Mediation in the Federal Service

Even though Executive Order No. 10988 did not exactly encourage the use of mediation, the Federal Mediation and Conciliation Service (FMCS) did experiment with its use after 1965.

Public employee unrest prompted the FMCS to re-evaluate its lack of activity among federal employees in the latter year, and discussion with Civil Service Commission personnel and union and agency representatives led to a policy and procedure for considering mediation requests. In part the policy included:

1. All requests for mediation had to be screened and decided upon at the FMCS office in Washington, D.C.
2. No request would be considered unless made jointly by both parties and usually in writing.
3. No request would be considered unless, following genuine bargaining efforts, both parties agreed that an impasse had been reached.
4. In the event a joint request was approved, the FMCS would select and assign the individual mediator.
5. The mediator assigned would be available only for a limited period of time and for a limited number of joint meetings, as the situation dictated.[5]

This policy pronouncement resulted from the inadequate executive order provisions for dispute settlement. On the whole, however, mediation was only mildly successful in contract dispute cases because mediators faced a different set of circumstances than in private industry. The strike is not permitted by federal employees and thus the strike deadline is not available to assist mediation efforts. Some negotiations, moreover, had been in progress for as long as fifteen months before mediation efforts were initiated.[6] Another weakness was in the mediation policy itself. A single-party mediation request was not honored. In some cases, one of the parties refused to enter into a joint request for mediator services. A more logical approach would have been to permit the FMCS to enter a case upon the request of either party.

Deficiencies in Executive Order No. 10988

A major weakness of meaningful bargaining in the federal service is the comparatively limited scope of bargaining subjects. Bargaining issues were limited not only by the 1962 executive order, but also by the Civil

---

[5] Abner Willoughby, "The FMCS and Dispute Mediation in the Federal Government," *Monthly Labor Review,* May 1969, pp. 27–29.

[6] *Ibid.,* p. 28.

Service Commission and various agency rules and regulations. Even though the parties were forbidden to bargain on certain items, many of them are sources of employment irritation and could lead to unwholesome labor relations. As stated, many matters were considered lawful issues of bargaining. However, those that were not imposed a limitation which is not found in the private sector. It is possible that bargaining on some of the prohibited subjects could be permitted without impairing the efficiency of the federal government.

Another important shortcoming was that no independent and impartial agency was established to administer and develop labor relations policies. The Civil Service Commission was entrusted with the responsibility of implementing labor-management policy under the order. Some observers contended that the Civil Service Commission is management-oriented and its responsibility for federal employee relations resembles a situation that would exist if the Board of Directors of U.S. Steel had been entrusted with administration of the Taft-Hartley Act.

The executive order was most defective, however, in the dispute settlement area. When mediation failed to bring about an agreement on the issues, the only available procedure was to appeal to a higher level of the agency's management. This has the effect of dampening meaningful negotiation.

Despite the weaknesses of the executive order, considerable activity has taken place among employee organizations. As of 1970, exclusive bargaining rights had been designated for 2,305 separate units in 35 agencies covering about 1,400,000 employees—52 percent of the federal labor force subject to the order. Organizational activity has been heaviest in the postal service where close to 90 percent of workers are members of unions with exclusive bargaining rights. The postal employees are by far the largest federal group of organized employees.

Impact of Executive Order No. 11491

As stated, Executive Order No. 11491, styled "Labor-Management Relations in the Federal Service," became effective on January 1, 1970. It resulted from studies of the operation of President Kennedy's order which highlighted some areas for improvement. In several ways, the deficiencies of the original order have been corrected. In the first place, only exclusive recognition is now provided for unions representing federal employees. The informal and formal categories have been abolished. This is a wholesome change since these two types had little meaning. Under the present order, a union to gain exclusive recognition must be selected by a majority of the employees in a bargaining unit through a secret election.

Under the original order, unions were able to secure exclusive recognition by the use of signed union membership authorization cards. This procedure has been eliminated, and undoubtedly the reason for this change has been the criticism of the NLRB policy which permits the use of authorization cards under certain circumstances as the basis of bargaining orders. Note that the basis of the NLRB policy is employer unfair labor practices calculated to destroy a union's majority. Since government officials are not likely to engage in such practices, the requirement that the election be used as the sole basis of gaining bargaining rights is probably a correct policy.

As we have noted, under the original order the Civil Service Commission and the various federal agencies were given the power to oversee and implement the policies and procedures contained in the document. The new order creates a three-member Federal Labor Relations Council to administer the program, decide major policy matters, and issue rules and regulations. This group is composed of the chairman of the Civil Service Commission, the Secretary of Labor, and an official to be named from the President's Executive Office. In a way, the Federal Labor Relations Council for purposes of the order stands in the same relationship as the NLRB for purposes of Taft-Hartley. It is likely that the Federal Labor Relations Council will be more objective and independent in its action than was true under the old system, under which the Civil Service Commission and the government agencies interpreted and applied the former order.

In addition, the new order gives the Assistant Secretary of Labor for Labor-Management Relations authority to resolve disputes over the make-up of bargaining units and representation rights, to order and supervise elections, and to disqualify unions from recognition because of corrupt or undemocratic influences. Formerly, these matters were handled by the particular federal agency and its final judgment on them was not subject to appeal. Though there still may exist a "community of interest" between the Labor Department official authorized to make these determinations and the heads of federal agencies, it is a safe prediction that he will make his decision on a much fairer basis than when sole power was lodged in the federal agencies. Decisions of the Assistant Secretary for Labor-Management Relations may be appealed to the Federal Labor Relations Council.

Another entirely new feature is contained in the new order. Unions representing government employees are required to furnish essentially the same kind of information (election, bonding, and financial reporting) as is required from unions operating in the private sector. In short, a good share of the information required in the Landrum-Griffin Act is now made mandatory for government unions. Though there has been no evidence that such unions have been marked by corrupt or undemocratic practices, it may be argued that consistency demands application of the Landrum-

Griffin requirements to unions representing federal employees. Since there is now assurance that government unions must operate free from corruption and undemocratic practices, it is questionable that the prohibition against the union shop should have been carried over to the new order. As before, government unions may not negotiate a requirement of union membership as a condition of employment. This means, of course, that nonunion employees in the bargaining unit receive the same benefits as those federal employees who support the unions by membership and dues payments.

In the area of grievance arbitration, the new order strips federal agencies of the power to refuse to honor the award of an arbitrator. Now the Federal Labor Relations Council has the authority to issue binding arbitration decisions on grievance disputes and questions of interpretation of contracts. Private arbitrators still will be used to deal with grievances not settled by the parties. Under specified circumstances, the decisions of the private arbitrators may be appealed to the council. The decisions of this body become final and binding. The new procedure overcomes one of the greatest defects of the original order. No longer is the head of a federal agency empowered to turn down an award issued by a private arbitrator. If there is to be any appeal from his award, it will go to the Federal Labor Relations Council. Though there still exists some difference even under the new order on grievance arbitration as compared to arbitration in the private sector, the present system certainly demonstrates improvement. At least it removes from the head of a federal agency the power to refuse to abide by an arbitration decision when he feels inclined to do so. Of course, to make the new system work fairly and in a manner such as to maintain the integrity of the arbitration process, the Federal Labor Relations Council must act in a strictly judicial and objective manner on any appeal made to it. If it acts in this fashion, it is entirely possible that in effect the decision of the private arbitrator will be final and binding.

Unfair labor practices for government unions and agencies are specified by the new order. In a way, these unfair labor practices reflect those established in the Taft-Hartley law. For example, a government agency violates the terms of the order if it interferes with the right of employees to join unions; encourages or discourages membership in a union by discrimination in regard to hiring, tenure, promotion, or other conditions of employment; refuses to recognize a union qualified for recognition; and refuses to negotiate with a union which has secured exclusive bargaining rights. Under the new order, a union engages in an unfair labor practice if it interferes with the right of employees not to join a union; coerces or fines a member as punishment for the purpose of impeding his work performance, his productivity, or his duties as a government employee; engages in strikes or showdowns or fails to take appropriate action to prevent or stop a strike; and refuses to bargain collectively.

As stated, the Federal Labor Relations Council will interpret these unfair labor practices in the same way as the NLRB interprets the Taft-Hartley law. Undoubtedly, the council will use some of the precedents of the NLRB in the execution of this duty.

Finally, but of crucial importance, the new order establishes a procedure to break impasses in contract negotiation disputes. As stated, except for mediation the old order provided for no impartial procedure to break deadlocks in matters of contract negotiation. Employees could not strike, and the old order strictly prohibited arbitration as a forum for the settlement of disputes. In fact, realistically viewed, the only procedure available under the old order was to have disputes of this kind resolved by the federal agency involved in the negotiations. It was the same as if a private employer would unilaterally determine contract negotiation disputes involving himself and the union!

Under the new order, the President appoints members to a Federal Impasse Panel. This group is authorized to consider negotiation impasses and "may take any action it considers necessary to settle an impasse." The panel at its discretion may, indeed, use arbitration to settle a contract negotiation dispute and, subject only to appeals to the Federal Labor Relations Council, a decision of the Federal Impasse Panel is binding upon the union, employees, and agency involved. Since under the new order, as was true under the original order, federal employees are not permitted to strike, the system for final and binding arbitration is equitable and realistic.

It will be interesting to follow the activities of the Federal Impasse Panel. If unions and the federal agencies bargain realistically and in good faith, it is entirely possible that not many disputes will be referred to the group for final and binding arbitration. Another point to watch is the number of disputes the panel accepts for arbitration. Note that it is not compelled to arbitrate contract negotiation issues. It has the discretion to do so if in the judgment of its members such a procedure is deemed necessary. Clearly, the purpose and intent of the new system will be defeated if the panel refuses to arbitrate. On the other hand, it would be proper for the panel to refuse to arbitrate small and unimportant matters that the parties themselves should handle in direct negotiations. Finally, aside from the quantity of work of the panel, attention should be paid to the quality of its decisions. What kind of decisions will be handed down by the group? What standards will it use in the discharge of its arbitration function? Will it be judicial in its decisions, using accepted standards of arbitration, or will it be persuaded by considerations not relevant to the merits of a dispute?

On the whole, the changes in the new order are worthwhile. They should do much to strengthen the right of federal employees to organize and bargain collectively. The evidence is not yet available as to the activities of the new groups established to implement the new order. In large measure, how they operate will determine the success or failure of public policy in bestowing upon federal employees and their unions rights similar to those enjoyed by employees in the private sector. If the groups operate fairly and objectively, a long step forward will have been taken by government to extend to its own employees the same rights which government has long conferred on employees in the private sector.

COLLECTIVE BARGAINING AT THE STATE AND LOCAL LEVELS

At the close of 1967, it was estimated that approximately 22 percent of five million state and local government employees were members of either unions or associations, excluding those in education.[7] The American Federation of State, County, and Municipal Employees, an AFL-CIO affiliate, reached a membership of 275,000 in 1967. The Assembly of Governmental Employees, a federation of 36 independent public employee associations, reached a total membership of 504,000 in 1968.[8] Combined, the two organizations represent about three-quarters of all such members.

Unions and associations compete for members. Traditionally, the latter have been less militant than the former on such issues as collective bargaining and strikes. More recently, the procedures and objectives of both have been converging. If the tendency toward common tactics continues, competition for members may depend largely upon the comparative pressure that one group can bring upon public employers. This seems particularly possible in light of a 1969 circuit court of appeals decision.

RIGHT OF PUBLIC EMPLOYEES TO JOIN UNIONS. The Eighth Circuit Court of Appeals in 1969 gave its opinion of the right of public employees to join unions.[9] The issue presented to the appellate court in the *Woodward* case was whether public employees discharged because of union membership have a right to seek injunctions and sue those public officials who discharged them for damages. A solution to the basic issue required a determination of whether public employees have a constitutionally protected right to belong to a union.

[7] James E. Young and Betty L. Brewer, *State Legislation Affecting Labor Relations in State and Local Government,* Labor and Industrial Relations Series No. 2 (Kent, Ohio: Kent State University, Bureau of Economic and Business Research, 1968), p. 5.

[8] *Ibid.,* p. 8.

[9] *American Federation of State, County, and Municipal Employees, AFL-CIO v. Woodward,* 406 F. (2d) 137 (1969).

The court ruled unanimously that union membership is protected by the right of association under the First and Fourteenth Amendments, quoting an earlier ruling that the right of assembly protects more than the right to attend a meeting. It includes

> the right to express one's attitudes or philosophies by membership in a group or by affiliation with it or by other lawful means.[10]

Public officials who violate the public employee's constitutional right of association are subject to court action for damages under Section 1 of the Civil Rights Act of 1871. A different appellate court decision was quoted in reaching this conclusion. It stated:

> It is settled that teachers have the right of free association, and unjustified interference with teachers' associational freedom violates the Due Process clause of the Fourteenth Amendment.... Public employment may not be subjected to unreasonable conditions, and the assertion of First Amendment rights by teachers will usually not warrant their dismissal. ... Unless there is some illegal intent, an individual's right to form and join a union is protected by the First Amendment.[11]

The guaranteed right to join a union may be important to a worker, but that right is not effective if there is a lack of procedures to protect it such as required recognition of a labor organization representing a majority of bargaining unit workers and, thereafter, good-faith collective bargaining. Also, all the other appellate courts will not necessarily rule the same as the above-cited circuit courts of appeals. Conflicting rules may eventually result in a Supreme Court decision on the issue. In the meantime, however, the states vary widely in their interpretation of public employee collective bargaining rights.

CURRENT STATUS OF STATE LAWS

State policy toward public employee bargaining is far from uniform. Alabama expressly denies state employees the right to organize into labor organizations; however, at the local level firemen have the right to organize. North Carolina prohibits public employee affiliations with a national or international union. Some other states deny certain categories of employees the right to join unions. Georgia, as one example, prohibits policemen from joining unions. A Virginia Senate resolution declares public employee union membership to be contrary to public policy. At the other end of

---

[10] *Ibid.*, at 139.
[11] *McLaughlin v. Tilendis,* 398 F. (2d) 287 (7th Cir., 1968).

the spectrum, nine states make it mandatory for some classes of public employers to bargain with unions representing a majority of employees.[12] Some of the laws are limited only to municipalities while others include the state and county levels, or exclude municipalities.

Most of the other states lie between the two extremes of mandatory bargaining and outright prohibition of union membership. Sixteen states have enacted legislation authorizing the right of *all* public employees to join unions. Six others have extended the same right through either court decisions or attorney general opinions.

Even though nine states make it mandatory for the public employer to bargain with majority unions and to reduce negotiations to written agreements, limitations are associated with most of these laws. Connecticut and Vermont laws apply only to municipalities. In Delaware, municipalities must elect to participate in collective bargaining proceedings. Civil service employees in Michigan are excluded from the requirement and in Wisconsin and Massachusetts state and local workers are covered by separate laws.

Four other states make collective bargaining permissive.[13] Employers have authority to bargain with majority unions, but there is no requirement for them to do so. Three additional states—California, Hawaii, and Minnesota—require only that employers meet and confer with majority unions. There is no penalty, however, for refusals to meet and confer. Obviously, some states encourage power conflicts between public employees. Work stoppages may be required to force employers to meet and confer. Once meetings and conferences are held as a result of pressures, it may be difficult to establish laboratory conditions within which constructive negotiations prevail.

Some states have neglected to define the collective bargaining rights of public employees. Mississippi and Nevada have not set forth guidelines by administrative determination, statute, or court decision. A South Dakota court has declared only that city workers have the right to organize. Ohio, South Carolina, and Tennessee have merely provided that public employees do not have the right to strike.

Considerable uncertainty regarding actual bargaining rights also faces public employees in a large number of states. In some cases, rights are spelled out for certain categories of workers, but not for others. Even if public employees are dealt with uniformly in a particular state or lesser political jurisdiction, the mere difference of treatment in other states is enough to create instability in employment relations. This situation may

[12] The states are Connecticut, Delaware, Massachusetts, Michigan, New York, Rhode Island, Vermont, Washington, and Wisconsin.
[13] Permissive bargaining exists in Alaska, Missouri, New Hampshire, and Oregon.

be termed a "demonstration effect." Public workers in a municipality in a state which does not permit collective bargaining among its workers become malcontents when they observe that bargaining rights exist in other states among those performing similar tasks. Indeed, the ability of federal employees to engage in bargaining activities within the same state also serves to frustrate state and local employees deprived of the same right.

Agitation for equal bargaining rights is likely to persist among public employees as long as a relatively high level of employment continues in most labor markets. In this regard, the loss of jobs because of union activities is less serious than would be the case if fewer job alternatives were available to such workers. Not only does a relatively high level of employment provide workers with more alternatives, it also has the effect of decreasing the number of job applicants from which public employers may choose. High turnover rates become especially damaging during such periods of high economic activity. Public pressure forces government agencies to maintain a constant flow of public services. Indeed, there is considerable pressure to expand and improve services when per capita income rises. It is difficult to adhere to traditional practices in the face of widespread employee dissatisfaction. Disruption of services could invoke the wrath of the general public, which in turn could lead to losses at the polls and eventually to new public employers. These factors, including widespread strikes among public employees, probably will result in more and more recognition of public employee unions.

DE FACTO BARGAINING. Despite the existence of restrictive laws or court and administrative decisions, state and local employees are exerting pressure on public employers to obtain bargaining arrangements. The assassination of Martin Luther King in Memphis, Tennessee, was the essential ingredient that forced the city to yield to garbage collection employee demands for union recognition and collective bargaining. The Indiana University administration, as another example, decided under pressure to meet and confer with employee representatives although the same is not true among the other universities in that state. Thus, even though specific legislation does not exist to support collective bargaining relationships in many jurisdictions, employee and third-party pressures are often enough to force employers to yield to certain pacifying demands. Civil rights groups are beginning to devote considerable attention to public workers in urban areas. Such a situation has been described as multilateral bargaining.[14] Its very existence forces both unions and public employers to yield their traditional positions in favor of the demands of the special community interest groups. In the meantime, a bargaining relationship is in the process of development.

[14] See Kenneth McLennan and Michael H. Moskow, "Multilateral Bargaining in the Public Sector," *Monthly Labor Review*, XCII, No. 4 (April 1969), 58–60.

Such pressures have led to reconsideration of a wide range of traditional practices in the public sector.

STUDY COMMISSIONS. Some governors have responded to various pressures by appointing special commissions to study public employment relations. Governor Rockefeller of New York appointed the Taylor Commission on January 15, 1966, to study the public labor problems of the state. It was charged with the responsibility of proposing legislation which would protect the public from illegal strikes as well as the rights of workers to engage in union activities. The crisis which climaxed the need for a revision of the outmoded Condon-Wadlin Act was the New York City Transit Authority employees strike in 1966. The commission's efforts resulted in recommendations which were included in the Taylor Act. Not only were employees given the right to organize but collective bargaining was required on a mandatory basis. The Public Employment Relations Board was created to administer the provisions of the New York act. It was also provided with machinery to deal with impasses.

The governors of Maryland, New Jersey, and Illinois have also utilized commissions to study public employment problems. This device should serve to bring special problems to the attention of the general public in an unbiased form whereby adequate legislation may result. Otherwise, the states will increasingly be forced into a crisis evaluation of the rights of the general public relative to those who provide public services. The explosive potential of public workers seems irreversible if machinery is not established to resolve disagreements before they arise.

THE RIGHT TO STRIKE

The right of public employees to strike is prohibited by statute or court decision in practically all states. Prohibition of the right to strike, however, has proved ineffective. Evidence demonstrates that despite legal prohibitions and even serious penalties against employees who strike, many public employees have engaged in strikes. Indeed, the rate of public employee strikes increased sharply in the latter part of the 1960s.

An increasing number of unions and employee organizations are changing their traditional policy of no-strike pledges. In 1963, the American Federation of Teachers issued a policy statement supporting strikes under certain conditions. Even the traditionally conservative and nonmilitant National Educational Association, in which most public school teachers hold membership, has revised its policies and supports teacher strikes under some circumstances. The American Federation of State, County, and Municipal Employees Union also followed this trend in 1966. In one study, it was found that of 20 unions composed primarily of public employees, eight have constitutional bans on strikes and eight others do not refer to the issue in their union constitutions.[15]

Public employee union leaders contend that without the right to strike employers will not negotiate in good faith. A former union official speaking for the International Association of Firefighters has remarked:

> Certain arbitrary public officials knowing that we cannot and will not strike because we voluntarily gave up the right in 1918 when we were founded, have certainly taken advantage of the professional firefighters across the land. As a matter of fact, the record will show we have been exploited by such arbitrary public officials who oft time dared us to strike, knowing that we would not.[16]

Various penalties have from time to time been imposed upon striking employees. In 1947, New York passed the Condon-Wadlin Act which permitted re-employment of strikers, but eliminated pay increases for them for a period of three years. Reinstated strikers were also considered temporary employees for a period of five years. The 1967 New York Taylor Act eliminated the pay raise ban feature, but provided instead for dismissal or fines. A labor organization is subject to loss of dues checkoff privileges for as long as 18 months and fines for engaging in strikes.

In Michigan, state employees are subject to discharge or financial penalties for striking. Massachusetts provides that striking municipal workers may be fined $100. Most states reserve the right to discharge striking public employees although this is not clearly spelled out in legislation.[17]

Laws prohibiting public employee strikes have not been successful in their objective. In 1966, the first full year after Michigan amended its public employee relations act, there were 23 strikes in the public sector. This number of strikes was more than had occurred in the previous 20 years.[18] In the next year, 1967, the number of strikes in Michigan almost doubled. Other states have experienced increased strike threats even if actual work stoppages have not materialized.

Employee strike idleness at all levels of government amounted to 1.2 million man-days in 1967, over twice the .5 million man-days recorded in 1966.[19] In 1967, there were 181 government strikes involving 132,000

---

[15] Young and Brewer, op. cit., p. 16.

[16] William Buck, former president of the International Association of Firefighters, as quoted by Eric Polisor in "Strikes and Solutions," *Public Employee Relations Report No. 7,* Public Personnel Association, 1968.

[17] See Anne M. Ross, "Public Employee Unions and the Right to Strike," *Monthly Labor Review,* XCII, No. 3 (March 1969), 15.

[18] John Bloedorn, "The Strike and the Public Sector," *Labor Law Journal,* XX, No. 3 (March 1969), 157.

[19] John T. Hall, Jr., "Work Stoppages in Government," *Monthly Labor Review,* XCI, No. 7 (July 1968), 53.

workers. It has been estimated that as many as 250 work stoppages occurred in 1968.[20]

Teacher Work Stoppages

There were several issues that brought about the above work stoppages, but teachers accounted for most of them. Salaries and supplemental benefits or professional standards were the major sources of teacher dissatisfaction. Disputes over union recognition or security ranked second in importance as causes of teacher strikes. However, it should be noted that union recognition as the identified source of dispute can hardly be separated from other problems such as concern over salary levels.

In 1966, a sharp increase in teacher strikes occurred. Thirty-three stoppages were recorded in that year.[21] In 1967, the number more than doubled to a total of 76. Most teacher work stoppages are in the form of protests to the public or legislature. This fact seems apparent from the short duration of the stoppages. In 1966, the average time lost per teacher amounted to 1.8 days compared with 14.1 days lost per employee for all strikes.[22] Even so, the loss of classroom time due to teacher protests may have a more dramatic impact upon the public than a greater number of average days lost in other occupations.

It is important to note that twelve of the 33 teacher stoppages in 1966 were in Michigan. The state had just enacted its Public Employment Relations Act in 1965. The act provided machinery for mediation and resolution of bargaining impasses. It appears that work stoppages may increase significantly when laws are first passed protecting the right to organize and bargain collectively. The response may well be due to the inexperience of the parties in collective negotiations. After the parties become more mature in collective bargaining, the number of strikes should decrease. This has been the experience in private industry. Clearly, refusal of states to enact statutes authorizing and compelling collective bargaining in the public sector will not prevent public employee strikes. In recent years, many such strikes occurred in states that had no legislation.

Union Security

Only twelve states explicitly deal with the issue of union security for public employee organizations. Generally, the laws provide that workers have

---

[20] Allen Weisenfeld, "Public Employees are Still Second Class Citizens," *Labor Law Journal*, XX, No. 3 (March 1969), 140.
[21] Ronald W. Glass, "Work Stoppages and Teachers: History and Prospect," *Monthly Labor Review*, XC, No. 8 (August, 1967), 43.
[22] *Ibid.*

the right to refrain from union activities. However, it has been reported that the American Federation of State, County and Municipal Employees had negotiated about 75 union-shop agreements prior to 1960.[23] The number of such agreements was undoubtedly much higher in 1970. There may be many other forms of union security negotiated at the state and local level, but most probably take the form of tacit understandings as opposed to written agreements in a majority of cases. The state of Vermont automatically grants municipal employee unions the right to negotiate union security agreements. This feature stems from the fact that public employees are covered under the same labor relations act as are workers in private industry.

The agency-shop arrangement is valid in the states of New Hampshire and Michigan. State courts have reviewed the agency-shop provisions for public employees and have held the device legal in both states. The Michigan case deserves special attention.

MICHIGAN: A SPECIAL CASE OF UNION SECURITY. The state of Michigan does not have a right-to-work law which makes the agency-shop arrangement attractive to unions in general industry. It does have a Public Employees Relations Act which grants employees the right to organize and belong to unions. As is the case under Taft-Hartley, workers have the right to refrain from engaging in union activities. Public employers and unions are prohibited from encouraging or discouraging union membership.

One town in Michigan signed a contract with its fire department containing an agency-shop clause. Some of the firemen refused to join the union or to tender the equivalent of union dues. The union requested their discharge for nonpayment of equivalent dues. A state circuit court ruled that it was within the authority of the town to discharge the workers.[24] This decision was justified as being consistent with the requirement that unions must represent all bargaining unit employees without regard to union membership. Benefits received, the court reasoned, should be paid for by all bargaining unit workers.

The decision to validate the agency-shop arrangement and in turn enforcement by discharge from employment was not held to be a conflict between the law permitting public employee bargaining and the Civil Service Act. The Michigan Civil Service Act prohibits employee discharge for any reason other than those associated with performance of work. However, this law was held to be a general one while the Public Employment Relations Act was deemed a special one. Special laws, the court held, prevail over general laws. The majority of employees had decided to choose the terms of the special law and not those of the general one.

[23] Arnold S. Zander, "Trends in Labor Legislation for Public Employees," *Monthly Labor Review*, LXXXIII, No. 12 (December 1960), 1295.
[24] *City of Warren v. International Association of Fire Fighters* (Michigan Circuit Court, Macomb County, July 24, 1968).

Essentially the same decision was reached in a bargaining unit of teachers. A teachers' union negotiated an agency-shop arrangement and later requested the discharge of those who refused to render the equivalent of union dues. Discharge of such teachers was ruled permissible under state law despite the existence of the Michigan Teachers' Tenure Act.[25] The tenure act, decided the court, is a general law that may be partially replaced by a collective bargaining agreement under the special Public Employment Relations Act.

Other Michigan courts may or may not follow the logic used by the Macomb County Court. At this writing, the state supreme court has not yet had the occasion to deal with the issue.

Resolution of Disputes

One of the most significant issues facing the public sector is machinery for resolving disputes in the face of prohibitions on the right to strike. Twenty-four states have some limited provisions for dispute settlement. Some limit machinery to specific categories of workers such as firemen or teachers. When legislation has been passed, it almost always states that there can be no conflict with civil service provisions or other statutes setting employment standards. The major difficulty seems to come from legislative bodies even when economic issues are negotiable. These bodies have to appropriate funds to cover the agreements and are usually unwilling to abide by decisions denied outside the traditional legislative processes.

There are at least three types of disputes in the public employment field. The first is organizational, which involves the issue of determining employee desires for union representation. Some states have labor relations boards to make bargaining unit determinations.

The second type of dispute involves the terms and conditions of employment, usually included in written collective bargaining agreements. Resolution may result from such devices as mediation or fact-finding boards with authority to offer recommendations.

The third type of dispute involves interpretation and enforcement of existing collective bargaining agreements. The usual method of resolving such disputes in private industry is an internal grievance procedure with impartial third-party arbitration as a final step.

Strikes in the public sector could be decreased if certain steps are clearly provided. Some of the possible steps which may result in better labor-management relations are:

> 1. The right of employee representation by a union of their own choice, and compulsory recognition of the union by the public employer.

[25] *Clampelt* v. *Board of Education* (Michigan Circuit Court, Macomb County, July 19, 1968).

2. Independent third-party mediation; fact finding to deal with bargaining impasses; and arbitration.
3. Written contracts with detailed clauses dealing with wages and other working conditions.
4. Voluntary final and binding arbitration as the final step in a grievance procedure involving contractual interpretation.

It is still too early to assess the success of dispute-resolving machinery enacted by some states during the latter 1960s. However, it is safe to say that the problem of public employee collective bargaining, and the growing restlessness among public employees, cannot be dealt with successfully by ignoring the problem. Undoubtedly, the results of inaction will be an increasing number of public employee strikes, a lowered morale among public employees, and the deterioration of services from government agencies. In the last analysis, the public will pay a stiff price if the federal and state governments do not face up to reality.

A Concluding Observation

The public sector has largely ignored its labor relations problems until confronted by crisis conditions. Not only has government at all levels become a relatively larger employer of labor than in the past, but there is every indication that the total will increase in the future. Public workers do not accept the traditional attitudes used to describe their employment rights such as "the sovereign can do no wrong." Increasingly, unilateral determination of wages and employment conditions is being questioned by government employees. Employers are finding their decisions questioned not only by unions representing their employees, but also by associations that have traditionally been somewhat passive in the area of collective bargaining. Competition between unions and associations has resulted in the use of more aggressive tactics to obtain wages and other working conditions that more nearly approach those of the private sector.

Several years of sustained high levels of employment coupled with increased demand for public services have placed public employers in a position where they must re-evaluate their traditional management practices. The general public is intolerant of inconveniences resulting from stoppages in the flow of services performed by the various agencies of government. The situation of being placed squarely between their employees and the general public has prompted a growing number of state and local governments to spell out more clearly the collective bargaining rights of workers. Once the process begins, there is little possibility of reversing it. The rights established in one state may be expected to spill over into adjoining states and then spread even farther.

The process may be expected to continue for as long as relatively high levels of employment exist. Otherwise work stoppages and high turnover rates may be expected to persist. The general public may react more against work stoppages than against high turnover rates, although both are costly in terms of taxes. The public may not approve of government employee strikes, and, therefore, may treat such workers in harsh fashion. But the greatest cost of a failure to provide a workable labor-management policy is likely to fall on the elected officeholders. Thus, there are incentives for state and local governments to deal with their employees on a basis that is more comparable with the private sector.

Index

Index

A

Abel, I. W., 161
Ad hoc arbitration, 233–34
Administration of agreement, 210–58
  arbitration in, 218–34
    characteristics of hearings, 225–26
    limits to, 224–25
    responsibilities of arbitrator, 226–31
    selection of arbitrator, 231–34
    "Trilogy" Cases, 220–24
  grievance procedure in, 212–18
    arbitrability, 247–58
    flexibility, 215–17
    harmonious labor relations, 217–18
    time limits under, 236–47
Administrative changes, 118–19
Administrative issues, 409–88
  automation, 426–34
    advance notice of layoff or shutdown

Administrative issues (*cont.*)
    due to, 429–30
    "attrition principle," 430
    funds, 431–32
    restriction on subcontracting, 432–33
    retraining, 430–31
  discharge and discipline, 419–22, 450–74
  manning, 423–26
  production standards, 423–26, 474–88
  safety and health of employees, 422–23
  seniority, 410–19
    exceptions to, 416–18
    filling of job vacancy, 436–50
    limitations upon, 413–15
    in transfer, 415–16
    units for, 412–13
Advisory arbitration, 514
AFL-CIO, *see* American Federation of Labor–Congress of Industrial Organizations
AFL-CIO News (periodical), 146, 149

533

Agency shop, 382
Agreement, administration of, see Administration of agreement
Agricultural workers, unionized percentage of, 8
Air Line Pilots Association, 85, 150
Amalgamated Association of Iron and Steel Workers, 62
Amalgamated Clothing Workers of America, 72, 76, 159
Amalgamated Meat Cutters and Butcher Workmen, 206, 431
American Arbitration Association, 226n, 231-32, 233n
American Federationist (periodical), 146
American Federation of Labor (AFL):
  Atlantic City Convention (1935), 72-73
  autonomy of national unions in, 59
  CIO and:
    conflict, 73-75
    merger, 78-79
  exclusive jurisdiction within, 60, 87
  Executive Council, 70
  fight for industrial unionism within, 72-73, 74
  formation, 58-61
  lobbying and, 66
  political parties and, 60
  strikes and, 60
American Federation of Labor–Congress of Industrial Organizations (AFL-CIO), 125, 272, 384n
  conflict between craft and industrial unions in, 148-50
  conventions, 148, 159
  departments, 142-43; see also Congress of Industrial Organizations; *specific departments*
  discrimination and, 81-86
  enforcement of rules, 135-37
  Executive Committee, 139
  Executive Council, 139-41, 142, 146, 269
  expulsion of national unions from, 79, 135-37, 143-44
    Teamsters, 135
  foreign labor movements and, 146-48
  functions and problems, 144-48
  General Board, 139-41
  government, 138-41
  Internal Disputes Plan, 146
  loose structure, 39
  membership, 145
  national union autonomy in, 133-37
  non-raiding policies, 137-38
  organizing and, 146
  politics and, 144-45, 157-58
  publications, 146
  public employees in, 520

American Federation (*cont.*)
  research programs, 146
  sanctions on unions in, 149-50
  standing committees, 141; see also *specific committees*
  state and city bodies, 143-45
  withdrawal of UAW from, 12, 79, 135, 143, 150
American Federation of Musicians, 431
  long-term officers in, 163
American Federation of State, County and Municipal Employees, 9, 509, 520
  strikes and, 524
American Federation of State, County and Municipal Employees, AFL-CIO v. Woodward, 520
American Federation of Teachers, 9, 509
  strikes and, 524
American Home Products, 202
American Machine Foundry Company, (38 LA 1085), 348, 352-53
American Manufacturing Company, 222
American Motors Corporation, 186, 263
American Plan, 68
American Railway Union, 62
Anti-Communist affidavits, 117
Apprenticeship Outreach program, 84
Arbitrability of grievances, 247-58
Arbitration, 218-34
  characteristics of hearings in, 225-26
  limits to, 224-25
  responsibilities of arbitrator in, 226-31
  selection of arbitrator for, 231-34
  "Trilogy" Cases and, 220-24
Armour and Company, 206, 263
Assembly of Governmental Employees, 520
Associationists, 52
"Attrition principle," 430
Automation
  advance notice of layoff or shutdown due to, 429-30
  "attrition principle" and, 430
  funds, 431-32
  restrictions on subcontracting and, 432-33
  retraining and, 430-31
Autonomy of national unions, 59

B

Babbitt (Lewis), 4
Baer, George F., 4
Bakke, E. Wight, 25
Basic wage rate, determination of, 261-70
Beck, Dave, 11, 13, 162, 207
Bendix Aviation (26 LA 540), 304-5

Berg Metals Corporation, 348
Bethlehem Steel Company, 262
B. F. Goodrich Rubber Company, 263
Black workers, 81–86; *see also* Discrimination
Bloom, Gordon F., 115, 174
Blue-collar workers, wage increases of, 14–16
Blue Cross, 332
Boeing Company, 115
Bok, Derek C., 85–86, 127–28, 203, 430
Borden's Farm Products (3 LA 607, 608), 458
Boulware, Lemuel R., 182*n*
Boulwarism, 182*n*
Boycotts, secondary, 123
Boys Market v. *Retail Clerks* (38 U.S. L.W. 4462, 1970), 390, 391
Braniff Airways, 134
Bridges, Harry, 207
Broadcast Engineering (trade journal), 455
Brotherhood of Locomotive Engineers, 134
Brotherhood of Locomotive Firemen and Engineers, 134
Brotherhood of Railroad Trainmen, 134
Brotherhood of Railway Carmen, 150
Brotherhood of Railway Conductors, 134
Brotherhood of Switchmen, 134
Building and Construction Trades Department, AFL-CIO, 83, 142
"Business unionism," 39

C

Campbell Soup Company, 202
Carey, James, 163
Carnegie Steel Company, 62
Carpenters' union, *see* United Brotherhood of Carpenters and Joiners
Census Bureau, U.S., 273
Chamber of Commerce, U.S., 267
Chase Manhattan Bank, 283
Checkoff, 386–88
Chicago Coalition for United Community Action, 83
Chrysler Corporation, 325
City central labor unions, 51, 52
City Worker's Budget (Bureau of Labor Statistics), 271–72
Civil Rights Act (1871), 521
Civil Rights Act (1964), 81, 82, 85, 136, 279, 280
Civil Service Commission, 516–17
Civil War, 53–54
Clayton Act (1914), 66, 68
Cleveland, Grover, 62

Closed shop, 381
Collective bargaining:
 administrative issues under, 409–88
  automation, 426–34
  discharge and discipline, 419–22, 450–74
  manning, 423–26
  production standards, 423–26, 474–88
  safety and health of employees, 422–23
  seniority, 410–19
 coordinated, 202–4
 crisis situations in, 197–200
 economic supplements under, 322–77
  dismissal pay, 333–34
  health insurance plans, 331–33
  holidays with pay, 330–31, 354–62
  pension plans, 323–27
  reporting pay, 334–35
  supplementary unemployment benefits, 335–40
  vacation with pay, 327–29, 345–53
 government intervention in, 207
 health of economy and industry and, 205–6
 institutional issues under, 378–408
  checkoff, 386–88
  managerial prerogatives, 393–99
  union membership as condition of employment, 376–86
  union obligations, 388–92
 national unions in, 151–53
  multi-employer, 154
 preparations for negotiations in, 184–90
 reciprocal character, 204–5
 stages of process
  counterproposals, 194–95
  early, 190–92
  final, 195
  later, 192–94
  trading points, 194
 on state and local levels, 520–21
 technological innovations and, 206
 testing and proofreading of contract in, 200–202
 wage issues in, 259–321
  determination of basic wage rate, 261–70
  job evaluation and job comparison, 284–86
  Truitt decision, 270–73
  wage differentials, 279–81
Colorado Fuel and Iron Company, 64
Commerce Department, U.S., 187, 273
Committee for Economic Development, 100–101
Committee on Ethical Practices, AFL-CIO, 141

Committee on International Affairs, AFL-CIO, 148
Committee on Political Education, AFL-CIO, 145
Commons, John R., 88
Commonwealth v. *Hunt* (1842), 50
Communications workers, unionized percentage of, 8
Communications Workers of America, 333
Communist-dominated unions, 78, 147
Community activities of local unions, 172
Company seniority system, 412
"Company unions," 71
Computer Technology, 134
Condon-Wadlin Act (1947), 524, 525
Congress of Industrial Organizations:
  American Federation of Labor and:
    conflict between, 73-75
    merger of, 78-79
  Democratic Party and, 76
  expulsion of Communist-dominated unions by, 78, 147
  Political Action Committee, 76
  Steel Workers Organizing Committee, 74
Construction workers, unionized percentage, 8
Consumer Price Index, 274, 276-77
Contracts:
  suits for violation, 118
  termination or modification of existing, 118
  testing and proofreading of, 200-202
Contributory pension plans, 326
  Landrum-Griffith Act on, 160
  of national unions, 158-60
Conway, Jack T., 11
Coolidge, Calvin, 94
Cooperatives, producers', 54-55
Coordinated collective bargaining, 202-4
Cost of living, 273-79
  escalator clauses for, 274-77
  reopener arrangements for, 277-79
Cox, Archibald, 128
Coxe (Assistant Secretary of the Treasury), 49
Craft unions
  conflict between industrial unions and, 148-50; *see also* American Federation of Labor; *specific unions*

D

Darrow, Clarence, 156
Deadlines, strike, 195-97

De facto bargaining, 523-24
Democracy in local unions, 165
Democratic Party, 76
Departmental seniority system, 412
Depression, the, 69-75
Direct referendums, 159
Dirksen, Everett M., 384*n*
Discharge, 419-22, 450-74
Discipline, 419-22, 450-74
  of members of local unions, 168
Discrimination
  AFL-CIO and, 81-86
  charges, 441-42
  national unions and, 151
Dismissal pay, 333-34
Dubinsky, David, 72
Dues:
  checkoff, 386-88
  local union, 174-75
Dulles, Foster Rhea, 53
Dunlop, John T., 85-86, 182, 190, 203

E

East and Gulf Coast longshoremen, *see* International Longshoremen's Association
East and Gulf Coast Shipping Operators, 206
Economic health, 205-6
Economic supplements, 322-77
  dismissal pay, 323-24
  health insurance plans, 331-33
  holidays with pay, 330-31
  nonscheduled workday, 354-62
  pension plans, 323-27
    contributory, 326
    noncontributory, 325-26
  reporting pay, 334-35
  supplementary unemployment benefits, 335-40
  vacation with pay, 327-29
    eligibility for, 345-53
Education:
  local unions and, 173
  national unions and, 158
Eighth Circuit Court of Appeals, U.S., 520
Elections, union, 120, 122, 158-60
  regulations on spending in, 117
Electrical workers, *see* International Brotherhood of Electrical Workers; International Union of Electrical, Radio and Machine Workers
Eliot, Charles W., 63
Engle, Earl L., 204

Enterprise Wheel and Car Corporation, 223
Erdman Act (1898), 64
Escalator clauses, 274–77
Evans, George Henry, 52
Exclusive jurisdiction, 89
Executive Order No. 10988, 510–16
Executive Order No. 11491, 516–20

F

Fair Labor Standards Act, 281–82
Falcone, Nicholas S., 98, 118
Faulkner, William, 190
Favoritism, 441–42
Federal Communications Commission (FCC), 454, 455, 459–60
Federal employees, organizations of, 510–12; *see also* Public employees
  exclusive recognition, 512
  formal recognition, 511–12
  informal recognition, 511
Federal Impasse Panel, 519
Federal Labor Relations Council, 517–19
Federal Mediation and Conciliation Service, 118–19, 200, 207, 230n, 231–32, 515
Federal pre-emption doctrine, 384
Federal Reserve Board, 273
Federation of Organized Trades and Labor Unions (FOTLU), 58–59
Finances of local unions, 174–75
Financial workers, unionized percentage of, 8
Firestone Rubber Company, 263
Fitzpatrick, P. F., 59
Fleming, Robben W., 100
Food and Beverage Department, AFL-CIO, 142
Ford, Henry, 47
Ford Motor Company, 159
  1967 strike, 493
  UAW agreement with, 324
Foreign labor movements, 146–48
Frankfurter, Felix, 129
French, Wendell, 284–85
Furriers union, 147

G

Gannon, James P., 12
Garment unions, 39; *see also* Amalgamated Clothing Workers of America; International Ladies' Garment Workers Union
General Electric Company, 34, 138, 182, 191, 430
  coordinated bargaining with, 202–3
General Motors Corporation, 263, 274
Goldberg, Arthur J., 156, 397, 510
Gompers, Samuel, 13, 17, 59–61, 64, 66, 68, 87
Government intervention in collective bargaining, 207
Government workers, *see* Federal employees; Public employees
Great Depression, 69–75
Green, William, 68, 70, 72, 78, 79
Grievance procedure
  arbitrability in, 247–58
  flexibility of, 215–17
  harmonious labor relations and, 217–18
  in local unions, 167–68
  time limits under, 236–47

H

Hardman, J. B. S., 11
Hazard, Leland, 342
Health of employees, 422–23
Health insurance plans, 331–33
Healy, James J., 8, 28, 36, 41–42, 182, 190, 381, 432–33
Heller, Walter W., 268
Hildebrand, George H., 204
Hilgert, Raymond L., 109
Hill, James, 344
Hillman, Sidney, 13, 72
Hoffa, James, 11, 13, 189
Holidays with pay, 330–31
  on nonscheduled workday, 354–62
Homestead lockout (1892), 62
Hoover, Herbert, 94
Horlacher, John P., 114
House Un-American Activities Committee, 76
Hutcheson, William L., 73, 163

I

"Independent" unions, 132, 156
Individuals, rights of employees as, 110–11
Industrial health, 205–6
Industrial Union Department, AFL-CIO, 138, 142

Industrial unions; *see also* Congress of Industrial Organizations; Industrial Workers of the World; *specific nationals*:
  conflict between craft unions and, 148–50
  fight within AFL for, 72–74
Industrial Workers of the World (IWW), 65, 68, 69, 88
Initiation fees, 174–75
Inland Steel Corporation, 431
Institutional issues, 378–408
  checkoff as, 386–88
  managerial prerogatives in, 393–99
  union membership as condition of employment as, 379–86
  union obligations in, 388–92
Insurance, health, 331–33
Internal Disputes Plan, 146
Internal Revenue Service, 332
International Association of Firefighters, 525
International Association of Machinists, 53, 142, 430
  direct referendums in, 159
  size, 9
International Brotherhood of Electrical Workers, 9, 133, 142
  dismissal pay, 333
International Brotherhood of Teamsters & Chauffeurs, 74, 206–7
  autocratic rule in, 132
  "business unionism," 39
  expulsion from AFL-CIO, 79, 135
  legal teams, 189
  locals, 143
  long-term officers in, 163
  salary of president in, 162
  size, 9
  white-collar workers in, 10
International Confederation of Free Trade Unions, 147
International Labor Organization, 147
International Ladies' Garment Workers Union (ILGWU), 66, 72, 206, 394
  dismissal pay, 333
International Leather Goods, Plastics and Novelty Workers Union, 150
International Longshoremen's Association (ILA), 206, 431
International Longshoremen's and Warehousemen's Union (ILWU), 431
International Teamster (magazine), 15–16
International Typographical Union, 150
International Union of Electrical, Radio and Machine Workers, 76, 133, 182n, 183n, 203
Iron Molders' union, 53

J

Job evaluation and job comparison, 284–86
  wage rate for new job and, 307–21
Job vacancy, seniority in filling, 436–50
Johnson, Lyndon Baines, 115, 282–83
Jones and Laughlin Steel Corporation, 134, 262
Journeyman Cordwainers of Philadelphia, 50
Judicial control of labor disputes, 92–94
Judicial procedures for local unions, 168
Jurisdiction, exclusive, 60
Justice Department, U.S., 61, 121

K

Kaiser Steel Corporation, 37, 186
Karsh, Bernard, 18, 23
Kassalow, Everett M., 14n, 17
Kelliher, Peter, 245
Kelly v. *Montour Railroad Company*, 348
Kennedy, John F., 115, 510–12, 514, 516
Kennedy, Thomas, 431
Keynes, John Maynard, 428
Kheel, Theodore W., 38, 90
Kimberley Clark (39 LA 216), 305–6
King, Martin Luther, 523
Knights of Labor, Noble and Holy Order of, 56–58, 59
Knights of St. Crispin, 56
Knutson, Donald T., 15
Kohler strike (1954–60), 155
Korean War, 274
Kossoris, 430

L

Labor Department, U.S., 84, 147n, 162, 231, 327
  Bureau of Labor Statistics, 186, 271, 326–27
  Consumer Price Index, 274n, 276–77
  study of collective bargaining contracts by, 381
Labor laws, 92–130; *see also specific laws*
Labor-Management Relations Act (1947), 77, 220, 277–78, 381–84, 387, 390–91, 517–19
  administrative changes in, 118–19
  anti-Communist affidavits under, 117
  contracts under, 118

Labor-Management Relations Act (*cont.*)
  election spending regulated by, 117
  national emergency strike provisions, 111–17
    applications, 114–16
    extralegal measures and, 115–17
  rights of employees as individuals under, 108–10
  rights of employers under, 110–11
  suits for violation of contract under, 118
  termination or modification of existing contracts under, 118
  union unfair labor practices under, 105–8
Labor-Management Reporting and Disclosure Act (1959), 81, 93, 119–25, 162, 169–70, 517–18
  Title VII of, 122–25
    picketing, 123–24
    recognition votes, 124–25
    secondary boycotts, 123
    small employers, 122, 124
  on "trusteeships," 120–21
  on union elections, 120, 122
    conventions, 160
    secret ballot provisions, 159
  unlawful employer actions under, 121–22
Labor movement, history of, 47–91
  of AFL, 58–66
  black workers in, 81–86
  city central labor unions in, 51, 52
  during Civil War, 53–54
  cooperatives in, 54–55
  eighteenth-century, 48–49
  of first unions, 50–51
  formation of nationals in, 52
  during Great Depression, 69–75
  of Knights of Labor, 56–58, 59
  1946 strike wave in, 79
  secret societies in, 56
  workingmen's parties in, 52–53
  during World War I, 66–69
  during World War II, 75–76
LaFollette Seamen's Act (1915), 66
Landrum-Griffin Act, *see* Labor-Management Reporting and Disclosure Act
Lapham-Hickey (3 LA 327), 246
Lasser, David, 203–4
Lawrence strike (1912), 65
Layoff
  due to automation, advance notice of, 429–30
  temporary, seniority and, 418
Legal obligations of unions, 253–54
Legal staffs of national unions, 155–56
Lester, Richard A., 81
Letter Carriers' union, 9, 10

Levine, Solomon B., 18
Levinson Steel (23 LA 135), 246
Lewis, John L., 13, 17, 71–76, 136, 163
Lewis, Sinclair, 4
Lincoln, Abraham, 54, 66–67
Ling-Temco-Vought, 134
Livernash, E. Robert, 8, 28, 36, 41–42, 285–86, 381, 432–33
Lobbying, 66
Local unions, 164–75
  attendance at meetings, 173–74
  borderline grievances in, 167–68
  community activities, 172
  democracy in, 165
  discipline of members in, 168
  education and, 173
  finances, 174–75
  functions, 166–68
  judicial procedures for, 168
  negotiation of grievances by, 167–68
  national unions and, 150–51
    charters, 165
    sanctions, 151
  officers, 164–66
    duties, 165–66
    salaries, 165
  politics and, 170–72
  trial committees, 168–69
London, Jack, 23
LTV Aerospace, 134
Ludlow massacre (1913), 64

M

McClellan Committee, 18
McCoy, Whitley, 245
McDonald, David J., 161, 163
McGuire, Peter, 59
Machinists' union, *see* International Association of Machinists
McKersie, Robert B., 197
Maintenance-of-membership arrangements, 382
Management:
  philosophies toward unions, 31–38
    accommodation, 31, 35–36
    armed truce, 34
    collusion, 37–38
    conflict, 32–34
    cooperation, 36–37
    power bargaining, 34–35
  prerogatives, 393–99
  resistance to unions by, 24–30
Manning, 423–26
Manufacturing workers, unionized percentage of, 8

Maritime Department, AFL-CIO, 142
Maslow, A. H., 19–21, 89
Maternity leave, 345–55
Mazey, Emil, 12
Meany, George, 79, 150, 269
Meetings of local unions, 173–74
Membership
  of AFL-CIO, 145
  as condition of employment, 379–86
  dues, 386–87
Metal Trades Association, 62–63
Metal Trades Department, AFL-CIO, 142, 143
Michigan Civil Service Act, 527
Michigan Public Employment Relations Act (1965), 526–28
Michigan Teachers' Tenure Act, 528
Milwaukee Spring Company (39 LA 1270), 348, 352, 353n
Mine workers, unionized percentage of, 8; see also United Mine Workers
Minnesota Mining and Manufacturing Company, 336
Mitchell, Clarence, 82, 114–15
Molly Maguires, 56
Morse, Wayne, 115
Multi-employer collective bargaining, 154
Murray, Philip, 13, 76, 78, 79
Musicians' union, see American Federation of Musicians

N

National Academy of Arbitrators, 232
National Association of Manufacturers, 64
National Car Rental, 134
National Education Association, 524
National emergency strike provisions, 111–17
National Founders' Association, 63
National Industrial Recovery Act (1933), 70–71, 73
National Labor Relations Act (1935), 71, 95–102, 379
  employee representation elections under, 101–2
  employer unfair labor practices under, 95–101
National Labor Relations Board, 93, 103, 278, 382–83
  enlargement of, 118–19
  federal employees and, 517, 519
  formation of, 72
  recognition votes and, 124–25
  small employers and, 122, 124

National Labor Relations Board (*cont.*)
  on union safety and health demands, 422
National Labor Relations Board v. *Gissel Packing Company* (395 U.S. 575), 102
National Labor Relations Board v. *Truitt Manufacturing Company* (1956), 270–71
National Labor Union, 55, 87–88
National Maritime Union, 150
National Trades' Union, 52, 87
National Typographical Union, 53
National unions:
  autonomy, 59
  in AFL-CIO, 133–37
  charters for local unions, 165
  in collective bargaining, 151–53
  multi-employer, 163–64
  constitution, 158–60
  conventions, 158–60
  departments, 153
  discrimination and, 151
  district or regional offices, 153–54
  education projects, 158
  expulsion from AFL-CIO, 79
  formation, 52–54
  government, 52–54
  legal staffs, 155–56
  locals and, 150–51
    sanctions, 151
  officers, 161–64
    term of office, 162–64
    salaries, 162
  organizing by, 156–57
  politics and, 157–58
  staff representatives, 152–54, 163–64
  strike benefits from, 155
National War Labor Board, 75, 327
Negotiations, preparation for, 184–90
New York City Transit Authority, 524
New York Journal of Commerce, 3–4
Nixon, Richard M., 114–15, 269, 283, 511
Noncontributory pension plans, 325–26
Non-raiding policies of AFL-CIO, 137–38
Norris–La Guardia Act (1932), 70, 94–98, 390
Northrup, Herbert R., 115, 174
No-strike clauses, 389–91

O

Occupational seniority system, 412
Officers
  local union, 164–66

Officers (cont.)
   duties, 165–66
   salaries, 165
   national union, 161–64
      length of terms, 162–64
      salaries, 162
Oil, Chemical and Atomic Workers Union, 336
Olin Mathieson Chemical Corporation, 202
Olin Mathieson Chemical Corp. (37 LA 588, 1961), 245
Order of Railroad Telegraphers, 430
Organizing:
   AFL-CIO and, 146
   by national unions, 156–57
Overtime:
   contract provisions for, 294
   deliberate violation, 294–97
   rates of pay for, 281–84
   rotation, 288–307
Owen-Keating Act (1916), 66

P

Pacific Maritime Association, 207
Paid holidays, 330–31
   on nonscheduled workdays, 354–62
Paid vacations, 327–29
   eligibility for, 345–53
Paterson strike (1913), 65
Penn-Dixie Cement (29 LA 457), 458
Pension plans, 323–27
   contributory, 326
   noncontributory, 325–26
Perlman, Selig, 88
Permanent arbitrators, 234
Peterson, Florence, 175
Petrillo, James C., 163
Philadelphia Plan, 84
Picketing, 123–24
Pittsburgh Plate Glass, 303–4
Plantwide seniority system, 412
Politics
   AFL-CIO and, 144–45, 157–58
   local unions and, 170–72
   national unions and, 157–58
   UAW, 157, 171
Postal Clerks' union, 9
Post Office, U.S., 246
Powderly, Terrence V., 57, 58–59, 88
Preferential shop, 382
President's Council of Economic Advisors, 115, 268, 269
Producers' cooperatives, 54–55
Production standards, 423–26, 474–88

Public employees:
   right to strike, 524–30
      resolution of disputes, 528–29
      teacher work stoppages, 526
      union security, 526–28
   state laws governing, 521–24
      de facto bargaining, 523–24
      study commissions, 524
   unionization, 16–17
      federal, 510–12
      percentage, 8
   rights, 420–21
Public Interest in National Labor Policy, The (Committee for Economic Development), 100–101
Public utilities workers, unionized percentage of, 8
Pullman Palace Car Company strike (1894), 62
Purcell, Theodore V., 29*n*

R

Racial discrimination, *see* Discrimination
Railway Employees Department, AFL-CIO, 142
Railway Labor Act (1926), 112*n*, 114
Railway unions, *see specific brotherhoods and unions*
Raskin, A. H., 12
Rayback, Joseph G., 68
Reciprocal character of collective bargaining, 204–5
Recognition:
   of Federal employees organizations, 510–12
   exclusive, 512
   formal, 511–12
   informal, 511
   votes on, 124–25
Rees, Albert, 111
Referendums, direct, 159
Reopener arrangements, 277–79
Reporting pay, 334–35
Representative elections, 101–2
Republic Steel Company, 262
Research Institute of America, 78
Research programs, AFL-CIO, 146
Resolution of disputes, 528–29
Retail, Wholesale and Department Store Union, 9
Retail Clerks International Association, 9–10
Retraining, 430–31

Reuther, Walter B., 39, 79, 150, 162, 163, 190, 206
Reynolds, Lloyd G., 31, 113
Rights of union, 253–54
 to file grievances, 254–55
"Right-to-work" laws, 109, 384
Rockefeller, David, 283
Rockefeller, Nelson A., 524
Roosevelt, Franklin D., 70–71, 75
Rotation of overtime, 288–307
Rubber Workers' union, 262–63

S

Safety of employees, 422–23
St. Sure, J. Paul, 207
Sanctions on AFL-CIO unions, 149–50
Sayles, Leonard R., 13
"Scanlon Plans," 37
"Scientific Management," 63, 88
Secondary boycotts, 123
Second Circuit Court of Appeals, U.S., 203
Secret ballot provisions, 159
Secret societies of workers, 56
Seidman, Joel, 23
Selekman, Benjamin M., 32–35, 37
Seniority, 410–19
 exceptions to, 416–18
 filling of job vacancy and, 436–50
 limitations upon, 413–15
 in transfers, 415–16
 units for, 412–13
Service workers, unionized percentage of, 8
Seward, Ralph, 245
Shutdown due to automation, 429–30
Sinclair Refining v. *Atkinson* (370 U.S. 195, 1962), 390
Slichter, Sumner H., 8, 22, 28, 36, 41–42, 381, 432–33
Socialist Labor Party, 65
"Social unionism," 39
Southern Pacific Railroad, 430
Staff representatives:
 of national unions, 152–54, 163–64
 of UAW, 158
Standard Lime & Cement Co. (26 LA 469), 305
Standard of living, 271–73
State laws governing public employees, 521–24
 de facto bargaining in, 523–24
 study commissions in, 524
Steel Fact-Finding Board, 323n
Steel Workers Organizing Committee, CIO, 74

Stevens, Carl M., 195, 196
Strasser, Adolph, 60
Strauss, George, 13
Strike benefits, 155
Strikes:
 AFL and, 60
 deadline for, 195–97
 national emergency provisions for, 111–17
 1946 wave, 79
 by public employees:
  resolution of disputes, 528–29
  teacher work stoppages, 526
  union security, 526–28
 by UAW:
  of Ford Motor Company, 493
  during World War II, 75
 in violation of no-strike clause, 389–91
 wildcat, 391–92
Strong, George E., 200
Study commissions, 524
Subcontracting, 432–33
Supplementary unemployment benefits, 335–40
Supreme Court, U.S., 64, 66, 71, 72, 81, 93, 102, 183n, 203
 decision on wage-reopening by, 278–79
 no-strike clauses upheld by, 390–91
 "Trilogy" Cases in, 220–24, 369
 Truitt decision in, 270–71
 on Wagner Act, 125
Swift & Company, 206, 263
Swift & Company (12 LA 108), 458
Sylvis, William, 54–55

T

Taft, Philip, 58
Taft, Robert A., 77, 78, 108
Taft-Hartley Act, *see* Labor-Management Relations Act
Taylor, Frederick W., 63
Taylor, George W., 112
Taylor Act (1967), 524, 252
Taylor Commission, 524
Teachers' unions, *see* American Federation of Teachers; National Education Association
Teacher work stoppages, 526
Teamsters' union, *see* International Brotherhood of Teamsters and Chauffeurs
Technological innovations, 206
Temporary layoff, 418
Texas Company (19 LA 709), 354n

Time limits of grievance procedure, 236–47
Tobin, Daniel, 73, 163
Trade workers, unionized percentage of, 8
Transfers, seniority in, 415–16
Transportation workers, unionized percentage of, 8
Trial committees, 168–69
"Trilogy" Cases, 220–24
Truitt Manufacturing Company, 270
Truman, Harry S., 77, 323*n*
"Trusteeships" in unions, 120–21
Twain, Mark, 19
Typographers' union, *see* International Typographical Union

U

Ulman, Lloyd, 69
Unemployment benefits, supplementary, 335–40
Unfair labor practices:
  employer, 95–101
  union, 105–8
Union bureaucrats, *see* Officers
Union Carbide, 202, 204
Union Label Department, AFL-CIO, 142, 143
United Auto Workers, 205, 268, 394
  Communists in, 76
  compulsory retirement of officers in, 163
  departments, 153
  funds for Kohler strike from, 155
  opposition to arbitration of production standards, 425
  politics and, 157, 171
  Public Review Board, 170
  salary of president, 162
  size, 9
    of locals, 159
  "social unionism," 39
  staff representatives, 158
    laying off, 175
  supplementary unemployment benefit plan, 335
  withdrawal from AFL-CIO, 12, 79, 135, 143, 150
United Brotherhood of Carpenters and Joiners, 9
  long-term officers, 163
  politics and, 157
United Glass and Ceramic Workers Union, 339
United Mine Workers, 66, 71–73, 136, 431
  elections in, 122
  long-term officers in, 163

United Mine Workers (*cont.*)
  strikes during World War II by, 75
United Shoe Workers of America, 206
United States Pipe and Foundry (28 LA 777), 246
United States Potash Co. (30 LA 1039), 458
U. S. Rubber (13 LA 839), 305
United States Steel Corporation, 74, 262
United Steelworkers of America, 74, 206, 207, 262, 397
  autocracy in, 161
  direct referendums in, 159
  dismissal pay, 333
  district 30, 153
  organizing by, 157
  size, 9
  staff representatives, 158
  supplementary unemployment benefit plan, 335
  "Trilogy" Cases involving, 220–24
  vacation plan, 328
  white-collar workers in, 10
United Steelworkers v. *American Manufacturing*, 222–23
United Steelworkers v. *Enterprise Wheel and Car Corporation*, 223
United Steelworkers v. *Warrior and Gulf Navigation*, 221–22
United Transportation Union, 134
Upholsterers International Union, 170
Urban League, 82

V

Vacation with pay, 327–29
  eligibility for, 345–53
Vietnam war, 269

W

Wabash Railroad strike (1885), 57
Wage differentials, 279–81
Wage increases, 14–16
Wage issues, 259–321
  cost of living as, 273–76
    escalator clauses, 274–77
    reopener arrangements, 277–79
  determination of basic wage rate in, 261–70
    ability to pay, 264–70
    comparative norm principle, 261–64
  job evaluation and job comparison in, 284–86

Wage issues (cont.)
   wage rate for new job, 307–21
   overtime rates of pay as, 281–84
   rotation of overtime, 288–307
   Truitt decision and, 270–73
   standard of living, 271–73
   wage differentials as, 279–81
Wagner Act, *see* National Labor Relations Act
Wall Street Journal (newspaper), 148, 391
Wallace, Henry A., 78*n*
Walton, Richard E., 197
Warrior and Gulf Navigation Company, 221–22
West-coast Longshoremen, *see* International Longshoremen's and Warehousemen's Union
Westinghouse Electric Company, 138
West Virginia Pulp & Paper Co. (10 LA 117, 118), 458
White-collar workers, unionization of, 9–18
   blocks to, 11–14
   women and, 14

Wildcat strikes, 391–92
Willkie, Wendell, 76
Wilson, Woodrow, 66–67
Wilson and Company, 134
Wilson Pharmaceutical, 134
Wilson Sporting Goods, 134
Wirtz, W. Willard, 112
"Wisconsin School," 88
Wobblies, *see* Industrial Workers of the World
Women:
   maternity leave for, 345–55
   as white collar workers, 14
Workingmen's parties, 52–53
Work loads, *see* Production standards
Work stoppages of teachers, 526
World War I, 66–69
World War II, 75–76, 322, 332

Y

Young, Jerry D., 109
Young, Whitney, 82